This is the first comprehensive history of Russian theatre in English. Written by an international team of experts, the book brings together the fruits of recent research into all areas of Russian theatre history. Of particular interest are the chapters written by senior Russian academics, who not only reveal previously unpublished documentation but also offer new insights into their subject areas. The *History* covers the whole range of Russian dramatic experience, from puppet theatre to ballet and grand opera, but its emphasis is on the practice of theatre, especially acting, and the final chapter puts Russian theatre into the wider context of Western performance and the stage.

The *History* begins with the earliest endeavours, with rituals and entertainments, and moves through to the emergence of established drama in the eighteenth century. The careers and activities of the playwrights as well as the actors are highlighted in each chapter, and the volume also includes information on the provincial, amateur and popular theatres. The Imperial Theatre and Imperial Ballet are also examined and a complete chapter is devoted to the development of Russian opera. The history of twentieth-century Russian theatre is a special feature of the volume, with chapters following the progress of drama and performance from the revolution, through communism, and up to the present day. A key feature of the *History* is the collection of rare photographs, some of which are published for the first time.

Robert Leach is Reader in Drama at the University of Birmingham and Victor Borovsky is at the School of Slavonic and East European Studies, University of London.

A history of Russian theatre

Edited by Robert Leach and Victor Borovsky
Associate editor Andy Davies

CAMBRIDGE
UNIVERSITY PRESS

PUBLISHED BY THE PRESS SYNDICATE OF THE UNIVERSITY OF CAMBRIDGE
The Pitt Building, Trumpington Street, Cambridge CB2 1RP, United Kingdom

CAMBRIDGE UNIVERSITY PRESS
The Edinburgh Building, Cambridge CB2 2RU, United Kingdom
40 West 20th Street, New York, NY 10011–4211, USA
10 Stamford Road, Oakleigh, Melbourne 3166, Australia

First published 1999

Printed in the United Kingdom at the University Press, Cambridge

Typeset in Monotype Columbus 11/13.5pt   [SE]

A catalogue record for this book is available from the British Library

ISBN 0 521 43220 0 hardback

In order to give a precise definition of what art is, it is most important that we should avoid regarding art as pleasure, and look at it instead as one of the necessities of human life. If we take this view of art, we cannot help but see that it is a way of communicating between people.

Lev Tolstoy, What is Art?

Contents

Illustrations

All illustrations reproduced by courtesy of the St Petersburg Museum of Theatrical and Musical Arts, except for illustrations 19, 20 and 21, which are reproduced by courtesy of the Maria Ermolova Theatre Museum, Moscow and illustration 31, which is from the collection of Robert Leach.

Contributors

ANDY ADAMSON is Director of Dance at the University of Birmingham. He is active as a choreographer and views research as integral to his work as a theatre practitioner. Publications include *Kurt Jooss: 60 years of The Green Table* (with Dr C. Lidbury) and CALABAN a system for digital documentation and dissemination of Labanotated dance scores.

PROFESSOR ANATOLY ALTSCHULLER (1922–1996) was an eminent theatre historian. After serving in the Second World War, he entered the Ostrovsky Theatre Institute and graduated in 1948. In 1954, he became a research fellow in the Leningrad Institute of Theatre, Music and Cinematography. He is the author of more than 140 articles and the following books: *Aleksandr Martynov, History of the Aleksandrinsky Theatre, Julia Linskaya, Pavel Svobodin, A Critical History of the Russian Theatre*, Volumes III and IV, and *Five Portraits of Famous Russian Actors*.

JEAN BENEDETTI trained as an actor at Rose Bruford College, and pursued a career in theatre, film and television as actor, director, writer and translator. In 1970 he returned to Rose Bruford College as principal. From 1979 to 1987 he was President of the Theatre Education Committee of the International Theatre Institute (UNESCO). His published works include translations of Brecht's *Eduard des Zweitens* and *Die Kleinebuergerhochzelt*, and *Stanislavski: an Introduction, Stanislavski: a Biography, The Moscow Art Theatre Letters, Dear Writer, Dear Actress* (the correspondence of Anton Chekhov and Olga Knipper), *Stanislavski and the Actor*. He is currently working on a biography of David Garrick.

BIRGIT BEUMERS is a lecturer in the Russian Department of Bristol University. Her book on Yury Lyubimov at the Taganka Theatre (1964–94), was published in 1997. She specialises in Russian culture and has published articles on contemporary Russian theatre and film.

VICTOR BOROVSKY is a Russian theatre historian. Author of *The Moscow Private Opera of S. I. Zimin, Chaliapin*, and co-author of *Stravinsky on Stage*, as well as many articles, he is currently completing 'A Triptych of the Russian Theatre', on the Russian theatrical family, the Komissarzhevskys. He taught the history of Russian theatre and opera for eighteen years at the Leningrad Institute of Theatre, Music and Cinematography, and at the Leningrad Conservatory. At present Dr Borovsky teaches at the School of Slavonic and East European Studies, University of London.

A. D. P. BRIGGS is Professor of Russian at the University of Birmingham and has written widely on Russian literature, including four books on Aleksandr Pushkin. He has also recently published a new edition of the poet Edward Fitzgerald.

SPENCER GOLUB is Professor of Theatre and Comparative Literature at Brown University (Providence, Rhode Island, USA). He is the author of *The Recurrence of Fate: Theatre and Memory in Twentieth-Century Russia*, which was awarded New York University's Joe A. Callaway Prize for the Best Book on Drama and Theatre, 1994–5, as well as of *Evreinov: The Theatre of Paradox and Transformation*. His current book concerns apparitional *mise en scene* and performance anxiety in theatre, film and narrative fiction.

CATRIONA KELLY is Reader in Russian and Tutorial Fellow of New College, University of Oxford. Her publications include *Petrushka, the Russian Carnival Puppet Theatre* (Cambridge University Press, 1990), *A History of Russian Women's Writing 1820–1992* (Oxford University Press, 1994), and *An Anthology of Russian Women's Writing 1777–1992* (Oxford University Press, 1994). She is co-editor (with David Shepherd) of *Constructing Russian Culture in the Age of Revolutions and An Introduction to Russian Cultural Studies* (Oxford University Press, 1998), and is General Editor of Cambridge Studies in Russian Literature. She is currently working on a history of conduct guidance in Russia, *Refining Russia: Gender and the Regulation of Behaviour in Russia after 1760*.

ROBERT LEACH is Reader in Drama at the University of Birmingham. Earlier books on Russian theatre include *Vsevolod Meyerhold* and *Revolutionary Theatre*. He is also a poet and playwright, as well as a freelance theatre director.

CYNTHIA MARSH is Senior Lecturer in Russian at the University of Nottingham. In addition to her work on Russian literature, she has published several articles on Russian theatre, a book on Gorky as playwright (*File on Gorky*), and is currently writing a full-length study of Gorky's plays.

ARKADY OSTROVSKY was born in 1971 in Moscow and received his first degree in theatre history and criticism from the Russian Academy of Theatre Arts (GITIS). He did his Ph.D. at the University of Cambridge and is presently completing his thesis on Stanislavsky's productions of English drama. Since January 1997 he has been working as a journalist for the Financial Times in London.

KATE SEALEY RAHMAN is a curator in the Slavonic and East European Collections of The British Library. A graduate of the Department of Russian at the University of Birmingham, she recently completed her doctorate there on Aleksandr Ostrovsky. Her monograph on Ostrovsky – *Ostrovsky: Reality and Illusion* (Birmingham Slavonic Monographs) – was published earlier this year.

PROFESSOR ANATOLY SMELIANSKY is a literary director of the Moscow Art Theatre, a theatre historian and a critic. Born in 1942 he graduated from the University in Gorky (Nizhnii Novgorod) before moving to Moscow. His academic interests cover Mikhail Bulgakov, the history of the Moscow Art Theatre, and contemporary Russian theatre. He is the author of several acclaimed books including *Mikhail Bulgakov at the Moscow Art Theatre*, published in Russian in 1986 (this book has been translated in English as *Is Comrade Bulgakov Dead? Mikhail Bulgakov at the Moscow Art Theatre*, 1993) and *The Russian Theatre After Stalin*, 1999. He is the editor of the new collected works by K. S. Stanislavsky and a co-editor/author of a two-volume History of the Moscow Art Theatre.

PROFESSOR INNA SOLOVYOVA is one of Russia's most prominent theatre historians and critics with particular expertise in the history of the Moscow Art Theatre. Born in 1927 into the family of a playwright she graduated from the State Theatre Institute, GITIS in 1949. The same year she began to be published by the national newspapers and specialist theatre journals. In 1967 she joined the research department of the Moscow Art Theatre where she has edited several volumes of Stanislavsky's director's plans and note-books. She is the co-editor of the new collected works by K. S. Stanislavsky and the author/editor of the two-volume history of the Moscow Art Theatre. Her own works include biographies of K. S. Stanislavsky (1984, 1985) and Vl. I. Nemirovich-Danchenko (1979).

JOHN WARRACK was formerly University Lecturer in Music and Fellow of St Hugh's College at Oxford, where he taught courses on Russian opera. He has also written widely on Russian music, his publications including a book on Tchaikovsky.

Acknowledgements

The creation of a book such as this takes several years, and involves many people. Some of those whose work has helped to make it possible have dropped out, others have come on board late and exerted themselves indefatigably. To all of them, and to those who have simply stuck with it throughout, the editors would like to proffer warm and sincere thanks.

Sarah Stanton and Dr Victoria Cooper of the Cambridge University Press have steadfastly supported us throughout the years of preparation. To them above all does this book owe its existence. We record cordial thanks especially to our assistant editor Andy Davis whose unobtrusive labours, understanding and forebearance were fundamental to the production of this book, and to Dr Kate Sealey, whose advice and input into this volume have been extremely valuable and highly valued. Special thanks go to Professor Anatoly Altschuller for his advice on structure and format at the conception of this project. We also thank each other for dedication to the original idea and for the friendship which was born out of this work and which survived despite sometimes differing views.

Victor Borovsky would first like to record his indebtedness to all the teachers and mentors, many of whom have now passed away, who throughout his life in the Soviet Union taught him to understand theatre and who instilled in him a great love for theatre history. He is also grateful to his colleagues from the St Petersburg Museum of Theatrical and Musical Arts for their efforts in locating and selecting illustrations for the volume. Finally, he thanks Peggy Marshall for her invaluable help and support.

Robert Leach would especially like to thank colleagues, and former colleagues, from the Drama and Russian departments at Birmingham University, notably the late Jocelyn Powell for his constantly stimulating challenges, and Tony Briggs and Mike Pushkin, for years of encouragement and support. He would like also to record thanks to those Russians with whom he has worked, especially Mark Rozovsky, Svetlana Sergienko and the members of the Teatre u Nikitskikh Vorot; Tamara Garamova; and the late Tatyana Tretyakova. He also thanks Alison Nott for hours of argument and discussion, which have helped to clarify many issues connected with the development of Russian theatre. Finally, he is proud to record his thanks to Joy Parker, without whose patience and sympathetic support this book – and much else – could never have come about.

Russian theatre in world theatre

ROBERT LEACH

This book aims to put the history of the Russian theatre from its inception to today into a modern perspective. Such an attempt is less easy to bring to fruition than might be imagined, for even today, years after the collapse of the communist system, suspicions, difficulties and misunderstandings still arise.

Nevertheless, collaboration between East and West is now possible, and this book deliberately boasts contributors both from the Russian tradition of theatrical-historical scholarship, as well as from the different traditions of Western scholarship. It should come as no surprise, therefore, to discover that this volume by no means offers a new consensus, the writers and editors do not necessarily agree with each other about everything, and the reader who would find emerging here some sort of orthodoxy in interpreting the history of the theatre in Russia will be disappointed. However, with the collapse of repressive communism in Russia, new archives have been opened and Russians especially have begun to enjoy the freedom to express unexpected or original thoughts. Hence this seems a good moment to try to open up the history of the theatre in that most extraordinarily artistic and most politically devastated country.

The book is founded on the premise that developments in contemporary theatre practice probably owe more to what has happened in Russia than to any other country. This is perhaps most noticeable in the field of mainstream acting, where the influence of Konstantin Stanislavsky is pervasive throughout the world. Stanislavsky spent a lifetime struggling to discover how to achieve the effect of spontaneity on the stage, and although he constantly rejected his own ideas and work, and sought new and ever more promising ways of reaching his crock of gold, at each point in his career he threw off brilliant and effective ideas which his friends, followers and disciples took up and developed. Even today, many of the most creative or effective theatre and film directors employ something akin to Stanislavsky's 'round-the-table' procedures, or a derivation of his 'method of physical action'. Similarly, actors of all styles in theatres around the globe analyse their role by employing techniques very much like those developed by Stanislavsky, such as identifying the character's 'objectives' and 'actions', noting and understanding as many of the 'given circumstances' as can be found, and releasing the imagination through the 'magic if'. These are the methods of the modern stage, and they derive almost entirely from Stanislavsky's attempts to codify his own practice, and that of his actor-colleagues at the Moscow Art Theatre.

Stanislavsky was embraced by Stalin, whose artistic commissars promulgated a perversion of his method as 'socialist realism'. At the same time, Westerners who saw or even suspected anything of the riches of the Russian theatre in the 1920s or 1930s all regarded Stanislavsky as the most significant Russian theatre practitioner of the time and learned what they could, often in garbled or second-hand form, of his procedures. It is no wonder then that his work had such an influence. Much more surprising is the continuing influence of Stanislavsky's younger contemporary, bitter rival, and most respected – even loved – colleague, Vsevolod Meyerhold.

Where Stanislavsky worked from within the actor's psyche, so that he or she responded to a series of impulses that were then blended or modified to create the performance, Meyerhold worked in the opposite way. For him, the theatre was an artificial medium in the best sense, and great acting was that which employed 'antics appropriate to the theatre'. Nothing was to be spontaneous or apparently haphazard, nothing was to give the impression of 'real life'. For Meyerhold, a production was more like a carefully constructed symphony, in which each element – theatrical equivalents of violins, oboes, percussion or French horns – was synthesised and given expressive force by a director-conductor. While each actor (player) was a creative artist in his or her own right, just as any musician is clearly a creative artist, and while the author, designer, and lighting designer were also artists deserving the respect such work should evoke, it was nevertheless Meyerhold's view that the finished production was the opus of the director, the ultimate theatre artist who was to be considered the 'author' of the production.

Thus, it is arguable that the two main streams of twentieth-century theatre practice flow from the work of Stanislavsky and Meyerhold, who bestride the modern theatre like colossi. This in itself is sufficient justification for this book. Yet in other ways, too, Russia's influence has been incalculable. The absurd and surrealist style of theatre which has had a long life through the twentieth century, for example, has at least one of its roots in the anti-naturalism of Nikolai Evreinov. His 'theatre for oneself', which dissects and toys with our perceptions of illusion and reality, stage truth and living lies, predates the not dissimilar theatrical trickery of Luigi Pirandello by a decade or more; and if Evreinov is less well known than the Italian playwright, that may be because, like so many others, he was trapped, and his career blasted, by the scatter-gun destructiveness of the Russian revolution. From being one of the most brilliant stars in the St Petersburg theatrical sky in the 1910s, Evreinov lost his place in the 1920s and emigrated to the West. Although his work was occasionally staged, and often admired, he never found an adequate niche from which to disseminate his ideas successfully. Yet his productions in Russia before 1917, especially at the Distorting Mirror Cabaret, were often sensational and scandalous, as well as challenging, and several of his plays were certainly in advance of their time.

Similarly, there is little doubt that twentieth-century ballet is largely the creation of Russian dancers and choreographers, and we still see what are effectively Marius Petipa's *Swan Lake*, *Sleeping Beauty* and other works being performed in theatres around the world. The development of ballet was significantly altered and moved forward by Petipa's successors, most notably Mikhail Fokin and Vaslav Nijinsky, and later, and perhaps even more significantly, by George Balanchine in the USA. Tchaikovsky, whose music was so important to Petipa, is a key figure in the history of opera, and his greatest interpreter, Fyodor Chaliapin, brought the dramatic actor's techniques to bear on operatic roles. It is no accident, therefore, that this book on the history of Russian theatre should include chapters on opera and ballet; it is also a mark of Russia's influence on the development of these theatre forms.

The absolute importance of these – and other – practitioners is obviously a valid reason why Russian theatre should be studied and known in the West. But the question of how they came to achieve what they did, is one that cannot be answered without some understanding of the history of the theatre in Russia. In other words, the work of these giants of the twentieth century can only be fully comprehended if the work of their predecessors is also understood.

One of the most intriguing and rewarding comparisons which can be made between Russian theatre and that of Britain, France, America and other Western countries is in their respective manifestations in the nineteenth century. The comparison revolves around the place of ideas in the drama. For while English, French and American theatres were setting a premium on spectacle and melodrama, farce, music hall and pantomime – forms that admittedly are full of theatrical life, but that are not capable of handling philosophical or sophisticated ideas – Russian theatre was trying to grapple with the real problems of social living, human relationships and emotions, and political and economic realities. The plays of Gogol and Ostrovsky especially, seem far in advance of almost anything that was being created contemporaneously in the West. And of course, plays such as these demand a commitment to acting that was rare indeed in the West. While Henry Irving in London had no contemporary drama better than Leopold Lewis's *The Bells* or Lord Tennyson's *Becket* in which to exercise his art, Russian actors such as Mikhail Shchepkin had plays like Turgenev's *The Bachelor*, and Maria Ermolova parts like Larisa in *The Dowerless Girl*, in which to hone their talents.

This is clearly significant, because it was the seriousness with which Russian theatre artists for generations approached their work, and the intelligence which their audiences consequently brought to bear on it, that created the conditions in which a Stanislavsky or a Meyerhold could thrive. To Russians of the nineteenth century, theatre was a serious art form, and had to be approached accordingly. The contrast with England is instructive. Edward Gordon Craig, a restless genius and personally difficult man, was quickly frozen out of the English theatrical world, and for most of his life he was a largely ignored, marginal figure whose ideas meant little or nothing in the land of his birth. In Russia, the major theatre practitioners were widely known and admired, their ideas were pored over and discussed, and their productions were the subject of popular open debates, vast numbers of newspaper and magazine articles, and even in some cases whole books.

Yet in the end, the dead hand of dictatorship all but smothered the spark of Russian theatrical genius in the twentieth century. By the 1990s, although there was much interesting and indeed original work going on in Moscow and St Petersburg, in truth it largely lacked bite and resonance. Partly this may have been because the sudden freedoms that were offered to Russian theatres with the demise of communism knocked many companies and theatre workers off balance. But it is also true that gradually, as the century had proceeded, the persistance with which the communists had suppressed and repressed originality had taken an inevitable toll. By relentlessly insisting – or trying to insist – on a monotonous conformity to externally imposed, ideologically driven artistic 'principles', the strength and sap of even the most vigorous theatre environment will become diluted or poisoned, and will wither and die.

This is precisely what happened to the Russian theatre in the late stages of communism: although the spirit of many practitioners was willing, in truth the performance standards generally were no higher, and no more original, than those of many countries in the West. Sometimes they were distinctly lower. Of course, resonances, nuances and double meanings which hinted at the rife corruptions of the power elite and their lackeys abounded, and always gave a *frisson* to watching plays in Moscow or Leningrad. But the spark and sparkle had gone, and the brilliance which had characterised Ostrovsky's Maly Theatre in the 1860s, the Moscow Art Theatre in the 1900s or the Meyerhold Theatre in the 1920s was no longer in evidence.

But while this book rightly celebrates those glories that have been, it is also written in the belief that a positive future can be built on a thorough understanding of the past. It is therefore to the future of Russian theatre that the following discussion of its history is dedicated.

Russian theatre in Russian culture

VICTOR BOROVSKY

This book is the first attempt in the West to produce a joint work on the history of the Russian theatre, from its origins to the present day. The chapters offered here for the reader's consideration in no way claim to provide an exhaustive account of the evolution and current state of the art of theatre in Russia. Fourteen specialists, from Great Britain, Germany, the USA and Russia, have participated. Robert Leach was responsible for the original idea and initial plan for the project; subsequent discussions with the Russian authors resulted in the final structure and content of the volume as a whole, which shows the process of this evolution in its cultural context. Above all, it is concerned with what, exactly, a critical study of the Russian theatre contributes to the concepts of theatre and theatre history.

Despite the undoubted importance of dramatic, and sometimes prose literature in the progress of the professional art of the stage, theatre research is essentially the study of the interpretation of plays in performance, together with an analysis of the changes that have occurred over time in the practice of the actors, directors and designers who create those performances.

For a number of reasons, Russian theatre did not pass through all the natural stages of self-development, rooted in folklore and ritual forms of acting, as happened in many countries. Only towards the end of the seventeenth century did Russia really begin to assimilate the Western-European theatrical system together with achievements in other forms of art and in science.

Theatre in Russia, in a strictly functional sense, was almost entirely borrowed from the West. (It is interesting that the words *teatr* and *drama* entered the Russian language only in the eighteenth century. Before then, what is generally included in the concept of theatre was defined in quite different terms.) More than that, the type of entertainment exported to Russia belonged to a relatively late stage of theatrical development. By the time of the first performance at the court of Tsar Aleksei Mikhailovich

Romanov (in 1672), let alone the decree by Peter the Great's daughter, the Tsarina Elizavera, concerning the creation of the first professional troupe in Russia (in 1756), the English stage had long been familiar with Shakespeare, Marlowe and Ben Jonson; Spain was renowned for the plays of Calderón de la Barca, Lope de Vega and Tirso de Molina; and France resounded with the names of Corneille, Racine and Molière.

However, starting from the imitation of foreign models in dramatic writing, production methods, stage design and acting technique, the Russian theatre grew rapidly, and acquired its own distinctive character-istics over an extraordinarily short span of time. This was primarily the result of the cultural ideals and tastes of the aristocracy – which had estab-lished professional public theatre in Russia – meeting the counter-flow of a native, popular theatrical movement.

The centuries-old history of popular theatre included orally transmitted plays, with origins in *khorovye igrishcha* (song-and-dance games and ritual celebrations), the art of *skomorokhi* (strolling players), liturgical drama, the scenarios and stage experiments of school theatre (performances by stu-dents at church educational institutions), and, finally, the numerous attempts, albeit often short-lived in terms of results, to create municipal theatres with Russian actors. Thus, a theatrical form taken ready-made from Western Europe, and the professional expertise of foreign actors, singers and dancers, began gradually to be applied to a new, national content.

The fortunes of Russia's dramatic theatre proved to be closely linked with the activities of opera and ballet not only because the serf actor was required to have all-round mastery of every genre, but also because a system of managing the Imperial Theatres had evolved which brought all its companies under one direction.

Right up till the middle of the nineteenth century, many Russian actors could one day perform a play by Shakespeare or Gogol, and the next sing an opera by Cherubini or Mozart. Partly for this reason, historians of the Russian theatre never studied the work of opera and ballet companies in isolation, but examined the achievements of the dramatic and musical thea-tres within the complex system under which they interacted and influenced each other.

Those familiar with the biography of Konstantin Stanislavsky know that in his youth he dreamed of a career as an opera singer, and studied with the famous tenor Fyodor Komissarzhevsky. His sessions with Komissarzhevsky were not confined to voice exercises: in lengthy conversations with the future innovator, the teacher imparted his ideas on new goals and as yet undiscovered possibilities for the theatre. Years afterwards, Stanislavsky wrote of the unquestionable importance of the discussions with Komissarzhevsky in shaping his own views on the art of the stage. A little later, Stanislavsky also astonished his followers by declaring that he had based his system on the work of the opera singer Fyodor Chaliapin.

He was a regular spectator at the Bolshoi Theatre, and in his earlier years was often lost in rehearsals at the Moscow Private Opera of Savva Mamontov. At the end of his life Stanislavsky worked mainly on operas, and it is worth noting that other eminent directors in the dramatic theatre were also highly successful opera directors, including Vsevolod Meyerhold, Fyodor Komissarzhevsky the younger, and Vladimir Nemirovich-Danchenko.

The Moscow Art Theatre created by Stanislavsky and Nemirovich-Danchenko in 1898, and the famous 'system', based partly on an under-standing of the art of great opera singers, proved to have an indelible influence on all aspects of the Russian theatre. That influence was not always acknowledged in discussions of the methods and style of the Art Theatre (although, as time showed, its traditions remained central to the subsequent development of a national theatre): Meyerhold's early experiments as a director arose from his active rejection of what Stanislavsky was seeking at that time.

Since we have touched on 'director's theatre', it is worth noting that there is now general recognition of the enormous contribution made by Stanislavsky's revelatory work as director (and later, by Meyerhold, Komissarzhevsky the younger, Aleksandr Tairov, Yevgeny Vakhtangov and others) to the development of twentieth-century world theatre. Their productions are the subject of careful research; their writing becomes a basic source of inspiration in the education and thinking of those who have seriously committed their lives to the stage. Stanislavsky, first and foremost, is rightly saluted as an innovator.

But Stanislavsky did not, of course, invent what we now call director's theatre. The art of the director, in the present-day sense of that term, origi-nated in Western Europe. It is noteworthy, however, that, within a single decade, having absorbed the legacy of the West, the work of the director in Russia was raised to an essentially new level of artistic thinking, offering at once both a method of approach to a role and to a production, and its theoretical basis. Many native theatre historians were drawn to speculate on the reasons for such a transformation. Traditional opinion inclined to argue that the influence which Russian concepts of production exerted on the world stage had its origins deep in past decades of the life of Russian theatre. A multiplicity of changes culminated by the turn of the century in an explosion of ideas, and work of a new quality.

Sometimes, the prime significance of the director was attributed to the literary centrism of Russian culture and to those improvements which literary reform in the theatre brought about for itself. Not least important in these arguments was the place assigned to the influence of 'new drama' by writers such as Zola, Ibsen, Maeterlinck, Strindberg, Hauptmann and, especially, Chekhov. In this connection the role of Vladimir Nemirovich-Danchenko merits particular attention. Critic, dramatist, teacher, director, he brought with him the perception, important not only for Stanislavsky but also for the future of all Russian theatre production, that 'the contemporary stage and its conventions are decades behind literature'.[1]

Others argued that the director's pre-eminence was the result of social forces at work in the country. Thus, the work of the director, as the leading profession in the theatre of the twentieth century, from its very beginnings demanded a single, overriding authority. A series of new ideas had to be assimilated, such as that of the unity of the company, the creation of a theatre of like-minded people, and a different conception of the acting ensemble, now based not on a casual association of those taking part in a performance, but on the discipline of a single design, essential for coherence in the production as a whole. Russians, so this argument asserted, were, by reason of their psychological make-up, particularly inclined to unite around a single idea and submit totally to a leader.

The private theatres and amateur theatrical groups also proved to be breeding-grounds for the new kind of strong director. Despite all their problems and limitations, they proved to be the soil, the environment, in which, in contrast to the Imperial Theatres, new thinking could not only emerge but also survive.

Much has been written about the exceptional talent of Stanislavsky, who was opportunely chosen by fate to transform the work of the director into an art. His career as an actor and as a director, which began ten years before the founding of the Moscow Art Theatre, bore the mark of a unique individuality, which was reflected in his creations on the stage. '"Great production", "brilliant production", "controversial production", "thought and poetry of the production" – people did not speak in those terms before the advent of Stanislavsky,' Inna Solovyova perceptively noted.[2]

In Russia, the new thinking was further stimulated by the challenge and opportunity presented by the plays of Anton Chekhov. An innovative concept of the very nature of stage performance began to emerge, which placed hitherto unknown demands on actors and ensemble playing. The Moscow Art Theatre, responding to those demands, discovered means of interpretation which made it possible to create the atmosphere of real life, where the human being exists not in isolation but in complex relationships with the world and with other people in it. The theatre continued to develop those methods of interpretation in productions of plays by other authors, both classical and contemporary.

It is important to emphasise the exceptionally high position which the theatre occupied for many years in Russian society. Oliver Sayler, on returning from a visit to Russia during the terrible winter of 1917–18, wrote of his astonishing encounter with the theatre and its audience:

> There was no evidence in distant America that the Russian theatre
> had survived three years of war and six months of revolution . . . The
> serious theatre, the theatre as an art and not a pastime or an industry
> has persisted through the anxious and constraining days of the
> Russian upheaval because that has been its firmly established spirit for
> a hundred years. The fact that it has weathered the storms of the class
> struggle, of the Terror and of starvation proves that it is the honest
> expression of Russian character and illuminates the imaginative and
> spiritual quality of Russian life . . . To the Russian, the theatre is rather a
> microcosms, a concentration and an explanation of life. If life cannot
> be explained at least its inexplicability can be faced.[3]

That position began to weaken only with the advent of *perestroika*, when the changed situation in the country no longer required the theatre to function simultaneously as a wise teacher and as the allegorical voice of thoughts, aspirations and feelings forbidden by the political regime. The former role of the Russian theatre in its ceaseless effort to enlighten its audience is now disappearing, more and more consigned to past history. In the new Russia, theatre tends increasingly to be viewed by its changing public, as it more generally has been in the West, as part of the entertainment business.

Early in the nineteenth century, Prince Aleksandr Shakhovskoi had already formulated the tasks facing the theatre: 'To strive to refine taste, to soften manners, to eradicate vices, to rouse the spirit and a sense of patriotism.'[4] The Russian stage of those years, continuing the tradition of the preceding epoch, educated its public through the improvement of taste. Human behaviour, it was believed at the time, was reformed by contemplating the beauty of a fine and noble spectacle. Hence even instructive maxims had to be imparted to the audience not harshly, but in a pleasant and amusing manner.

Surviving contemporary memoirs and letters often refer to *teatr-prazdnik*, theatre as a festive occasion, and to the exhilarating atmosphere prevailing in the house, even before the performance started. Acting skill, polished and elegant, was knowledgeably analysed in the finest detail. Habitués of the theatre rarely sat through a show from beginning to end. They came to watch some particularly striking item, the technically difficult performance of a scene, or to listen to the dizzying embellishment of an aria, crowned by the ultimate top note. Personal acquaintance with the actors and actresses became an obligatory mark of interest in the theatre. Obligatory, likewise, was discussion of theatre in the fashionable salon: it was the mark of good form, a characteristic of the well-bred, respectable lady or gentleman.

However, beyond an outwardly frivolous and superficial attitude to theatre were hidden indications of serious changes to come. Belief that impeccable technique was an essential requirement for the performer would become the basis on which the famous Russian school of acting was created, and the concept of 'the actor' was invested with new meaning.

But attachment to lavish spectacle and festive entertainment, as opposed to theatre reflecting real life, was to enjoy a revival in the first decade of the twentieth century, when questions would be raised about the seriously critical situation of the Russian stage, despite its splendid achievements.

Apart from that, an undiminished, passionate interest in the art of the theatre was transmitted from one century to the next. By the third and fourth decades of the nineteenth century, it had become the centre of intellectual life for significantly wider sections of the population, and this would remain the Russians' attitude: 'Our theatres', wrote a St Petersburg newspaper in 1902, 'are cultural centres, fixed points, on which people's thoughts are concentrated.'[5] 'For us, plays and theatres are what parliamentary affairs and political speeches are for Western Europe,' reflects the journal *Theatre and Art*, on the same theme.[6]

A belief in theatre as a powerful instrument of education had been inherited from the past. In the nineteenth century, with increasing urgency, attention was focused not on lessons in correct, fashionable behaviour being taught from the stage, but on an awareness of social ideals. Purely aesthetic criteria gradually lost their importance, and the prescriptions for beauty determined by the strict rules of late classicism were only for a limited circle of theatrical devotees.

In theatre notices and press reviews, in critical articles by Vissarion Belinsky, and in the reminiscences of Aleksandr Herzen, theatre stood out as a vital necessity of life. It seemed that answers to the most serious and difficult questions of the time were expected of it. Imperceptibly, the reaction of the audience was changing, and along with it the whole system of relationships between theatre and public. Better productions and actors' performances now combined to give a sense of being part of something very important and essential. It was as though in the course of the action on stage a meaning was revealed of unprecedented significance for everyone sitting in the theatre.

'Every anxiety troubling the age . . . bursts out on stage and is discussed with the terrible logic of events which come and go before the eyes of the spectators. We emerge from the theatre burdened with painful and uncomfortable thoughts. Naturally enough. The theatre is the highest authority for resolving vital questions.'[7] So wrote Herzen about this period of Russian culture.

Gogol gave a similar but even more passionate evaluation of the purpose of the theatre. For him, it was 'a pulpit, from which much good can be told to the world'.[8] The value of art (including that of theatre) lies in the ability to teach people how to live, 'when through a vivid representation of a man's lofty deed, the spectator, as though enlightened by it, on leaving the theatre sets about his tasks with new energy, seeing before him that heroic deed thus portrayed'.[9]

It can be argued that such significant changes in Russian theatre and its new alliance with the public essentially derived from the great models of European and national drama. In actual fact, the repertoire of theatres in both the two capitals (Moscow and St Petersburg) and the provinces was composed largely of plays by mediocre writers, now utterly forgotten. Molière, Shakespeare and Schiller accounted for an insignificant proportion of theatre playbills. What is now known to the civilised world as classic Russian drama was as yet practically non-existent. Its first great examples, the dramatic works of Griboedov, Pushkin and Gogol, either did not reach the stage at all, or, because they were so few, could not yield satisfactory box-office takings.

Nevertheless, it was precisely during the second quarter of the nineteenth century that the actor grew into a central, almost all-embracing figure in Russian life. The idea also took shape of a production as a combination of separate performances by individual actors. Such a production surveyed the world exclusively from the point of view of man and only in terms of its relationship to man, as the chief and absolute measure of all things. The environment in which the hero existed did not change of itself; it did not appear, as it would in director's theatre, as a leading character. On stage, it was man who was portrayed, and his struggle with the realities of life at every level. One of the most outstanding actors at the end of the nineteenth century, Vladimir Davydov, clearly defined the basis of this theatre: 'Man operates within an environment, but he is the centre of life, the master of that environment. That is why in the theatre man must occupy pride of place. Theatre is, above all, Man, and consequently, above all, Actor.'[10]

It is very easy to accuse the actors' theatre of the nineteenth century of limited vision and aesthetic deafness. Such accusations were heard in plenty when, towards the end of the century, concern began to be expressed about the crisis of the Russian stage. The Russian actor, with the full and unreserved support of the public, saw him or herself not as a mere performer, but as a teacher, a proclaimer of goodness, justice and truth. The Russians' reason for going to the theatre and their expectations shaped the actor's ideology and sense of his or her own significance. In exceptional cases, actors were put on a par with authors by their contemporaries, but not for giving an interpretation of some familiar and dearly beloved play that matched exactly the public's understanding of the work. One of the greatest actors in Russian theatre, Pavel Mochalov, was regarded as Shakespeare's peer, for creating from the material of the playwright's tragedies his own images, and for adding to Shakespeare's characters his personal features. The audience looked forward to seeing Mochalov because it wanted to hear his judgements on the world, and to look at that world they had in common through his eyes.

Often an actor assumed the role of co-author, creating characters and producing ideas that went far beyond the limits of the written text. Together with the troubled audience, he or she looked into the hearts of the characters portrayed and easily evaded the barriers of censorship through which a play had to pass before it could reach the stage. In intonation, colouring and timbre of voice, in the rhythm of the acting, in a glance, a turn of the head, in pauses between words or actions, he or she expressed what everyone felt but was strictly forbidden to say openly. Innocuous material, approved and published after careful checking, then took on a meaning alarming to the authorities.

The Russian theatre and its public rapidly mastered a system of allusions. This ability to speak and comprehend a subtext became an integral feature of performances. It was not only in the second quarter of the nineteenth century that the dramatist provided actors with themes for their variations. During the Soviet period, the audience often expected a performer to 'enliven' a character constructed according to the blueprint of socialist dogma, contrary to elementary logic and inspiration, let alone the actual reality of a communist state, and then and there, according to inclination and the promptings of conscience, to reveal by his or her interpretation candid, sometimes bitter reflections on life. Soviet authority fought relentlessly against such shows, on many occasions closing them down straight after the dress rehearsal.

But, however paradoxically, the Soviet period of Russian theatre has entered the history of the stage as an important and fruitful phase in its development. In its finest manifestations (and there were many), people who were committed to the theatre in a constant, often acutely dangerous, struggle with the system, continued to preserve and develop what had accrued from preceding generations. The theatre of the Soviet era created great productions, maintained the tradition of the Russian school of acting, enhanced the art of the director, and was, above all, an inseparable element in the spiritual life of the thinking part of the population. In the productions of Georgy Tovstonogov, Yury Lyubimov and Anatoly Efros, in the operas staged by Boris Pokrovsky, and the ballets by Yury Grigorovich, the audience found continual confirmation of the astonishing fact that, even under the most intolerable conditions, the old themes of love, understanding and compassion could still evoke a response, and human beings could still retain their essential humanity.

But let us return briefly to the actors' theatre of the nineteenth century. Converting literary characters into stage characters always requires the involvement of both actor and author if it is a question of genuine art, and not merely a substitute variety show with turns by actors in costume, loosely linked to the plot of a play. The greatness of an actor is distinguished by depth and originality in interpreting a role, but it means, inevitably, introducing the performer's own judgements into a character created by someone else. During this period, writers, critics and theatre experts began to devise, after their own fashion, a scale of acting values, a kind of 'table of ranks'. The aesthetic principles developed during those years, as a means of assessing the strengths and weaknesses of professional acting, did not lose their importance for future generations. Much of what Pushkin, Gogol and Belinsky wrote became the basis of many of Stanislavsky's conclusions.

Russian theatre criticism of that time clearly divided actors into two categories. To one, belonged artists who had attained such a high degree of technical skill that, like Proteus, they could astound the spectator with a rapid succession of extraordinary transformations into dozens of persons quite unlike one another. These masters of their craft knew how to develop a stage character with rare thoroughness and accuracy of detail, and usually they were excellent teachers, founders of schools, and formulators of rules and standards of professional acting. Their own art was marked by distinctive, inimitable features; their vivid, graphic and brilliant talent amazed in its every manifestation. They avoided both the depths of tragedy and the extremes of satirical denunciation. Historians of Russian theatre include among their number Vasily Karatygin and Ivan Samarin, Glikeria Fedotova and Maria Savina, Vladimir Davydov and Konstantin Varlamov.

On the other hand, there were actors whose passionate sincerity, whose missionary and prophetic zeal burned with fiery brilliance in the theatre; artists who played only one tune, but that the most enthralling. Solitary fanatics, they were reckless spendthrifts of the gift bestowed on them. As a rule they had no disciples or direct successors. Their talent was unique, and their place in the Pantheon of art belongs only to them. Comparisons and parallels with them are impossible. As well as belonging to theatre history, these people also belong to the history of Russian thought. Memories of them are preserved even by those with no special predilection for the theatre, who rank the supreme achievements of these individuals among the cultural landmarks of their time. Such were Pavel Mochalov and Aleksandr Martynov, Maria Ermolova and Polina Strepetova, Pavel Orlenev and Vera Komissarzhevskaya.

There were, of course, also those who unintentionally shattered established stereotypes, instinctively combining in their performance widely differing styles and trends. Among them were Mikhail Shchepkin,

Aleksandr Lensky, Fyodor Chaliapin and Konstantin Stanislavsky. But any categorisation looks convincing only where contrasting features are over-simplified. On closer analysis, there may prove to be a greater number of such artists. Theatre historians, researching the testimony of contemporaries, are able to detect what had been missed, to reappraise the artistic means employed, and to point to previously undiscovered aspects of life which actors of the past have raised from the depths of oblivion and brought to general view.

During the Soviet period, such a review was inadmissible. In every sphere of human activity figures were set up by the state, to be regarded as points of reference. This was all the more possible because for decades after the 1917 revolution thousands of people disappeared from Russian culture, some into the torture cells of the secret police, others into emigration. The most important events and people of the Russian theatre, violently excised, were gradually forgotten. Whole generations of Soviet theatre students received specialist education without any real knowledge of Vsevolod Meyerhold or the younger Fyodor Komissarzhevsky, Nikolai Evreinov or Michael Chekhov, Alexandre Benois or Mstislav Dobuzhinsky.

However, the tragic exodus to the West of leading figures of Russian culture had its positive sides. Above all, by leaving, many saved their lives. Their art also continued to live, albeit not always on the same scale or with the same intensity as in prerevolutionary Russia. Furthermore, the encounter with Russian culture, and with its theatre in particular, proved to be an important influence on the performing arts in Western Europe and America.

'A significant period of time had to elapse, after Russians forsook their native land', wrote the literary critic and memoirist Valentin Bulgakov in 1938, 'for it at last to become clear that this period, historically speaking, was a whole epoch, and that educated Russians have a duty laid on them to ensure the collection and preservation of evidence of that epoch.'[11]

'Preservation of evidence' is particularly difficult in relation to theatre, where everything that gives it life begins, finishes and dies before our eyes. Nothing survives of a performance, as it does in the other arts – in literary texts, – on canvas, musical scores or sculptures. Hence the value of eye-witness accounts, without which the theatre has no past. But the theatre has something else – a spiritual dimension, which is transmitted through the work of actors and directors. In this case it is not primarily a matter of discipleship. Not all masters are capable of handing on their experience, and not all pupils can assimilate what they are told.

Tradition in the theatre survives and exerts a fruitful influence on the future through continuity. Unlike the Soviet authorities, who ruthlessly distorted art and forced it to serve its political doctrines, physically eliminating anyone thought to be 'unreliable', the Western world helped to preserve that continuity. Unfortunately, it was not possible for Russian people at the time to respond to Valentin Bulgakov's appeal. But again, thanks to the West, priceless records of the past of Russian theatre have survived, and Russian and Western theatre historians have begun to carry out joint research, which was not previously possible. Eminent examples of this collaboration are the Harvard Theatre Collection, and the volume of essays edited by Laurence Senelick, *Wandering Stars. Russian Emigré Theater, 1905–1940*. Our book is a further step in that direction.

Notes

1. V. I. Nemirovich-Danchenko, *Izbrannye pis'ma* (2 vols., Moscow, 1979), vol. I, p. 86.
2. Inna Solov'eva, 'Rabota Khudozhestvennovo Teatra nad p'esami A. K. Tolstovo', in *Rezhisserskie ekzempliary K. S. Stanislavskovo* (Moscow, 1980), p. 10.
3. Oliver M. Sayler, *The Russian Theatre under the Revolution* (Boston, 1920), pp. 2, vii, 7–8.
4. Cited in B. Alpers, *Teatra Mochalova i Shchepkina* (Moscow, 1979), p. 249.
5. O. Dymov and O. I. Perel'man, 'Zametki ob iskusstve', *Birzhevye Vedomosti*, 16 January 1902.
6. I. O. Ivanov, 'O sovremennoi nevrastenii i starom geroizme', *Teatr i iskusstovo*, 50 (1899), 900–1.
7. A. I. Gertzen, 'Kaprizy i razdum'e', *Sobranie sochinenii*, vol. II (Moscow, 1956), pp. 50–1.
8. N. V. Gogol', *Polnoe sobranie sochinenii*, vol. VIII (Moscow, 1952), p. 268.
9. Ibid. p. 277.
10. V. N. Davydov, *Rasskaz o proshlom* (Leningrad and Moscow, 1962), p. 93.
11. V. F. Bulgakov, *Russkoe iskusstvo za rubezhom* (Prague and Riga, 1938), p. 41.

1 The origins of the Russian theatre

CATRIONA KELLY

'The theatre', in its central Western sense of scripted drama staged by paid performers in specific arenas for a paying audience, is not a cultural institution indigenous to Russia. *Teatr* (or its popular corruptions *kiatr* and *featr*) retained an exotic ring to working-class ears as late as the nineteenth century; in the sixteenth century, even aristocrats would not have understood the word. Of the concepts which it now embraces, the only one that would have been familiar at that period was that of 'paid performers', which a Russian could have glossed as *skomorokhi*. The idea of a dramatic repertoire was introduced to Russia in the seventeenth century, along with the literary culture (*literatura* – also a foreign borrowing) with which it is intimately connected. Regular theatre troupes and permanent purpose-built performance spaces arrived rather later, becoming institutionalised only in the second half of the eighteenth century.

But if the theatre was very definitely a foreign seed, it was not one that fell on altogether stony ground. Russia before Peter the Great, like any pre-modern or early modern society, was a culture where the spoken word was far more important than the written. Performances of all kinds – processions, sermons, readings from the Bible and the lives of the saints, story-telling, games and entertainments, and rituals for religious, occult, social and political occasions – had a central role. In this chapter, I shall briefly survey the types of early Russian performance that can most readily be described as 'theatrical', before going on to analyse the influence of the West on some of the genres of entertainment that were to be the basis of the popular theatre when it eventually became properly established, in the late eighteenth century. My main sources are contemporary documents: ecclesiastical pronouncements and royal decrees, and the accounts of early foreign travellers to Russia, some of whom set down detailed descriptions of the Russians' 'crude' and 'barbarous' manner of amusing themselves, as well as of the more seemly rituals of Church and court festivals. I have used later documents, such as nineteenth-century records of folklore, only where these appear to reflect earlier practice, as is the case with the agricultural rites and seasonal festivals of Russian villages, which had apparently changed as little over the centuries as had the work practices of peasant life.[1]

Revels and rituals: performance traditions before 1648

There can be few important social groups in medieval and early modern Europe that are as tantalisingly ill-documented as the *skomorokhi*, the professional entertainers of Old Russia. Until the end of the seventeenth century, Russia's written culture was dominated by the Orthodox Church, and the vast majority of books and manuscripts were religious in character. Since Russian Orthodoxy was also characterised by an extreme ascetic distaste for the things of the world, and most particularly for 'devilish' secular entertainments such as music and dancing, the only Russian-language sources relating to the *skomorokhi* are those in which their activities are condemned as sinful. Though references to the *skomorokhi* go back to at least the eleventh century, a large number of the documents in which they are mentioned date from the sixteenth and seventeenth centuries, a period during which anxieties about Western influence enhanced the sense of proper Orthodox belief as a necessary part of 'Russianness'. In the *Stoglav*, the proceedings of the Church Council called by Ivan IV in 1551, the entertainments of the *skomorokhi*, and other social practices seen to subvert the interests of church and state, were branded as 'Hellenic devilry'.[2]

In fact, the anger of churchmen and rulers was oddly misdirected; so far from the *skomorokh* shows being evidence of Western influence, they were examples of the indigenous practices that were later to be displaced or transformed by westernisation. By the late seventeenth century, the *skomorokhi* had disappeared from polite society; by the mid-eighteenth century, they were no more than a memory even amongst the lower strata of Russian society. Up to the mid seventeenth century, however, the *skomorokhi* were the nearest thing to a class of professional theatrical performers that might be found in Rus or Muscovy, and so it is important to piece together what evidence we have about their activities.

Contemporary sources overwhelmingly suggest that the *skomorokhi* were first and foremost musicians. A thirteenth-century ecclesiastical document speaks disapprovingly of 'whistling, bawling, and wailing'; churchmen of later generations were to condemn the 'vile tooting' of the *skomorokhi*, and the English interpreter Richard James, who visited Northern Russia in the late sixteenth century, translates 'skomoroke' as 'fidler'.[3] Accordingly, *skomorokh* is frequently rendered as 'minstrel' in English; however, this translation, with its suggestion of refined music performed by epicene young men in tights, as in a pre-Raphaelite painting, does not adequately convey the rough and coarse character of the entertainments that the *skomorokhi* offered their audiences. As one English visitor to Russia in 1557 recorded:

> In the dinner time there came in six singers, which stood in the midst of the chamber, and their faces towards the Emperour, who sang there before dinner was ended three severall times, whose songs or voices delighted our eares little or nothing.[4]

Other travellers, such as the early-sixteenth-century German visitor Petrus Petreus, made it clear that the words of the songs were as unpolished as their musical values:

> At weddings they set their dogs on great bears, and they also have many musicians in attendance, who sing numerous shameless and unchaste songs, sounding their trumpets and sackbuts, pipes and cymbals the while, and beating their kettle drums to make a strange and wonderful music, that falls on the ear as charmingly as the howling of dogs; but the Muscovites are delighted to hear this music and make merry with it, holding it the best and most charming in the world, since they have heard no other; however, any stranger can only be overcome with disgust.[5]

Besides executing the bawdy songs for which they were most famous (the word *skomoroshina*, meaning a comic song of scabrous inclination, survived in dialect use as late as the nineteenth century), the *skomorokhi* also performed as jesters and tumblers. The English traveller Giles Fletcher has recorded that such shows were an inevitable part of the evening entertainments enjoyed even by the relatively pious and mild-mannered Tsar Fyodor Ivanovich:

> After his sleep he goeth to evensong and, thence returning, for the most part recreateth himself with the empress until suppertime with jesters and dwarfs, men and women that tumble before him and sing many songs after the Russian manner.[6]

1. A *lubock* showing a Russian round dance.

Not all the songs that *skomorokhi* performed were necessarily obscene: their repertoire appears to have included paeans to rulers, and also the epic poems later known as *bylinas* or *starinas*; these latter were always chanted, rather than merely recited, and *skomorokhi* occasionally appear in them as characters.[7]

The *skomorokhi*'s suggestive lyrics were often accompanied by gesticulations and dances that rammed the suggestions home. According to a famous verbal description made by a German traveller, Adam Olearius, who visited in 1637, during performances the *skomorokhi* would flourish their bare posteriors at the audience, and represent acts of sodomitic or bestial intercourse, sometimes using small hand puppets manipulated by an operator concealed from his waist to well over his head by a sack (a form of puppetry also recorded in Central Asia).[8] Whether any of the *skomorokh* performances went beyond gesticulatory accompaniment to songs, and turned into the performance of actual plays without music, is harder to say. The customary word used in church documents for the *skomorokh* acts was *pozorische*, spectacle, a term that could signify simply a musical or acrobatic performance.[9] Speaking of the *skomorokhi*'s puppet-show, Olearius uses the German word *Posse*, glossed as the Dutch *klucht*, which could refer merely to a rough jest, though it is also possible that Olearius had in mind a short comic sketch or a rudimentary farcical playlet. Evidence is equally ambiguous for other genres. References to the fact that the *skomorokhi*'s accoutrements included 'masks and hobby-horses' may imply that they performed short comic scenes – acting out, say, comic weddings or funerals, as the similarly accoutred mummers, *ryazhenniki*, would do in Russian nineteenth-century villages.[10] But such references could also suggest no more than a costumed ritual dance, like the morris-dancing of English tradition. Those *skomorokhi* who 'led bears about' may also have put on short verbal shows, instructing their bears to perform certain human actions ('Marusya, comb your hair'), as some bear-trainers did in the nineteenth century; but their bears may equally well have been trained to do no more than prance to the skirl of the pipes.[11]

Sixteenth- and seventeenth-century accounts indicate that there was a high degree of resemblance between the professional entertainments offered by the *skomorokhi*, and those that Russians of the lower classes organised for themselves: comic songs were vital in 'amateur' entertainments too. Sigmund von Herberstein writes of Russian women in the early sixteenth century: 'They often stand and sing before their houses, clapping their hands so they resound'; a more detailed description of such activities survives in the writings of Petrus Petreus:

> They also have a most curious dance which they perform at weddings or suchlike feasts: two women will stand clutching one another, and sing songs of most impolite content. From time to time as they are singing they will leave hold one of the other, then clap their hands, and smack their hands on each other's, leaping in the air and turning towards one another, now with their faces, now with their rears, and then standing still and moving their hindmost parts as though they were grinding mustard or lentils, and the one who sings the loudest, and moves her body and hindmost parts most vigorously, will be accounted the winner, and win high praise for her efforts.[12]

It is possible that the resemblance between professional and amateur entertainments partly depended on diffusion. Whilst some of the *skomorokhi* were evidently employed as full-time entertainers in the households of princes and boyars, others led an itinerant existence for at least part of the time. Petrus Petreus, again, states that 'these jesters wander up and down, travelling the land from place to place, with their bears and their musical instruments, earning much money with their dancing, singing, wailing and playing, for the Muscovites are much delighted by their efforts and have themselves much merriment withal'.[13] According to some records, the *skomorokhi* might descend on towns and villages in large numbers, perhaps at traditional festival seasons such as Christmas, Shrovetide and Easter.[14]

Whatever the importance of the *skomorokhi* in livening up the existence of towns and villages, though, it is clear that their shows were by no means the only available form of entertainment. Other peripatetic performers included the *kaliki-perekhozhie*, the wandering cripples and blind men who, in return for a small donation of alms, would give performances of religious songs, such as 'The Mother of God's Visit to Hell', or 'The Tale of St George'.[15] There was also a strongly dramatic flavour to the appearances of the *yurodivye*, 'holy fools' or 'fools for Christ's sake', who would appear in towns and villages and castigate the local population, including local dignitaries, for their sinful ways.[16]

The face that the *yurodivye* and the *kaliki-perekhozhie* appealed to piety in order to survive gave them a very different status from the *skomorokhi*, but all these groups were alike in that they were made up of social outsiders who expected to be rewarded, in financial or material terms, for their efforts. In contrast, other activities in pre-Westernised Russia that could be described as 'theatrical' were the responsibility of people from within an urban or rural community, or else of the community as a whole. Some such activities involved an individual giving a recitation in front of an audience, much as the 'social outsiders' did. But, while the local performer might use his or her skills to earn some small windfalls in the way of gifts or favours, these skills were not fundamental to existence in the way that the talents of *skomorokhi* or *kaliki-perekhozhie*, or the wiles of *yurodivye*, were; whilst skilled individuals might have a peculiar, and often marginal, status in their own community, they did not lead peripatetic lives.[17]

Among the important performances that were given by skilled 'insiders' was the formal lament, a complicated paean of praise to a dead person which was sung in the presence of his or her relatives and friends as part of the secular rites surrounding a funeral. Lament-singers in Russia, as in other countries where similar rites have been recorded, such as Greece or Ireland, were always women of the locality: as Fletcher puts it, 'When any dieth they have ordinary women mourners that come to lament . . . and stand howling over the body after a profane and heathenish manner.'[18] Other vital genres mediating between life and death included spells and charms (*zaklinaniya, zagovory*), which to a large extent depended for their efficacy on the performance skills of the wise man or woman (*znakhar, znakharka*) who uttered them.[19] If spells and laments were elevated above ordinary life, the *skazka*, or folk-tale, a prose text narrated to entertain, rather than impress or astonish, definitely belonged to the world of its listeners; but here, too, success greatly depended upon a narrator's dramatic skills.[20]

For all the importance of performances by gifted individuals, by far the most significant place in pre-Westernised popular life seems to have been occupied by prototheatrical activities that were carried on in a collective or group form. Apart from the singsongs that were mentioned earlier, one of the most important types of such activity was the ritual game. The most elaborate of these were associated with certain seasonal festivals, such as the spring and summer festivals of *Semik* (held seven weeks after Easter) and *Kupala* (the feast of St John the Baptist on Midsummer Day). On *Semik*, women of the village would get dressed up, some in men's clothing, and ritually 'murder' a straw-stuffed dummy to signify the end of the old season; *Kupala*, a mixed-gender festival, was the occasion for the building of a huge bonfire, around which rumbustious games, involving much coarse banter, were played by large groups of villagers.[21] These ritual games were generally linked to agricultural practices, being believed to ensure crop fertility and economic success for the rest of the year; but Russian peasants and other members of the lower classes also played a large number of other games for their own sake, without any such ulterior motive. Most consisted of some form of tig, or trial of strength, accompanied by simple dialogues. One game called 'The Radish', for example, was an elaboration of the tug-o'-war principle. A group of villagers would gather in an open space: two would act the speaking parts of 'The Merchant' and 'The Old Woman', whilst the rest squatted down in a long line, each person sitting on the knees of the person behind. Then the following dialogue took place:

MERCHANT: Here, grandma, sell us a radish!

GRANDMA: Surely, your honour.

[*The Merchant gropes several of the people in the line, pretending to 'feel' the radishes.*]

MERCHANT: Here, grandma, these feel a bit squashy to me.

GRANDMA: How can you, your honour; they're all young and sweet, every one; why not pull one out and taste it?

[*The Merchant grabs hold of a 'radish' and starts pulling for all he is worth.*]

MERCHANT: Here, grandma, it doesn't seem to want to come out: must've bolted. Give me a trowel, will you, so I can dig out the root.

GRANDMA: No need to cast aspersions on my radishes, dearie. They'll slip out as easily as ice from water, just you see.

[*The Merchant manages to tear one 'radish' free: then he shakes it about, pretending to clean the dirt off. All the other radishes jump to their feet and chase him away, flailing at him with their fists.*][22]

The rough play on which these games depended was also evident in contexts less formalised by ritual. Foreign travellers record that even high-class Russians of the sixteenth and seventeenth centuries tended to a certain crudity of speech; on the streets or amongst the common people, there was no reticence whatever. Banter and sharp talk was ubiquitous, particularly as part of the rituals of buying and selling. The elaborate sales jingles that were later to be used by merchants and traders in Russian cities (see chapter 6) do not seem to have been current in the days before westernisation, but many accounts suggest that coarsely jovial exchanges of insults were frequent. Richard James records that an acquaintance of his said to a woman trader '*Dai etti*' (Give us a fuck) rather than '*Dai yaits*' (Give us some eggs), 'for which shee', understandably, 'did well revile him'.[23] Wedding processions also attracted a good deal of crude humour. James recalls a scandal created when some lads in the street called out '*Priyobonna*' (She's been fucked before) in the wake of a bridal procession; the bride's husband was only too inclined to believe the accusation.[24] According to an English contemporary of James's, after weddings there was a ritual resembling the *charivari* of Western Europe: 'the boyes in the streets cry out and make a noyce in the meanetime, with very dishonest words'.[25]

From all this different material we can understand the importance to medieval and early modern Russian society of performance in the broadest sense. However, whilst the games, entertainments and rituals that I have described could certainly be called 'prototheatrical', and whilst they do indicate that Russians before the time of Peter the Great would have been receptive to performances of drama, they do not provide firm evidence for any tradition of such performances. There is in fact only one unambiguous record of a dramatic performance in Russia before westernisation. Rather ironically, given the Russian church's hostility to the theatre, this was of a religious play, *The Burning Fiery Furnace*, which was traditionally put on during the third week of Advent.[26] As the play's name indicates, it was an adaptation of the tale in the Book of Daniel, chapter 3, which describes how the three noble youths, Hananiah, Mishael and Azariah, refuse to worship the 'golden image', supplication to which has been decreed by Nebuchadnezzar. The play's provenance and antiquity are not recorded – the earliest accounts of it date from the sixteenth century, but it quite possibly goes back to some much earlier, perhaps even Byzantine, prototype. However, relatively elaborate details of its performance survive. The 'furnace' itself, or three-sided curved box with gilded representations of flames carved upon it, would be set up in church, with tall candles beside it, the pulpit being specially dismantled for the occasion. The main actors in the drama, the 'Chaldeans', or Babylonian sorcerers, and the three youths, would make their first appearance at Saturday vespers; the play itself was performed at Mass the following day. At the end of the seventh verse of the Canon, a further series of verses paraphrasing the Book of Daniel's narration of the youths' history would be sung. Then followed the play itself, which consisted of a series of dialogues in which the Chaldeans threatened the youths, and the latter responded that they were not afraid to die:

CHALDEAN 1: My friend!
CHALDEAN 2: What?
CHALDEAN 1: Are these the children of a king?
CHALDEAN 2: They are.
CHALDEAN 1: Will they obey our king?
CHALDEAN 2: They will not.
CHALDEAN 1: Will they worship the golden image?
CHALDEAN 2: They will not.
CHALDEAN 1: Shall we cast them into the furnace?
CHALDEAN 2: Yes, and scorch 'em and burn 'em![27]

When the youths were being placed in the furnace, the officiating deacon cried, 'Praise be to God our Father! May His name be praised unto endless ages!' and the boys repeated his words. Eventually, the youths having been bound and cast into the furnace, a *deus ex machina* angel descended in a blast of thunder and lightning; his arrival disarmed the Chaldeans both literally and figuratively, and they released the youths from the furnace unharmed.

As the above description makes clear, *The Burning Fiery Furnace* was rather like the mystery plays popular in the medieval West, having a similar dependence upon spectacular stage effect and gesture, though the number of characters was more limited and the plot more concentrated. Like the medieval mystery play, too, *The Burning Fiery Furnace* appears to have been a scripted drama: as Fletcher jadedly recalls, it depended upon 'the same matter played each year without any new invention at all', a comment suggesting fidelity to a manuscript text.[28] Despite the solemn religious character of the spectacle, it appears to have touched off a genuine resonance in secular life: during the festival season, apparently, the Chaldeans would run about town in costume letting off fireworks and making 'much good sport'.[29] Other religious ceremonies which depended on particularly elaborate celebrations also often spilled over into street life. Perhaps the most important of these was the Palm Sunday procession, described here by Robert Best:

> First, they have a tree of a good bignesse, which is made fast upon two sleds, as though it were growing there, and it is hanged with apples, raisins, figs, and dates, and with many other fruits abundantly. In the midst of the same tree stand five boyes in white vestments, which sing in the tree before the procession. After this there follow certaine young men with waxe tapers in their hands, burning, and a great lanterne, that all the light should not goe out. After them folowed two with long banners, and six with round plates set upon long staves. The plates were of copper, very ful of holes and thinne. Then folowed six, carying painted images upon their shoulders; after the images follow certain priests, to the number of 100 or more, with goodly vestures . . . after them followed one half of the Emperours' noble men. Then commeth the Emperours maiestie and the Metropolitane.
>
> First, there is a horse covered with white linnen cloth down to ye ground, his eares being made long with the same cloth like to an asses ears. Upon this horse the Metropolitane sitteth sidelong like a woman; in his lappe lieth a faire booke, with a crucifix of Goldsmiths worke upon the cover, which he holdeth fast with his left hand, and in his right hand he hath a crosse of gold, with which crosse he ceaseth not to blesse the people as he rideth.[30]

Of a similar spectacularity were the royal processions on occasions such as coronations; even more ordinary days might see the tsar's servants process through the streets, taking dinner to one of his subjects who could not attend a banquet in the palace, or the progress of a nobleman and his retinue.

Whilst 'theatrical' enough, however, all these processions, whether religious or royal or both together (the Russian state before Peter the Great followed the Byzantine model, in which ecclesiastical and temporal power were at once autonomous and fused), were fundamentally different to the theatre in that they were manifestations, not of artistic skill for its own sake, but of the symbolic authority vital in a society where to make a show of power is to be at least halfway to having it. Similarly, the performances that surrounded seasonal rites, funerals, weddings and so on were always instrumental to the final purpose of the ritual, which was strictly functional (the attempt to ensure the productivity and viability of the community). And, whilst the entertainments of medieval Russia had some affinities with those of Western fairgrounds, they were more ad hoc and ephemeral even than these. Therefore, the importation of Western theatre under Tsar Aleksei Mikhailovich was to wreak profound changes in every stratum of Russian society, from the upper echelons of the aristocracy right down to townspeople and peasants, changing both the character of theatrical forms, and the general context in which they were understood.

The popular theatre after westernisation

As befitted a tsar whose epithet was 'The Most Pacific' (Tishaishii), yet who caused popular revolts to be put down with a ferocity worthy of Peter I or Ivan IV, Aleksei Mikhailovich's reign (1645–76) was rich in paradoxes. A ruler who gave the dictates and traditions of the Orthodox Church a pious prominence in his actions, Aleksei was at the same time no fundamentalist. During his reign, wide-ranging liturgical and doctrinal reforms were instituted, provoking traditionalist 'Old Believers' to a schism with the mainstream church; relying heavily on convention to legitimise his rule, Aleksei at the same time discarded the chauvinistic obscurantism of his predecessors, and encouraged contacts with Europe and European culture, thus beginning the slow westernisation of Russia, and laying the foundations for Peter I's more radical, and more notorious, rebuilding of the country.[31]

In terms of the development of the theatre, Aleksei's policies were equally contradictory. Deferring to the Orthodox Church's hostility to the impious shows of the *skomorokhi*, in 1648, the third year of his reign, Aleksei issued two decrees banning these shows, forbidding the *skomorokhi* from the practice of their profession under pain of severe penalties, and dictating the destruction of their instruments. Yet Aleksei himself was to encourage – at first hesitantly, but later with growing enthusiasm – the importation of Western theatrical forms along with new styles of painting and architecture, music and dance. In the 1640s and 1650s, the tsar's court was to be intrigued by numerous dramatic performances, and in 1660 the English merchant John Hebdon was commanded to recruit large numbers of German puppeteers to work in the Russian theatre.[32]

Whilst Aleksei's right hand put an end to 'Hellenic devilry', his left hand was encouraging this 'devilry', albeit in a new and different form. But, whatever the contradictions in his approach – which were to be seized upon by such hostile contemporary commentators as the Old Believer Archpriest Avvakum – their effects on theatre and entertainment history were coherent. Traditional Russian genres of performance art were gradually replaced by, or at any rate transformed by, imported Western genres. Late-seventeenth-century travellers – who inevitably mixed in urban and upper-class society first and foremost – make no reference to shows by the *skomorokhi*, describing instead performances by visiting foreign troupes.[33] From the 1650s until the revolution, but especially between 1700 and 1840, foreign performers and entertainers, among them mechanical-theatre operators, acrobats, puppeteers, animal-trainers, clowns and pantomime artistes, as well as 'straight' actors, were to flood into Russia, some travelling in groups, and some as individuals. From the fusion of foreign influence and native enthusiasm and talent was to grow the remarkable, varied and sophisticated tradition of theatrical entertainments that thrived in Russia between the late eighteenth and early nineteenth centuries.

The technical terms for entertainments that are given in eighteenth-century wordlists and dictionaries of the Russian language allow one to form some appreciation of the chronology according to which genres of theatrical entertainment became established in Russia. Early- to mid-eighteenth-century lexicons provide entries for rope-dancers, conjurers and puppeteers alongside their listings for such high-theatrical terms as 'playhouse', 'comedy' and 'tragedy'; only in the late eighteenth to early nineteenth centuries, however, do more specialised words such as 'marionette' (*marionetta*), 'peep-show' (*rayok*) and 'circus' put in an appearance.[34] The delay in Russifying such terms suggests that the activities they denominated became accessible to a wider audience, as distinct from the small Francophone elite, only in the last few decades of the eighteenth century. This suggestion appears to be confirmed by other evidence. The advertisements placed by foreign entertainers in Russian newspapers, and the depositions which they were forced to make about their activities to the

Russian police, indicate that individual performers of small-scale theatrical entertainments, such as mechanical theatres and marionettes, generally performed in the private houses of rich St Petersburgers and Muscovites during at least the first two-thirds of the eighteenth century.[35] By the late eighteenth century, however, according to I. G. Georgi's detailed and reliable 1794 account of St Petersburg, lower-class city-dwellers 'would invite [to taverns and dwelling-places] Italians and other such who go about the streets with portable organs and lanterns for shadow plays, or marmots, dancing dogs, trained monkeys and so on, who show their wonders for very low sums'.[36]

By the late eighteenth century, foreign entertainers had also begun to have a significant impact on the celebrations that were traditionally organised in Russia at Shrovetide and Easter, and on certain saints' days, especially those of the patron saints of Moscow monasteries. These festivities had long been associated with the erection of ice-hills and swings, amusements once enjoyed by all classes but increasingly understood to be, as the Russian Academy of Sciences Dictionary, published in the 1790s, put it, for 'the common people' alone.[37] In the vicinity of these traditional constructions, the equally traditional customs of fighting, drinking, swearing and bawdy singing had perpetuated their lowly existence. From the early years of the eighteenth century, groups of seminarians, clerks and apprentices had put on occasional performances of plays and farces in makeshift wooden theatres, or premises rearranged as theatres, during the festive seasons. This practice had been accorded a certain official recognition in 1769 when the Russian government organised a series of performances of acrobatics and *intermedii* (interludes, farces) in a wooden theatre placed on the Devichye Field, an established site for popular junketings.[38]

The available evidence does not indicate exactly when Italian, French and German clowns and entertainers began giving performances at the Shrovetide and Easter funfairs. But accounts by Russians and foreigners make it clear that such players were already well established at the fairs by 1810. Logically, therefore, they must first have appeared at fairgrounds in about the 1760s or 1770s. Indeed, there is evidence that the Italian giant Bernardo Gigli was showing at Devichye Field during a festival held there on 13 May 1765,[39] whilst Elizaveta Yankova, born in 1768, recalls that she was taken as a child of about twelve to the fairground to see the antics of the *payatsy* (clowns, from the Italian *pagliaccio*).[40] The increasing familiarity of lower-class Russians with foreign entertainments is also indicated by the playwright Vladimir Lukin's satirical account, in the preface to his *The Fancy Goods Seller* (1765), of an imaginary plebeian play-goer expecting to see 'oriental French tricks done in the Russian manner'.[41] And in the 1770s and 1780s, the performances of Signor Brambilla's harlequinade troupe in St Petersburg were accompanied by the publication of dozens of harlequinade booklets, all very accessibly priced at 10 kopecks.[42]

The origins of the Russian theatre are traceable not only to the direct dissemination by foreign entertainers of foreign material, but also to the diffusion of foreign material in Russian adaptations. This came about through several routes. The necessarily limited numbers of members of touring companies meant that help with backstage work and acting had to be sought from locals; given the dubious social status of the theatre in Russia, these locals were generally drawn from the lower classes.[43] And, as interest in the theatre began to spread outside the highest circles of Russian society, as it did in the early eighteenth century, companies began to establish themselves in temporary theatres set up in public open spaces, or in private houses. Whilst the boxes in such theatres were expensive and intended for the rich and fashionable, the stalls and especially the gallery (known by the French term *paradis*, or by the Russian equivalent *rayok*) were open to clerks, traders and even factory workers, whose boisterous responses to the spectacles they attended are widely recorded.[44] Not surprisingly, it was the *intermedii*, the farces played between the acts, or at the end of tragedies and melodramas that were most popular with the *rayok* spectators. These pieces depicted male clowns who went by the names of Gaer (probably from the French *gaillard*, or German *Geiger*) and Arlekin, and female clowns who bore such names as Lizeta and Darikin; they were usually represented as streetwise servants, who during the course of the play succeeded in abetting their mistresses in adultery, and cheating their masters both financially and sexually. Like all rough farces, including those of the commedia dell'arte and Hanswurst traditions on which they were based, the *intermedii* abounded in crude and often cruel wit, and in physical comedy: characters were regularly whacked or inundated in water, or discovered cramped up in uncomfortable and humiliating hiding places such as dower chests.[45]

Another instrument for the diffusion of a Westernised theatrical tradition amongst the Russian lower classes, though one of a very different character, was the so-called 'school play': an allegorical and didactic drama of religious and moral content, modelled on the baroque dramas that Polish

Jesuits had used as an instrument of the Counter-Reformation in the Ukraine. Introduced by Orthodox churchmen who had observed with trepidation the relentless, and successful, proselytism of their Catholic counterparts, the school play had spread from seminaries in Kiev to those in Russia itself, notably the Slavonic–Greek–Latin Academy of Moscow. The propaganda aspirations of the school play meant that the widest possible audiences were encouraged to watch it, and the elevated and scholarly character of the earliest dramas, such as Simeon Polotsky's *The Comedy of the Prodigal Son* and *Tsar Nebuchadnezzar*, written in syllabic verse, was soon displaced by more humble versions in which verse was interrupted by prose, and which had incongruous elements of low farce interspersing, or even intruding upon, the devotional scenes.[46]

If the arrival of the theatre per se made vast differences to Russian popular entertainments, so too did changes to the aspects of the general social background that I earlier classified as 'prototheatrical'. The secularisation of Russian society, begun by Peter I, reduced the significance of religious processions in Russian cities, and altered the language of royal processions, in which classical divinities, Latinate allegorical figures, and clowns from the Western theatre, now became prominent. The parade to celebrate victory over the Swedes in 1722 included a capering Harlequin; four decades later, the vastly more complicated procession organised in Moscow for Catherine II's coronation, 'The Triumph of Minerva', involved deities such as Venus and Mars, allegories such as 'Profligacy and Penury', and positive shoals of Western fools, among them Mommus, Pantaloon and Silenus. On one especially picturesque float, the 'World Upside Down' was represented, with musicians in coats turned inside out, walking backwards or mounted on oxen or donkeys, piping for the delectation of bottle-sucking old women in cradles, attended, and viciously castigated by, terrifying prepubescent nannies.[47]

All these revels provided Russians with a more sophisticated carnival vocabulary than had been available in the *skomorokh* shows; wider social changes also fostered a new appreciation of the carnival as a privileged site of riotous amusement. As Peter I and his successors, notably Catherine II, strove to introduce orderly Western city culture to Russia, a different attitude to public space also evolved. Rather than being so everyday and ubiquitous as hardly to be noticed, swearing, fighting and the singing of bawdy songs now became subversive, and hence also furtive, activities, which might be practised only at special seasons (Shrovetide, Easter and

Christmas) or in special places (parks, pleasure gardens, markets, funfairs or lower-class districts of town).[48] The effect was to reinforce the social stratification of entertainment that had begun with Aleksei's reforms. If the *skomorokhi* had offered much the same bill of fare to boyars, burgers and peasants (though often in different places), the Western and Westernised entertainers of the eighteenth and nineteenth centuries prepared their offerings to suit the consumer, and their shows reflected the fact that a taste for refined entertainment was increasingly understood as a prerequisite of seeming a refined, and therefore a socially elevated, person.[49]

In the nineteenth century, the stratification of entertainments was to become a burning issue, as the refined and socially elevated anxiously contemplated the pleasures enjoyed by 'the people', and found them strange, exotic and attractive, or more often peculiar and repellent. These persons' attempts to provide the kind of spectacles that they thought their social inferiors should watch, together with the growing commercialisation of the popular theatre as Russian cities grew larger, and their inhabitants' demands for leisure activities more varied, were to encourage many further changes in the nature of Russian theatrical entertainments. These changes will be discussed in chapter 6. Here, though, I shall give a short outline of the specific effects of early westernisation on the texts and dramatic practices of the Russian popular theatre, looking first at some plays and farces performed in the nineteenth century that appear to date back to the first half of the eighteenth century, and then at the puppet-shows and peep-shows, which appear to have reached their final form early in the nineteenth.

Serious Western plays, whether classic or contemporary, appear to have had remarkably little impact on Russian popular tradition, and the same was true of the work by Russian authors which imitated them. However, the allegorical and didactic school play orientation did leave some marks. One of the traditional plays of the nineteenth-century popular theatre, *Tsar Maksimilian and his Disobedient Son Adolf,* represents a conflict between a wicked pagan ruler and his God-fearing son, a subject close to that in such school plays as *Tsar Nebuchadnezzar, The Frightful Representation of the Second Coming,* and *The Glorious Queen of Palestine,* as well as their remote ancestor *The Burning Fiery Furnace.*[50] Saints and Roman divinities (Venus and Mars) appear in *Tsar Maksimilian,* as they had in the school play, and, as in the school play, the action was frequently interrupted by stylised fights: formulaic challenges would be followed by foot-stamping and head-tossing, and then by the noisy clashing of wooden sword on sword. However, the actual dialogue of *Tsar Maksimilian* retained few of the school play's elevated locutions, and the (rather leaden) comic scenes are much closer to those performed in mummers' shows than to the Westernised traditions of farce evident in the comic interludes of the school play, or even the *intermedii* themselves.

Another type of theatrical performance closely related to the school play was the *vertep*, a nativity drama of Ukrainian origin that also spread to some parts of Russia proper.[51] The term *vertep*, like the Polish *szópka*, referred to a Christmas crib with wooden figures, but also, by extension, to a type of popular drama played out with rod puppets in a wooden box like a crib. The canonical subject was King Herod's massacre of the innocents; to this was ordinarily appended a secular drama of a low farcical kind, whose disconnected episodes presented local jester heroes and quarrelsome married couples. The *vertep* was equally common in a form with human actors (known as the 'live vertep'); one of the characters in Gogol's 1834 story 'Viy' is a hulking seminarian who specialises in playing the female roles in the drama.[52]

If the *vertep* and *Tsar Maksimilian* were instances of popular dramas whose theatrics, if not texts, had fossilised practices of the first quarter of the eighteenth century, other popular dramas were derived from later stages in the westernisation of the Russian theatre, most particularly, from the spread of small-scale entertainments in the late nineteenth century. Amongst the most popular miniature shows of Russian fairgrounds and streets in the nineteenth century were the *Petrushka* show, a puppet farce of the *Punch and Judy* kind, and the *rayok*, a peep-show, in which spectators gazed through a prismatic lens at an image, usually a cheap print, displayed at the end of a long box so as to give the illusion of depth vision, whilst the showman recited a comic monologue describing some element of the scene, or constructed a narrative that was tangentially related to it.[53]

In both cases, the technological elements of the staging were undoubtedly of Western origin. The *Petrushka* show, like Western street puppet-shows, but unlike the puppet-shows of the *skomorokhi*, was performed by an operator who, rather than masking his or her body in a sack, stood behind a three-sided screen, sometimes with a proscenium-arch top; where the *skomorokhi* had used rod puppets, their nineteenth-century equivalents used marionettes, or more often glove puppets. The mechanics for the *rayok* (prints, lenses and perspective boxes) were also quite unambiguously of Western origin. Prints first began to appear in Russia during the seventeenth century, and imported perspective boxes, as an exotic luxury, in about the mid-eighteenth.[54] So far as their texts go, the small-scale fairground shows, like *Tsar Maksimilian* and the *vertep*, appear to be the result of a complicated fusion between the native and the foreign. Some aspects of the fairground farces are almost certainly traceable to long-established Russian tradition. The most favoured kind of joke in the shows was the 'carnival pun', a device linking innocent and everyday subjects with obscene and otherwise unmentionable ones. This universal and international tradition requires no diffusion theories to explain its presence (and Richard James's anecdote about the eggs illustrates that it was perfectly at home in Russia before westernisation).[55] Equally, the association of the fairground dramas with scabrous jokes, insults and mockery need not be explained by westernisation, since these elements, in one form or other, were undoubtedly popular parts of the *skomorokhi's* shows too. What Western influence did was to provide concrete forms of expression for mockery and punning, to supply the scenarios and characters with which mockery and punning might be associated. The *Petrushka* show, whose hero was frequently known as Polichinel, Porchinel or Polishinel in the first half of the nineteenth century, borrowed from the West the idea of an episodic drama dealing with the misadventures of a working-class boy, and also certain key characters in this drama (the doctor, the soldier, the policeman, the arrogant foreigner). The *rayok* shows appropriated from the West the idea of accompanying optical displays with humorous commentary, giving age-old comic strategies a new pseudo-scientific and topical function. And in another popular type of fairground performance, in which clowns appeared on the balconies outside roundabouts or theatres to harangue the passing crowds, traditional jokes were narrated by performers whose costumes and characters mediated between Russian and Western tradition (the tow beard of the *payats* was allied to the straw decorations of the *pagliaccio's* costume on the one hand, and the traditional masks of the Russian mumming shows on the other).

Besides modelling themselves on Italian, French and German showmen directly, Russian performers also drew extensively on other genres of entertainment that had been naturalised before the arrival of these showmen. From the *intermediya*, for example, they took certain comic characters (Gypsies, Jews), and also certain formulaic jokes (such as spiels about raffles for useless items and dowries of junk). They interlaced their performances with popular songs, such as 'I shall leave these lovely places/and go into the wilderness', that were ultimately derived from literate culture, having appeared in the *pesenniki* (printed songbooks) of the eighteenth century. The showmen also drew their material from the world around them, besprinkling the shows with local and topical references to the changing character of Russian cities. Such references were especially frequent in the *rayok* shows, which, by the early twentieth century, had begun to include satirical allusions to such phenomena as gaslighting, motor-cars, mains drainage, and even the 'decadent' movement. Topical considerations also had a negative effect, dictating the exclusion of some material. For example, the adulterous dramas in which eighteenth-century *intermedii* had specialised fell out of favour in the nineteenth; the same was the case with female trickster figures. The reason for this is that the rise in population in Russian cities during the nineteenth century led to an increasing disproportion between men and women, which did not begin to be corrected until the early twentieth century. The single young men who made up the most significant group in cities generally, and whose presence was especially evident at entertainments, saw their tastes reflected in what they watched.

Russian folklorists of the nineteenth, and even of the twentieth century, often argued that the fairground shows and popular dramas of the nineteenth century were of very ancient origin, and that they were timeless emanations of the national character. In this chapter I have demonstrated that these shows were, by contrast, neither ancient nor peculiar to Russia. The arrival of Western theatrical techniques had huge effects not only on the elite theatre, but also on the Russian popular theatre. And, far from being static or fixed for all time, the post-Western popular theatre was, as we shall see in due course, itself to prove sensitive, even vulnerable, to social change.

Notes

1. On orality in early modern culture, see Peter Burke, *Popular Culture in Early Modern Europe* (London, 1978). For accounts of medieval Russia using folklore, see A. Famintsyn, *Skomorokhi na Rusi* (St Petersburg, 1889), A. A. Belkin, *Russkie skomorokhi* (Moscow, 1975), and especially Russell Zguta, *Russian Minstrels* (Oxford, 1978).

2. See *Stoglav*, ed. D. E. Kozhanchikov (St Petersburg, 1863; reprinted Letchworth, 1971), p. 265.

3. N. I. Kostomarov, *Ocherk domashnei zhizni i nravov velikorusskogo naroda v XVI i XVII stoletiiakh* (St Petersburg, 1860), pp. 140–1; cf. Belkin, p. 171, and the

manuscript dictionary of R. James in V. A. Larin (ed.), *Russko-angliiskii slovar'-dnevnik Richarda Dzheimsa 1618–1619* (Leningrad, 1959), p. 65. M. Fasmer, *Russisches etymologisches Wörterbuch* (3 vols., Heidelberg, 1950–8) suggests *skomorokh* may be linked with the Slovenian verbs *skomucati*, 'to make unintelligible noises' and *skomudrati*, 'to whistle'.

4. Richard Best, in E. D. Morgan and C. H. Coote (eds.), *Early Voyages and Travels in Russia by Anthony Jenkinson and Other Englishmen* (2 vols., London, 1886), vol. I, p. 357.

5. Petreus in *Skazaniia inostrannykh pisatelei o Moskve, izdannye arkheograficheskoi komisseiu* (St Petersburg, 1851), vol. I, p. 313.

6. Fletcher in L. E. Berry and R. O. Crummey (eds.), *Rude and Barbarous Kingdom: Russia in the Accounts of Sixteenth-Century Travellers* (Madison, Milwaukee, 1968), p. 238.

7. Zguta, pp. 82–3, 88–9.

8. A. Olearius, *The Voyages and Travels of the Ambassadors, rendered into English by John Davies of Kidwelly* (London, 1662), p. 81.

9. For the use of *pozorishche*, see for example Stoglav, p. 266, and Aleksei Mikhailovich's first decree of 1648, quoted in Belkin, p. 176.

10. See for example 'Chelobitnaia nizhegorodskikh popov' (1636), 'Izvestnaia chelobitnaia Gavrily Malysheva' (1648), and the two Aleksei Mikhailovich decrees, in Belkin, pp. 168–80. 'Hobby-horse' (*kobylka*) appears in these documents and is also listed by James (in Larin, ed., p. 67). Mumming shows (as well as other rustic entertainments) are discussed in Elizabeth Warner, *The Russian Folk Theatre* (The Hague, 1977), pp. 3–17, and texts are given in N. I. Savushkina and A. F. Nekrylova (eds.), *Narodnyi teatr* (Moscow, 1991), pp. 23–32.

11. On the *skomorokhs* and bears, see for example T. Fenne's 1607 wordlist, which glosses *skomorokh* as men with dancing bears, in L. L. Hammerich and R. Jakobson (eds.), *Tönnies Fenne's Low German Manual of Spoken Russian, Pskov 1607* (4 vols., Copenhagen, 1961–70), vol. II, MS p. 54; Aleksei Mikhailovich's second decree (Belkin, p. 179). A number of performing bear shows appear in Savushkina and Nekrylova (eds.), *Narodnyi teatr*, pp. 403–14.

12. S. von Herberstein, *Description of Moscow and Muscovy* (1557), trans. J. B. C. Grundy (London, 1969), p. 42; Petreus in *Skazaniia*, vol. I, p. 314.

13. Petreus in *Skazaniia*, vol. I, p. 313.

14. Kostomarov, p. 140; Zguta, pp. 47–8, 59.

15. On the *kaliki-perekhozhie*, see P. Bessonov (ed.), *Kaleki-perekhozhie: sbornik stikhov i issledovanie* (Moscow, 1861).

16. On the *iurodivye*, see D. S. Likhachev, A. M. Panchenko and N. V. Ponyrko, *Smekh v drevnei Rusi* (Leningrad, 1984), pp. 81–116; A. M. Panchenko, 'Iurodstvo kak zrelishche', *Trudy otdela drevnerusskoi literatury AN SSSR*, 29 (1973), 144–53.

17. On the lives of 'insider' performers see for example G. Beloretskii, '"Skazitel" – gusliar v ural'skom krae', *Russkoe bogatstvo*, 1902: 11, 33–55; *Entsiklopedicheskii slovar' izd. Brokgauza Efrona*, ed. I. E. Andreevskii (41 vols., St Petersburg,

1890–1907), vol. xxx, pp. 161–2, under *Skaziteli*; ibid. vol. xii, pp. 620–1, under *Znakhari i znakharki*; the introduction to *Prichitaniia* (Leningrad, 1960).

18. Fletcher in Berry and Crummey (eds.), p. 235.

19. See the comments of A. K. Baiburin in L. V. Maikov, *Velikorusskie zaklinaniia* (1862; reprinted St Petersburg, 1992), p. 168.

20. On the *skazka* performers see *Entsiklopedicheskii slovar'*, vol. xxx, pp. 162–5.

21. On the agricultural seasonal festivals, see Warner, pp. 22–38.

22. I. Sakharov, *Skazaniia russkogo naroda* (first publ. 1841), (St Petersburg, 1885), pp. 213–14.

23. James in Larin (ed.), p. 177.

24. Ibid. p. 121; on popular insults, see also Hammerich and Jakobson (eds.), vol. ii, MS pp. 481–93. On pre-Petrine street life in general, see V. V. Nechaev, 'Ulichnaia zhizn' Moskvy XVI-XVII vekov', *Moskva v ee proshlom i nastoiashchem*, no. 3 (Moscow, 1910), pp. 58–79.

25. Best in Morgan and Coote (eds.), p. 357.

26. See the detailed summary in Kostomarov, pp. 150–2. Eisenstein's film *Ivan the Terrible*, part I, includes a breathtaking performance of *The Burning Fiery Furnace*.

27. Kostomarov, p. 151.

28. Fletcher in Berry and Crummey (eds.), p. 234.

29. Ibid.

30. Best in Morgan and Coote (eds.), p. 343.

31. On the reign of Aleksei Mikhailovich, see P. Dukes, *The Making of Russian Absolutism 1613–1801* (London, 1982); G. Vernadsky, *The Tsardom of Muscovy 1547–1682* (2 vols., New Haven and London, 1969); Lindsey Hughes, *Sophia, Regent of Russia 1657–1704* (New Haven, 1990), pp. 3–43.

32. Zguta, p. 119.

33. Samuel Collins's description of a Russian wedding, published in *The Present State of Russia* (London, 1671), for example, refers to improper songs sung by a choir, rather than *skomorokhi*: A. Cross (ed.), *Russia under Western Eyes, 1517–1825* (London, 1971), pp. 112–16; see also Berngard Tanner, *Opisanie puteshestviia pol'skogo posol'stva v Moskvu v 1678*, translated from Latin and ed. I. Ivankin (Moscow, 1891); Augustin von Meyerberg, *Relation d'un voyage en Moscovie* (1661; reprinted Paris, 1858); Baron de Manstein, *Memories of Russia from the Year 1727, to the Year 1744*, tr. anon., 2nd edn (London, 1773); Bergholz in P. E. Mel'gunova, N. P. Sidorov and K. V. Sivkov (eds.), *Russkii byt vo vospominaniiakh sovremennikov: XVIII vek*, part I (Moscow, 1916), pp. 108–10.

34. Lexical sources include I. I. Sreznevskii, *Materialy dlia slovaria drevnerusskogo iazyka* (3 vols., St Petersburg, 1893–1903); H. Klueting (ed.), *Das Leidener russisch-deutsch Gesprächswörterbuch von c. 1730* (Amsterdam, 1978); G. A. Poletika, *Slovar' na 6 iazykakh [...] izdannyi v pol'zu uchashchegosia russkogo iunoshestva* (St Petersburg, 1763); and contrast *Frantsuzskii podrobnii leksikon [...] s nemetskim i latinskim, prelozhennyi na rossiiskii iazyk*, 2nd edn (2 vols., St Petersburg, 1779); P.

I. Zhdanov, *Novyi slovar' angliiskii i russkii* (St Petersburg, 1784); J. Heym, *Novyi rossiisko-frantsuzskii i nemetskii slovar'* (Moscow, 1799).

35. On handbills and police records, see L. N. Starikova, 'Teatral'no-zrelishchnaia zhizn' Moskvy v seredine XVIII veka', *Pamiatniki kul'tury: novye otkrytiia. Ezhegodnik 1986* (Moscow, 1987), pp. 133–88; L. N. Starikova, *Teatral'naia zhizn' starinnoi Moskvy: epokha, byt, nravy* (Moscow, 1988); L. N. Starikova, 'Novye dokumenty o deiatel'nosti ital'ianskoi truppy v 30-e gody XVIII veka v russkom liubitel'skom teatre etogo perioda', *Pamiatniki kul'tury: novye otkrytiia. Ezhegodnik 1988* (Moscow, 1989), pp. 67–95; 'Khronika obshchestvennoi zhizni v Moskve s poloviny XVIII stoletiia' in I. Zabelin, *Opyty izucheniia russkikh drevnostei i istorii* (2 vols., Moscow, 1872–3), vol. II; M. I. Pyliaev, *Staryi Peterburg: rasskazy iz byloi zhizni stolitsy* (St Petersburg, 1889); M. Burgess, 'Fairs and entertainers in eighteenth-century Russia', *Slavonic and East European Review*, 38 (1959–60), 95–113.

36. I. G. Georgi, *Opisanie stolichnogo goroda Sankt-Peterburga i dostopamiatnostei v okrestnostiakh ego* (St Petersburg, 1794), p. 656.

37. *Slovar' Akademii Rossiiskoi* (6 vols., St Petersburg, 1789–94), vol. II, col. 230, under *Gora*; ibid. vol. III, col. 464, under *Kachel'*.

38. On performances by apprentices etc. at the fairgrounds, see the notes and introduction to *Ranniaia russkaia dramaturgiia XVII-pervaia polovina XVIII veka*, ed. A. N. Robinson et al. (5 vols., Moscow, 1972–6), vol. IV; Burgess, 'Fairs and entertainers in eighteenth-century Russia'; V. D. Kuz'mina, *Russkii demokratich-eskii teatr XVIII veka* (Moscow, 1958); on the 1769 'theatre for the people', I. Inozemtsev, 'Narodnyi teatr XVIII veka', *Istoricheskii vestnik*, 89 (1902), 555–62.

39. Zabelin, p. 407.

40. D. Blagovo, *Rasskazy babushki: iz vospominanii piati pokolenii* (Leningrad, 1989), p. 154.

41. Lukin's play appears in A. V. Kokorev (ed.), *Khrestomatiia po russkoi literature XVIII veka* (Moscow, 1965), p. 271.

42. On harlequinade booklets, see I. Inozemtsev, 'Obshchestvo ekvilibristov: kartina iz istorii razvlechenii XVIII veka', *Istoricheskii vestnik*, 84 (1901), 274–9.

43. See Liubov' Gurevich, *Istoriia russkogo teatral'nogo byta* (Moscow, 1939), chapters 2, 3, 6 and 7.

44. See Starikova, 'Teatral'no-zrelishchnaia zhizn''; O. E. Chaianova, *Teatr Maddoksa v Moskve 1776–1805* (Moscow, 1927), p. 102; M. Burgess, 'Russian public theatre audiences of the eighteenth and early nineteenth centuries', *Slavonic and East European Review*, 37 (1958–9), 160–83.

45. A selection of Russian harlequinades appears in *Ranniaia russkaia dramaturgiia*, vol. IV.

46. For Polotskii's plays, see his *Izbrannye sochineniia* (Moscow-Leningrad, 1953); other and later 'school plays' appear in *Ranniaia russkaia dramaturgiia*, vols. III and IV. On the tradition in general, see A. I. Beletskii, *Starinnyi teatr v Moskve I: Zachatki teatr v narodnom bytu i shkol'nom obikhode Rusi-Ukrainy* (Moscow, 1923).

47. M. I. Pyliaev, *Staraia Moskva: rasskazy iz byloi zhizni pervoprestol'noi stolitsy* (St Petersburg, 1891), pp. 110, 18–21.

48. On legal regulation of the Russian city, see *Slovar' iuridicheskii, ili svod rossiiskikh uzakonenii po azbuchnomu poriadku*, comp. F. Langas (Moscow, 1788), for example *bran', p'ianstvo*; the philosophy behind such legislation is stated in Catherine II, *The Grand Instructions to the Commissioners Appointed to Frame a New Code of Laws for the Russian Empire* (the Nakaz), (London, 1768), paras. 552–3.

49. On refined entertainments, see for example the comments quoted by Chaianova, pp. 107–8, and Burgess, 'Russian public theatre audiences'.

50. For *Strashnoe izobrazhenie vtorogo prishestviia*, see *Ranniaia russkaia dramaturgiia*, vol. III, pp. 88–123; for *O premudroi Iudife* and *Akt o preslavnoi palestinskikh stran tsaritse*, ibid. vol. IV, pp. 437–65, 404–36. For texts of *Tsar Maksimilian*, see Savushkina and Nekrylova (eds.), *Narodnyi teatr*, pp. 131–213. A rather different account of the play's origins appears in Warner, pp. 155–83. The classic account of staging techniques in the popular theatre is P. I. Bogatyrev, *Cheshskii kukol'nyi i russkii narodnyi teatr* (Berlin and Prague, 1923); see also his 'Stage setting, artistic space and time in the folk theatre', tr. L. M. O'Toole, *Russian Poetics in Translation*, 3 (1976), 33–8.

51. For texts of the *vertep*, see Savushkina and Nekrylova (eds.), *Narodnyi teatr*, pp. 300–16; on the techniques of the show, see especially P. Gorbenko, *Revoliutsiinii lial'kovii teatr* (Kiev, 1924). A definitive modern analysis of the *vertep*'s history remains to be written: classic studies include Nikolai Vinogradov, 'Velikorusskii vertep', *Izvestiia otdeleniia russkogo iazyka i slovesnosti Imperatorskoi Akademii Nauk*, 10: 3 (1905), 360–82, and the relevant parts of V. N. Peretts, 'Kukol'nyi teatr na Rusi', *Ezhegodnik imperatorskikh teatrov* (1894–5), Supplement, Part I, 84–185.

52. N. Gogol', 'Vii', *Polnoe sobranie sochinenii*, vol. II (Moscow, 1937), pp. 175–219.

53. On the *raek* see A. M. Konechnyi, 'Raek: narodnaia zabava', *Dekorativnoe iskusstvo*, 346 (1986), 13–14, 34–5; A. M. Konechnyi, 'Raek v sisteme peter-burgskoi narodnoi kul'tury', *Russkii fol'klor*, no. 25 (1989), 123–38; on *Petrushka* see Catriona Kelly, *Petrushka: The Russian Carnival Puppet Theatre* (Cambridge, 1990). Texts of the dramas appear in Savushkina and Nekrylova (ed.), *Narodnyi teatr*, pp. 225–316, and also in the same editors' *Fol'klornyi teatr*.

54. On the history of popular prints, see A. Sytova (ed.), *The Lubok* (Leningrad, 1984); an early reference to a perspective box appears in A. Bolotov, *Zhizn' i prikliucheniia Andreia Bolotova, opisannye samym im dlia svoikh potomkov*, vol. I (Moscow and Leningrad, 1931), pp. 468–9.

55. See note 23. For general observations on the history of carnival language in Russia, see Kelly, *Petrushka*, chapter 3.

2 The organisation of the Russian theatre 1645–1763

VICTOR BOROVSKY

In 1645, at the age of sixteen, Aleksei Mikhailovich Romanov became tsar of Russia. He had received a good education, and was guided by the culture of the royal courts of Western Europe. The Russian historian, Vasily Klyuchevsky, noted that 'foreign culture, with its wealth of experience and knowledge, began to exert an influence' on Russian society from the mid seventeenth century.[1]

In 1660 the tsar sent John Hebdon abroad with various commissions, and ordered him to bring 'from foreign lands skilled people to make a comedy'.[2] It is not known whether this order was fulfilled, but the idea of theatrical productions remained with the tsar. He ordered Johann Gregory, a protestant clergyman in the German suburb of Moscow, to organise a theatre. Gregory had lived abroad for many years; he had seen stage performances and was an educated man. He engaged assistants, painters in particular, and arranged for young men to study theatre. Russian customs of the time made it inadmissible for women to appear on stage, so all the female roles were played by men.

The first performance of the court theatre took place in 1672. *The Play of Artaxerxes* was performed in the village of Preobrazhenskoe, near Moscow, to mark the birth of Prince Peter, the future tsar, who would later be known as Peter the Great. The script of the play was thought lost, but relatively recently, in the 1950s, two copies were found, one in Russia, in the Vologda town library, and the other in France, in a library in Lyons.[3]

Based on a biblical story, the play was a topical adaptation of an English comedy published in Germany in 1620. The plot may be summarised as follows. King Artaxerxes marries the virtuous Esther, and her uncle, the wise Mardokhei, becomes close to the king. But Aman, a wily and wicked man, tries to destroy him. Mardokhei can readily be identified with the boyar, Artamon Matveev, who was the tutor of Prince Peter's mother, Tsarina Natalya Kirillovna Naryshkina. Matveev was a distinguished diplomat, the head of the Ambassadorial Office which implemented Russia's foreign policy. He was a man with Western inclinations who loved theatre and music, and was the inspiration behind Tsar Aleksei Mikhailovich's court theatre which existed from 1672 to 1676.

Only nine plays were ever staged at the court theatre. The complete texts of two of them are extant, and fragments of another three have survived, and from these it is quite obvious that the court theatre supported absolute monarchy and glorified Christianity. *The Play of Temir-Aksak*, staged at the court theatre, was an adaptation of Christopher Marlowe's play *Tamberlaine the Great*. It was performed at the time of the Russo-Turkish War, allegedly waged in defence of Christianity.

The theatre functioned for two months each year, either in October and November, or in January and February. Performances, which would start late at night and finish at four or five o'clock in the morning, were treated as very important events and were attended by the tsar and his large retinue of courtiers. As many as 150 people might take part in them, and their staging was marked by their magnificence, and by the effects. These included Boyar Matveev's own court musicians, who played on violins, flutes, clarinets and trumpets.

In 1676, Tsar Aleksei Mikhailovich died and was succeeded by his eldest son, Prince Fyodor Alekseevich. However, he was still a minor, and power was seized by boyars opposed to Matveev, who was removed from his post at the head of the Ambassadorial Office and exiled. The theatre, which owed its existence to his enthusiasm, was closed. But short-lived though it had been, it proved to be highly significant in the history of the Russian stage, and the court theatre of Aleksei Mikhailovich may be said to have paved the way for the development of Russian theatre in the time of Peter the Great who succeeded his half-brother, Fyodor, on the latter's death in 1682.

The age of Peter's reforms was a turning-point in the history of Russian culture. Tsar Peter imposed new customs and a new way of life with ruthless determination, overcoming the backwardness and inertia of Muscovy. He campaigned against the prevalent medieval ideology and religious dogma, guided by the experience and achievements of the developed countries of Western Europe. His innovations affected everything: clothing, manners, upbringing and language. Special attention was paid to education. New schools came into being, free from the traditional influence of the church. A School of Navigation was established, which trained men for the fleet, and a School of Surgery was opened in the Moscow hospital. The Zaikonospassky School in Moscow, which had served largely ecclesiastical purposes, was turned into the Slavonic–Greek–Latin Academy, where the Russian scholar, Mikhail Lomonosov, was to study in the early 1730s. In 1724 the Russian Academy of Sciences was founded. New educational establishments played an important role in the development of a national theatre.

In Peter's view, culture, which included theatre, had to have a didactic purpose and at the same time strengthen the Russian empire and glorify its ruler. He had become convinced of the power of theatre during his travels in Western Europe in 1697–8 when he had met different forms of theatrical culture. He had been to the ballet in Amsterdam and the Italian opera in Vienna; in London he had seen a performance of Nathaniel Lee's tragedy *The Rival Queens, or The Death of Alexander the Great* with Thomas Betterton in the cast. Theatrical life in late seventeenth-century England was lively, and the two months Peter spent there influenced his attitude to theatre. Mikhail Alekseev wrote: 'There is no doubt that Peter fully understood the importance of theatre in English life, and was able to appreciate its great social and educational influence.'[4] According to the memoirs of a contemporary, 'the tsar found that theatrical shows are useful in a large town'.[5]

At the start of the eighteenth century, on Peter's direct orders, a company of German actors was invited to Moscow; it consisted of nine people, including its manager, Johann Kunst, and one woman, Kunst's wife. The company arrived in the summer of 1702 and with German thoroughness spent a long time in preparation for the opening of the theatre. Twelve young Russian men were selected to be trained in it.

This was a time of important events. In October 1702 the Russian army recaptured the fortress of Noteburg from Swedish occupation. Kunst was immediately commissioned to write a play to celebrate this victory. He complained about the urgency of the order and presented his own terms, which included additional payment, but nevertheless he took on the task. Kunst composed a comedy, called *About the Fortress Grubeton, with Alexander of Macedon as the Leading Character*, in which Grubeton represented the fortress of Noteburg (formerly called Oreshok, now renamed Shlisselburg), and Alexander the Great recalled Tsar Peter. The performance of the play, on 16 December 1702 in the Lefortovo Palace on Red Square, was heavily punctuated by cannon fire and musket shot, drum rolls and marches; and there were about twenty musicians from Germany, Holland and Poland in the orchestra. Scenes of combat and councils of war alternated with farce: comic characters played vulgar tricks, making crude remarks. Peter, who attended the performance, was delighted with Kunst, and he was particularly flattered by being compared with Alexander the Great.[6]

Kunst's management of the theatre was of brief duration. He died in 1703, and was succeeded by Otto Fuerst, a goldsmith. This was Moscow's first public theatre, and it has been known since then as the Kunst–Fuerst theatre. Fuerst, in his turn, also tried to indulge the tsar's tastes, producing the comedy *Two Conquered Cities, with Julius Caesar as the Leading Character*, where the 'leading character' could not fail to recall Peter.

The theatre's repertoire, however, consisted chiefly of foreign plays reworked and adapted for a Russian audience. It was this theatre that introduced the public to Molière's works, staging among them *The Comedy of the Beaten Doctor* (a new version of *The Doctor In Spite Of Himself*) and *The Race of Hercules, with Jupiter as the Leading Character* (a new verison of *Amphitryon*). Besides these, the theatre produced Russian adaptations of comedies by Calderón de la Barca, Gryphius and others, as well as dramatisations of tales of chivalry. But the theatre did not live up to Peter's expectations, primarily because the plots of the plays tended to be beyond the comprehension of the Russian audience.

In 1706, the Kunst–Fuerst theatre ceased activity after less than four years' existence, and Otto Fuerst returned to his former profession of goldsmith. Though short-lived, the theatre had a lasting effect on the subsequent development of theatre in Russia: it had laid the foundation for the theatrical undertakings which were already starting in Russia's new capital, St Petersburg.

When the Kunst–Fuerst company's theatre on Red Square came to an end, its actors dispersed, and some of them joined the private theatre of Natalya Alekseevna, (the tsar's favourite sister), which was situated in Preobrazhenskoe, outside Moscow. Princess Natalya, who loved theatre and herself wrote plays, bought the remaining properties of the Kunst–Fuerst theatre and the playscripts. The Central State Archive of Ancient Acts still preserves the files dealing with the transfer of the costumes and scenery from Red Square to Princess Natalya Alekseevna's theatre.[7] The latter was patronised by members of the city's public, as well as by courtiers. It did not last long, however, since soon afterwards the tsar ordered the court to move to the new capital.

Natalya Alekseevna brought all her theatrical property to St Petersburg, and plays were performed in her palace on Kamenny Island, where they were free for 'all and sundry' to see. Peter himself often visited the theatre, whose repertoire included the plays which had been performed by the Kunst–Fuerst company, some plays written by the princess herself (mainly based on the Bible), and some adaptations. Boccaccio's story of Griselda, reworked as *The Comedy of Daniel, the Prophet*, was a success; there were female actresses and some highly frivolous scenes which appealed to Peter's tastes and were in keeping with the moral code he was introducing.[8] The theatre remained in existence for a total of ten years, from 1707 to 1711 outside Moscow, and from 1711 to 1716 in St Petersburg, but came to an end on Natalya's death.

Apart from the court theatre, privately owned public theatres made their appearance in the first half of the eighteenth century, not only in Moscow and St Petersburg, but in many other cities too. These were open to the general public for a low admission fee. Plays were performed in specially adapted barns, sheds and other premises. Gentlemen's houses in important towns usually had a large hall, which many owners leased out for performances. Productions were organised by merchants, students, retired army officers and even serfs. It would seem that the staging of the plays performed in these theatres was modest, according to stage directions in a number of surviving playscripts.

Two plays typical of the repertoire of these theatres were *The Comedy of Count Farson* and *The Play of Prince Peter Golden-Keys*. The former tells how Count Farson travels to Portugal to learn 'the science of warfare'. The queen of Portugal falls in love with him, and after a series of court intrigues Farson dies, the queen stabs herself, and their son succeeds to the throne. The play was published and, presumably, performed, in 1738 in Penza.[9]

The Play of Prince Peter Golden-Keys is a dramatisation of a tale of chivalry about a young prince who journeys abroad. The play sings the praises of love and fidelity and ends with the wedding of Peter and a Neapolitan princess, Magilena. This play, which is also extant and has been published, was performed in city theatres and also in Natalya Alekseevna's court theatre.[10] Obviously, young Prince Peter's travels abroad could not fail to recall Peter the Great's journeys overseas.

A specific type of eighteenth-century theatre was the so-called 'school theatre', that is, theatre under the auspices of educational establishments of all kinds, both religious and secular. School theatre came about as early as the seventeenth century, and reached a high standard in the Kiev Religious Academy. One pupil of this academy, Simeon Polotsky, court poet to

2. An illustration of Simeon Polotsky's *The Comedy of the Prodigal Son*, 1685.

Aleksei Mikhailovich and tutor to his children, was one of the pioneers of school theatre in Moscow.

In the eighteenth century the Slavonic–Greek–Latin Academy in Moscow maintained a school theatre of its own. The actors were students of the academy, and the plays they staged belonged to the genre of the medieval European morality play, which was religious and didactic. Since it was a religious institution, its repertoire consisted predominantly of religious subjects and plots: episodes from the Bible alternated with scenes of allegory and myth. However, the School of Surgery, a secular institution attached to the Moscow hospital, staged plays of a more democratic nature.

Archbishop Feofan Prokopovich, a strong supporter of Peter and a highly gifted and cultivated man of his time, made a valuable contribution to the development of school theatre. He was the author of *Vladimir* (1705), based on the historical theme of the introduction of Christianity into Russia, and one of the best plays in the school theatre's repertoire. *Vladimir* is an allegorical play and politically topical: the struggle of Prince Vladimir of Kiev against the heathen priests was intended to remind the audience of Peter the Great's struggle with the church authorities. Moreover, from the mouth of one of the characters comes a prophecy foretelling Russia's victory over Sweden. Feofan Prokopovich made use of devices from popular comedy, for example in his satiric portrayal of the heathen priests. It is known that *Vladimir* was performed at the Kiev Religious Academy.

A theory of acting for school drama was developed by a German director, Francisk Lang, in his book *A Discourse on Stage Acting* (1727). Lang proceeded from the rules of classical aesthetics, and dealt with effective poses, illustrative gestures, and melodious declamation. This book was popular in Russian theatre during the first half of the eighteenth century.

Of the many theatres that were organised by the pupils of various academic institutions, including those in the provinces (Novgorod, Kazan, Smolensk, Tver, Irkutsk and other towns), the Land Forces Cadet School Theatre played a major role in the development of Russian stagecraft. This educational establishment was founded in St Petersburg in 1731 to educate the sons of the nobility, and its pupils took part in the life of the court, performed interludes and recited poetry at court functions. They staged the tragedies composed by Aleksandr Sumarokov, and performed Voltaire's tragedy *Zaire* in the original language, to improve their French. The court cadet theatre was officially opened at the beginning of 1750, and remained in being until 1752. Sumarokov must take most of the credit for the creation of this theatre; some years later, he became (in association with Fyodor Volkov) the director of the first public state theatre in Russia.

In the middle of the eighteenth century, theatre at the royal court took on a new character. It was no longer intended purely for the diversion of the public at court, but also to hymn the power and splendour of the Russian empire. The companies appearing at court were predominantly foreign – Italian, French, German and English. These foreign companies put on performances of different types – opera, comic opera, ballet, commedia dell' arte and drama. Between 1730 and 1783, there were seventeen foreign companies at the St Petersburg court.[11] Of this number, eight were Italian, four were French, three were German, and two were British, and they included opera, ballet and drama companies, and some performing in a variety of genres.

In spite of the fact that the court performances were private, they nevertheless became famous and influenced the overall development of the theatre. An Italian company, managed by Francesco Araia, the conductor and composer of the Neapolitan school, enjoyed enormous success. It came to St Petersburg in 1735, and Araia's debut in the capital was his opera seria *The Power of Love and Hate*. This was one of the first operas performed in Russia, and it was a magnificently sumptuous spectacle. The basis of the plot is a complicated intrigue, with military and amorous encounters. Anna Ioannovna was present at the performance, and as the *St Petersburg News* wrote, 'she evinced much pleasure'.[12] Araia's company performed in the theatre of the Summer Gardens in summer, and in the Winter Palace in winter, seats being allocated free of charge 'according as to rank and title'. Later, in 1755, during the reign of Elizaveta Petrovna, Araia composed the opera *Cephalus and Procris*, with a Russian libretto by Sumarokov. It was extremely successful, and the empress paid the composer 500 roubles and a sable coat for it.[13]

Araia worked in the Russian capital for almost a quarter of a century, staging operas, ballets and commedia dell'arte. His company, which numbered almost forty people, included the actor, teacher and choreographer Antonio Rinaldi (nicknamed Fossano), who produced and performed the ballet interludes in *The Power of Love and Hate*. In 1748 Rinaldi Giovanni became head of the court ballet, and Gina Casanova, the mother of the traveller and adventurer Casanova, was an actress in the company. Productions were extravagant and magnificent – the company was granted great privileges. According to the evidence of one contemporary, the actors of Araia's company 'lived like persons of quality'.[14]

Among other foreign companies, those of the German Caroline Neuber and the French Charles Serigny deserve mention. Both performed plays by Molière, Voltaire and Regnard.

The rise of the Russian ballet school dates from the time of Empress Anna Ioannovna (1730–40), whose court was exceptionally splendid and brilliant. A French dancer, choreographer and teacher, Jean Baptiste Landé, came to Russia in the early 1730s. In 1734 he was invited to the Land Forces

Cadet School to teach dancing, and in 1738 he was accepted for court service to teach dancing to Russian pupils who were subsequently to become professional artists. This was the beginning of the first Russian ballet school which is now known as the St Petersburg Vaganova Academy of Dance.

Courtiers did not find drama enjoyable. Their attendance at theatre was compulsory, but many found this irksome and, frequently bored by it, would devise various pretexts to escape the 'obligation'. And when there were few members of the court in the theatre, the 'lower classes' were admitted. In 1751, Tsarina Elizaveta noticed that there were very few spectators in the theatre when a French comedy was being performed, and in consequence she ordered that 'members of both sexes of the distinguished merchant class should be allowed admission to the opera house when comedies, tragedies and interludes are to be performed, only upon condition that they be not offensively dressed'.[15]

The foreign companies at court most commonly staged an opera combined with a ballet, on a historical or a mythological theme, showing the achievements of the gods or the nobility, and extolling beneficent monarchs. These performances would be decked out with ornate sets and elaborate stage effects.

In the middle of the eighteenth century, the dominant aesthetic theory in the Russian theatre was that of classicism. In Western Europe, classicism and the prevailing ideology of absolute monarchy were closely associated. Exponents of classicism proclaimed reason to be the highest principle, requiring that all human passions, intentions and actions be subordinate to its laws. Classicists asserted the rationality and inviolability of the structure of the state, made personal life subservient to the interests of society, and insisted on the unquestioning fulfilment of civic duty. In drama and theatre, classicism reached its zenith in seventeenth- and eighteenth-century France. Classical aesthetics required that the dramatic genres should be strictly distinguished from one another, the two main genres being comedy and tragedy; that the three-fold unity of action, time and place should be observed; and that the characteristics of the dramatis personae should be monolithic. Classicism found its fullest expression in tragedy.

The founder of Russian classical drama, and one of the outstanding figures in eighteenth-century Russian theatre, was the author and dramatist Aleksandr Petrovich Sumarokov. His tragedies, which occupied an important place in the theatre of the time, were almost always based on two interwoven themes: politics and love. The conflict between emotion and

3. A lithograph of Aleksandr Sumarokov by P. Borelia, 1860.

duty was invariably settled in favour of duty in accordance with the tenets of classicism, whereby the hero willingly sacrificed his personal happiness for his country's good.

Sumarokov wrote nine tragedies and twelve comedies. All the former and most of the latter were staged. His first tragedy, *Khorev* (1747), is set at the time of Kievan Rus; the eponymous hero is a man of noble birth and spirit who is in love with Osnelda, the daughter of his enemy Zavlokh, the former prince of Kiev. In the tragic denouement, Osnelda is put to death and Khorev commits suicide. But the tragic situation is not brought about by the classical conflict between duty and emotion, but by the tyrannical actions of Kiy, Khorev's brother. The play was published and performed in 1750 by the pupils of the Kiev Military School. News of the extraordinary success that met the performance reached Elizaveta Petrovna, who commanded the pupils to put on a performance of *Khorev* at the palace. Many of the young pupils who acted in this play were later to become men of distinction in Russia. Nikolai Beketov, who had played Khorev, became a lieutenant-general; Pyotr Melissino, who acted Kiy, was appointed director of the Second Military School; Pyotr Svistunov, who had performed as Osnelda, became a high-ranking statesman. That night was Sumarokov's triumph. The tsarina invited him into her box and lavished praise upon him. *Khorev* became a favourite topic of conversation in St Petersburg, and it became a fashion to recite monologues from the play.

In his second tragedy, *Hamlet* (1748), Sumarokov used the characters and plot from Shakespeare's tragedy, but since he knew no English, he acquired his knowledge of the play from a French version by La Place. Sumarokov rendered Shakespeare's philosophical masterpiece as a purely political tragedy that turned on the struggle of the lawful heir to a throne against a usurper and his accomplices. Sumarokov presents the mutual love between Hamlet and Ophelia, but makes Polonius one of the murderers of Hamlet's father. Thus, the woman whom the hero loves is the daughter of his enemy – a typically classical situation. In the end, Hamlet kills the villain, Claudius; Polonius commits suicide; and the conspirators are defeated. Using a legend from ancient Danish history, Sumarokov created a political play with recognisable, topical allusions. We find here a despot's rule, a tyrant's enmity towards the people, their sympathy for the lawful heir who has been cheated of his rights, and a revolt. A shrewd spectator would find that the characters of Sumarokov's tragedy could be linked with historical personages, Anna Ioannovna and Ernst Biron, for example.

The political sensitivity of the play inevitably affected its stage life. In the 1750s *Hamlet* was successfully performed in many theatres, but afterwards it disappeared from the stage for a long time, because it coincided too closely with the actual course of events in the country. After the assassination of Peter III (1762), and Catherine II's accession to the throne, a number of unexpected and undesirable parallels became evident.

> The real, not the stage, tragedy of Prince Hamlet was taking place before the eyes of all Russian society; its hero was the heir to the throne, the future tsar, Paul I. Prince Paul Petrovich was Hamlet, Peter III the assassinated king, and Catherine II was Queen Gertrude; the murderers' accomplice, Grigory Orlov, who had taken an active part in the court revolt of 1762 and was almost the official spouse of the queen mother, was Claudius [in Sumarokov's tragedy he is not the king's brother but a courtier].[16]

Sumarokov's *Hamlet* was published in 1748, and in the same year his *Two Epistles* came out, in which he mentions the 'English tragedian and comedian', Shakespeare, thus marking perhaps the first appearance of Shakespeare in Russian culture.

Sumarokov's tragedy *Sinav and Truvor* (1750) was a great success. It is set in ancient Novgorod, where the tyrant, Sinav, and the noble hero, Truvor, were two brothers opposed to each other as rivals in love. The typical characters in Sumarokov's tragedies are kings, princes and courtiers, and the action revolves around the throne. The dramatist conforms to the rule of the classical unities of time, place and action, and devotes much space to dialogue, sometimes to the detriment of the action. Sumarokov's plays formed a considerable part of the repertoire of the contemporary theatres; *Sinav and Truvor*, for example, was performed over fifty times in St Petersburg and Moscow between 1750 and 1800.

His comedies showed the unmasking of noblemen who had breached the rules governing the behaviour expected of persons of high rank: he derided cruel, greedy and ignorant landowners; he satirised functionaries who accepted bribes. But his depiction of wily servants who gave help to young lovers was sympathetic. Sumarokov based his plays on well-established patterns, and frequently took plots for his comedies, and even characters' names, from Molière, whose work he greatly admired. Nevertheless, Sumarokov introduced into his dramatic works genuine features of Russian life and customs, and sometimes even portrayed real people.

Sumarokov's earliest comedies date from 1750, when he wrote four within a year: *Tresotinius, Monsters, An Idle Quarrel* and *Narcissus*. The first two contained a literary attack, on Vasily Trediakovsky in particular, who was satirically portrayed as Tresotinius. In *An Idle Quarrel* we meet Dyulizh, a Francophile whose every other word is French, and who proudly announces that he does not care a jot for Russian. In contrast to the impersonal and abstract language of Sumarokov's tragedies, the language of his comedies is vivid and colloquial and is specific for every character in the play. The comedies, which were all written in prose, were less influenced by the canons of classicism than his tragedies, which were all written in Alexandrines – rhyming pairs of iambic hexameters.

The satirical comedies, with their colourful and vivid reflections of real life, strongly influenced the subsequent development of Russian comedy. The image of the ignoramus, depicted by Sumarokov, was later elaborated by Denis Fonvizin in his comedy *The Minor*. Sumarokov's mockery of the Gallomania which was then sweeping through Russian society was continued in Ivan Krylov's plays. Sumarokov's comedies were highly esteemed by the nineteenth-century dramatist Aleksandr Ostrovsky.

Sumarokov's younger contemporary, Fyodor Grigorevich Volkov, a

stepson of the Yaroslavl merchant and manufacturer Polushkin, was fascinated by the theatre from an early age. At thirteen he had been sent to
Moscow to study commerce, where he stayed for eight years. In Moscow
during the 1740s he developed a strong interest in the theatre, just at the
time when Sumarokov's first tragedies were being published and attracting
public attention. Volkov, then a complete unknown, could scarcely have
imagined that he would not only soon make the acquaintance of the
famous playwright, but that the two would jointly run the Russian national
theatre in the capital.

On his return to Yaroslavl, Volkov organised a theatre for which he converted an old tannery. Besides Volkov, the company comprised his brothers
Gavrila and Grigory, a student seminarist Ivan Narykov (who became the
famous actor Ivan Dmitrevsky), a barber Yakov Shumsky, and others. In
1750 this amateur theatre became a professional town theatre selling tickets
for admittance, but its cramped premises soon proved inadequate. A fund-
raising campaign was launched, and a new building, seating one thousand
spectators, was eventually built. During the construction of this theatre,
Volkov, who was a man of many parts, was architect, painter and stage engineer; and when the new building was ready, he became the theatre's director and its leading actor.

Rumours of the Yaroslavl theatre reached Peter the Great's daughter,
Tsarina Elizaveta Petrovna, and she issued an edict on 5 January 1752 that
'Fyodor Volkov, Grigory's son (otherwise known as Polushkin) with his
brothers Gavrila and Grigory (who keep a theatre in Yaroslavl and perform
comedies) and such of their people as they may need, are to be brought to
St Petersburg.'[17] The royal edict was executed without delay. The departure of the company was fixed for 13 January, and the twenty-year-old
Fyodor Volkov had the onerous task of organising the move. A gifted artist,
he was also a highly resourceful and capable theatre manager – abilities of
crucial importance in the practical life of the theatre. Still extant is a list
drawn up by Volkov which records the number of carts, sledges, and so on,
needed for this move.

The Yaroslavl actors arrived in Tsarskoe Selo, the royal residence outside
St Petersburg where they performed Sumarokov's tragedy *Khorev* for the
tsarina. They later performed the play in St Petersburg in the premises of a
private German theatre, but by the summer of 1752 the company had been
disbanded. Some of the members returned to Yaroslavl but eleven leading
actors, including Fyodor Volkov, his brother Grigory, Ivan Dmitrevsky,

Aleksei Popov and Yakov Shumsky, were retained in St Petersburg. Some of them were enrolled in the Land Forces Cadet School, where they were taught by Sumarokov. The Yaroslavl actors' style of performing differed from that of the cadets: it was unaffected, 'natural', not circumscribed by classicist rules, unlike that taught at the Cadet School. When the Yaroslavl actors had completed their course of instruction, on 30 August 1756, the tsarina issued an edict which read:

> We have now commanded that a Russian theatre should be formed for the performance of tragedies and comedies. For this purpose Golovkin's stone house on Vasilevsky Island near the Cadets' House is to be used. And it is decreed that actors and actresses should be put under contract for the same. The actors are to be chosen from among the singers and the Yaroslavl actors who are being trained in the Land Forces Cadet School, as many as are needed, and in addition actors are to be recruited from among those not in government employment, and as many actresses as are necessary. The maintenance costs of this theatre established pursuant to this decree, are to be assessed in the sum of up to 'five thousand roubles a year, counting from the present moment ... We entrust Brigadier Aleksandr Sumarokov with the management of this theatre.[18]

This edict is momentous in the history of Russian culture. The theatre was thereby declared to be a state institution, the public purse being charged with its upkeep. However, in order to give an idea of the attitude of the Russian court to the Russian theatre, it should be added that while this theatre was assigned 5,000 roubles a year, the French theatre was receiving 20,000 roubles a year and the Italian theatre as much as 25,000.

Although the decree mentioned specifically the necessity of engaging actresses, there were initially no women in the company, and the female roles were performed by men. In 1757 the *St Petersburg News* printed a notice about the recruitment of actresses for the state company. As a result, the first actresses made their appearance in the company, among them Agrafena Musina-Pushkina, who later married Ivan Dmitrevsky, and Avdotya Mikhailova. In 1761, the classical actress Tatyana Troepolskaya, who had played previously at the University Theatre in Moscow, became a member of the company. Troepolskaya played leading roles in Sumarokov's tragedies – typically, heroic women capable of great deeds. Aleksandr Ablesimov, a young man who later became a famous playwright, was employed in the theatre to copy out the actors' parts.

In 1759, the theatre was put under the jurisdiction of the Court Department. This strengthened its financial position and improved the situation for creative work. Its repertoire included tragedies by Sumarokov, and Molière's plays and operas. Fyodor Volkov was the leading actor of the company. According to a contemporary, his acting was equally good in tragedies and comedies; he also sang Italian arias. Volkov is known to have been an actor of fiery temper, but we have scant information as to which parts he actually played. It is quite certain that in Sumarokov's plays he acted Mars in the prologue to *New Laurels*, the American in the drama-ballet *The Refuge of Virtue*, and Oskold in *Semira*. There are gounds for thinking that he also played Hamlet. Sumarokov's plays served as a whetstone for Volkov's art. In the roles of young heroes struggling against tyrants he performed with great force and conviction.

In 1761, after Sumarokov's retirement, Volkov became the director of the Russian theatre, but not for long. In 1763 in Moscow, on the occasion of the coronation of Catherine II, he produced a splendid pageant, 'The Triumph of Minerva'. Tragically, during the performance of this pageant, Volkov caught a severe cold, fell seriously ill, and within a few days was dead.

With Catherine II's coronation, Russian culture and the Russian theatre entered a new phase.

Notes

1. V. O. Kliuchevskii, *Neopublikovannye proizvedeniia* (Moscow, 1988), p. 13.
2. I. Ya. Gurliand, *Ivan Gebdon: Komissarius i rezident* (Yaroslavl', 1903), p. 49.
3. For the text of the drama and commentaries on it, see: I. M. Kudriavtseva (ed.), *Artakserksovo deistvo – pervaia p'esa russkogo teatra XVII veka* (Moscow and Leningrad, 1957).
4. M. P. Alekseev, *O sviaziakh russkogo baleta s angliiskim v kontse XVII – nachale XVIII vekov* (Uchenye zapiski Leningradskogo Gosudarstvennogo Universiteta, 1943), no. 87, pp. 123–140.
5. 'Zapiski Grafa Bassevicha', *Russkii arkhiv* (1865), p. 601.
6. See L. Starikova, *Teatral'naia zhisn' starinnoi Moskvy* (Moscow, 1988), pp. 87–90.
7. *Tsentral'nyi gosudarstvennyi arkhiv drevnikh aktov (TsGADA)*, opis' 139, papki 18, 22.
8. See I. A. Shliapkin, *Tsarevna Natal'ia Alekseevna i teatr ee vremeni* (St Petersburg, 1898).
9. See N. M. Petrovskii, *K istorii russogo teatra. Komedia o grafe Farsone* (St Petersburg, 1900).
10. See G. P. Georgevskii, 'Dve dramy petrovskogo vremeni', *Izvestiia russkogo iazyka i slovesnosti Akademii nauk, 1905*, I, pp. 255–9.

11. G. A. Mordison, *Istoriia teatral'nogo dela v SSSR. Gosudarstvennyi teatr XVIII veka (1730–1783)* (Leningrad, 1987), p. 5.

12. *Sankt Peterburgskie vedemosti,* 10 (1736).

13. P. Arapov, *Letopis' russkogo teatra* (St Petersburg, 1861), p. 47.

14. A. A. Gozenpud, *Muzykal'nyi teatr v Rossii ot istokov do Glinki* (Leningrad, 1959), p. 42.

15. *Zhurnaly Kamer-Furierskie 1751 goda,* (St Petersburg) pp. 67–8.

16. A. Bardovskii, 'Russkii Gamlet', *Vosemnadsatyi vek. Russkoe proshloe. Istoricheskii sbornik,* 4 (Petrograd, 1923), p. 142.

17. Iu. A. Dmitriev (ed.), *F. G. Volkov i russkii teatr ego vremeni* (Moscow, 1953), p. 84.

18. Ibid.

3 The emergence of the Russian theatre 1763–1800

VICTOR BOROVSKY

Catherine II ascended the throne in 1762 and died in 1796. The thirty-four years of her reign witnessed a notable expansion of the Russian empire, and great progress in the economic, political and military spheres as well as in the sciences, education and culture. Although many objective factors condition the course of a country's historical evolution, nevertheless the personal will of the head of state is of paramount importance. Two centuries have passed since her death, but the interest in Catherine II's character has continued to grow.

The famous monument to Peter the Great in St Petersburg, Falconet's Bronze Horseman (1782), bears on its pedestal the inscription *Petro Primo – Catharina Secunda* ('To Peter the First from Catherine the Second'): the tsarina wanted to establish her succession and the great historical connection with her illustrious predecessor. This assertion met with varying responses among her contemporaries. Princess Ekaterina Dashkova, the President of the Russian Academy of Sciences, considered that Catherine's reign outshone even that of Peter, but her opponents' admiration of Peter and glorification of his reign were regarded as an implicit slight on Catherine. The comparison between the two even found its way into the theatre. It can be detected in a veiled form in Denis Fonvizin's comedy, *The Minor*.

Catherine reigned in a period which experienced momentous historical upheavals, the greatest of which were the peasant wars in Russia, and the French Revolution. The Russian enlightenment, which had sprung from Peter's reforms, now reached its zenith. The ideal of an enlightened aristocracy was prevalent in Russian social thought of that time, as can be seen in the work of Nikolai Novikov, writer and publisher, and Aleksandr Radishchev, author of *Journey from St Petersburg to Moscow* (1790), both notable representatives of the Russian enlightenment movement of the late eighteenth century. The ideas of the enlightenment also found voice in the works of such prominent dramatists and critics as Fonvizin, Knyazhnin, Kapnist and Krylov.

In the last third of the eighteenth century, classicism lost its dominant position in literature and theatre, and a new school, sentimentalism, emerged. The latter is the opposite of classicism, to the extent that it calls upon the human being to be guided in his actions by natural feelings and emotions, rather than by reason or sense of duty. Sentimentalists held that human feelings were the same in all people, irrespective of any social inequality. Denying the distinction between the high and low genres in art, they endeavoured to bring art as close to life as they could. The foremost of the Russian sentimentalists, the writer and historian Nikolai Karamzin, insisted that the centre of artistic interest should be the individual life of the 'common man'. This led to two distinct approaches to theatre. For some, theatre was richly significant as a reflection of the social values and political ideology of the times. Others were more interested in aesthetics and art, and concentrated on the theatrical work itself. It is evident that these two concerns were not mutually exclusive; they had areas in common, and the one enriched the other. However, they were essentially different. The first may, conventionally, be termed 'publicistic', and the second 'aesthetic'. Plavilshchikov and Krylov were typical representatives of the first movement, whereas Karamzin was spokesman for the second.

Pyotr Alekseevich Plavilshchikov, actor, playwright and art critic, was one of the first dramatists to set out his artistic ideas in literary form. In the journal *Spectator*, published by Krylov in 1792, he wrote an article entitled 'The theatre', in which he presented his programme for the development of a stagecraft that would be purely Russian: 'A spectacle is a public entertainment which improves human morals,' he stated. The principal aim of the article was to defend the national culture. It is an accepted fact that the Russian theatre of the time was greatly influenced by Western European theatre; hence one of Plavilshchikov's objectives was to free it from foreign affectation. He was strongly opposed to the prevalence of plays in translation on the Russian stage and saw no good in presenting Molière, Beaumarchais, Schiller or Shakespeare. He believed that these plays portrayed a life that was unknown to the Russian people and consequently left the audience indifferent. He wrote, 'Why should we watch some Dido languishing with love for her Aeneas, while Iarbas rages in jealousy?' (The reference here is to Knyazhnin's *Dido*.) 'Why should we care about the implacable enmity depicted in *The Tombs of Verona*?' (Mercier's rendering of

Romeo and Juliet.) 'We would be better off learning first what has taken place in our own country.' And further on, as examples worthy of performance, Plavilshchikov mentioned the merchant Minin and Prince Pozharsky, national heroes of the seventeenth century. Despite the evident narrowness of his aesthetic views, his efforts hastened the development of a distinctive national character in the Russian theatre.

Ivan Andreevich Krylov found his vocation as a writer of fables. As a youth he had met Dmitrevsky and Plavilshchikov, who soon became his friends. For Krylov the theatre was an effective and powerful political force. He edited the journals *The Spirits' Post* (1789) and *Spectator* (1792), where he wrote about theatre's social aims, insisting that 'the theatre is a school of morals, a mirror of passions, and a court for trying errors'.[1] Like Plavilshchikov, Krylov was against the dominance of translations of frivolous plays, and he strove for a theatre which could expose public vices, and for the satirical drama, the genre he favoured. Krylov notably increased the country's appreciation of the significance of the Russian theatre.

Nikolai Mikhailovich Karamzin, a connoisseur of the theatre, represented the other approach. While Krylov and Plavilshchikov were chiefly occupied with general issues, Karamzin was interested in concrete matters: for him, a theatrical performance was a piece of art in its own right. Karamzin first set out his theoretical views in 1787 in the foreword to his translation of Shakespeare's *Julius Caesar*. He admired Shakespeare and argued with those who criticised his artistic methods. In the late eighteenth and early nineteenth centuries, Karamzin was Shakespeare's most consistent advocate in Russia. He was interested in the life of Russian, French, English and German theatre, and devoted many pages of his *Letters of a Russian Traveller* (1791–5) to drama and the stage.

Criticising classicism in the theatre as an archaic style, Karamzin based his aesthetic principles on man, his thoughts, feelings and experiences. According to him, human nature is the basis of all drama. Each man's fate demands a special, individual interpretation and analysis. Karamzin never doubted the link between the life of society and theatre, but he put art before social demands.

The Russian State Theatre, founded in 1756, gave performances mainly for the court and nobility. In addition, for the ordinary people of St Petersburg, there were 'folk theatres' (*narodnye teatry*). According to Derzhavin, the folk theatre on Brumberg Square near the River Moika performed 'all sorts of farces, and comedies by Molière in translation'. Among the latter were *The Miser* and *The Doctor In Spite of Himself.* But the state theatre and the folk theatres could not satisfy the demands of the rapidly growing capital city. In 1779, on Tsarina's Meadow, near the Summer Gardens, the impresario Karl Kniper opened a private theatre, the Free Russian Theatre.

This new company was formed from the inmates of the Foundlings' Hospital (for orphans and children of the poor). It put on stage performances of plays, and its drama teacher was a well-educated actor, Ivan Kaligraf. Twenty-eight actors and twenty-two musicians joined Kniper's theatre from the orphanage. In 1780, Dmitrevsky came to work in the Free Russian Theatre as its stage director and teacher, and in 1782 he became its director. In the same year, the theatre gave a benefit performance for Dmitrevsky of Fonvizin's *The Minor*: this was the first performance of the play and proved to be a significant artistic event. Dmitrevsky played the part of Starodum (The Old Thinker), who was the author's mouthpiece. The theatre's repertoire also included the comic operas *The Miller as Magician, Trickster and Match-maker, Misfortune Through a Coach,* and *The St Petersburg Emporium.* Dmitrevsky worked extensively with young actors, among them Anton Krutitsky, who was to become a well-known comic actor.

The theatre on Tsarina's Meadow was popular among the middle and lower classes. The wooden building itself was attractively unusual: it had no circles or galleries to break up the audience into their class divisions, but instead was constructed along the lines of an amphitheatre, and all its seats gave a good view of the stage. The people of the time likened it to the theatres of antiquity. In 1783 the Free Russian Theatre passed into state jurisdiction and treasury control, and was renamed the Maly Theatre to distinguish it from the Bolshoi Kamenny Theatre. The Maly Theatre operated until 1797, when it was pulled down at the new tsar's instruction. Paul I decided that it impeded the military parades on Tsarina's Meadow.

In the theatrical life of late-eighteenth-century Moscow, the private theatre established by Michael Maddox was an important entity. Maddox had come from England in the 1760, and, being a highly qualified mechanic, put on 'engineering' performances in St Petersburg and Moscow. We still have a description of one of his masterpieces, a clock with multiple moving figures: it was exhibited a century later at the Moscow Polytechnical Exhibition of 1872.

In 1780 Maddox had a new theatre built, called the Petrovsky Theatre, since it was situated on the corner of Petrovka Street and Petrovskaya

Square, the present location of the Bolshoi Theatre. It had 20 rows of stalls, 3 circles of boxes and galleries, and could seat 1,500. The boxes were hired annually by the rich; the stalls were occupied by the nobility, merchant class, or state officials; and the galleries were for the poorer spectators. The stage was inclined towards the auditorium and had all sorts of technical devices to create stage effects and fantastic sets. According to the testimony of contemporaries, its artistic standards were high. Among other actors, the company could boast such stars as Vasily Pomerantsev, Yakov Shusherin, Andrei Ozhogin, Pyotr Plavilshchikov and Maria Sinyavskaya.

Its repertoire was varied to include tragedies, comedies, operas and ballets. An important part of the repertoire consisted of plays by familiar European playwrights. This theatre was the first in Russia to stage Beaumarchais's *The Marriage of Figaro*. It also staged *Romeo and Juliet*, Voltaire's *Mahomet*, Lessing's *Emilia Galotti*, and Molière's *The Miser* and *The Misanthrope*. Among the Russian dramatists whose works it performed, it numbered Fonvizin, Sumarokov, Knyazhnin and Plavilshchikov. It also put on many comic operas. Sergei Glinka, a writer and pamphleteer who closely followed the work of the Petrovsky Theatre, observed that 'When authors or translators brought their works to Maddox, he invited his actors to consult together on whether the plays should be accepted or not.'[2] Maddox always discussed with the actors important professional questions, such as the casting, rehearsals and dates of first performances, which greatly enhanced the high artistic level of the theatre's work. Unfortunately, in 1805 a fire destroyed the theatre's premises.

In the late eighteenth century, the so-called serf theatres became quite numerous. They were organised by the rich nobility in their country houses or city mansions, and employed serfs as actors, musicians and artists. Most of the productions were extremely lavish, since this was one way in which the owners could parade their wealth, as well as display their cultural sophistication. The serf theatre was a part of the nobleman's household, and many of the wealthy competed with the royal court attempting to outdo it in style and elegance.

Documentation exists about the serf theatres, particularly those of the famous Sheremetyevs on their estates outside Moscow at Kuskovo and Ostankino. Count Pyotr Borisovich Sheremetyev was one of Russia's richest men, who owned extensive estates in many provinces, as well as a colossal number of serfs – almost 150,000. To put this figure in perspective, a man was considered rich if he owned 1,000. Among the army of

Sheremetyev's serfs there were whole regiments of carpenters, builders, painters and plasterers. A great connoisseur of art and music, and the owner of a superb art collection, which included major works by Rembrandt, Rubens and Van Dyck, Sheremetyev created a magnificent world at Kuskovo, with palaces and parks, marble statues, alleys of exotic trees, and French, Italian and Chinese pavilions. But pride of place belonged to the theatre, and it was the object of the utmost attention on the part of Count Pyotr and his son Nikolai.

Between 1769 and 1773, young Count Nikolai Sheremetyev studied the theatre of France, England and Switzerland. A gifted musician, he took lessons with Ivar, the best cellist of the Paris Grand Opéra, and not infrequently Nikolai acted as conductor of his own orchestra. When Nikolai returned home in 1773, his father handed him sole management of the theatre; this would mark the high point in the history of the Sheremetyevs' theatre.

Nikolai Sheremetyev never lost contact with his old music teacher in Paris, and the correspondence between him and Ivar from 1784 to 1803 still survives. Ivar also carried out numerous commissions entrusted to him by Sheremetyev in connection with his theatre. With his help, Sheremetyev received new French plays, books, periodicals, opera scores, information on materials and methods for creating special stage effects, and sketches of stage scenery, costumes and theatre sets.

Serf musicians and actors took lessons from the famous foreign composers, singers and dancers who worked in Russia, and Russian celebrities, such as Shusherin and Plavilshchikov of Maddox's theatre, were also invited to give them instruction. Some of Sheremetyev's serf actors were even sent to St Petersburg to study under Dmitrevsky. The names of the actors and the repertoire of the Sheremetyev theatre have been preserved in archives. In 1789 the company numbered 115, of whom 19 were actors, 26 were dancers (male and female), 41 were singers, 23 were technicians and there were also 6 stage hands. The company grew constantly and by 1792 it had 212 members.[3] Sheremetyev understood the theatre and theatre organisation better than any other owner of serf theatres: for a period in 1799 he served as the Director of Imperial Court Theatres.

The most distinguished actress of the Sheremetyev theatre was Praskovya Zhemchugova-Kovaleva, the daughter of a serf. While still a child she was marked out for work in theatre. She was exceptionally beautiful; she had a distinctive dramatic talent and a fine lyrical soprano voice. In her youth she occupied the leading position in the Sheremetyev theatre – in both plays and operas. Her best role was as the maiden-warrior Elyana in Grétry's opera, *Samnite Marriages*. Now Sheremetyev's mistress, Zhemchugova-Kovaleva was given her freedom at the age of thirty, and soon after, despite the gossip and disapproval of society, the count married her. Such were the paradoxes of Russian life at that time: a blacksmith's daughter became the Countess Sheremetyeva.

There were many talented artists among Sheremetyev's serfs, including the conductor Sergei Degtyaryov; the violin-maker Ivan Batov; and the painter Ivan Argunov. There is at present a museum at Ostankino which contains the work of serf artists. The Sheremetyev theatre performed some 116 works, of which 91 were operas or ballets and 25 were dramas.[4] It was mostly the high nobility who visited the theatre and they included at some time or other Catherine II, Paul I, and the last king of Poland, Stanislaw Poniatowski.

Among the serf theatres at the end of the eighteenth century, Count Aleksandr Vorontsov's holds a special place. He was a high-ranking official under Catherine II, and in the 1760s he was ambassador to England. He objected to much in Catherine's rule and, as a sign of protest, he quitted the capital for his country residence Alabukha in Tambov Province. Here in 1792, he founded a theatre which he then moved to another of his estates, Andreevskoe in Vladimir Province.[5] The theatrical season extended through the autumn and winter, and there were performances three times a week. The company consisted of serfs, but there were also free artists who were paid a salary. It counted forty-eight actors, seventeen actresses and thirty-eight musicians among its personnel. The chief difference between Vorontsov's theatre and other serf theatres was its repertoire. Unlike the vast majority of aristocratic serf theatres, which preferred elaborately grand operas or ballets, this theatre based its repertoire on plays. Ninety-three shows are known to have been performed in Vorontsov's theatre, of which seventy-two were plays. They included Fonvizin's *The Minor* and *The Brigadier*, Krylov's satire *The Jokers*, and Mikhail Verevkin's *Word for Word* – a politically risky play about Emelyan Pugachyov's peasant revolt. Of foreign plays, the most popular were Molière's *The Miser*, *The Critique of the School for Wives*, *Georges Dandin*, and *The Imaginary Invalid*, Goldoni's *Servant of Two Masters*, and Sheridan's *The School for Scandal*. The theatre went out of existence in 1805 on the death of its founder.[6]

Many eminent eighteenth-century figures maintained a serf theatre including, for example, the poet Derzhavin and Field-Marshal Suvorov, and many nineteenth-century actors were born into serfdom, most notably Mikhail Shchepkin. The serf theatre was referred to by many Russian writers, including Turgenev, Herzen, Saltykov-Shchedrin and Leskov. Herzen's story 'The Thieving Magpie' (1846) was based on a true story narrated by Shchepkin, which describes the tragic fate of an actress who fell victim to the whim of a landowner. Despite the appalling conditions in which the actors lived and worked, serf theatres made an important contribution to the evolution of the Russian theatre.

Professional theatre companies began forming in the provinces in the early eighteenth century. For the most part, they took the form of performances in ecclesiastical and secular schools, in Novgorod, Rostov, Smolensk, Tver and other towns. There were amateur performances too, but in 1775 a decree was issued 'On Establishments for Provincial Administration' which led to many theatres being erected at the initiative of local administrations. One after the other, theatres came into being in Kaluga (1776), Kharkov (1781), Tambov, Voronezh and Irkutsk (1787), Kazan (1791) and other towns. The introduction to the *Dictionary of Dramatic Art* (1797) reads: 'Everywhere one hears of theatres in the course of construction or already in existence, and actors of good standing are appearing in them.'

Even in those towns where no special theatres were built, people were eager to attend theatrical performances. For example, on 17 July 1787, on the occasion of Catherine II's passing through the town of Orel, local amateurs put on a play in the governor-general's house in her honour. They chose Favart's comedy *Suleiman II, or The Three Wives of the Sultan*, which had had a great success in Maddox's theatre in Moscow, and also the comic opera *The Fortune-Teller*. These were the first dramatic performances in Orel recorded by historians and they became the starting point of the development of theatre life there.

In some towns, public theatres arose on the foundations of serf theatres. Thus, Prince Nikolai Shakhovskoi, who used to spend the winter in Moscow and the summer on his country estate in the province of Nizhny Novgorod, organised his own serf theatre with about 100 performers, singers, musicians and actors. They played both in his Moscow mansion and in his country house near the provincial town. From 1798 Shakhovskoi lived in Nizhny Novgorod permanently, and in the same year he moved his theatre company and all its considerable property into the town. One of his town houses was rebuilt as a theatre, with 120 seats. In winter, the company played in the town, and in summer, at the Trade Fair centre located outside, where it attracted large and enthusiastic audiences. Partly because of this commercial support, but largely, still, owing to the generosity of Shakhovskoi, in 1811 a new, public theatre was built in Nizhny Novgorod which sold tickets to the public, and was able to maintain three companies, for drama, opera and ballet. The serf theatre here, as elsewhere, thus played a significant part historically in the development of professional public theatre in Russia.

The serf theatre of the landowner Pavel Esipov developed into the Kazan Town Theatre. In the remote Siberian town of Irkutsk, a town theatre was organised in 1787 by an amateur actress, Troepolskaya, who was the wife of a powerful official in the judiciary. Her theatre was named the Theatre of the Nobility, and was intended for the enjoyment of provincial officials and the local gentry. The traveller T. Sievers visited Irkutsk in 1789 and recorded his impressions: 'the theatre has made a particularly large contribution to the morals and manners of the young people. A theatre? – I hear you ask. In this distant land? – Yes, indeed. You will be even more puzzled when I tell you that all the actors are local people who had never before seen a theatre in their lives. Nevertheless, their performances are excellent.'[7]

The development of the theatres in provincial towns depended to a large extent upon the governor. Governors were supposed to promote culture in their provinces. In Tambov the first performances started when the poet Derzhavin was appointed governor. The local nobility and both amateur and professional actors, took part. The repertoire of the provincial theatres was much the same as that of the St Petersburg and Moscow theatres: tragedies by Sumarokov and Knyazhnin, comedies by Fonvizin, comic operas, and plays by Molière all figured prominently on the billboards.

The most outstanding Russian playwright of the eighteenth century was Denis Ivanovich Fonvizin. His comedy *The Minor* led the way for nine-teenth-century Russian satirical drama, and he influenced writers such as Griboedov, Gogol and Saltykov-Shchedrin. Pushkin called this play a 'monument of national satire', and Fonvizin 'a friend of freedom'. Herzen wrote that Fonvizin's laughter 'was heard long afterwards; it called forth a cohort of great comic writers; it is to their laughter through tears that our literature owes its achievements and its influence upon the Russian people'.[8] *The Minor* has remained continuously in the Russian repertoire for over two centuries. Many of the characters' names have become common nouns, while numerous lines from its text have become sayings. Its central character, Mitrofan, is familiar to every Russian from childhood.

Fonvizin was born in Moscow to a noble family of moderate means. He studied at the University Gymnasium where he first encountered theatre. In 1760 he enrolled at Moscow University. There nearly all the students loved theatre, but Fonvizin also studied Latin, German and French diligently. In 1762 he moved to St Petersburg to serve as an interpreter at the Ministry of Foreign Affairs. A year later he changed his job and went to work for an important official and man of letters, Elagin, who was a minister of Catherine II's cabinet and her close associate. Elagin was also the first director of the Imperial Theatres and held this position from 1766 to 1779. As a result of his connection with Elagin, Fonvizin was accepted into theatrical circles, where he met Dmitrevsky who became his friend for life. Fonvizin's literary and theatrical endeavours began in earnest in the 1760s. He translated Voltaire's tragedy *Alzire, or The Americans* and adapted for the Russian audience the sentimental play *Sidney* by Gresset, calling it *Korion* after the hero. He gave a very sympathetic portrayal of the servant, Andrei, who contrived the heroes' fates, and he made references to the hard lives of the serfs. The play was staged in St Petersburg in 1764.

Fonvizin's first original work was a comedy, *The Brigadier* (1769). It was put on by an amateur company at the court theatre in 1772, but it did not find its way into the professional repertoire until 1780, at the Free Theatre on Tsarina's Meadow. The play's pronounced satirical slant had delayed its presentation before a wider audience. Two groups of characters are in opposition: the ignorant, immoral and hypocritical; and the well-educated, decent and honest. The play exposes rude, ignorant landowners; the corrupt; and high-society Francophiles who indiscriminately worshipped everything emanating from France. As is true of most satires, the negative characters in *The Brigadier* are highly coloured, while the positive characters, such as Dobrolyubov (Lover of virtue) and Sofia (Wisdom) seem pallid in comparison. *The Brigadier* is clearly a classical comedy with the emphasis on the speeches, rather than the action. An important feature of the play is that the author introduced characters who resembled people with whom he was familiar and made use of real, everyday situations. Contemporary reviewers compared it to a pamphlet and noted its faithfulness to life.

It took Fonvizin a long time to write his chief work, *The Minor*. He embarked upon it in the 1760s and completed the last rewrite in 1782. The author was not merely trying to improve a play that he had long since conceived: he turned a play about the upbringing of children into a comedy about the life and mores of the nobility.

The essence of the play is the conflict between the forward-thinking noblemen Pravdin (Truthful) and Starodum (Old Thinker), and the brutal and primitive Prostakov (Simpleton) and Skotinin (Beast), whose savage behaviour, stupid ideas and low morals are born of the serf system. The comedy shows the petty tyranny and blindness of serf-owners: during the period of the enlightenment, when education and personal betterment were universally accepted values, Fonvizin portrayed Mitrofan, the uneducated noble, the minor, as one who, far from seeing his own deficiencies, was completely self-assured and confident. His most famous line, which has entered colloquial speech, is: 'I don't want to study, I want to get married.' These words are reminiscent of Peter the Great's edict that prohibited young noblemen from marrying in order to avoid studying. All the countless Mitrofans were eventually to become serf-owners, officials and officers, with catastrophic consequences for Russia, according to Fonvizin. The main positive character, Starodum, is the author's mouthpiece. He condemned serfdom: 'Oppression by enslavement of people who are like yourself is unlawful.' Starodum advocates the old rules. His father had served Peter the Great and had brought up his son 'according to those times'. Starodum had been an officer and had fought in the wars, but he was indignant about the mode of life and behaviour in the army of Catherine II. He had served at court, but realising that decent people were not wanted there, he had left for Siberia where he had made a fortune 'through his own labour and honesty'.

Starodum speaks of the 'wisest ruler who enriches the souls of his subjects'. By this he meant an ideal monarch, whose high standards would have been beyond the reach of the present occupant of the throne. These were also Fonvizin's own ideas, expressed through the stage character.

The Minor follows the classical rules of the three unities and consists of the traditional five acts; the characters are depicted according to the principles of classical rationalism. But at the same time, Fonvizin broke the strict canon by intermingling the comic and the serious, a device of sentimentalist drama. He also included his own observations on everyday life, and minor touches showing how people lived.

Even before the play's completion, Fonvizin and Dmitrevsky gave readings in private houses. It had its premiere on 24 September 1782 at the

Kniper-Dmitrevsky Free Theatre in St Petersburg. The performance was given as a benefit for Dmitrevsky, and proved to be an outstanding event in the theatrical life of the capital. The title page of the 1783 edition of the play lists all the actors in that production. The beneficiary, who was also the director, played Starodum, thus making this the central part in the play. Starodum's soliloquies, which account for a fifth of the play's text, came across in Dmitrevsky's delivery as a damning indictment of evil and social injustice. In his preparatory work on his role he consulted with his friend the author, and Fonvizin had no doubts that the first night owed its succes primarily to Dmitrevsky. Young Karamzin attended the premiere and wrote later in his memoirs that the audience was held enthralled by the 'serious' scenes involving Starodum. When in 1788, after finishing *The Minor*, Fonvizin decided to publish a magazine, he named it *The Friend of Honest People, or Starodum, a Periodical Dedicated to Truth*, but the magazine was never to come out: the police banned it.

The comic actor Yakov Shumsky, a former member of Volkov's Yaroslavl company, shared the success of the first night with the beneficiary. He played the part of Eremeevna, the nanny. Also in the cast were the young Plavilshchikov, who played Pravdin, and Sokolov, in the part of Skotinin. Now forgotten, the actor and writer Sokolov was the author of a satire called *The Judge's Birthday*, which influenced Kapnist's *Slander*. Vasily Chernikov played Mitrofan; he had made a name for himself playing young heroes in comic operas. He went on to play Eremeevna in that same play. The first to act the ignorant Mitrofan, Chernikov was an educated man with a range of talents, who could translate Italian and French, and was later the first director of the Russian opera.

In 1783 a very successful production of *The Minor* was staged at Maddox's Petrovsky Theatre. The play entered the repertoire of many professional and amateur theatres, and in 1786, when Derzhavin was governor there, it was performed in Tambov. It was also put on at Count Vorontsov's serf theatre. In the last years of his life, Fonvizin wrote a three-act comedy *The Selection of the Tutor*, about the education of the young nobility, but as a work of art, this comedy falls far short of the standard of *The Minor*, which was the best Russian dramatic work of the eighteenth century and secured Fonvizin's place in the history of Russian culture.

Yakov Borisovich Knyazhnin was a representative of the classicism of the Russian enlightenment, a follower of Sumarokov and a writer of tragedies, comedies and comic operas. In the theatre, his most successful works were comic operas, while in literature he was famous as the author of the 'revolt' tragedy, *Vadim Novgorodsky* (1789), which was never staged. Almost all his plays were based upon literary sources, which prompted Pushkin to call him 'Knyazhnin the Borrower'.

His first verse tragedy, *Dido*, derived from Vergil's *Aeneid*, was written in 1769. Academics have interpreted it in various ways: some have considered the tragedy to be a glorification of Catherine the Great; others saw in it a lesson for the tsarina and a criticism of her rule. In view of Knyazhnin's later activities, the latter view seems the more plausible. In his tragedy *Vladimir and Yaropolk* (1772), based upon Racine's *Andromaque*, Knyazhnin depicts a loss of faith in an enlightened monarch, which was open to interpretation as an appeal to save the motherland through a coup d'état. In a decree dated 1789, the year of the French Revolution, Maddox's theatre was forbidden to stage the play.[9] Nevertheless, the theatre succeeded in performing it twice.

Knyazhnin's best known comic opera, *Misfortune Through a Coach* (1779) is discussed later in the chapter. For the plot of his tragedy *Vadim Novgorodsky*, the author drew inspiration from the works of Catherine II, who used to write plays and who, in 1786, published her drama *From Ryurik's Life*, a weak attempt at a Shakespearean historical play. Its interest lay in the fact that this was the first time that Vadim Novgorodsky occurs as a theme in Russian literature. According to the old chronicles, Vadim was killed by Ryurik after the Novgorod insurrection had been suppressed. Catherine's play offers a different interpretation: she has Ryurik say that Vadim's courage can serve the state, and pardons him. Moved close to tears, Vadim kneels before Ryurik and says, 'I am your loyal subject for ever.' A critic of that time wrote, 'In her attempt to prove the historical inevitability of a monarchy in Russia, Catherine reinforced this idea by confirming the Russian people's age-long innate humility and obedience to their monarch.'[10] In Knyazhnin's tragedy, Vadim, who is the opponent of tyranny, tries to arouse in his fellow citizens hatred toward those who flouted their 'liberties and freedoms'. But after the rebellion is quelled, Vadim stabs himself. Although Knyazhnin's version resolves the political conflict in favour of the monarch, the author's sympathy evidently lies with Vadim, whose suicide is seen as a protest against triumphant autocracy.

The St Petersburg Theatre started rehearsals of the play with Plavilshchikov playing Vadim and Shusherin as Ryurik; but the author quickly decided against staging the play since it might have been too indiscreet for the times. Knyazhnin did not want an open conflict with the tsarina. The tragedy was published in 1793, but on Catherine's orders it was banned from distribution, and all copies were burnt. The full version of the tragedy issued in 1793 was published only in 1914.

The St Petersburg and Moscow theatres successfully staged Knyazhnin's satires *The Braggart* (1786) and *The Cranks* (1790). Both are renderings of French plays with Russian characters substituted. The former tells the story of a young man of noble birth who becomes a favourite at the court. The theme of favouritism, of the unexpectedly quick rise in rank, was topical in Catherine's reign, and considered risqué. Its heroes, as well as some of the situations portrayed, anticipate those of Gogol's *The Government Inspector*.

The Cranks is a comedy that ridicules the arrogance of the nobility, their atrocious upbringing and their obsession with all things French. These comedies continued on stage into the early nineteenth century: Pushkin knew them well, and he used lines from *The Braggart* as the epigraph to the first chapter of *The Captain's Daughter*.

Russian classical verse drama reaches a peak of achievement in Kapnist's *Slander* (1796). Kapnist enlarged on his own experience of a lawsuit against a local landowner to create a satirical work of much wider significance. The theme of the struggle against the machinations of court officials had been introduced into Russian theatre by Sumarokov: *Slander* expanded this theme into a picture of the absolute corruption of the whole class of court officialdom and of universal bribery. To protect the play from the censors, Kapnist dedicated it to the tsar, Paul I. In 1798 it was published as a separate work and staged in St Petersburg for the benefit of Anton Krutitsky, who played the hero, Krivosudov (Bent Judgement). The author and the beneficiary were courageous enough to disregard the rumours that flooded the capital about the play's unheard-of scurrility; nevertheless, it was banned after only four performances and the printed copies of the text were confiscated and burnt. *Slander* and *Vadim Novgorodsky* shared the same fate. Not until the nineteenth century did this play return to the stage.

This review of eighteenth-century drama would be incomplete without reference to Ivan Andreevich Krylov. He was a writer whose verse fables every Russian knows from childhood. The monument to 'Grandpa Krylov', who sits in the Summer Gardens in St Petersburg, is a favourite place for children to play. Unlike his fables, which are very well known, his theatrical works have not been so widely recognised. Critics often remark that his fables are for the most part small dramas, scenes expressed in dialogue, comedies in miniature, and essentially offshoots of his works for the theatre.

Krylov had not received any systematic education but, being a man of outstanding ability, he taught himself and became one of the most cultured persons of his time. He had a good command of the major European languages, and at the age of fifty he mastered classical Greek.

In 1783, aged fourteen, he wrote the comic verse opera *The Fortune-Teller*, made the acquaintance of Dmitrevsky and through him was introduced to the capital's theatrical circles. Three years later he wrote the comedy *A Crazy Family*, depicting a very old woman, Gorbura (Hunchback) Ivanovna, who made amorous advances to a young man. The voluptuary and her excessive passions could not fail to suggest comparisons with the tsarina. In 1786, when the play was written, Catherine the Great, then fifty-seven, was paying close attention to the twenty-eight-year-old Dmitrev-Mamonov, whom she had promoted to the rank of aide-de-camp and moved into the palace.[11] The obvious question here is how it came about that plays of this sort, with their barbed allusions, were not suppressed at the very start, but were allowed to be staged. The reason is simply that the attempt to prove the similarity between the character satirised in the play and a high-ranking individual could be as damaging for the person who drew attention to the resemblance as it was for the playwright.

Other comedies by Krylov, for example *The Writer in the Ante-Room* and *The Mischief-Makers*, contain features of caricature and parody, exaggeration and hyperbole. They all satirise contemporary behaviour. In 1800 Krylov wrote the 'buffoon-tragedy' *Podshchipa* (*Trumf*), a savage attack on the military regime at the court of Paul I. The play was intended for an amateur theatre, and it was staged not far from Kiev in the home theatre of Prince Sergei Golitsyn, whom Krylov was serving at that time, but it was not published abroad until 1859. Krylov's chief comedies, *The Fashion Shop* and *A Lesson for Daughters*, were composed at the beginning of the nineteenth century.

In the 1770s a new and popular genre appeared in the Russian theatre: comic opera. It was a combination of dramatic performance and music, accompanying arias, duets, a chorus and dances. Comic opera was essentially different from the serious opera already well known to Russian audiences. In opera, the composer of the music is the author, while the librettist is of secondary importance, whereas in eighteenth-century comic opera, the playwrights were the authors, and the actors were dramatic actors who could also dance and sing. Comic opera was popular with Russian audiences for several reasons: its plots were based on contemporary life depicting family relationships and on love stories with happy endings; its characters were ordinary people – peasants, merchants, the middle classes and petty officialdom; it contained many folk dances and songs, and the language of its librettos was lively and accessible. In many comic operas peasants received a sympathetic portrayal, and in view of the fact that during 1773 to 1775 Russia was experiencing a peasant uprising, the social significance of such plays is evident.

The first comic opera known to us is *Anyuta* (1772) by Mikhail Popov: the name of the composer of its music is unknown, but some sources suggest it was written by Vasily Pashkevich. Essentially the plot is a love story. Miron, a peasant, wants his daughter Anyuta to marry Filat, a farmhand, but Anyuta is in love with a young landowner, Viktor, who returns her love. It turns out in the end that Anyuta is also of noble birth and that there are therefore no obstacles to her marriage to Viktor, which duly takes place. The young landowner gives thirty roubles to Filat by way of recompense. This simple plot contains serious social themes. The peasants Miron and Filat are hostile towards landowners; in the course of the action Filat and Viktor quarrel and abuse each other. Filat answers Viktor's threats with proper dignity: 'Bear in mind that peasants can also defend themselves, just like the nobles.' Popov's *Anyuta* set the way for a series of operas based on folk life, the most popular being Nikolai Nikolev's *Rozana and Lyubim* (1776), Aleksandr Ablesimov's *The Miller as Magician, Trickster and Matchmaker* (1779), Mikhail Matinsky's *The St Petersburg Emporium* (1779) and Knyazhnin's *Misfortune Through a Coach*.

The action in *Rozana and Lyubim* is set not far from Moscow. The peasant, Rozana, and Lyubim, a fisherman, love each other and want to marry, but the landowner, with the aid of his serfs, abducts Rozana, intending to make her his mistress. Rozana's father, the old soldier Izlet, Lyubim and others break into the landowner's villa but a violent confrontation is avoided. The landowner is ashamed of his actions: he repents, asks forgiveness of the peasants, and wishes Rozana and Lyubim happiness. Nikolev gave the play a happy ending in order to appease the censors. Izlet is an interesting character because, although he is an old soldier, he does not submit to the will of the landowner, but is ready to go before the tsarina to appeal for her protection. The image of the noble-minded father was always well-received on the Russain stage, as witness the success of Russian translations of two classical plays: *Eugenie* by Beaumarchais (which preceded *Rozana and Lyubim*) and *Emilia Galotti* by Lessing, which followed. The Moscow composer and conductor Ivan (also known as Iosif) Kertselli wrote the music for *Rozana and Lyubim*, and the score is still extant. Analysis shows that the composer softened the dramatic force of the play by filling his music with sentimental, lyrical and harmonious melodies. *Rozana and Lyubim* was staged both in St Petersburg and Moscow, but it enjoyed particular success in Moscow where it was performed until 1800.

Another comic 'peasant' opera which was very popular was Ablesimov's *The Miller as Magician, Trickster and Matchmaker*. The play's main character is a cunning and guileful miller, Faddei, whom the village believes to be a sorcerer, and who helps loving couples to get the girl's parents' permission for her marriage. The music by Mikhail Sokolovsky, which incorporated Russian folk songs and popular melodies of the time, contributed to its long-lasting and great success in St Petersburg and Moscow. The miller was played by such famous comic actors as Ozhogin in Moscow and Krutitsky in St Petersburg. One contemporary critic wrote: 'It would be impossible to represent the miller more naturally than does Mr Krutitsky. His accent, mannerisms, jokes, and dances to the accompaniment of his own folk singing, indeed everything down to the minutest detail, are typical of our Russian millers.'[12] There were stories that during the performances admiring spectators threw purses of money on to the stage for Krutitsky as a mark of their appreciation of his performance as the miller.

Matinsky, the author of *The St Petersburg Emporium*, wrote in his foreword to its second edition (1792) that the quality of his comic opera was 'close to the miller Faddei'. The affinity between the two works is evident primarily in the portrayal of everyday life, with a specifically national colouring. In Matinsky's play, the ritual of the wedding, the paying of respect to the bride and other songs are performed according to very detailed and ethnographically precise stage directions. The audience admired the picturesque and boisterous presentation of a folk festival. The music by Pashkevich was 'a serious step forward in the development of realist art . . . The text and the music are in perfect accord.'[13] *The St Petersburg Emporium* is noteworthy not only for its vivid and lyrical episodes: it has also a strongly satirical tendency, with such characters as the greedy knave, the merchant Skvalygin (Huckster), and the swindler and bribetaker, the official Kryuchkodei (Pettifogger), symbolic names which follow the conventions of classicism. The swindlers are exposed and plead guilty; in the comic opera tradition, the play ends happily.

Knyazhnin's *Misfortune Through a Coach* was also performed to the music of Pashkevich. The plot is very simple: Firyulin, a landowner who is obsessed with French fashions, intends to sell his serfs into the army to raise money to buy a coach from Paris. Among them is Lukyan, a young man and Anyuta's fiancé. Luckily he escapes the fate of being sold, and the lovers marry. But as the landowner remarks, 'I still own many men.' The play exposes the petty wilfulness of the landowner and ridicules the widespread passion for French possessions and extravagance. In his music the composer not only followed Knyazhnin's text and reinforced it, but he sometimes invited a different interpretation. For example, according to the text, Lukyan and Anyuta beg the landowner to have mercy on them, but the accompanying music has a tone of indignation and protest. *Misfortune Through a Coach* was first staged in the Kniper-Dmitrevsky theatre on Tsarina's Meadow at the end of 1779. Subsequently it was frequently performed in St Petersburg and Moscow.

In summary, a few conclusions can be made about comic operas. The comic opera depicted the ways and manners of the Russian peasants, gentry, petty clerks and officials, and was thus able to arouse the interests of a wide audience. Nevertheless, of these social groupings, the most important was the peasants. At a time when the peasant problem was becoming increasingly acute in Russia, any sort of discussion about the position of the serfs, who were completely without rights, was in keeping with the social climate and the progressive ideas of the period. An interest in the national culture and the habits and manners of the people stimulated a corresponding interest in the collection and study of folklore, folk songs and folk rituals, all of which were fully reflected in the music. These elements, taken together, furthered the democratic tendencies manifest in the theatre in Russia at this time.

The second half of the eighteenth century witnessed the rise of Russian professional acting skill. An outstanding actor of this time, Ivan Afanasevich Dmitrevsky, was one of the founders of the national theatre: he was also a stage director, teacher, translator and theatre historian. He translated plays from the French and German, many of which were staged. A man of broad education and general knowledge, Dmitrevsky was elected a member of the Russian Academy in 1802. His was a unique example in the history of Russian culture of an actor becoming an academician.

Dmitrevsky was well acquainted with the theatre of Western Europe, and in 1765 he was sent to Paris and London to study the art of acting in those countries. He was abroad for more than a year, attending performances at the Comédie Française and watching the acting of Lekain, Clairon and Dumesnil. Together with Lekain he went to London to meet David Garrick and held discussions with him.[14] In 1767, a year after his return, he was again sent to Paris, this time to invite Lekain and Clairon to St Petersburg with the French court company. Although both agreed to come, in the end neither actually did. Dmitrevsky's trips abroad had a perceptible effect on his aesthetic views and his acting style. From his youth he had followed the tenets of classicism. The Comédie Française represented high classicism, but the general atmosphere of French theatrical life and culture had shifted away from a static and declamatory style towards a more natural and human one. 'Naturalness' and 'simplicity' could be noticed in Dmitrevsky's acting after his return from his study tours abroad.

In 1768 in Leipzig, the magazine *New Library of Belles Lettres and the Liberal Arts* published an article by an unknown Russian traveller, entitled '*Report by a Russian author with a brief account of the Russian theatre*'. The article is a biographical dictionary of forty-two eighteenth-century Russian writers, including twenty-four playwrights and translators of plays. In 1771 this article was translated into French and published in Italy; this item is now a bibliographical rarity. Its authorship has been intensively discussed by researchers into the Russian theatre, and many candidates have been proposed as the author; but not long ago incontestable proof was produced that its author was Dmitrevsky.[15]

Dmitrevsky had links with many distinguished writers: he worked with Sumarokov and had close friendships with Knyazhnin, Krylov and Fonvizin. A talented teacher of dramatic arts, Dmitrevsky constantly helped his stage associates to perfect their acting techniques, and in 1784 he was officially appointed a teacher at the St Petersburg Theatrical School. In 1787, after thirty-five years' service, he retired from office but continued working. According to his own testimony, he took part in sixty-two performances between 1791 and 1799, excluding benefits for the directorate. In 1791 he was appointed the 'chief director for all sections of theatre', with responsibility for supervising all Russian performances. At the end of his life, Dmitrevsky was fully justified in writing: 'I have been teacher, mentor and inspector to the Russian company for thirty-eight years ... There has not been, nor is there, an actor or actress who has not had the benefit of my

4. An engraving of Fyodor Volkov by P. Borelia, 1860.

teaching and instruction. In the years when I was in charge, not a single play appeared on the stage, but I had made some contribution to it in the form of advice or comment.'[16]

Dmitrevsky's stage career spanned more than sixty years, his first performances being in 1750 when, aged seventeen, he acted in Volkov's Yaroslavl theatre, and his last in 1812, when long retired from the stage, he returned to take part in the patriotic play *All to Arms* by Stepan Viskovaty, to the general delight of the St Petersburg audience. In Vsevolod Vsevolozhsky-Gerngross's list of the roles which Dmitrevsky was known to have played,[17] the most prominent are Khorev, the eponymous hero of Sumarokov's play; Sinav, from *Sinav and Truvor*, and Dmitry in *Dmitry the Impostor* by the same author; Iarbas in Knyazhnin's *Dido*, the Misanthrope in Molière's play; Dobroserdov in Lukin's *The Rake Reformed by Love*; Clarendon in *Eugenie* by Beaumarchais; the hero in Saurin's play *Beverley*, Starodum in *The Minor*; and Sir Peter Teazle in *The School for Scandal* by Sheridan. He was successful in tragedies and comedies alike. At a time when actors were strictly divided into one genre or the other, Dmitrevsky was beyond such limitations. In the performance of tragedies, he changed the convention of chanting declamations, typical of the classical style, to a natural and simple delivery. *Beverley*, a tragedy taken from the life of the lower middle classes, was translated by Dmitrevsky himself. In 1772 he played the part of Beverley, whose suicide was a protest against the injustice of life. His performance produced a tremendous response. Its overwhelming emotional impact upon the audience was described by Radishchev.

When acting in comedies, Dmitrevsky again displayed brilliant technical skill, eloquence and the ability to create a role. His young contemporary, the art critic and memoirist Stepan Zhikharev, appraised his role in the Russian theatre as follows: 'We owe it to him, and to him alone, that the Russian stage has acquired a noble demeanour . . . He is the first to set the standard of how a true artist should behave and to show how an actor may be respected for his great knowledge, impeccable manners and profound understanding of his responsibilities.'[18]

Yakov Danilovich Shumsky began his professional acting career with Dmitrevsky in Yaroslavl. He came to St Petersburg in Volkov's company, and was admitted to the court theatre with the permanent role of the 'comic servant'. The image of the witty and clever servant, who treats his master with ironic respect, but who assists him in his romantic and financial affairs, has a long-standing tradition in European comedy. Shumsky added to this image features characteristic of Russian serfdom. His comic talent evolved from traditional folk buffoonery. In the comedy *Henry and Pernilla* by the Danish playwright Ludvig Holberg, Shumsky played the part of a roguish servant who presents himself as a fashionable member of high society. Playing the servant in Regnard's *The Gambler*, he humorously commentated on the actions of his young master, who was played by Dmitrevsky. This duet was a memorable occasion on the Russian stage. Vladimir Lukin greatly admired Shumsky's performance as Vasily. The innovative element of Shumsky's characterisation was that he played a Russian serf as a positive hero.

Shumsky also performed in female roles, mostly comical old women. In the first presentation of *The Minor* (1782) he enjoyed a great success as the serf nanny, Eremeevna, a part which Fonvizin, who held Shumsky's acting in high regard, personally insisted that he should play.

Dmitrevsky and Shumsky, each in his own way, strove to overcome the constraints of classicism. The former tended towards the naturalistic in his acting, while the latter turned to folk traditions for his comic performances.

Nonetheless, both of them kept within the classical framework. This shift in the principles of play-acting was first observed in the work of the Moscow actor Vasily Petrovich Pomerantsev. His acting was positively appraised by Karamzin and many other writers. Karamzin's support had aesthetic grounds, in that Pomerantsev was the first Russian actor to embody sentimentalism in his work in the theatre.

Pomerantsev's artistic career began when classicism was at its height, but even so he never managed to conform to its rules. He could not subordinate his art to reason; he did not chant his lines, nor did he assume statuesque poses. He was uncomfortable in classical tragedies; his talent flourished in sentimental dramas drawn from the life of the lower middle classes, with free gestures and uninhibited expression of emotions. Among Pomerantsev's best parts was that of Harley, from *Eugenie*, in which he played an impoverished noble whose daughter is deceived by a high-society ne'er-do-well. The scene where the old man bares his chest covered with war scars and demands justice from the king is instinct with great dramatic force. Pomerantsev played another type of 'noble father' in Lessing's tragedy *Emilia Galotti*. The image of Odorado killing his daughter to save her from shame met with delighted approval by Karamzin: 'What grandeur and what valour are revealed in his actions and in the movements of his body when he appears on stage! His ordinary talk is as full of high art as are his ardent speeches. Could an actor be found who could surpass Pomerantsev in the play of his eyes, or in the fleeting changes of his face and voice?'[19]

In this connection, Dmitrevsky's skill as a teacher should be given its due: he worked much with Pomerantsev without compelling him to adopt the techniques of classicism which were alien to his nature: rather he encouraged an emotional style of acting that was congenial to his talent. In the early nineteenth century, Pomerantsev took part in sentimental plays by his friend Nikolai Ilin. Theatre critics of later periods saw him as a precursor to Pavel Mochalov.

The development of theatre in Russia was much assisted by a multi-volume series devoted to the theatre, *The Russian Theatre, or the Complete Collection of all Russian Theatrical Compositions*. It came out in St Petersburg in parts during 1786–91 and 1793–4, and was published by the Russian Academy of Sciences and edited by its president, Ekaterina Dashkova. The complete work, amounting to 43 volumes, covered 175 plays in different genres and did much to promote the development of theatre in Russia.

In 1796 the death of Catherine II ended an epoch of intensive development in Russia; an epoch of enlightenment, of science and art, and of serfdom. Her son, Paul I, succeeded her and after he was enthroned, he introduced strict regulations into every sphere of Russian life – 'the severity of rules', as Pushkin wrote. Firm prescriptions were issued concerning everything from what words might be uttered, and at what time dinner should be eaten, to which clothes should be worn and what dances danced. They extended to the theatre. During the thirty-four years of Catherine II's reign the Directorate of Imperial Theatres received in all 340 instructions (an average of 10 annually), but none of these interfered directly with the theatre's creative work. During the four years of Paul's rule, 234 instructions were promulgated, which was an annual average of almost 60. Some of these did directly affect the staging of plays and other professional functions of the theatre.[20]

The theatres were closed for ten months in mourning for Catherine's death, and they resumed only in the autumn of 1797. In particular, performances recommenced in the town of Gatchina, near St Petersburg, at the tsar's residence. 'The Tsar Paul was fond of the theatre, but he required that performances should not be long, especially when he attended them. The plays to be presented at Gatchina were selected by the ruler himself; five-act comedies, such as The School for Scandal and A Word of Honour, were cut down to an hour and a half.'[21] In 1800, Paul ordered performances in the public theatres to start at 5 p.m. and finish before 8 p.m. A special edict prescribed that everywhere lights should be extinguished at ten o'clock. People were employed for the express purpose of walking down streets and crying out, 'Put out the lights, lock the doors and go to bed!' People were to sleep and to rise early, and punishment awaited the law-breakers. Strict discipline was to be observed in the theatre, and two non-commissioned officers were to be constantly on guard both in front of the stage and behind the scenes. All actors and musicians were ordered to wear uniforms.

During the reign of Paul I, the plays of the German playwright August Kotzebue, who was then working in Russia, appeared, and they became immensely popular. In 1797, after the period of mourning, the Gatchina court theatre premiered Kotzebue's melodrama Misanthropy and Repentance in St Petersburg, where it was highly successful. The tsar sat in the first row of the stalls, immediately in front of the orchestra.

The plot of this play, which enjoyed a great vogue on the Russian stage, is as follows: the wife of Baron Meinau deserts her husband for one of his friends; Meinau then becomes a misanthrope and a recluse, but does good deeds anonymously. His wife subsequently repents and, after a series of complex peripeteias, the married couple reunite. Aside from its tense plot, the play has emotional episodes, moments of suspense, and unexpected turns. The central parts were played by Aleksei Yakovlev (Baron Meinau) and Aleksandra Karatygina-Perlova (Eilalia). Karatygina, the mother of the nineteenth-century actors Vasily and Pyotr Karatygin, had been Dmitrevsky's pupil; she was the ideal actress for plays that 'abounded in sentiment'. Years later, the role of the baron became one of Mochalov's most famous roles.

Classical plays were still being performed at this time, as, for example, Sumarokov's tragedy *Dmitry the Impostor*, which was popular both in Moscow and in St Petersburg. But the tastes of the audience were changing. Chanting declamation was giving way to everyday colloquial speech. Instead of the gods, tsars and heroes of classical tragedies, the demand was for plays about common people. The heroic fervour of classicism was replaced by a concern for ordinary individuals and for their inner world. This shift of social interest became apparent by the end of the eighteenth century and it was evident that sentimental drama was widely accepted.

The period of sentimentalism in Russia, short-lived though it was, served as an important link in the development of the Russian theatre. Sentimental drama, centred on the idea of a universal human nature, helped to undermine the old-fashioned and obsolete canons of classicism and was a forerunner of the new aesthetics. It was soon followed in its turn by a sharply defined artistic style which also became widely accepted in the Russian theatre – romanticism.

Russian theatre was traditionally very responsive to important historical events: thus, the Russo-French wars of the nineteenth century inspired several plays. The historical context was not directly described but was hinted at by all sorts of allusions and metaphors. Thus, when in 1806 Vladislav Ozerov wrote the tragedy *Dimitry Donskoi*, he was not thinking about the hero of the Battle of Kulikovo between the Russians and Tatars. Readers and spectators were expected to substitute Alexander I for Dimitry and Napoleon for Mamai. The analogies were regarded as self-evident. The staging of a play which expressed the patriotic feelings of the Russian nobility whose self-esteem had been profoundly shaken by Russia's defeat at Austerlitz turned out to be a triumph. Zhikharev has left a detailed account of the performance, presented on 15 January, 1807 in St Petersburg: 'What a fine tragedy *Dimitry Donskoi* is, and what a Dimitry Yakovlev makes! The impact upon the audience is inconceivable and unbelievable. At the words "The time has come to pay the enemy his due!" the audience burst into such applause, foot-stamping and shouts of "Bravo!" etc. that Yakovlev had to break off. The storm lasted for a good five minutes before abating, but hardly had Dimitry (replying to Count Belozersky's attempts to persuade him to agree to a peace with Mamai) pronounced "Ah! Better is death in battle, than a dishonourable peace", than the pandemonium broke out again, with increased vigour if anything.'[22]

During the Napoleonic Wars, the numerous plays which ridiculed the aping of French customs were even more successful than hitherto. 1807 also marked the appearance of Krylov's comedy *A Lesson for Daughters*, a play imbued with deep anxiety for the fate of the national Russian culture. The theme of love for the motherland, its language and its customs are the play's leitmotif.

The early nineteenth century was a period when many representatives of the intellectual élite from high society worked for the theatre. One of the brightest figures was Prince Aleksandr Shakhovskoi, an outstanding dramatist and a member of the Russian Academy. Pushkin referred to him in *Eugene Onegin*, in his description of a Russian theatre at the start of the nineteenth century:

> Where Shakhovskoi's caustic pen
> Brought forth a swarm of comic plays.

Shakhovskoi's comedies constituted a significant proportion of the repertory of the Moscow and St Petersburg theatres from 1810 to the 1820s. His comedy *The New Sterne* (1805) was a successful parody of sentimentalism as a trend in art. Shakhovskoi founded vaudeville in the Russian theatre and embedded patriotic sentiments in this genre – for example, in *The Cossack Poet* (1812), *Peasants, or the Meeting of the Uninvited* (1814). *A Lesson for Coquettes, or the Lipetsk Waters*, staged in 1815, gave a picture of the society of his time, and many of his plays contained allusions to his contemporaries. He wrote one hundred dramas in all, including adaptations of Molière, Shakespeare and Scott; and the language of his comedies – piquant, witty, colloquial and studded with aphorisms – anticipated the language of

Griboedov's comedy *Woe from Wit*. Shakhovskoi had a thorough knowledge of the theatre; he worked as a stage director and did much to create a harmonious actors' ensemble. 1825 saw the issue of the 'Resolutions and Rules for the Internal Administration of the Imperial Theatres Directorate', which Shakhovskoi had elaborated. Among other innovations, he introduced the word '*rezhisser*' – stage director – together with a description of his duties. Shakhovskoi was the artistic director of leading actors and actresses such as Ekaterina Semyonova, Pyotr Karatygin, Ivan Sosnitsky, Yakov Bryansky and Maria Valberkhova.

The history of stage decoration in the early nineteenth century is dominated by two names: Pietro Gonzaga and Antonio Kanopii. Sketches of Gonzaga's theatrical sets reveal both the architectural motifs of classicism and romantic landscapes with 'mysterious moonlight' or 'enigmatic reflections' of the crescent-moon in water, and the like. Kanopii's sketches are the more colourful and effective. Theatrical settings from this time generally tended to evolve from classical forms in the empire style to the romantic and picturesque.

This period in the Russian theatre is also marked by major developments in opera and ballet. The first Russian choreographer Ivan Ivanovich Valberkh started his career in the late eighteenth century. In 1799 he staged *The New Werther* to the music of Titov. This was a sentimental ballet with melodramatic overtones, in which the dancers were dressed in contemporary tail-coats; this was the first example of a feature of Russian urban life being reflected in ballet. Some of Valberkh's ballets have a didactic character and a complicated plot portraying fierce passions and the struggle between nobility and vulgarity, such as *Clara, or an Appeal to Virtue* (1806), and *Raoul the Blue-Beard, or the Dangers of Curiosity* (1807). A special niche in Valberkh's *oeuvre* belongs to patriotic ballets about incidents in the Napoleonic Wars. Among them is a pantomine-ballet set to the music of several composers, *A New Heroine, or the Woman-Cossack*, staged in 1810. The leading part is played by a young woman dressed as a cavalry officer who, following her fiancé, went off to fight in the war. In 1813, together with the French choreographer Auguste, Valberkh staged the ballet *The Russians in Germany, or the Consequences of Love for the Fatherland*, in which the characters in the drama tried to reunite in Germany, accomplishing meanwhile an assortment of heroic deeds.

After Valberkh, a new and highly talented choreographer appeared, Didelot, who quickly achieved supremacy in the Russian ballet in the first quarter of that century. Charles Louis Didelot was a Frenchman born in Stockholm who had studied ballet in Paris. In 1788 he put on his first ballets in London; in 1792–95 he was working in Paris and Lyons; and in 1796–1801 he danced in, and staged, ballets at the Royal Ballet Theatre in London. From 1807 he had lived in St Petersburg. He started with the Anacreontic ballets *Apollo and Daphne* (1802), *Zephyr and Flora* (1804) and *Cupid and Psyche* (1809). Owing to the Franco-Russian War, Didelot had to interrupt his activities in St Petersburg, and in 1812–15 he was working again in London. But the years 1816–29 saw him in Russia once more, and witnessed a change in his artistic tastes: in particular, themes from mythology were succeeded by historical, literary and fantastical ones. Pantomine-ballets became prevalent, as mime was an easier medium for the expression of psychological drama. Important productions of this period are the tragic and heroic ballets *Acis and Galatea*, set to music by Cavos (1816), *Raoul de Cresquis, or the Return from the Crusade* (1819) and *Phaedra and Hippolytus* (1825), which Cavos also put to music. In 1823 Didelot staged Cavos's ballet *The Prisoner of the Caucasus, or the Bride's Shadow*, based on the poem by Pushkin who greatly appreciated the choreographer's talent. When the ballet was performed in the St Petersburg Bolshoi Theatre, Cavos himself conducted the orchestra, while the leading roles of the Cherkess girl and the captive were performed by Didelot's pupils Avdotya Istomina and Nikolai Golts. Didelot's work at the St Petersburg Theatre brought Russian theatre to the forefront of world art. His innovations were later developed in the ballets of Marius Petipa.

Caterino Albertovich Cavos, who composed the music for many of Didelot's ballet's, was an Italian who in 1797 went to live and work in Russia. For many years he headed the Russian opera and was as famous as a conductor as he was as a composer and singing master. Many of his operas drew on Russian history and folklore, for example *The Invisible Prince* (1805), *Ilya Bogatyr*, libretto by Krylov (1807), and *Ivan Susanin*, libretto by Shakhovskoi (1815). He made a great contribution to the development of Russian opera and the training of the first Russian opera singers. Having admitted the superiority of Glinka's opera *Ivan Susanin* (1836) over his own on the same subject, Cavos himself conducted the first performance of Glinka's masterpiece.

In the early years of the nineteenth century, St Petersburg had only state theatres in operation. In 1801 the architect Vincenzo Brenna fitted out the Maly Theatre, near the Anichkov Palace. A German company, directed by the playwright Kotzebue, worked in a theatre on Palace Square. Later, Russian companies also performed in this latter theatre, which became known as the New Theatre and existed until 1819, when it was demolished in the process of general replanning of the square by Carlo Rossi. He designed a new theatre in the city, which was opened in 1832 and called the Aleksandrinsky Theatre in honour of the wife of Emperor Nicholai I.

Moscow had no state theatres for a considerable period. It was not until 1806 that the Moscow imperial theatres were organised on the basis of the combined companies of the Petrovsky Theatre, the ballet group of the Foundling Hospital, Stolypins' serf actors, and others. Plays were performed on Mokhovaya Street in Pashkov's riding school, which had been converted into a theatre. At the same time, Rossi was building a theatre near the Arbat Gates: it was opened in 1808. The Moscow State Company performed right up to the summer of 1812, i.e. almost until Napoleon's troops were at the gates of Moscow. Their performances were resumed in 1814. In 1824 the Moscow Company moved to the building erected by Osip Bove and took the name of the Maly Theatre. The two greatest Russian theatres, the Maly in Moscow and the Aleksandrinsky in St Petersburg, which are still operating today, to a great extent determined the development of Russian theatre during the nineteenth and twentieth centuries.

Notes

1. *Pochta dukhov* (1789), part 2, p. 247.
2. *Zapiski S. N. Glinki* (St Petersburg, 1885), p. 181.
3. N. A. Elizarova, *Teatry Sheremet'evykh* (Moscow, 1944), pp. 258–9. This book contains many archive documents and has not lost its significance for researchers.
4. Ibid. p. 113.
5. *Tsentral'nyi gosudarstvennyi arkhiv drevnikh aktov* (TsGADA), fond 1261, opis' 1, papka 3016.
6. A. S. Shcheglova, 'Vorontsovskii krepostnoi teatr', *Iazyk i metafora*, vol. 1 (Leningrad, 1926), pp. 323–50.
7. T. Sievers, *Breife aus Siberien Neue Nord Beitrage*, vol. VII (St Petersburg and Leipzig, 1796), p. 151.
8. A. I. Gertzen, *Izbrannye sochineniia* (Moscow, 1937), pp. 420–1.
9. TsGADA, fond 16, papka 578, line 5.
10. Iu. Stennik. 'Dramaturgiia russkogo klassitsizma', *Istoriia russkoi dramaturgii XVII – pervaia polovina XIX veka* (Leningrad, 1982), p. 98.
11. See M. Gordin and Ia. Gordin, *Teatr Ivana Krylova* (Leningrad, 1983), p. 39.
12. *Sovremennyi vestnik* (1804), part 1, p. 217.

13. A. S. Rabinovich, *Russkaia opera do Glinki* (Leningrad, 1948), pp. 107–8.
14. B. Malnich, 'David Garrick and the Russian Theatre', *Modern Language Review*, 1: 2 (1955), 173–5. There are papers on the visit of I. A. Dmitrevskii to Paris and London in TsGADA, fond 466, opis' 1, papka 112.
15. E. A. Dinerstein, 'Leipzigskoe Izvestie o nekotorykh russkikh pisateliakh i ego avtor', *Zhurnalistika i literatura* (Moscow, 1972), pp. 72–81.
16. I. F. Gorbunov, *Sochineniia*, vol. III (St Petersburg, 1910), p. 42.
17. V. N. Vsevolodskii-Gerngross, *I. A. Dmitrevskii* (Berlin, 1923), pp. 56–8.
18. S. P. Zhikharev, *Zapiski sovremennika* (Moscow and Leningrad, 1955), p. 568.
19. N. M. Karamzin, *Sochineniia v dvukh tomakh* (Moscow and Leningrad, 1964), vol. II, pp. 87–8.
20. N. Ia. Eidelman, *Gran'vekov* (Moscow, 1982), p. 81.
21. P. N. Arapov, *Letopis' russkogo teatra* (St Petersburg, 1861), p. 136.
22. S. P. Zhikharev, *Zapiski sovremennika* (Moscow and Leningrad, 1955), pp. 323–5.

4 Writers and repertoires, 1800–1850

A.D.P. BRIGGS

From Oedipus to Belyaev

A new play, *Oedipus in Athens*, a 'Tragedy in Five Acts, in Verse, with Choruses', opened in St Petersburg on 23 November 1804. Its author was Vladislav Ozerov.[1] His work had sailed serenely through the public censor's office and was now staged in a spectacular production for which nothing had been spared. Kozlovsky had written music for an overture and chorus work; the sets were by the celebrated Pietro Gonzaga; costumes had been designed by Olenin and Ivanov; and the best actors and actresses were on display, including Shusherin, Yakovlev and Semyonova. The printed text boasted a long and florid dedication to Gavriil Derzhavin; the play itself, although written in flawless Alexandrines, began in tetrameters, with a Chorus of the People who sang as follows:

> How brightly does the sun, ascendant,
> All nature quicken in the spring!
> The good tsar comes, no less resplendent,
> And in their hearts the people sing.

The story, borrowed from Sophocles and his French adapters, centred on incidents taken from the end of Oedipus's career. Its measure may be taken from the fact that the last piece of action sees Creon struck down by a thunderbolt, after which there is just time for the High Priest to pronounce a short monologue calling the tsar and people alike to a life of repentance and innocence. *Oedipus in Athens* found instant and enduring success; it ran for nearly five years and, following a revival in 1816, it stayed in the repertoire until the 1850s. Nowadays it is remembered only by a few specialists.

Scarcely four decades after the opening of *Oedipus in Athens*, Ivan Turgenev (who would soon become better known as a novelist) wrote *A Month in the Country*, a very different sort of play which had a different fate. Announced in the press as early as 1849 (under another title), the play was completed the following year and sent to the censor, who immediately banned it. The ban stayed in place for five years, when it was circumvented only at the expense of drastic changes to the script.[2] Twenty years after its creation, in 1869, the author was finally permitted to publish the original version. The first performance (at the Maly Theatre) was delayed for another three years, and the play achieved lasting success only in the twentieth century, following a famous production by Stanislavsky in 1909. Its popularity continues today both at home and abroad.

Although the two plays are separated chronologically by a mere generation and a half, it would be hard to imagine a better example of polar opposites. While Ozerov's play clearly looks back to the eighteenth century, Turgenev's anticipates the twentieth. Their only common feature is that each consists of five acts. Although they appear to be written in the same language, the linguistic differences are substantial. Ozerov was writing a decade before Pushkin began his modernisation and democratisation of literary Russian; he used diction which was high-flown, pretentious, artificial, remote from that used even in the cultivated drawing room, let alone on the streets of Moscow or in any provincial backwater. Ozerov felt constrained to write in verse, and he chose the noblest form available. Turgenev, by contrast, wrote in prose, using the normal Russian language, as spoken by educated, though provincial, people, and even by lower-class elements and a funny foreigner with bad pronunciation. The comic utterances by Shaaf with which the play begins provide perhaps the most startling contrast with Ozerov's exalted opening chorus. From there on the disparities between 1804 and 1849 regard each other across a yawning gap. *Oedipus in Athens* was stylised, poetic, historical, histrionic, foreign, aristocratic, metropolitan, politically correct, immediately performed, instantly successful, though ultimately insubstantial. *A Month in the Country* was natural, down to earth, modern, realistic, Russian, democratic, provincial, subversive (at least in the censor's view), proscribed, delayed, slow to gain acceptance, but eventually received as a lasting masterpiece.

The distance traversed from the former play to the latter is remarkable in itself. More surprising is the speed with which such a radical change occurred; a similar transition in France, say from Corneille to Sardou, took two full centuries. What happened during the first half of the nineteenth century to make such rapid development possible? By what stages did it proceed? Who were the main protagonists in this real-life drama? In providing the answers to these questions we shall have to consider not only those theatrical forms that were developed, in particular historical drama, comedy and comic opera, but also those that were imported and Russified – especially melodrama and vaudeville. This was an age in which individual actors and actresses became figures of almost legendary importance, and their careers will be discussed in the next chapter. The immense popularity and importance of the Russian theatre will become apparent, as will the mediocrity and transience of much material that, in its own day, seemed to be significant. It will be rewarding to note the emergence, from an outgrowth of largely inglorious entertainment, of three or four plays that broke the rules of the day and in doing so established themselves as indisputable masterpieces.

Historical drama

From roots put down in the seventeenth century and nourished in the eighteenth by Sumarokov and Knyazhnin, historical drama grew to enormous popularity in the period 1800–40. Far from advancing the cause of Russian dramaturgy, however, it represented a step backwards. Its huge acclaim at the time stands in inverse proportion to its actual merits. Dozens of historical plays were written, produced and applauded, and most are now only of interest as museum pieces. Many minor writers dabbled with the genre – Glinka, Shakhovskoi, Kryukovsky, Zotov, Polevoi, Khmelnitsky and others – but the undisputed champions of this field are Ozerov and Nestor Kukolnik. They demonstrated better than anyone how to win favour and (short-lived) fame by misapplying the resources of the genre, for reasons which are as meretricious as they are understandable, while ignoring its virtues and potential values.

A good example is provided by Ozerov's play, *Dmitry Donskoi* (1807). The genesis of this work seems to have had more to do with Napoleon's charge through Europe towards Russia than with any spontaneous interest on the dramatist's part in the Mongol invasion of 1380 which he chose to depict. Certainly the audience saw it that way. They packed the theatre well beyond the limits of safety, cheered the opening lines so enthusiastically that the speaker, Yakovlev, was silenced for more than five minutes, and thundered such applause at the end that the St Petersburg Bolshoi Theatre seemed to be in danger of collapsing.[3] What they were acclaiming, however, was not a great play, good acting or an impressive production or set; they were cheering for Russia and the tsar. The play was an overt political allegory. Whereas the action ostensibly treated Dmitry Donskoi's great victory over Mamay, leader of the oppressing Mongol forces, no-one had any difficulty in equating Dmitry with Aleksandr I, Mamay with Napoleon, and the Russian princes with Aleksandr's foreign and military staff. The work itself is unremarkable: its two-thousand-odd hexameters roll down the page now as they must have rolled out into the audience then, in tedious waves of unoriginal grandiloquence. True, there was some interest in a subplot which was meant to relieve the political–historical intensity by depicting a love-match between the great hero and Princess Ksenia. Even this, however, is stock material, predictable in its outcome despite being historically inaccurate. Already well known, Ozerov was raised to glory by this play; when the tsar rewarded him with the gift of a jewelled snuffbox that must have been the high point of his career, and perhaps of his whole life.

A generation later, under the next tsar, there was worse to come. Historical and patriotic drama had always been separated by the thinnest of lines; Nestor Kukolnik was to leap across it into outright chauvinism. He managed to out-Ozerov Ozerov by taking a line from *Dmitry Donskoi*, 'The hand of the Almighty has saved our fatherland,' and using it as the title for a play, again in verse, which made its predecessors seem almost lukewarm in patriotic and political enthusiasm. *The Hand of the Almighty* took its subject matter from the 'Time of Troubles' (1598–1613), one of the most agonising periods of Russian history when the nation suffered every imaginable ill: famine, rebellion, invasion and one unsuccessful tsar after another. Kukolnik showed how the country was brought from chaos into order, the enemy expelled, the rabble put down, and happiness brought to the people by military success and firm control delivered by the first of the Romanov rulers. More than that, as the title indicated, all of this had come about by God's will; Russia, and the Romanovs, emerged as nothing less than a chosen people. Nikolai I, much impressed when he saw an early performance, went further than Aleksandr, not only inviting the author to the Winter Palace for an audience, but also supplying him with a list of proposed improvements, all of which Kukolnik obediently worked into the text. His fame was now assured. Performances of his play became ritualised state occasions, with top people in attendance and thunderous applause, as genuine from the gallery as it was from the best seats. The poetry of this play was an advance on Ozerov; Alexandrines had by now given way to blank verse, though hardly of Shakespearean plasticity. However, the action, the dialogue and, worst of all, the characters lacked any vestige of life or originality. The tightly gripping hand of the Almighty had squeezed out all human inspiration. Despite the obvious appeal of the play to patriotic sentiment there were those who saw through its tawdry attractiveness. Polevoi, the editor of the *Moscow Telegraph*, wrote a negative review, for which he paid dearly; taken under armed guard to St Petersburg, he was subjected to rigorous questioning and was lucky to get away with a minimal penalty – the closure of his journal. Not for the first or last time the Russian theatre had been drawn into real-life politics at the price of freedom curtailed.

It is against these examples of historical drama – extreme but not atypical – that the attempts at improvement in the genre by Aleksandr Pushkin and, later in the century, Aleksei Tolstoy should be gauged.

Comedy

The Russian theatre has known little success when attempting anything of high seriousness; it has no classical, tragic or historical drama of unalloyed quality and international standing. Its true strength lies in comedy, of one form or another, and Russian comedy came into its own during the first half of the nineteenth century, gathering confidence, flourishing in all directions and improving all the time. Although to begin with much was derived from the past and from abroad, indigenous quality soon began to show itself, as Russian subject matter and the everyday Russian language were asserted with increasing assurance. The progression decade by decade may be measured against clear landmarks: 1802 saw Sudovshchikov's *A Marvel Unheard-of, or An Honest Secretary*, which was a competent rehash of ideas and characters from the previous century; in 1815, Aleksandr Shakhovskoi created the comedy of high life, *A Lesson for Coquettes, or Lipets Spa*; in 1823 Aleksandr Griboedov wrote the first acknowledged Russian dramatic masterpiece, *Woe from Wit*; thirteen years later, Gogol produced the unsurpassed *The Government Inspector*, and in 1849–50 Turgenev created what was perhaps the first modern Russian play, *A Month in the Country*.

If progress is one characteristic of this period, another is diversity. Comic opera, *comédie larmoyante*, satirical drama, melodrama, vaudeville and every kind of comic translation and adaptation all came together in a rich brew. From the 1820s onward the theatre-going public delighted in a broad range of popular and light entertainment on the stage; hundreds of plays were put on in thousands of performances, in the provinces as well as the metropolitan centres, and the people turned up in large numbers to enjoy them.

Among the most popular of genres was vaudeville. Created by comic opera out of French comedy, and rapidly descending from courtliness to common realism, this consisted of verse plays, usually in one act, but sometimes in two acts (and up to five as the years went by), with a story including interpolated songs and dances, as well as some improvisation. It was light-hearted, gently satirical and sometimes rather racy. Vaudeville was one of the few media in which some gentle criticism of the government and aristocracy was tolerated by Nikolai I. He must have seen the risk as one worth taking. In this genre what mattered most was laughter; there was simply too much fun for anything subversive to take root. Meanwhile, in an age of heavy-handed censorship and spiritual darkness, if the population could be encouraged into increasing flippancy, so much the better for the authorities; this was a welcome safety-valve after the failure of the Decembrist rebellion of 1825.

In vaudeville little premium was placed on the verse medium, the music, the characters or the ideas; what counted were the fast-moving story with its sting in the tail, the jokes and innuendos, and the sense of snappy topicality which gave them life. The poetry was amusing but banal, consisting of so-called *kuplety*. Couplets they may have been in France, but in Russia they became short quatrains not unrelated to the *chastushka*, a popular, comic, four-line song. The music was incidental and second rate; when this genre was succeeded later in the century by Viennese operetta a steep rise in musical quality was one of the welcome new features. Many hundreds of vaudevilles were performed, either adapted from the French or written in original Russian. They varied enormously in quality, from dire vulgarity to a style and sophistication which has kept one or two in the repertoire up to the present day.[4] Among the best-known authors of vaudeville were Nikolai Khmelnitsky, Aleksandr Pisarev, D. Lensky, Pyotr Karatygin (brother of Vasily, the famous tragic actor) and F. Koni. But the father of the genre must be said to be the author of the first Russian vaudeville, Aleksandr Shakhovskoi, who wrote what he called a 'bastard child of comedy and comic opera', *The Cossack Poet*, as early as 1812.[5] He could scarcely have known that he was bringing into the Russian theatre one of its most enjoyable and popular forms; in any case his greatest achievement was to lie elsewhere, in a more elevated form of comedy.

High comedy

In the whole of this period no name holds greater overall significance for the Russian theatre than that of Aleksandr Shakhovskoi. A man of many parts living in an age of rapid transition, he had more than his fair share of talent and originality. He was lucky enough to go abroad in his early twenties to study acting, production and management in Paris, after which all of his adult life was devoted to the theatre. In a career spanning five decades – his first play was staged under Catherine II in 1795 – he served as impresario, director, theatre manager, talent-spotter and eventually elder statesman of the profession. He also wrote, or adapted from other sources, more than a hundred plays, including at least four or five of high quality.[6] Always at the centre of the vigorous debates of the day, especially those concerning Russian culture, he was no stranger to controversy. In both character and achievement he personifies better than anyone else the turbulent progression of Russian dramaturgy in this age. The importance of this man of the theatre, undermined during his lifetime as much by his own indiscretions as by ideological enemies, is now clearly established.

For all his versatility, Shakhovskoi is best remembered for the contribution that he made to high comedy. His first real mark was in *The New Sterne* (1805), a satirical prose comedy in one act directed against the excesses of sentimentalism. Intelligent, commonsensical and funny in equal proportions, it was warmly received in St Petersburg, then in Moscow and beyond, though popularity was bought at the cost of some resentment. In lampooning artificiality and affectation the author came near to pouring scorn also on those who were seeking conscientiously to modernise Russian customs and the Russian language, particularly Karamzin. This did Shakhovskoi no favours, but his career, fuelled by popular acclaim, still prospered. Another prose comedy, *A Semi-lordly Escapade, or The House Theatre*, this time in five acts, gave him his next success in 1808. In this play much amusement derives from the bungling attempts of a parvenu landowner to enhance his standing by following a popular fashion; he tries to set up a serf theatre without knowing the first thing about serfs or theatres. But Shakhovskoi was no revolutionary or iconoclast. His masterpiece, *A Lesson for Coquettes, or Lipets Spa* (1815), reverts to poetry and the observance of the classical unities. This apparent volte-face may seem to be backward-looking but it concerns only structure. In its action, story, characters and language, *Lipets Spa* is innovative and modern. It is also full of ideas. Running through the machinations of a rather complicated love-match, which nearly comes to grief at the hands of a scheming coquette, are Shakhovskoi's usual thoughts on the need for good sense to rule human conduct, on the greater importance of honesty than social rank and, most importantly, the natural superiority of all things Russian over anything imported. This rather reactionary attitude is itself counterbalanced by the play's greatest single quality, its sensitivity to language. *Lipets Spa* is the first Russian play in which the verse medium permits plausible-sounding conversation, using the very words and – this is the real secret – more or less the word *order* employed by real people in their everyday lives. This play is a delightful paradox, half-archaic, half-modern. The manner in which it reconciles contradictions and keeps the audience entertained while doing so attests to the sensitivity of a gifted artist trying to find his way through a changing cultural landscape. It is a splendid accomplishment of transitional drama, arching between Fonvizin and Griboedov.

If Shakhovskoi had written nothing more he would still have made a singular contribution to the Russian theatre. In fact he continued to write for another quarter of a century and left behind a solid corpus of further achievement. Among his subsequent successes were *All in the Family, or The Married Bride* (1818) (a remarkably well-integrated collaborative work with some scenes by Griboedov and Khmelnitsky), *Don't Listen if You Don't Want To, But Don't Stop The Lies* (1818), and *The Cockatoo, or The Consequences of a Lesson for Coquettes* (1820). Shakhovskoi's was not a lone voice; a number of contemporaries and immediate successors followed his several examples with varying degrees of ability and success, particularly F. Kokoshkin, Mikhail Zagoskin, Khmelnitsky himself, and the gifted but short-lived Aleksandr Pisarev.

Four famous plays

The first two-and-a-half decades of the nineteenth century were years of expansion, experimentation and creativity in the Russian theatre, but they did not give rise to any outright masterpiece destined to conquer the Russian stage and stay on it, let alone impress the outside world. In the second quarter of the century, however, such works did begin to appear. Many playwrights had sown the seed and the fruits were harvested by a small number of exceptionally gifted writers. All of them wrote from a negative impulse. A combination of qualities – imagination, talent, courage, originality and sheer perversity – enabled them to seize the rich opportunity presented by an age of energetic cultural reform. They were all dissatisfied with things as they stood, in the country at large, or in the theatre, or both, and they had in common not only a desire for improvement but also the ability to innovate while working to the highest artistic

5. A lithograph of Aleksandr Griboedov by P. Borelia, 1860.

standards. Aleksandr Griboedov, Aleksandr Pushkin, Nikolai Gogol and Ivan Turgenev each wrote a play of such striking quality that, in one form or another, it still appears regularly on the national stage. With the single exception of Fonvizin (whose redoubtable comedy, *The Minor*, has never lost its deserved popularity), they were the first Russian dramatists to achieve such a distinction.

Griboedov, a soldier and then accomplished diplomat, led a life busier in narrowly professional terms than most of his artistic contemporaries. Nevertheless, he was drawn to the theatre and spent much of his spare time writing for it. Working in comedy and vaudeville, mainly as an adapter and in collaboration with several other writers (notably with Shakhovskoi and Khmelnitsky on *All in the Family*), he took some time to become fully confident and develop his individuality. When he did so, in *Woe from Wit* (1824), he transcended them all.

This play (which appears in English under several other titles, such as *The Misfortune of Being Clever, Wit Works Woe* and *Chatsky*) might not seem distinctive at first sight. In some respects it appears even to put the clock back. A glance at the first pages will show that it is written in verse (free iambic lines, though almost half of them are hexameters) and contains characters with funny names in the tradition of the previous century: Famusov (Mr Famous), Molchanin (Mr Taciturn), Skalozub (Mr Grinning) and others. The opening speech is made by a servant girl called Liza; the fact that she has just woken up in an armchair indicates early morning – a clear sign that the unity of time is about to be invoked. These are hardly original touches. Furthermore, the plot and characters are derivative; Molière's *The Misanthrope* is one obvious precursor and it has been shown recently that Shakhovskoi's *A Lesson for Coquettes* must be considered another.[7]

The story concerns a young nobleman, Aleksandr Chatsky, who returns to Moscow after three years' absence, spent partly abroad. He has two purposes in mind: to pick up the threads of a relationship with a young lady, Sofia, and to speak out against the atrocities of contemporary Russian life that have become painfully apparent to him during his travels. After a series of outspoken denunciations and confrontations he is taken to be insane and rejected by Sofia. Her fate, however, is little better, for the odious Molchalin's wooing of her is exposed as an attempt on his part to ingratiate himself with her father and, in passing, to try his luck with Liza, her maid. Chatsky departs, presumably to continue his travels and take his complaints elsewhere. There is much that is unsatisfying in this story. It lacks verisimilitude, dramatic shape and any sense of resolution. Chatsky has been complaining to the wrong listeners; these old conservatives are too obviously immovable. Several of the people who appear before him in a parade of self-seeking mediocrity and reactionary smugness are one-dimensional characters borrowed from Fonvizin; this is a mark of the play's old-fashioned attitude. Also in the eighteenth-century manner its speeches are directed not so much between the players as out across the stage to the listening audience. The plot, and most of the people in it, make no lasting impact on the imagination.

Significantly, this is the only one of the four masterpieces of this period which has made no strong impression on the foreign stage and is unlikely ever to do so. A bold attempt in this direction, mounted in 1993 when a new English translation of the play was performed in London and several provincial English cities, cannot be described as an unqualified success. Yet for once things were done properly. The translation was written by a man of real talent and reputation, the novelist Anthony Burgess; the director and the cast came from the front ranks of the British theatre. But even Burgess's literary strength proved insufficient for the task. Some of the linguistic cleverness was transported from Russian to English, creating moments of delight, but the shortcomings of the play as a whole left most reviewers and audiences rather bemused. It is improbable that this work, which could hardly hope for a better English version, will now begin to rival even Gorky or Turgenev, let alone Chekhov or Gogol, as an accepted Russian masterpiece regularly produced on the London stage. Of all the Russian favourites, *Woe from Wit*, which is utterly dependent for its quality on a knowledge of the original language and the historical background of the play, must be described as the least universal and exportable.

For all that, the play has one or two remarkable qualities which have raised it to unshakable heights of popularity and significance for the Russian people. First of all, hidden among the stereotypes is some unforgettable characterisation: Chatsky and Famusov present wonderful opportunities for the accomplished actor, and Sofia possesses more subtlety than may at first be realised. Then there is the humour, covering a wide range but consistently shot through with venomous ironies; the tone of the play is much sharper than anything in Fonvizin. Satire worthy of Juvenal at his most mordant, and the bitterest sarcasm known to Russian letters pour out together in monologue and dialogue as the political rhetoric of *Woe from Wit* strikes time and again with vituperative directness. One or two of Chatsky's set-piece addresses are among the most memorable instances of declamatory power in Russian verse or prose. The actual language of the play, that element which most strongly defies transposition on to the foreign stage, amounts to a unique achievement. Pushkin recognised its distinctiveness at a single reading of the unpublished manuscript, issuing a famous prediction that every other line would become a Russian proverb. Dozens of them have done so; they now lie deeply buried in modern Russian speech, mostly unrecognised as coming from this play. Despite the constraints imposed by their iambic medium, Griboedov's cleverly turned expressions shine with aptness, intelligence, epigrammatic sharpness and sardonic humour. It is like Oscar Wilde without the showmanship. In terms of language alone, and on a much smaller scale, the achievement of this play may be properly described as Shakespearean.

Having completed the first version of *Woe from Wit* in 1824, Griboedov kept on polishing it almost to the end of his short life. Already well known in manuscript, it was banned while being prepared for publication and performance in 1825, and had to wait until 1831 for its premiere at the St

Petersburg Bolshoi Theatre. By then the author had been dead for two years.

It was in 1825 that Aleksandr Pushkin completed his historical drama, *Boris Godunov*, which also failed to pass the censor. Published eventually six years later, it was kept off the stage until as late as 1870. *Boris Godunov* has been seldom performed in Russia, let alone abroad, for both technical and artistic reasons, but it has been reborn in the hugely impressive operatic version by Musorgsky. The play is set, like Kukolnik's *The Hand of the Almighty*, in the early seventeenth century, a time of political crisis for Russia, with the dynastic succession uncertain following the death of Ivan the Terrible, who left no suitable heir. Boris Godunov accepts the regency, to which he has long aspired, with a great show of reluctance. In the event, his reign fails to bring the desired peace and prosperity; he is blamed by the people for everything that goes wrong, even natural disasters. Part of the trouble is ascribed by Pushkin to Boris's illegitimacy. He has risen to power over the dead body of Ivan's young son, Dmitry, the victim of a murderous plot several years earlier. (Pushkin accepted Karamzin's version of events which held Boris guilty of this crime, though this is far from certain historically.) Now the shadow of the dead tsarevich returns to haunt the usurper. A young novice, Grigory, leaves his monastery, passes himself off as Dmitry, the legitimate pretender to the throne, and attacks Russia from the west. This would appear to be promising dramatic material: the build-up to a titanic confrontation between two illegitimate contenders for ultimate authority. Unfortunately that was not how things worked out. The two contenders never met and the issues were settled with disappointing messiness, with Dmitry temporarily assuming power following Boris's sudden death. The arbitrary mischances of real history left the story of the play without any sense of climax and resolution, which remains one of its incorrigible disadvantages.

Another drawback is the apparent shapelessness of this work. Twenty-three tableaux are strung together successively, with no division into acts and scenes. They take place in twenty different settings. There is no list of dramatis personae; people come and go in profusion; there are about forty speaking parts, though many are small. A number of significant characters appear in only one scene. What can Pushkin, by now a mature and accomplished writer, be playing at?

The dramatist has a number of clear aims in mind, and may have taken some of them too seriously. For one thing, he is disgusted with the artificiality of contemporary historical drama, and determined to cast its conventions into outer darkness. The stilted hexameters, the false characters, all those speeches and choruses of nauseating praise for the rulers of Russia, the unlifelike unities of time, place and action – all of these outdated paraphernalia have been dismissed with contempt. The extent and audacity of Pushkin's single-handed attempt at reform are breathtaking. His reading of classical and European dramatists has taught him a clear lesson: the only model worthy of respect is Shakespeare. The English playwright holds all the secrets of historical conviction, persuasive characterisation, psychological truth, philosophical awareness and human warmth.[8] The spirit of Shakespeare alone will save the Russian theatre, and only a gifted poet will be equal to his example.

But Pushkin has tried to do too much, too quickly. One particular decision may have altered the entire fate of his play. Close examination suggests that he may have planned *Boris Godunov* in five acts; four long time-spans appear to divide the play in this way. By removing any indication of acts and scenes he may have asserted at a stroke his independence from all predecessors, Shakespeare himself included; unfortunately, Pushkin has also exaggerated the amorphous character of his work. The play has more unity – of purpose, tone, personality and even action – than is commonly suspected. It deserves better, and more frequent, productions. It contains several scenes of impressive quality – miniature dramas in themselves which opera-goers will easily recognise. The characterisation is of a very high order, consistent and authentic throughout, from the grand Patriarch to the hostess at an inn, from a toping priest to Boris himself; the personalities are strongly individualised and cover a broad range. The achievement deserves recognition in its own right; in comparison with the characters presented in any other Russian play of the period it looks particularly outstanding. The poetry of this play is nothing less than sumptuous. Pushkin's blank verse, despite being inhibited by a second-foot caesura borrowed unnecessarily from France, flows majestically, well suited to the impressive rhetorical outpourings of the ageing chronicler-monk, Pimen, as well as to the Patriarch and the great tsar himself. Contrasting with the verse are scenes of rapid dialogue, some of them in prose. It is evident throughout the play that one of the true masters of the Russian language is at work. *Boris Godunov* is generally regarded as a disordered failure of a play with some surviving residue of quality material.

The reverse is true; here we have a splendid piece of theatre somewhat devalued by a number of drawbacks and difficulties which are not insuperable and should not be exaggerated.

Gogol's famous 1836 comedy, *The Government Inspector* (sometimes called *The Inspector General*), is commonly described as the best Russian play ever written.[9] Simplistic though such judgements may appear to be, it is not easy to think of a serious rival for that accolade. This play never fails. At all times and in all countries it is accepted as topical, its comic characters provide revulsive delight, and its humour finds immediate audience response. It has the capacity to survive translation, adaptation and the wildest attempts by critics of every hue to explain its hidden meanings.[10] If these exist, they are of little interest to most audiences; the appeal of the play is direct and primitive rather than intellectual or spiritual. The immediacy of its humour probably accounted for its unusual fate when first written. Although overbrimming with a satirical spirit which could be interpreted all too easily as direct criticism of contemporary Russian life, and officialdom in particular, nevertheless it was passed by the censor for public performance. On this occasion mere arbitrariness is not the explanation. Tsar Nikolai saw the play himself at an early stage and amazed everyone by approving it. He is said to have exclaimed, 'What a play! Everybody copped it, me most of all.'

The story was probably suggested to Gogol by Pushkin, who had once been mistaken for a government official travelling incognito. This simple idea was developed into a five-act prose comedy, the leading figure of which is a minor civil servant from St Petersburg, Ivan Khlestakov, who fetches up, penniless and living on his wits, in a small town. By chance the local officials, corrupt to the last man, have just learned that a government inspector is on his way to visit them for a close scrutiny of their affairs. They assume that Khlestakov must be the inspector. This misunderstanding releases a flow of marvellous dramatic irony. Khlestakov, astonished at the sudden reversal of his fortunes when, one by one, the worthies of the town begin to fawn upon him, just manages to avoid giving the game away. His good luck is nicely balanced by their stupidity, and he rides it well. First he cadges more and better food for himself and his grumbling servant, Osip; then he goes on to greater things, accepting bribes on a rising scale and making promising advances both to the mayor's daughter and to his wife. Khlestakov is saved not by his own resourcefulness but by Osip, who persuades him that they ought to leave quickly before the deception is discovered. This they do, Khlestakov accepting a few hundred roubles more as they depart, not a moment too soon. A gloating letter from Khlestakov to a friend has been intercepted and the truth is out. But it is too late for the gawping officials to recoup their losses, and there is one more shock in store for them. The real inspector has arrived.

In this play humour strikes at many levels. Slapstick and pantomime fun coexist with satire, which itself covers a broad range, from gentle chastisement of feminine fussiness in the mother–daughter relationship to a round condemnation of corruption and inefficiency in the town's hospital, court, police station, schools and town hall. At all times Horace speaks louder than Juvenal; laughter prevails over the corrective spirit. There are plenty of barbs, but they are unvenomed, and there is not a decent villain to be had. This is Gogol's main point. He was struck by the awful quality of pettiness, vulgarity and self-centred smugness which the Russians call *poshlost* – the same spiritual deficiency which he would return to in his novel, *Dead Souls*, one which is most unattractive but hardly repellent or dangerous. These pitiful characters are as daft as any you will meet, but there is nothing ominous about them. Their world is also peculiarly Gogolian, filled with delicious illogicalities, hyperbole and angular juxtapositions which, although ridiculous, seem somehow half-believable. When we hear that one of the judge's assistants, who reeks like a distillery, is beyond medical help because his nanny bumped him when he was a baby and he has given off a slight odour of vodka ever since, who is going to question the diagnosis? This is Russia; more than that, it is Gogol's Russia.

Another secret of the play's success is its excellent construction. It is beautifully shaped and styled down to its last detail, with a satisfying overall cyclic movement, from the announcement of the impending visit of an inspector to his actual arrival at the end, and the ranging of the characters either in neat little pairings or else in wonderful processions as, one by one and on several occasions, they parade themselves, hilariously exposing their little rivalries, their fears and their faults.

The first performances of the play, and the reviews, were bad. Gogol left Russia, smarting from the hostile criticism. Partly with this in mind, and partly as a result of growing religious mania, the author revised his play many times and left us with a clear exegesis of it. He wanted it to be seen as a universal allegory treating the subjects of immorality and conscience; the real inspector is a reminder that all of us will one day be called to judgement. This may be worth a passing thought; it is not the reason why so many people watch this play with enjoyment and remember it for a long time afterwards.

A Month in the Country (1849–50) appeared much too early for its own good. Given the relatively crude state of the Russian theatre in the 1840s, despite the innovations just described, Ivan Turgenev's intention to introduce psychological drama (without naming it as such) must count as one of the greatest cultural innovations of the century. At the time, of course, it seemed like nothing of the kind; the would-be dramatist was castigated for writing a play with no action or interest. Modest to a fault, he was only too ready to believe the negative criticism. He went to his grave, decades later, with no full appreciation of his own outstanding ability as a playwright, and certainly no idea that *A Month in the Country* would gain international standing and remain popular for many generations to come. As a novelist Turgenev was strong on character, atmosphere and dialogue; he was less impressive on plotting and the general manipulation of his personalities. He worked best with small groups in confined areas. A good case could be made for considering him to be a kind of dramatist *manqué* rather than a natural novelist who, at one stage of his career, strayed on to the stage.

A Month in the Country looks for all the world like Chekhov half a century early. The action takes place on a country estate in summer; indoor and outdoor scenes alternate. People go about rather aimlessly, commenting on the weather and indulging in trivial occupations. The arrival and departure of an outsider circumscribe the action, such as it is. The newcomer, Belyaev, is a likeable young man who soon turns the heads of two women: Natalya Islaeva, the mother of the boy he has come to tutor, and her ward, a seventeen-year-old girl called Vera. Rivalry develops between Natalya and Vera, but the younger girl is no match for her protectress; she ends up married off to an unappealing fifty-year-old neighbour. Belyaev leaves in some confusion and all the other characters are left to pick up the pieces of lives that have been overturned by events, even though little enough seems to have happened to anyone.

This work is prosaic in every sense. The medium is prose; the characters, dialogue and incidents are normal and workaday. Nothing strains against credulity; no allowances have to be made. This was the problem with the play when it first appeared. Audiences still wanted to be impressed, to be taken out of themselves, stirred up, entertained by extraordinary people and circumstances. What Turgenev wished to do was to show how ordinary people react psychologically to emotional shocks. He was interested in states and processes of mind, rather than external events. His characters are remarkably successful. Authentic and individual, they grow, mature and undergo change even as the story makes its slow progress. This kind of play, as later audiences would learn to appreciate, has a kind of organic self-sufficiency which leaves the mind disturbed but satisfied. There are certainly no villains, monsters, saints or heroes on view; if such people exist in real life, Turgenev has no interest in them. Vera's plight moves us all the more because she is such an ordinary girl, and even Natalya, who deliberately consigns her to unhappiness, seems in some respects almost as pitiable as her victim. She is, after all, brought down by two uncontrollable forces: the ageing process, which is just beginning to tell on her, although she is not yet quite thirty, and the power of erotic passion, which we know to have ruined stronger persons than her. She is also trapped in an unrewarding marriage. Her unforgivable behaviour can at least be understood. The pull towards sympathy which Turgenev exerts upon us in relation to this ostensibly shameful character demonstrates his deep knowledge of human personality and his interest in the complexities of motivation and behaviour.

The undoubted sophistication of the play is hidden behind a veil of casual conduct and a covering of humour. Turgenev had a good sense of humour, which is often underestimated, and it serves him well here. Directors succeed best, in both amateur and professional productions of *A Month in the Country*, when they allow the comedy a free rein; the sadness will always speak for itself. The comic characters, in any case, outnumber the serious ones; the plain-speaking Dr Shpigelsky who woos a rather prim and pretentious old maid, Lizaveta Bogdanovna, in a couple of memorable scenes; the sadly out-of-touch husband, Islaev; the outrageous Bolshintsov, Vera's eventual husband-to-be; Shaaf, the amusing middle-aged German tutor, and so on. Little of the comedy is overt, but it is there in abundance and it deserves gentle emphasis.

There is rather more to this play than can be found in Chekhov; more story, more development, more comedy. Chekhov on the other hand will bring the study of inactivity, lost potential and failed communication to an even finer art. But the similarities between the two dramatists are remarkable. Anyone who doubts them should make a careful comparison of the cast lists in *A Month in the Country* and *Uncle Vanya*, and of the relationships existing between the various characters. These people are not stock personalities, nor are they set in familiar patterns (like, for instance, the eternal triangle), yet the characters and the grouping of them in the latter play strongly recall the former. Chekhov denied any influence, but in doing so he was being disingenuous. That influence certainly exists, though it remains still to be fully documented.[11]

A turning-point in the Russian theatre had now been reached. The legacy of the eighteenth century had been fully assimilated and at last outgrown. Major new developments had taken place, and significant plays were now being written. Following a period of sustained expansion, turmoil, development in all directions, controversy and experiment, the age of artificiality had been laid to rest; the attention switched from Oedipus to Belyaev. As in the other arts, realism had become the new order.

Notes

1. See V. A. Ozerov, *Tragedii: Stikhotvoreniia* (Leningrad, 1960). Details of the production appear on p. 419.
2. I. S. Turgenev, *Sobranie Sochinenii*, vol. IX (Moscow, 1962), p. 410.
3. Ozerov, pp. 421–2.
4. A good example is D. Lenskii's *Lev Gurych*; see S. Karlinsky, *Russian Drama from its Beginnings to the Age of Pushkin* (Berkeley, 1985), p. 275.
5. Karlinsky, p. 232.
6. No fewer than 111 dramatic works and translations are listed in A. Shakovskoi, *Komedii: Stikhotvoreniia* (Leningrad, 1961), pp. 817–25.
7. Karlinsky, pp. 288ff.
8. Further details are to be found in two prefaces to *Boris Godunov* written by the author; translations are available in T. Wolff, *Pushkin on Literature* (London, 1986), pp. 220–4, 245–50.
9. The clearest expressions of this view are by D. S. Mirsky, *A History of Russian Literature* (New York, 1960), p. 154, and V. Nabokov, *Nikolai Gogol* (London, 1961), p. 40.
10. The following article, which discusses images of sterility and sexuality, may be taken as an example of a rather extreme view of the play: J. Bortnes, 'Gogol's *Revizor* – a study in the grotesque', *Scando-Slavica* (1969), 44–64. There are many others.
11. But see A. D. P. Briggs, 'Two months in the country: Chekhov's unacknowledged debt to Turgenev', *New Zealand Slavonic Journal* (1994), 17–32.

5 Actors and acting, 1820–1850

ANATOLY ALTSCHULLER

Theatre reached a peak of popularity in Russia during the second quarter of the nineteenth century, when new kinds of public fascination focused on actors, playwrights and almost anything to do with the theatrical world. Actors suddenly found they had ardent fans, and the newspapers printed all sorts of snippets of news and gossip, while serious dramatic criticism may be said to have been born. Ordinary theatre-goers became interested not only in the performances themselves, but also in the actors' lives. They found new pleasure in discussing backstage intrigues, and in discovering which actors and actresses were protected by which important state personages, and why. Thus, tongues were wagging when in 1822 the well-known poet and translator, Katenin, was expelled from the capital because he had demonstrated against the actress Azarevicheva, who was the favourite of Miloradavich, the governor-general of St Petersburg.

Almost all the leading writers of the period, including Pushkin, Lermontov, Gogol and Belinsky, were attracted to the theatre, and contemporary correspondence, diaries and memoirs contain many references to the stage and its leading practitioners and personalities. The influence of the theatre upon the social and spiritual life of the country owed at least as much to the appearance of a constellation of brilliant actors as it did to the writings of any of the authors who are perhaps better known to history.

For most of the first half of the nineteenth century, the actor was regarded as the central figure in the theatre. Even in weak or unimportant plays, many actors managed to create striking and memorable performances. If the text of the play was of no help, the actor drew on material taken from real life to make a role expressive (or so it was claimed). Belinsky described actors as the 'authors' of their roles. During the period under review, however, this situation underwent a significant change. Whereas in 1820 it could be said that many characters were created as much by the actors as by the playwright, by about 1850, when Ostrovsky's plays began to appear, the persona of the author had become central in the creation of theatre. This was the most significant development in what was a transitional period in the history of Russian theatre, and it can be illustrated by noting the change in style between the most popular actors of the 1820s – the romantic Mochalov, for instance – and the more moderate and subdued style of Shchepkin, the best loved actor of the 1840s. It is worth noting, however, that this development can also be detected in the way drama itself changed during these years: the classical tragedies of the 1820s, dissociated from real life, gradually gave way to the more 'realistic' drama associated with Ostrovsky, which portrayed the life of the bourgeoisie.

An evening at the theatre in St Petersburg or Moscow in the 1820s, as elsewhere in Europe, consisted of a series of entertainments, often the more mixed the better. Thus, a classical tragedy might be juxtaposed to a comic singer; a dance act followed by a vaudeville. These latter were especially popular, and produced a number of actors who achieved great fame and popularity. Among them was Nikolai Osipovich Dyur, who played Khlestakov in the original production of Gogol's *The Government Inspector* in 1836. Tall, slender and agile, Dyur had attended Didelot's famous master-class in dance, and he was a good singer as well. He was also a virtuoso quick-change artist. All this endeared him to vaudeville audiences, for his personality, rather than his acting skills, was his strength. His best-known partner was Varvara Nikolaevna Asenkova. While Dyur largely confined his appearances to vaudeville, Asenkova, despite her early death at the age of twenty-four, became a highly-praised actress at the Aleksandrinsky Theatre, albeit for a brief period. Her stage debut was in January 1835 and her last performance in February 1841, but she filled those six years with triumph and disappointment, rapturous audiences and political scandal. All over St Petersburg, people gossiped about her rejected admirers, who apparently included Tsar Nikolai I himself. The actress's contemporaries declared later that Asenkova had no longer been able to tolerate the baiting and persecution from Nikolai's entourage, and had taken poison.

Like Dyur, Asenkova was tall and graceful, and her popularity initially blossomed when, with natural ease and inventiveness, she played disobedient teenage daughters of state officials, or else ingenious fiancées who outwit their fathers to secure the husband of their choice. But soon this was eclipsed by her success in travesty parts, including, on the vaudeville stage, Cadet Lelev in *The Hussar's Station*, the Marquis de Cresquit in *The Old-Time Colonel*, and Hussar Lazov in *The Military Citizens*. Dressed as a young officer, she sang boldly of heroism, bravery and the glorious Russian army. Her song as Hussar Lazov in praise of the military feats of Mikhail Kutuzov was an especial success. But besides these vaudeville parts, Asenkova also performed in more legitimate drama, and was indeed the original Maria Antonovna in Gogol's *The Government Inspector*, as well as a successful Sofia in Griboedov's *Woe from Wit*. Her powerful dramatic gift was perhaps best revealed in her performance as Esmeralda in an adaptation of Victor Hugo's *Notre Dame de Paris*, and this contrasted impressively with her melancholy and touching Ophelia, whose memorable mad scene was the inspiration for Nekrasov's poem, *Ophelia*, written in 1840. Asenkova was thus both a brilliant vaudeville performer and also an actress who could reveal a woman's inner world, and show her suffering, dreams and hopes with the piercing force of her talent.

Another master of vaudeville was Vasily Ignatevich Zhivokini. Stanislavsky recalled how Zhivokini 'appeared on stage and advanced straight towards the audience, stopped at the edge, at the footlights, and said his personal greetings to the audience. An ovation ensued, after which he started to perform.'[1] Famous for his ad libs and his buffoonery, Zhivokini was said to 'ignite an electric sparkle of fun in the house' when he appeared on stage. His best-known parts in vaudeville included Sinichkin in Lensky's *Gurych Sinichkin*, Jeauvial in *The Scrivener under the Table* by Teolon and Chauquar, and Mordashov in Fyodorov's *Az and Fert*. As vaudeville gave way to a new stage repertory, Zhivokini turned to more serious acting in plays by Turgenev, Ostrovsky and others. For example, he was the poor landowner in Turgenev's comedy, *The Bachelor*, greatly to the author's approval. Nevertheless, vaudeville was at the heart of Zhivokini's art, and he remained above all a brilliant performer on the vaudeville stage.

On the legitimate stage, romantic acting may be said to have reached its apogee in the 1820s and 1830s. The most notable female performer in this period was perhaps Ekaterina Semyonova who, until her retirement in 1826, created a series of strong, independent women – heroic, passionate, ready for self-sacrifice, unable to compromise. Thus she embodied admirable figures of the romantic imagination who also gave a whiff of defiance against tyranny, which her audiences found highly stimulating. Her performances as Iphigenia, Medea, Theodora, and Gertrude in an adaptation of *Hamlet*, as well as Zarema in Pushkin's *The Fountain of Bakhchisarai*, were all widely acclaimed. According to Medvedeva, Semyonova's biographer, her 'acting style in heroic parts was classico-romantic, or, to be more exact, it was in the style of romanticised classicism'.[2] This may suggest some traces of the austere acting style of earlier decades, but in fact Semyonova's emotional sincerity undermined the old rational style. If the predominant characteristic of her style seemed to be a kind of classicism, it was a complicated, fragmented version, penetrated by newer trends. Ekaterina Semyonova was also perhaps the first to try to coordinate the actors on the stage in a way which today we would regard as the job of the director. In a long memorandum *On Improving Dramatic Performances* to the Directorate of the Imperial Theatres, she wrote 'Just as a perfect musical composition cannot be played by the most skilful orchestra without a general agreement among the players, so a dramatic play, perfectly written and performed by reasonably talented actors, cannot be successful without a preliminary attempt at the coordination of all the participants by a conductor, who achieves a musical harmony through rehearsals at which he harmonises the playing of the individual musicians into a general agreement, and then directs the performance when it is actually presented.'[3] This is probably the earliest explicit appeal for a stage director in the Russian theatre.

Romantic acting reached a new peak, however, in the performances of Pavel Stepanovich Mochalov. He was not only an outstanding actor, but also, according to the poet and critic Apollon Grigoriev, a great teacher to a whole generation. Mochalov made his debut in 1817 as Polynices in Ozerov's *Oedipus in Athens*, and soon the young actor's potential was apparent. It was clear early in his career that Mochalov would introduce a new note of emotion onto the Russian stage: 'tempestuous inspiration, ardent, scorching passions, deeply emotional feelings, a wonderful face, a voice either resonant or low but always harmonious and melodious – these are his acting techniques', wrote Belinsky.[4] All his contemporaries agreed, however, that Mochalov's performances were unpredictable: when Mochalov was inspired, he was a genius, but when inspiration left him he was no more than ordinary. Those who had a chance to see Mochalov on stage in the hours and minutes of his inspiration were lucky. Fortunately these hours and minutes were not rare.

In the 1820s, Mochalov acted largely in melodramas, the two most interesting of which were perhaps Kotzebue's *Misanthropy and Repentance*, and Duchange and Dinot's *Thirty Years, or A Gambler's Life*. The former had appeared originally in the late eighteenth century, but became newly popular in the 1820s when Mochalov started to act in it. Commentators tended to agree that the most telling moment in his performance as Baron

6. Pavel Mochalov as Meinau in August Kotzebue's *Misanthropy and Repentance.*

Meinau was the long monologue telling the story of his unhappy life. Emotions rose as his speech progressed, and by the end not only was the audience weeping, but the actors on stage with Mochalov could not keep back their tears either. Equally notable was his performance as Georges Germenie in *Thirty Years, or A Gambler's Life.* In the first act, Georges is young, impulsive, spontaneous. The play encompasses, however, thirty years of his life, and by the third act, the climax of the play, he is a humble old man, living with his family in squalid surroundings. He now realises the absurdity and the criminal wastefulness of his life. Mochalov cleverly but unexpectedly did not make this reprobate a totally dark character, but showed carefully the moments when light gleamed in his soul – this was one, and perhaps the best, of Mochalov's many Byronic images of lonely and disappointed people, rejected by society.

In 1831 the full version of Griboedov's comedy, *Woe from Wit*, was staged for the first time at the Maly Theatre in Moscow, with Mochalov as Chatsky, Shchepkin as Famusov and Lvova-Sinetskaya as Sofia. Mochalov was not sure that his casting was appropriate: 'I feel out of place,' he told Lvova-Sinetskaya, 'out of my line. The frivolous Chatsky, with his playful chatter, his laughter and biting sarcasms . . . is something I have never played and do not know how to play.'[5] The laughter and 'playful chatter' in Mochalov's performance were unfortunately too unobtrusive, and he was criticised because the play lost its comic effect.

Nevertheless, the 1830s were the peak of Mochalov's career, and in this decade he created his most impressive Shakespearean characters – Richard III, Othello, Hamlet and King Lear. His attitude to Shakespeare was expressed in his reverent remark: 'We actors are only small tools in the hands of this greatest of all masters.'[6] Mochalov's Richard III was a malevolent figure with fiery eyes and convulsive gestures, whose desperate cry: 'A horse! A horse! My kingdom for a horse!' implied that this Richard, if he did manage to escape, would again assemble an army and bring further bloodshed to the land. The villainous figure of the limping Richard staggered the audience with its monstrous criminality, and at the same time attracted it with its brazen power and indomitable will.

As Othello, Mochalov made an unforgettable impression. More than half a century after the actor's death, Veinberg recalled: 'Never will I forget (Mochalov's) Othello weeping over the dead body of Desdemona, the expression on his face (his strongest and greatest feature!) when he rushed at Iago, never will I forget the whisper which replaced the expected cry – "O blood, blood, blood!"'[7] Mochalov's Hamlet was a triumph. Choosing to use Polevoi's translation of the play, he performed the role for his benefit performance on 22 January 1837. Polevoi's version departs to some extent from the original in that the hero seems to be an irritable, nervous person, full of unrest and discontent. Denmark is very seldom mentioned in the translation; often the word 'fatherland' is substituted, so that there is an implication that it is not Denmark which is a prison, but Russia. Mochalov chose to emphasise this interpretation by making Hamlet no weak and uncertain ditherer, but rather a fierce and heroic avenger. Instead of a suffering and meditative hero, this Hamlet was someone full of vitality and energy, and somehow this seemed to turn the thoughts of the spectators to contemporary Russian life and the military regime of Nikolai I, which stifled so many talented and free-minded people. Belinsky saw Mochalov as Hamlet eight times before writing his well-known article, 'Hamlet, Shakespeare's Drama; Mochalov as Hamlet'. In this, he analyses Mochalov's performance act by act, and is forced to admit that it was not until he saw Mochalov that he understood the profundity of the tragedy.

Mochalov's major roles on stage tended to show lonely, proud and pro-testing personalities, and most of his characters were rebels or fighters. His contemporary, Vasily Andreevich Karatygin, the other great exemplar of Russian romantic acting, was more methodical than Mochalov, less inspira-tional, more intellectual. Karatygin, who dominated St Petersburg's stages in the 1820s and 1830s much as Mochalov did Moscow's, began as partner to Ekaterina Semyonova, and carried something of her classicism with him throughout his long career. Karatygin and Mochalov were rivals who appeared together in Moscow in 1833 and 1835, provoking a lively contro-versy. The review of their performance in Schiller's *Mary Stuart* in the magazine *Molva* indicates something of their respective talents: 'The higher-ranking members of the audience were for Mr Karatygin; the middle classes were divided fifty-fifty; and the lower orders were for Mr Mochalov.'[8] Though Belinsky admired Karatygin's technique, he preferred Mochalov's enormous natural talent.

Early in his career, Karatygin was known for his romantic revolution-aries – regicides, avengers, rebels. He was especially admired by, and even was a member of, a group of progressive young people in St Petersburg in the 1820s. He knew Pushkin and Griboedov as well as several of the would-be revolutionists known as the Decembrists. But after the defeat of the 1825 Decembrist uprising, Karatygin changed completely. He realised that his connection with the group could ruin him, and he immediately swore alle-giance to the new tsar, Nikolai I. Suddenly he began to appear in chauvin-istic propaganda pieces which were dominating the Aleksandrinsky stage, and he never meddled in politics again.

Karatygin's approach to Shakespeare, always a supreme test of an actor, eschewed psychological sophistication: he tended to focus on the single major passion, and pour all his effort into creating an image of that. Thus, his Othello was jealous and only jealous; his Hamlet focused almost entirely on his struggle to gain the throne; and in *King Lear* Karatygin mesmerised the audience with his grandeur, and his elaborate, even noble, madness.

Being well aware that any talent requires constant polishing, Karatygin worked continually on his roles. He was the first Russian actor to make consistent use of literary and iconographic sources in his preparation for any role. It was said that the walls of his rehearsal room at home were covered with mirrors so that he could perfect every movement – every gesture, pose and turn of the head. Hard and systematic work, elaboration of many fine details, and a declamatory, decorative and dramatic style were the hallmarks of Karatygin's art.

In the mid-1830s, Karatygin was joined, and then perhaps overtaken, as the capital's most popular actor by Aleksandr Evstafyevich Martynov, who worked with him as the Aleksandrinsky's leading male actor for eighteen years, during which time the pair appeared in more than thirty plays together. Each was considered a genius, and each seemed to complement the other. Where Karatygin's art was considered 'elevated', Martynov's was regarded as 'low', and where the former played kings, courtiers, generals and noblemen, the latter presented servants, petty officials and janitors. Karatygin was about two metres tall, of solemn bearing and statuesque posture, with a powerful voice and an elaborate declamatory manner. But Martynov was small, had a dull-sounding voice, seemed often to articulate indistinctly, and frequently used tricks such as stammering or local accents to induce the audience to laugh. Karatygin seemed to glorify heroism, valour, honour; Martynov reminded people of suffering, misery and ill fortune. Karatygin's art was majestic and grand; Martynov's manner was matter-of-fact and modest. Karatygin was sometimes called the last representative of classicism, the style of the eighteenth century, whereas Martynov may be regarded as having something of the impressionism and psychological effects more usually associated with the twentieth century.

Vasily Karatygin was at the height of his fame when, in 1836, the twenty-year-old Martynov started his career at the Aleksandrinsky Theatre. It was the year of the first performance of Gogol's *The Government Inspector*, in which Martynov had the minor role of Bobchinsky. Gogol's artistic perception of the world, where the funny and the sad were blended in a full-blooded character, was close to Martynov's own. Perhaps this explains why some of Martynov's greatest successes came in Gogol's dramas, including his performance as Podkolyosin in *Marriage*, the Postmaster in the stage version of *Dead Souls*, and Khlestakov in *The Government Inspector*, which Lev Tolstoy admired. Indeed, Martynov's was the first true Khlestakov, according to Tolstoy. In these roles, Martynov presented a series of 'unimportant people' who were simultaneously funny and touching: attempts to create Gogol's 'smiles through tears' were never more successful than here. Martynov was also conspicuously successful in his playing of five different roles in four plays by Turgenev. Though unalike in character, all five had one thing in common – they contributed to the fashionable contemporary theme of the 'superfluous man'. Martynov presented humiliated dignity and the forlorn fight for personal respect through characters such as a petty provincial official, a poor landowner and an aged serf-servant. In the foreword to the first edition of his dramatic works, Turgenev wrote: 'With a feeling of deep gratitude I want to record that Martynov, this genius of an actor, bestowed merit upon four of the plays in this collection by acting in them.'[9]

Everyday happenings, impressions of people around him, the facts of contemporary life – these were significant sources of Martynov's work. He used to wander through crowds, drop into shops, stroll around the bazaars and haggle with vendors with no intention of buying, just for the sake of starting a conversation or catching an interesting speech intonation or linguistic idiom. Dandyish hussars, bribe-seeking officials, lazy landlords, affected provincial beauties and others afforded him raw material for his art, and he tried to memorise their gestures and manners for later – often humorous – use on the stage. Indeed, many of Martynov's most striking creations could be described as 'comic–serious'.

Martynov's partnership with Karatygin reached its apogee, perhaps, in two plays about actors which they performed together in the 1840s. The first was *Kean*, Alexandre Dumas's portrait of the great English actor, Edmund Kean, written for the French star, Frederick Lemaitre. The play is highly effective on stage, and not surprisingly attracted the attention of Karatygin, who decided to translate it himself. Under the title he gave it, *Genius and Disorder*, the play was presented at the Aleksandrinsky and was a notable success for Karatygin. Despite the fact that Kean is presented at one moment as a drunkard in a dirty pub, then as a man of the world, then as the sublime and inspired artist of the stage, the critic Grigoriev noticed the 'simplicity' of Karatygin's performance.[10] He was no longer the cold technician of earlier years, and was now more honest and direct in his acting.

Martynov, too, performed in *Genius and Disorder*. He played Salomon, the old prompter who loves the great actor unquestioningly, and remains endlessly devoted to him. Kean trusts Salomon who cares for the actor, helps him out of trouble and nurses him back to sobriety after his drinking bouts, so that Kean considers Salomon his only true friend. This friendship between the great actor and the insignificant prompter, however, is far from a partnership of equals. It smacks more of a master–servant relationship. And servants, of course, often see the weaknesses of their masters, and may take advantage of them, or at least regard them with irony. Martynov did none of this: his Salomon helped Kean to realise his romantic heroism as part of the stage life to which he was wedded. The leading actor and the unimportant prompter were in accord; Martynov followed Karatygin, supported him, and, excising his own quirkiness and individual style, presented a Salomon whose emotions and moods reflected those of his idol.

The Great Actor, or The Love of a Debutante, the second play about an actor in which Karatygin and Martynov appeared together, followed hard upon their success in Genius and Disorder, and indeed Kamensky, the author, was clearly influenced by Dumas's play. This time, Karatygin played another great English actor, David Garrick, and Martynov, the stage painter, Tom. The poetic world and elevated feelings associated by the romantic imagination with the world of the theatre came into direct conflict with the prosaic realities of everyday life: when Tom cannot pay his rent, his landlady ejects him from his lodgings despite his theatricalised appeal to her better feelings: 'But you go to the theatre! The theatre is a school for morals. It teaches how pleasant is the fruit of every good deed.'[11] When Garrick visits the scene-painter in his squalid lodgings and sees his misery, he reproaches him with hiding his poverty. Thus, the romanticism of the world of the theatre is interspersed with the everyday difficulties of ordinary people, high art with an apparent naturalism. Despite its frequently overheated melodrama, the play did manage to juxtapose Tom's sufferings and his miserable fate with Garrick's monologues and – a high point in the performance – the scene from King Lear acted by Karatygin as Garrick.

The partnership between these two actors flourished in such relationships. There was, for instance, Truth is the Tsar's Best Friend by Kukolnik, in which Karatygin played Prince Dolgorukov, valiant and noble, while Martynov was his tricky and mean-spirited antagonist; or Zotov's The Barge Skipper, in which Karatygin's solemn and elevated skipper was set against Martynov's provincial carpenter. The naive, fairytale performance showed again the opposition between the majestic and the simple, the important and the ordinary, the ideal and the natural – those classic ingredients of Karatygin and Martynov's 'duets'.

In 1846, Turgenev wrote: 'Ten years have passed since The Government Inspector was first performed. A wonderful change has come about since then in our ideas and in our demands.'[12] He was correct: in those ten short years the theatre was transformed, and by the end of them realism, the 'natural school', was predominant. These were the ten years of partnership between Karatygin and Martynov, but it should be noted that during them Karatygin passed his peak, while Martynov was yet to reach his. Had it not been so, had each been at the height of his career, their collaboration might not have been so productive, or so easy.

A new kind of spectator invaded the theatre in these years, demanding a new kind of experience. Fewer people came to the Aleksandrinsky simply to marvel at Karatygin's art. Luxurious coaches at the entrance became something of a rarity, and French was heard in the stalls more and more infrequently. The theatre was filled with officials, clerks, merchants and students: democratisation of the audience was taking place, and the repertoire was changing accordingly. For Karatygin, there was less and less scope, whereas Martynov became busier and busier. In 1844, Karatygin acted in thirteen new plays, Martynov in twenty-six; the following year Karatygin had only seven new roles, while Martynov had twenty-five. Karatygin could see the changes in theatre aesthetics and artistic styles developing, he was aware of the advent of realism, and though he modified his acting to something more simple and even natural, yet he remained within the realm of his magnificent past, among the famous and noble heroes, the parts which had brought him fame. Martynov, on the other hand, was one of the first Russian actors whose work was imbued with the spirit of contemporary reality: his characters might almost have stepped from the pages of Gogol or even Dostoevsky's St Petersburg tales.

Critics of later years could not envisage Karatygin and Martynov acting together; the artistic, psychological and social differences between them seemed too great. But the theatre, even before the advent of the director, is always capable of uniting and blending heterogeneous and seemingly incompatible elements. In a sense, the theatre itself acts as a director. This is what happened in the case of Karatygin and Martynov. Yet by the 1840s, the theatre of Karatygin's youth, the theatre that was spectacular, a show, a festival in its own right, was giving way to the 'theatre-pulpit'. The age when the Maly Theatre would become Moscow's 'second university' had almost arrived, and in 1853, the year of Karatygin's death, Ostrovsky's play, *Out of Place*, was staged at the Aleksandrinsky, prompting A. I. Wolf to assert that 'From that day, rhetorical insincerity and Gallomania gradually began to disappear from Russian drama.'[13]

Ostrovsky's dramas required a new kind of actor, and especially one attuned to the needs of the ensemble. For Martynov, to step in this direction was not only feasible but also liberating, and he became the dramatist's associate and friend. Up to 1860, the year of Martynov's death, the Aleksandrinsky staged no fewer than ten of Ostrovsky's plays, and Martynov appeared in eight of them. His most successful role was probably that of Tikhon in *The Storm*, whom he interpreted as a man broken by the Domostroi regime (the strict rule of household and social etiquette), feeble and timid in his protests, but in the last scene a passionate exposer of such inhuman domination of ordinary life. For Ostrovsky, Martynov remained one of Russia's outstanding actors, one of the best representatives of 'the natural and expressive manner'.[14]

Martynov was able to make the step from romanticism to realism – indeed he was a significant catalyst for this change – but his success in this latter style never matched that of Mikhail Semyonovich Shchepkin, whom many still regard as the greatest Russian actor of all time. While the careers of many important actors have given rise to argument and controversy, Shchepkin's art has been unanimously accepted, and his talent never doubted. People of widely opposing political and aesthetic views were in agreement when they came to appraise Shchepkin's great gifts. He had an enviable reputation for hard work, and this, and the fact that he was known as a staunch friend, family man and fighter for social justice, made him attractive to many. He radiated kindness and optimism, and placed his faith in people and progress. He died at the age of seventy-five, having spent sixty-three of those years on the stage. Born a serf, he made his debut in Sumarokov's comedy, *The Quarreller*, at the age of twelve while still at Sudzhensk High School, while only a month before his death he appeared as the Mayor in *The Government Inspector*.

Shchepkin's career began in the provinces: he worked in Kursk, Kiev, Poltava and other towns. Only in 1821, when he was already a well-known provincial actor, did he manage to obtain liberation for himself, his wife and his two elder daughters. In the summer of 1822 in Romna in the Ukraine, he appeared in Sudovshchikov's comedy, *An Experience of Art*, in which he had seven roles, including a soldier, a member of the gentry, a German woman and a match-maker. A representative of a Moscow theatrical agency saw this surprising piece of virtuosity and offered to secure Shchepkin a place in a Moscow company. Shchepkin accepted, and that autumn he made his debut there. As the *Moscow Gazette* of 20 September

1822 announced, 'Today, Imperial Russian actors of the Mokhovaya Street Theatre present the debut of Mr Shchepkin, who has come from Tula and before that played in Poltava, in *Mr Bogatonov, or A Provincial in the Capital.*' The play, a loose Russian adaptation of Molière's *The Would-be Gentleman*, provided Shchepkin with one of his best parts, so that from his very first performance in Moscow Shchepkin's eminence was assured.

Soon the former serf became one of the most respected actors in Russia, and a familiar name in the circles of the progressive Moscow intelligentsia. Thus, when he studied the part of Famusov in *Woe from Wit* it was with the help of the author himself. Pushkin urged Shchepkin to write his auto-biography, and even wrote the opening lines for him. Shchepkin's friends included Gogol, Belinsky, Shevchenko and Herzen, as well as, later, Nekrasov, Turgenev, Ostrovsky and many other outstanding figures in the Moscow of his time.

During his long stage career, Shchepkin played about 600 roles. It is impossible to classify such a vast number, whose variety was staggering, but his contemporaries seemed to perceive two main trends: satirical characters and 'unimportant people'. Major roles of the first kind included the Mayor in *The Government Inspector* and Famusov in *Woe from Wit.* He first per-formed Famusov on 31 January 1830, and kept the role in his repertoire for over thirty years. Despite his immense popularity in the part, and the critics' constant enthusiasm, he himself felt his interpretation wanted nobility. It may be that Shchepkin did indeed lack grandeur and lordliness – his Famusov was perhaps not a man of the nobility – but on the other hand he was, as Griboedov specified in the stage directions, 'a manager of an official place'. This Famusov's haughtiness and arrogance towards his inferiors existed side by side with an obsequiousness and an excessive admiration for the titled nobility. Shchepkin had a perfect feeling for Griboedov's poetics, and written descriptions of his monologues as Famusov show that he brilliantly combined the poetic rhymes with the psychological interpretation of the comic character.

Shchepkin's Mayor in *The Government Inspector* came over as 'true to life' and full of vitality. Belinsky wrote that 'the actor has understood the poet's idea: he too wants to show something which is to be found in real life, but something which is also characteristic and typical'.[15] 'Watch his behaviour in the fifth act, in the episode with the merchants,' wrote Grigoriev. 'This is no longer the Mayor who was like a rain-soaked chicken in front of the imaginary inspector; now he is Prometheus, a genuine Prometheus! . . .

How can this man, full of rough and rampant energy, delighting in the pleasures of revenge and relaxing on imaginary laurel leaves, suddenly be turned into nothing when he reads Khlestakov's letter? His energy becomes feverish, yet within this there is still room for comic pathos.'[16]

The second major trend within Shchepkin's work consisted of images of 'unimportant people'. In an article on the Aleksandrinsky Theatre, Belinsky wrote: 'Without doubt Shchepkin is wonderful as Famusov or as the Mayor, but it is not these roles that form his true line. Whoever has seen him in the small part of the sailor in the play of the same name (and who hasn't?) will easily understand his real strength. That lies in his portrayal of people of the lower middle classes, ordinary people, parts that require not only comic effect but also an element of deep pathos.' And later in the same article, Belinsky added: 'The part of the sailor seems to have been written especially for him, it is a triumph of his talent.'[17]

Why was this particular part so remarkable? The one-act play, *The Sailor*, by Sauvage and Desluriet, is an example of the so-called 'dramatic vaudeville', in which traditional vaudeville is combined with a dramatic plot. Shchepkin first played the sailor, Simon, in 1835, and continued with it until 1860. The play tells the story of Simon, a peasant who is drafted into the armed forces a year after his marriage, becomes a sailor, is captured and imprisoned, and after twenty years of roaming the world, returns home. Everything has changed: his wife received notification of his death long ago, and has married Simon's oldest friend; and his daughter is already a young woman. Simon realises that his appearance would ruin the happiness of his former family, so after some cogitation he leaves his native village. This simple and sentimental story was turned into a heartbreaking dramatic creation by Shchepkin's acting. The playwright Diachenko wrote:

> Throughout the performance you watch a sailor who loves his fatherland, glory and the people dear to him. How fine is his entry, how wondrously he expresses the happiness of returning, and at the same time his secret sorrow at the thought that his wife and daughter may no longer exist! Soon he learns that his wife is alive, but married. Poor Simon! How shocked you are at the murderous news! You do not say a word, nor utter a single complaint, but you are in a terrible state, your wild crazy eyes glisten with tears, and the audience can understand what is happening in your soul. No, in this horrifying minute,

Shchepkin did not speak, but his beautiful face expressed all he felt, and the whole theatre, in reverence, did not dare applaud, so great was the power of his talent.[18]

Shchepkin's heroes in Turgenev's plays *The Parasite* and *The Bachelor* were also 'unimportant people'. The central figure in the first of these, Kuzovkin, is a humble man, totally without rights, a poor member of the gentry who boards in his benefactor's house without paying. Early Dostoevskian influence can be perceived in this character, and since the play was banned by the censors, Shchepkin read scenes from it in private houses in Moscow and St Petersburg to invited audiences. But perhaps because it was banned from print and from public presentation, the play almost inevitably aroused great interest. Herzen and Nekrasov thought highly of it, and after the abolition of serfdom it was permitted a stage production. Shchepkin, at the age of seventy-four, played Kuzovkin in the first performance in Moscow on 30 January 1862, and to great acclaim. For his benefit performance in St Petersburg on 14 October 1849, Shchepkin chose Turgenev's comedy, *The Bachelor*, in which he acted the part of Moshkin for the first time. Nekrasov, who was present at the performance, wrote: 'Difficult as this part is, it is absolutely no problem for Shchepkin's strength and talent. Throughout the third act, starting with the episode when the old man worries about the fate of his ward, Shchepkin triumphs . . . The applause never stopped.' Nekrasov concluded his article with an expression of gratitude to Shchepkin for presenting this new Russian comedy.[19]

Shchepkin was also responsible for raising to new heights Russian performances of West European classics, especially by Shakespeare, but also by Molière, Schiller and others. Panaev was sure that 'no other Russian actor knows and understands Shakespeare as well as Shchepkin'.[20] Perhaps part of the reason for this was his close friendship with Ketcher, one of the best translators of Shakespeare, whose versions he urged for performance. The actor was also keen to promote a more profound understanding of Shakespeare among his colleagues, and persuaded his friend, Professor Granovsky, to read a lecture on *Hamlet* when the play was to be produced.

Shchepkin performed notably in many of Shakespeare's plays. Often he chose Shakespeare for his benefit performances, as when he appeared as Shylock in *The Merchant of Venice* in 1835, as Ford, the jealous husband, in *The Merry Wives of Windsor* in 1838, as the Fool in *King Lear* in 1859, and

Brabantio in *Othello* in 1861. Perhaps his most interesting Shakespearean performance was as Polonius in *Hamlet* to Mochalov's Prince. Belinsky wrote:

> The part of Polonius is played by Shchepkin, whose mere name guarantees something close to perfection. In fact, half the second scene of the first act and most of the second act were a real delight for the audience, even though Mochalov did not appear on the stage. Best of all was the episode in the second act when the two actors came together . . . Polonius and Shchepkin merge into one as Hamlet and Mochalov merge. If our spectators did not fully appreciate Shchepkin as Polonius, it is for two reasons: firstly, their attention was concentrated completely on Hamlet, and secondly they perceived only the comical in Shchepkin's acting, rather than the evolution of the character, which was his particular triumph. A large part of the audience was prepared to laugh whenever they saw Shchepkin, be it in the part of Shylock, so deep in sorrow and so representative of universal ideas, or in the role of the sailor, which provokes tears rather than laughter.[21]

It had for long been usual for audiences to divide actors into comic or tragic, and to respond accordingly. Shchepkin opposed this notion vehemently throughout his career, and his success was to be seen in another line in which he excelled, namely the portrayal of misers. Besides Shylock in *The Merchant of Venice*, he created other memorable 'mixed' characters such as Harpagon in Molière's *The Miser*, Sir Giles Overreach in Massinger's tragedy, *A New Way to Pay Old Debts*, and the Baron in Pushkin's 'little tragedy', *The Covetous Knight*.

Shchepkin is rightly considered to be the founder of 'realism' in Russian acting. Having started his career attempting to create verisimilitude simply in speech, he came to realise that the truth of acting lies in the inner logic of the character. He became more and more convinced that it was of major importance for the actor to feel that the character presented by him was true to real life. Shchepkin was sure that the actor must penetrate into the soul of the character, and get under the skin of the person he was playing. In the years when acting technique was abstract, superficial, and effect-oriented, Shchepkin consistently fought for the character's truth to life. 'It was he who created truth on the Russian stage. He was the first to become non-theatrical in the theatre, his presentations were without any affectation or exaggeration.' That is how Herzen defined his significance.[22]

7. Mikhail Shchepkin in Kotlyarevsky's vaudeville *The Charming Muscovite* (with Kotlyarevsky himself in the centre).

Shchepkin was renowned as a man of high morals and firm friendships, and he was never afraid to promulgate his beliefs or behave according to his principles. Thus, he did all he could to distract his friend Gogol from his gloomy moods, and he defied the danger of attracting the attention of the police by travelling to Nizhny Novgorod to visit his friend, the Ukrainian poet Taras Shevchenko, when he returned from exile. Shchepkin liked to amuse his friends with stories about the old-time theatre and its ways, and writers sometimes transplanted these into their own works. Thus, Shchepkin's tale of the tragic fate of a talented serf actress found its way into Herzen's 'The Thieving Magpie', and Gogol, Sukhovo-Kobylin, Nekrasov and Ostrovsky, among others, were all similarly indebted to Shchepkin.

In 1853, at the age of 65, Shchepkin travelled to London to meet the writer and political exile Herzen, who was agitating Russian society with his revolutionary magazine *The Bell*. Herzen described how, at the time:

I was completely isolated in a crowd of strange and semi-familiar faces
. . . Russians at the time rarely travelled abroad, and most were afraid of

me . . . The first Russian who came to London and was not frightened to stretch his hand out to me as in previous years was Mikhail Semyonovich Shchepkin. I could not wait until he came to London, and on the morning of his arrival, I took the express train to Folkestone . . . When the ship approached the land, the stout figure of Shchepkin stood out from the crowd on board. I waved my handkerchief at him and rushed down . . . We went to London together, I urgently enquiring about minute details concerning my friends, small things without which faces are no longer alive . . . He told me all sorts of nonsense, we laughed until we cried.[23]

Some of his Moscow friends long remembered Shchepkin's attempt, doomed to failure, to persuade Herzen to give up his editorial activity and return to Russia. As might have been expected, Herzen did not take this advice, but nonetheless they parted on extremely good terms.

At least one subsequent event revealed the impact Shchepkin's trip to London had on him, and it showed how he had understood what Herzen was doing, and how he himself could put this knowledge to use. In 1857, a few years after Shchepkin's visit to London, Turgenev described the incident to Herzen: 'Action was taken against Moscow actors: they were not paid the money they had earned. They sent old Shchepkin to Gedeonov, the head of the Imperial Theatres, in pursuit of justice, which would be like trying to milk a billy goat, no chance at all. Naturally, Gedeonov would not listen. "Then we shall have to complain to the minister," said Shchepkin. "Don't you dare!" replied Gedeonov. "In that case, I will complain to *The Bell*." Gedeonov turned red in the face, and agreed to give the actors their money. See what fine tricks your *Bell* plays!'[24]

Finally, it must be recorded that Shchepkin also exercised great influence on the development of acting as an art in Russia. During his lifetime, a number of outstanding Moscow actors, mostly from the Maly Theatre, regarded themselves as his disciples. One such was Samarin, also a former serf, who had worked in the theatre since 1837, and who had particularly distinguished himself in the role of Chatsky in *Woe from Wit*. But he also won acclaim for his performance as Famusov in the same play, a role in which he closely followed Shchepkin's interpretation. Samarin was also a notable Mayor in *The Government Inspector*, again using many of Shchepkin's innovations. In the 1860s, on Shchepkin's initiative and under his direction, the Maly Theatre staged Shakespeare's *The Taming of the*

Shrew and *Much Ado about Nothing* with Samarin as Petruchio and Benedick. Since Samarin also taught Shchepkin's methods at the Moscow School of Acting, and among his students were Nikullina and Fedotova, it is possible to see how Shchepkin's traditions lived on into the twentieth century. Again, in 1839, on Shchepkin's insistence, the Maly Theatre company admitted to its ranks Sadovsky, the first of a notable family of Russian actors, who specialised in simple and true-to-life roles, such as those provided by Ostrovsky. Meanwhile in St Petersburg, at the Aleksandrinsky Theatre for example, Shchepkin could count among his followers Martynov, Sosnitsky, Vasilev and others, the actors who brought about the complete victory of realism on the Russian stage. It was a trend which had been introduced and asserted by Shchepkin. Indeed it can be argued that Shchepkin laid the foundations of the system of acting which would be brought to its finest fruition in the work of Stanislavsky.

Thus it was that in a mere three decades Russian theatre was utterly changed by the transformation of acting styles. The capering comicalities of the vaudeville theatre, and the morbid intensity of romanticism, were alike extinguished, and something approaching a realistic style such as we would recognise today had replaced it.

Notes

1. K. S. Stanislavskii, *Sobranie sochinenii,* vol. 1 (Moscow, 1954), p. 36.

2. I. N. Medvedeva, *Ekaterina Semenova: zhisn' i tvorchestvo tragicheskoi aktrisy* (Moscow, 1964), p. 6.

3. A. Ia. Altschuller, 'Mnenie aktrisy Kateriny Semenovoi ob uluchshenii dramaticheskikh predstavlenii', *Teatr,* 2 (1952), 36.

4. V. G. Belinskii, *Polnoe sobranie sochinenii,* vol. VIII (Moscow, 1955), p. 530.

5. *Pavel Stepanovich Mochalov. Zametki o teatre, pis'ma, stikhi, p'ecy. Sovremenniki o Mochalov* (Moscow, 1953), p. 357.

6. P. I. Veinberg, *Iz moikh teatral'nykh vospominanii. Ezhegodnik Imperatorskikh Teatrov,* 1894/5, supplement, book 1, p. 84.

7. Ibid. p. 83.

8. N. I. Nadezhdin, 'Pis'ma k g. izdateliu "Teleskopa"', *Molva,* 19 (1835), col. 319.

9. I. S. Turgenev, *Polnoe sobranie sochinenii i pisem,* vol. III (Moscow and Leningrad, 1962), p. 245.

10. A. A. Grigor'ev, *Teatral'naya kritika* (Leningrad, 1985), p. 49.

11. P. P. Kamenskii, *Velikii akter liubov' debiutantki. Rukopisnyi ikz.* From a collection of the St Petersburg Theatre Library. Quote from Act 1, scene 3.

12. Turgenev, vol. XI (Moscow and Leningrad, 1960), p. 258.

13. A. I. Vol'f, *Khronika Peterburgskikh teatrov s kontsa 1826 do nachala 1855 goda*, part 1 (1877), p. 156.

14. A. N. Ostrovskii, *Polnoe sobranie sochinenii* (Moscow, 1978), vol. x, p. 86.

15. Belinskii, vol. vii (Moscow, 1978), p. 229–30.

16. Grigor'ev, p. 119.

17. Belinskii, vol. x (Moscow, 1978), p. 86.

18. V. A. D'iachenko, *Kharkovskii teatr* (Pribavleniia k *Kharkovskim gubernskim vedomostiam* – Supplement to the *Kharkov Province News*), 2 October 1843, p. 3.

19. 'Kholostiak, komediia v 3–x deistviiakh Ivana Turgeneva', *Sovremennik,* 11 (St Petersburg, 1849), p. 142.

20. I. I. Panaev, 'Zametki o Peterburgskoi zhisni', *Sovremennik,* 12 (St Petersburg, 1855), p. 267.

21. Belinskii, vol. ii (Moscow, 1977), p. 86.

22. A. I. Gerzen, *Polnoe sobranie sochinenii*, vol. xvii (Moscow, 1959), p. 268.

23. Ibid.

24. Turgenev, vol. iii, p. 181.

6 Popular, provincial and amateur theatres 1820–1900

CATRIONA KELLY

In 1827 Tsar Nikolai I instituted the Theatrical Monopoly – a decree placing public theatrical performances in St Petersburg and Moscow under the control of the state-run Imperial Theatres. He intended this measure, in the first place, as an instrument of censorship within the elite theatre. By dictating that all plays for public performance in the two capitals should have their suitability scrutinised by a special board, Nikolai hoped to ensure that the theatre would continue to be, as Catherine II and other eighteenth-century opinion formers had envisioned it, the place where appropriate political views would be expressed, and decorous behaviour encouraged.[1] The fate of the popular theatre concerned Nikolai not at all. Yet, for all that 1827 was, for the popular theatre, nearly as significant a date as 1648, the year when Tsar Aleksei banned the *skomorolchi*. The date was important, not because it changed the character of popular entertainment, as the decree of 1648 had done, but because, until its suspension in 1882, the Theatrical Monopoly artificially stifled the growth of a central, metropolitan theatrical tradition in Russia. Consequently, the marginal theatres – the theatres of urban fairgrounds and pleasure gardens, the street shows and cabarets, the amateur theatricals of drawing rooms and salons, and the theatres of the provinces – had an especially important role in the development of the Russian theatre, a situation which led to some agonised discussions. Russians who wished to see their country develop a national theatrical tradition, fully reflecting and participating in literary life, were repeatedly brought up against the contradiction between the Imperial Theatres' symbolic role as spearhead of this national tradition, and the practical limits on their influence, given that they were inaccessible to most of Russia's population. Compared with the central Imperial Theatres, the marginal theatres employed and gave seating space to vast numbers of people. But on the other hand, their very size and commercial success made them amorphous; they were not immediately responsive to the dictates of literary taste. Certainly, some marginal theatres, such as the major provincial theatres and the amateur performances got up in the drawing rooms and salons of intellectuals and aristocrats, staged texts refused by the Imperial Theatres, and so furthered the cause of high literature. But in others, theatrical performance was primarily associated with entertainment, and literary aspirations were scarcely recognised. This was especially the case with the popular theatres of big cities.

The history of the popular theatre in the nineteenth century is closely bound up with the struggle to impose on the lower classes of Russian society the idea that the theatre should be mainly, if not exclusively, an instrument of education and enlightenment. This struggle was marked by an insistence, on the part of those who wished to direct the taste of the lower classes, that what is 'popular' in the sense of familiar and well-loved amongst the masses, is not necessarily the same thing as 'popular' in the sense of 'expressing the true spirit of the people'. If the terms of the debate were often similar to those invoked in other Western countries, the debate's intensity was often rather greater. The wholly undemocratic nature of Russian society meant that 'the people's will' could not be objectively determined; yet at the same time this unknowable quantity was constantly evoked as a legitimation for radicalism or reaction. The question of what ordinary Russians wanted to watch in the theatre, therefore, was an inflammatory topic. Any preparedness in them to watch 'quality' material (for example, plays by Pushkin or Shakespeare) was felt to indicate a desire for self-betterment, a desire which might be threatening or uplifting, depending on the observer's point of view. A taste for low entertainments, on the other hand, might indicate, again depending on a commentator's ideology, either a pleasing loyalty to quaint and folksy pastimes, or else a fatuous conservatism of outlook, fostered and manipulated by members of the reactionary elite (and, in the late nineteenth century, by the grasping capitalists whom Russian radicals assumed to be that elite's natural allies).

Views 'for' and 'against' the popular theatre did not split radicals and reactionaries once and for all, but depended on the relative status of populism within these opposing parties. Before 1840, serfdom seemed so entrenched that most Russians, even if opposed to absolutism, could hardly imagine 'the people' to be an active political force. The gentlemen and aristocrats who then made up the opposition shared the general views of their class. Occasional flashes of proprietorial irritation, contempt or pity for the 'people' or 'the common herd' did not curdle the vague and generalising benevolence that had been warmed by the sense of the part 'the people' had played in defeating Napoleon.[2]

Between 1812 and the late 1830s, members of the upper classes in St Petersburg and Moscow continued to amuse themselves at such elegant venues as the Elagin and Kamenny Islands, or the Tverskoy Boulevard.[3] As in the eighteenth century, they would also pay visits to the places where 'the people' traditionally disported themselves. The difference was that they did not now merely observe from their carriages (as had been the custom), but walked amongst the crowds, and even participated in some of the amusements. Pyotr Svinin's 1814 account of grand St Petersburg ladies tobogalning down the ice-hills with fur pelisses over their gauzy gowns is perhaps apocryphal, but the woman poet Evdokia Rostopchina nostalgically recalled, in 1839, the seasonal funfairs of 1820s Moscow as a time when the classes mixed freely:

For a single day, for one brief hour,
The rumbustious merriment of the common herd
And the frigid grandeur of the aristocrat
Mingled, making show one for the other.[4]

The cross-class carnival did not last, however. The upper classes soon returned to their own exclusive pursuits; and, with the arrival, after 1840, and especially after 1860, of new kinds of populism, informed by socialist visions of egalitarian societies, the established lower-class entertainments of Russian cities began to be seen by radicals as detrimental to progress.[5] The nineteenth-century Russian state, less interventionist than its twentieth-century successor, was slow to accept that popular entertainments were anything other than benign. But from the 1880s, the tsarist authorities, confronted with the need to provide leisure activities other than drinking for an expanding urban population, became converted to the 'rational leisure' movement, encouraging the development, both on a commercial and on a philanthropic basis, of low-cost amusements aimed at the working population, and then beginning to organise such amusements themselves.[6]

This short résumé of nineteenth-century institutional and ideological history is intended to function as a kind of chronological carapace for the survey of the marginal theatres' specific theatrical traditions that follows. I shall deal first with the popular theatrical entertainments on offer in Russian cities, before giving a briefer account of the rather different traditions of the provincial theatres and amateur theatres of Russia.

The urban popular theatre

By 1820, the small genres of the Russian popular theatre – the peepshow, the clown monologue and the *Petrushka* show – were already established entertainments. These were to remain fairly stable in outline, if not in detail, throughout the nineteenth century. The larger genres of the Russian fairground, however, were all established, and underwent significant changes, during the nineteenth century itself.

One important early development affected the circus. Occasional acrobats and animal-trainers had begun appearing in Russia, as individuals and as members of troupes, from the early eighteenth century, but the nineteenth century was to see a shift to a new understanding of the circus as a fixed institution offering a mixed programme of acrobatics, animal acts, clown shows and often also pantomimes or spectaculars, in a dedicated building. In 1827, the first permanent circus was founded in St Petersburg; from then on, circus acts were to be amongst the best-loved theatrical entertainments in Russia. The Russian state's attempt to cash in on the success of commercial initiatives by establishing an Imperial Circus proved short-lived; but all over the Russian Empire, private fixed or touring circuses, most famously the Ciniselli Circus in St Petersburg, kept up an internationally admired tradition until (and in their nationalised form even after) the revolution.[7]

With its mixed programme of entertainments, all more or less 'theatrical', but depending to a different degree on spoken dialogue and narrative (from clown shows at one extreme to liberty horses and trapeze acts on the other), the circus was typical of nineteenth-century traditions of popular entertainment. It was flexible in overall structure, readily allowing the absorption of independent shows once these became popular (the clown show, the harlequinade and the hit song all being examples). Other popular genres displayed just as much freedom of adaptation. With some, such as the 'variety show' or 'cinema miniatures' (a mixture of variety numbers and film shorts), admixture of genres was an essential characteristic; but even those which were apparently more unified were usually in practice susceptible to the *bricolage* principle. Popular songs might start life in a vaudeville, before moving on to an independent existence as 'standards' performed on request by street and tavern singers; from there they might make their way into puppet-shows or clown shows, with or without the assistance of printed songbooks. A notorious murder might first be captured by the doggerel street balladeers who were as common in Russia as in other nineteenth-century European countries, before becoming the subject for a melodrama, an anecdote, or a joke. Witticisms moved freely from genre to genre, and from the printed word to the spoken word, and back again. Anything new, anything interesting, was grist to the performer's mill. But so, too, was anything already known to work, the new and the well-worn being fashioned into a curious and beguiling patchwork.[8]

The popular theatre mixed media as freely as it mixed genres. Even in the humble puppet-shows, the sharp, punning dialogues were offset by gaudy costumes and booths wrapped in bright printed fabric, and musical accompaniment was provided by a barrel-organ. Small-scale shows that primarily depended on visual effect, such as the panorama or the peepshow, were furnished with a verbal commentary (in the latter case), or background music (in the former). Melodramas allowed scope for lurid sound and lighting effects. The extremely popular full-length genre of vaudeville, much favoured in *cafés-chantants* and pleasure gardens long after it fell out of fashion in the Imperial Theatres, interrupted its comic dialogue with stretches of visual comedy, and comic songs (*kuplety*), often of mildly risqué content. The most spectacular visual and musical effects of all, elaborating a straightforward narrative line, were used in the harlequinades of the early nineteenth century, and the grandiose pantomimes and *feerii* (fairy shows) that succeeded them. In the harlequinades, predictable love intrigues and dramas of mistaken identity were performed with multiple costume transformations and disguises, mechanical effects, light illusions, and other 'magic' tricks. In the pantomimes of the mid nineteenth century, patriotic subjects such as *The Battle of Sinope* or *The Conquest of the Caucasus* were acted out by dozens of horses and actors, and perhaps even by boats on real lakes, to the accompaniment of thundering cannon, flashing lights, and wafting gunpowder. Finally, the *feerii*, elaborations of the simpler panorama, displayed pseudoscientific subjects such as *A Trip to the Moon* or *A Voyage Round the World*, each scene using different light effects and music to create an appropriate atmosphere.[9]

My account so far has concentrated on the similarities of urban popular entertainments, whether performed at the traditional Shrove and Easter fairground sites (which in the nineteenth century were the Admiralty, and later the Field of Mars and then the Semyonov Platz in St Petersburg, and the Podnovinskoe Field, and later the Devichye Field, in Moscow), or at summer pleasure gardens (such as the upmarket Elagin and downmarket

Krestovsky Islands in St Petersburg, or the Hermitage in Moscow), in expensive restaurants, cheap taverns, or on the street. There were also similarities in the lives of Russian popular entertainers, no matter where they worked. Many artistes moved from position to position seasonally, spending the Shrove and Easter seasons at the fairgrounds having done the rounds of bars, restaurants and courtyards in the winter, and then finding a patch at some pleasure garden, or near the dachas of holidaying city-dwellers, in the summer. Wherever itinerant artistes lived, their existence was hard – a fact that the romantic and post-romantic sentimentalisation of *saltimbanques* and hurdy-gurdy players should not allow us to overlook. Certainly, there were some remarkable success stories. The turn-of-the-century gypsy singer Varvara Panina, for example, became one of the most famous women in Russia; whilst her fabulous triumphs were beyond most people, many competent performers, even street performers such as the puppeteer Zaitsev, did well enough in a quiet way, and lived respectable lives. Others, however, were overworked, dishevelled, perpetually harassed, and lived in cramped and bug-ridden lodgings with little food and fewer comforts. Worst off, perhaps, were the actors and circus artistes in low-quality troupes, since their pay often depended on a share of the profits assigned at whim by the entrepreneur; solo performers, such as street singers, *Petrushka* players, and peep-show owners, had more direct control over their earnings, especially if they owned their own equipment.[10]

Over-stretched, underpaid, and with insufficient leisure time, performers lived no better, in a material sense, than the working classes in general. However, they also lived no worse, and no doubt enjoyed a greater sense of freedom and job satisfaction – even if, to outside observers, their demeanour on occasion suggested the sulky boredom of jaded office workers rather than the painted cheerfulness of Petit Trianon milkmaids, as in Maurice Baring's evocative description of a group of gypsy singers:

The gipsies are not raggle-taggle people in shabby and gorgeous clothes. They are a chorus of men and women in ordinary dress who, though swarthy in complexion, look like the audience in the upper circle at a Queen's Hall concert. [They] show signs of the boredom and fatigue common to professionals engaged in the performance of their professional duties. They yawn. One of them has got a toothache and a swollen face. They carry on an undercurrent of irrelevant conversation amongst themselves, whilst they automatically sing.[11]

Whatever the overall similarities in the urban entertainments of Russian cities, and in the lives of the entertainers, there were also, of course, important differences depending on the exclusivity, or otherwise, of a venue, and the economic resources of its clientele and management. The more expensive the venue, the more spectacular the show, was the obvious rule – and often, too, the better the performers. However, the cheapest shows, with their strings of double entendres and malicious insults, could offer a compensatory rough energy and collusive rapport between performers and spectators. An account in Bakhtiarov's encyclopedic study of Russian low-life, *The Belly of Petersburg*, effectively conveys the electricity generated by a roundabout clown show in the 1880s:

> 'Ladies and gents, roll up, roll up for the lottery! Win an ox's tail, win half a dead whale! Oooh look, here's a teapot: no bottom, no top and no sides – but the handle should make a fine prize! Nice teapot, eh?'
> 'Yes! Yes!'
> 'And look here, gents: who wants to buy my estate? Fine heap of stones in Smolenskoe cemetery: been two hundred years in the family! And a dozen hankies for blowing your nose – made them out of me old underclothes!'
> 'Ha, ha, ha!'
> 'Here, but what am I doing?' bawls the clown, whacking himself on the head as if he'd just remembered something. 'I haven't introduced my mates to you!'
> He makes a big show of rushing back into the roundabout building, and drags out three girls. They all have snub noses, and cheeks thickly painted in red and white; they are wearing short skirts, silver-braided velvet jackets, and small round hats. They smile brightly at the crowd, ogling them invitingly.
> 'Will you look at her, making a real present of herself, eh!' says someone in the crowd.
> . . .
> The clown starts dancing the quadrille, the mazurka, and all sorts of other dances with the girls, making erotically suggestive movements with his body all the while.
> 'Not bad for an old 'un, eh!'
> 'There's juice in the old boy yet!'
> Encouraged by the crowd's shouts, the clown stops every now and

again and puts his arm round one of the girls, planting a smacking kiss on her lips.

. . .

'Eh, lads, have a look over there: I do believe a skoobent has turned up. He's finished at college, got his degree, now the Poor Law Board pays his sal–a–ry!'

Discomfited by this witticism, the young man beats a hasty and embarrassed retreat.[12]

Unlike their sleeker counterparts in expensive restaurants, the fairground and street performers lived close to the ordinary lives of their audiences. Their shows drew from the repartee of the Russian streets; in turn, the badinage of market traders (some of whom worked as clowns during the festival season) acted as another kind of street theatre. One memoirist recalls that, during his childhood in the 1860s, boy candle-sellers would sing a verse running, 'Candles made of real tallow!/Lovely and yellow!/They shine so nicely!/Lovely and brightly!' Rival traders would respond with their own verse: 'They drip and smell funny!/Don't waste your money!'[13]

It was the unseemly commercialism of the popular theatre, as well as its unseemliness in other ways, that was to disconcert and even disgust many concerned Russian radicals, who were both high-minded and anti-capitalist. During the late 1860s, as radical groups got to grips with the aftermath of the 1861 Emancipation of the Serfs, the question of suitable and proper entertainment for the lower classes came under increasing scrutiny. Philanthropic groups, such as the Moscow Society for the Welfare of Working People, argued that the provision of appropriate leisure activities, most particularly a 'people's theatre', or a 'theatre for all', was essential if workers' lives were to be improved. The imperial authorities were suspicious, seeing in such measures a covert attempt to subvert the Theatrical Monopoly, as well as to sow radicalism and discontent amongst the lower classes. But in 1872 they bowed to pressure and allowed the construction of a low-price theatre in Moscow, on a site next door to the Polytechnical Exhibition that had been set up to celebrate the bicentenary of Peter I's birth. This theatre was, however, allowed to remain open only a few months. The 'people's theatre' movement was refused permission for a more permanent institution; a so-called 'theatre for all' in the Moscow suburbs, allowed by the authorities, was in fact too expensive to fulfil its role.[14]

In St Petersburg, an early and interesting experiment in the 'people's theatre' movement was represented by the Entertainment and Benefit Theatre, begun by A. Ya. Alekseev-Yakovlev in 1878, which played on the Shrovetide fairground, and which represented a half-way stage between the popular theatre and the 'people's theatre'.[15] But the 'people's theatre' movement did not really take off until after the end of the Theatrical Monopoly in 1882. The Nevsky Society for Popular Entertainments, founded in 1885, set up the first St Petersburg theatre for working people in 1887, in an industrial section of the Vasilevsky Island; other theatres, sponsored by similar societies, were set up shortly afterwards, in places such as the Vyborg District, the Imperial Porcelain Factory, and Krestovsky Island.[16] In Moscow, development was to be even slower. The Skomorokh Theatre (which ran from 1882–3, and then from 1885–91) offered cheap places and attractive programmes, but was not a 'people's theatre' in the sense of those at Vasilevsky Island or Vyborg. Although interest in the 'people's theatre' movement was high during the 1880s, it was only in the late 1890s that the cumbersomely entitled Society for the Furtherment of the Organisation of Generally Educational Entertainments for the People, set up 'rational leisure' centres all over Moscow and its suburbs.[17]

The notion that one might offer workers cheap leisure activities on or near the site where they lived and worked appealed to industrialists as well as philanthropists; the extent to which entrepreneurs participated can be sensed from Chekhov's story 'A Doctor's Case-Notes', in which the *bien-pensant* protagonist's cynical doubt about the actual benefits of organised leisure schemes is an indication of the extent to which employers now accepted them as necessary.[18] However, by no means all rational leisure schemes included full-scale theatres, since the cost of maintaining these was enormous. The fairground theatres, which had always charged prices low enough to allow working-class people to attend, had operated over a very short season, with as many as sixteen or twenty performances a day, and had therefore turned in a good profit. The pleasure gardens were also seasonal, operating over the summer months, and offered a range of entertainments amongst which consumers could select according to pocket. The people's theatres, on the other hand, aimed to offer a full dramatic programme at prices that were as low as those of traditional entertainments, or indeed even lower: in order to tempt factory workers, the St Petersburg people's theatres began by offering free tickets through the workplace.[19] The very large subsidies required if people's theatres were to be viable meant that the real turning-point in their history came with the Tsarist government's decision to place its full weight behind the temperance movement. In 1895, an official agency, the Directorate of Popular Temperance, was set up to manage propaganda for the cause. The directorate duly took over the management of the traditional seasonal funfairs of St Petersburg until these were run down in the early twentieth century; it also instituted a number of 'people's palaces' (narodnye doma), offering programmes of theatrical entertainment, as well as tea rooms and lending-libraries, to the working classes.[20]

If finance was one problem for the 'people's theatre' movement, another was constructing a programme that would be suitably edifying, yet not entirely alienate potential spectators. The organisers' first objective was to offer their audiences quality material (which meant above all Russian realist drama), but they had to contend with the fact that factory workers who had worked a sixty- or seventy-hour week did not always want a lengthy session of communing with high culture. A questionnaire circulated by the Nevsky Society for Popular Entertainments in the 1890s revealed that workers, whilst appreciative of the theatre's edificatory function in an absolute sense (they recognised that occupiers of theatre seats were prevented from excessive boozing), were often bemused by the actual programme on offer. 'I'm not sure if Ostrovsky's The Storm is really the kind of thing you want to watch on a warm summer's night,' one respondent commented, whilst another pointed out that watching plays about life in factories, 'however well done', was an activity that held limited appeal for those who had just spent the week working in one themselves.[21] The organisers' solution was usually to offer a mixed programme, in which classic Russian drama, performed in whole or in part, and adaptations of famous prose works alternated with dramatisations of popular literature (such as Bova the King's Son, a fabulous romance), vaudevilles, folk-dancing and feerii.[22] Given that the people's theatre organisers mostly espoused the anti-urban and anti-capitalist views typical of Russian populism, the only material from the oral tradition generally on offer was adaptations of suitably heroic and decorous folk-tales and epics. Pressing home the point, the drop-curtain of the Vasilevsky Island people's theatre displayed a view of a Russian village complete with church and school, and embellished with the following jingle: 'The Russian people will be truly grateful/If you sow what is rational, lasting and tasteful.'[23]

In combination with like-minded activists in the workers' education

'Sunday schools', and with the co-ordinators of cheap libraries, museum displays, and popular lectures, the members of the people's theatre movement laid the foundations for the immensely successful literacy and cultural propaganda drive embarked upon by the Soviet government in the 1920s. Their efforts must be given due recognition, although it is easy to mock the slightly humourless earnestness which occasionally characterised populist philanthropy. At the same time, there is no denying that the limitations in the philanthropists' vision – the timid conservatism of their own artistic tastes, and their emphasis on autodidacticism as the primary virtue in their audiences – had some unfortunate long-term results. Just as the elite theatre, enthused by the modernist movement, began appropriating the stage techniques of the traditional popular theatre, the people's theatre movement was trying to ensure that these techniques were effaced by realism. In this respect, the efforts of the movement can be said to have prepared the ground for the isolation of the avant-garde theatre in the 1920s, and, arguably, also for the extreme artistic impoverishment of the self-vauntedly national-popular 'socialist realist' theatre of the late 1930s and 1940s.

The provincial theatre

On a superficial appraisal, the theatre of the Russian provinces during the nineteenth century had many resemblances to the popular theatre of Russian cities. For one thing, in the provinces as in the capital, it was the seasonal fairground theatres (*balagany*) and circuses that provided the main – in some cases the only – experience of the theatre that those less than comfortably off were likely to have.[24] The importance of the fairground theatre also meant that *balagan*-like shows and techniques often found their way on to the stage of the provincial theatre proper, as entrepreneurs and actors struggled to satisfy the tastes of a public used to mixed-genre, mixed-media performances and to energetic, but rather unsubtle, playing. In the provincial theatre, as in the popular theatre of Russian cities, melodrama and vaudeville were the mainstays of the repertoire; variety numbers were well-loved here too. During the prolonged intervals, as stage hands heaved about the heavy painted backdrops and lumpish props, entrepreneurs would usually stage a programme of such numbers in front of the curtain. 'I adored the interval shows,' wrote one nineteenth-century actor, Vladimir Davydov. 'The things I used to do in them! Telling jokes, singing soulful ballads, doing conjuring tricks, dancing the polka, the can-can, and all kinds of other foreign dances.' No wonder that, as Davydov also recalled: 'No one accepted "I can't" as an excuse. If you'd decided to go on the stage, you had to do anything – including walking on your hands, if need be.'[25]

In fact, some actors were so infected by the *balagan*-like atmosphere of the provincial theatre that they would start playing to the gallery quite brazenly. Even when acting in classical verse dramas, the Kazan player I. Vykhodtsev would enter with cries of 'Oh ho ho!' 'Here I am!' or 'Get an eyeful of this!' When taking curtain calls, he would don outrageous animal costumes and enter on all-fours, or have himself wheeled on-stage in a baby carriage.[26] According to actors' memoirs, the acoustics and lighting of provincial theatres often left much to be desired; this no doubt enhanced the preference of actors for large histrionic gestures and exaggerated declamation. Such playing had its own dangers, however. The well-known actress N. A. Smirnova, who began her career on the provincial stage in the late nineteenth century, recalled one disaster when she was acting a kept woman in a melodrama, and had to play a scene in which she tore off all the gaudy jewels presented to her by her *souteneur*:

> Suddenly, at the high point of my speech, when I was sure that I had the public eating out of my hand, I heard a titter coming from the audience. The more jewels I tore off, the louder the titter grew. It turned out that, in my frenzied gesticulation, I had been snatching at everything within reach; not content with tearing off the jewels, I had been bombarding my horrified fellow-actors with ringlets from my wig ... When I came to myself and saw their dinner-plates heaped to the brim with hair, I fled the scene in confusion.[27]

The tendency of provincial actors to exaggeration was enhanced by conditions backstage. Rivalry between stars was intense, partly out of pride, and partly because earnings depended on an actor's place in the pecking order. Those at the bottom, having struck their contract with the troupe's entrepreneur in one of the Moscow taverns that was used as a theatrical labour exchange or elsewhere, often earned scarcely enough to cover their lodgings and costumes. Success on the stage could make it possible for an actor to transfer to a better place in another troupe, if not to move up the hierarchy within the one where he or she had started. There is no doubt, too, that the octane of applause was some compensation, in the provincial theatre as in the *balagan*, for the exigencies of living in grim and squalid lodgings, and struggling through muddy streets to perform in an under-heated shack.[28]

The conditions of the provincial stage were haphazard: entrepreneurs rarely combined both artistic talent and business acumen, and were in any case subject to uncertain market demands and unreliable subsidies, even in such wealthy and cultivated towns as Kazan, Kharkov and Odessa. All this meant that the art of coarse acting had every occasion to flourish. But for all that, artistic standards were often markedly different from those of the *balagan* stage. For one thing, theatre-going was not only or even mainly a working-class and petit-bourgeois leisure activity in the provinces. In the late eighteenth and early nineteenth centuries, most provincial theatrical programmes were put on, and attended, by upper-class amateurs, or were performed by serf theatre troupes whose owners fixed them up in make-shift theatres on town squares in an attempt to recover some of the troupe's running costs. Only around 1815 or so did such troupes start to be replaced by companies of free-born actors, or of serfs temporarily released on quit-rent.[29]

Although the audience of provincial theatres became socially more mixed over the course of the eighteenth century, one of its most significant components, from the 1840s, was made up by provincial intellectuals, all of whom seethed with ideas borrowed from such radical thinkers as Belinsky, Chernyshevsky and Dobrolyubov. If entrepreneurs allowed their shows to become too much like the *balagan*, they risked alienating this part of their audience, which wanted to see politically committed, socially critical drama; at the same time, they had to contend with the fact that the gallery occupants might quite easily desert the theatre for any passing flea circus, or other such attraction, that happened to offer itself.[30] And so, whilst entrepreneurs did sometimes pack their programmes with vaudevilles and operettas, intellectual tastes often also played a part in determining the selection of material. The massive repertoires of local theatres (as many as three new productions might be offered in a week) found room for foreign classics in translation, Russian classics, and modern Russian plays, as well as for the latest popular successes. Admittedly, there was little inde-pendence of taste in evidence: the provincial theatres did not usually culti-vate their own local playwrights; but, before the Theatrical Monopoly ended, they sometimes staged plays that had been refused permission for performance in the capitals.[31]

After the monopoly ended, traffic between the provinces and the capital became more intense, as actors and directors from the new private theatres, and sometimes from the Imperial Theatres as well, toured the provinces performing, occasionally giving impromptu master-classes, and also taking talented young actors from the provinces back with them to the capitals. The insights of such contacts with metropolitan practice were often consolidated by the efforts of actors' *sociétés*, or fraternities, which began to take an increasingly important role in organising tours and productions from the mid 1880s. The result of these different processes was a gradual assimilation not only of repertoire, but also of acting technique; up until the 1890s, provincial actors had often practised their own, alternative tradition of stagecraft; from then on, the straightforward opposition of 'city' and 'province' began to be dissolved by the formation of different 'schools'. From the 1880s also, provincial theatres, especially those in such long-established theatrical towns as Kazan or Kharkov, were often owned and subsidised by the local administration, providing much more secure material and better artistic conditions for theatre troupes, whether resident or touring. By 1900, then, the provincial dramatic theatre was effectively wholly integrated with the artistic practices of the Imperial Theatres in the capitals. For their part, however, the provincial fairground theatres, which the dramatic theatres had once tried so hard to beat or even to join, continued their performances more or less unaffected either by these changes, or even by the expansion of leisure activities in the capitals, as they were in fact to do until the Soviet nationalisation of popular entertainments in the 1920s and 1930s.[32]

The amateur theatre

No more than the provincial theatre does the amateur theatre fit entirely easily into a study of the Russian popular theatre. Certainly, there were some connections between amateur and popular traditions. Some branches of the amateur theatre – the performances by soldiers of traditional plays such as *Tsar Maksimilian*, or the plays and entertainments put on by Russian prisoners in their labour camps – were extremely close to the popular theatre in techniques, repertoire and social location. (Indeed, the soldier troupes themselves used to perform – for money – in fairground booths on occasion, indicating how indistinct the divide between 'amateur' and 'professional' generally was in the popular theatre.)[33] In the late nineteenth century, other branches of the amateur theatre did important work for the 'people's theatre' movement. In 1902, for example, white-collar railway workers from the Moscow–Yaroslavl Line gave a performance of a play based on the traditional ballad *Vanka-klyuchnik* as a free Easter entertainment for the line's management and workers.[34] Amateur theatres also performed a hugely important role in taking the message of the people's theatre to groups of Russians, most particularly peasants in outlying villages, who had never had access to professional theatres, but who now had the chance to learn about theatrical performances from the inside.[35]

The more familiar manifestations of the Russian amateur theatre, however, were spectacles organised not by or for Russian workers, but by and for members of the upper and middle classes, with varying degrees of competence and regularity, in their salons and drawing rooms, in the halls and classrooms of schools and other educational establishments, and on the premises of clubs and art societies. Certainly, the amateur theatre, even that organized by the aristocracy and bourgeoisie, did sometimes share the popular theatre's emphasis on theatre as entertainment, and also its propensity for improvisation and 'making do' on a shoestring budget, with simple home-made costumes using one or two readily identifiable features to symbolise roles and professions, a small selection of humble props, and a performing space rigged up in premises that were often less than ideal. Davydov, for example, recalls how in his childhood he improvised a performance at home, contriving costumes and curtains from bed-linen, and purloining his nanny's soldier-boyfriend's sword and helmet as props.[36] For the most part, though, the Russian amateur theatre took itself rather seriously, and the performances that it gave were often hardly distinguishable, in terms of repertoire and technique, from those of the most sophisticated professional theatres.

If one discounts the seminarians, clerks and petty traders who moonlighted as actors, sometimes against their own will, in the seventeenth century, the earliest Russian amateur theatricals appear to date from the late eighteenth century, when Russian schoolboys and schoolgirls would perform at masques and recitations for the edification of their parents. One such spectacle was the masque organised by the poet Gavrill Derzhavin, then governor of Tambov, for Catherine II's coronation anniversary in 1786. A group of youthful 'sons and daughters of the nobility', dressed in white chitons and garlands, recited verse tributes to 'Minerva' before presenting the province's military commander with a wreath (in the boys' case), and a basket of flowers (in the girls').[37] Records from other provincial towns indicate that adult members of the aristocracy sometimes banded together and performed plays for the delectation of peers: Madame Yankova had warm memories of the Lipetsk *amatyory*, for example.[38]

However, at this stage theatrical amateurism seems mostly to have found an outlet in the serf theatres, whose organisers were generally dabbling dilettante aristocrats, but whose actors were subjected to very rigorous programmes of training. Only upon the decline of interest in the serf theatre do adult aristocrats in the capitals seem themselves to have become interested in acting. The heyday of their enthusiasm was between 1815 and 1840, when the dominance of the literary salon meant that there was an emphasis on all literature as performance, and when there was also a mania for masquerades, costumed balls, and dressing-up of all kinds. Princess Zinaida Volkonskaya, an early woman author and famous beauty, was, for example, much celebrated for her acting and singing in aristocratic salons during 1815–16. Whilst living in Rome in 1820, she took the lead part in an opera of her own composition, *Giovanna d'Arco*; upon her return to Moscow in the early 1820s, she organised performances in her house of Marivaux, Racine and Molière.[39] Griboedov's famous comedy, *Woe from Wit*, initially banned from public performance in the capitals, was given its first airing by a group of officers who staged scenes from the play in Erevan in 1827; it also became widely known to Moscow and Petersburg aristocratic circles through readings in private houses.[40]

After 1840, the rise of Russian radicalism for a time damped enthusiasm for private theatricals: reading parties, with intense and prolonged discussion of socialist ideas, now became a more favoured occupation. In the 1860s and 1870s, however, the upsurge of interest in the theatre as a forum for political and social discussion led to the reappearance of the amateur theatre in a new and purposeful form – the well-organised, committed group with the overt objective of making good the shortcomings of the Imperial Theatres. An important group of this kind was the Society of Artistes, whose activities were encouraged by Ostrovsky, and which gave the first performances of his plays *A Nice Earner* and *Seek and You Shall Find*, and of Pisemsky's *A Bitter Fate*. Although this particular group was soon more or less taken over by young professional actors, other similar associations of amateurs were to play an important role in later decades. The most significant of these was Moscow's Society for Art and Literature, under whose aegis Stanislavsky made his directorial debut in the 1880s.[41]

In provincial towns, the relative underdevelopment of professional theatrical activity made amateurism just as important in the nineteenth century as it had been in the eighteenth. The famous actor N. N. Khodotov's earliest experiences of the theatre were the *tableaux vivants* and amateur theatricals organised by his parents at home, whilst Davydov recalled that the plays staged by the group of amateurs managed by his parents constituted the only artistically respectable form of the theatre available to residents of the small provincial garrison town where he was brought up.[42] The importance of the amateur theatre is also confirmed by Chekhov's story 'My Life', in which a woman from the haute bourgeoisie in a large provincial town gets involved in a very serious and time-consuming amateur theatrical group, and eventually opts for a life on the professional stage.[43]

Until the end of the nineteenth century, then, the amateur theatre in a sense compensated for the deficiencies of the mainstream theatre, much as the provincial theatre sometimes had, by facilitating the performance of plays outside the accepted repertoire. It also acted, for those involved in it, as an introduction to theatrical life, as is evident from the instances of Davydov and Stanislavsky, and also of Tairov and Evreinov.[44] With the vast and accelerating expansion of theatrical activity both in and beyond mainstream theatres after 1890, the amateur theatre began to make a rather different contribution: it no longer made up the shortfall in the mainstream theatre, but instead reinforced its strength. As the amateur authors of 'album verse' during the 1810s and 1820s had fostered and disseminated the poetic culture of that time, so post-1900 amateur theatricals, from school performances of Greek tragedy in the original language and manner to the *kapustniki* (parties with jokey pantomimes that Russian institutions, right up to avant-garde art organisations, traditionally put on for Christmas) all in their different ways contributed to the extraordinarily rich theatrical culture that was one of Russia's glories between 1900 and 1917.[45]

1820 was a historical turning-point for Russian marginal theatres, marking the beginning of an era in which they played an extremely vital role, both as complements and alternatives to elite tradition. This era came to an end around 1900, for various reasons. By this date a Western-style appreciation of the theatre's literary function had spread out from educated metropolitan and provincial society: it was being actively propagandised by the 'people's theatre' movement, and had begun to influence even some aspects of the popular theatre. At the same time, from 1900 new forms of entertainment, potentially devastating to theatrical tradition, began to make their mark. These, the gramophone and the cinematograph, helped to preserve some of the performance styles of the popular theatre for posterity, and ensured some entertainers huge success and vast incomes, but at the same time they began an inexorable erosion of the traditions of live performance.[46] And so the opening of the twentieth century left the theatre in a paradoxical position. On the one hand it now had, for the first time in Russian history, the potential to become, in its literary form, the prerogative of the masses. On the other hand, live performance arts were beginning to lose the position they had had for centuries, as forms of mechanical and recorded forms of popular entertainment attracted large numbers of spectators. These new forms provided shows that represented situations and characters that the inhabitants of Russian villages or working-class districts in towns found familiar, sympathetic and interesting. This uneasy and contradictory situation was to develop, in the course of the following decades, into a central, albeit mostly unrecognised, problem for theorists of the theatre and cultural politicians alike.

Notes

1. The first step towards the monopoly was in 1803, when Aleksandr I gave the Imperial Theatres the sole right to organise masquerades. It was extended still further by Aleksandr II, who banned new private theatres in the capitals (in 1856) and then, in 1862, banned private theatres altogether. On its effects, see A. Ostrovskii, 'Klubnye stseny, chastnye teatry i liubitel'skie spektakli', *Polnoe sobranie sochinenii v 12 tomakh*, vol. x (Moscow, 1978), pp. 114–26.

2. See for example P. Viazemskii, *Staraia zapisnaia kniga* (Leningrad, 1929), passim; Pushkin's *Evgenii Onegin*, chapter 2, stanza 4, and chapter 3, verse 4 are lightly ironical treatments of such views from the outside.

3. See M. I. Pyliaev, *Staraia Moskva: rasskazy iz byloi zhizni pervoprestol'noi stolitsy* (St Petersburg, 1891) and *Staryi Peterburg: rasskazy iz byloi zhizni stolitsy* (St Petersburg, 1889).

4. P. Svinine, *Sketches of Russia* (London, 1814), p. 98; E. Rostopchina, 'Dve vstrechi', *Stikhotvoreniia, proza, pis'ma* (Moscow, 1986), p. 94.

5. See for example A. I. Levitov, 'Tipy i stseny sel'skoi iarmarki', in *Rasskazy i ocherki* (Voronezh, 1980), pp. 23–63; V. A. Sleptsov, 'Balagany na Sviatoi', in *Sochineniia v 2-kh tomakh* (2 vols., Leningrad, 1933), vol. II, pp. 461–4.

6. On the official 'popular theatre' movement, see the end of the Popular Theatre section later in the chapter.

7. On the circus, see Iu. A. Dmitriev, *Tsirk v Rossii ot istokov do 1917* (Moscow, 1977); *Malen'kaia entsiklopediia: Tsirk*, ed. A. Ia. Shneer and R. E. Slavskii (Moscow, 1973); A. Vsevolodskii-Gerngross, 'Nachalo tsirka v Rossii', in *O teatre: sbornik stat'ei: Vremennik otdela istorii i teorii teatra Instituta istorii iskusstv, 2*

(Leningrad, 1927), 66–107; on the Petersburg circus, see *Konnyi tsirk: vystavka na temu 'konnyi tsirk'* (catalogue of an exhibition mounted by the Muzei tsirka i estrady, Leningrad, 1930); A. M. Konechnyi, 'Peterburgskaia gorodskaia zrelishchnaia kul'tura: tsirk, zoologicheskii sad, narodnye teatry: materialy k ekspozitsii Muzeia [Istorii Leningrada] "Staryi Peterburg"', unpublished typescript of a paper presented at the Museum of the History of Leningrad Conference, 2 July 1990, cited by kind permission of the author.

8. On popular entertainments generally, see R. Stites, *Russian Popular Culture: Entertainment and Society since 1900* (Cambridge University Press, 1992), ch. 1; C. Kelly, '"Better halves"? Representations of women in Russian urban popular entertainments, 1870–1910', in Linda Edmondson (ed.), *Women and Society in Russia and the Soviet Union* (Cambridge University Press, 1992), pp. 5–31; Konechnyi, 'Peterburgskaia gorodskaia zrelishnaia kul'tura'; B. Nijinska, *Early Memories*, tr. and ed. I. Nijinska and Jean Robinson (London, 1982); A. Benois, *Reminiscences of the Russian Ballet*, tr. M. Britnieva (London, 1941), ch. 3; M. L. Schlesinger (ed.), *Langenscheidts Sachwörterbuch: Land und Leute in Russland* (Berlin and St Petersburg, c. 1910), under *Maslenitsa*; N. S. Anushkin (ed.), *Ushedshaia Moskva: vospominaniia sovremennikov o Moskve vtoroi poloviny XIX veka* (Moscow, 1964), pp. 89, 92, 99, 143, 146–52, 337–58; P. I. Shchukin, 'Iz vospominanii', *Shchukinskii sbornik,* 10 (1912), 140–2, 146–51, 164–6, 274–5, 394–5; V. N. Davydov, *Rasskaz o proshlom* (Leningrad and Moscow, 1962), pp. 13–14, 32–46. On the funfairs, see A. V. Leifert, *Balagany* (Petrograd, 1922); A. Ia. Alekseev-Iakovlev, *Russkie narodnye gulian'ia* (Leningrad and Moscow, 1948); A. M. Konechnyi, 'Peterburgskie balagany', *Panorama iskusstv,* 8 (1985), 383–95; A. M. Konechnyi, 'Garderob peterburgskikh razvlechenii', in *Garderop: vystavka sovremennykh karneval'nykh kostiumov* (St Petersburg, 1992: catalogue of exhibition at the St Petersburg Manège, 26 December 1992 – 26 January 1993), pp. 23–30; on the pleasure gardens, cafés-chantants, etc., see M. Baring, *The Mainsprings of Russia* (London, 1915), pp. 169–72; T. M. Lycklama a Nijeholt, *Voyage en Russie, au Caucase, et en Perse* (4 vols., Paris, 1872–4), vol. 1, pp. 102–9; A. Rostislavov, 'O teatrakh miniatiur: starye i novye shablony', *Russkaia mysl',* 4 (1913), section 3, 39–43. On artistes' lives, see also Iu. A. Dmitriev, 'Na starom moskovskom gulianii', *Teatral'nyi al'manakh VTO,* 6 (1947), 345–57.

9. On the texts, repertoire and theatrics of the popular theatre, see Kelly, '"Better halves"?'; C. Kelly, *Petrushka: the Russian Carnival Puppet Theatre* (Cambridge, 1990); A. M. Konechnyi, 'Raek: narodnaia zabava', *Dekorativnoe iskusstvo,* 346 (1986); A. M. Konechnyi, 'Raek v sisteme peterburgskoi narodnoi kul'tury', *Russkii fol'klor,* no. 25 (1989); A. Ia. Alekseev-Iakovlev, 'Vospominaniia', Saltykov-Shchedrin State Public Library, St Petersburg, f. 1130 arkh. A. P. Gershuni, no. 317 – publication forthcoming as A. M. Konechnyi (ed.), 'Peterburgskii balagannyi master A. Ia. Alekseev-Iakovlev', cited by kind permission of the editor; Alekseev-Iakovlev, *Russkie narodnye gulian'ia*; E. M. Uvarova, *Estradnyi teatr: miniatiury, obozreniia, miuzik-kholly 1917–1945 gg.*

(Moscow, 1983); Leifert; and the repertoire lists in vols. v and vi of *Istoriia russkogo dramaticheskogo teatr* (7 vols., Moscow, 1977–87).

10. On artistes' lives, see Dmitriev, *Tsirk v Rossii*; Dmitriev, *'Na starom moskovskom gulianii'*; Kelly, *Petrushka*, ch. 1; Alekseev-Iakovlev, 'Vospominaniia'; and Nijinska.

11. Baring, pp. 170–1.

12. A. Bakhtiarov, *Briukho Peterburga* (St Petersburg, 1888), pp. 312–3.

13. Shchukin, p. 140.

14. Ivan Inozemtsev, 'Narodnyi teatr v 1872 godu', *Istoricheskii vestnik*, 91 (1903), 694–8; *Istoriia russkogo dramaticheskogo teatr*, vol. v, pp. 244–53.

15. Alekseev-Iakovlev, 'Vospominaniia'; Alekseev-Iakovlev, *Russkie narodnye gulian'ia*.

16. Konechnyi, 'Peterburgskaia gorodskaia zrelishchnaia kul'tura'; Iu. V., 'Razvlecheniia dlia naroda', *Entsiklopedicheskii slovar' izd. Brokgauza Efrona*, ed. I. E. Andreevskii (41 vols., St Petersburg, 1890–1907), vol. XXVI, pp. 130–1. On the ideology and history of the popular theatre, see also I. Shcheglov, *Narodnyi teatr* (St Petersburg, 1898); I. Shcheglov, *Narod i teatr* (St Petersburg, 1911); B. V. Varneke, 'Chto igraet narod', *Ezhegodnik imperatorskikh teatrov*, 4 (1913), 1–40; Anon., 'The theatre in Russia', *Proceedings of the Anglo-Russian Literary Society, February-April 1916* (London, 1916), pp. 100–101.

17. *Istoriia russkogo dramaticheskogo teatr*, vol. vi, pp. 239–40; Iu. V., 'Razvlecheniia dlia naroda', p. 131.

18. A. P. Chekhov, 'Sluchai iz praktiki', *Polnoe sobranie sochinenii i pisem v 30 tomakh*, (Moscow, 1974–) vol. x, pp. 75–85.

19. On the economics of the popular theatre, see Iu. V., 'Razvlecheniia dlia naroda'; N. Mikhailovskii, 'Literatura i zhizn'', *Russkoe bogatstvo*, 6 (1896) section 2, 51–61.

20. On the Directorate of Popular Temperance, see Patricia Herlihy, *Strategies of Sobriety: Temperance Movements in Russia 1880–1914* (Kennan Institute for Advanced Russian Studies Occasional Paper 238, Washington, DC, 1990); *Entsiklopedicheskii slovar'*, vol. IIL, 547–8; Daniel Brower, *The Russian City: from Tradition to Modernity* (Berkeley, 1990), pp. 170–87.

21. Mikhailovskii, pp. 54, 58.

22. On the repertory of the people's theatres, see Mikhailovskii; Konechnyi, 'Peterburgskaia gorodskaia zrelishchnaia kul'tura'; Alekseev-Iakovlev, 'Vospominaniia'.

23. Konechnyi, 'Peterburgskaia gorodskaia zrelishchnaia kul'tura'.

24. On the provincial balagans and circuses, see Dmitriev, *Tsirk v Rossii*; V. E. Meierkhol'd, *Stat'i, pis'ma, rechi, besedy* (2 vols., Moscow, 1968), vol. I, p. 309.

25. N. V. Davydov, *Iz proshlogo* (Moscow, 1913), pp 78–9.

26. *Istoriia russkogo dramaticheskogo teatr*, vol. IV, p. 225.

27. N. A. Smirnova, *Vospominaniia* (Moscow, 1947), p. 27. An intriguing record of acting techniques in the popular and provincial theatres is offered by early

films such as Larin's *Merchant Bashkirov's Daughter* (1913), Bauer's *Silent Witnesses* (1914), and Puchalskii's *Antoshka Ruined by a Corset* (1916). (All these films, and many others, are available in the British Film Institute's 10–cassette video anthology *Early Russian Cinema*, released in 1992.)

28. On provincial actors' living conditions, see the memoirs of N. V. Davydov, Smirnova, M. Savina, (*Goresti i skitaniia*, Leningrad, 1983) and N. N. Khodotov, (*Blizkoe – dalekoe*, Moscow, 1932). The hardships that could be suffered by actors' families are made clear by Savina; however, the recollections of Avdot'ia Panaeva (*Vospominaniia*, Moscow, 1956) indicate that conditions were not necessarily better for Imperial Theatre performers.

29. On amateurs in the provinces, see the section on amateur theatre later in the chapter; for a detailed study of the provincial theatre before 1825, see *Istoriia russkogo dramaticheskogo teatr*, vol. II, ch. 3.

30. See especially N. V. Davydov, pp. 82–3.

31. On the repertoire of the provincial theatres before 1882, see the inventories in *Istoriia russkogo dramaticheskogo teatr*, vols. III, IV, and V.

32. On the later history of the provincial theatre, see Smirnova; B. A. Babochkin et al. (eds.), *Russkii provintsial'nyi teatr: vospominaniia* (Leningrad, 1937); *Istoriia russkogo dramaticheskogo teatr*, vol. VI, ch. 4; on the *balagans*, see especially Shcheglov, *Narodnyi teatr*, pp. 8–35, 232–68.

33. On performances by soldiers, see Elizabeth Warner, *The Russian Folk Theatre* (The Hague, 1977), pp. 75, 148–9, 218–9; on performances in the camps, see Dostoevskii, *Notes from the House of the Dead (Zapiski iz mertvogo doma)*, Polnoe sobranie sochinenii, vol. IV (Leningrad, 1972), part 1, ch. 11, pp. 116–30; V. Doroshevich, *Sakhalin* (St Petersburg, 1901), pp. 128–43.

34. See the short report in *Russkie vedomosti*, 11 April 1902, which also makes it clear that this was an annual event.

35. On amateur performances in the popular theatre, see *Narodnyi teatr: sbornik* (Moscow, 1896); *Istoriia russkogo dramaticheskogo teatr*, vol. VI, pp. 283–90; Iu. V., 'Razvlecheniia dlia naroda'.

36. N. V. Davydov, pp. 30–1.

37. G. Derzhavin, *Sochineniia* (9 vols., St Petersburg, 1864–83), vol. IV, pp. 3–6.

38. D. Blagovo, *Rasskazy babushki: iz vospominanii piati pokolenii* (Leningrad, 1989), p. 146.

39. On Volkonskaia see Nadezhda Gorodetsky, 'Princess Zinaida Volkonsky', *Oxford Slavonic Papers*, 5 (1954), 95–7.

40. See *Teatral'naia entsiklopediia*, chief ed. S. S. Mokul'skii (6 vols., Moscow, 1961–7), vol. I, under 'Griboedov'.

41. *Istoriia russkogo dramaticheskogo teatr*, vol. V, pp. 235–44; ibid. vol. VI, pp. 258–61; K. Stanislavskii, *Moia zhizn' v iskusstve, Polnoe sobranie sochinenii v 8 tomakh*, vol. I (Moscow, 1954), pp. 101–86; on his earlier activities as a member of the 'Alekseev circle', see pp. 75–82. Another important group, the St Petersburg

Circle of Litterateurs and Artistes (Literaturno-artisticheskii kruzhok), is described in *Istoriia russkogo dramaticheskogo teatr,* vol. VI, pp. 273–83.

42. N. V. Davydov, pp. 29–30.

43. Chekhov, *Moia zhizn'*, *Polnoe sobranie sochinenii,* vol. IX, pp. 192–280.

44. N. N. Evreinov, *Teatral'nye novatsii* (Petrograd, 1922), p. 99; A. Tairov, *Zapiski rezhissera, stat'i, besedy, rechi, pis'ma* (Moscow, 1970), pp. 67–8.

45. In 1893, for example, Euripides' tragedy *Rhesus* was staged by the Number Eight Boys' Gimnaziia in St Petersburg, under their director I. F. Annenskii (See V. Krivich, 'Innokentii Annenskii po semeinym vospominaniiam', *Literaturnaia mysl',* 3 (1925), 253). On *kapustniki,* see for example Stanislavskii, pp. 360–5.

46. On early films, see note 27 above. The technologisation of Russian popular culture is described in Kelly, '"Better halves"?', and also in the opening chapters of Stites.

7 Realism in the Russian theatre, 1850–1882

CYNTHIA MARSH

In the latter half of the nineteenth century realism was the major force in Russian culture: it embraced literature and painting as well as theatre. The Russian novel became internationally recognised, and Russian painters established a school of art on a par with their European counterparts for the first time. Critics of various persuasions fought in print over the meaning of realism, setting an agenda for twentieth-century thinking. The theatre responded, developing texts and standards of décor of unprecedented acclaim. As a publicly conducted activity, however, the theatre was subject to a stricter censorship than either literature or painting, which may have inhibited it from gaining the international recognition awarded the other two art forms.

One of the foremost distinguishing factors of realism in Russia during this period lay in the need to understand and explore the nature of Russianness. Brought close to the West by Peter the Great after 1700, Russia had made European culture and values her own. Attention to matters Russian had begun in the 1830s and 1840s, laying the foundation of a realist school. Realism meant an examination of Russian society, her history, her customs and her people. In its realist achievements theatre provided a window on Russian life, deflecting the need to depend on Western works.

It was a period of immense change. Opening during the final difficult years of Nikolai I's oppressive rule – he died in 1855 – the first crisis came with the end of the Crimean War in 1856. As much as defeat put paid to the reactionary ethos of the previous regime, so it delivered a heavy blow to the Russian psyche, initiating the desire for political and cultural self-contemplation. The swift move into reform brought sweeping changes to Russian life. The following years introduced new freedoms to Russia, including the Emancipation of the Serfs in 1861, but they were also marked by an unprecedentedly vociferous movement of opposition, impatient with the slow pace and apparent timidity of the reforms introduced, so that opinion in the country became polarised. The establishment's attempts to quell dissent brought curtailment of some of the new freedoms, and led to ever more desperate measures on the part of the opposition. First, they resorted to propaganda, then to illegal activity, and finally to terrorism in pursuit of their aims. The period closed with the assassination of the tsar in 1881, an event which brought cultural stagnation for a decade as every sign of independent creativity was stifled. However, that is only one aspect of the picture: in the wake of reform Russia began a transformation of her economy. She drew closer to her European counterparts and began the change from a peasant economy into a modern industrial nation. The complexity of realism stemmed from its attempts to reflect all this political and social diversity.

Why the year 1882? It is a date of crucial significance to the theatre; the Imperial Monopoly in the two capital cities was lifted, and commercial theatre was possible for the first time. Under the monopoly, a legacy of the introduction of theatre to Russia through the royal court, the theatres of St Petersburg and Moscow had been placed under Imperial control. During this time the showcases of Russian drama, the Aleksandrinsky and the Maly Theatre, were supervised by a governor on the direct appointment of the tsar. Obviously in these circumstances power over the repertoire was complete. There was a minimal compensation in that funding was guaranteed. For the most part, however, the controlling aristocratic taste preferred opera and ballet: drama by comparison was under-resourced.

A play had to go through two different stages of scrutiny in its passage through the censorship. Firstly it had to be submitted for approval for publication, and then a separate application had to be made for it to be performed. A list of the dramas which were allowed to be performed was published; sometimes the licence only applied to the capital cities, and excluded the provinces. In addition, sanction also had to be sought locally from the police with regard to ticket prices and advertising material.

Occasionally, censorship prevented plays already published from being performed, thereby creating a paradoxical perception of the theatre as outwardly tame but inwardly potentially explosive. Thus some plays that rightly belong in the realist period only reached the stage well beyond it. The frustration born of this situation was channelled into a movement for change, the first victory of which was the lifting of the Imperial Monopoly, the second was the great improvement in standards and opportunities for training which mark the 1880s as a decade. These changes undoubtedly paved the way for the high point of theatrical realism which came at the turn of the century with the Moscow Art Theatre, Chekhov and other play-wrights, and not least, in the performance of previously censored works.

Private theatres had operated on a small scale in the provincial towns, on the country estates of the wealthy, and in the temporary summer theatres in the capital cities, and with the rise of capitalism, theatre was seen as an area ripe for private enterprise and investment. Perhaps unfortunately for any would-be entrepreneurs, however, the organs of censorship were not removed at the same time as the lifting of the monopoly, and state control of the repertoire was retained. For a couple of decades at least, therefore, the authorities were able to feel relatively secure in the knowledge that the fast-growing urban population with a little more money in its pockets and time on its hands would be provided with conservative and unadventurous theatrical fare. A theatre commercially driven by audiences used only to such acceptable dramas would be unlikely to risk confronting the censor-ship laws.

The European links were not broken in the realist period. Private com-panies from abroad had visited Russia by invitation since the 17th century: their presence had ensured a highly European-oriented theatrical culture. Examination of the repertoire of the Imperial Theatres for those decades shows that half of the plays were foreign or adapted from foreign sources. The plays performed, however, were the classics of an earlier age or the works of popular theatre designed to provide escapist entertainment rather than discussion of social issues. The writers who created the new drama of Europe do not figure. Zola's writings were translated and discussed in the 1870s, but his plays were not seen, and Ibsen's influence came later.

As far as Russian realism was concerned, preoccupation with national issues and exploration of areas of Russian life provocatively free from Western influence have made much of this work inimical to Western tastes. As a result the familiar, recognisably European values of a Turgenev or a Chekhov have been taken as the essence of Russian realism. However, the pursuit of realism in the form of a national repertoire drew dramatists to new subject areas, which supply the focus of this chapter: the vast mass of the Russian peasantry; the Russian grotesque as the essence of fantastic realism; and Russian history, the theatricalisation of which was to have great implications for set design. By concentrating on these areas and on a discussion of the changing social structure of the audience and the implica-tions for realism, and by analysis of the repertoire to show the relative weight of realist works within it, one can gain an unusually rich view of the texture the realist theatre provided for Russian culture.

The peasantry, previously frequently idealised, offered unplumbed depths for discussion of contemporary issues and national character. Three plays and their performances illustrate the development and fate of this theme in the realist period and beyond: Aleksei Potekhin's *The People's Judgement, not God's* (1854), Aleksei Pisemsky's *A Bitter Fate* (1859), and Lev Tolstoy's *The Power of Darkness* (1886).

The People's Judgement, not God's was Aleksei Potekhin's first play: he had begun his literary life as a prose-writer shortly before. The heroine of the play, Matryona, in love with an unsuitable boy in the eyes of her pious father, is cursed by him when he discovers the extent of their relationship. After a period of madness, during which Matryona flees and lives as a 'holy fool', she swears to God that if she is saved she will obey only Him and her father and will deny her love. Meanwhile, father and suitor are reconciled, then find Matryona, but too late to retrieve a happy outcome, and the suitor Ivan, resolves to serve tsar and country as a soldier. This tragedy of peasant life, expressed in a language that Potekhin knew well and reproduced without constraint or artificiality, brought peasants to the stage with an unprecedented dignity. In his early years an ardent Slavophile associated with the journal *The Muscovite*, that was the platform of Slavophilism, Potekhin approved of the traditional patriarchal values the play clearly expressed. He asserted peasant values and morality against the loose behaviour of a passing 'gentleman' whose only interest in the peasantry is the prettiness of the womenfolk. Published in 1854,[1] and performed in April of the same year at the Aleksandrinsky, Potekhin's play drew comments for its closeness to reality, with references to the new science of photography never far absent.[2] Less favourable reviews referred to Potekhin's 'coarse' talent and his 'naturalism'.

Always overshadowed by Ostrovsky in the theatre, Potekhin had made his mark in this instance with his choice of milieu. Although he wrote much about rural and provincial Russia, Ostrovsky was never able to write with conviction about the peasants. The Russian movement of naturalism, if it may be called such, was in its early stage almost entirely rooted in studies of the peasantry. A savage review in *The Contemporary* found Potekhin's play excessively melodramatic and overdependent upon imagination, which was seen to be a contradiction in a piece of national drama.[3] In their day Potekhin's plays were popular repertoire pieces. He

moved with the times and changed the setting of his plays to the bureaucratic world, and the theme to an exploration of the incipient capitalist
Russia of the 1870s. He refused, however, to use his work as a political
vehicle to accuse and expose as demanded by the radical view of realism,
and was neglected by subsequent influential scholarship of the Soviet
twentieth century. Potekhin wrote twelve plays in all, but his work is now
largely forgotten.

Aleksei Pisemsky suffered a similar neglect.[4] Best known for his play *A
Bitter Fate*, he was a popular and highly regarded prose-writer, producing
stark material about peasant life. He was in dispute with the formulators of
radical opinion who congregated on the journal *The Contemporary*. So
bitter did the invective become that Pisemsky was challenged to a duel,
which fortunately did not take place. In fact, Pisemsky had few friends. He
lived out the kind of coarse behaviour shown by some of his peasant characters in his own life. The radicals saw the potential of this subject matter
but objected to the apolitical manner in which it was handled. Naturalism
was further marginalised and was frequently the object of critical scorn.

Published in 1859, *A Bitter Fate* was performed at the Aleksandrinsky in
October 1863 and a month later at the Maly in Moscow after considerable
efforts by Pisemsky with the censorship. The play concerns Lizaveta, a
peasant girl, who falls in love with the local gentry landowner during her
husband's prolonged absence working in St Petersburg. She has a child.
When her husband, Anany, returns, he is unable to control his jealousy and
murders the child. Anany tries to run away, but comes back, confesses his
guilt, begs the forgiveness of his fellow-villagers and accepts punishment.

In a review of the St Petersburg production, the writer Mikhail
Saltykov-Shchedrin devoted a final desultory paragraph to the performance, which he regarded as 'coarse' and 'false', serving only to
increase the audience's vocabulary of swear-words and 'not very clever
ones at that'. In the long, preceding discussion of his version of realism he
branded Pisemsky's characters as 'mere organisms who can therefore only
utter one note in all the circumstances and incidents the author forces them
through in order to create their existence'. With this simplistic and dis-
missive definition of naturalism Saltykov-Shchedrin denied it a place in the
school of realist art he proposed. Realism, he argued, should always carry a
notion of the ideal, should indicate a healthy authorial point of view, and
should serve to 'remind man of his humanity'.[5]

Critics more radical than Saltykov-Shchedrin, such as Dobrolyubov, had been heartened by Ostrovsky's masterpiece, *The Storm*, also written in 1859. The play's suffering heroine was seen as an emblem of the wrongs of Russian society. She triumphed over injustice by committing suicide, an expression of her refusal to accept what society unjustly asked her to bear. This was a work which responded to demands for literature to serve society's needs rather than reproduce its ills.[6] Pisemsky's play uncovers the violence and abuse common in peasant life but, unlike *The Storm*, does not allow the people, the peasants, a way out of their situation.

As if to confound the ostracising view of several critics, *A Bitter Fate* took on a life of its own in the repertoire and in criticism. The role of Lizaveta in the hands of two actresses – E. N. Vasileva-Lavrova in the original Maly production, and subsequently Polina Strepetova, who took over the role in 1876 – became an icon of the oppression of women and a call for female emancipation.[7] In 1888, Stanislavsky immortalised the role of Anany in a production by the semi-professional Society for Art and Literature.[8] Finally, Innokenty Annensky responded to Saltykov-Shchedrin's harsh criticism in an article of 1906 in which he pointed to the classic simplicity of the play's structure and the profundity of its ideas, and identified the work as the beginning of the 'new drama' in Russia.[9]

Together, Potekhin's and Pisemsky's presentation of the peasantry for the Russian stage paved the way for a work which has been acknowledged internationally as a masterpiece, although it was slow to achieve this status in Russia. Lev Tolstoy's *The Power of Darkness* (1886) was first performed at the Théâtre Antoine in Paris in 1888. The play was banned in Russia and was only performed in 1895 after the ending had been rewritten.[10] The play has clear echoes of the two former works, and references in his own writings suggest Tolstoy knew the Pisemsky play, and was acquainted with Potekhin.[11] All three plays operate within a religious framework, although Tolstoy manipulates *The Power of Darkness* to express his own views on Christianity. In each case the male peasant hero provides the wayward subject, who is subsequently brought to face the consequences of his wrongdoing. The female counterparts suffer in the course of each play, in two cases losing a child, and in two cases being, or becoming, a simpleton or holy fool. In each play judgement is brought by a collective of peasants to whom the wrongdoers admit their crimes, and before whom they accept their suffering.

All three plays have been associated with naturalism, and criticised for their crudity and violence. Together they provide characteristics of the gem, or in this case the rough diamond, of naturalism in the Russian theatre, Gorky's *The Lower Depths*, performed at the Moscow Art Theatre in 1902. The setting is no longer a peasant one, but the sense of collective remains. The play is similar in other respects: the language caused a furore because of a coarseness not dissimilar in its impact from the predecessors; there is an itinerant religious figure of peasant origin, Luka; and an internal play of domestic violence, the murder of Kostylev, mirrors the violence of the earlier plays. By 1902, however, a politically aware audience made capital of Gorky's observations. This underside of realism, so frequently denounced, marked a clear path in the Russian repertoire, and the ideas naturalism expressed, as well as the implications attention to environment had for set design, were felt for several decades.

At another extreme of realism, the obscure playwright Aleksander Sukhovo-Kobylin developed the 'fantastic', but influential radical realists found his work inimical to their programme and tended to ignore it.[12] Of Sukhovo-Kobylin's trilogy of plays, only one was performed, but that with considerable success. The subject matter of the three dramas was the bribery and corruption of legal and bureaucratic practice, which brought considerable difficulty with the censorship, added to which Sukhovo-Kobylin was under some suspicion for the murder of his wife. It is important to remember his work: the Gogolesque tradition of fantastic realism has surfaced occasionally in twentieth-century Russian theatre only to be denounced as unacceptable. The nineteenth-century radical realist critics placed Gogol high on their list of acceptable writers on the basis of his implied criticisms of Russia, preferring to ignore his acceptance of the inexplicable and the grotesque within realism.

Sukhovo-Kobylin's trilogy begins with a grotesque comedy, *Krechinsky's Wedding* (1854). Old Muromsky, with the help of his sister, is trying to find a suitor for his daughter, Lida. He disapproves of Krechinsky, who has deceived Lida into thinking he loves her, while he is really seeking to augment his position and fortune. A penniless gambler, Krechinsky has an elaborate strategy to use a diamond brooch belonging to Lida to deceive a money-lender into advancing him funds. Krechinsky plots with intensity and demonic attention to detail, employing his sidekick Raspluev to do the dirty work. However, Krechinsky is finally confronted by the police, the money-lender and the innocent lad who really loves Lida. The play ends on an unfinished note as father and daughter rush out, and Krechinsky addresses sardonic comment to the audience. The second play (1861), *The*

Case continues the Krechinsky-Lida story as Lida is investigated for complicity in the plot to steal the diamond brooch. Muromsky is introduced to corrupt officials, Tarelkin and Varravin, who are susceptible to bribes as he tries to extricate his daughter from the affair. In the final play, *Tarelkin's Death* (1869), Tarelkin decides to fake his own death and disguise himself as his recently deceased neighbour. Tarelkin's aim under his new identity is to blackmail Varravin with some stolen correspondence which proves his corruption. Varravin, however, realising Tarelkin's identity, adopts the same tactic and assumes a disguise. The police arrive in the person of Raspluev, who has undergone meteoric promotion, and all witnesses are interrogated. Raspluev is convinced that the disguised Tarelkin is an agent of the devil. Tortured by being deprived of water, Tarelkin is driven into submission by Varravin, who has abandoned his disguise. Tarelkin hands over the letters but is allowed to retain his assumed identity.

Without the famous production of *Tarelkin's Death* by Meyerhold in 1922, Sukhovo-Kobylin's reputation might have died. However, brilliant and innovative as it was theatrically, with acrobatics often caused by furniture sprung to surprise actors and audience by their collapse, and with torture machines in the police-station scenes constructed to grind up the innocent on stage, Meyerhold's version imposed a modernist perspective on a play from the past. As a result, precisely those aspects intrinsic to the original play which pursue the fantastic as a legitimate element of realist theatre were distorted, and the whole production became an exercise in surreal staging. Meyerhold's 'circusisation' of the action made the play 'look back with horror to the past'.[13] He made political capital out of the play as a diatribe against prerevolutionary Russia in a way the author could never have foreseen. But Sukhovo-Kobylin's fortunes in Russia endured: films were made of his plays in the 1950s and 1960s.[14]

Krechinsky's Wedding was first performed to popular acclaim at the Maly in November 1855, with S. V. Shumsky as Krechinsky, Mikhail Shchepkin as Muromsky, and Prov Sadovsky as Raspluev, bringing together actors who were to provide the backbone of realistic performance at the Maly.[15] The premiere was given as a benefit night for Shumsky, and his performance created a memorable model with which many of his subsequent interpretations of other roles were compared. At the Aleksandrinsky in May 1856, V. V. Samoilov played Krechinsky, initiating by his very different interpretation a debate as to how the role should be performed. The public relished the contemporary resonance, in contrast to their usual diet of classics and adaptations of foreign plays. In comparison to Ostrovsky who always believed in the ultimate good of human beings, in Sukhovo-Kobylin's characters there is a realistic touch of the demonic.[16] Other critics make frequent reference to the French boulevarde theatre, to Scribe and the 'well-made play': in their comparisons Sukhovo-Kobylin is praised for his convincing characters and his 'sensitivity to the demands of the stage and his sense of proportion'.[17] Little reference is made to the grotesque characters Sukhovo-Kobylin created, nor to strange passages where people are able to change their physical shape. It is known that Sukhovo-Kobylin was particularly impressed by French actors such as Pierre Levassor, who would play multiple parts in the same play, changing his physical shape and facial expression as the occasion demanded.[18] In the first play, in a fit of violent rage, Krechinsky becomes grotesque and unrecognisable, and is described by Raspluev as either demonic or mad.[19]

The stage fate of the other two plays was less happy: *The Case* was published in 1861 but only reached the stage in 1882 at the Maly after a long battle with the censor and in an adaptation, *Times Gone By*, while *Tarelkin's Death* was published as part of the trilogy in 1869, was given an amateur premiere in adapted form in 1900, and performed in full in 1917, in a staging of the trilogy by Meyerhold and Andrei Lavrentev at the Aleksandrinsky.[20] Where the fantastic in the first play was used as an engaging theatrical device to suggest the demonic and demonstrate the physical skills of the actor, by the final play it had become a recognised force in itself.

Historical drama enjoyed a new vogue in the realist period. Some argue that it was confronted as a test case for realism: actors had established a new style, and now wished to make their excursions into the past fit the realistic mould. Others argue that the popularity of historical drama lay in its ability to address contentious political issues under the guise of a discussion of events long past, that it was a response to the Russian need to discover roots and national identity in a fast-changing world after the Crimean War. Whatever the reasons for its popularity, historical drama both developed and catalysed the realistic movement in the theatre in a number of ways. The search for truth and verisimilitude brought historians and archaeologists into the theatre as advisers; and new thoughts on the connection between character and environment brought artists in as designers, moulding their materials for set and costume in relation to the characters' mood and changes in their psychology.

The 1860s and 1870s saw historical drama gain widespread popularity in the hands of Ostrovsky and Aleksei Tolstoy, who established the genre as a formidable part of the Russian repertoire. Lev Mey, a dramatist from the 1850s, Ivan Lazhechnikov, and Dmitry Averkiev, who made his debut in the 1860s, were writers also in demand. The latter dramatists popularised and to some extent vulgarised the genre. Aleksei Tolstoy, however, his fate always overshadowed by the successes of Ostrovsky, not only created an outstanding trilogy of historical plays, but also explored theatrical concerns in his texts and in his involvement in their production.

After a promisingly satirical start as a contributor to the collective creation of the fictitious poet and dramatist Kozma Prutkov,[21] Tolstoy surprised the theatrical world with his production of the first play of the trilogy *The Death of Ivan the Terrible* in 1867 at the Alexandrinsky. Tolstoy stated his priorities in an article of 1866 directed at the artists who would be working on the production.[22] He defined the general idea of his play, gave detailed expositions of the characters and how he saw them reacting at specific moments in the play, how changes in their mood, their attitudes and self-knowledge could be reflected in the design of costumes and décor; he explained how he had created the play so that each act fell into two parts requiring a different décor, and laid out his aesthetic beliefs on author–performer relationships. Placing the author at the pinnacle of the theatrical process, he regarded all others as agents in revealing the writer's will. In his view, this hierarchy must lead to a harmonising of everyone's activities towards the creation of a unified concept for the play. Some of these ideas were startling in their originality. Much classical drama was simply played in contemporary costume, and its décor conventionalised under the influence of the chief theatre designer in the 1850s, A. A. Roller.[23] The choice of costume and décor was determined by whether the action was inside or out, foreign or Russian, concerned peasants or gentry, and so on.

Tolstoy's change of approach was helped by the budget he was given. The Directorate of Imperial Theatres had been consistently generous to opera and ballet at the expense of drama. This was because the influential classes preferred the two former art forms, to which as a result lavish sets and costumes were deemed necessary. Tolstoy's closeness to court circles and the interest of the tsarina in this particular project ensured that he received ample means. Historical scholarship was also making great strides due to technological progress and to its alliance with the growing science of archaeology. A play which had imperial patronage brought scholars into the theatre to work on the production and proved a great show-piece for a new generation of scene-painters and costume designers, some of whom had made their mark as artists. Matvei Shishkov and Mikhail Bocharov worked on the designs, N. I. Kostomarov gave historical advice, Vyacheslav Shvarts worked on costume design, and Aleksandr Serov on the musical interludes.

Not a little of this new interest in authenticity of representation of people and place can be seen as a response to the work of the Itinerants. Earlier in the 1860s a group of painters had rebelled against the programme and ethos offered by the Academy of Arts and had set up their own organisation of itinerant exhibitions. Their vivid representations of Russia, her landscape and her people had formed an audience with a developed sense of the visual. This sense of place and of physical character also typifies the school of realist prose of this period. The public was being prepared for the new assault on the visual sense being made in the theatre. Here lies the beginning of a period of cross-fertilisation of the arts which makes the turn of the century in Russian culture such a memorable one.

The actors, too, were challenged. They had developed a more realistic style for the contemporary repertoire, but historical realism demanded further skills, the absence of which this production emphasised. Shvarts' magnificent costumes hung badly on actors unused to historical dress. Historical tragedy of this new kind had to abandon the gestural traditions of the past. Shumsky, who played the role of Ivan the Terrible at the Maly Theatre in 1868, solved many problems by the simplicity of his style. The apparent ease of his performance was underpinned, however, by a detailed study and mature understanding of this demanding role. Anticipating Stanislavsky's system, he found a logical line of development for the character which allowed Ivan to grow in stature as the tragedy proceeded.

Such was the impact of this production that it can be seen as the starting point of the great theatrical efflorescence of the end of the century, not solely within the genre of historical tragedy but in the theatre as a whole. It gave rise to the production of a long-neglected classic, Pushkin's *Boris Godunov*, in 1870, and its standards and aesthetic agenda of teamwork, and the incorporation of designers and composers who were artists in their own right, percolated into other theatrical genres, notably opera. In the 1870s similar attention to theatrical design began to be applied to contemporary plays: settings for plays about the peasants or the minor impoverished bureaucracy of the capital cities benefited enormously.[24] The search for authenticity in acting style, in décor, and in costume, regarded as characteristic of the achievements of the Moscow Art Theatre, is usually traced to the visits of such enterprises as the Meiningen Company in 1885 and 1890. It had, though, been initiated much earlier in Russia, largely as a response, and contribution, to the movement of realism across the arts from the 1860s onwards.[25]

Despite the popularity and discussion of this production, subsequently Tolstoy was not so successful. *Tsar Fyodor* (1868) and *Tsar Boris* (1870), the second and third dramas of the trilogy, had difficulty gaining permission to be performed although both were published. The implied debate about autocracy the plays conduct proved too challenging for the kind of public presentation afforded by theatre, in the view of the censoring authorities. *Tsar Boris* was not performed until 1881. The Moscow Art Theatre chose the unperformed *Tsar Fyodor* to open its first season in 1898, attesting to its recognition of its heritage.

Perspectives on the nature of realism altered in response to a changing audience. There was a notable difference between the audiences of the 1850s and the 1880s, mirroring changes in society as a whole. The population of the cities grew: in 1852, 336,000 people were estimated to live in Moscow, and 532,000 in St Petersburg,[26] and these figures grew by a third between 1860 and 1880.[27] It was not simply a matter of a rise in the birth-rate; numbers were swelled by an influx of immigrants from the countryside, particularly after the emancipation. Former serfs came as artisans, traders and factory workers. What had been predominantly an aristocratic audience in the preceding period became more socially diverse. Greater opportunities in education led to a large increase in the number of students, and to greater diversity in their social origins. The merchant classes began to patronise the theatre, enticed by the success of one of their greatest sons, Ostrovsky. The severity of the censorship which has already been noted in the fate of several plays was a response to this function of the theatre as almost the only forum which brought together such a diverse public. The intelligentsia fast became the driving force behind drama: one source remarks that the Maly was in effect Moscow's second university in the 1870s.[28] Theatre was patronised as much by the radical writers and students as by other less politically active groups and individuals, distinguishing it considerably from the 'aristocratic' theatre with which the period opened. Theatre criticism made a lively contribution to the pages of the popular monthly 'thick' journals, reaching an even wider urban and rural population.

Amateur groups in the capital cities were another important source of theatre, particularly in the 1860s. They operated as clubs, providing performances for their membership only. Amateur theatres tended to mirror the repertoire of the professional theatres and were not seen as experimental venues. They offered opportunities for actors from provincial theatres to perform in the capitals which otherwise was difficult as the professional theatres tended to recruit for life. There are instances where the amateur groups functioned as training grounds, enabling talented individuals to turn professional. Occasionally, the clubs scored theatrical coups by performing plays banned from the professional stage but seen as appropriate for societies with their closed memberships. In addition, the clubs were not barred from performing during Lent and could give performances on Saturdays and public holidays.

Although under the monopoly commercial theatre was not allowed in the capital cities, it flourished in the provinces. It was also possible to set up a theatre just beyond the city limits, and enterprises were often run for a summer season. These summer theatres made an initial contribution to the foundation of a commercial theatre, which marks the following period. The movement for a 'people's' (*narodnyii*) theatre, however, demonstrated that not all the population was catered for, and it introduced an important notion of accessibility into theatrical thinking.

In 1872 a theatre was erected for the Polytechnical Exhibition in Moscow. Theatre practitioners were conscious of their lack of provision for the uneducated working classes of the capitals. The need for a special repertoire was also discussed: some argued for the classics, others for a moral, didactic repertoire, and the authorities insisted it should be subject to strict censorship. Funded by the Moscow merchant class and the City Council (Duma), the theatre had a capacity of about 1,600 with more than 1,000 seats available at a cheap rate. As an enterprise it was a great success, and it was visited by the tsar (although he disliked the production that he saw of Gogol's *The Government Inspector*). Most importantly the theatre's existence initiated a debate over repertoire. Its focus was on Russian plays, a brave but important step when so much of the repertoire of the established theatre consisted of foreign plays or adaptations. The following year the theatre was run as a private enterprise, and gradually lost its initial accessibility to a wide audience, largely because it did not retain its policy of cheap seats, and because it was restricted to the performance of extracts.[29] By 1876 it had closed, but the beginning of a move towards a private commercial theatre was underway. There is also reference to one or two examples of successful enterprises that catered mostly for the Moscow intellectual community just before the lifting of the monopoly in 1882.[30] Consciousness of accessibility for a socially diverse audience was now seen as desirable theatrical practice, and was consequently high on the agenda of the Moscow Art Theatre when it was formed in the 1890s.

The professional theatre was prohibited from performing during Lent, on public holidays and on Saturdays. There were strict rules relating to the representation of religious material on stage and the playing of religious characters. In many respects the censorship was as sensitive to this issue as it was to political infringements. Actors were taken on much in the manner of apprentices and had a contract with an individual theatre. Some performances, sometimes premieres, were given as benefits for individual actors, allowing them to augment their incomes by receiving a substantial amount of the box-office takings. Actors were largely responsible for supplying their own costumes and props, and frequently therefore performed in contemporary costumes. This was particularly the custom before the concept of an overall design was introduced, as in the Tolstoy production of 1867 described above.

Many think the period under discussion was primarily a time of actors' theatre. Rehearsals and preparations focused on their efforts and as yet the director had not achieved the central, organisational and interpretative role of the next period. The major example of house style is that developed at the Maly, mainly through the work of Ostrovsky on his own plays. The model production of Tolstoy's *Death of Ivan the Terrible* was coordinated mostly by the *author*. It is certainly true that the success of the realist theatre owed a great deal to the strides made by actors such as Shchepkin, Samoilov, Sadovsky, Shumsky, Ermolova, Fedotova, Savina and Strepetova, among many others, in adapting the received gestural style to the more natural ways now demanded. The great actors developed style dynasties of their own. Training facilities were scarce: most learning was conducted on the job, with young actors gaining expertise from the established stars. Such schools as there were tended to rely on well-tried methods and styles: students had to memorise texts and declaim them, despite a number of different proposals for change.[31] A commission for the reform of actor training, of which Ostrovsky, Potekhin and Averkiev were members, was set up at the very end of the period. New drama schools emerged as theatre proliferated in the capitals with the lifting of the

8. Maria Ermolova as Ophelia in *Hamlet*. Maly Theatre, 1878.

monopoly in 1882. However, the contribution made by the actors of the 1860s and 1870s to the concepts worked out subsequently by Stanislavsky in his school of realist acting should not be underestimated.

The repertoire consisted of a constantly alternating body of productions, with no concept of the continual run of modern Western theatre. Plays were sometimes given again after an interval of several months, and the same production would stay in the repertoire for several years. Actors acquired roles which they kept, and frequently their individual interpreta-

9. Maria Savina as Verochka in Turgenev's *A Month in the Country*. Aleksandrinsky Theatre, 1879.

tions became famous and performances sought after. Strepetova was still performing as Lizaveta in Pisemsky's *A Bitter Fate* well into the 1890s.[32] Bequeathing a role to a younger actor was often a difficult process.

Analysis of the repertoire of the leading Imperial Theatres gives an idea of the theatrical diet of the realist period.[33] For example, for the years 1862–81, 1,227 plays are recorded in the repertoire of the Alesksandrinsky and Maly theatres. Of these, 607 were translations or adaptations of foreign plays. Of the remaining 620 Russian plays, some 500 were popular vaudeville pieces or the work of dramatists who have sunk without trace. The 120 plays that are left have had an enduring reputation, 30 of them being classics from a former era, 49 being attributable to Ostrovsky or to his collaborations with others, and some 40 being by realist writers such as those we have already discussed, as well as by Saltykov-Shchedrin, Leskov, and one or two writers whose reputations have not endured, such as N. A. Chaev or V. A. Krylov.

Of the classics, the most frequently staged Russian play was Gogol's *The Government Inspector,* performed approximately 200 times during this period. Gogol's presence was further bolstered by productions of his other plays and by adaptations of his prose works. This influence may arguably be responsible for satire and comedy being by far the most popular genres. Gogol was followed by Turgenev in popularity (9 different works figure), with Griboedov a close third (153 performances of his one play, *Woe from Wit,* were given between 1862–81). The works by the realist Saltykov-Shchedrin were mainly adaptations from his prose writings; Leskov is credited with one major play, *The Wastrel* (1867), more popular for its melodrama than for its realism. Saltykov-Shchedrin and Leskov made original and substantial contributions to the realist school through their prose works, but their impact on theatre, while important for demonstrating their interest, was not of great consequence for theatrical realism in comparison to the writers and productions discussed earlier in the chapter.

What is the character of realism that emerges from this panorama, disregarding for the moment the contributions of Ostrovsky, Turgenev and Chekhov? There were differing views of what realism could project. The radical critics sought a form that could be harnessed to the exposure of society's ills; and others wanted a perception of contemporary Russia that incorporated an ideal. At the other extreme, writers such as Pisemsky or Potekhin wanted to convey what they knew was true about the brutality and corruption of Russian life. In peasant plays, the problem lay in whether or not to destroy the sacred image of the people, as dear to the radical critic as to the Slavophile, but in which writers with naturalist tendencies were uninterested. Plays about the urban bureaucracy and the changes brought about by the rise of capitalism disenchanted the influential radical critics unless the plays conformed to their programme. As for the 'fantastic' theatre of Sukhovo-Kobylin, hampered by the censorship, only his first play was performed. His view of the grotesque remained a matter for literary perception and failed to make its mark with the increasingly extreme radical critics. As these latter became the saints of the literary and theatrical critical world, what they neglected in the nineteenth century remained so in the twentieth. Naturalism and the fantastic as the acceptable extremes of realism were denied their rightful place.

Realism demanded truth, but censorship operated to prevent some areas of truth from being revealed. Post-Crimean War reform highlighted the principles whereby Russia was governed: dramatists resorted to history to conduct their discussion of Russian government, and in so doing brought the underlying principles of realism, verisimilitude and authenticity to the treatment of Russia's past. Perhaps here is a clue to the discovery of the clearest and most lasting consequence of the realist movement: the new audience expectations of staging and acting. Henceforward, realist theatre was rarely able to survive without rising to these expectations. The following period in the Russian theatre takes the standards of realism to exacting levels, while also generating an antithesis. Russia goes on to create a modernist experimental theatre, unmatched in contemporary Europe. Likewise the realist achievements of the turn of the century were without parallel. The period 1850–82 laid the foundations in some measure for both.

Notes

1 *Moskvitianin*, 23 (1854).
2 See *Panteon*, book 2, section IV, p. 2, as quoted in A. I. Zhuravleva (ed.), *Russian drama epokhi A. N. Ostrovskogo* (Moscow, 1984), p. 445.
3 *Sovremennik*, 49, (1855), pp. 226–7.
4 Pisemskii, Aleksei Feofilaktovich, 1821–81. Russian novelist, short story writer and dramatist. He wrote fifteen plays, many of which were banned by censorship. For the best biographical and critical study in English, see Charles Moser, *Pisemsky. A Provincial Realist* (Cambridge, Mass., 1969).
5 'Peterburgskie teatry', *Sovremennik*, 11 (1863); M. E. Saltykov-Shchedrin, *Sobranie sochinenii*, vol. V (Moscow, 1966), pp. 183–98.
6 N. A. Dobroliubov, 1836–61. Critic and publicist. See his article 'Luch sveta v temnom tsarstve' (A ray of light in a realm of darkness), *Sovremennik*, 10 (1860). English version in N. A. Dobrolyubov, *Selected Philosophical Essays*, tr. J. Fineberg (Moscow, 1948) pp. 543–628.
7 A. F. Pisemskii, *Sobranie sochinenii*, vol. IX (Moscow, 1959), p. 609.
8 Constantin Stanislavski, *My Life in Art*, tr. J. J. Robbins (London, 1980), p. 169.

9 I. Annenskii, 'Gor'kaia sud'bina', *Knigi otrazhenii* (Moscow, 1979), pp. 44–63.

10 1895 brought a rash of productions of the play in the Imperial and commercial theatre. The MAT production of 1902 was the first to present the play in its original version.

11 For references to *A Bitter Fate* see L. N. Tolstoi, *Polnoe sobranie sochinenii*, vol. LI (Moscow, 1952) p. 98; vol. LX (Moscow, 1949), p. 217; Tolstoy had to deal with A. A. Potekhin in the 1880s as head of the repertoire committee when trying to arrange for performance of *The Power of Darkness* (see vol. LXIII (Moscow, 1934), pp. 455, 407), but there is no direct reference to Potekhin's plays.

12 Sukhovo-Kobylin, Aleksandr Vasil'evich, 1817–1903. The only full-length study in English is Richard Fortune's , *Alexander Sukhovo-Kobylin* (Boston, Mass., 1982).

13 K. Rudnitsky, *Russian and Soviet Theatre*, tr. R. Permar, ed. L. Milne (London, 1988), p. 95.

14 Fortune, p. 126.

15 N. G. Zograf, *Malyi Teatr vtoroi poloviny XIX veka*, (Moscow, 1960), pp. 78–80.

16 S. A. Pereselenkov, 'A. V. Sukhovo-Kobylin', *Ezhegodnik Imperatorskikh gosudarstvennykh teatrov*, 1918–19 (Petrograd, 1920(22)), p. 135.

17 *Moskovskie vedomosti*, 152 (1855) p. 629 as quoted in I. Kleiner, *Dramaturgiia Sukhovo-Kobylina* (Moscow, 1961), p. 29.

18 L. Grossmann, 'A. V. Sukhovo-Kobylin: Zhizn', lichnost', tvorchestvo', in L. P. Grossmann (ed.), *A. V. Sukhovo-Kobylin: Trilogiia*, (Moscow and Leningrad, 1927), pp. 29–30.

19 *The Trilogy of Alexander Sukhovo-Kobylin*, tr. and introduction by H. B. Segel (New York, 1969), pp. 45–7.

20 V. G. Sakhnovskii, 'Teatral'naia sud'ba trilogii Sukhovo-Kobylina', in Grossman (ed.), p. 548.

21 Prutkov was presented as a writer with a bureaucratic outlook, not very intelligent but well meaning. He was used to lampoon pretentious attitudes. His works were published between 1859 and his 'death' in 1863, in the journals *Iskra* (The Spark) and *Sovremennik*. His collected works were published posthumously.

22 A. K. Tolstoi, 'Proetkt postanovki na stsenu tragedii *Smert' Ionanna Goznogo* (1866), *Sobranie sochinenii*, vol. III (Moscow, 1964), pp. 454–95.

23 Roller, Andrei Adamovich, 1805–91. German by birth, Roller joined the Imperial Theatre in St Petersburg in 1834. The peak of his career came in the 1850s after which a school of Russian stage designers began to emerge.

24 F. Ia. Syrkina, *Russkoe teatral'no-dekoratsionnoe iskusstvo vtoroi poloviny XIX veka* (Moscow, 1956), pp. 175ff.

25 Ibid. p. 144–5.

26 *Istoriia russkogo dramaticheskogo teatra*, (7 vols., Moscow, 1977–87), vol. IV, p. 24.

27 Ibid. vol. V, p. 7.

28 Syrkina, p. 156.

29 *Istoriia russkogo dramaticheskogo teatra*, vol. v, p. 252.

30 Ibid. pp. 253–5.

31 Ibid. p. 32.

32 Pisemskii, p. 609.

33 Full repertoire for 1862–81 in *Istoriia russkogo dramatischeskogo teatra*, vol. v, pp. 412–537.

8 Aleksandr Ostrovsky – dramatist and director

KATE SEALEY RAHMAN

Russian theatre of the mid and late nineteenth century was all but synonymous with one man – the playwright Aleksandr Nikolaevich Ostrovsky (1823–86). While other great figures of nineteenth-century Russian literature made ventures into play-writing, Ostrovsky was the sole nineteenth-century Russian writer of note who was purely a dramatist. (Even Chekhov, who stands firm in the minds of Western audiences as the embodiment of Russian drama, was known in his day as primarily a writer of comic short stories.) The author of nearly fifty original plays – principally comedies, but also tragedies, historical plays and a fairy-tale drama in verse – as well as seven collaborative works and numerous translations (including works by Shakespeare, Goldoni, Cervantes, Calderón and Seneca), Ostrovsky created a Russian national repertory all but single-handedly. His plays provided actors with more than seven hundred different characters. They formed the basis of libretti for operas by Janáček, Rimsky-Korsakov, Tchaikovsky, and Serov. As the novelist Ivan Goncharov was prompted to declare in a letter to Ostrovsky in 1881: 'You have given Russian literature a whole library of works of art and you have created a world of its own for the Russian stage. You have completed the building for which Fonvizin, Griboyedov and Gogol laid the foundation stones. It is only after you that we Russians can proudly claim to possess a national theatre of our own – a theatre that can justly be called the Theatre of Ostrovsky.'[1]

His literary works aside, Ostrovsky devoted his entire life to the theatre, working to improve the position of actors and playwrights and developing new techniques of stage-setting, acting and directing. As one critic and translator of his plays has noted: 'In a word, Alexander Ostrovsky *was* the Russian theatre of his day.'[2]

Ostrovsky was born on 31 March 1823 in a two-storey wooden house at 9, Malaya Ordynka, in Zamoskvoreche, the merchants' quarter of Moscow.

His grandfather, Fedor, was a priest in Kostroma, who later moved to Moscow to become a monk at the Donskoy monastery. Ostrovsky's father, Nikolai, also trained for the priesthood, studying at the Moscow Theological Academy. However, on graduating, he chose not to join the clergy, instead taking up a position in the judiciary branch of the civil service. He rose through the ranks with rapid speed, eventually achieving the level of Collegiate Assessor – a rank elevating him to the hereditary nobility. A substantial private law practice ensured him of the wealth to accompany his title. In 1820 Nikolai married Lyubov Ivanovna, the sister of a former classmate. M. Wettlin describes her as 'handsome, accomplished and with good connections'.[3] Aleksandr was their third child (their first two sons died in infancy). They were to have three more children before Lyubov's death from tuberculosis in 1831, when Aleksandr was eight years old. Five years later, in 1836, Nikolai married Baroness Emiliya Andreevna von Tessin, the granddaughter of a Swedish nobleman, bringing further wealth and status to the family.

By all accounts Ostrovsky was a gifted child, particularly skilled as a musician and a linguist. In 1840 he graduated from secondary school with *magna cum laude* – granting him automatic entrance into Moscow University. Despite his desire to pursue an Arts education, pressure from his father led Ostrovsky to enrol in the Law Faculty. His subsequent university career was not a success. Ostrovsky's love of the theatre meant that his interest lay more in frequenting theatrical productions than in attending to his university studies. In 1843, after his second failure at examinations and following disagreements with his professor, he left university. His father secured him a position as a clerk in the Moscow Court of Conscience. Two years later, in 1845, he took up an appointment at the Moscow Commercial Court.

Despite his passion for theatre, Ostrovsky's earliest literary endeavours were in narrative prose. His first known literary work, a short story entitled *The Tale of How the Police Superintendent went on a Binge, or From greatness to ridicule is only one step*, was written in December 1843.[4] The work parodies Pushkin's famous narrative poem, *Count Nulin*, transposing events to a small wooden house in 'one of those squalid, narrow, little lanes, of which there are so many between Myasnitskaya and Sretenkaya streets' and taking as its hero a timid, downtrodden civil servant. Unmistakably influenced by the works of Gogol, *The Tale...*, with its emphasis on verisimilitude, and portrayal of life in the lower middle classes, is characteristic of the physiological sketch, a genre which rose to prominence in Russia in the 1840s. Yet even in this early work Ostrovsky's interest in the theatre is clearly apparent: sections of dialogue are written in the style of a playscript.

Ostrovsky's first published works – an incomplete cycle of physiological sketches under the title *Notes of a Zamoskvoreche Resident* and a fragment of a play, entitled *The Bankrupt* – appeared in *The Moscow City Flysheet* in 1847. It was also in 1847 that Ostrovsky achieved his first real literary success: the public reading of a one-act play, *A Family Picture*, at the apartment of Professor S. P. Shevyrev on 14 February. Ostrovsky was later to refer to this day as 'the most memorable day in my life . . . From this day on I began to consider myself a Russian writer and believed in my calling without doubt or hesitation.'[5]

A Family Picture was published (again in *The Moscow City Flysheet*) in March 1847. However, its negative portrayal of the corruption endemic in the Moscow business world meant that it was almost immediately banned from performance on the stage. A similar fate befell Ostrovsky's first full-length play, *It's All in the Family*. This was published in *The Muscovite* in 1850 to great critical acclaim, yet was once more banned from stage production. (A decision famously upheld by Tsar Nikolai I himself.) Given a revised 'moral' ending, the play was eventually staged in 1861. It was not until 1881 that the work was performed in its original form.

The consequences of Royal disapprobation were severe. In June 1850 Ostrovsky was placed under police surveillance, leading to his dismissal from government service the following year. (The surveillance itself lasted until 1856.) Disinherited by his father in 1849 for refusing to end his relationship with his common-law wife, Agafya Ivanovna,[6] Ostrovsky was, in effect, forced to rely on his writing for a living.[7] From this point on, until his death in 1886, he was to publish at least one play (sometimes two) a year.

Critical discussion of Ostrovsky's plays typically divides his work into two broad categories: those written up to and including *The Storm* in 1860 – generally referred to as 'the early works' or 'merchant cycle' – and those written between 1860 and his death in 1886 – 'the late works'. Despite the fact that Ostrovsky wrote the bulk of his drama in the later period – thirty-three original plays as opposed to the fourteen he wrote in the years 1847–60 – the accepted critical view of his work is based largely on the

10. A scene from Aleksandr Ostrovsky's *It's a Family Affair – We'll Settle it Ourselves*. Aleksandrinsky Theatre, 1907.

debates among critics which raged around reception of his earlier works. Ostrovsky's first two plays – *A Family Picture* and *It's All in the Family* – were hailed by his contemporaries as opening a new chapter in the history of Russian literature, bringing to the forefront a class of people never before seen in Russian writing – Moscow merchants. This critical acclaim (Turgenev famously dubbed Ostrovsky 'The Shakespeare of the merchant class') gave rise to the myth – frequently promulgated in modern critical analysis of his work – that Ostrovsky was purely a playwright of the merchant class. The reality could not be more different. The critic N. Henley has noted that: 'In actuality only a small number of Ostrovsky's plays deals to any great extent with merchants, and in those the merchant's significance is as a human being, not as a businessman.'[8] Indeed, it is the diversity of his characterisation which provides one of the most striking features of Ostrovsky's work. His plays explore a whole spectrum of humanity from peasants to the nobility. A brief examination of the principal characters in his early works alone reveals civil servants, noblemen, landowners, peasants, teachers and servants, depicted alongside the merchants. His later works would go on to portray members of 'high society', provincial actors and representatives of the emerging capitalist class.

Perhaps the greatest injustice inflicted on subsequent critical interpretation of Ostrovsky's work was the emphasis placed by his contemporaries on the realism of his plays, and the view that his works constituted a form of social protest. This analysis of Ostrovsky's drama was largely formulated by the critic N. A. Dobrolyubov, whose two articles on Ostrovsky (entitled *The Kingdom of Darkness* and *A Ray of Light in the Kingdom of Darkness*, and published in 1859 and 1860 respectively) have coloured critical discussion of his work ever since.[9] In these Dobrolyubov argued that the primary value of Ostrovsky's plays was as a form of social documentation. He emphasised that the essence of Ostrovsky's works was 'their unadulterated truth', their 'faithfulness to reality', before going on to argue that the underlying motive for Ostrovsky's work was social criticism, the desire to challenge Russian life: 'if our readers, after pondering over our observations find that . . . the artist has indeed challenged Russian life . . . then we shall be satisfied, no matter what our scholars and literary judges might say'.[10] Ostrovsky's plays, Dobrolyubov asserted, were a protest against the tyranny to be found in this 'Dark Kingdom' (namely Russian society).

Dobrolyubov's interpretation of Ostrovsky's work contains many elements of truth. Ostrovsky did undoubtedly play a crucial role in the development of realism in Russian drama. His plays did indeed depict everyday life to a far greater extent than ever before seen on the Russian stage (as we shall see below, he frequently stressed the importance of authenticity in stage production). And his work did contain elements of social protest: a number of his plays include calls for greater social justice. However, the continual emphasis on this aspect of Ostrovsky's work – advocated time and again in modern critical works – has served to root it firmly in the narrow sphere of nineteenth-century Russian society. It has given rise to the commonly expressed view that Ostrovsky has little to offer to audiences in the West

This in turn provides the answer to the paradox which lies at the centre of any discussion of Ostrovsky: namely, that this man, universally acknowledged as the central figure of nineteenth-century Russian theatre, is so little known and studied in the West. Calls for greater recognition outside Russia for Ostrovsky's work date back to William Ralston's famous essay on Ostrovsky in 1868,[11] yet thus far they have gone largely unheeded. In the West, professional productions of Ostrovsky's plays remain rare, few of his works have been translated, and there is very little critical comment. Ostrovsky's plays are often overlooked in major anthologies of Russian drama. To date there is only one full-length publication in English devoted to Ostrovsky's life and works.[12]

Explanations for this paradox often emphasise the complexities of Ostrovsky's language. Critics highlight his frequent use of local speech and idiom, and note the difficulties this poses for successful translation. However, a more likely explanation for the playwright's obscurity in the West is the continued promotion of Dobrolyubov's interpretation of his plays. It has led critics to view Ostrovsky's plays solely in terms of their nineteenth-century context, giving rise to the view that Ostrovsky is somehow too 'Russian' to be of interest to Western audiences.

Quotations from Western literary criticism which illustrate this view are overwhelming in their number. To quote just a few: D. Magarshack (a scholar who has done much to introduce Ostrovsky's work to Western readers) notes that many of Ostrovsky's plays 'deal exclusively with the life of the Russian Merchant class in the middle years of the last century, whose traditions, patriarchal customs and dark superstitions are unintelligible outside Russia'.[13] A. V. Knowles states that Ostrovsky 'established a tradition of realism on the Russian stage', noting that he 'bequeathed a wide and varied repertory which dealt in the main with particularly Russian themes and national problems'.[14] L. Hanson talks of Ostrovsky's 'essential Russianness'.[15] *The McGraw-Hill Encylopedia* notes that 'his work is so closely tied to a specific Russian milieu that it is difficult for foreign audiences to penetrate the wealth of local colour and typically Russian characterization'.[16]

Such views are echoed in works by Soviet and Russian scholars. In Russian and Soviet criticism the words most frequently used to describe Ostrovsky include '*realist*', '*bytovik*', and '*bytopisatel*'' ('depictor of everyday life'). V. Lakshin talks of Ostrovsky's plays providing 'information on the realities of life in the mid nineteenth century'.[17] (Indeed, the belief in the accuracy of Ostrovsky's portrayal of nineteenth-century social mores is so strong that some writers even refer to Ostrovsky for historical details.[18]) V. Setchkarev notes that: 'Ostrovsky's plays are so intimately bound up with Russian social conditions that for all their excellent qualities it is unlikely that they will ever attract much of an audience outside Russia.'[19] Even contemporary writers asserted the peculiar 'Russianness' of Ostrovsky's work. The novelist Fedor Dostoevsky, writing in 1873, noted that 'at the very least, three-quarters of his comedies remain completely beyond European understanding'.[20]

The net effect of such assertions is that criticism of Ostrovsky's work has, in general, focused on issues of a narrow, contemporary nature, overlooking those of universal concern. Yet the universal content of Ostrovsky's drama is considerable. His plays overflow with themes of a universal nature; posing social, psychological and philosophical questions of worldwide concern. The critic E. K. Bristow has noted the presence in Ostrovsky's work of such universal questions as: 'How should the family complex be governed? What alienates parents and children? What are the rights of women? Does education eliminate prejudice and vulgarity?'[21] To these should be added, at a minimum, a concern with the corrupting influence of money and the relationship between realism and idealism. Not least, Ostrovsky's plays raise questions about the nature of reality itself. The world depicted in his plays is a complex web of deception and illusion, fantasy and realism. Throughout his work there are constant reminders about the superficiality of appearance and the dangers of taking things at face value. Like many playwrights, Ostrovsky was clearly fascinated by the relationship between reality and illusion.[22]

Paradoxically, *The Storm*, Ostrovsky's best-known play, and certainly the one which has most frequently made its way into Western anthologies, is perhaps his least accessible work. Certainly the traditional view of the play as a protest against the oppressive mores of mid-nineteenth-century provincial Russian society (Dobrolyubov's 'Dark Kingdom') has served to fix it in the minds of many Western scholars as a particularly 'Russian' play.[23] Yet *The Storm*, too, which charts a young woman's struggle to break out of a loveless marriage and oppressive home life, clearly explores themes of universal concern. The central character, Katerina, is a highly complex figure, and viewed as psychological (rather than a social) study, the play takes on an entirely new, more universal, slant. A number of directors (among them Meyerhold, as early as 1916) have staged radically unconventional productions of *The Storm*. K. Rudnitsky, discussing Meyerhold's 1916 staging, noted: 'By avoiding fidelity to life, rejecting the idea of a direct depiction of "The Kingdom of Darkness" and by transforming the prosaic and wild Kalinov into a fairy-city Kitezh, Meyerhold removed the dramatic situation of "The Storm" from the specific historical environment of mid-nineteenth-century Russia. This made obvious the significance for the early twentieth century. Poeticized, it gained the significance of universality. Instead of the specific merchant's dark kingdom and dark life, there stepped forth the power of dark spiritual forces . . . what was essentially Russian stepped forth in a generalized and threatening form.'[24]

The position of *The Storm* as the play most commonly associated with Ostrovsky is perhaps surprising, as it is hardly representative of the majority of his work and gives no indication of his considerable skill as a comic writer.[25] Once more, the explanation lies largely with Ostrovsky's contemporaries, many of whom viewed *The Storm* as the pinnacle of Ostrovsky's achievement. Some even went so far as to suggest that after creating *The Storm* Ostrovsky had written himself out. Certainly there was a feeling that Ostrovsky had passed his prime as a playwright. By 1875 the critic N. Shelgunov was writing 'the time of Ostrovsky has finished. He is insufficient in the new world, he is not familiar with the new world and does not depict it.'[26] Again, this view – often repeated in modern critical accounts – does Ostrovsky great injustice. Over two-thirds of Ostrovsky's plays were penned in the years following *The Storm*, including among them many of his best works. The charge that Ostrovsky 'is not familiar with the new world and does not depict it' is particularly unjust. Ostrovsky's plays remained remarkably in tune with the changes wrought in Russia by the emancipation of the serfs in 1861 and the great reforms of the 1860s. Several of his later plays reflect the changing social structures of the time – the declining role of the gentry and the emergence of a new capitalist class. (This is particularly noticeable in *The Forest* (1870), where a former serf, Vosmibratov, is shown buying up the forest of the local landowner – a plot-line later echoed in Chekhov's *The Cherry Orchard*; and *Easy Money* (1870), which contrasts a hardworking and successful entrepreneur with the impoverished and frivolous nobility.)

In the sixties, Ostrovsky wrote a number of historical dramas – *One-Armed Minin* (1862), *Voevoda* (1865), *The False Dmitry and Vasily Shuisky*

(1867) and *Tushino* (1867) – not generally considered to be among his best works. It was during this time that he underwent a period of disillusionment with the theatre, even contemplating a break with it altogether. In a letter to the actor F. Burdin in 1866, he stated:

> I am informing you in secret that I'm giving up the theatrical world completely. My reasons are these: I receive almost no profits from the theatre (although all the theatres in Russia live by my repertory). Those in charge of the theatres are not well-disposed towards me ... Believe me, I shall gain far greater respect – which I deserve and am worthy of – if I break with the theatre. Even after giving the theatre twenty-five original plays I am treated no differently than if I was some inferior translator. At least I will have peace and independence, instead of constant worry and undeserved humiliation.[27]

Ostrovsky recovered from his despondency and between 1868 and 1878 he wrote some of his finest works, among them a number of satirical plays mocking the hypocrisy to be found in high society and the landed gentry: *Even Wise Men Err* (1868) – Ostrovsky's famous portrayal of an ambitious young man on the make in Moscow high society; *Easy Money* (1870); and *Wolves and Sheep* (1875). During this period he also wrote two plays depicting the life of actors – *The Forest* (1870) and *A Seventeenth-Century Comic* (1873) – and his fairy-tale play, *The Snowmaiden* (1873).

In his last years Ostrovsky turned again to plays depicting life in the theatre – writing *Artists and Admirers* (1882) and *Guilty Without Guilt* (1884) – as well as creating another deeply effective psychological drama, *Without a Dowry* (1879), and the plays often dubbed 'the sad comedies'[28] – *A Last Sacrifice* (1878), *The Heart is not Stone* (1880), *The Unfree* (1881).

A brief period as an editor of Pogodin's *The Muscovite* (1850–5), during which he wrote three plays – *Stick to Your Own Sleigh* (1853), *Poverty Is No Vice* (1854) and *You Can't Live Just As You Please* (1855) – which broadly conformed with Slavophile philosophy in their positive portrayal of ordinary Russian people, has led some critics to label Ostrovsky as a Slavophile. Yet Ostrovsky was not a polemical playwright and there is no real indication that he shared Pogodin's views. Despite his early connection with *The Muscovite*, Ostrovsky went on to publish works in journals as diverse as *The Russian Herald*, *The Contemporary*, *Time*, *The Messenger of Europe*, *A Library for Reading* and *Fatherland Notes*. Indeed much of Ostrovsky's difficulty with his

11. Olga and Mikhail Sadovsky in Aleksandr Ostrovsky's *Wolves and Sheep*, Maly Theatre, 1894.

critics – particularly in later years – lay in the fact that, during this time of fiercely held ideologies, he never adopted a specific ideological stance. Throughout his life, Westerners vied with Slavophiles to label him as one of their own. Yet as early as 1851, in a review of the Pisemsky story 'The Simpleton', Ostrovsky argued that ideology simply 'confuses high artistic value'.[29] His plays sought to pose questions rather than to answer them and they rarely contain clearly defined 'heroes' and 'villains'.

If Ostrovsky avoided polemics in his literary works, he was a more than willing participant in debates relating to the practicalities of theatre, and wrote a number of notes and memoranda on the condition of contemporary Russian drama. He involved himself in theatrical life on every level, even conducting a series of statistical surveys at the Maly Theatre to determine the precise social make-up of his audience. He campaigned actively for improvements in the terms and conditions for actors and playwrights, founding two influential societies for reforming the rights of actors and composers. He was similarly concerned with the lack of formal training for actors, writing essays on acting technique and advocating the development of drama schools.

The success of any playwright is heavily dependent on the actors who perform his or her plays and Ostrovsky formed a lasting relationship with the actors of the Maly Theatre, numbering many of them as among his closest friends. He himself directed several of the Maly productions of his plays, paying close attention to stage-setting and design. (E. K. Bristow has described him as 'the first modern stage director in the Russian theatre'.[30]) The declamatory techniques employed by the great actors of the past – Mochalov and Shchepkin – were no longer appropriate for the greater realism emerging in Russian drama, and Ostrovsky was influential in introducing a greater authenticity in acting style. He believed strongly that actors should bring their own experiences and recollected emotions to their roles. (In this, he was an early exponent of a system not unlike that which was later developed by Stanislavsky.) In a telling scene in *Guilty without Guilt*, Ostrovsky has the theatre patron Dudukin state: 'In order to give a true representation of a situation, it seems to me you have to have lived through it yourself, or at least something similar.' However, Ostrovsky was equally concerned that actors should receive formal training in acting technique, noting that 'People are not born actors any more than they are born violinists, opera singers, painters, sculptors or playwrights. They are born with capabilities and proclivities. The rest is acquired through education, hard work and a thorough mastery of technique.'[31] (Such sentiments were later echoed by the director Vsevolod Meyerhold: 'To be an actor it is not enough to know, remember and imagine, one must also know how [to express it].'[32])

Central to Ostrovsky's work in the theatre was his belief in its social role. He viewed theatre as a great educative force in society. To that end, he was a life-long campaigner for the establishment of a national 'people's' theatre. He never realised this ambition, but was undoubtedly influential in bringing to an end the Imperial monopoly in theatres in Moscow and St Petersburg. It was the 1882 Decree allowing the establishment of private theatres in these cities which eventually paved the way for Stanislavsky and Nemirovich-Dancheko to form the Moscow Art Theatre – in many ways the embodiment of Ostrovsky's dream.

Despite the enormity of Ostrovsky's work for the theatre, official recognition was scarce. In January 1886 he was eventually appointed Director of Repertoire for the Moscow Imperial Theatres. (His delight in receiving this appointment was great. He wrote to his wife: 'I have never been so happy in my life! . . . How much suffering have I endured for the sake of the theatre! For the past five years I have thought of nothing else and my thoughts have driven me almost crazy. I wrote petitions in favour of private theatres, I drew up projects for the Imperial Theatre, I sat on commissions, I covered mountains of paper with writing. All to no avail. The level of art fell lower and lower, millions of roubles were wasted, the gulf between me and the theatre grew wider and wider. And here all of a sudden I have a theatre, my own theatre, completely my own, of which I am solely in charge, answering to no-one.'[33]) However, he was to die just five months after taking up his post.

Ostrovsky's legacy to the Russian theatre continued long after his death. As a campaigner, he set in motion the chain of events leading to the creation of the Moscow Arts Theatre, and succeeded in establishing a proper system of royalty payment and copyright for future generations of playwrights. As a director, his system of stage production closely resembled techniques adopted by future directors. Stanislavsky, in particular, was undoubtedly influenced by Ostrovsky's work at the Maly Theatre. The critic Magarshack notes that: 'When one compares Ostrovsky's and Stanislavsky's system of stage presentation there is very little to distinguish them from each other . . . Ostrovsky's view on scenery, gesture and stage diction are in all essentials identical with those of Stanislavsky.'[34] Elements of Ostrovsky's system are also apparent in the works of Nemirovich-Danchenko, who shared Ostrovsky's belief in the 'invisible' role of the producer; and Meyerhold, who like Ostrovsky, emphasised the importance of acting technique. As a dramatist, Ostrovsky's influence can be seen in the works of future playwrights – aspects of his dramatic technique are clearly evident in works by Tolstoy and Chekhov, for example. Yet it is his plays themselves which represent Ostrovsky's greatest legacy. In Russia, his works have been more frequently performed that those of any other playwright and his popularity remains unrivaled. In the years following his death until the 1917 Revolution, Ostrovsky's plays were performed on average 1,358 times a year. After 1917, his popularity increased even further – in 1939 over 11,000 performances of his plays appeared on the Russian stage.[35] Even today, after perestroika, his plays continue to dominate the Russian repertoire. A cursory glance at the Moscow newspapers reveals that in the two-week period between 29 April and 13 May 1997, no fewer than ten different productions of Ostrovsky plays were being staged in Moscow in seven different theatres.[36]

It is this enduring popularity which provides the greatest challenge to the traditional interpretation of Ostrovsky as a narrowly realist writer. If he was indeed concerned solely with depicting the lives of Moscow merchants in the mid nineteenth century, then, surely, as Yu. Aikhenval'd claimed as early as 1909, he would have 'lost meaning as the conditions he describes disappear from Russian life'.[37] In Russia, as well as the West, Ostrovsky's plays would contain little of significance. The enduring presence of his plays in the Russian repertoire demonstrates that they offer something of value and relevance to today's audience.

Ostrovsky has not yet won the recognition in the West that his pivotal role in the development of nineteenth-century Russian theatre – as both dramatist and director – deserves. Yet the lasting popularity of his drama provides hope for the future. As the playwright himself wrote in 1881 in a *Note on the Condition of Dramatic Art in Contemporary Russia*: 'Only literary works which have had truly popular appeal in their own country have stood the test of time. Such works in the course of time become intelligible and valuable to other nations also, and finally to the whole world.'[38]

Notes

1. See David Magarshack, 'He created Russia's National Theatre: Alexander Ostrovsky – 1823–1948', *Anglo-Soviet Journal*, 9 (1948), pp. 6–10 (p. 6).
2. Margaret Wettlin, 'Alexander Ostrovsky and the Russian Theatre before Stanislavsky' in *Plays*, tr. Margaret Wettlin (Moscow, 1974), pp. 7–79 (p. 8).
3. Ibid. p. 9.
4. This work was never published in Ostrovsky lifetime. It first appeared in print in *Ostrovskii. Novye mater'ialy. Pis'ma. Trudy i dni. Stat'i* (Leningrad, 1924).
5. See A. N. Ostrovskii, *Polnoe sobranie sochinenii v 16 tomakh*, ed. I. Shiryaev (Moscow, 1949–53), vol. XIII, p. 302.
6. Agafya Ivanovna (surname unknown), lived with Ostrovsky from 1849 until her death in 1867. Their four children all died young. In 1869 Ostrovsky married an actress of the Maly Theatre, Marya Vasil'evna Bakhmetova. They had six children together.
7. Ostrovsky struggled financially throughout his life. His letters to friends frequently include requests for loans to carry him through times of financial difficulty and he campaigned vociferously for proper remuneration for playwrights. It was not until 1884 – two years before his death – that Tsar Aleksandr III granted him an annual pension of 3,000 roubles.
8. Norman Henley, 'Introduction', in Alexander Ostrovsky, *Without A Dowry & Other Plays*, tr. and ed. Norman Henley (Ann Arbor, 1997), pp. 11–14 (p. 13).
9. Dobrolyubov's hold over the critical interpretation of Ostrovsky's drama is evident from a recently published edition of selected works, which has, as its only critical comment on the plays, a reprint of Dobrolyubov's article, 'A Ray of Light in the Kingdom of Darkness'. See. A. N. Ostrovskii, *Izbrannye sochineniya* (Samara, 1996).
10. N. A. Dobrolyubov, *Selected Philosophical Essays*, tr. and ed. J. Finsburg (Moscow, 1948), pp. 238, 240, 628.
11. William Ralston, 'Art VI. *Sochineniya A. N. Ostrovskogo*. [The Works of A. N. Ostrovsky.] 4 vols. St Petersburg: 1859–67', *The Edinburgh Review*, 261 (July 1868), 158–90.
12. The work referred to is: Marjorie L. Hoover, *Alexander Ostrovsky* (Boston, 1981).
13. David Magarshack, 'Introduction', in *Alexander Ostrovsky: Easy Money and Two Other Plays*, tr. David Magarshack (London, 1944), pp. 6–11 (p. 8).
14. A.V. Knowles, 'Introduction', in *Groza*, by A. N. Ostrovskii (Oxford, 1988), pp. x–xxi (pp. x–xi).
15. L. Hanson, 'Introduction', in *Career Woman. Artistes and Admirers*, tr. Elisabeth Hanson (New York, 1976), p. xxiii.
16. *The McGraw-Hill Encylopedia of World Drama,* IV, ed. S. Hochman (New York, 1984), p. 54.

17. V. Ya. Lakshin, 'Mudrost' Ostrovskogo', in *P'esy*, by A. N. Ostrovskii (Moscow, 1993), pp. 5–12 (p. 11).

18. I. Beasley notes that Shashkov's *History of Women in Russia* refers to Ostrovsky for historical detail. See Ina Beasley, 'The Dramatic Art of Ostrovsky' (unpublished doctoral thesis, University of London, 1931), p. 101.

19. V. Setchkarev, 'From the Golden to the Silver Age (1820–1917)', in *Companion to Russian Studies,* ed. R. Auty and D. Obolensky, 2 vols. (Cambridge, 1977), vol. ii, pp. 133–85 (pp. 152–3).

20. F. M. Dostoevskii, 'A. N. Ostrovskii', *Grazhdanin*, 13 (26 March 1873).

21. Eugene K. Bristow, 'Introduction', in *Five Plays of Alexander Ostrovsky*, tr. and ed. Eugene K. Bristow (New York, 1969), p. 21.

22. For further discussion of reality and illusion in Ostrovsky's plays, see Kate Sealey Rahman, *Ostrovsky: Reality and Illusion* (Birmingham, 1999).

23. Henley suggests that *The Storm* 'may have hurt Ostrovsky in the West by giving him the reputation of writing plays too "Russian" to be understood readily by non-Russian audiences'. See Henley, p. 12.

24. Konstantin Rudnitsky, *Meyerhold the Director* (Ann Arbor, 1981), pp. 222–3. A 1997 production of *The Storm* at the Moscow TYUZ, directed by Genrietta Yanovskaya, also dispensed with the usual 'Kalinov' setting. Yanovskaya transposed the action to the cramped confines of a Soviet-style communal flat.

25. Again, N. Henley is one of the few critics to have noted this point, stating that *The Storm* 'is hardly a leading candidate for Ostrovsky's most typical play'. See Henley, p. 12.

26. Shelgunov's comments appeared in *Delo*, 2 (1875). See A. N. Ostrovskii, *Polnoe sobranie sochinenii v 12 tomakh*, ed. G. I. Vladykin et al. (Moscow, 1973–80), vol. iv, p. 466.

27. See A. N. Ostrovskii, *Polnoe sobranie sochinenii v 16 tomakh*, vol. xiv, p. 138.

28. See Henley, p. 13.

29. See A. N. Ostrovskii, *Polnoe sobranie sochinenii v 16 tomakh*, vol. viii, p. 157.

30. Bristow, p. 18.

31. See Wettlin, pp. 60–1.

32. See Hoover, p. 30.

33. See Wettlin, p. 72.

34. See Magarshack, 'Alexander Ostrovsky: the founder of the Russian theatrical tradition', in A. N. Ostrovsky, *The Storm* (Ann Arbor, 1988), pp. 8, 12.

35. Ibid. p. 5.

36. See *Kul'tura*, no. 16 (7127), 29 April–13 May 1998. The productions were as follows: at the Maly Theatre: 1, 8 May, *It's All in the Family*; 3, 9 May, *Not a Copper, then Suddenly Gold*; 5, 10, May, *The Forest*; 13 May, *Wolves and Sheep*; at the Stanislavsky Theatre: 3 May, *Artists and Admirers*; at the Mayakovsky Theatre: 1, 10 May, *Truth is Good, but Luck is Better*; at the Moskovsky Theatre: 8 May,

Wolves and Sheep; at the Teatr na Perevskoi: 7 May, *It's All in the Family*; at the Aleksandra Kalyagina Theatre: 13 May, *An Old Friend is Better than Two New Ones*.

37. Yu. Aikhenval'd, *Siluety russkikh pisatelei* (Moscow, 1909), p. 172.
38. See A. N. Ostrovskii, *Polnoe sobranie sochinenii v 16 tomakh*, vol. XII, p. 123.

9 The Russian Imperial Ballet

ANDY ADAMSON

The Russian Ballet was the culmination of that astonishing renaissance which in less than a century, from Glinka to Stravinsky, from Dostoevsky to Soloviett, raised Russia from obscurity to the foremost ranks of the world's artistic and philosophic thought.[1]

That we have a classical tradition of dance practice and an accompanying repertoire of ballets, some over 150 years old, is thanks largely to the Directorate of the Russian Imperial Theatres. Although the directorate showed little interest in the art of ballet itself, being mostly concerned with pleasing its royal masters, it enabled the development of a stable environment, over a long period of time, during which ballet as art and science could develop and finally flourish.

The first professional ballet appeared in Russia in 1736, as part of Francesco Araia's opera *The Power of Love and Hate*. The performance was given by more than 100 Russian dancers who, since 1734, had been trained under the guidance of the French ballet-master Jean Baptiste Landé. Landé was also responsible for founding the first professional dancing school, which opened in St Petersburg in 1738. When the Imperial Theatres became state run, in 1758, their remit included responsibility for ballet.

The eighteenth century saw a favourable climate for dance in both Moscow and St Petersburg, the two centres of Russian cultural life. The new ideas of *ballet d'action* were welcomed by the Russian public. They were attracted by this style of theatre, based on the ideas of Jean-Georges Noverre,[2] in which dance and dramatic mime were fused together to unfold a wordless plot, and which sought the emancipation of the dramatic ballet from its former position as mere divertissement. A steady stream of gifted foreign innovators, including Franz Hilverding and Gasparo Angiolini, found support in Russia, while talented Russian dancers and mime artists proved worthy of the new challenges.

In a sense ballet was just another foreign import. Throughout the eighteenth and nineteenth centuries French, Italian, Austrian, German, Danish and Swedish artists were all enticed to Russia. The financial rewards could be considerable, but many of these artists chose to stay well beyond their initial contracts, and often became 'naturalised' Russians, attracted both by the working conditions, and by the enthusiasm and talent of Russian dancers.

From Landé onwards the essential techniques of ballet training were French. Steps from the *danse d'école* formed the basis of Russian training. But Russia already had its own distinct national dance – traditional dances with a strong sense of rhythm, an innate musicality and a wide variety of dynamic qualities. Thus, as Russian dancers absorbed the French techniques they did so in a way that retained a distinctly Russian accent.

Before the twentieth century native choreographic talent was largely overshadowed by foreign ballet-masters. Ivan Valberkh, a pupil of Angiolini, became director of the St Petersburg Ballet in 1794, staging thirty-six ballets in the manner of Noverre. His work included early attempts at dealing with Russian themes; for example, his patriotic ballet of 1812, *A New Heroine, or The Woman Cossack*, was based on the story of Nadezhda Durova, heroine of the Napoleonic Wars. Earlier, in 1803, he had tried his hand at contemporary subject matter with *The New Werther*, dressing the dancers in frock-coats, much to the scorn of Russian critics.

But it was Charles-Louis Didelot's arrival in St Petersburg in 1801 that heralded a new epoch for Russian ballet. Didelot, a pupil of Vestris, Dauberval and Noverre, was primarily concerned with a style of theatre that formed a synthesis of dancing and acting. This ideology inevitably led to a preponderance of narrative ballets, but on the whole it seems that Russian audiences preferred to see dance which conveyed a dramatic narrative. During his first period in Russia from 1801–11 Didelot staged only revivals of earlier works. These included *Apollo and Daphne* (1802), *The Shepherd and the Hamadryads* (1803), and most notably *Zephyr and Flora* (1804), which contained the famous 'flying scenes', with dancers suspended from wires. He introduced considerable costume reforms, which were in turn to influence the development of dance technique. Gone were the stiff and panniered costumes typical of the eighteenth century – instead he introduced flowing tunics influenced by contemporary fashion, encouraging a more fluid style of dance. Gone also were the wigs and buckled shoes, the latter replaced with light slippers, which enabled dancers to rise onto three-quarter pointe, and for women to poise momentarily on full pointe.

During this first Russian period Didelot concentrated great efforts into training young dancers, particularly women. In an era when the ballet stage was dominated by men he wanted female dancers to acquire the attributes of strength, flexibility and stamina (which had hitherto been exclusive to the domain of men) while preserving qualities of lightness, poise and grace, which he saw as being distinctively feminine. He was known as a ruthless teacher, but seemingly only in his enthusiasm to obtain the best from his students: 'Didelot had a fiery and often quite ungovernable temper – and yet he was loved and even adored by everybody.'[3] Indeed his efforts were well rewarded, forming many fine pupils, notably Maria Danilova through whom he may have first introduced pointe dancing.[4] A baby ballerina aged fifteen, she enjoyed much success in *The Loves of Venus and Adonis, or Mars's Revenge*, and was regarded by many as the brightest hope of the Russian ballet.

Despite the talents of native-born dancers, preferential treatment was awarded to foreign artists. Typically a Russian dancer received less than half the salary paid to a foreigner. Didelot took up the cause of his protégés and in 1809 a significant improvement in conditions of dancers' training and employment followed. However, Didelot's support for the Russian dancers made him some important enemies and in 1811, quite suddenly, he and his wife were dismissed. A notable decline in standards followed and by 1816 Didelot was back, having negotiated favourable terms of employment for himself and his wife. During this second Russian period he created many original works and became increasingly drawn toward Russian themes. *The Prisoner of the Caucasus* (1823) was based on a poem by Pushkin, and included elements of Russian dance. Didelot's identification with Russian culture was not, however, embraced by court circles, and eventually, in 1829, he was forced to resign.

After Didelot's retirement there followed a period of stagnation. Various attempts to build a national repertoire were unsuccessful, mostly consisting of pale imitations of Paris productions. Marie Taglioni's St Petersburg appearances in 1837 stirred a brief revival, but excitement was somewhat cooled by the time of a fifth successive season of similar repertoire and the auditorium remained half empty.

In 1847, Marius Petipa and his father (Jean) arrived in St Petersburg to stage two Western novelties, *Paquita* (based on a production by Maziliev) and *Satanella*. Despite their success, in a dawning age of nationalism they were viewed as un-Russian, and on the order of Nikolai I a search began for an original choreographer to raise the standards of Russian ballet to a level higher than those in the West. Jules Perrot was found. He brought with him to St Petersburg productions of *Esmeralda, Catarina, Naiad and The Fisherman, La Filleule des Fées, La Fille mal Gardée* and an associated wealth of world-renowned dancers, including Fanny Elssler, Carlotta Grisi and Fanny Cerrito. Perrot, co-choreographer of *Giselle,* considerably reworked this ballet for Russian audiences, strengthening the dramatic action and emphasising realism, particularly in the mad scene. Contemporaries of Perrot remark on his skill in handling large ensembles. For example, in the Dance of the Corsairs from Act I of *Le Corsaire* he considered that the purpose of the dance was to act out the incidents of work, such as the motion of the sailing ship, hoisting the sails and rowing.

Perrot soon encountered trouble with the imperial censors, guided by the dicta of Gendarme Dubbelt: 'A Prince must be a defender of virtue and not its seducer . . . The theatre must be a school of morals; it must show vice punished and virtue rewarded.'[5] However, in Perrot's first St Petersburg *Esmeralda,* an army officer was shown as a scoundrel and pure love was 'rewarded' by the execution block. His ballet *War of Women* provoked a classical decision from Dubbelt: 'if this were a play I would not have passed it.'[6] Perrot's work, which was formulated on realistic themes, was branded 'anti-Russian'. The contemporary press declared: 'Ballet is the same as a dream . . . the further it is away from every verisimilitude the more captivating it is.'[7] Perrot was forced to resign in 1859, by a directorate who considered his work both dangerous and out-moded.

He was succeeded by another Frenchman, Arthur St Léon. A talented entertainer, both dancer and violinist, he seemed to fit perfectly the bill set by the directorate. St Léon readily invented charming and lightweight ballets, full of new effects, which were really little more than protracted divertissements. Unlike Didelot or Perrot, who sought artistic independence, St Léon was happy to satisfy his masters, altering libretti or changing titles as required. A notable success came with *The Little Humpbacked Horse* (1864), based on the fairytale by Yershov. But with music by Pugni (adapted from Rossini) and a very safe adaptation of the original tale by St Léon, the Russian elements remained superficial. Nevertheless, the work became a popular favourite and stayed in the repertoire for many years. Later works were less successful. *The Goldfish* (1867) was a feeble adaptation of Pushkin's poem, and *The Lily* (1869) offered little more than novelties. St Léon's work never found favour with the growing intelligentsia, who in the late 1850s and 1860s were seeking greater dramatic depths than it seemed his ballets could offer. His general popularity also waned and his contract was not renewed in 1869.

The French-born Marius Petipa came from a family of dancers. His brother, Lucien found fame partnering Carlotta Grisi in the premier of *Giselle* (1841). In 1847 Marius was offered a one-year contract in St Petersburg and remained there for the rest of his life, devoting fifty-six years to the Russian stage. The so-called 'Era of Petipa' dates from his appointment as ballet-master in 1869. He became identified with the very idea of Russian ballet and was to sustain it as a flourishing art while the remainder of European dance was in decline. Petipa's creative energy seemed to mature in old age. He produced his greatest work, *The Sleeping Beauty*, when in his seventies. At best his work creates a marvellous fusion of emotional content expressed in dance and music, though at worst he degenerates into banal bad taste, pandering to the demands of his aristocratic patrons.

As a young choreographer, despite his early successes, Petipa had fallen under the shadow of Jules Perrot, appointed ballet-master in 1848. Petipa spent the next twelve years dancing dramatically charged roles in Perrot's ballets. He danced with Fanny Elssler, earning a reputation for utter reliability, both as a partner and as a talented mime. But his determination to become a choreographer remained steadfast, as he studied avidly all the ballet libretti he could acquire, sent by his brother Lucien from Paris. In 1850, Petipa produced *Giselle*, after Perrot's instruction, introducing his own material to the dances of the Wilis in Act II. It is thanks to Petipa that *Giselle* survives to this day, since he revived the production in 1884, adding the 'Grand pas de Wilis'.

Arthur St Léon's brief spell as ballet-master in St Petersburg again thwarted Petipa's ambitions, but did expose him to a style of dance composition in which divertissements and large-scale *ballabili*[8] were all important. His first real opportunity came in 1862, with St Léon briefly in Paris and the Imperial Directorate in need of a new ballet for the Italian ballerina Caroline Rosati. The result, *The Pharaoh's Daughter* (1862), was a grand spectacle in five acts based on Gautier's *Le Roman de Momie* and produced in an astonishingly short six weeks of rehearsal. The theme was immensely topical, for almost the entire civilised world was following the near-daily revelations from Egyptian excavations. The plot was pure fantasy, with English gentlemen transplanted back to the time of the pharaohs, and exotic scenes beneath the River Nile. With its numerous dances, processions, *ballabili*, monkeys, camels and lion chase it became a long-term favourite.

Rosati, in the role of Aspicia, the pharaoh's daughter, wore the typical tutu, flesh-coloured tights and pointe shoes that were to become the uniform of the ballerina for the next forty or so years. The music, by Cesare Pugni (the staff ballet composer of the Imperial Theatres), was written to the choreographer's exact specifications. Rhythms and tempi were designed to fit already created dances with no attempt to convey national character or psychological motivation. The composer was merely to provide 'danceable' accompaniment. However, the plot provided a variety of dramatic situations and opportunities for fantastic divertissement and exotic theatricality. The ballet's success led to Petipa's appointment as second ballet-master, and subsequently, at St Léon's departure in 1869, to full ballet-master. This *grand spectacle* of a first ballet was to provide a model, repeated frequently by Petipa with few changes.

Many of his works were created on a truly grand scale, lasting four or five acts, but often with only the slightest of stories to tell. To sustain an audience's interest during these vast visual panoramas he developed a style that was almost kaleidoscopic in its never-ending variety. Characters paraded around the stage ceremoniously, or arranged themselves in tasteful groupings, as a backdrop for an array of contrasting dances. These might include national dances evoking the spirit of some far-off land, or fantastic character dances inspired by fairytales. He absorbed the tastes of the court and took a strong interest in the traditional folk dances of Russia, incorporating their typically complex and symmetrical patterns into his own choreography for large ensembles. The story as such was usually very thin and was conveyed through stylised mime, which had lost any real connection with expressive gesture. Petipa saw the plot as little more than a framework on which to hang his dance compositions. He found himself composing according to a formula, in which it was necessary to have a certain number of ensemble scenes, at least one *pas d'action* per act, and most importantly, the balanced number of dances for coryphées, soloists and the ballerina. The *première danseuse* became all important, and Petipa became particularly adept at creating variations which suited the talents of individual dancers. The highlight of each ballet came in the *pas de deux* created for the ballerina and her male partner. Here, Petipa's adherence to a formula became almost regimented – an adagio introduction with lifts and complex balances led to a solo variation for each of the two principles; a concluding allegro coda showed off their virtuosity in brilliant steps, turns and leaps. Almost everything was created in sixteen-bar phrases.

From 1869–76 Petipa's work had mixed success with some dismal failures. The great August Bournonville, former fellow pupil of Vestris, visited St Petersburg in 1874 and was horrified by what he saw:

> I sought in vain to discover plot, dramatic interest, logical consistency, or anything which might remotely resemble sanity . . . I could not possibly suppress these and similar observations during my conversations with Johansson and the Balletmaster Petipa. They admitted that I was perfectly right, confessed that they privately loathed and despised this . . . that they were obliged to follow the current of the times, which they charged to the blasé tastes of the public and the specific wishes of the high authorities.[9]

Petipa was evidently concerned with his failure to please the Russian public as he sought a collaboration with Sergei Khudakov, publisher of the *St Petersburg Gazette*. In 1877, Petipa staged *La Bayadère* based on a libretto by Khudakov. Although this was something of a strange mixture of styles it contained some individual masterpieces. Most notably, the scene in the 'Kingdom of the Shades' where a simple, endlessly repeated choreographic image creates a sense of timelessness and wonder. This is Petipa at his finest, for here we are seeing the birth of symphonic ballet.

Nineteenth-century dance had been dominated by the ideology that ballet should be the synthesis of acting and dancing. It seemed that all dance must stem from some literal starting point. Petipa's achievement was in releasing dance from its links with dramatic imitation. Much of his work is best seen in terms of pure dance. Often his attempts to convey narrative seem artificial or over formal. But it must be recognised that the strict limitations of Petipa's aesthetic were largely externally imposed. In the 'Shades' we see an outstanding example of pure lyricism, with Petipa moving towards an abstract language of dance completely devoid of programmatic context. This was to be the forerunner of abstract, plotless ballets, such as Fokin's *Les Sylphides*, and the symphonic ballets of Massine and Balanchine. Petipa's own creations in this vein continued with the 1881 addition to *Paquita*, and the 1884 'Grand pas de Wilis'. In these he succeeded in creating fine and lasting gems of pure classicism.

His compositional structures were always simple – the minimum of

12. Marius Petipa, 1880.

ideas exploited to the full. Each section would contain just three or four movement motifs which were repeated and moulded into a rhythmically intricate structure. Each variation thus created would have had its own dynamic. Petipa masterfully juxtaposed a simplicity of compositional construction with a complexity of virtuosic performance.

1881 saw the appointment of Ivan Vsevolozhsky, 'one of the most enlightened and energetic directors who was ever in charge of the Russian Imperial Theatre'.[10] Petipa recalled: 'It was a wonderful time when art flourished on the Imperial stages of St Petersburg.'[11] But this was the year of Aleksandr II's assassination. A reactionary period followed. Even more than before, ballet was to provide safe entertainment for the aristocracy. Petipa's public was a power elite, and his dancers' world with its strict hierarchy of ballerinas, soloists, coryphées and corps de ballet reflected the ordered hierarchy of court society. The parades, grand entrances and large ensembles affirmed the power of ceremony.

Technical advances in ballet now reflected audience taste as much as choreographic demand. The first fleeting moments on pointe had been performed for expressive reasons. But now audiences became obsessed with the ballerina's ability to perform complex feats and balances on pointe. (In 1885 Virginia Zucchi enchanted audiences by performing an entire solo on pointe.)

It was often said of Petipa that he had little time for male dancing. Indeed the role of the male dancer declined significantly during Petipa's reign. If he was short of ideas for a male variation he would visit the class of his co-teacher at the school, Christian Johansson. A Swede by birth, Johansson had trained with Bournonville, and remained throughout his career a devotee of the French School of Vestris. The advantage of this system of dance was that it introduced a scientific method into the training of dancers. Over the years it was developed and refined to meet the needs of the Russian school with its 'soaring, soulful flight'.[12] It was Johansson who introduced the so-called *Classe de perfection*, for artists who graduated from the school to maintain or continue to develop their technical ability. Johansson's method was based on observation of the individual, spotting faults and correcting them, but allowing distinguishing traits to give character to individual dancers. For example, he did not attempt to change Pavlova's lack of turnout, considering it a feature of her personality.

The function of male dancing was also transformed as the male dancer took on the role of *porteur*, supporting the ballerina in her difficult balances and pirouettes on pointe. A complex system of lifting and partner work evolved, with the male dancer elevating the ballerina and sometimes changing her pose in the air two or three times before returning her to earth on pointe again. Photographs from the late nineteenth century all show ballerinas in rock-solid poses on steel-like pointes. The image is one of stability or permanence, just what the court wanted to see, and in stark contrast to the transcience and pursuit of unattainable dreams typified by the fleeting use of pointe-work in earlier ballets.

The new surge in technique was strongly influenced by the Italian School. Carlo Blasis had been in Moscow from 1861–4 teaching his method, but from 1885 Petipa was forced to submit to the engagement of Italian ballerinas. He had long resisted using foreign stars, preferring dancers from his own school. But in fact the Italian influence was to be the final factor in the forging of a truly Russian style of ballet. Until now, so-called Russian ballet had been dependent on the methods of the French School, admittedly danced with Russian ardour.

The acrobatic style of the Italians was unknown to Russian audiences, who flocked to see their accomplishments. The most important of these dancers found their way into starring roles in Petipa's ballets. Carlotta

13. A scene from Tchaikovsky's *Sleeping Beauty*, choreographed by Marius Petipa. Maryinsky Theatre, 1890.

Brianza made her Russian debut in *The Tulip of Harlem* (1887) and created the role of Aurora in *The Sleeping Beauty* (1890), impressing the Russians with her double pirouettes, performed unaided, and her *jetés en tournant*. Pierrina Legnani's influence, however, was much greater, for she spent eight years in Russia, from her debut in *Cinderella* (1893) to her farewell benefit performance in *La Camargo* (1901). Her technique was regarded as faultless, and particularly impressive was her execution of thirty-two *fouettés*, which were incorporated in the 1895 production of *Swan Lake*. She became a role model for future stars such as Anna Pavlova and Tamara Karsavina. Male dancing received a boost, with the arrival of Enrico Cecchitti, who, in *The Sleeping Beauty*, performed the double roles of Carabosse (*en travesti*) and The Bluebird, with its soaring leaps and *brisés*.

The relationship between Russian and Italian dance styles was not entirely one-sided. Russian dancers were absorbing the Italian 'tricks' and were in turn able to offer advice:

> Brianza was the first Italian dancer on whom the Russian School exerted a beneficent influence. When criticised for the extreme angularity and brittle quality of her dancing . . . she introduced into her performance greater softness, roundness and elasticity, i.e. those very features . . . of the Russian school.[13]

Creatively, the 1880s were years of comparative inactivity for Petipa. He concentrated on a series of safe revivals. In 1881, *Paquita* was given a much developed third act and a children's mazurka, regarded by many as the finest opportunity for children's dancing within the classical repertoire. There followed successful restagings of *Coppélia* (1884) and Perrot's *Esmeralda* (1886), to which Petipa added a *pas de six* with music by Drigo.

All this was under the watchful gaze of Vsevolozhsky, who was determined to shape Petipa into a true *maître des menus plaisirs* of the Imperial Court – like the ballet-masters of Louis XIV. Vsevolozhsky made no attempt to conceal this, writing to Petipa that: 'It would be rather nice to begin the season glamorously. The court will arrive in St Petersburg early, and you know yourself how fond it is of novelties ... Whatever it will cost, we must have something new.'[14] Petipa dutifully turned out *The Magic Pills* (1886), a French *féerie* ballet, using the opportunity to create some varied novelty dances. In 'The Games' scene he used thirty-two 'playing cards' wearing velvet costumes and wigs to match the appropriate suit. In the 'Spinning Tops Dance' the brilliant young Russian, Zinaida Frolova, showed some Italian 'tricks' consisting of rapid turns, in the course of which multicoloured ribbons sewn to her costume flowed out and became blurred into a single pattern, the dancing ending as the spinning top fell over.

It was Vsevolozhsky who had the idea for using Perrault's *La Belle au Bois Dormant* for a ballet. He liked to involve himself artistically, offering suggestions for costume and scene design, but this was his first involvement with the libretto of a ballet. Petipa must have seen it as yet another *féerie*. However, Vsevolozhsky had engaged Tchaikovsky, by now a well-known composer, but with limited experience in composition for ballet. His only previous attempt had been *Swan Lake*, produced in Moscow in 1877, but with such poor choreography by Reisinger, and an audience unused to symphonic music at the ballet, that it met with disaster. Tchaikovsky, it seems, was nervous of writing music for dance, aware of its special needs, but unsure as to how to provide them. We learn from his brother that: 'before embarking on the composition of the music he requested of ballet-master M. Petipa designations of the dances in the most exact way, the number of bars, the character of the music, the amount of time of each number'.[15] Petipa's instructions to the composer, so often held up as the definitive outline of the ballet, are in fact but a sketched starting point for Tchaikovsky.[16] By no means did Tchaikovsky feel obliged to follow his instructions, often providing more music than required, or making subtle changes to the rhythmic structures requested (waltzes, polkas, galops) which he may have seen as too stereotypical.

Both musically and choreographically *The Sleeping Beauty* is the crowning glory of Russian nineteenth-century ballet and includes some of Petipa's finest work. For example the 'Rose Adagio' for Aurora and the four suitors, which ends Act I, may be seen as pure virtuosic display for the ballerina (Legnani). But this material is also rich in allegory. A young woman is becoming aware of her charms, and how to use them to control the attention of men.

The resounding success of *The Sleeping Beauty* led to another collaboration with Tchaikovsky, this time on *The Nutcracker*. The choice of theme again came from Vsevolozhsky but this time he prepared the libretto jointly with Petipa. Petipa once more provided the composer with detailed instructions and was to have started the ballet early in the season of 1892–3. A sudden onset of illness provided the second ballet-master, Lev Ivanov, with a unique opportunity to work alone with Tchaikovsky, but committed to the structure as already devised.

The libretto of *The Nutcracker* provided a difficult challenge for choreographer and composer. There seems little opportunity for good theatre, and there are obvious defects in the structure. Act I, so full of action, is followed by an almost static Act II. Although there is a certain logic to the magical events of Act I, the endless divertissements of the second act seem to lead nowhere. The heroine takes a magical journey from a Christmas party to the land of sweets, but never returns, and the audience is left wondering just what it was all about. Modern revivals have emphasised the theme of Clara's growing sexual awareness, but are still challenged by the stream of divertissements. In the 'Waltz of the Snowflakes' Ivanov was at least able to create one masterpiece of symphonic choreography, creating the illusion of falling snow. Images of quivering snowflakes formed intricate groups, moving across the stage in a variety of symmetrical patterns forming now a star, now a huge snowball. A corps de ballet of sixty dancers was headed by eight soloists.

Ivanov became jointly responsible with Petipa for the St Petersburg version of *Swan Lake*, which had much reworking of the original music by Drigo. In 1894, Ivanov's choreography for Act II was staged as a tribute to Tchaikovsky who had died in 1893. The full ballet was revived in the following year. Petipa created the first scenes in each of Acts I and II, but it is

Ivanov's choreography for the lakeside scenes that have gained this ballet a lasting reputation. The variation for four little swans provides a charming, unforgettable moment, while the lyrical high point of the ballet is formed by the love duet. Ivanov departed radically from the Petipa formula for *pas de deux*, emphasising the intensity of the scene by making it one long, lyrical adagio.

To Petipa's misfortune, Vsevolozhsky left the theatre in 1899. He was briefly succeeded by Sergei Volkonsky, whose interest in Delsarte and Dalcroze was well ahead of his time. It was Volkonsky who, in 1902, gave brief employment at the Imperial Theatre to Sergei Diaghilev. Diaghilev was later dismissed when he demanded sole authority over a production of *Sylvia,* an opera by Delibes. Telyakovsky became the new director in 1902, making his principle concern the modernisation of opera and ballet. Subsequently, in February 1903, Petipa was informed that his contract as ballet-master would not be renewed. Petipa's memoirs[17] recall the bitterness he felt toward Telyakovsky, and he lived on until 1910 planning yet more revisions of his old ballets.

During his long reign as ballet-master in St Petersburg, Petipa had created a repertoire of original works for the Russian court. While the Imperial School had produced many fine Russian dancers, a native-born choreographer had eluded it. But a new age of Russian ballet was dawning, one which rejected the stasis of nineteenth-century ideals and reflected new ideas from the contemporary theatre. Aleksandr Gorsky, a pupil of Petipa, became interested in the Moscow Art Theatre, which had been opened by Stanislavsky and Nemirovich-Danchenko. Gorsky was invited to Moscow in 1898 by the Directorate of Imperial Theatres to revive *The Sleeping Beauty,* which had been recorded using the Stepanov system of notation and in 1900 he accepted a post as director at the Bolshoi company in Moscow, an opportunity which gave him greater freedom than if he had stayed in St Petersburg. As far as Russian ballet was concerned St Petersburg had always been the principal centre. Moscow was seen as somewhere to send lesser or undesirable artists. Consequently it was the artists of St Petersburg who received the greatest 'guidance' from the directorate.

Gorsky's first task in his new appointment was to restage Petipa's *Don Quixote* with licence to make changes as he saw fit. So he embarked upon a production based on the new principles of the Art Theatre. Thus, Gorsky became the first choreographer to treat the entire stage ensemble as members of a choreographic drama, in the manner of Stanislavsky. Instead of frozen symmetrical lines, typical of Petipa's corps de ballet, each performer was given an individual action, to form a living crowd. Designs by Korovin and Golovin represented real-life settings. Gorsky's work clearly anticipated Fokin's *Petrushka*, but met with strong criticism: 'Gorsky's new version was vitiated by the abhorrent lack of organisation that is typical of amateur performances. Its "novelties" consisted of making the crowds on the stage bustle and move about fitfully and aimlessly.'[18]

Gorsky was not the only young choreographer to criticise the outmoded traditions of nineteenth-century ballet. Mikhail Fokin, destined to become a driving force in Diaghilev's Ballet Russe, was an outspoken critic against what he saw as: 'the artificial form of dancing'.[19] In 1904 he presented the directorate with a proposal for a two-act ballet on the theme of Daphnis and Chloe. His scenario contained a memorandum in which he outlined the principles to be observed in the proposed ballet. Nothing came of these plans, but the first opportunity to test his ideas came at a school graduation production of Ivanov's *Acis and Galatea* which he staged in 1905. However, as part of his preparation for *Daphnis and Chloe* he had made extensive study of the sculpture and bas-relief of Ancient Greece, preparing to use this style of 'plastique' in his choreography before Russia had seen the dancing of Isadora Duncan. While, superficially, Fokin may seem to have had much in common with Duncan, it is clear that while she was determined to abandon classical dancing, Fokin preferred a process of revitalisation in which the 'older' ballet was invigorated to become the so-called 'new ballet'.

Fokin's ideas were later clearly formulated in his famous letter to *The Times* of 6 July 1914. In this he complained that:

> The art of the older ballet turned its back on life and all the other arts and shut itself up in a narrow circle of traditions. According to the old method of producing a ballet the ballet-master composed his dances by combining certain well-established movements and poses, and for his mimetic scenes he used a conventional system of gesticulation, and endeavoured by gestures of the dancers' hands according to established rules, to convey the plot of the ballet to the spectator.[20]

His solution came in the form of five principles which may be outlined as follows:

1 Not to depend on 'ready-made' steps from the *danse d'école* but to create them as necessary in a way that is relevant to the subject matter, character and context.

2 The function of dance and mimetic gesture is to serve as an expression of dramatic action, not as a divertissement or entertainment.

3 The whole body should be used in the creation of the gesture. This should not be limited to movements of the hands.

4 Attention should be given to the expressiveness of stage groups and ensembles, which should not be seen as mere ornamentals.

5 Dancing should be allied to the arts. It should not provide preconditions which dictate to the composer or scenic designer the terms of their contribution to the dance. Their creative imagination should be given free rein.

A key factor in Fokin's formative years was his association with The World of Art, a group of cultured men including Benois, Bakst, Korovin and Nouvel, but most notably the founder Sergei Diaghilev. *The World of Art* magazine was largely devoted to painting, although it claimed to reflect art in all its realms. During its six years, from 1899–1906, it devoted pages to literary and musical review, so it is perhaps surprising that it spoke little of reforms in the world of ballet.

Fokin's *The Pavilion of Armide* (1907), a collaboration with Benois, was a cautious first step away from the 'old' ballet. But in *Chopiniana* (*Les Sylphides*) of 1908 he brought to life lost images from the romantic era. Sylphs dressed in long white tutus moved with ethereal lightness, and dancing on pointe seemed to have been reunited with its original airy poeticism. Most important of all, for Fokin, the dancers were totally absorbed in the creation of a mood. There was no attempt at virtuosic display. This return to the image of the sylphide was in itself an allegory, by which Fokin implied that academic ballet had stagnated, and should rediscover lost principles from its history. *The Dying Swan* (1907), a choreographic miniature lasting only two minutes and danced by Anna Pavlova, reaffirmed this idea. *An Egyptian Night* (1908) saw Fokin exploring even further into the past, with images inspired by ancient wall inscriptions, murals and hieroglyphs.

1909 saw the most significant event for the Russian Imperial Ballet, but not one that was to take place in Russia. Under Sergei Diaghilev's management, the finest artists of the Imperial Theatres burst forth their talents on an unsuspecting Parisian audience. Paris was delighted by the choreography of Mikhail Fokin and thrilled by the décor of Benois and Bakst. They were inspired by the expressive dancing of Anna Pavlova and Tamara Karsavina, and male dancing, all but forgotten in the West, was revitalised by Adophe Bolm and the incomparable Vaslav Nijinsky. Working in Paris in an environment of artistic liberation, this combined wealth of talent produced a series of masterpieces for four seaons running. These included many distinctly Russian works, like the 'Polovtsian Dances' (1909) from *Prince Igor*, full of virile male dancing, and *The Firebird* (1910), with its modern score by the young Stravinsky. Fokin's triumph came in collaboration with Stravinsky in *Petrushska* (1911), with Nijinsky in the title role. The following season saw Nijinsky's debut as a choreographer with *L'Après-midi d'un faune*, which signalled a radical departure from the traditions of classical ballet favoured by Fokin. Fokin resigned and returned to work at the Imperial Theatres in St Petersburg, but the artistic environment could never compare with that of Paris, and his subsequent choreography lacked lustre.

Sergei Diaghilev's Russian seasons were intended to make the cultural world of Western Europe marvel at the theatrical secrets of Russia. The Soviet historian Slonimsky suggests that it was Diaghilev's long-term intention to regain a foothold in the Imperial Theatres and ultimately to gain the directorate for himself.[21] The events of 1917 were of course to make this impossible, and a company of itinerant dancers who gained their freedom found they had lost their homes. Many of these artists were at the onset of their careers and eventually they became scattered around the world. But wherever they went, they took with them the now fully formulated principles of the Russian ballet.

Notes

1. Paul Dukes. Preface to Nadine Nicolaeva-Legat, *Ballet Education* (London, 1947), p. xv.
2. Noverre (1727–1810) published his reforms as *Lettres sur la danse et les ballets* (Stuttgart, 1760).
3. Rafail Zotov, 'My reminiscences of the theatre', *Repertory of the Russian Theatre for 1840*, vol. II, book 7, p. 34. Quoted in Natalia Roslavleva, *Era of the Russian Ballet* (London, 1966), p. 43.
4. According to Yuri Bakhrushin in *Istoriia russkogo baleta* (Moscow, 1965), p. 74. Quoted in Mary Grace Swift, *A Loftier Flight* (London, 1974), p. 103.

5. N. Drisen, *Dramatic Censorship of Two Epochs*, pp. 8–9. Quoted in Yuri Slonimsky, 'Jules Perrot', *The Dance Index*, vol. iv (New York, 1944), 222.

6. Ibid.

7. *Panteon i repertuar Russkoi szeny*, vol. ii, book 3 (1850), p. 44. Quoted in Slonimsky, 222.

8. *Ballabile* (pl. *ballabili*) denotes a dance for a large group or corps de ballet, without solos.

9. August Bournonville, *My Theatre Life* (London, 1979), pp. 581–2.

10. Serge Lifar, *A History of the Russian Ballet* (London, 1954), p. 130.

11. Marius Petipa, *Russian Ballet Master: The Memoirs of Marius Petipa*, ed. Lillian Moore (London, 1958), p. 60.

12. Aleksandr Pushkin, *Eugene Onegin*, tr. James E. Falen (Carbondale, Ill., 1990), p. 22.

13. Serge Khoudekov, *History of Dancing* (Petrograd, 1918). Quoted in Roslavleva, p. 119.

14. Khoudekov, *History of Dancing*. Quoted in Slonimsky, vol. vi (New York, 1947), p. 116.

15. *Zhisn' Petra Il'icha Chaikovskogo*, vol. iii, pp. 288–9. Quoted in R. J. Wiley, *Tchaikovsky's Ballet* (Oxford, 1985), p. 108.

16. See Wiley, pp. 109–11.

17. Petipa, p. 67.

18. Alexandre Benois, *Reminiscences of the Russian Ballet* (London, 1941), p. 222.

19. Mikhail Fokine, *The Times*, 6 July 1914, p. 6.

20. Ibid.

21. Slonimsky, Yuri (ed.), 'Fokine in his time', in *M. Fokine. Against the Current. Memoirs of the Ballet Master, Articles, Letters* (Leningrad, 1962), pp. 5–80. Quoted in Roslavleva, p. 180.

10 Russian Opera

JOHN WARRACK

For the last century and a half, the familiar judgement on Russian opera has been that it was born with the twin achievements of Glinka's *A Life for the Tsar* (1836) and *Ruslan and Lyudmila* (1842). Mikhail Glinka indeed towers over his predecessors, and nineteenth-century Russian composers were united in looking back to him as their founding father. For them, he set standards for historical and fairytale opera, which appealed to those who were seeking to establish a national identity in opera, and he brought distinctive Russian musical techniques into his idiom: this in turn lent force to a Soviet line wishing to devalue earlier contributions by foreign composers as well as the role played by royal patronage.

However, Glinka's talent would never have found realisation without the century of work that preceded it. Russia's musical isolation, with church chant and folk music the only indigenous traditions, and her lack of a broadly based theatre-going public meant that opera's first appearance was as court entertainment, summoned from Italy, long recognised as the home of the best opera. One of Tsarina Anna Ioannovna's first acts on her accession in 1730 was to welcome to Moscow a company under Giovanni Ristori; and his comedy *Calandro* became, at the Kremlin in the following year, the first opera to be heard in Russia. Four years later, she had a company recruited for St Petersburg under Francesco Araia, whose opere serie included, under her successor Elizaveta Petrovna, *Cephalus and Procris* (1755): this, to a text by Aleksandr Sumarokov, is the first opera known to have been sung in Russian. Sumarokov also wrote the libretto for *Alceste* (1758), by Hermann Raupach, the only German to have held the position of musical director; he also wrote, for the public theatre, a very successful singspiel, *The Good Soldiers* (1779). The only other German of importance to work in Russia was Mathias Stabinger, who conducted at Michael Maddox's theatre in 1782, and, following a return visit in 1785, wrote the successful *Lucky Tonya* (1786) and *Baba Yaga* (1786).

The Italians' court popularity confirmed what became, from 1762, a long and distinguished succession of *maestri di cappella*: Manfredini, Galuppi, Traetta, Paisiello, Sarti, Cimarosa and Martín y Soler. Meanwhile, from 1757 comic operas were presented to paying audiences in both Moscow and St Petersburg, initially under Giovanni Battista Locatelli (who opened a private theatre, the Krasny Kabak, in Moscow in 1763). On her accession in 1762, Catherine had imported a French opera troupe under Jean-Pierre Renaud, and its success in 1764 with Favart's celebrated *Annette and Lubin* led to a Russian-language comedy, *Anyuta* (1772), with numbers set to music by an unknown composer. The first surviving complete Russian opera, however, is *Rebirth* (1777), by Dementy Zorin, which confronts for the first time the problem of how to accommodate the modal nature of Russian folk music to Western harmony. The second Russian opera, *The Miller as Magician, Trickster and Matchmaker* (1779), with music by Mikhail Sokolovsky, tackles the problem by modifying the tunes; it is also notable for its balalaika imitations on pizzicato strings and for the first appearance of the *devichnik*, or female wedding chorus, which was to be an enduringly popular feature of Russian opera.

In the late 1760s two composers, Maksim Berezovsky and Dmitry Bortnyansky, were sent to study in Italy, where their Italianate operas were performed. Others were engaged to provide music for the five opéras comiques which Catherine, with her French inclinations, saw as instruments of instruction and political comment, and for which, with some assistance, she wrote the texts. These included an attack on Gustav III during the Swedish war, *The Woeful Knight Kosometovich* (1789), with music by Martín y Soler. Her preferred composer, however, was Vasily Pashkevich.

Pashkevich's first opera, *Misfortune Through a Coach* (1779), had satirised the craze for French manners; his second, *The Miser* (1781), also to a text by Yakov Knyazhnin, made some musical response to the mobile stress of the Russian language. He further wrote, in *The St Petersburg Emporium* (1782), a satire on petty crooks which draws on town music and opens its second act with a remarkably effective sequence of *devichniki*. To Catherine's libretto, he composed a fairy opera, *Fevey* (1786), which not only contrasts a Russian musical idiom with an 'Oriental' one, but makes some use of the idea of accompanying a repeating folk melody with a changing background – a technique that arises from Russian folk music and was brought to prominence by Glinka. For another opera, Catherine employed Raupach's pupil Evstigney Fomin, whose later works include the very striking melodrama, *Orpheus* (1791), and a successful Italianate opera, *The Americans* (1800).

In these, and in other eighteenth-century works, there can be seen some of the features and tendencies that were to mark Russian opera as it grew to maturity. The lack of interest in German opera was a reflection of that genre's own immaturity, but also part of the Russian instinct for Latin artistic values. Though eighteenth-century Russian opera is to some extent marked by Italian methods, the more significant influence is French, in that opéra comique (as in Rousseau's influential *Le Devin du Village*) rested upon plots connected to real life that touched on some moral issue, using a vernacular text and set to music drawing on the folk tradition.

The most important of all the visiting Italians was Caterino Cavos. Born in Venice, he went to Russia in 1798 to conduct the Italian company and, profiting by Aleksandr I's reorganisation of the St Petersburg theatres in 1803 into Russian, French, Italian and German houses, became director of the Italian company at the Maly Derevyanny Theatre and of opera and ballet at the Russians' Bolshoi Kamenny Theatre. The Italian company quickly collapsed, and while the French company continued for the few years until Napoleon's invasion with a repertory of opéras comiques and other French works (and with, among others, Boieldieu as director), Cavos strengthened his position by composing music for *The Dnepr Water Nymph* (1804), a popular Russian version of Ferdinand Kauer's *Das Donauweibchen*. Then, as well as directing the Russian theatre, he trained singers and conductors at the theatre school, developing for Russia by precept, practice and leadership the first systematic, professional schooling in the craft of opera.

Cavos's operas draw on Russian subjects. *Ilya Bogatyr* (1807), for which the fabulist Ivan Krylov wrote the libretto, is a Romantic magic opera continuing the line of Catherine's *Fevey* text and anticipating Glinka's *Ruslan and Lyudmila*. A few, such as *The Firebird* (1822), treat the Oriental themes that had become fashionable with Russia's expansion, and thus also anticipate *Ruslan and Lyudmila* and Borodin's *Prince Igor*. Cavos's main librettist, however, was Aleksandr Shakhovskoi, Director of the Imperial Theatres. Shakhovskoi's text for *The Cossack Poet* (1812) invokes the patriotic sentiments of the times; and so, even more, does his text for *Ivan Susanin* (1815), a 'rescue opera' owing much to French example. When Glinka's own opera about Ivan Susanin, the hero who misleads the invading Poles so as to assure the coronation of the tsar, was produced in 1836, it was Cavos who

14. A scene from Mikhail Glinka's *A Life for the Tsar.*

conducted; but though Cavos generously declared that his work was now superseded, it continued in the repertoire until 1854.

Hitherto, opera in St Petersburg had been given principally at the Hermitage Theatre in the Winter Palace, and at the Bolshoi Kamenny Theatre, built in 1783 and the city's main opera house until 1885; it was also presented in other imperial residences and at the Maly Derevyanny Theatre, later renamed the Volny Theatre. In Moscow, opera was first produced in Maddox's theatre on the Znamenka, then from 1780 in his new, 1,500-seat Petrovsky Theatre. When the latter burnt down in 1805, the company came under the Imperial Theatres, and after various vicissitudes moved into the Bolshoi Theatre in 1825. Opera was also given in the private theatres of various aristocratic families.

The Bolshoi's new director, a part of his role as Inspector of Music for the Imperial Theatres, was Aleksei Verstovsky. His first works, often in collaboration with Aleksandr Alyabyev, had been in the immensely popular genre of vaudeville. The career of Alyabyev's own works was frustrated by Verstovsky's notorious jealousy, which was later in turn to deny performance to Glinka's works in Moscow.

Verstovsky was an admirer of Méhul and Cherubini and of their influence on Weber, and his operas are significant for their tendency towards a national style suggested by the success of Der Freischütz in Moscow in 1825. Pan Tvardovsky (1828), once hailed as the first truly Russian opera, reflects these interests, which take on stronger Russian colour in Vadim (1832). However, his most famous work is Askold's Tomb (1835), which transfers from Der Freischütz effects such as folk-influenced songs and choruses, and an incantation scene indebted to Weber's Wolf's Glen. With this work, Verstovsky claimed precedence over Glinka as the founder of Russian national opera; but though it remained popular throughout the nineteenth century, it later dropped from the repertoire completely.

The first performance of Glinka's A Life for the Tsar in St Petersburg in 1836 was epoch making in a dual sense: it concluded an epoch, and it opened a new one. Many ideas and techniques explored by Glinka's predecessors are brought into new focus, thanks to his vastly superior talent and to his strong theatrical instinct. Yet the work is hybrid. Russian idioms play an important part: there is the opening folk polyphony (podgolosok) absorbed into the composition, the devichnik brought into a stronger dramatic function, and the scene in which the balalaika is not merely imitated but taken as inspiration for descriptive writing on pizzicato strings. Glinka is, in fact, not simply citing Russian techniques, ideas and sounds, but taking them as inspiration for a new kind of music. But for want of a secure Russian vocal style he also falls back on Italian example; the orchestral amplitude owes much to Germany; and there are ingredients from French opéra comique, while the shape of the work is that of French Grand Opera, with multiple soloists and choruses, panoramic scenes, clashing dynastic ambitions, and an epic sweep to the action. Given its title by the tsar's intervention, instead of Glinka's original *Ivan Susanin*, *A Life for the Tsar* became an automatic choice to open seasons at the Imperial Theatres; and the convention endured into Soviet times with a rewritten *Ivan Susanin* that managed to exclude all mention of tsars. *Ruslan and Lyudmila* takes up the fairy tradition, in a work whose notorious dramatic muddle does not prevent Glinka from writing his most inventive music. There is a stronger Russian idiom, including the use of the changing background technique for a Finnish bard and Persian dancing girls, and harmonic ideas that were to prove fruitful to Glinka's successors. There is also the most vivid contrast yet explored between Russian, Oriental and magic worlds.

In the year in which *A Life for the Tsar* seemed to promise new hope for Russian composers, Cavos conducted a performance of Rossini's *Semiramide* whose triumph turned fashion firmly towards Italian opera, not least since there was so little in the way of native Russian opera to compete. Nikolai I promptly established an Italian company in St Petersburg, and in 1843 this ousted the Russian company from the Bolshoi to the lesser Aleksandrinsky Theatre. The Russians gave fewer performances, and decamped to Moscow, not effectively returning except for occasional visits, while the German company gave fewer performances still and then closed. Although with this move Nikolai damaged the chances of Russian composers, he made the Italian opera at St Petersburg one of the most important in Europe, drawing the greatest Italian singers of the age and staging the premiere of Verdi's *The Force of Destiny* in 1862. The Italian domination even affected Moscow, where the restored Bolshoi Theatre was opened for Aleksandr II's coronation in 1856 – with Italian performances.

However, Cavos's work had begun to bear fruit in the 1830s with the emergence of a new generation of Russian singers. The greatest of them was Osip Petrov, who, with his performance as Glinka's Ivan Susanin, set a style that was to influence subsequent roles in Russian opera and who thereby founded the great dynasty of Russian operatic basses. A prime characteristic of the latter has been not only the profundity that can be heard even with ordinary singers in church choirs; the style has included a sonorous elegance and a wide range of colour, encompassing romantic passion and tragic brooding but also a wild, grotesque humour. Scarcely less significant was the appearance of Cavos's pupil Anna Vorobyova, who sang Vanya to Petrov's Susanin, and later married him. She in turn set an example to subsequent generations of Russian contraltos, whose voices have often possessed extraordinary depth and richness, with a capacity for both the sinister and the comic (sometimes simultaneously). A third influential singer to appear in the first *Life for the Tsar* was Maria Stepanova, whose lines suggest a soprano able to respond with the lyrical grace deriving from the French *romance* that was a prime influence on Russian art song (which indeed tends to use the word *romans* rather than *pesn*), and also a forceful, declamatory manner suitable for moments of high drama. The fourth leading voice in this performance was the tenor Leon Leonov (natural son of the Irish pianist John Field): all were to confirm their success, and their styles, in *Ruslan and Lyudmila*. Though they were obliged to appear mostly in French and especially Italian opera, for want of a Russian repertory, Glinka enabled these singers to reveal characteristics that touched on something essentially Russian, inspiring and colouring the responses of composers of many different natures.

Nikolai's policy towards opera proved so discouraging to Russian composers that little, and virtually nothing of importance, was written during the two decades following the appearance of *Ruslan and Lyudmila* in 1842. Aleksandr's accession in 1855 brought with it a new initiative, but time was needed for this to be realised. The new tsar's wish to encourage native talent led to the construction in St Petersburg of the magnificent new Maryinsky Theatre (with Cavos's son Alberto as architect), replacing the inconvenient Tsirk Theatre in which the Russians had been obliged to play. A public move against the Italians' domination, in part caused by resistance to their expense and the niggardly treatment of Russians, came to a head with the extravagant production of *The Force of Destiny*, and a growing patriotic mood aroused greater interest in the Russian company.

More importantly in the longer term, musicians depressed about the condition of opera, and that of the arts in general, had begun to consider what was to be done – *Chto delat?*, in the title of Chernyshevsky's influential novel of 1863. Among the artists and intellectuals concerned with art as an expression of life, what was seen as the essentially decorative nature of Italian opera proved less and less satisfying; and the stagnation of Russian opera in mid-century, by comparison with all that had been achieved in the West, was more and more frustrating. Thus, by their nature, efforts at reform sought to correct what was imposed by authority, a fact that did not escape the tsar's watchful Second Section. A crucial figure in the movement of new ideas was Russia's first great music critic, Vladimir Stasov, who had been fired with the ideals of Belinsky and took these into his forceful and articulate discussions and correspondence with the young musicians of his circle.

The only composer of interest to complete an opera in the 1850s, as Stasov's influence was beginning to make itself felt, was Aleksandr Dargomyzhsky. Wealthy by birth, he had been encouraged to compose by Glinka (who had fallen silent after *Ruslan and Lyudmila*), and had first turned his attention to Italian opera. However, *Esmeralda*, completed in 1841 to a translation of Victor Hugo's own libretto, ran into difficulties with the Italian hegemony, and was not produced until 1847. In the enduringly popular *Rusalka* (1856) he tried to move beyond Glinka, and set beside Romantic vocalism a more vivid, immediate declamatory manner. Its value was fully appreciated by the only other significant composer attempting opera in these years, himself an important critic, Aleksandr Serov; and Dargomyzhsky also came to the attention of a younger group led by the composer Mily Balakirev. However, his only other opera was *The Stone Guest* (1872). The plan here was to set Pushkin's 'little tragedy' word for word, avoiding arias, duets, ensembles and so on, as being operatic forms that by their nature intervened between the listener and the poem, whose 'truthfulness' he sought to heighten with a kind of continuous musical recitative. In practice, two songs are included; and the opera avoids the threat of monotony through skilful use of the orchestra and a well-judged balance between declamatory recitative and a more lyrical involvement with the verse. Dargomyzhsky did not live quite to complete *The Stone Guest*, but it was played through at private meetings of friends (with Musorgsky singing Leporello); the completion was undertaken by Cui and Rimsky-Korsakov.

As well as encouraging Dargomyzhsky, Aleksandr Serov had interested himself in composing operas in the 1840s and 1850s, and had considered several projects, but none came to fruition. He was independent of factions, and never taught, but his sharp intelligence and sharper critical tongue made him an influential figure in these years. He shared the concern for considering opera as a form of drama, and sought to reconcile Italian and German examples. It was a reading of Wagner's *Opera and Drama*, and then the experience of seeing *Tannhäuser* and *Lohengrin*, that rekindled his interest in opera. His championship of Wagner cost him Stasov's friendship and aroused the suspicions of those for whom Wagner represented a threat to

Russian values. Serov's first completed opera, *Judith* (1863: in Wagnerian fashion, to his own text), has in it some of the elements of French Grand Opera which Wagner himself had absorbed, but inherits from Glinka the type of motive employed, crowd scenes functional to the drama, and a musical contrast between two conflicting peoples, here Hebrews and Assyrians.

The success of *Judith* brought Serov into contact with Dostoevsky's circle, whose nationalism coloured a second opera, *Rogneda* (1865). The conflict here is between Orthodox Christianity and paganism, with the triumphant establishment of Byzantine caesaropapism. The work is a considerable muddle, but its popular success aroused the curiosity of the tsar, who went to a performance and awarded Serov a life pension on the spot. Encouraged by this new royal interest in Russian opera, Serov began work with Ostrovsky on *The Power of the Fiend* (1871), but progress was delayed by quarrels, and Serov did not live to complete his most ambitious work. There remains the substance of a very remarkable opera that integrates folk material and town music, separate numbers and elaborate structures, melodic originality and earthily realistic declamation, in a manner close to Musorgsky.

A practical initiative of enormous significance had meanwhile come from the composer and pianist who was to dominate Russian musical life for much of the remainder of the century, Anton Rubinstein. One of the great virtuosos of the age, he was taken up by the tsar's sister-in-law, the Grand Duchess Elena Pavlovna, and given the full support of her wealth and influence. With her backing he founded in 1859 the Russian Musical Society, whose regular concerts he conducted, and then in 1862 the St Petersburg Conservatoire; his brother Nikolai followed by setting up a Moscow branch of the society in the 1859/60 season and the Moscow Conservatoire in 1864. At last in Russia not only were concerts given regularly but there were two training establishments in which composers and performers could study their art at the highest level, and from the best teachers the Rubinstein brothers could attract.

Anton's own contribution to opera made him an equivocal figure in Russia. His international fame won him the attention and respect of musicians including Liszt, to whom he was compared as a pianist and who staged a number of his operas at Weimar. He completed eighteen operas, more than any of his countrymen, although he regarded opera as inferior to absolute music; and only one survives in any repertory. Three of his

early operas written for the grand duchess concerned various national-
ities (Siberian, Ukrainian and Georgian), and make only decorative use of
folk music. However, his touch with musical Orientalism is revealed with
Feramors (1863), the first of the works in the genre of the 'sacred opera'
which he went on to cultivate in rivalry to Wagner; he even considered
building a special festival theatre for their performance. It was, however,
The Demon (1875) which proved his masterpiece. Its Caucasus setting gave
him free rein with his gift for Oriental colour, and the struggle between
the damned soul of the title and the suffering heroine Tamara has continued to exercise a powerful appeal to Russian audiences. Among the
opera's originalities is the long 'love duet' in which the Demon calls to
Tamara in seductive tones which only she can hear, while, with her
companions, she mourns the bridegroom he has killed. The vocal style is
close to the French *romance* manner of Russian song – which was to
influence Rubinstein's devotee Tchaikovsky – and is far distant from the
ideals of the group of composers who emerged into a dominant position
in the 1860s.

In an article in the *St Petersburg Gazette* in 1867, Stasov referred to the few
composers whom he regarded as Russia's most significant as a 'mighty little
heap', a term he intended to describe a slightly larger group than five; but
'The Mighty Handful' (in the conventional English phrase) now refers to
'The Five': Balakirev, Borodin, Cui, Musorgsky and Rimsky-Korsakov. All
were based in St Petersburg; all were amateurs, initially with other professional careers; all were virtually self-taught. The exception was Balakirev.
The dominating (not to say domineering) member of the group, he was also
the only one not to write an opera; but with his intellectual perception, his
forceful personality and his practical resistance to the authoritarian standards of the Conservatoire in founding his rival Free School of Music, he
strongly influenced their ideas.

The first of their operas came from Cesar Cui, with *William Ratcliff*
(1869). As a critic – one with a notoriously sharp tongue – Cui attacked the
resident Italians, seeing greater inspiration for Russia as coming from
Germany (Wagner always excepted). He admired Weber and Schumann;
and *William Ratcliff*, the most important of his fifteen operas, was taken as
embodying the group's ideals, especially in its approach to a 'fate' tragedy,
in its handling of motive, and above all in its Dargomyzhskian use of what
Cui described as 'melodic recitative' – that is to say, music arising directly
from the text.

After initial hostility, Cui was to praise these qualities in the work of Modest Musorgsky. The chaos of Musorgsky's private life is reflected in the condition in which he left his operas, one of which, *Boris Godunov*, is among Russia's greatest dramatic masterpieces. Before embarking upon it, he began a setting of Gogol's *Marriage* in the manner suggested to him by Dargomyzhsky, who was then busy with *The Stone Guest*. In connection with this, he set forth realist ideals of music conveying the sounds of human speech as an external manifestation of inner thoughts and feelings. *Marriage* remained unfinished, and not surprisingly was found extreme in its attention to naturalistic speech-melodies even by Dargomyzhsky and the 'handful'.

Turning his attention to *Boris Godunov*, Musorgsky completed seven scenes in 1869, to some extent modifying his declamatory ideas and also making use of more lyrical musical numbers in a mixed-genre manner, respecting Pushkin's conscious modelling of the original drama on Shakespeare (the other main source of his libretto was Karamzin's history). When the Imperial Theatres turned the work down on the grounds that it lacked love interest, Musorgsky added a so-called Polish act, introducing Marina Mniszek as lover for the False Dmitry, but also recast the opera by shuffling scenes, making cuts, adding extra numbers and even important whole scenes, and turning the opera in a more traditional, tragic direction. Though this gave greater stature to the role of Tsar Boris, one of the greatest characterisations in Russian opera and the ambition of every Slavonic bass, it also brought to the fore the role of the crowd, on whose rebellion the opera ends. Musorgsky's realism has, moreover, moved beyond any kind of literalism, and skilfully reinterprets the strengths of Italian convention in purely Russian terms. Examples of this may be found in the crowd choruses, the opening one of which serves, in Italian fashion, to set a colourful scene but does so with the fragmented, haphazard utterances of a real crowd, and in Boris's death scene, which is no aria but a steady disintegration of his vocal line, against steady chanting and chiming, into nullity. Eventually the newly completed opera was performed in 1874, to a warm reception.

Musorgsky never completed another opera before his death from alcoholism, although he left enough of *Khovanshchina*, on the revolt of the *streltsy* in the time of Peter the Great, for Rimsky-Korsakov to be able to orchestrate it and supply what was necessary to make the work performable. Rimsky-Korsakov could do little for the folk comedy *Sorochintsy Fair*;

other composers who tried to complete it included Cui. Rimsky-Korsakov's services to his friend included a revised version of *Boris Godunov*, softening the harmony and orchestration and placing Boris's death at the end, all of which was designed as a temporary measure to win the opera Western acceptance. Most opera houses now prefer the greater strength and originality of Musorgsky's final version.

Rimsky-Korsakov, Cui and Musorgsky all wrote music for the collaborative opera-ballet *Mlada* (1872), which was more than touched by an attempt to find a Russian response to Wagnerian ideas about the *Gesamtkunstwerk*. However, the major contribution came from the fourth member of the group, Aleksandr Borodin. Operatically, he was not close to their ideals, which indeed are lampooned in his early pastiche *The Bogatyrs* (1867). As is evident in *Prince Igor* (1890), he preferred a more lyrical and prominent vocal line and did not resist closed forms. He claimed ancestry for the work in *Ruslan and Lyudmila*, though his broadly drawn historical epic owes as much to *A Life for the Tsar*. He died with it unfinished, leaving another task of completion to the indefatigable Rimsky-Korsakov.

No-one did more to establish Russian opera as a genre of national and international significance than Nikolai Rimsky-Korsakov – as a chronicler and teacher, through his selfless assistance to his colleagues, and as the composer of fifteen operas. In the first, *The Maid of Pskov* (1873), he plunged in with the group's ideology and produced a crowd scene comparable in approach to those of Musorgsky, with whom he was sharing lodgings. This was about the furthest he went in support of the group's ideals, and the brilliant polish of most of his later works provides a dazzling surface to rather plainer substance.

With two exceptions, all are on Russian themes. *May Night* (1880) is based on Gogol, the inspirer of many Russian composers, from Musorgsky to Shostakovich and beyond, who found in his stories and plays the local colour, humour and fantasy that lent themselves well to operatic treatment. Rimsky-Korsakov made copious use of *devichniki, rusalki*, and the *skomorokhi* whose tumbling antics he helped to make a popular feature of the divertissement scenes in Russian opera of a kind which showed that Glinka was still casting a long shadow. In *The Snow Maiden* (1882), fairy and human worlds impinge, and there is a skilful use of motive to reinforce the ancient ritual elements that absorbed him, though the heroine is characterised as touching but hardly sympathetic. This weakness was underlined when he returned to Gogol's village comedy *Christmas Eve* (1895), which also emphasises the fantastic element at the expense of the human. From the panoramic, exotic *Sadko* (1898) he suddenly turned back to the group's ideals with *Mozart and Salieri* (1898), based on a literal setting of Pushkin's 'little tragedy' and drawing again on the manner of Dargomyzhsky (to whom the opera is dedicated). But feeling that this was not a way forward, he returned to historical costume drama with *The Tsar's Bride* (1899) – a work underrated in the West and his most popular in Russia – and to magic opera with *The Tale of Tsar Saltan* (1900). He did not develop seriously in his few remaining operas: the most popular abroad, though not the finest, has been the last, *The Golden Cockerel* (1909), another Pushkin setting that mixes the fantastic elements, for which his marvellous orchestral gifts were so well suited, with a sharpness of satire that got him into trouble with the censor. Despite being based on Pushkin, the work was read as a comment on the incompetent conduct of the Russo-Japanese War. Among his later services to musicians, for whom he had become a mentor, was his brave public support for the students demonstrating in the 1905 revolution, which led to his dismissal from the Conservatoire and a temporary ban on his music.

To identify the group of Five's ideals with the Slavophiles would be as simplistic as to label Rubinstein and his followers Westernisers. The group's community of interests gave its members a cause which led them to put forward a well-argued, certainly much-argued, agenda for a specifically Russian operatic genre. To this extent, it formed a corpus of critical thought, and of creative work, referring to essential Russian values and drawing on Russian musical techniques. It was a centre of activity as the history of Russian opera moved from the 1860s towards the end of the century. But within it there was much that embraced Westerniser ideals, just as in the work of the international Rubinstein there was much that was nationalistic, even superficially Slavophile. The situation is still more complex in the work of the greatest composer who firmly distanced himself from the group of Five, Pyotr Tchaikovsky.

To refrain from writing operas was a heroism he did not possess, Tchaikovsky once wrote. He completed ten, one of which is lost and another of which survives in two versions. As a child he had been overwhelmed by a performance of Mozart's *Don Giovanni*, which, he said, made him resolve to be a musician; and he took full advantage of the teaching he was able to receive at the new St Petersburg Conservatoire. He thus became the first major Russian composer to have a professional training in his own country; and he immediately went on to teach harmony at the Moscow Conservatoire (until the patronage of a wealthy widow, Nadezhda von Meck, rescued him from his obligations). His affiliations were thus to the Rubinstein brothers and the new official life they established, and he remained in awe of them, particularly of Anton, throughout his and their lives. Nikolai was the stronger supporter, and conducted the premiere of *Eugene Onegin* (and many of the concert works); Anton's wounding reluctance to offer praise may well have been based on jealousy, in particular for the younger man's operatic achievement.

Tchaikovsky's first opera, *Voevoda* (1869), was to a text partly by Ostrovsky, who withdrew after the composer first lost some of the text and then proved in other ways difficult. The outcome was an awkward work, as modern reconstruction from orchestral parts has shown; for Tchaikovsky destroyed the score, after salvaging some of it for later use. The same fate befell his second opera, *Undine*, for which no original material survives. *Oprichnik* (1874), a historical drama with a powerful love interest, could be said to take the group on at its own game, and certainly its members' hostile reaction suggested that they thought as much; but in it Tchaikovsky found his individual touch, which included a melodic richness that was Russian but not ruled by speech inflections. As with other contemporaries, the next genre he tried was a Gogol folk comedy, *Vakula the Smith* (1876). His vein of dramatic music is further developed in this, his only comedy, which includes some lyrical love music, some delightful dances, and a skilful contrast between peasant vigour and urban, aristocratic elegance. The work was later revised as *Cherevichki* (1887).

It was the experience of seeing *Carmen* in Paris in 1876, in the same year that he had been an unenthusiastic reviewer of the first Bayreuth Festival, that turned him back to opera, but opera of a personal kind. A chance suggestion of *Eugene Onegin* caught his imagination, but, although more sympathetic to the Italians than most of his contemporaries, he professed himself glad to get away from 'all the routine pharaohs, Ethiopian princesses, poisoned cups and all the rest of these tales about automata'.[1] He called the work 'lyrical scenes', and concentrated on seven, describing Onegin's rejection of Tatyana, Lensky's death in the duel, and Onegin's belated recognition of his love for Tatyana. There are occasions for local colour, as in the peasants' *podgolosok* and in the contrast between their own dancing, that at the country house party and that at the St Petersburg ball. But the vocal lines are once more closer to the Russian art song than to folk-coloured or speech-inflected melody, and far removed from Italian example. Indeed, Tchaikovsky had by now come to fear that current stage conventions would maim his opera: 'how Pushkin's captivating picture will be vulgarised when it is transferred to the stage with its routine, its senseless traditions, its veterans of both sexes who, without any shame, take on, like Aleksandrova, Komissarzhevsky and *tutti quanti*, the roles of sixteen-year-old girls and beardless youths!'[2] He solved his problem by giving the first performance to the students of the Moscow Conservatoire; but the opera, his greatest, has long since entered international repertoires, and its roles are those which not only Russian singers covet dearly.

In an attempt to further his international career, Tchaikovsky next took on the most important theatre in Europe, the Paris Opéra, with *The Maid of Orleans* (1881). This Joan of Arc setting is cast in French Grand Opera style, for which it was duly pounced upon by Cui with almost personal malice. *Mazeppa* (1884), a return to Pushkin and to a national subject, is a gloomy but a much stronger work, and Tchaikovsky then lost his way with its successor, *The Enchantress* (1887), before successfully taking up Pushkin again in *The Queen of Spades* (1890). Though echoes of *Carmen* are strong, parts of the work look forward to an Expressionist manner that he never lived to explore. His last opera was the one-act *Iolanta*, commissioned in a unique (and not very practical) theatrical enterprise as companion to the ballet *The Nutcracker* by his long-time supporter at the Imperial Theatres, Ivan Vsevolozhsky.

The first conductor of *Iolanta* and of five more of Tchaikovsky's operas was a Czech who spent his professional life in Russia, Eduard Nápravník. He also conducted the premieres of major works by Dargomyzhsky, Serov, Rubinstein and all the group of Five, as well as his own operas. It was not, however, as a composer that his reputation was made and his great work for Russian opera done: his only success, and a limited one, was *Dubrovsky* (1894), to a text based on Pushkin by Tchaikovsky's brother, Modest. Nápravník's contribution to the establishment and development of opera in Russia rested on the skill with which he formed, prepared, maintained and directed a brilliant company of singers and musicians at the Maryinsky Theatre from 1868, when he was appointed chief conductor after five years as assistant, until his death. Though he was never an exciting conductor, his cool, professional efficiency was a more important characteristic in these years. 'With all his pedantry, with all his inexorable dryness, he was an inspirer, he was a constructor,' wrote one admirer. 'His hand moved like a metronome without volition, but under this seeming indifference there was an iron will.'

For all its Italian influence, the style of the Imperial Theatres was really closer to that of Parisian Grand Opera, with its emphasis on sumptuous sets, star singers, a large chorus, powerful scenes of action, and vivid décor evoking local colour. This was to remain so even when the royal monopoly ended in 1882, for after the disbanding of the Italian company in 1885, Aleksandr III saw to it that generous funds were transferred to the Maryinsky. In the world of ballet, this consciously French emphasis on prettiness and virtuosity created difficulties even for Tchaikovsky when he tried to give music a more functional role; with opera, the conventions were more dramatic, but were still artificial enough to give the group reasons for hostility. However, an 'official' style that is the descendant of this can still be seen in the monumental productions of Russian nineteenth-century classics at the Moscow Bolshoi and the St Petersburg Maryinsky. Similarly, the need to project emotions in a grand manner could lead to a degree of exaggeration and formalisation in the acting style, transfigured by the genius of Chaliapin but in the hands of his imitators often merely crude.

Under Nápravník, the opera continued to foster the great singers who contributed much to the development of Russian opera in the latter decades of the century. Tchaikovsky's favourite baritone was Ivan Melnikov, also the first Boris Godunov and Prince Igor, who was universally admired for his development of strong character-singing on a basis of sound bel canto training. Fyodor Stravinsky, father of the composer, was a bass in the line of Osip Petrov, whose attention to dramatic detail and character helped to pave the way for Chaliapin. Pavel Khokhlov was another baritone of bel canto training who, until an early decline, sang most important roles (including the first public Eugene Onegin). Nikolai and Medea Figner were a gifted tenor and soprano husband and wife; they were also much admired by Tchaikovsky, who wrote the parts of Hermann and Lisa for them in *The Queen of Spades* and counted himself lucky to have their friendship and professional support. Ivan Ershov was another fine singer-actor, who sang many Russian roles and whose Heldentenor tones did much to help the cause of Wagner in Russia. Fyodor Chaliapin himself sang briefly in St Petersburg, but really gained his experience in the private opera company of Savva Mamontov. In Moscow, one of the most striking artists was the tenor Leonid Sobinov who became famous as a Lensky more realistic than in Figner's romantic portrayal. Sobinov was in later life to

15. Tchaikovsky's *The Queen of Spades* with Medea and Nikolai Figner. Maryinsky Theatre, 1890.

16. Fyodor Chaliapin as Ivan the Terrible in Rimsky-Korsakov's *Maid of Pskov*, on tour in Monte Carlo, 1907.

work with Stanislavsky, who regarded him as one of the great actors of the Russian stage. To draw conclusions from only a few of the great singers of these decades would be wrong; but it is fair to say that they were the leading representatives of a tradition of Russian singing that moved from a Romantic style, based on bel canto training and a more French lyricism, in the direction of powerfully realistic singing-acting, with great attention to costume and make-up as part of a strong characterisation. The style was, at its best, a successful fusion of the old Romantic manner with the group's realism.

A consequence of the ending of the royal monopoly was the formation of a number of private opera companies by various wealthy Moscow merchants. The most important was the first of these, the Moscow Private Russian Opera Company, formed in 1885 by Savva Mamontov, a railway millionaire with well-informed artistic tastes. The company was conducted by a pupil of Rimsky-Korsakov, the composer Mikhail Ippolitov-Ivanov, later by Rakhmaninov, and it was here that Chaliapin had his first substantial opportunity. The company played in the Solodovnikov Theatre, and its experiments included bringing in a stage designer, often the painter Viktor Fasnetsov, on equal dramatic terms with the production, which was sometimes a collaborative effort by the entire cast. Other important private companies, notably the Zimin Company in the years after the collapse of the Mamontov Company, were to follow in the new century. It was by them that the most enterprising work was generally done, a legacy that was inherited by Stanislavsky and Nemirovich-Danchenko. More recently (1972), the Kamerny Opera Theatre, under Boris Pokrovsky and with Gennady Rozhdestvensky as music director, has not only explored new works and production methods that would not gain acceptance at its parent Bolshoi, but given serious attention to Russia's eighteenth-century operatic origins.

Notes

1. From a letter Tchaikovsky wrote to Nadezhda von Meck in December 1877. Published in Pyotr Tchaikovsky, *Literaturnie proizvedeniia i perepiska*, vol. VI (Moscow, 1961), p. 308.
2. Ibid.

11 Imperial and private theatres, 1882–1905
ARKADY OSTROVSKY

1. Moscow

It is a paradox of Russian history that periods of cultural vitality seldom coincide with times of political and economic reform. The 1880s clearly exemplify this absence of cohesion.

After the turbulent 1860s and 1870s, notable for their social and political changes, came the retreat and quietism of the 1880s. Aleksandr II was assassinated on 1 March 1881 and a period of reaction set in. Rehearsing Chekhov's *Ivanov* in 1904, Vladimir Nemirovich-Danchenko recalled the late 1880s when the play was written: 'Bans, exiles, oppression began. As I remember it, one good newspaper went to hell after another, men of integrity and intellect hid like snails in their shells.'[1] *Ivanov* provides a depressing portrait of the lost generation of the 1880s: 'You see a man exhausted at the age of thirty-five . . . Heavy-headed, dull-witted, worn out, broken, shattered, without faith or love, with no aim in life, I moon around more dead than alive.'[2] Yet it was during this time that Chekhov wrote most of his plays, Tchaikovsky composed his best operas, Tolstoy wrote *The Death of Ivan Ilyich* and *Kreutzer Sonata*, and the best Russian actors created their most famous roles.

In 1882 there were five Imperial Theatres altogether – two in Moscow and three in St Petersburg. Drama was mostly performed at Moscow's Maly Theatre and St Petersburg's Aleksandrinsky, and opera and ballet were at the Bolshoi in Moscow and the Maryinsky in St Petersburg. There was also the Mikhailovsky Theatre in St Petersburg where the aristocracy could see touring French companies. The Imperial Theatres had their own schools with ballet and drama classes.[3] On 24 March 1882, Aleksandr III finally signed a decree abolishing the monopoly of the Imperial Theatres, opening the way to private (commercial) theatres. Contrary to expectations, however, Russian theatre did not change significantly.

Attempts to open private theatres had been made before the end of the monopoly. In 1865 a group of actors and playwrights supported by

Ostrovsky founded an Artistic Circle and often used its stage for professional productions. In 1880 the actress Anna Brenko was granted permission to open her 'Dramatic Theatre in Malkiel House', better known as the Pushkin Theatre because of its proximity to the Pushkin monument. It had famous actors from the provinces and a high-quality repertoire which included plays by Ostrovsky, Turgenev, Sukhovo-Kobylin, Griboedov, Shakespeare and others. Brenko was popular with the Moscow intelligentsia, but that did not help her theatre to survive financially and it had to close two years later. Its disappearance changed as little in the Russian theatre scene as its appearance.

Many private theatres were launched by women with an eye on their careers. In 1889 a young provincial actress, Maria Abramova, opened her own theatre using the proceeds from a recent inheritance. It closed a year later as a result of bad management, a weak repertoire, poor acting – and lack of artistic purpose. The same year another actress, Elizaveta Goreva, set up a theatre with a repertoire of Western plays already produced at the Imperial Theatres. Despite a good company, that, too, closed after eighteen months. Private theatres improved the quantity, not the quality of performances. None of them challenged existing traditions or introduced new artistic ideas. Most of them (except for the Moscow Art Theatre) were mediocre copies of the Imperial theatres with similar repertoires and, very often, the same acting techniques.

Of all the private theatres of this period, by far the most successful and long-lasting was launched by a stage-struck lawyer, Fyodor Korsh. He owned the cloakroom in Brenko's theatre[4] and, when it closed, took over her troupe and the building, and opened his Russian Drama Theatre. This was always known, however, as the Korsh Theatre. Like Brenko before him he opened with a mainstay of the Imperial Theatres, *The Government Inspector*, on 30 August 1882. Korsh was not interested in theatrical experiments and new art forms. He put on Ostrovsky and Gogol because Ostrovsky and Gogol were the most popular dramatists at the Maly. In the first season there were twenty-two performances of Ostrovsky's plays and fourteen of Gogol's, out of a total number of seventy.

Encouraged by a profitable first year, Korsh decided to mount a spectacular production in his second season, a play which was almost as long as its title: *The Tsar and the Grand Duke of All Russia, Vasily Ivanovich Shuisky,* (a chronicle in five acts with a prologue) by Nikolai Chaev. It had breathtaking scenery with views of medieval Novgorod, period costumes, stunning theatrical effects and rousing monologues declaimed by famous actors. But the audience was unimpressed and the production failed to break even. Having spent over 20,000 roubles, Korsh found himself on the brink of a financial crisis. He could not pay the rent and had to move out of Gazetny Street and sell off all his costumes and scenery. 'It seemed that the Russian Drama Theatre had died, disappeared for ever. But no . . .'[5] Korsh somehow managed to find money, and in 110 days 'owing to everybody's friendly and enthusiastic work' a new theatre designed by Chichagov in a popular style *á la Rus* appeared in Bogoslovsky Street.

Korsh concluded that the sympathies of the new bourgeois audience lay with light and elegant comedy or vaudevilles, rather than long plays with complicated plots and dramatic endings. Thereafter, every Friday, audiences were guaranteed a new comedy or farce – cheap to produce and easy to watch. The posters resembled a menu. Shows were called by different names, but concocted from the same ingredients.

On 10 January 1886 the audience was offered: *Fofan*, a comedy in three acts by Shpazhinsky; *Little Devil*, a comic farce in two acts by Zazulin; and *A Comedy Without a Title*, a comedy in one act by Kugushev, all in one evening. A comedy without a title is almost a metaphor for the repertoire of Korsh's theatre. Korsh's spectators 'decide to go to the theatre on the spur of the moment, when they feel like it, without choosing or knowing the play, simply because they find some fun in it'.[6]

However, the Korsh theatre had an important educational role. On Sundays and during the holidays Korsh offered cheap matinée performances of classics for grammar schools. Korsh's matinees not only cultivated young people's tastes for theatre but also prepared a future audience for evening performances. Several great actors such as Moskvin, Leonidov and Ostuzhev began their careers in the Korsh theatre.

Although Korsh did not have a permanent troupe, his theatre was rich in talents and soon established its own acting style. New plays had to be rehearsed in four to five days, which demanded considerable technical proficiency from Korsh's actors. They had to be extremely versatile and able to improvise. Yartsev defined their main characteristic as a 'talented carelessness': 'one must have a talent to be able to play after three to four rehearsals'.[7] But if one-act French vaudeville hardly needed more rehearsals, Chekhov's plays certainly suffered from this method of work. In 1887 the theatre premiered Chekhov's *Ivanov* which Korsh had commissioned. Performed as a double bill with a French vaudeville, Chekhov's play seemed out of place: audience reaction was mixed, but nobody was indifferent.

In 1887 Chekhov was not yet a famous writer and Korsh in commissioning him to write a play displayed a fine sense of intuition. Although not particularly interested in experiments, Korsh was flexible and attentive to the interests of his times: if in the beginning his theatre was a copy of the Maly, after 1898 it was trying to react to the newly opened Moscow Art Theatre. Korsh realised that like Stanislavsky he needed a professional director and a new play. In 1901 Korsh invited Nikolai Sinelnikov to become director of his theatre. Sinelnikov was one of the most dedicated directors from the provinces and pre-empted some of Stanislavsky's ideas. Sinelnikov's production of *The Children of Vanyushin* by Sergei Naidenov was a major event and had thirty-seven performances in one season. Naidenov's play, which described the disintegration of a patriarchal family, had autobiographical roots. Naidenov grew up in a merchant family, was expelled from school, ran away from home to study in Moscow, and was in the middle of his final examinations when his father committed suicide. Chekhov wrote to Nemirovich-Danchenko: 'Contemporary plays which I have to read have no author, as though they are all produced at the same factory, by the same machine; in Naidenov's plays, on the contrary, there is an author.'[8] The same could be said about Sinelnikov and his producton. Yet Sinelnikov's serious productions, like Chekhov's and Naidenov's plays, were drowned in a welter of comedies and vaudevilles.

In the 1880s and 1890s life in both Russian capitals was becoming more diverse, rich and dynamic. Capitalism was growing fast. People were selling their country houses and moving to Moscow and St Petersburg looking for new opportunities. The new rich demanded new entertainments and were prepared to pay. The theatre enterprise launched by Mikhail Lentovsky best expressed the taste and scope of the emerging capitalist class – and also its spirit. Chekhov, ironic as ever, remarked: '[Lentovsky] is a remarkable man. When he dies they're bound to put up a monument to him. He is everything: an actor, an impresario and the proud possessor of several decorations. He is eternally busy: acting, running around his garden, reading romantic poems from the stage, shooting pigeons, beating trouble-makers flat.'[9] Lentovsky, in fact, was a monument to himself. His picturesque image was inseparable from his enterprise. Stanislavsky remembered him as a large and very strong man, with wide shoulders and a black abundant beard: 'his hair cut long in ancient boyar fashion. A Russian coat of thin black cloth, and high lacquered boots gave his figure knightly grace. He wore a thick gold chain bedecked with all sorts of knick-knacks and gifts from famous persons and – even royalty.'[10]

Lentovsky was one of Shchepkin's last students and began his career at the Maly, mostly singing in operettas and playing the parts of dare-devils (Ostrovsky even wrote a special part for Lentovsky – the gypsy Ilya in *The Dowerless Girl*). But for the Muscovites in the 1880s the name Lentovsky was associated with the Hermitage Garden. A man of feverish energy and wild imagination he turned the Hermitage Garden into a wonderland, replete with ingenious fireworks, water battles, tightrope walking, performing animals and bathing nymphs. In 1882 he opened an open-air theatre, appropriately named the Fantastic Theatre and inspired by his personal fantasy: 'an unknown family comes in summer to their estate, situated near the ruins of an old castle. Young people go for a walk to inspect the castle. One part of the castle looks like a theatre: a big amphitheatre, surrounded by huge boulders with some climbers.'[11]

The Fantastic Theatre specialised in most elaborate extravaganzas (or *féeries*) which owed much of their popularity to extraordinary stage devices. Lentovsky's *féeries* resembled Jule Verne's tales with their combination of adventure and popular science. The plots of Lentovsky's *féeries* were based on supernatural journeys to distant lands and covered most of the globe and sometimes space: 'An unbelievable trip to the Moon,' 'In the forests of India, on the shores of the Ganges, in the land of white elephants,' 'Travelling in Africa or the events in Egypt' and so on. The shows were filled with explosions, fires, army battles, landslides, waterfalls, earthquakes and other disasters (natural and unnatural). Lentovsky was a brilliant impresario, a true man of the 1880s and an idealist and eccentric at the same time. He was called 'a magician and enchanter', but though he could charm the audience, his magic power had little effect on his creditors. In spite of his great popularity Lentovsky was constantly losing money and increasing his already gigantic debts: even playing to full houses could not cover the costs of his shows.

Despite this, in 1885 he opened another theatre – the Skomorokh – intended for the working class. It was for this theatre that Tolstoy wrote *The Power of Darkness*, a naturalistic tragedy about peasant life, which was banned by the censors. Lentovsky originally planned to put on melodramas and plays about the life of simple people, but soon the spirit of the magician took over and he began to mount vaudeville productions with fantastic stage effects which could only increase his debts. In 1891 he had to give up the Skomorokh, and a year later he sold the Hermitage Garden. Lentovsky burned bright and fast, like a firework in his *féerie*, but by 1894 he was completely broke.

The abolition of the monopoly in 1882 did not change the pace of the Imperial Theatres' life: they were subsidised by the state, had a solid reputation and did not have to compete with private theatres either for audience, or for good actors. The Imperial Theatres were often referred to as 'exemplary', an adjective indicative of their position as 'model' for private theatres as well as their high artistic qualities. For the Moscow intelligentsia the Maly was more than just a theatre, it was the 'Second Moscow University', a place of great cultural importance. According to Stanislavsky, 'The Maly Theatre defined our intellectual and spiritual life . . . I can safely say that I have received my education not in a grammar school, but in the Maly Theatre.'[12] Muscovites had a special pride in their theatre: 'Wherever Sergei Flerov, a critic of the *Moscow Gazette* wrote Theatre with a capital "T", he meant the Moscow Maly Theatre. When he spelled theatre with a lower case "t", it meant any other ordinary theatre.'[13]

In the 1880s the Maly had the best and most varied company of actors, including Maria Ermolova, Glikeria Fedotova, Aleksandr Lensky, Aleksandr Yuzhin, Olga and Mikhail Sadovsky. They were not united by one artistic idea, like the company of the Moscow Art Theatre, rather they formed a big workshop, where there was enough room and work for everyone. If in the 1860s the Maly Theatre had been known as the home of Ostrovsky, in the 1880s it stopped being anybody's house. It did not belong to any one actor or actress or any one playwright or theatre director. It was administered by Pavel Pchelnikov, the director of the Moscow office of the Imperial Theatres, but he had little influence on artistic matters.

It is important to remember that the role of theatre director as artist and author of the production was only introduced by Stanislavsky in 1898 with the opening of the Moscow Art Theatre. In the 1880s, the stage manager cast the play and 'wrote the "staging", i.e. filled in the blanks under the rubrics: Cast, setting, furniture, costumes, wigs, properties . . . Costumes were described as "civilian" or "historical" . . . The standard sets for all plays were: drawing room – rich and poor, likewise studies, prison, forests . . . The classic plays of Shakespeare, Schiller and Hugo were served by notorious "Gothic" sets.' At the rehearsals, the stage manager 'distributed positions, i.e. it was agreed that x would stand there and y sit here. Ten or twelve

17. Aleksandr Lensky, 1900s.

was the largest number of rehearsals.'[14] Rehearsals had a merely technical role. The main artistic work was outside the rehearsal room. Actors created their characters at home and only verified them at rehearsals. The system of benefit performances, by which all the takings went to a particular member of the company, allowed actors to choose their favourite plays and create their best roles. 'About sixteen to eighteen plays were staged each year. Four were brought out at benefits and it must be said, all the best and most worthwhile plays appeared at these benefits.'[15]

Acting was the main and only element of a theatre production that did not fall into a set pattern. The audiences were used to conventional sets and costumes and paid little attention to them – only actors and their roles mattered. The theatre history of this period is mainly the history of great actors and actresses – not designers, directors or even playwrights. Actors had supreme power on stage. Describing the Maly Theatre in the 1880s and 1890s, Nemirovich-Danchenko remarked: 'At the head of the company stood Fedotova and Ermolova; later – Ermolova and Fedotova.'[16]

Glikeria Fedotova made her first appearance in *The Child*, a play by Boborykin, when she was sixteen and still a student. Her teachers were two of the great actors of the Maly – Ivan Samarin and Mikhail Shchepkin. Her debut was a great success, but after the performance Shchepkin came up to her with words she remembered for the rest of her life: 'Pay no attention to this success. They are all applauding your youth and prettiness. The talent which God gave you brings with it a responsibility. Remember this and work hard all your life.'[17] After this production Fedotova went to live with Shchepkin at his old manor-house like an apprentice in a workshop learning the basics of theatre craft. Many years later Fedotova herself started teaching. Among her pupils was Konstantin Alekseev (later known as Stanislavsky). One of the professional secrets which Fedotova passed on to him was a rule she had learned from Shchepkin: 'When you play an evil person, always try to find his kind sides.' From Shchepkin Fedotova also inherited strict discipline and a strong will, qualities for which she was famous at the Maly Theatre. Actors and theatre producers alike feared Fedotova, who always 'kept her vigilant eye on the whole production, listening to the rehearsals of even those scenes in which she did not appear. Fedotova did not allow any complacency or laziness.'[18]

A combination of imperiousness and cheerfulness was also characteristic of the stage characters she played. Her most famous roles were Queen Elizabeth in *Mary Stuart*, Lady Macbeth, Cleopatra, Beatrice in *Much Ado about Nothing*, and Katharina in *The Taming of the Shrew*. One critic wrote that Fedotova 'was an ideal actress for the major roles in Shakespeare's plays, for women full of strength, vitality, action; either *joie de vivre* or almost villainous aggressive energy. Intelligence, intellect, imperiousness – these qualities she played best. She was less inclined towards passive and sacrificial characters. Maybe the romantic heroism of sacrificial women, which Ermolova loved so much, was less fascinating for Fedotova than roles of sovereigns, victors, jovial or dark.'[19] Relations between the two great actresses, Ermolova and Fedotova, were surprisingly good. They did not compete, rather they complemented each other, they were a partnership.

Maria Nikolaevna Ermolova stands out among actors of the Maly Theatre. Like Salvini and Duse, she was one of the great tragediennes in theatre history. Like Dostoevsky and Tolstoy, she represented a whole era in late nineteenth-century Russian culture. Unfortunately, unlike a great writer, she did not leave any permanent trace of her art.

Although critics of her time unanimously recognised her as a 'tragic actress of genius', 'a symbol of our time', they found it almost impossible to define and describe that genius. Even such a perceptive critic as Aleksandr Kugel gave up and confessed: 'I could see a great talent, but it was clear that I could not find a formula for this actress . . . Words like "good", "wonderful", "artistic" are helpless to give the impression of her and I do not know what words should be used here. I could only say: it was truth.'[20]

In an attempt to define the Ermolova phenomenon, Nemirovich-Danchenko began with her background: 'All her inner life was different from that of Western actresses. Even her childhood was typical for a Russian actress: daughter of the prompter at the Maly Theatre, student of a theatre school, she retained her childhood memories of a Russian village. A little house in the Karetny riad (street) near a small church with its grave-yard, clergy house, was the source of her first impressions of life.'[21] Nemirovich-Danchenko defined here Ermolova's artistic genealogy, and interestingly enough placed her between the Maly Theatre and a small church-yard. Ermolova's childhood was mythologised in her time almost like the childhood of her favourite stage character, Joan of Arc, and became part of the actress's hagiography. The culmination of this legend was the evening of 30 January 1870 when Fedotova, who was supposed to play the leading role in Nadezhda Medvedeva's benefit performance of Lessing's *Emilia Galotti*, fell ill and Medvedeva decided to try the young student, Ermolova, in her stead. Medvedeva did not have much hope for the prompter's daughter, but when, at the rehearsal, 'Ermolova ran onto the small stage and with her low chest-notes spoke through the tears of emotion just the first few words "Thank God! Thank God!" it gave me the chills. I shuddered.'[22] Audience reaction was similar. Ermolova took twelve curtain calls. After the performance she wrote in her diary 'I am an actress.'

There were few roles in the Maly Theatre repertoire which gave full scope to Ermolova's capacity for tragedy. Nemirovich-Danchenko, who wrote plays specially for her, confessed: 'We were even embarrassed sometimes when Ermolova appeared in our plays. Her talent was so much richer than the parts we could offer her, that at times it seemed as if the roles split at the seams when Ermolova filled them with her genius.' But even in contemporary plays Ermolova looked for an opportunity to develop tragic motives. As Inna Solovyova has pointed out, Ermolova's characters always had some sense of perfection, something reminiscent of Dostoevsky's

18. Maria Ermolova as Laurencia in *The Star of Seville* by Lope de Vega, 1886.

image of Russian woman: 'In our woman one observes more and more sincerity, perseverance, seriousness and honour, sacrifice and search for truth.'[23] These were probably the most important elements in Ermolova's acting and the qualities that made fanatical young revolutionaries identify her with their beliefs and ideals. Soon after her debut as Emilia Galotti she was drawn into a revolutionary circle. For students and young people

Ermolova was more than an actress, she was a moral leader. The talented journalist Vlas Doroshevich portrayed a typical scene:

> Small room on Bronnaya.
> Three o'clock in the morning.
> Smoke everywhere.
> In a dense fog – ten dark figures.
> And talking . . . No!
> Screaming about Ermolova.[24]

When, in 1876, Ermolova held her first benefit performance she chose the role of Laurencia in *Fuente Ovejuna*. Ermolova's friend, Nikolai Storozhenko, recalled: 'When Laurencia with flowing hair, pale, shivering with shame and indignation came running to the square and, with her powerful speech roused the people to revolt against the governor, the excitement of the audience was almost hysterical. It was as if an electric circuit connected the actress with the audience.'[25] The political resonance of the play made the directors uncomfortable, and the production was soon removed from the repertoire. This only increased Ermolova's heroic image. Nemirovich-Danchenko felt that her success in those years 'was not only the success of a very talented actress. With her appearance, the very art of theatre was raised to a special, moral height; both from the artistic and social point of view.'[26]

Yet in real life Ermolova was no Laurencia: she was shy, modest and indecisive. She was often identified with her characters, and her art was considered to be a form of self-expression, but in answer to a questionnaire Ermolova said that real-life events never served her as material for her roles. Instead she often used literary and artistic sources.[27] The strength of Ermolova's acting was in her capacity for total transformation on stage. The life of her characters belonged to a different reality which was more vital and important for Ermolova than her own daily life. It was this gift of metamorphosis that linked her with Joan of Arc in Schiller's *The Maid of Orleans*, which she played in 1884. This is what Ermolova's daughter meant when in her unpublished memoirs she drew parallels between Joan of Arc and her mother 'with her impoverished childhood at the church-yard . . . with her belief in her vocation, with her gentle love for her mother and sisters.'

> She and Joan had much in common: the same extraordinary simplicity, the same obedience to the one "who sent her", the same amazement at

"what had descended upon her", the same recognition of her own insignificance and acceptance of your gift as if it was the Eucharist. Nobody knows what voices mother heard when, wrapped in her warm shawl, she went away from people to her own corner; what kind of visions she had . . . She never shared her inner world with anyone . . . In mother's acting there were no questions, no hesitations or doubts about the supernatural voices Joan heard, the visions she saw, the commands she received. For mother as for Joan it was all more than real life . . . that is why she was so convincing and why the enchanted audience lost any ability to think logically and to comprehend reality. She literally hypnotised people.'[28]

The audience could only repeat the words of Joan: 'There are miracles!' Ermolova played Joan of Arc for eighteen years. In 1886 she played Schiller's Mary Stuart to Fedotova's Queen Elizabeth, but besides the European romantic repertoire, she also performed in many Russian plays. Amongst her best roles were Negina in *Artists and Admirers* and Larisa in *The Dowerless Girl*, and in later life, Kruchinina in *Guilty Without Guilt*. Ermolova worked at the Maly Theatre until 1921. For the last seven years of her life she hid in her big house on Tverskoi Boulevard, no longer saw people, retreated deeper into religion and almost stopped speaking.

If Ermolova was the embodiment of an 'ideal' woman in the 1880s to 1890s, the embodiment of the 'ideal' man was Aleksandr Lensky, Ermolova's partner in many productions. If Ermolova's childhood reminds one of Joan of Arc, Lensky's youth resembles a Dickensian story: the illegitimate son of Duke Gagarin and Olga Vervitsiotti, an opera singer who was Corsican by birth and British by nationality, Lensky lost both his parents at the age of ten. He was adopted by Kornely Poltavtsev, a tragedian of the Maly Theatre, who was married to another of Gagarin's illegitimate children. After several difficult years in the provincial theatre, Lensky came to Moscow, where he joined the Maly Theatre in 1876.

Lensky was an object of admiration and a role model for a whole generation of young people in the 1880s. 'I admired Lensky: I admired his languishing, melancholy big blue eyes, his gait and movements, his incredibly expressive and handsome hands; I loved his charming tenor voice . . . Of course I tried to imitate his virtues (unavailingly!) and his mistakes (successfully!)' wrote Stanislavsky.[29] Young men of the 1880s imitated Lensky's acting and his famous 'velvety voice' in real life: 'Even courting ladies and winning women's hearts, young people acted like Lensky, trying to acquire his melancholy glance and slightly frowning brow – just like Lensky in *Hamlet!*'[30]

Lensky first played Hamlet for his benefit performance in 1877 – almost ten years after the play had last been produced at the Maly. It was definitive for its generation. 'His poetic Hamlet attracted young people like a magnet,' remarked Amfiteatrov.[31] Lensky's Hamlet was too gentle, too vulnerable and too intelligent for his own time. He knew too much about the vileness of the world around him and the uselessness of action; and this knowledge only increased in him the bitter sense of his own weakness. Lensky's Hamlet was disappointed in the world around him, but he was not cynical.

It was probably this Hamlet that Chekhov's Ivanov referred to when he exclaimed: 'I'm dying of shame at the thought that I, a healthy, strong man, have somehow got transformed into a sort of Hamlet, or Manfred, or one of those "superfluous" people.'[32] In spite of all the differences, Chekhov's Ivanov and Lensky's Hamlet both suffered from the realisation of duty and an inability to perform it at the same time. These themes of Lensky's Hamlet were the main preoccupations of the Russian intelligentsia in the 1880s and 1890s. Vsevolod Meyerhold named Lensky as the best actor he had ever known: 'Lensky had a rare gift of *lightness* – this does not mean that he was lightweight or superficial, it means that even in the most difficult situations, he could effortlessly show all the nuances; even at a slow tempo, he was in constant motion. Even playing Hamlet he was light. He could be serious, tragic, deep and – light at the same time.'[33]

This gave Lensky a very wide range: from Hamlet to Benedick in *Much Ado about Nothing* and Famusov in *Woe from Wit*, a role he first played in 1887. Lensky was not too concerned with the political or social significance of Famusov. A plump old man with chubby cheeks, a double chin and a tuft of hair, Lensky's Famusov was a typical comic father 'in a dressing gown' – extremely talkative, not clever, rather harmless. His main concern was to find a good husband for his daughter; when he asked Chatsky about his marriage plans, fear and doubt were transparent in his question. Lensky was probably one of the most influential actors at the end of the century. The actors of the following generation not only admired Lensky, but also took a lot from him. His *Actor's Notes and Notes about Facial Expression and Make-up* were essential reading for anyone interested in theatre at the time.

Stanislavsky studied and annotated Lensky's articles and imitated his performance in *Much Ado about Nothing*.

In many ways Lensky paved the way for Stanislavsky, and it is symbolic that in 1898, when Stanislavsky and Nemirovich-Danchenko started the Moscow Art Theatre, Lensky opened the New Theatre, where he intended to work with his students and young actors. The New Theatre was formally a branch of the Maly Theatre, though in fact Lensky had hoped it would overcome the routine of the Imperial Theatre system. He directed several brilliant productions including Shakespeare's *The Tempest* (1905) and *A Midsummer Night's Dream* (1899), and he had plans to put on *The Merchant of Venice* and Aleksei Tolstoy's *Tsar Fyodor Ioannovich*. However, in 1907, a year before Lensky died, the New Theatre was closed.

For all its reputation for conservatism, the Maly was tolerant to different acting talents and styles. One of the best examples of this pluralism was the coexistence of the two leading actors, Aleksandr Lensky and Aleksandr Yuzhin, who differed in everything – temperament, style and background.

Aleksandr Yuzhin-Sumbatov was descended from the aristocratic Georgian family of Prince Sumbatov. His passion for the theatre started early, when he and his friend Vladimir Nemirovich-Danchenko played in amateur productions at Tiflis Grammar School. After a few years studying law at St Petersburg University, young Prince Sumbatov became an actor, and in 1882 he appeared as Chatsky in *Woe from Wit* at the Maly Theatre under the name of 'Yuzhin' which in Russian means 'from the south'. About the same time he began to write plays. Kugel has suggested that the best epigraph to Yuzhin's life and his acting would be the words written above Shakespeare's Globe Theatre: '*totus mundus agit histrionem*'. 'Acting was not his "second", but his first nature. At home, in his study, on stage, at dinner – he was the same man. He delivered speeches in real life just as he did on stage. A brilliant and talented actor, Yuzhin perceived life through the prism of the theatre.'[34]

'Yuzhin was demonically hard working, every step he made was filled with energy, persistence and determination,' remarked Nemirovich-Danchenko.[35] These were also the features of Yuzhin's stage characters. Yuzhin belonged to the world of Shakespeare, Schiller and Hugo. Yuzhin's Richard the Third, Dunors in *Joan of Arc*, and Hernani and Ruy Blas in Victor Hugo's romantic dramas, had something in common: they were men of action, with strong wills and intellects. Even his Hamlet 'was not a weak-willed, poetic and melancholy prince, but a nervous man with a strong spirit who hesitated only because he was not sure whether he should take vengeance on the King or not. But as soon as the King's guilt is proven Hamlet stops hesitating and becomes a man of action, just as he had been a man of ideas before.'[36]

'Between the two concepts of the world: "to be" or "to seem", Yuzhin chose the latter. Although quite short in real life Yuzhin always seemed very tall, grand and monumental on the stage. This optical illusion always amazed me. Or rather it was his real height that amazed me,' remarked Kugel.[37] Yuzhin's theatricality was best expressed in his own plays, which were 'melodramatic like the Caucasus itself'. Kugel vividly depicted a scene from one of Yuzhin's plays, *The Chains*:

> Yuzhin sees a character as a stage image: he stands, half turned to the stalls. Half of his face is hard as stone while the other half of his face lights up with triumph. He wears a tie with a large pearl . . . Yes, a pearl . . . A cane . . . His eyelids are densely pencilled with heavy dabs of Indian ink on his eyelashes. And he says . . . What does he say? He says:
> 'These are not arms, they are chains . . . (*through his teeth* – "tchains"), iron manacles . . .' (*shakes his hands as though threshing*).
> How many actors anticipated this phrase like the Blessing! How many storms of applause were evoked . . .! Do you want to analyse this speech and ask why his tiepin sticks out? It is possible. But what for? Do not touch the wonderful world of theatrical illusion. It may crumble . . .[38]

The finale of Yuzhin's life was no less theatrical than his plays. He died in Nice, on his seventieth birthday, sitting at his desk and finishing his play *Rafael*. The last word he wrote was '*Konets*' (The End). *Totus mundus agit histrionem.*

The company of the Maly in the 1880s to 1890s could be best described as a constellation of great personalities. They were not ensemble actors, but having spent so many years acting together they became like a big family in the 'House of Shchepkin', as the Maly was known. Yury Yuriev, who started his career at the Maly, wrote: 'The company was notable for its cohesion, its sense of responsibility and its serious attitude to work. This resulted in a unity of style in productions and a mutual understanding on

19. Vasily Samoilov as Shylock in *The Merchant of Venice*. Maly Theatre, 1894.

the stage. There were no directors at that time, yet there was *collective* directing by the first-rate actors.'[39]

The best example of the Maly family acting was the 1893 production of Ostrovsky's comedy *Wolves and Sheep* where all the stars gathered together for Mikhail Sadovsky's benefit performance. *Wolves and Sheep* also revealed one of the most sophisticated actresses of the new generation: Elena Leshkovskaya, who played Glafira. Critics called Leshkovskaya 'the best grande-coquette of Russia'. In her sharp and often bitter portrayals of seductive and vicious coquettes there was always a Wildean irony and a strong sense of *fin de siècle*. Leshkovskaya, however, was the only new voice in the Maly Theatre at the turn of the century. The family of great actors was growing old, and productions like *Wolves and Sheep* were becoming more and more rare. The troupe was suffering from increasing size, traditionalism and lack of fresh blood. With the opening of the Moscow Art Theatre, the Maly could no longer play the dominant role in Russian theatre and was generally becoming a backwater for cultivated conservatism.

2. St Petersburg

On 15 August 1893, Yury Yuriev arrived in St Petersburg. He had graduated from the Maly Theatre Drama School a few months earlier and was about to join the Maly Theatre, when against his will he had been appointed to the Imperial Aleksandrinsky Theatre by its director Viktor Krylov. Once in St Petersburg, Yuriev set out to familiarise himself with the city:

> With mixed feelings I walked around the Aleksandrinsky Theatre and went back to the Nevsky Prospect. I walked to The Admiralty, then through the arc to the Winter Palace and to the Neva River. Petersburg amazed me: the palaces, the massiveness of its cathedrals, the width of the Neva, the general stateliness of the northern capital. The traffic was much more lively than in Moscow at that time. And even the people in the street looked completely different. There was more shine and elegance to them. A lot of military officers in most varied the chic uniforms were walking along the streets.[40]

'Shine', 'elegance', 'chic' – those words perfectly describe the Aleksandrinsky Imperial Theatre in St Petersburg. Unlike the Maly, which was only formally called Imperial, the Aleksandrinsky Theatre had every right to this noble title. 'Its closeness to the court set a particular seal to its profile.'[41]

For young Yuriev, a disciple of the 'Second Moscow University', St Petersburg seemed alien: 'For most of the Petersburgers the theatre was just an entertainment and had little cultural importance.'[42] The audience consisted mostly of servants and bureaucrats, people who were not interested in advanced liberal ideas or political movements, and preferred light and elegant French comedies to the tragedies of *Joan of Arc* or *Mary Stuart*. 'There is enough drama in real life,' was their motto. The repertoire of the Aleksandrinksy Theatre consequently consisted mainly of classical Russian comedy (such as Gogol's *The Government Inspector*, Griboedov's *Woe from Wit*, and Fonvizin's *The Minor* and contemporary Russian and French plays and vaudevilles depicting the manners of modern society. The plays most successful at the box-office included Viktor Krylov's *The Society for the Encouragement of Boredom*, adapted from a French comedy, and V. Rodislavsky's *For Bread and Water*, from a French vaudeville.

St Petersburg was more European than Moscow, not only in repertoire and attitude to theatre, but even in stage equipment. Yuriev was amazed: 'For the first time in my life I saw electric lighting in a theatre. Only last spring I played on the stage of the Maly Theatre which was lit by gas.'[43] Moreover, actors at the Aleksandrinsky were more skilful and effortless, and had greater flexibility, subtlety and sense of style and rhythm. According to Yuriev:

> The style of rehearsing was very different from the Maly . . . Everybody rehearsed more or less on their own: they cared only about themselves, their own role and position on the stage with no regard to the scene as a whole . . . This . . . obviously affected the production and the acting of even most talented actors. There was no cohesion among the actors so the logical links between the scenes were missing. Yet there were brilliant individual performances; one could see a whole range of deep and colourful characters, but mostly like the unconnected . . . talented appearances of great touring actors, who happened to play in the same performance.[44]

In fact, many actors at the Aleksandrinsky learned their craft touring in provincial theatres. Thus, in 1881, the legendary Pelagea Strepetova emerged from the provinces and joined the Aleksandrinsky Theatre. Unattractive and suffering from a congenital illness, she was a foundling and had grown up in poverty. Strepetova's physical weakness was matched by her spiritual fervour. Her characters reminded the audiences of *narodniks*, women-terrorists and martyrs. Strepetova's sense of tragedy was as innate as her talent. Tragedy was at the very core. She played Katerina in Ostrovsky's *The Storm* and Lizaveta in Pisemsky's *A Bitter Fate* as characters driven by a frantic sense of sin and guilt, who were possessed by the desire for self-sacrifice. Although Strepetova never played Dostoevsky's characters on the stage, she was one of the them in reality. One critic wrote: 'When Strepetova played Katerina she did not have to pretend. When she talked about angels and the Last Judgement, she experiened that religious ecstasy and rapture. Her acting was never on one level, it scaled the heights and plumbed the depths.'[45] Strepetova's gifts ran counter to the very nature of the Aleksandrinsky Theatre, which, as one of its actors put it, was 'congested with comedians'. Ostrovsky was right when he wrote: 'Strepetova is superfluous here, she seems like a stranger who came to play in five or six productions . . . the plays in which she can show the best side of her talent must have sincerity and strength, they must also be adjusted to suit her abilities. Such plays do not appear often.'[46] In 1890 Strepetova left the Aleksandrinsky Theatre; the audience, 'fed up with tragedies in every-day life', preferred Davydov, Varlamov and Savina who brought optimism and vitality.

Konstantin Aleksandrovich Varlamov was adored by his audience and known in St Petersburg as 'Uncle Kostya', a name which represented his personality as well as his stage persona. 'Uncle Kostya' was a man of Rabelaisian appearance with an enormous paunch, elephantine legs – and a talent to match. In 1891 Nemirovich-Danchenko noted: 'Varlamov is a colossal talent. In terms of the gifts nature gave him, it is hard to find an actor of equal talent in the whole of Russia.'[47] 'Varlamov essentially embodied many typically Russian qualities and peculiarities. He was good-natured, warm and simple, considerate and benevolent. He accepted people and the world for what they were. Everybody was his friend and he was prepared to feed everybody till they were full.'[48] This created the impression that he personally knew everyone in the audience and that everyone knew him – just as he was 'Uncle Kostya', so his characters were all relatives and friends for the audience.

Varlamov's characters were usually simple, practical and down-to-earth; people who did not worry much about the universe. He was ideal as Dogberry in *Much Ado about Nothing*, and the merchant Bolshov from Ostrovsky's *It's a Family Affair*, as Bottom in *A Midsummer Night's Dream*, and the fantastic and kind Tsar Berendei in Ostrovsky's fairytale *The Snow Maiden*. Varlamov accepted the characters he played with all their weaknesses – they were all relatives. In his performance, even such crooks as Groznov in *The Truth is Good, but Happiness Better* were not really evil, they 'simply did not recognise the difference between good and bad, just like Eve before the Fall'.[49]

Varlamov was one of the most versatile actors at the Aleksandrinsky Theatre: he felt at home in Chekhov's world playing Semenov-Pishchik in *The Cherry Orchard*, and in Meyerhold's stylised production of *Don Juan* where he was Sganarelle. Varlamov had a unique and intuitive sense of style: 'his ad libs and gags never sounded alien to the author's text . . . but merged with it'.[50] Like a commedia dell'arte actor, Varlamov improvised on behalf of his character, combining the role he played with his own personality. But because Varlamov knew the audience loved him whatever he did, he only used one tenth of his potential. 'An embodiment of Russian qualities,' Varlamov was also the embodiment of Russian laziness – 'jolly Oblomov', as Kugel called him. He was not ambitious, never worked on his parts, and as a result mostly played minor roles. He lived a quiet life, grew fat and cared little about his 'colossal' talent. He was simply 'the darling of the audience': that was his fortune and his drama.

Vladimir Nikolaevich Davydov was the direct opposite. He was conscientious, hardworking and took his talent seriously. If Varlamov was a wild plant and usually played by intuition, Davydov worked long and hard on his characters and recognised the importance of cultural tradition. If Varlamov portrayed his characters with a few broad strokes, Davydov's roles resembled a carefully laid mosaic. His part-books were covered with detailed pencil notes about the character. Although Davydov did not have Varlamov's spontaneity and genius, his characters were more precise, finished and polished. 'As an actor he was more restrained: discretion and moderation were his definitive features.'[51] Unlike Varlamov, Davydov always put some distance between himself and his characters. Davydov was an actor with a very wide range – from Figaro in *The Barber of Seville* to Akim in Tolstoy's *The Power of Darkness* and Firs in *The Cherry Orchard* – yet it was in classical Russian comedy that he made his name. From Shchepkin and Samarin, Davydov inherited the roles of Famusov in *Woe from Wit*, the Mayor in *The Government Inspector*, and Podkolyosin in *Marriage* – roles which were a touchstone for any Russian actor. To this family line Davydov added a new classical role – Raspluev in *Krechinsky's Wedding* by Sukhovo-Kobylin. As Raspluev or as Chebutykin in *The Three Sisters*, Davydov portrayed the 'little man'. Even when playing Chekhov, he retained the nineteenth-century literary and theatrical traditions. He treated all of Meyerhold's director's experiments at the Aleksandrinksy Theatre with great hostility. For him, the Aleksandrinsky was a theatre of great actors: Martynov, Samoilov, Varlamov, Davydov; and of course Savina.

From the 1880s the dominant position at the Aleksandrinsky Theatre belonged to Maria Gavrilovna Savina. It was Savina who was the real tsarina

20. Maria Savina as Maria Antonovna in *The Government Inspector* by Gogol, 1881.

in the Imperial Theatre. 'Maria Gavrilovna Savina reigned on the stage. She loved it, she could do it. Whatever happened, she always came out on top.'[52] Good brains and a winning spirit were the features Savina shared with her characters. Savina's success began in 1879, as the result of two roles: Varia in Ostrovsky and Solovyov's *The Shy Girl*, and Verochka in Turgenev's *A Month in the Country*. In *The Shy Girl* Savina created a new type of Russian *ingénue* – no longer sentimental, weak and suffering, but sharp, energetic, wilful and obstinate. Savina's Verochka was a subtle mixture of youthful inexperience and the awakening resolve of a real woman. Amfiteatrov wrote: 'From her first appearance you can see the type; extremely charming, graceful, half adolescent, half woman; not yet quite mature, but already very attractive. She is already in love, but does not realise it. Her youthful impulses change like April weather; from heavy showers to hot sun.'[53] Turgenev, who came to congratulate Savina in the interval, was astonished: 'Verochka . . . have I really written this Verochka? I did not even pay attention to her when I was writing . . . the focal point of the play is Natalya Petrovna . . . your Verochka is alive!'[54] It was this dark-complexioned girl wth large black eyes that the 61-year-old Turgenev fell in love with.

For Savina, 'understanding' a character was always based on physical experience rather than on abstract ideas. Trying to find a clue to the role of Maria Antonovna, the mayor's daughter in Gogol's *The Government Inspector*, Savina 'one day just put on a short dress, made her face up and came up to a big mirror and suddenly felt like making a curtsy. She did so like a young girl, smiled at her own reflection and immediately found the right feelings. She recognised the real Maria Antonovna in the mirror.'[55] Savina played the mayor's daughter in 1881 and it remained one of her best roles for twenty years. Her Maria Antonovna was extremely dynamic, fresh, neatly dressed, and prepared to provoke her rival mother. Evtikhy Karpov, the director of the Aleksandrinsky Theatre, recalled: 'She was a typical provincial girl who seemed to have just stepped down out of an old engraving. She was a naive, uneducated, affected creature of the 1820s who read too many novels and was filled with romantic dreams curiously mixed in a funny way with petty practicalness.'[56]

Yuriev regarded the role of Maria Antonovna as Savina's 'Joan of Arc'. This remark was not only the highest praise one could get from Ermolova's admirer, but also a definition of the nature of Savina's talent. If Ermolova was the embodiment of the tragedy in Russian theatre, 'Savina was primarily an actress for comedy. This does not mean that she was a comic actress, but, rather, that she was a non-tragic actress.'[57] She was unable to play tragedies not because of insufficient talent, but because she did not have a tragic sense of the world. Even in Tolstoy's *The Power of Darkness*, the play Savina chose for her benefit performance, she played the non-tragic role of Akulina. To some extent, Savina's Akulina was a dark variation of her Maria Antonovna. Kugel wrote: 'Savina only used two gestures: her dumb Akulina had one eye half-closed, which gave her a particularly heavy, stupid and animal look; and during the lyrical conversation between Nikita and Akim, being unable to understand its meaning, she slightly swung her right leg. It was immediately apparent that she was as distant from any moral questions as she was from the star Sirius.'[58] Yet plays of this quality were rare in Savina's repertoire. She was much more interested in women of her own time and mostly appeared in contemporary plays often written specially for her by second-rate playwrights. She played tomboys who took their lives into their own hands; energetic, cold, greedy careerists and adventuresses; unfaithful wives and flirtatious mistresses. They all had common sense and were willing to compromise. Savina was the complete opposite of Pelagea Strepetova. If Stepetova lacked rationality on the stage, Savina was 'the common sense of Russian theatre' as Kugel called her.

Savina and her characters grew old together: when she returned 24 years after her debut to perform in *A Month in the Country* in 1903, her 25-year-old Verochka grew into a 49-year-old Natalya Petrovna. 'Savina's Natalya Petrovna resembled the old family portraits, that were usually hung over a big sofa in the studies of aristocratic manor-houses . . . Her manners, her walk, the way she spoke showed the time and milieu of Turgenev's characters.'[59] *A Month in the Country* was directed by Aleksandr Sanin who worked at the Moscow Art Theatre until 1902, and it was hardly surprising that the play reminded many in the audience of Stanislavsky's productions of Chekhov. But although *A Month in the Country* was the most Chekhovian production of the Aleksandrinsky Theatre, Chekhov himself remained alien to the Aleksandrinsky Theatre. In 1896 Savina very wisely turned down the role of Nina in the first production of *The Seagull*. Her Arkadina in the 1902 revival of the play was not a success. Perhaps Savina was too much of Arkadina in real life to be able to play the character on the stage. She did not belong to Chekhov's world; she did not feel the tragedy of people for whom time is slipping by. Savina was Turgenev's actress and belonged to the nineteenth century. Chekhov's plays belonged to the twentieth century and required a new type of actress.

And a new actress emerged. She came to the Aleksandrinsky Theatre in 1896, the year that *The Seagull* was premiered, and there was something symbolic in this 'joint' appearance. Her name was Vera Fedorovna Komissarzhevskaya. 'She was a child of our century, with its exposed nerves and sharp spiritual bent . . . her pain hacked into the audience. There was a frightening closeness to life, and a frightening agreement between audience and stage. She did not cry out in anguish, these were the quiet and suppressed moans of our contemporaries.'[60] Komissarzhevskaya felt and expressed the quality of the approaching twentieth century with a force similar to the poetry of Aleksandr Blok. When she died it was a national tragedy and Blok wrote a poem in which he compared Komissarzhevskaya to 'the Promised Spring'.[61] She was not a tragic actress, like Ermolova, rather, 'she was the great dramatic actress of this century.'[62]

Vera Komissarzhevskaya was born into a highly artistic family. Her father, Fyodor Komissarzhevsky, was a famous opera tenor and one of the founder members of the Society for Art and Literature, where Stanislavsky enjoyed his first success. Yet, despite her background, Komissarzhevskaya's theatre career started unusually late, when she was nearly thirty. 'Komissarzhevskaya became an actress all of a sudden, as if someone woke her up from a deep sleep and called her to the stage.'[63]

After taking several lessons from Davydov in St Petersburg, Komissarzhevskaya moved to Moscow in 1890. She played in several amateur productions at the Society for Art and Literature, including Tolstoy's *The Fruits of Enlightenment* directed by Stanislavsky, but she soon left Moscow and in 1893 signed a contract with one of the best provincial theatres run by Nikolai Sinelnikov in Novocherkassk. In 1894 Komissarzhevskaya joined Nezlobin's company in Vilno. Two years later she was invited to join the Aleksandrinsky Theatre. Komissarzhevskaya took her repertoire with her: Varia in *The Shy Girl*, Rosie in *The Battle of Butterflies*, and Klerkhen in *Sodom's End* by Hermann Sudermann. In these roles she reminded some of the young Savina: the same type of *ingénue* – bright, fresh, sincere. Yet something was different. As Lunacharsky noticed, 'the bright wings of these fluttering "butterflies" were touched by black edging'.[64]

The sense of doom and anxiety which the audience sensed in Komissarzhevskaya's girls became particularly apparent in her next two roles: Larisa in *The Dowerless Girl* and Nina Zarechnaya in *The Seagull*.

'Komissarzhevskaya linked Larisa with Nina: in both characters she saw an impassioned desire and a tragic impossibility to break from the deadening routine of daily life.'[65] Komissarzhevskaya's Larisa 'seemed strange and abrupt in the splendour of the Aleksandrinsky Theatre'.[66] The audience saw not a melodramatic story of the life of a poor provincial girl in some remote Russian town, which was the usual interpretation, but a story which was happening here and now: the tragedy of an intelligent modern woman. It was this sense of the present in her acting, that disturbed the audience. 'She paints her watercolours with real blood,' remarked Kugel.[67]

On 17 October 1896 Komissarzhevskaya played Nina in *The Seagull*. The fiasco of the first performance of *The Seagull* is one of the best documented legends in Russian theatre.[68] The actors loved the play, and although they only had nine rehearsals, they felt confident. Karpov, who directed the play, recalled Chekhov saying at rehearsal: 'Komissarzhevskaya plays Nina as if she were in my soul and had overheard my intonations. What a subtle and sensitive actress.'[69] Disaster struck where it was least expected. The play was announced as a benefit performance for a much-loved comic character-actress, Elizaveta Levkeeva. She was particularly popular with the low-brow audience who gathered in the Aleksandrinsky Theatre to greet their favourite actress and enjoy a new comedy (the playbill stated clearly: '*The Seagull*, a comedy in four acts'). The audience felt cheated, for not only was Levkeeva not to appear on the stage, but 'the comedy' was not funny either. Nina's speech in Treplev's play evoked jeers, guffaws and loud remarks from the first rows of the auditorium. The morning papers unanimously savaged the play. 'Unprecedented scandal' and '*The Seagull* turned out to be a turkey' were the mildest remarks.

However, Komissarzhevskaya reported to Chekhov after the second performance: 'I've just returned from the theatre, dear Anton Pavlovich. Victory is ours. The play is a complete, unanimous success, just as it ought to be, just as it had to be. How I'd like you . . . to hear the unanimous cry of "Author". Your – no – our Seagull, because I have merged with her for ever heart and soul – is alive; her suffering and her faith are so ardent that she will compel many others, to have faith. "Think of your vocation and have no fear of life."'[70] Even if Komissarzhevskaya exaggerated the general success of the performance, which was far from 'ideal' (the letter was written at midnight in a state of high excitement), she had every reason to say that she merged

21. Vera Komissarzhevskaya as Ophelia in *Hamlet*, 1900.

with Chekhov's character, and not only when she was on the stage. In Nina, the seagull, Komissarzhevskaya recognised her own self. Her Nina was not the naive country girl with dreams of the stage whom we usually see, but a talented actress who was born to appear in Treplev's symbolist play. For her, Treplev's play was the key to the whole part; she related to it so that when she was reciting: 'I am lonely. Once in a hundred years I open my lips to speak and in this void with none to hear me my voice echoes mournfully' (Act I), she saw these words as a perfect description of her own place in art.

Komissarzhevskaya's personality was inseparable from her roles. Her letters, often signed with her characters' names, not only contain many hidden quotations from *The Seagull*, but their very tone and language resemble Nina's soliloquy about 'the universal soul'. Indeed, the word 'soul' is repeated in these letters with extraordinary frequency, even for a Russian actress. In 1902 she wrote to Nikolai Khodotov, an actor at the Aleksandrinsky Theatre:

> In my soul I am standing on the threshold of great events. My destiny is at stake. This is my faith: 'Art should only reflect the eternal, and the only thing which is eternal is the soul.' That means the only important thing is the life of the soul in all its forms. Do you remember I told you that there is no need to create typical characters? I did not explain it then, but that was what I meant.[71]

Komissarzhevskaya's acting technique (if it can be called a technique) differed from all other actresses of her time. Some critics called her a symbolist, some a realistic actress. In fact her acting, just like Chekhov's drama, was an inseparable mixture of symbolism and realism. She considered what she called 'truth' to be the only criteria of art: 'I can say the same thing about the artist's soul as Jesus said about himself: "I am the truth."'[72] The confessional, homiletic elements were as strong in Komissarzhevskaya's acting as they were in her letters. A sense of love and compassion for her ever-suffering characters dominated Komissarzhevskaya's life on stage. 'Was it not this predominance of the ethical element in Komissarzhevskaya's acting that made her so exceptionally popular (100,000 people came to her funeral!)?' wondered Kugel.[73]

Contemporaries were startled by the contrast between the physical fragility and tenderness of Komissarzhevskaya's characters and their spiritual stoicism.

> Komissarzhevskaya's characters believed in a wonderful future for the whole of humanity. But they were impatient. They wanted it now. They did not want to wait, just as Komissarzhevskaya's young contemporaries who came to her theatre in the midst of the revolutionary events of 1904–5 did not want to wait either. 'Give me my Kingdom, my kingdom on the table!' Komissarzhevskaya demanded as Hilda in

Ibsen's *The Master Builder*, and the whole audience burst into applause responding to this form of civic and spiritual maximalism.[74]

Komissarzhevskaya was 'all or nothing and no compromise'. This purely Russian concept of 'spiritual maximalism' determined all her endeavours. In spite of a good repertoire (Ophelia, Desdemona, Margarete in *Faust*, Aglaya in the adaptation of Dostoevsky's *The Idiot*) and the great success she had at the Aleksandrinsky Theatre, Komissarzhevskaya felt restless and constrained. In 1902 she left the Imperial stage and went on tour – in search of a new and ideal 'kingdom'.

In 1904, in the electric atmosphere that preceded the first Russian revolution, Komissarzhevskaya opened her Drama Theatre in St Petersburg. Her passionate desire for changes both in art forms and in 'life forms' made her join the group of revolutionary playwrights who were led by Maksim Gorky and his publishing house, Znanie. Their plays were supposed to make up the repertoire of the Drama Theatre. The revolution for Komissarzhevskaya had ethical, rather than political meaning. It was the romantic symbol of a new and better life, not a power struggle. At the beginning of 1905, Komissarzhevskaya could often be seen at revolutionary gatherings 'in a very simple black dress with white button-up collar, silent and pale'. Her face expressed extraordinary seriousness and almost childlike reverence for what was happening. At charity concerts she often read Gorky's 'Song of the Falcon' and 'Song of the Stormy Petrel'. An idealist, fascinated by the works of Nietzsche and the concept of an 'ideal man', it was hardly surprising that Komissarzhevskaya found Gorky so attractive. In 1904 he symbolised the Stormy Petrel. In 1904 Komissarzhevskaya's theatre premiered Gorky's *Summer Folk* and the storm broke: the production turned into a political demonstration, the play was banned after only twenty performances. Shortly afterwards Gorky was arrested for his revolutionary activities. Yet, neither *Summer Folk* nor the 1905 production of *Children of the Sun* were great artistic achievements, though both had an incendiary effect on their audiences.

During her first two seasons, Komissarzhevskaya played Varvara in *Summer Folk* and Lisa in *Children of the Sun*, as well as Ibsen's Nora and Hilda. However, revolutions and 'thunderstorms' never last for long and Komissarzhevskaya's first theatre, which opened on the eve of the 1905 revolution, ceased to exist almost immediately after its end. In 1906 Komissarzhevskaya's theatre changed its address and direction. The

Drama Theatre became the famous Theatre on Ofitserskaya, and Gorky was replaced by the symbolist poets of Blok's circle, and directors like Meyerhold and Evreinov. This theatre was equally short-lived. None of these theatres became a permanent home for Komissarzhevskaya. An inability to settle down and live 'like others' was one of her main characteristics, as it was of her characters. She appeared at a moment of transition in Russian life and art, and spent her life accordingly – in perpetual transition.

In 1908 Komissarzhevskaya renounced the stage. Her ambition was to found a drama school, where she wanted to teach first of all 'new people' and after that actors. This was not to be. In 1910, touring in Tashkent, where she was trying to earn money for her school, Komissarzhevskaya caught smallpox, Meyerhold remarked: 'She died not of smallpox, but of the same illness as Gogol – silent despair.'[75]

Towards the end of the century the need for a new type of theatre became obvious in Russia and elsewhere. New 'free' and 'independent' theatres opened all over Europe, and in St Petersburg such a theatre was that of Aleksei Sergeevich Suvorin, a journalist, publisher, playwright and theatre critic who was one of the most controversial figures of the period. The son of a soldier, Suvorin began his career as a history teacher in a village school. In the 1860s he started to publish articles in liberal Russian papers and acquired a reputation as a progressive journalist. In 1876 he bought *The New Times*, a St Petersburg daily newspaper, and soon he became a media magnate with editions of *The New Times* and its supplements selling across the country. Notorious for its chauvinistic and conservative views, Suvorin's newspaper was nonetheless one of the most popular papers in Russia. It was also the paper in which Chekhov first published his short stories. *The New Times* was aimed at a middle-class readership, or rather it aimed to shape a new middle class and their tastes.

> The newspaper addressed itself to each of its readers in a personal and polite way ... It did not call: 'Rise up, Russian man!' The tone of the newspaper was completely different: 'Think for yourself, dear Nikolai Ivanovich' ... It appealed to people's common sense ... and proclaimed the superiority of privacy over civic duty. Suvorin advised his readers: 'Do not worry so much about the fate of the universe and how to save your country, be simpler and think more about your own home and work!'[76]

22. Lidiya Yavorskaya in Berton and Simon's *Zaza*, 1898.

Suvorin's own plays were also written to suit middle-class tastes. They varied from historical dramas (*Tsar Dmitry the Imposter and Princess Ksenia*) and tragedies (*Medea*) to a comedy of manners (*The Question*) and vaudevilles, but most of them were rather mediocre. Yet, paradoxically, Suvorin as a person was not one of the members of 'his audience'. He had refined tastes in art and literature and his critical articles were highly respected by his contemporaries. He was one of the first to notice young Chekhov and the only person who publicly supported him after the premiere of *The Seagull*. Many Russian intellectuals who loathed Suvorin's newspaper kept close personal contact with its publisher.

The new Theatre of the Literary and Artistic Society, acquired by Suvorin in 1895, was originally planned not as a commercial enterprise, but as a rather elitist independent theatre for the Russian intelligentsia. Unlike other private theatres of the time Suvorin's tried to be different from the

Imperial stage. Nemirovich-Danchenko advised Suvorin to find plays first, then form a company: 'If you would manage to get the censors' permission for two of the most interesting plays in the Russian repertoire – *The Power of Darkness* and *Tsar Fyodor Ioannovich*, you should then try to find not a *jeune premier*, an *ingénue*, a *grande dame*, etc., but specific actors for these plays.'[77] Using his powerful connections, Suvorin managed to get the censorship lifted on both plays. (Three years later this enabled Nemirovich-Danchenko and Stanislavsky to open the Moscow Art Theatre with *Tsar Fyodor*.) Suvorin was under no financial constraints and managed to gather a talented company, including Yavorskaya, Orlenev, Domasheva, Strepetova, Sudbinin, Dalmatov and others. Evtikhy Karpov, *narodnik* and the author of several naturalistic plays about the hardship of peasants' personal lives, was invited to be artistic director. Karpov worked in Suvorin's theatre for only one year (in 1896 he was invited to the Aleksandrinsky Theatre), but it turned out to be a most promising period.

The number of premieres in the first season – thirty-four – and their diversity, was astonishing. The season, which started with Ostrovsky's *The Storm*, included: *The Power of Darkness, Hannele*, three productions of Turgenev (including an adaptation of his novel, *The Smoke*), Ibsen's *A Doll's House*, Schiller's *The Maid of Orleans*, Rostand's *Princess Lointaine*, Victor Hugo's *Angelo, Tyrant of Padua* and Maeterlinck's *Interior*. Each of these plays may have been a masterpiece in its own right, but the combination of Tolstoy's naturalistic tragedy with Rostand's neoromantic play and Maeterlinck's symbolist drama was bewildering. The first season demonstrated two trends: a taste for good literature and an all-devouring appetite. The first trend soon disappeared; the latter unfortunately remained. After the first season of high-quality plays, the theatre became flooded with pot-boilers. Suvorin's theatre was turning into yet another 'supplement' of *The New Times* catering for an audince with similar tastes. In 1903 Chekhov wrote to his wife: 'I would not give my play [*The Cherry Orchard*] to Suvorin even if he offered me 100,000 roubles. I despise his theatre.'[78] Suvorin's theatre largely owed this negative reputation to the 1900 production of an anti-Semitic play, *The Sons of Israel* by Litvin and Krylov, which produced an outcry from the Russian intelligentsia so that at the opening night the actors were pelted with apples, galoshes and other missiles.

Yet this scandal helped one of the actresses of Suvorin's theatre, Lidia Yavorskaya, to promote her own career. Originally recommended to

Suvorin by Chekhov, Yavorskaya became one of the leading actresses of Suvorin's theatre. She was particularly good in plays by Rostand and the younger Dumas, where she combined neoromanticism with the features of art nouveau and fin de siècle. In *The Lady of the Camellias* and in *Princess Lointaine*, Yavorskaya tried to imitate Sarah Bernhard. In her search for fame, Yavorskaya used everything, from her somewhat extravagant lifestyle to affiliation with left-wing playwrights such as Gorky and Chirikov. If Komissarzhevskaya genuinely believed in liberal ideas, for Yavorskaya they were merely a way to gain publicity. After the scandal of *The Smugglers* Yavorskaya made a spectacular exit from Suvorin's theatre and, with her husband, Prince Baryatinsky, opened the New Theatre, 'where for the next five years they presented a mixed repertoire of contemporary "problem" plays, boulevard comedies and vehicles for Lidia from the prolific pen of her husband'.[79] After the 1905 revolution Yavorskaya left Russia and toured in France and England.

One of the most important actors in Suvorin's theatre was Pavel Orlenev (known as Orlov). Together with his stage partner Domasheva, Orlenev first appeared in short comic scenes and vaudevilles. They played two grammar school pupils who, whilst spending their summer vacation in the country, begin to discover 'new' feelings. This image of an 'adolescent with a soul of Childe Harold', which Orlenev created, was so strong that everyone was surprised when Suvorin suggested giving Orlenev the role of the vulnerable and weak-willed Tsar Fyodor Ioannovich in Aleksei Tolstoy's historical drama (1898). Orlenev's Fyodor writhed in despair, trying but unable to find solutions. His state of mind was irremediably fractured, his nerves were frayed. In Tsar Fyodor, Orlenev created a new theatrical role, the angst-ridden neurasthenic, a type which became extremely popular at the end of the century: his Raskolnikov and Mitya Karamazov launched the twentieth-century tradition of stage adaptations of Dostoevsky. Orlenev's Raskolnikov was not an intellectual, 'all his ideas were born and bred by the suffering of his soul, whereas in Dostoevsky's novel Raskolnikov's will to commit a crime derives from the anguish of his proud intellect . . . Orlenev's Raskolnikov was touching and pitiable . . . in a way he was closer to Marmeladov and Myshkin . . . than to Napoleon.'[80] In 1901 Orlenev left Suvorin's theatre, feeling 'constrained and bored in Suvorin's theatre, just as Komissarzhevskaya had felt restrained and bored in the Aleksandrinsky Theatre.'[81] And like Komissarzhevskaya, Orlenev was a wandering star. He toured in America, England, Sweden and

Norway, trying to earn money for his own theatre, and ultimately wasting his talent.

Kugel, concluding an article about Orlenev and expressing his concern about 'homeless' actors, wrote: 'An actor must have his "winter quarters", a permanent home, where he can settle down. This "home" can be just a modest ordinary theatre, with a real theatre director, with a precise timetable of rehearsals on the board, for which actors turn up on time, where everybody rehearses in accordance with each other . . . It may not be a mansion on Broadway, but it is a home where an actor can live.'[82]

Writing these lines Aleksandr Kugel paid hidden tribute to a theatre which opened a new era in the history of European culture, a theatre with a precise rehearsal schedule on the board and real theatre director: the Moscow Art Theatre.

Notes

1. Vl. I. Nemirovich-Danchenko, 'Iz rezhisserskogo ekzempliara "Ivanona"', *Teatr*, 1 (1960), 149.
2. A. Chekhov, *The Oxford Chekhov*, tr. and ed. Ronald Hingley (9 vols., London, New York and Toronto, 1964–80), vol. II, p. 225.
3. For management and administration at the Imperial Theatres in the 1880s and 1890s see Laurence Senelick (ed.), *National Theatre in Northern and Eastern Europe, 1746–1900* (Cambridge, 1991), pp. 381–4.
4. In this period it was customary to subcontract the ownership and management of the cloakroom.
5. *Kratkii ocherk dvadtsatipiatiletnei deiatel'nosti teatra Korsha* (Moscow, 1907), pp. 28–9.
6. *Teatr i iskusstvo*, 7 (1902), 154, quoted in *Istoriia russkogo dramaticheskogo teatra*, ed. E. G. Kholodov et al. (7 vols., Moscow, 1982–7), vol. VII, p. 278. Henceforth: *Istoriia*.
7. *Istoriia*, vol. VII, p. 275.
8. Anton Pavlovich Chekhov, *Polnoe sobranie sochinenii i pisem v tridtsati tomakh* (30 vols., Moscow, 1974–83), vol. XI (*Pis'ma*), p. 246.
9. Ibid, vol. XVI (*Sochineniia*), p. 47.
10. Stanislavski, Constantin, *My Life in Art*, tr. J. J. Robinson (London, 1962), p. 120.
11. Quoted in Iu. A. Dmitriev, *Mikhail Lentovskii* (Moscow, 1978), p. 116.
12. K. S. Stanislavskii, *Sobranie sochinenii v deviati tomakh*, ed. A. M. Smelianskii et al. (9 vols., Moscow, 1988–), vol. I, pp. 85, 518.

13. A. R. Kugel', *Teatral'nye portrety* (Leningrad,1967), p. 205.
14. Nelidov, quoted in Senelick, p. 383.
15. Ibid, p. 382.
16. Vl. I. Nemirovich-Danchenko, *Rozhdenie teatra: vospominaniia, stat'i, zametki, pis'ma* (Moscow, 1989), p. 56.
17. Fedotova, *Vospominaniia*, in N. Abalkin (ed.), *Maly Teatr SSSR 1824–1927*, vol. I (Moscow, 1978), p. 257.
18. Nemirovich-Danchenko, *Rozhdenie teatra*, p. 282.
19. A. V. Lunacharskii, 'Glikeriia Nikolaevna Fedotova', quoted in N. G. Zograf, *Maly Teatr vtoroi poloviny XIX veka* (Moscow, 1960), p. 528.
20. Kugel', p. 123.
21. Nemirovich-Danchenko, *Rozhdenie teatra*, p. 294.
22. Nikolai Efros, *M. N. Ermolova: dvadtsatipiatiletie stsenicheskoi deiatel'nosti* (Moscow, 1896), pp. 40–1.
23. F. M. Dostoevsky, *The Diary of A Writer*, tr. Boris Brasol (2 vols., London), vol. I, p. 142.
24. Vlas Doroshevich, *Rasskazy i ocherki* (Moscow, 1987), p. 253.
25. Storozhenko, in S. N. Durylin (ed.), *M. N. Ermolova: pis'ma, iz literaturnogo naslediia, vospominaniia* (Moscow, 1955), p. 330.
26. Nemirovich-Danchenko, *Rozhdenie teatra*, p. 290.
27. See Durylin (ed.), *M. N. Ermolova*, pp. 294–5.
28. The Memoirs of Margarita Zelenina in the Private Archive of M. N. Varlamova. I am grateful to M. N. Varlamova and the Ermolova museum for allowing me to consult this document.
29. Stanislavskii, *Sobranie sochinenii*, vol. I, p. 89.
30. A. V. Amfiteatrov, quoted in N. G. Zograf, *Aleksandr Pavlovich Lenskii* (Moscow, 1941), p. 13.
31. Ibid.
32. A. Chekhov, *Plays*, tr. Elizaveta Fen (Reading, 1959), p. 71.
33. Aleksandr Gladkov, *Meierkhol'd* (2 vols., Moscow, 1990), vol. II, pp. 324–5.
34. Kugel', pp. 108–9.
35. Nemirovich-Danchenko, *Rozhdenie teatra*, p. 71.
36. N. I. Storozhenko, letter to A. I. Iuzhin, quoted in Zograf, *Maly Teatr*, pp. 532–3.
37. Kugel', p. 116.
38. Ibid, p. 113.
39. Iu. M. Iur'ev, *Zapiski* (2 vols., Leningrad and Moscow, 1963), vol. I, p. 163.
40. Ibid, vol. I, pp. 314–15.
41. P. A. Markov, *O teatre* (4 vols., Moscow, 1974–7), vol. I, p. 204.
42. Iur'ev, vol. I, p. 356.
43. Ibid, vol. I, p. 330.
44. Ibid, vol. I, p. 353.

45. Sergei Iablonovskii (S. O. Potresov), *Gallereia stsenicheskikh deiatelei* (Moscow, n. d.), pp. 22–3.

46. A. N. Ostrovskii, *Polnoe sobranie sochinenii*, vol. xii (Moscow, 1952), pp. 213–14.

47. Vl. I. Nemirovich-Danchenko, *Izbrannye pis'ma*, ed. V. Ia. Vilenkin (2 vols., Moscow, 1979), vol. i, p. 63.

48. Kugel', p. 133.

49. Doroshevich, p. 321.

50. Iur'ev, vol. i, p. 424.

51. Ibid, vol. i, p. 444.

52. Ibid, vol. ii, p. 7.

53. Quoted in I. Shneiderman, *Mariia Gavrilovna Savina: 1854–1915* (Leningrad and Moscow, 1956), p. 119.

54. Nora Gottlieb and Raymond Chapman (eds.), *Letters to an Actress: The Story of Ivan Turgenev and Marya Gavrilovna Savina* (London, 1973), p. 31.

55. Iur'ev, vol. ii, p. 11.

56. Quoted in Shneiderman, p. 168.

57. Iur'ev, vol. ii, p. 11.

58. Kugel', p. 152.

59. Iur'ev, vol. ii, pp. 9–10.

60. Kugel', pp. 167–8, 171.

61. See Aleksandr Blok, *Sobranie sochinenii v vos'mi tomakh* (8 vols., Moscow and Leningrad, 1960–3), vol. v, pp. 419–20.

62. Meierkhol'd quoted in Gladkov, vol. ii, p. 326.

63. Boris Alpers, *Teatral'nye ocherki* (2 vols., Moscow, 1977), vol. i, p. 393.

64. Alpers, vol. i, p. 391.

65. Markov, vol. i, pp. 227–8.

66. Ibid.

67. Iur'ev, vol. i, p. 34.

68. See Ronald Hingley, *A New Life of Anton Chekhov* (London, 1976).

69. E. Karpov quoted in A. Ia. Al'tshuller (ed.), *Vera Fedorovna Komissarzhevskaia: pis'ma aktrisy, vospominaniia o nei, materialy* (Leningrad and Moscow, 1964), p. 216. Even after the Moscow Art Theatre's production of *The Seagull*, Chekhov continued to consider Komissarzhevskaia to be 'the ideal Nina'.

70. Michael Heim and Simon Karlinsky (eds.), *Letters of Anton Chekhov* (London, 1973), p. 283.

71. Al'tshuller, pp. 115–16.

72. Ibid, p. 81.

73. Kugel', p. 162.

74. Alpers, vol. i, p. 399.

75. Gladkov, vol. ii, p. 325.

76. Inna Solov'eva and Vera Shitova, 'A. S. Suvorin: portret na fone gazety', *Voprosy Literatury*, 2 (1977), 168, 174.

77. Nemirovich-Danchenko, *Izbrannye pis'ma*, vol. i, p. 80.

78. Ol'ga Leonardovna Knipper-Chekhova, *Vospominaniia i stat'i, perepiska s A. P. Chekhovym*, ed. V. Ia. Vilenkin (2 vols., Moscow, 1972), vol. 1, p. 223.

79. Kugel', pp. 253–4.

80. Ibid, p. 258.

81. Ibid, p. 264.

82. Kugel', p. 163.

12 Stanislavsky and the Moscow Art Theatre 1898–1938

JEAN BENEDETTI

The Moscow Art Theatre was created between 2 p.m. on 22 June and 8 a.m. on 23 June 1897 by two men who knew each other professionally but were not, and never became, close friends: Konstantin Stanislavsky, a textile magnate who, despite being officially an 'amateur', was the leading actor and director of his generation, and Vladimir Nemirovich-Danchenko, a prize-winning dramatist, critic and head of the drama section of the Philharmonic School.

It had been common knowledge that Stanislavsky was planning to launch a professional theatre company. For ten years he had been running and financing the Society for Art and Literature, which although only semi-professional, had set standards of performance that even theatres like the Maly could not match. Stanislavsky's productions were remarkable for their ensemble work, the meticulous accuracy of the sets and costumes, and their sense of period. They were not costume dramas but living representations of life as experienced in the past. His own performances were no less authentic. He refused to conform to the stereotypical view of well-known characters but presented contradictory human beings at grips with concrete problems. It was this combination of the historically specific with the humanly specific which gave his work its impact. Many saw in him the salvation of the Russian theatre, the artist who would recapture the once glorious tradition of the Maly and Shchepkin, and hand it on to future generations.

Nemirovich was at the height of his fame as a prize-winning writer of popular comedies, the darling of fashionable audiences, but, like the rest of the intelligentsia, his major concern was the reform of the Russian theatre, in particular the Maly. Like Ostrovsky before him, he submitted plans both for reorganising the management and for training young actors and, like Ostrovsky, he was thwarted by the inertia of the imperial bureaucracy. Stanislavsky's proposed new theatre might be a possible vehicle for his ideas. He wrote twice suggesting a meeting.

Stanislavsky, who was briefly in Moscow to collect his post, replied by telegram, inviting Nemirovich to lunch at the Slavyansky Bazar, the preferred restaurant of writers and intellectuals. Discussions began at two o'clock, continued on through dinner, and ended over breakfast at eight o'clock the next morning at Stanislavsky's estate in Lyubimovka. In those eighteen hours they defined the principle of an ensemble that, unlike other theatres, would be repertoire-led not actor-led. It would break with the tradition of 'types' – leading man, juvenile lead, character, the heavy, and so on – which had been established earlier in the century by imperial decree, and create a pool of actors who would play a variety of parts of varying importance ('today the lead, tomorrow an extra'). Only actors who could agree to this policy would be admitted to the company. The new theatre would, above all, play a social and educational role. It would be open to all, particularly to working-class audiences, who, if they could not afford the modestly priced seats, would attend special free performances. It would be a 'popular' theatre in everything but name since the term 'popular' caused political hackles to rise. 'Popular' meant 'subversive'.

The new theatre was thus founded on the twin pillars of the tradition of Russian realism advocated by Pushkin, Gogol and Shchepkin and the educational and social concerns of critics like Belinsky. It was the culmination of a nineteenth-century dream.

Stanislavsky and Nemirovich agreed that artistic responsibility should be divided between them: Nemirovich would have the last word in all questions of dramaturgy, and Stanislavsky in all matters of staging. This seemed an ideal arrangement. Nemirovich had an outstanding ability for dramatic analysis but recognised that he was somewhat pedestrian as a director. Stanislavsky had no literary pretensions but was a theatrical virtuoso.

Important practical questions remained to be negotiated by letter during the long summer break and it soon emerged that both men, without guile, had a hidden agenda.

What would the repertoire be? Modern or classical? A mixture of both? Nemirovich favoured an exclusively modern repertoire but recognised that there were not enough good contemporary plays to keep the theatre going. Stanislavsky wanted a mix, including light popular pieces which would be good training for the company. Nemirovich demurred. He was equally opposed to including what he called great men's trivia, such as *Twelfth Night* and *Tartuffe*.

More important was the question of finance. Nemirovich had assumed that Stanislavsky would finance the theatre out of his considerable fortune just as he had supported his Society for Art and Literature. He was disconcerted when Stanislavsky insisted on creating a public company, claiming his money was tied up in his textile business. Of the calculated Alekseev family fortune of 8m roubles only 300,000 was his.[1] Stanislavsky would invest 10,000, roubles. In this way he would protect himself against accusations that he was using his position to create a 'cheap commercial tyranny'. The new company must not only have, but be seen to have, an educational purpose. They should, therefore, look both for private investors and try to obtain a subsidy from the Moscow city council.[2]

The months preceding the opening of the theatre were a dispiriting experience for both men. Stanislavsky made a tour of his friends for support. He had not anticipated the indifference and outright hostility he was to encounter. Time after time he was rebuffed. It was only with great difficulty that the launch capital of 28,000 roubles was raised. Apart from Stanislavsky's 10,000, investments came in small sums of 1,000–2,000 roubles. The only other major investor was Savva Morozov, a wealthy industrialist who also subsidised Lenin's newspaper *Iskra*. Meanwhile, Nemirovich did battle with the bureaucracy. He drew up carefully worded applications to the authorities for a licence to perform, avoiding the word 'popular'. A society for the promotion of an 'open' theatre was created but the first season had already started by the time the inevitable refusal arrived.

Nemirovich was not happy with a public company; he mistrusted the Moscow bourgeoisie, Morozov included, and feared that at some moment artistic values would be sacrificed to commercial interests, and quality to profit. Stanislavsky's credentials were, on the other hand, above suspicion. But there was nothing Nemirovich could do so he unwillingly submitted to the inevitable.

Stanislavsky negotiated a lease on the Hermitage Theatre and rehearsals were scheduled to begin in June 1898. Unfortunately, or fortunately as it turned out, the theatre was not available during the summer and so the company assembled at Pushkino, outside Moscow, some thirty miles from Stanislavsky's country estate. Of the thirty-eight members that gathered, fourteen came from Stanislavsky's Art and Literature Society and twelve, including Meyerhold, Olga Knipper (Chekhov's future wife) and Moskvin, from the Philharmonic School.[3] They were lodged locally in the village while Stanislavsky rode over every day for rehearsals. Nemirovich was absent for the first few weeks, whilst he finished a book.

The company lived as a community, sharing domestic chores in which Stanislavsky insisted on participating, not always with happy results. Much of the solidarity of the group was created in these early summer days. Meyerhold was captivated by Stanislavsky, while Stanislavsky in his turn described Meyerhold as his 'darling'.[4]

Initially, much time was spent in discussion of the first three plays which were to be rehearsed. Meyerhold and others were deeply impressed by the seriousness of the enterprise, the attention to period and historical accuracy, and the organic nature of the productions, each of which was based on a central concept to which all other elements – design, lighting, costume – must be subordinated. Actors were tried out for various roles and casting was kept open.

The repertoire for the opening season was to consist of Aleksei Tolstoy's *Tsar Fyodor*, Shakespeare's *The Merchant of Venice*, Sophocles' *Antigone*, Goldoni's *La Locandiera*, two productions carried over from the Society for Art and Literature, *Twelfth Night* and Hauptmann's *The Sunken Bell*, and, finally, *The Seagull*.

Nemirovich arrived on 25 July 1898 and rehearsals proper began. A working method was established. Stanislavsky would prepare minutely detailed production plans, with all moves, and sometimes motivations, carefully indicated. Frequently, thumbnail sketches indicated the physical positions and relationships of the characters. Nemirovich would direct the play according to the plan, making whatever changes he thought appropriate. When confronted by *The Seagull*, Stanislavsky was at first bewildered by the half-tones, the lack of 'action'. His forte had always been crowd scenes, as is evident from the 'Yauza' scene in *Fyodor* where one stage direction is turned into a small play.[5] Nemirovich spent two days analysing and explaining Chekhov's text. Stanislavsky then retired to his brother's estate near Kharkov to work, full of misgivings. The resulting production plan was, according to Nemirovich, 'a supreme example of Stanislavsky's *creative genius* as a director'.[6]

For Nemirovich, work on *The Seagull* represented the perfect collaboration between him and Stanislavsky. It had been at his insistence that the play had been included in the first season. Stanislavsky's initial incomprehension was, in a sense, welcome. For Nemirovich the director's task was to transmit his understanding, his feeling for the particular 'flavour' of the play to the actors or, in Tolstoy's terms, to 'infect' them.

23. Anton Chekhov and Lev Tolstoy, 1900.

Now he had 'infected' Stanislavsky. He supplied the interpretation which Stanislavsky then embodied in theatrical form. This, to his mind, was the proper order of things.

The season was to open with *Fyodor*. Everything was ready; forays into the south had produced a rich variety of materials and objects to ensure historical authenticity. But the problem of censorship was still unresolved. The play contained scenes with ecclesiastics which were not generally approved of and might have to be cut. That would also throw out the extremely intricate pattern of casting across the season. The censors delivered their decision at the eleventh hour, contenting themselves with a few internal excisions which, Stanislavsky complained, mangled the verse.

The Moscow Art Open Theatre opened on 14 October 1898 in an atmosphere of latent hostility. Stanislavsky was acutely aware that many were waiting, and wanting him to fail. But he had chosen the opening play wisely. It enabled him to deploy all his acquired skills in presenting a 'spectacle'. One of his most original strokes, particularly admired by Meyerhold, was to place a cut-out of trees right across the footlights for the scene in Shuisky's garden, so that the audience saw the action through the branches.

The success of *Fyodor* was followed by a series of failures. *The Merchant of Venice* (21 October), in which Stanislavsky had Darsky play Shylock with a Jewish accent, provoked accusations that the theatre was anti-Semitic and caused Stanislavsky to abandon his intention to alternate in the role. He could not allow his reputation to reinforce an unfortunate impression. *The Sunken Bell* (19 October), *Twelfth Night* (30 October) and *La Locandiera* (2 December), fared no better. The theatre was in crisis. Although salaries were lower than in most other theatres, even for the older actors, the policy of specially through-designing each production was costly. The projected budget for the first season showed a deficit even with good houses.[7]

Everything then hinged on *The Seagull*. Tension was so great on the first night that the theatre reeked of the valerian drops everyone was taking to calm their nerves. Stanislavsky's staging was bold and original. If, in *Fyodor*, he had put a cut-out right across the front of the stage, in *The Seagull*, at the end of Act 1, he placed a row of spectators with their backs to the audience.

Initially, Nemirovich had questioned the detailed by-play suggested for this 'audience' but, as Stanislavsky pointed out, this was only a way of getting actors into the situation. Activity could be reduced once they had gained in confidence. Detailed physical actions prevented young actors falling into the trap of playing 'in general' with stereotyped gestures. It forced them to behave in a specific, natural, human manner, not like 'actors'.

There was also the question of the sound effects, such as croaking frogs, which have so obsessed theatre historians. This was not a whim on Stanislavsky's part. As he pointed out, the theatre is a noisy place. If you want to make the audience feel silence, you must focus their attention on a specific sound. The silence that follows is then properly registered and a mood is created, for actor and audience alike.[8] Interviewed in 1936, Meyerhold was quite clear that Stanislavsky's effects were poetic, bringing to the theatre the use of significant detail that had hitherto been the prerogative of literature.[9]

Following a difficult first night, played to a half-empty house, the production grew into a triumph. After the final curtain, the audience insisted a telegram of congratulation be sent to Chekhov. The theatre was saved and a stylised seagull became its logo.

But disappointments were to follow. *Antigone* played to empty houses. *Hedda Gabler* (19 February 1899) failed. The company's social policy also suffered a fatal blow. On 10 January 1899 it had given a free performance of *La Locandiera* to an audience of factory workers. The authorities were quick to point out that this had been illegal since they had omitted to obtain the approval of the fourth censor, whose task it was to vet material for presentation to working-class audiences. Any repetition could result in imprisonment. The notion of an 'open' theatre was thus effectively killed. At Chekhov's suggestion, the theatre became simply the Moscow Art Theatre (MAT).

The most wounding blow appeared to come from Chekhov himself. After *The Seagull* Stanislavsky and Nemirovich had assumed Chekhov would allow them to present *Uncle Vanya*, and were hurt and bewildered when he refused. Chekhov, however, had given an option to the Maly and considered himself honour-bound by it. Nemirovich, who was still officially on the Repertoire Committee of the Maly, then learned the management had upset Chekhov by making unacceptable demands for rewrites. He immediately approached Chekhov's sister, Maria, who handled all her brother's business affairs, with a request for permission to do the play unaltered. Permission was granted at the end of April.

Chekhov had still not seen *The Seagull* complete, he had only attended some early rehearsals, when Stanislavsky was absent. The company decided to give him a showing, without décor, at the Paradiz Theatre. This took place on 1 May. Chekhov was impressed by the production but had strong reservations about Stanislavsky's performance as Trigorin. Stanislavsky played the character in an elegant white suit and based his performance on the line 'I have no will of my own'. This interpretation had 'expert' approval; writing to Chekhov after the first night Nemirovich said that Stanislavsky had 'successfully captured the soft, weak-willed tone'. But Chekhov had seen the character quite differently, as a seedy character who 'wears check trousers and has cracked shoes', although nowhere is this indicated in the text. Six years later, when the play was revived, Stanislavsky radically revised his approach, as photographic records demonstrate.

Rather too much has been made of Chekhov's reaction, in an attempt to foster the legend of an antagonism between Chekhov and Stanislavsky which the facts do not bear out. Chekhov made a number of disparaging remarks about Stanislavsky the actor as opposed to Stanislavsky the director over the years but, in fact, hardly ever saw him act, except on this one occasion. Although he attended the first night of *The Cherry Orchard*, it is doubtful whether he saw much of the performance.[10] What is certain is that Chekhov endorsed the MAT as an institution and was willing to be identified with it, the more so since he married one of its actresses, Olga Knipper.

The 1899–1900 season opened, like the first, with a 'spectacular', Aleksei Tolstoy's *The Death of Ivan the Terrible* (29 September), followed by *Twelfth Night* (3 October), Hauptmann's *Drayman Henschel* (5 October), *Uncle Vanya* (26 October), and Hauptmann's *Lonely People* (16 December).

By the third season, 1900/1, a pattern was beginning to emerge. The opening play was usually a lavish production, in this case Ostrovsky's *Snow Maiden* (24 September), followed by works mostly of the kind that Stanislavsky later defined in his autobiography *My Life in Art* as the sociopolitical line: *An Enemy of the People* (24 October), and *The Three Sisters* (31 January).

The Three Sisters, specially written for the MAT, was the first Chekhov play Stanislavsky directed single-handedly, owing to the fact that Nemirovich was abroad on family matters. Chekhov also elected to spend the rehearsal period travelling in Italy and France, although this did not prevent him from bombarding the theatre with rewrites.[11]

24. Stanislavsky as Vershinin in the Moscow Art Theatre production of *The Three Sisters*, 1901.

25. A scene from the Moscow Art Theatre production of *The Three Sisters*, 1901.

By the time Nemirovich returned, Stanislavsky was far from happy. Knipper had proved very difficult; her wish to play Act 3 as a 'big' scene found favour with no-one, not even with Chekhov. By the first night she was still caught between two interpretations, and her Masha, although specially written for her, was not a complete success. Furthermore, Meyerhold was proving a lacklustre Tusenbach, despite all Stanislavsky's hard work, and Sudbinin was a dull Vershinin. With two major characters under par the play was at risk. Sudbinin had to be replaced. Stanislavsky took over, creating one of his greatest performances in just ten days.

The time had come to brave St Petersburg audiences. The rivalry between the two capitals was notorious; the St Petersburg aristocracy looked down on the money-making Muscovites. Critical reaction was, therefore, all too predictable. Only Stanislavsky, whose talent could not be denied, got good notices, both as actor and director, while the rest were dismissed as mediocrities.

Audiences were another matter. They responded to the social message in the repertoire. The MAT was seen as politically critical even if Stanislavsky and Nemirovich quite specifically eschewed, for aesthetic reasons, any overt ideological stance. *An Enemy of the People* provoked enthusiastic demonstrations on 26 February 1901, and an even greater outburst from students, many of whom had been at a demonstration, and some of whom had come straight out of jail, on 13 March. The many letters in the MAT archives demonstrate the extent to which audiences saw the MAT as a theatre of protest, condemning the inertia, the stultifying effect of Russian life.

The 'sociopolitical line' emerged even more strongly in Gorky's first two plays, *Small People* and *The Lower Depths*. It was Chekhov who encouraged Gorky to write for the stage, taking him to MAT rehearsals to see the creative process in action.

Small People was completed late and could not be included in the 1901/2 Moscow season, but Stanislavsky and Nemirovich took the bold decision to premiere it during the second St Petersburg tour of March 1902. They cut the play heavily but the censor insisted on further excisions, and on the first night the house was packed with policemen, although after much negotiation Nemirovich succeeded in having them suitably attired in evening dress so as not to frighten the audience.

The Lower Depths, which opened on 18 December 1902, represented an advance in working method. One evening in August the whole company went to the Khitrov market to mingle with the tramps and down-and-outs, and listen to their stories. The designer, Simov, took a large number of photographs, on which he then based the sets. Gorky also supplied detailed biographies for each character.

1902 was also a year of major reorganisation. The lease on the Hermitage Theatre ran out. With heavy financial backing from Morozov the Aumont Theatre was acquired. It was gutted, a new interior built and up-to-date equipment installed.

At the same time the company was restructured. In 1897 Nemirovich had predicted that the company could become a collective with the actors as shareholders. Morozov took over this idea, lent money to those members who could not afford to buy shares, and invested heavily himself with the proviso that no other shareholder should own a larger percentage than he. Chekhov, too, agreed to particpate. There was, however, a negative side. Some members, including Meyerhold, were deliberately excluded. Deservedly or not, Meyerhold had acquired the reputation of a 'troublemaker'. Certainly there was no love lost between him and Nemirovich. Some of the younger members, led by Meyerhold, felt the theatre should be more in tune with new developments in the arts like The World of Art group, led by Diaghilev and Alexandre Benois. Meyerhold denied being disloyal and asked for, or rather demanded, a meeting with Stanislavsky which was refused. An acrimonious exchange of letters took place. Meyerhold left before he was pushed out, taking some of the company with him to form a new, more experimental group.

The reorganised MAT company moved into the theatre in Kamergersky (now Art Theatre) Lane in the autumn. Far from feeling elated Stanislavsky was in a despondent mood. So was Nemirovich. In August he had written to Stanislavsky expressing his fears about the future. His anxieties mostly focused on the ever present, ever more influential Morozov. It seemed that all Nemirovich's fears were being confirmed. The theatre had sold out to the capitalists, to fashion. Because Morozov championed Gorky they were expected to stage the works of Gorky's imitators, the 'Gorkiad' as Nemirovich described them. They were being identified with one political tendency which was against everything they had stood for. If the theatre was successful, Nemirovich pointed out, it was because everyone could find something they liked and something they hated. Now the theatre was in danger of becoming Stanislavsky's 'club', with special facilities for his and Morozov's friends.

There was unease, too, in the productions themselves. For all the originality of Stanislavsky's initial approach to *The Lower Depths*, by the end of rehearsals the staging was hopelessly cluttered with detail so that the central meaning was lost. The same had been true of *The Power of Darkness* (5 November 1902). What had once been revelatory detail was now becoming a mannerism. In both instances Nemirovich had to clean the staging up to find the play behind the direction. It was as though, after four years of unremitting effort, exhaustion had set in.

Stanislavsky directed nothing in 1903. The only two plays premiered, *The Pillars of Society* (24 February) and *Julius Caesar* (2 October), were directed by Nemirovich. Neither was a happy experience for Stanislavsky, who found Nemirovich's dramaturgical approach no help in trying to achieve a rounded characterisation.

Nemirovich prepared *Julius Caesar* with infinite care. In accord with MAT's practice, he went to Rome with his designer in search of authenticity. His production plan was indistinguishable from Stanislavsky's plans of the period. The forum scene, with its large crowds, which Stanislavsky agreed to stage, slotted in harmoniously. Yet the resemblance was superficial. There was no agreement on basic approach: Nemirovich wanted to emphasise the political aspect to the play, the death of the republic, while Stanislavsky wanted to explore Brutus as a tragic hero. Stanislavsky, with an eye for historical truth, wondered why everyone, plebeians included, was so clean and why the clothes were so shining bright.

Successful as the production was, it was more famous as a piece of archaeology than as a theatrical experience. Parties of schoolchildren were brought to see a reproduction of Ancient Rome. For Stanislavsky a living theatre became a dead museum, an empty shell.

He kept silent, but three weeks into the run expressed his reservations to Nemirovich, unfortunately in the presence of Morozov. This provoked a furious letter from Nemirovich which marked the beginning of the real decline in their relationship and the battle for the heart and soul of the theatre.[12]

Work on *The Cherry Orchard* (17 January 1904) came as a welcome relief but its success was overshadowed by Chekhov's death in June 1904. A further blow came when Gorky severed all connection with the theatre after receiving a tactless letter from Nemirovich in which, with infinite expressions of goodwill, he demolished *Summer Folk*. Furthermore, Kachalov, the lead actor of the company after Stanislavsky, was restless and threatening to leave. Only personal loyalty to Stanislavsky stopped him.

In the new season the only real novelty was a Maeterlinck triple bill (shortly before he died Chekhov had urged Stanislavsky to stage Maeterlinck). Here Stanislavsky encountered a new aesthetic and a new set of ideas. He had to make the invisible visible, the inexpressible expressible, and turn his attention to inner processes and to the actor. However, in 1902 Valery Bryusov had published his seminal essay, 'Unnecessary Truth', a critique of the MAT style. He pointed out that realism in the theatre was in fact a matter of convention. The only 'real' thing on stage was the actor's irreducibly material body. 'The art of the theatre and the art of the actor are one and the same thing,' he stated, and, for good measure, 'The author is the servant of the actor.'[13] The Maeterlinck programme was not a success simply because Stanislavsky had not found a consistent new method of approach.

The Chekhov triple bill which followed (21 December 1904) was no more successful. Stanislavsky would have done better to revert to an earlier, original and forward-looking idea. In 1899 he had proposed an evening of short scenes, performed on an inner stage with boxes of props and costumes which the actors would dip into in full view of the audience, a kind of cinematic montage. Nemirovich had dismissed the project as impractical and Stanislavsky had not pursued it. A potentially fruitful opportunity was missed.

The last production of the 1904/5 season was *Ghosts* (31 March 1905), which Stanislavsky and Nemirovich were to co-direct. There were disagreements from the start. Stanislavsky had passed the stage of silent endurance and now openly declared that the MAT was too 'literary'. He could no longer go into rehearsal with everything cut and dried. He produced no detailed production plan, merely some notes, leaving a great deal to be explored in rehearsals. He brushed aside Nemirovich's early attempts at detailed discussion of character and changed the opening of the play on the grounds that Ekdal's entrance was insufficiently motivated in the script.

Nemirovich saw his world collapsing. The hierarchy of values that had informed all their joint work so far was being destroyed. The theatre, for him, was the servant of literature. For Stanislavsky, theatre was an independent art form of which the text was an important part. A great text should be scrupulously respected. But what if the script was less than marvellous? Or if improvements could be made, as with the last act of *The Power of Darkness*? For Stanislavsky, theatre was more than a staged 'reading'; scope must be given for the contribution of what Gogol had called the 'actor-creator'.

Stanislavsky's dissatisfaction extended beyond rehearsal method. For twenty years he had nurtured the idea of a network of theatres covering the whole of Russia, which would be controlled centrally by an institution like the MAT. On 13 February he called a board meeting to ask for agreement in principle to such a project. It was Nemirovich's unfortunate duty to have to point out that a theatre that was in severe financial difficulty could not embark on such a scheme. The plan was turned down.

It was at this juncture that Meyerhold returned to Moscow full of new ideas, essentially derived from Bryusov. It was just what Stanislavsky needed. Meyerhold had invented the notion of the studio-theatre. In April 1905 he submitted a plan which Stanislavsky welcomed with open arms. Stanislavsky tried to repeat Pushkino. He rented a barn at Mamontovka and recruited a young company to work under Meyerhold's direction on Hauptmann's *Schluck und Jau*, Maeterlinck's *The Death of Tintagiles*, and Ibsen's *Love's Comedy*. Stanislavsky was so impressed by the rehearsals he saw during the summer that he decided on a more public showing. With typical impulsiveness he rented a theatre on Povarskaya Street and proceeded to renovate it at enormous cost. Nemirovich could only wonder how Stanislavsky, who always insisted he could not risk putting more money into the MAT, could afford this private 'whim'. But the point was not lost. Stanislavsky could and would do what he wanted. The MAT was not his only option in life. He informed Nemirovich that when working on *The Drama of Life* in the next season, he would dispense with all preliminary discussion and analysis and rely initially on free exploration and improvisation. In other words he would build on his work with Meyerhold, failure notwithstanding. Analysis through action, through rehearsal, and through the actors, would replace cold dramaturgical analysis in the study.

During the summer, Nemirovich attempted to re-establish his authority. A letter, written on 10 June, ran to no less than twenty-eight tightly written pages and attempted to trace the history of their partnership. Much of the letter was an exercise in self-justification, an attempt to prove that he, not Meyerhold, was the truly original thinker but that he had not been listened to. The tone then became more personal: Stanislavsky was a capricious amateur, a wilful child playing with his toys, needing the professional skills which only he, Nemirovich, could supply.

Nemirovich was right in one respect. For all his skill in managing the family business, Stanislavsky appeared to suffer from total commercial amnesia the moment he passed through the stage door. It was Nemirovich who kept the theatre financially viable by careful programme planning, balancing new works with classics. The company was aware of this. But his claim to omniscience in artistic matters was as futile as it was desperate. The 1905/6 season opened badly. *The Seagull*, with Stanislavsky's revamped Trigorin, did not catch on, and *The Children of the Sun* (24 October), which Stanislavsky had persuaded Gorky to release despite the quarrel with Nemirovich, was too close to reality in a volatile political climate for audiences to take.

The theatre-studio's performance in October was also a failure. What had seemed impressive in a barn was less so in a barn of a theatre. Stanislavsky himself contributed to the failure by insisting that the Maeterlinck which Meyerhold had intended to be played in silhouette should be performed with the lights full up. The inadequacies of the young cast were all too painfully revealed. The studio was closed, much to the delight of Nemirovich and most of the MAT company. Meyerhold and Bryusov concluded that the MAT was a lost cause but also made a crucial distinction between Stanislavsky as a forward-looking creative force and the rigid attitudes of the MAT management, represented by Nemirovich. It was a perceptive judgement.

The 1905 season was abandoned when the general strike of 14–19

October turned into full-scale revolution. Morozov's suicide, following his depression over the failure and bloody consequences of the revolution, added to the general gloom, at least for Stanislavsky.

In an attempt to recoup their losses, Stanislavsky and Nemirovich decided to embark on their first foreign tour, which would take in Dresden, Leipzig, Prague, Vienna, Frankfurt and Berlin. The tour made its greatest impact in Berlin. The leading critic Alfred Kerr devoted long articles to it; Hauptmann and Schnitzler declared it a revelation; the young Max Reinhardt was inspired to create his Munich Kammerspiele on the MAT model. Duse was so impressed she suggested they should extend the tour to Paris, though Nemirovich's negotiations with Lugné-Poë came to nothing for financial reasons. Both Stanislavsky and Nemirovich were decorated by Kaiser Wilhelm II. The news of the MAT's success echoed across Europe.

A now exhausted Stanislavsky suffered a severe personal crisis in the spring of 1906. He felt he was artistically dead. On holiday in Finland that summer he began the first draft of what was later to become the 'system' in an attempt to take stock of his career and find new energy.

The 1906/7 season opened in a poisonous atmosphere. The theatre was divided into two camps: the cast of *Brand* (20 December 1906) directed by Nemirovich and the cast of *The Drama of Life* (8 February) directed by Stanislavsky. There were undignified squabbles over casting and the order in which the plays were to be presented. Nemirovich deliberately stayed away from the public dress rehearsal of *The Drama of Life*, a calculated insult which Stanislavsky described as 'theatrical filth'.[14]

Both Stanislavsky's excursions into symbolist theatre, Hamsun's *The Drama of Life* (8 February 1907) and Andreev's *The Life of Man* (12 December 1907), were successful but mainly due to his ability to exploit the techniques of staging rather than to any new discoveries in the art of the actor. The thumbnail sketches in the production plan show mysterious forms which no actor could embody.

Nemirovich came to the conclusion that he must take over complete management control to avert financial ruin. He had the support of most of the company. Stanislavsky's new ideas on acting were treated with hostility and suspicion, the more so since they did not appear to produce positive results, rather the contrary: Stanislavsky's own acting seemed to have suffered. But Kachalov was adamant that Stanislavsky must stay. Without him the MAT would still be a good theatre but it would not be the MAT.

Stanislavsky realised that either he or Nemirovich had to go, and that if Nemirovich went the theatre would indeed fall apart. In an agonised exchange of letters between November 1906 and February 1907 the two men attempted to work out a scheme whereby Nemirovich would control the management, while Stanislavsky would contribute artistically where he could be most useful.[15] Nothing was resolved. When, however, Stanislavsky learned, in 1908, that Nemirovich was being offered the management of the Maly he decided to resign from the board.[16] Under a new agreement Stanislavsky, in addition to his contractual duties, would be allowed to stage one production of his own choice a year, without interference.

Stanislavsky's last 'official' production for the MAT was one of his most celebrated, *The Blue Bird* (30 September 1908), which remained in the repertoire for many decades. It was more or less reproduced for Réjane in Paris and copied by Beerbohm Tree in London.

Thereafter Stanislavsky and the MAT essentially followed separate paths, a fact which Stanislavsky and Nemirovich were at pains to conceal. This cover-up was later perpetuated in the Stalinist period to promote the myth of the ideal theatre. The true facts did not come to light until 1962, and consequently all the sins of the MAT, its sometimes stodgy naturalism, have mistakenly been laid at Stanislavsky's door.[17] But the fact remains that all Stanislavsky's work in the last twenty-five years of his life was done on the margin of the MAT and sometimes in spite of it.

Stanislavsky's first independent production, the first demonstration of his new 'system', was *A Month in the Country* (9 December 1909). At the same time he began rehearsals for *Hamlet* (23 December 1911) on which he was to collaborate with Gordon Craig, who was specially invited by Stanislavsky.[18]

Nemorivich pursued his notion of a literary theatre by adapting Dostoevsky's *Brothers Karamazov* (12–13 October 1910). As he wrote to Stanislavsky, he believed he had evolved a new form, using a narrator to link scenes and episodes of varying length, thus breaking the tyranny of the traditional four-act structure. Original and forward-looking though it was, the production was not a commercial success, mainly because it was spread over two evenings.

In 1911 Nemirovich attempted a reconciliation and took the unexpected step of declaring Stanislavsky's new 'system', which he essentially disliked, the official working method of the company. This was an entirely cynical manoeuvre. Since he could not ban the 'system' he would accept it and jettison those parts he disapproved of. Nemirovich suggested he should attend the rehearsal of *Hamlet* and Stanislavsky should attend those of *The Living Corpse* (23 September 1911). However, seeing the 'system' applied to his own work Nemirovich was horrified and his true feelings surfaced.[19]

As Nemirovich tightened his control Stanislavsky turned to other, younger colleagues. He fulfilled his obligations to direct a play as contracted and turned in some notable acting performances, including Argon in *The Imaginary Invalid* and Ripafratta in *La Locandiera*, but his main interest was the newly created First Studio, where he could develop his 'system' with such exciting new talents as Vakhtangov, Boleslavsky and Michael Chekhov. This was a logical development. Stanislavsky's concerns were not compatible with a working commercial theatre that was only just breaking even. His rehearsals more and more became acting classes, so that each play took longer and longer to prepare at ever greater cost.

Without Stanislavsky as a driving force the theatre stagnated. In 1916 the board decided not to stage any new productions but to take stock of the situation. It was evident that Stanislavsky had to be drawn back into the fold, but all Nemirovich's attempts at reconciliation were rebuffed. Matters were not improved when, on the eve of the revolution, after months of rehearsal, Nemirovich took Stanislavsky out of the cast of *The Village of Stepanchikovo* (26 September 1917) on the grounds that he had failed to create a rounded character. Stanislavsky, for his part, blamed Nemirovich for not allowing him to develop the character in his own way and for foisting a 'literary' concept on him which he had been unable to assimilate.

A directionless, divided MAT was ill-equipped to face the consequences of the revolution. On the one hand there were the Proletkult, who wanted to abolish all previous art and the concept of the professional actor in favour of the most banal, incompetent, amateur theatre. On the other there was the avant-garde, bursting with talent and ideas, which could now be given expression.

A new generation of critics, notably Vladimir Blyum, led the assault on the MAT. Blyum condemned it as the 'standard bearer of the bourgeoisie'. Chekhov's plays, with which the theatre was identified, were dismissed as irrelevant. The situation was made more difficult by the loss of half the company, including Knipper and Kachalov, who were cut off by the Civil War and continued to tour Europe. Only Lenin's support and the refusal of

26. A scene from the Moscow Art Theatre production of *Hamlet* with Olga Knipper-Chekhova as Gertrude and Nikolai Massalitinov as Claudius, 1912.

Anatoly Lunacharsky, commissar for the arts, to commit the new government ideologically to any one trend saved the theatre from destruction.

Nemirovich's decision to stage *The Daughter of Madame Angot* (16 May 1920), an irrelevant musical trifle, did nothing to enhance the theatre's reputation. The only production that displayed any adventurousness was Stanislavsky's staging of Byron's *Cain* (4 April 1920), which failed mainly for technical reasons. Like *Angot*, it was a curious choice for new proletarian audiences but was registered by Meyerhold at least as a bold attempt to break new ground. In a crucial essay, *The Solitude of Stanislavsky*, he underlined the distinction between Stanislavsky's creative openness and the dead naturalism of the MAT. Both he and Vakhtangov made strenuous efforts to persuade Stanislavsky ('the Michelangelo of theatre') to leave the MAT and work exclusively with the First Studio. Stanislavsky refused out of loyalty to his old comrades and because he mistrusted the director's 'concept' theatre which Meyerhold and Vakhtangov seemed to favour.

The best solution to the MAT's difficulties appeared to be to take it out of the firing line by sending it on tour to Berlin, Paris and the USA. This would be impossible without the 'Kachalov group' who, after much pleading from Nemirovich, returned in the summer of 1921. The first American tour had two major effects. First it presented the image of a theatre that had stopped developing around 1904. The repertoire was virtually the same as the European tour of 1906, deliberately so. Stanislavsky did not wish to present works that would identify the theatre with the Bolshevik regime and also knew what the public expected: legendary productions like *Tsar Fyodor* and the plays of Chekhov. Second, it profoundly influenced ideas about acting, launching Lee Strasberg, under the tuition of Bolelavsky, on the path that would lead to the Method.

During Stanislavsky's absence on tour, and with his consent, Nemirovich had reorganised the main company and the studios, of which there were now four. The First Studio became the Second Art Theatre. Stanislavsky disapproved of the name since, in his view, the First Studio had betrayed everything the Art Theatre stood for. On Stanislavsky's return Nemirovich left Russia for two years.

Between 1925 and 1927 Stanislavsky relaunched a new 'Soviet' MAT. He had a new young company and forced the 'veterans' as he called them to rethink their approach. He also had a new author, a new Chekhov: Mikhail Bulgakov, whose *The Days of the Turbins* opened on 5 October 1926.

The Marriage of Figaro, which followed (28April 1927) was an astute choice. Beaumarchais's drama with its biting criticism of the *ancien régime* is the most revolutionary play of the eighteenth century. Stanislavsky was at his most brilliantly inventive. Designed by Golovin the set harked back to the days of The World of Art. By using a revolve, Stanislavsky turned the last act into a mad rush through the garden using four different locations. The production became a classic of Soviet theatre. Another classic of a totally different kind followed with *The Armoured Train 14–67* (8 November 1927), which set the style for later 'socialist realist' productions. *Untilovsk* (27 February 1928) found less favour since it dealt with corruption in the new regime.

Stanislavsky's intention was to contrast a theatre of the revolution, which showed people's experience of events, with a 'revolutionary' theatre (constructivism), concerned with formal experiments, in which the actor was reduced to a mere cipher, a feature of 'style'.

The 'rehabilitation' of the MAT did not, however, proceed altogether smoothly. Slowly, new censorship was being introduced in the form of the Repertory Committee (Repertkom) which had to approve every production. Powerful among its members was Vladimir Blyum, whose opposition to MAT had not diminished with the years. Strenuous efforts were made to prevent *The Days of the Turbins* being put on and, once it was on, to get it taken off. Meanwhile, Chekhov was more or less unacceptable to the new revolutionary regime, and the theatre's request to stage *Uncle Vanya* was denied. *The Cherry Orchard* was suggested as being more ideologically suitable. In the event the theatre staged neither.

In the autumn of 1928 Stanislavsky suffered a heart attack during the MAT's 30th anniversary celebrations, and he spent the following two years, 1929–31, abroad, convalescing. This was a period of radical change, the beginning of the Stalinist era, the Five-Year Plans and the drive for productivity. The theatre was not to escape this obsession with quantity. More turnover, more productions and more performances were demanded, whatever the quality. Once again, incompetent amateurism flourished in the name of a mythical 'proletariat'. One of the first victims of this new policy was Stanislavsky's production of *Othello*. He was to send a detailed production plan, scene by scene, from the south of France to Sudakov who was to stage it. Stanislavsky had not even completed his plan before he learned that the play had already been staged, after only three months rehearsal, with modified sets and only a passing regard for his intentions.

Other changes had taken place. In 1929 Lunacharsky was sacked, and the following year the revolutionary poet, Mayakovsky, committed suicide. A 'red' director was appointed to the board to ensure that the theatre followed the proper ideological line. Stanislavsky had no objection to this, provided the appointee understood the theatre and its pattern of decision making. The appointee, Heitz, did not.

On his return to Moscow in 1931 Stanislavsky went onto the attack on behalf of the theatre. He issued a direct challenge to the authorities: they could have quality, which took time, or they could have 'pot-boilers' which would do nothing to educate the taste of the masses.[20] He won his point. Within months the MAT had been made autonomous and Heitz had been removed. The moving hand behind this reversal of policy was certainly Stalin's. It was also Stalin who, indirectly, was responsible for restoring *The Days of the Turbins* to the repertoire. A red-faced Repertkom, having discovered that Stalin liked the play and had seen it some eighteen times, withdrew its ban.

The theatre was now safe, independent within limits but not in a healthy state. The younger members of the company were restless. There were too few productions and too few new roles. They wanted a 'career'. In his address to the theatre on its 35th anniversary in 1933, Nemirovich called the company to task. Where was the theatre going? It was achieving less with a total staff of almost 1,000 than it had in 1903 with a staff of 70. It was the most privileged theatre in the world, and it had everything – resources, money, status – everything except dedication and commitment. The real problem was that there was no unified leadership. Stanislavsky and Nemirovich were not communicating with each other except through the theatre's secretary, Bokshanskaya. In the autumn of 1935, Stanislavsky made a direct approach to Stalin.[21] He suggested, first that an administrator be appointed to mediate between himself and Nemirovich, and second that a 'production' company be formed for the malcontents. An administrator was duly appointed.

The MAT was gradually becoming a pawn of Stalin's artistic policy, expressed in the notorious speech of Zhdanov, then commissar for the arts, to the 1934 Soviet Writers' Congress. The avant-garde was systematically suppressed. The Second MAT, which had stemmed from the First Studio, and Meyerhold's theatre were both closed. A sleight of hand was being operated by which the glories of the great Russian realist tradition were being identified with the new, resolutely optimistic socialist realism.

Suddenly Stanislavsky's opposition to purely formalist experiments, and his championship of Chekhov seemed to coincide with the party line. Stalin decided that the MAT would be the emblem of his new policy. All Soviet theatres would be built on the MAT model. Actor training would follow the 'system', rigidly codified into a dogma.

Stanislavsky, isolated from the mainstream of events by his illness, continued to rehearse productions – Gogol's *Dead Souls* (28 November 1932), adapted by Bulgakov, and Bulgakov's own *Molière* (11 February 1936) – in the privacy of his own apartment, but, unfortunately, much of his work became meaningless when transferred to a large stage. For the rest of the time he continued to develop the 'system' in the new studio he created and to work on opera.

In the theatre itself there was a war for the succession. Who would be Stanislavsky's heir? Stanislavsky was quite clear. He had no great opinion of any of the younger generation. It was, rather, to the disgraced Meyerhold he turned, inviting him to take over the production of *Rigoletto* on which he had been working since 1930. During the last few months of his life he and Meyerhold spent many hours in private discussion planning a new kind of theatre and a new kind of acting. Stanislavsky's final pronouncement was, 'Meyerhold is my successor in *everything*.'

But Stanislavsky was only thinking in terms of theatrical talent. Meyerhold was arrested, tortured and shot, and the MAT confined within a narrow presentation style which was only redeemed by the virtuoso quality of the acting. Stalin's policy and Stalin's patronage were lethal. It was, in Anatoly Smeliansky's memorable words, 'a theatre killed with kindness'. No effective change was to occur until Oleg Efremov arrived 'on a white charger' in 1971.

Notes

1. Stanislavskii's real name was Alekseev.
2. See *The Moscow Art Theatre Letters* (MATL) (London, 1991), nos. 3–6.
3. Iu. M. Orlov, *Moskovskii Khudozhestvennyi teatr, novatorstvo i traditsii v organizatsii tvorcheskogo protsessa* (Rostav-na-Dony, 1989).
4. MATL, nos. 18, 19, 20.
5. See Jean Benedetti, *Stanislavski* (London, 1990), p. 72.
6. Quoted in the Introductory Essay to *The Seagull: Production Plan* (Moscow, 1938).
7. See Orlov's, *Moskovskii Khudozhestvennyi teatr*, and 'The foundation of the Moscow Art Theatre', in L. Senelick (ed.), *National Theatre in Northern and Eastern Europe 1746–1900* (Cambridge, 1991), pp. 414–17.

8. MATL, nos. 29, 32.

9. Published in *Novyi Mir,* no. 8 (1961), p. 221.

10. Viktor Borovsky, 'Discord in the cherry orchard', *Encounter* (January–February 1990), 65–72.

11. The script of *The Three Sisters* as presented by the MAT does not entirely correspond to the normally published text, which incorporated further cuts and revisions.

12. MATL, no. 212.

13. For a translation see Laurence Senelick, *Russian Dramatic Theory from Pushkin to the Symbolists,* (Austin, 1981).

14. In Russia, as in France, the most important event for a new production was not the first public performance but the public dress rehearsal (the *générale*), which critics attended.

15. MATL, nos. 285–90, 295–7.

16. MATL, no. 303.

17. Eighteen private letters were published without authorisation in the magazine *Istoricheskii Archiv* in 1962. The issue was seized and the magazine closed down.

18. For a full account of the *Hamlet* production, see Laurence Senelick's *Gordon Craig's Moscow Hamlet* (New York, 1982).

19. MATL, nos. 326–7.

20. MATL, no, 358.

21. MATL, no. 368.

13 The Silver Age, 1905–1917

SPENCER GOLUB

Russian artists of the period which succeeded the historically exhaustive nineteenth century and the historically exhausted *fin de siècle* inhabited a partially self-fashioned existential reality. The theatres of Moscow and St Petersburg closed temporarily following 'Bloody Sunday' (8 January 1905), a prelude to revolution, reactionary state politics and renewed and intensified government censorship of the arts. The depression and suicides of Russian intellectuals increased with Tsar Nikolai II's disbanding of the Second Duma (3 June 1907). Socially alienated and questing intellectuals sought relief, clarity and self-definition in retrospective and utopian, mystical and formalist, symbolist and futurist, elitist and popular 'solutions' to art and life.

Beginning in 1898, the end of a decade of rapid industrialisation, a network of temperance, factory, railway and soldiers' theatres supported by liberal intellectuals promoting revolution developed in Russia's provincial towns and villages. In 1907, the state sought to exercise greater control over popular theatres, but their activities continued to widen. In late 1915, a popular theatre congress brought 365 delegates (among them Bolsheviks and tsarist secret agents) to Moscow. By 1916, the number of producing popular theatres grew to almost 200.[1] However, this phenomenon contributed little to the theatre history of the Silver Age, as the intelligentsia largely dissociated itself from the masses and retreated into coterie – experimental theatres that constituted communities of interest and faith.

By 1909, when the critical anthology *Landmarks* offered its influential brief for the intelligentsia's personal and collective re-orientation from the sociopolitical to the spiritual, the process was already well under way. The Russian symbolists, most of whom wrote plays, sought to expand and deepen artistic understanding and representation of reality. The symbolists reclaimed primacy for human instinct and the subconscious, reintegrating inner and outer experience, the ideal and the material, the individual and the communal. Vyacheslav Ivanov's neo-Nietzschean Hellenic cult of 'the suffering [and feminised] god' Dionysus argued for performative consciousness, personal liberation and the reconciliation of psychological, behavioural (gender) and cultural (European and Asiatic) opposites. Theatre, which both expressed and sought to resolve what Ivanov called 'the pathos of individualism', transformed nineteenth-century Russian culture's moral imperative to unite the artist and the people, into the individual artist-intellectual's spiritual imperative to reconstitute his divided self.[2] This newly integrated self-consciousness was posited by the symbolists and others as an unselfish model for cultural renewal.

The symbolist effort to conceal the intellectual difference between artist and people with an overlaid common currency of 'creative ecstasy' (mystical anarchist Georgy Chulkov's phrase) coincided with both irrationalist trends and a popular religious revival, or 'God-seeking', in Russia.[3] Religious philosophical societies founded in Moscow and St Petersburg in 1908 continued the legacy of Russian symbolism's godfather, Vladimir Solovyov, who had offered 'God-manhood' as a constructive alternative to Nietzsche's anti-Christian concept of 'man-godhood', that is 'the superman'.

Although Ivanov's 'prophetic commune' nominally eschewed divisive politics, it further rarefied intellectual consciousness rather than coalescing 'the folk soul'.[4] In their pursuit of a social ideal of non-egotistical collective individualism, the Russian symbolists differed among themselves and by 1906 split over whether the new theatre's mysteries should be old or new, pagan or Christian (Ivanov's theorised Dionysus-Christ said both), direct, allusive or even obscure. Inevitably, symbolist drama posited the author as ideal spectator and, in the case of Fyodor Sologub's 'Theatre of One Will' (1908), in which the author read his text from the stage, the ideal performer. Nikolai Evreinov's theory of monodrama (1909), which vested authorial consciousness in a dramatic protagonist's scene- and character-altering vision, further demonstrated the terminal self-referentiality of symbolist and symbolist-influenced theatre.

In clubs, salons (especially, Ivanov's Tower apartment symbolist circle), newspapers and highbrow journals (*The Scales*, *The Golden Fleece*), Silver Age culture ubiquitously discussed and enacted its self-doubt in pursuit of self-awareness. Heated arguments ensued over theatre's 'quest', 'crisis', 'fall', 'death', and 'future', while traditional yet ambiguous masks traversed commedia and *balagan* (Russian fairground or showbooth) stages. As the interrevolutionary period progressed, even the faithful began to wonder whether theatrical transformation could ever be synonymous with spiritual and cultural transfiguration, and whether the artist's Faustian dream of a boundaryless reality and unfettered free will was attainable.

Influenced by Wagner's theories, symbolist theatre artists aspired to spiritualise matter and sensualise the spirit in a non-representational artistic synaesthesia imbued with the mythic potency and abstract aesthetic of music. Yet these artists instinctively knew that a fully and freely created conscious life transcends conscious art's ability to represent it. At the same time, they understood through the example of artists such as August Strindberg, whom they admired for his experimental, experiential, life, that unlimited self-experiencing and self-dramatisation lead to implosion and alienation from self, class and even coterie. Such knowledge before the fact resulted in intensified self-consciousness, a feeling of doubleness and the 'exhausting laughter of [romantic] irony', a theme treated in Blok's play *The Fairground Booth* (1906) and his essay 'Irony' (1908).

Under the influence of Otto Weininger's misogynist study *Sex and Character* (1903), which was translated into Russian in 1909 and widely disseminated by 1914, doubleness and irony were often presented in Silver Age culture in terms of ambiguous sexuality. The homosexual Mikhail Kuzmin wrote homoerotic poetry and drama and composed music for the avant-garde theatre. The androgyne Zinaida Gippius wrote under a masculine pseudonym, lived in an eccentric *ménage* and, with 'the Russian Nietzsche' Vasily Rozanov, propounded a relationship between sex and God.[5] The doubling and inversion of sexual types was personified by passive, effeminate, decadent men (Pierrots and homosexual masks) and masculine, libertine, predatory women (Columbine, Salomé, Cleopatra, Woman as Death), not only in fiction but in the paintings and scenic and costume designs of Leon Bakst, Konstantin Somov and Nikolai Kalmakov.

In 1908, Ivanov published 'Two Elements in Contemporary Symbolism' in which he linked realism with the receptive, non-creative female, and idealism with the active, creative male. Blok, who warned his fellow intellectuals of the perils of doubleness, promoted the Strindbergian idea of the destructive female muse and the tragic male sufferer. In *The Fairground Booth*, originally written for Chulkov's unrealised 'Torches' Theatre, a group of Mystics await the arrival of Solovyov's speculative 'Divine Sophia', a feminine Christ or World Soul who enthralled the Russian symbolists. However, the Eternal Feminine appears only in the guises of Columbine and Death, and mystery is displaced by theatricality. Theatre was for Blok both a repository of conventions, illusions and devices to be exposed (the set flies up at the play's end) and perhaps the sole means of restoring 'the wholeness of life'.[6] Blok and other Silver Age artists seemed to believe such wholeness could be expressed only in art that transcends the divisiveness while penetrating the mystery and power of sex and gender.

With the exception of such actress–managers as Vera Komissarzhevskaya, Lidia Yavorskaya, Vera Linskaya-Nemetti and Zinaida Kholmskaya in St Petersburg, Elizaveta Goreva in Moscow and the exotic dilettante Ida Rubinstein, who operated her vanity theatre mainly in Paris, the course the Russian theatre followed in the Silver Age was largely set by men. Virtually all employed Russian stage directors were male, and the vast majority of plays in the Russian theatrical repertoire were written by men. That the speculative 'theatre of the future' was also a male preserve was evidenced by the fact that all of the contributors to the seminal essay collection *Theatre: A Book on the New Theatre* (dedicated to Stanislavsky, 1908) and the respondent social-democratic anthology *The Crisis of the Theatre* (1908) were male. The mostly short-lived success of female-managed theatres, which depended upon male philanthropy and artistic aid, owed as much to a lack of business training as to the quixotic temperaments of those in charge. Except for the Distorting Mirror Theatre, which Kholmskaya co-founded and co-managed with her husband, theatre critic Aleksandr Kugel, and the Kamerny Theatre at which actress Alisia Koonen helped evolve the aesthetic of her director husband Aleksandr Tairov, only Komissarzhevskaya's symbolist stronghold (1905–9) could be said to be artistically progressive. Komissarzhevskaya was a highly individualistic actress attracted to 'new woman' roles. Her theatrical age was beginning to perceive bourgeois conservatism in MAT's social ethos of general audience education and its naturalistic ensemble acting of realistic drama. Komissarzhevskaya's theatre was closed owing to financial losses suffered when the Holy Synod banned its production of the Evreinov-directed *Salomé*, for which Kalmakov designed a giant scenic vagina.

The Silver Age accommodated a large variety of privately owned and operated theatres (nearly forty in St Petersburg alone), not all of which were run by or played to an intellectual elite. These year-round and seasonal enterprises, based in existing theatre structures, houses, halls and gardens, offered farces, comedies, vaudevilles, melodramas and even *grand guignol* to audiences composed of bourgeoisie, workers and provincial tourists. Some

27. Vera Komissarzhevskaya as Larisa in Ostrovsky's *The Dowerless Girl*. Aleksandrinsky Theatre, 1905.

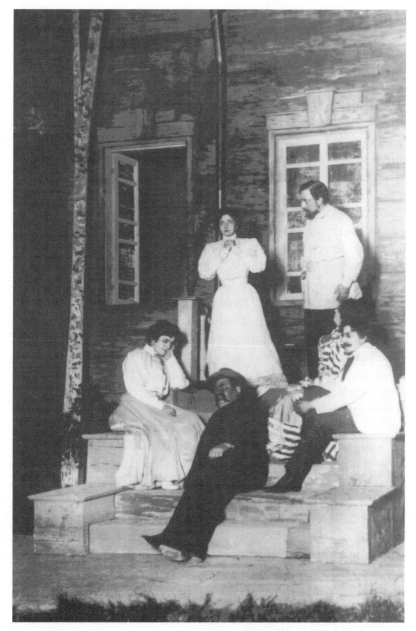

28. Vera Komissarzhevskaya as Liza (centre) in Gorky's *Children of the Sun*, Komissarzhevskaya Theatre, 1905.

of these theatres received financial support from wealthy merchants and nobles, and many shared and exchanged actors and directors. While most of these theatres had brief careers and closed prior to the revolution, the theatres founded in Moscow by F. A. Korsh and K. N. Nezlobin (Alyabyev) survived, only to be nationalised after 1917. Korsh's theatre, which opened in 1882 on the site and with the company of Anna Brenko's Pushkin Theatre, offered a typical mixture of farce, melodrama and Russian classics but also staged new Russian plays on Friday nights and sponsored low-priced student matinees. The Nezlobin Theatre, which opened in 1909, supported a strong acting company and the work of notable directors, including Konstantin Mardzhanov (Kote Marzhanashvili) and Fyodor Komissarzhevsky.

Along with their commercial dramatic fare, Korsh, Nezlobin and fellow theatrical entrepreneurs A. S. Suvorin (The Theatre of the Literary and Artistic Society, 1895–1917) and V. P. and E. M. Sukhodolsky (The Moscow Dramatic Theatre, 1914–19) introduced a more general audience to the plays of Zola, Hauptmann, Wedekind, Schnitzler, Wilde, Ibsen, Shaw, Strindberg and Maeterlinck. The New Theatre (1901–6), co-founded by Yavorskaya and V. V. Baryatinsky, was the first theatre to join the workers' strike in 1905. This theatre's personality reflected the provocative persona, inflammatory acting style and radical politics of Yavorskaya, who played Lulu in *Earth Spirit* and produced a banned version of *Danton's Death*.[7]

Within the realm of avant-garde experimentation, stage directors Meyerhold, Evreinov, Tairov and (especially after 1917) Evgeny Vakhtangov offered theatrical conventionalism or 'theatre as such' in place of symbolist obscurantism or 'theatre as temple'. Once theatre artists accepted the legitimacy of theatre's transparent mystery, its self-revealing symbolic reality, they began to investigate their art's history. In his theoretical texts *Theatre as Such* (1912), *Pro Scena Sua* (1914) and *Theatre for Oneself* (3 vols., 1915–17), Evreinov pursued the idea that a prepotent 'theatrical instinct' exists in mankind. Evreinov pursued this notion in 'creative reconstructions' of theatrical epochs and cultures at the Ancient Theatre (1907–8, 1911–12), which he co-founded with theatre censor, editor and Imperial Theatre director Baron Nikolai Drizen and co-directed with M. N. Burnashev and K. M. Miklashevsky.

In Silver Age Russia, cultural retrospectivism and theatrical reconstructionism, pursued in the name of societal renewal, became the shared concern of professional stages, scholarly journals, academic circles and antiquarian commissions. The investigation and recreation of theatrical audiences, performance conventions and conditions was part of the larger project of discovering the source and essence of theatricality, the personal and social will to transform. Beginning in 1890, Alexandre Benois convened the World of Art (*Mir iskusstva*) group of painters to study and depict theatrical cultures of the past. They were attracted to Ancient Egypt and Greece and especially to the artificial societies of Louis XIV's Versailles and Peter the Great's St Petersburg, to which they imparted mystical powers and fairytale qualities. Benois and his World of Art colleagues Nikolai Roerikh, Ilya Bilibin, Mstislav Dobuzhinsky, Vladimir Shchuko and Evgeny Lanseré designed for the Ancient Theatre. The presence of these and other World of Art painters (Aleksandr Golovin, Konstantin Korovin, Leon Bakst, Boris Kustodiev) was so ubiquitous in Silver Age stage design that in 1913 Dmitry Filosofov wrote '"the World of Art" has turned into "the World of Theatre".'[8] This world extended from St Petersburg and Moscow to Paris under the sponsorship of Sergei Diaghilev, editor of *The World of Art* journal and impresario of Russian art exhibitions beginning in 1906 and Russian ballet in 1909. The ballets, especially *Cleopatra* (1909), *Schéhérazade* (1910), *Petrushka* and *Narcissus* (1911), *L'Après-midi d'un faune* (1912) and *Jeux* (1913), communicated the World of Art's fascination with *balagan*, neo-primitivism, cultural reconstruction, the rhythmic body and the cult of beauty. At the same time, these productions provided studio painters turned set and costume designers with an additional forum for experimentation.[9]

With the exception of Somov, who employed commedia dell'arte and baroque motifs to expose theatrical sham in life and art, most World of Art painters evoked the past talismanically as the trace of life and art's lost unity. This was often cemented, as in the case of Bakst's Orientalist fantasies of Ancient Egypt, Greece and Persia for Diaghilev's ballets, by the natural force of eroticism. As alluring to Silver Age artists was the resacralisation of Eros by Christian Slavic and European cultures, in which life infused with ritual simultaneously sublimated the sexual, and accentuated the sensual. The first two productions in the Ancient Theatre's medieval cycle of plays (only the second was realised), Evreinov's street theatre performance *The Fair on the Day of St Denis* (1907) and the eleventh-century miracle play *The Three Magi* (directed by A. A. Sanin), mixed sensual and religious ecstasy, profane and sacred actions and locations (brothels and churches) in rambunctious town-square settings. The medieval mystery,

29. A scene from *The Miracle of Theophilus* at the Ancient Theatre, 1907.

miracle and morality plays, along with the farces and pastorale offered at the Ancient Theatre, stylised emotional, psychological and theatrical simplicity in neo-primitivist fashion, paying careful attention to often painterly stage composition, rhythmic control and dance, some of which was choreographed by Mikhail Fokin.

The Ancient Theatre directorate began with a medieval rather than a Greek cycle of plays, in part to acknowledge the link between Christian mystery and the Russian *skomorokhi*, who may originally have been priests.[10] There was little and widely dispersed written documentation for the early Russian folk theatre, although iconography and a tradition of storytelling and performance persisted in the provinces. Urban artists were tempted to aestheticise folk art in order to legitimise instinct in the context of current theory. By the 1910s what Viktor Shklovsky called 'counterfeit Russian provincialism' could be seen in plays, playbills, book illustrations, toys and dolls, stage design and theatrical performance. The neo-primitivist scenic designs by Natalya Goncharova and Mikhail Larionov, which impressed Parisian audiences in this era with their robust natural-ness, appealed to Russian artists as exercises in aesthetic stylisation and became subjects for Russian theatrical parody.[11]

'The reconstruction of the spectator,' performance intimacy that was conventionally achieved via the casting of onstage audiences and the col-lapsing of the boundary between stage and auditorium, practically extended the speculative performances suggested by Evreinov's mono-dramatic and theatre-in-life theories. Commedia dell'arte, Miklashevsky's academic speciality, was to have been the Ancient Theatre's third and final cycle following the Spanish Golden Age. Commedia best exemplified the desire to transcend conventional boundaries by invoking the self-defined, partially flexible, limits of conventional forms, that is, mask (the Nietzschean concealer of Dionysiac chaos), ritual, controlled improvisa-tion (*lazzi*) and real-life personae (for example, Evreinov and Meyerhold's personal identification with Harlequin and Pierrot).

In the hands of Evreinov, Meyerhold, and playwrights Blok, Kuzmin and Vladimir N. Solovyov (not to be confused with the philosopher), com-media and *balagan* darkened and became more ironically conscious of the unlimited human need to role-play and the artificially limited conventions of dramatic genre and theatrical performance. In modernist commedias like *The Fairground Booth* and Evreinov's *A Merry Death* (1908), life was pre-sented as a continuous performance which deepens man and woman's torment of self-doubt, sexual perfidy and gender imprisonment, and provokes the ironic questioning of all authority, authenticity and reality.

Many of the same Russian artists who tried in vain to see 'the big picture' through a theatrical filter were more successful at using thoughtful laughter and theatres of small forms, similar to German *Kleinkunst*, to provide perspective on serious issues.[12] Some of these Russian theatres retained a *conférencier*, or master of ceremonies, while others had artistic directors whose personalities largely shaped their programmes. Virtually all of the miniature theatres took their audiences and their artistic agendas seriously but were generally careful not to show it.

The actors in the theatres of small forms, many of whom (along with directors, classical musicians and composers) were drawn from the Imperial and private theatres, parodied the Russian tradition of great acting. The often absurd quick-sketch characterisations of 'small forms' actors undercut the serious contemporary debate over role preparation and performance technique. The theatres of small forms set out to prove that 'just as there are no small roles, there is no small art . . . only bad authors and actors'.[13]

The studied light-heartedness of these venues can be seen in their homely, self-parodying names, for example, the Crooked or Distorting Mirror (1908–31), the Bat (1908–20; evoking the Viennese café *Der Fledermaus* as well as MAT's seagull logo), the Stray Dog (1911–15) and the Players' Rest (1916–19). Such self-effacement seemed appropriate for enterprises which initially performed their divertissements after regular theatre hours in wine cellars, gambling casinos, borrowed theatres and other converted locales. Meyerhold's pretentious theatre of small forms, the Strand, which performed one-act plays and featured refined sets and costumes designed by Bilibin and Dobuzhinsky, closed less than a week after its 6 December 1908 opening at St Petersburg's Theatre Club. The satirical Distorting Mirror Theatre, which premiered with the Strand, benefited from the contrast in their programmes and saw its career launched as a result.

Russian theatres of small forms tried at first to protect their audiences of anti-bourgeois aesthetes and enlightened theatrical amateurs from the culturally status-conscious bourgeoisie, who sought admission. These philistines or 'pharmacists' were admitted on a limited basis, generally to advertised readings that were designed to raise money for the authors who performed them. Many theatrical miniatures stressed inversion, fragmentation and the collision of competing realities and elitist and anti-elitist points of view. They offered an outlet for the expression of personal and social anxiety, social (but usually not political) criticism and fantasy self-projection, that is theatrical rather than social role-playing, during a period when progressive satire caught the censor's eye. These semi-legitimate stages were home to Russian folk art and popular theatrical forms: commedia, *balagan* and puppet show, pantomime, vaudeville, circus clowning, fairytale and shadow play, opéra bouffe and parody grotesque, 'living sculpture' (painted, posed actors brought to life) presentations and one-act plays, monodramas and polydramas (which presented competing inner perspectives on 'reality'). Genuine specialists and those impersonated by actors lectured theatre audiences on serious and windy themes, illustrating the fine line separating sense and nonsense, authority and pedantry, intellectual ambitiousness and artistic egoism in theatre, which was then the most criticised and self-critical art. The purposely small scale and design of these enterprises questioned theatrical art's reality and social stature, and called the bluff of theatre artists who at times promoted their own interests above those of the society they were attempting to save. In their role as conscious distortions (not reductions) of their above-ground counterparts, the underground theatres parodied the naturalists' and symbolists' artistic goals of representing fully revealed sensory and spiritual states. However, these satirical venues largely served the same liberal intellectual audience attending the leading independent theatres in St Petersburg and Moscow, where these ideals were being pursued.

The intimacy of these non-chamber theatres was as much a practical function of space as of ideology. The Stray Dog, which occupied a cellar on Italyanskaya Street in St Petersburg, accommodated about eighty patrons seated at tables, on straw stools and floors for its six- to seven-hour entertainments. The Bat's original auditorium was about as small, although it included a balcony. Close quarters often required actors to play in the audience. Beginning as an after-hours and Lenten holiday ('cabbage-party' or *kapustnik*) showcase for MAT actors to indulge comic and musical talent and whimsy, the Bat became in 1912 an independent, professional theatre open to the public. The Bat's audience now sat in rows rather than at tables in the basement of Moscow's largest apartment building, on Bolshoi Gnezdikovsky Lane. Its inability to attract major writers led the Bat's co-founders, moon-faced *conférencier* Nikita Baliev and writer Nikolai Tarasov, to present an eclectic mix of variety and 'eccentric' acts, impressions, poetry readings, dramatic skits, gypsy romances, 'living-doll' presentations (for example, Vakhtangov's staging of 'The Parade of the Wooden Soldiers'), one-act plays, short-story adaptations of Russian classics, and parodies of MAT performances and productions. The Bat offered Vakhtangov's inter-pretation of Kachalov as Hamlet in Gordon Craig's 1911 monodramatic MAT production, as well as a parody of Nemirovich-Danchenko's mono-dramatic version of Dostoevsky's *The Brothers Karamazov*. The Bat parodied MAT's stagings of Schiller's *Mary Stuart* and Maeterlinck's fairytale *The Blue Bird*, the latter presented in puppet-show form with Stanislavsky and Nemirovich-Danchenko depicted in the leading roles.[14]

The Distorting Mirror's first and most enduring success was staff com-poser Vladimir Erenberg's opera parody *Vampuka, the African Bride* (libretto by Prince M. N. Volkonsky, 1908), which spoofed Meyerbeer, Verdism and the great Russian bass Fyodor Chaliapin and was conducted by a nervous Erenberg in a wig and false beard. In the same period, the real Chaliapin, wearing Oriental mufti, wrestled Leopold Sulerzhitsky, the leading teacher of the Stanislavsky system, at a MAT cabbage-party.

Under Evreinov's artistic directorship (1910–17), the Distorting Mirror dropped its *conférencier*, moved to the former Ekaterininsky Theatre (at 60 Ekaterininsky Canal), which contained a 750-seat auditorium and a fully rigged deep stage, and adopted a more legitimate curtain time of 8.30 p.m. The new Distorting Mirror's satires of opera, operetta and ballet (under Ilya Sats's musical direction), farce, melodrama and vaudeville, temperance theatre, 'pot-boilers' and pulp literature benefited from Evreinov's experi-ence in 1909 as co-founder with Fyodor Komissarzhevsky of the Merry Theatre for Grown-up Children. Evreinov and Komissarzhevsky, who were at that time artistic director and company manager of Vera Komissarzhevskaya's theatre, offered a programme of opera and opera parody, legitimate dramas and parody grotesques, including *A Merry Death*, during the parent company's provincial tour.

Under Evreinov's direction, the Distorting Mirror also spoofed the 'new drama' of Ibsen, the futurists and the quasi-expressionist Leonid Andreev, who nevertheless contributed plays to the Distorting Mirror repertoire. Of the fifteen original, co-written and adapted dramatic and musical composi-tions that Evreinov created for the Distorting Mirror (he was involved with a total of nearly 100 productions), the most popular was his reworking of Gogol's *The Government Inspector* (1912). Evreinov's version championed directors' authorial rights (a bone of contention with Kugel), while deflating the pretentious avant-gardism of Stanislavsky, Craig, Reinhardt and the silent cinema. Evreinov continued his attack on MAT-ism, the misapplication of psychological acting techniques and naturalistic scenography to variety theatre and opera, in his plays *The School for Stars* (1911) and *The Fourth Wall* (1915), both of which premiered at the Distorting Mirror. In the latter, a solid wall conceals from audience view the actor playing Faust in Gounod's opera, who allegedly drinks real poison for the sake of authenticity. This absurdly literal *mise en scène* illustrated what Valery Bryusov in 1902 had labelled the 'unnecessary truth' of MAT realism.[15]

The bohemian café the Stray Dog, conceived and organised by a consortium of artists, writers and directors and run by Meyerhold's theatre associate Boris Pronin, mixed an informal, sometimes rambunctious ambience with serious lectures and discussions. The club, which employed no waiters but offered a serve-yourself food and wine buffet, sponsored 'extraordinary' Saturday and Wednesday nights on which audiences were required to wear paper hats. Club habitués argued over the roles of verbal language, movement and dilettantism in the theatre, French impressionist painting and post-impressionist music. The Italian futurist Marinetti and the French symbolist Paul Fort visited the club on separate occasions in 1914. 'Musical Mondays' and literary evenings featured performances by the then little-known Igor Stravinsky and the celebrated poetess Anna Akhmatova, recitals of French music and scandalous futurist poetry readings which not infrequently erupted in fights. Vladimir Mayakovsky gave his first public reading at the Stray Dog on 17 November 1912, a month prior to delivering in print the futurist salvo 'A Slap in the Face of Public Taste'.

In a basement at St Petersburg's Field of Mars, Meyerhold, Pronin, Evreinov, Sudeikin, Boris Grigoriev and Nikolai Petrov opened the Players' Rest, the successor to the Stray Dog, which the police had closed for selling wine illegally. The Players' Rest is best remembered for its 'Hall of Gozzi and Hoffmann', a room whose walls were painted in a fantastic manner by Sudeikin, and for such exotic touches as a dwarf doorman dressed in parrot feathers, and waiters who wore Oriental turbans. The theatre-cabaret's repertoire included stagings of works by Schnitzler, Claudel, Maeterlinck, Tieck, Strindberg and Kuzmin, reflecting Meyerhold's original plan to follow the Stray Dog with a 'theatre of underground classics'.[16]

Theatres of small forms cast new light on Russian literary classics, which most often received stodgy stagings in the official theatres, and reclaimed neglected works from obscurity. They parodically explored the contemporary enthusiasm for puppetry (a self-contained 'other world') and living statuary (part of a cult of nudity), as well as significant theoretical texts of the period. Distorting Mirror polydramatist Boris Geyer adapted his 1910 play *The Evolution of Theatre* from the critical anthology *Theatre: A Book about the New Theatre*.[17] In general, the theatres of small forms joyfully collapsed a panorama of contemporary subjects and modes of thought, freely intermingling artefacts and conventions of high and low culture.

Meyerhold's prerevolutionary career outside the Imperial Theatres (of which he was the St Petersburg director) embraced the full range of Silver Age theatrical theory and experimentation and, as such, deserves closer attention. Originally a MAT actor, Meyerhold was drawn back into the fold in 1905 to stage plays by Maeterlinck, Hauptmann, Przybyszewski and Ibsen at the Theatre Studio on Povarskaya Street. However, unease over the revolution then breaking out in the streets, coupled with Stanislavsky's anxiety about Meyerhold's staging of Maeterlinck's *The Death of Tintagiles* and Hauptmann's *Schluck und Jau*, led to the studio being closed, nominally owing to a lack of funds, before the planned productions could be realised.

Like Evreinov, Meyerhold sought cultural reconstruction in order to awaken the audience's creative fantasy. His production of *Schluck und Jau* featured bewigged court ladies in crinolines mass-embroidering a long ribbon with giant needles (embodying the principle of 'multiple uniformity'), while seated in bowers stretching along the footlights, downstage of a painted backdrop of sky and clouds. This stage picture was meant to represent a stylised 'powdered-wig age'. Meyerhold staged *The Death of Tintagiles*, co-designed by Sudeikin (Acts I–III) and Nikolai Sapunov (Acts IV–V) and musically scored by Sats, as a series of bas-relief living frescoes. The director posed actors before a neo-primitivist pale painted backdrop, which reflected Sapunov's interest in the Russian *lubok*, a late form of folk woodcut. The production's actors had difficulty reconciling the stylised *plastique*, which Meyerhold demanded, with the emotional truthfulness to which their MAT training had conditioned them.[18]

Meyerhold's staging of *Tintagiles* offered a preview of his work at Vera Komissarzhevskaya's Dramatic Theatre on Ofitserskaya Street in St Petersburg. In only one and a half years as Komissarzhevskaya's artistic director (1906–7), Meyerhold staged fourteen productions of contemporary plays (as opposed to his largely classical repertoire at the Imperial Theatres) by Ibsen, Semyon Yushkevich, Maeterlinck, Przybyszewski, Blok, Gunnar Heiberg, von Hofmannsthal, Andreev, Wedekind and Sologub. Prior to Meyerhold's arrival, the repertory of Komissarzhevskaya's theatre, originally located in the Passage on Italyanskaya Street, mixed modern European and Russian classics with artistically thinner, popular fare. The directorial staff of A. P. Petrovsky, N. A. Popov, I. A. Tikhomirov and N. N. Arbatov (Arkhipov) imparted a vaguely understood Stanislavskian aesthetic to the acting company. In a theatre repainted white to mark a new, non-representational beginning, Meyerhold freed Komissarzhevskaya and company to explore the realm of the spirit conveyed in the new symbolist drama. The Bakst-designed stage curtain, featuring white nymphs dancing in front of the Doric columns of an Elysian temple, contributed to the theatre's timeless quality. Like Stanislavsky, Komissarzhevskaya began as a Meyerhold enthusiast but soon became a Meyerhold detractor, in her case owing to first-hand experience with his directorial restraint of the actor. In response to Meyerhold and Stanislavsky's directing, Fyodor Komissarzhevsky strove to create more actor-sensitive, humanly formalist and philosophically attuned *mise en scènes* at his own St Petersburg theatre (1910–18).

There were two common themes at work in Meyerhold's productions during his tenure as Komissarzhevskaya's artistic director. The first was a critique of contemporary stage realism, which represented the narrowness and hypocrisy of the bourgeois world. The second, related theme was the staging of the unreal in a 'theatre of mood' (aided by lighting effects and progressions), which, unlike Stanislavsky's, embraced the irrational and transcended the psychological and material. Meyerhold's inaugural production of *Hedda Gabler* (premiere 10 November 1906) depicted in a narrow stage space (the backdrop was hung only twelve feet upstage) a mermaid-like spiritual aristocrat drowning in a sea of bourgeois mundaneness, symbolised by Sapunov's mostly greenish-blue scenery. The characters entered and exited this watery world, which Sapunov framed in gold lace, through gold-net slits rather than doors.

In their next and most successful collaboration, Meyerhold cast Komissarzhevskaya, wearing an expensive long blonde wig, in the title role of Maeterlinck's *Sister Beatrice* (premiere 22 November 1906). The production featured bas-relief simplicity of action and décor, which was dominated by Sudeikin's Giotto- and Botticelli-inspired silver-gold tapestry.

The *mise en scène*'s uniformly choreographed choral rhythms and mono-chromatic choral attire underscored the play's theme of the individual's problematic relationship with the masses without directly alluding to contemporary Russian politics.

Amidst his stagings of symbolist and fate-driven dramas for Komissarzhevskaya – Przybyszewski's *The Eternal Fairy Tale* (premiere 4 December 1906), Maeterlinck's *The Miracle of Saint Anthony* and *Pelleas and Melisande* (30 December 1906 and 10 October 1907), Andreev's *The Life of Man* (22 February 1907) and Sologub's *The Victory of Death* (6 November 1907) – Meyerhold directed *The Fairground Booth* (30 December 1906), for which Kuzmin composed the music. Meyerhold's joyful dismantling of Sapunov's theatre-inside-a-theatre set and exposure of the 'real' theatre's onstage and backstage effects vanquished the symbolists' dour aesthetics and static drama. Despite its mixed critical and audience reception in St Petersburg and in Moscow, where it later played, this production was among the era's most significant theatrical events. It captured the substantial insubstantiality and menacing tragi-farce of the creative intelligentsia's inner and outer lives, suspended between social irrelevance and disabling fantasy.

Meyerhold's use of cardboard body façades for his Mystics in *The Fairground Booth* foreshadowed his replacement of Gogol's frozen characters with life-size wax figures at the conclusion of his *The Government Inspector mise en scène* (9 December 1926). Meyerhold's staging of Andreev's *The Life of Man* for Komissarzhevskaya (22 February 1907), which preceded MAT's production by six months, also looked forward to his work on Gogol's play. In both productions, Meyerhold used oversized symbolic (of type) objects, a complete lighting score, including area and spotlight-controlled character appearances and disappearances, exaggerated make-up and grotesque scenic tableaux. Meyerhold's episodic staging of Wedekind's *Spring Awakening* (15 September 1907) anticipated his director-ial montages of the 1920s.[19]

Rhythmic stage composition, an essential part of symbolist and expressionist stagecraft, was a natural function of musical education for Meyerhold and also Evreinov, who studied with the composers Nikolai Rimsky-Korsakov and Aleksandr Glazunov (1901–5). Wagner's theories, which were influential in Russia from the 1890s, became more accessible with the Russian publication of *Art and Revolution* in 1906. In 1910, Prince Sergei Volkonsky lectured on Emile Jacques-Dalcroze's system of eurhythmics, and Bakst designed his sensual, rhythmic costumes (after the model of Mikhail Vrubel's paintings) for the Russian Ballet's Paris production of *Schéhérazade*. In the same year, Meyerhold worked with the painted, rhythmic body, musical *mise en scène* and commedia masks at Pronin's and M. M. Bonch-Tomashevsky's St Petersburg House of Interludes, where he, Kuzmin and Sapunov constituted an artistic committee. His production of Schnitzler and Donany's *Columbine's Scarf*, which offered a playful deformation of *Romeo and Juliet*'s love suicide theme, was consistent with this venue's stated programme of offering 'ancient and new farces, comedies, pantomimes, operettas, vaudevilles, small forms and specialty numbers'.[20]

Meyerhold experimented with a Japanese-influenced gestural system in the St Petersburg studio on Borodinskaya Street which he founded in 1913. While the studio was seldom open to the public, it did produce a short run of Blok's *The Unknown* and *The Fairground Booth* (7–11 April 1914) at the Tenishevsky High School auditorium, which featured advanced students in the leading roles, Eastern-influenced stylised conventions, various performative inversions of illusion and reality, and a makeshift reconstruction of an Ancient Greek theatre. A second demonstration on the same site (12 February 1915) sought to express the essence of commedia, Spanish Golden Age and Russian classical traditions. Vakhtangov's 1922 production of Gozzi's *Princess Turandot* at MAT's Third Studio may have been influenced by his viewing of the first set of public performances by Meyerhold's students, although Vakhtangov may also have seen Komissarzhevsky's staging of Gozzi's play at the Nezlobin Theatre in 1913 or read about it in a 1914 review essay by Solovyov. Vakhtangov, an actor at MAT from 1911, began directing at MAT's First Studio, organised in 1912 and run by Sulerzhitsky until the latter's death in late 1916. Here Vakhtangov crossbred Stanislavsky's psychological realism with Meyerhold's theatricalism. The *études*, or improvised creative tasks which Vakhtangov developed at the First Studio, formed the basis of *Turandot*'s 'fantastic' or 'imaginative' realism. Meyerhold anticipated *Turandot*'s mixing of masks and formal evening dress in his staging of Solovyov's pantomime *Harlequin the Marriage Broker* at Sologub's home (*c.* 1911–12).

The first year's curriculum at Meyerhold's studio included Solovyov's course 'The Commedia dell'arte', the lectures for which were published in Meyerhold's *Love of Three Oranges: The Journal of Doctor Dapertutto* (1914–16). The journal's name cited a Gozzi play, and the subtitle referred to Meyerhold's experimental theatre pseudonym during his tenure as Imperial Theatres Director. In this journal, Meyerhold published play translations and adaptations (especially of commedia), a poetry section edited by Blok, critical and review essays on theatre and literature, studio announcements and news on Russian experimental theatre venues.

At Meyerhold's studio on Borodinskaya Street, composer Mikhail Gnesin offered a course entitled 'Musical Reading', which covered the musical notation of Greek tragedy as a performance medium and informed Meyerhold's production 'chronometrage' in the 1920s. Meyerhold's course 'Movement on the Stage' stressed the actor's physicality as the basis of theatre (a belief he formally proclaimed in 1914) and explored the ideas of the grotesque and pre-Brechtian *gestus* (the plastic and pantomimic summation of a role and a play).[21] In the essay 'Theatre: toward a history and a technique', part of his 1913 collection *On Theatre*, Meyerhold proposed *mise en scène* as a directorial *gestus* of the author's and the actor's soul.

Also important in seeking to synthesise music, drama and *plastique* on the stage during the Silver Age was Tairov. He and Koonen were trained at Moscow's Free Theatre, founded in 1913 by Mardzhanov and backed by wealthy patrons Madame and V. P. Sukhodolsky. The theatre's permanent stage curtain, designed by Somov, depicted romantic lovers rapturously approaching one another in Arcadia surrounded by commedia masks, many of whom, along with cupids and cherubim in 'glories' above, stared directly and unselfconsciously at the audience. Founded 'to revive artistic operetta and musical comedy', Mardzhanov transformed the Free Theatre into an eclectic 'collector of theatrical Russia', which employed 150 actors and, in addition to himself and Tairov, a directorial staff of Sanin and A. L. Zinoviev. In its sole season, the Free Theatre produced Offenbach and Munstein's operetta *The Beautiful Elena* (whose setting was transferred from Ancient Greece to Napoleonic-era Moscow), G. C. Hazelton and J. H. Benrimo's adapted Chinese folk-tale *The Yellow Jacket* (staged by Tairov), Musorgsky's comic opera *The Sorochintsy Fair* and *Columbine's Scarf* (staged by Tairov and starring Koonen). From the Free Theatre's masking, clowning and musical staging in both the Eastern and Western traditions, Tairov derived his own non-mask-driven 'mime drama'.[22]

Tairov's Kamerny (Chamber) Theatre opened its first Moscow season (1914) with a production of Kalidasa's fifth-century BC Hindu drama *Shakuntala*. The production was notable for Tairov's use of the painted 'revealed body' of the actor as a basic costuming principle, and his (and designer Pavel Kuznetsov's) adaptation of the Indian theatrical practice of harmonising the scenic backdrop's shifting colours with the changing moods of the play. Adopting the scenic principles of ballet performance, Tairov emptied the flat stage-floor (framed by four sculpted horses set atop vases) in order to accentuate the performers' dance-like movements. The Kamerny's first season also included a production of Goldoni's *The Fan*, elegantly designed by Goncharova and Larionov to resemble a brilliantly reflective Italian town square, and staged by Tairov with much mime and physical business derived from rehearsal improvisations. Tairov's *balagan* staging of Beaumarchais's *The Marriage of Figaro* in this same season was designed by Sudeikin, who in 1910 had worked on Meyerhold's reconstructivist staging of Calderón de la Barca's *Adoration of the Cross* at the Tower Theatre. Tairov's *Figaro* was reminiscent of Meyerhold's 1910 Imperial Aleksandrinsky Theatre staging of Molière's *Don Juan*, which attempted to capture the colourful spectacle of the author's theatrical era.

The Kamerny's 1916 production of Innokenty Annensky's *Famira Kifared* sought to reinvent the Dionysian 'theatre of ecstasy' via passages of unintelligible *zaum* (trans-sense) speech and a rhythmic synthesis of emotion and physical play. The actors, many of whom played satyrs and maenads, wore false breasts with painted nipples, and costumes which further counterfeited nudity by outlining muscles. Aleksandra Ekster's cubist 'sculpted décor', consisting of rectangular steps of varying widths, conical cypress trees and cube-shaped stones and cliffs, antedated Picasso's designs for *Parade* (Paris, 1917) by one year.

Tairov's production of Wilde's *Salomé* (9 October 1917), translated by symbolist poet Konstantin Balmont, featured a dramatic protagonist and a cubist scenic environment in a state of emotional flux. Koonen's Salomé, struggling to discover pure love through sensual yearning expressed in dance, seemed to symbolise the Kamerny's rhythmic cult of antique beauty and romantic heroism at the start of an era of downsized personal aesthetics and initiative. Ekster created a spatial choreography of ramps, staircases, platforms, heavy columns, free-standing geometric shapes and colour – and mood-shifting curtains and cloths. The geometrically costumed actor harmonised rhythmically with the scenic design, solving what had been realism's inability to reconcile figure and background. However, in the process the designer sacrificed the actor's human flexibility and individuality.[23]

Much as Renaissance artists solved the problem of the central vanishing point, Russian artists (c. 1910–17), several of whom like Ekster, Marc Chagall, Vasily Kandinsky and Vladimir Tatlin observed cubism abroad, attempted to physically represent the point at which previously separable dimensions of reality converge. Cubo-futurist painters (Kazimir Malevich, Larionov, the Burlyuk brothers) and poets (Elena Guro, Velimir Khlebnikov, Aleksei Kruchenykh, Vasily Kamensky, Vladimir Mayakovsky) applied their 'intuitive reason' and their taste for verbal and visual primitivism, abstraction, absurdity and punning to the creation of a new dimension in art. Larionov developed 'Ray(on)ism', a synthesis of cubism, futurism and Orphism, which focused on the lines in space that connect objects and the extension of the objects in space, rather than on the objects themselves. In 1913, Tatlin, influenced by Picasso's work with cubist collage, designed the first non-utilitarian constructions in Russia. Tatlin, whose fame rests mainly on his post-revolutionary constructivist creations, continued the artistic trend of exploding surface to release space, with his unrealised scenic designs for Glinka's opera *A Life for the Tsar* (1913–14) and Wagner's opera *The Flying Dutchman* (1915–18). The latter design centred around an enormous ship configured from abstract shapes with masts and sails for the actors to climb.

Malevich, Larionov, Tatlin and Khlebinkov were all influenced by Pyotr Uspensky's *Tertium Organum: Key to the Laws of the Universe* (1911), which theorised the discernible presence in life of a fourth dimension of space-time. Malevich, who proclaimed that 'the theatre is the pillar of art's decrepitude', designed a stage production of the futurist opera *Victory Over the Sun*,[24] which he hoped would respresent the fourth dimension. Malevich illuminated by way of shards of light a dynamic combination of painted box-within-a-box backdrops, diagonal lines and volumetric shapes, mechanical artefacts and robotic humans to force perspective on this new reality.[25]

Malevich's Act II, scene 5 curtain, which featured a large white square divided into black and white triangles (the prototype for his suprematist painting 'Black Square', c. 1915), suggested both the dark side of the moon (that is, mystery and irrationalism) and a solar eclipse. This hieroglyph was consistent with much Silver Age theatre, art and literature, which equated revelation with eschatology, the longed-for termination of the spiritually exhausted life of rationalism, materialism and realism in favour of the new, self-created life.

The designs by Pavel Filonov, Aristarkh Lentulov and I. S. Shkolnik for

Vladimir Mayakovsky, a Tragedy, which shared the bill with *Victory Over the Sun*, included a series of painted and illuminated panels backed by a rough cloth drop. The production's student actors held cut-out cardboard figures in front of them, like the Mystics in *The Fairground Booth*. These cardboard figures represented the deformed typical characters in Mayakovsky's play, each of whom lacked a body part or else possessed a distinguishing feature like 'two kisses' or 'a tiny tear'. Only the character of Mayakovsky, played by the author, largely ignored these phantasms and was 'real'.[26] This *zaum* collage of present and absent physical elements extended Mayakovsky's effort to infuse human consciousness with a new, synthetic visual and oral sense derived from painting, sculpture, poetry and graphics.

Physical abstraction on the stage extended the notion, espoused in 1916 by Ivanov, of 'the elasticity of the image'.[27] After 1917, the images presented on, off and of the stage struggled to remain elastic, abstract and ambiguous in the face of an evolving concrete aesthetic, which again made art not only socially but politically accountable.

Notes

1. E. G. Kholodov (ed.), *Istoriia russkogo dramaticheskogo teatra* (Moscow, 1987), pp. 298–9, 312–13; Gary Thurston, 'The impact of Russian popular theatre, 1886–1915', *Journal of Modern History*, 55: 2 (June 1983), 238–9, 262.

2. V. Ivanov, 'Ellinskaia religiia stradaiushchego boga', *Novy put'*, 1–3 (1904); James West, *Russian Symbolism: A Study of Vyacheslav Ivanov and the Russian Symbolist Aesthetic* (London, 1970), p. 100.

3. Georgy Chulkov, *VZh*, 9 (September 1905), 246, 248; Bernice Glatzer Rosenthal, 'Theatre as church: the vision of the mystical anarchists', *Russian History*, 4, Part 2 (1977), 125.

4. Viacheslav Ivanov, *Po zvezdom* (St Petersburg: Ory, 1909), p. 218; Rosenthal, 132.

5. A. L. Crone, 'Nietzschean, all too Nietzchean? Rozanov's anti-Christian critique', in Bernice Glatzer Rosenthal (ed.), *Nietzsche in Russia* (Princeton, 1986), pp. 95–112; Laura Engelstein, *The Keys to Happiness: Sex and the Search for Modernity in Fin-de-Siècle Russia* (Ithaca, N. Y., 1992), pp. 303, 383–96.

6. Aleksandr Blok, 'O teatre', in Blok, *Sobranie sochineniia v vos'mi tomakh*, ed. V. N. Orlov, A. A. Surkov and K. I. Chukovskii, vol. v; (Moscow and Leningrad, 1962), p. 261; West, p. 142.

7. Kholodov, pp. 302, 321; S. S. Mokul'skii and P. A. Markov, *Teatral'naia entsiklopediia* (6 vols., Moscow, 1961–7), vol. III, pp. 222–3, 546–7, 934; ibid. vol. IV, pp. 11, 1122; Catherine Schuler, 'Female theatrical entrepreneurs in the Silver Age: a prerevolutionary revolution', *Theatre History Studies*, 13 (1993), 79–94;

S. Golub, *Evreinov: The Theater of Paradox and Transformation* (Ann Arbor, 1984), pp. 221–2.

8. Kholodov, p. 151.

9. J. E. Bowlt, 'Stage design and the Ballets Russes', *The Journal of Decorative and Propaganda Arts*, 5 (Summer 1987), 28–45.

10. Edward Stark, *Starinnyi teatr* (Petrograd, 1922); Golub, pp. 107–43.

11. Viktor Shklovsky, *Zoo, Or Letters Not About Love*, tr. Richard Sheldon (Ithaca, N. Y., 1971), p. 89.

12. Laurence Senelick, 'Boris Geyer and cabaretic playwriting', in Robert Russell and Andrew Barratt, *Russian Theatre in the Age of Modernism* (London, 1990), p. 36; Iu. Dmitriev, 'Teatry-miniatiur', in *Russkaia khudozhestvennaia kul'tura kontsa XIX-nachala XX veka (1908–1917)* (Moscow, 1977), pp. 191–207; Anthony Pearson, 'The cabaret comes to Russia: "theatre of small forms" as cultural catalyst', *Theatre Quarterly*, 9 (Winter 1980), 31–44; Harold B. Segel, 'Russian cabaret in European context: preliminary considerations', in L. Kleberg and N. A. Nilsson, *Theater and Literature in Russia, 1900–1930* (Stockholm, 1984), pp. 83–100; Harold B. Segel, *Turn-of-the-Century Cabaret: Paris, Barcelona, Berlin, Munich, Vienna, Cracow, Moscow, St Petersburg, Zurich* (New York, 1987), pp. 255–320.

13. Actor V. N. Davydov, quoted in N. N. Khodotov, *Blizkoe-Dalekoe* (Moscow and Leningrad, 1962), p. 220.

14. Alma Law, 'Nikita Balieff and the Chauve-Souris', in Laurence Senelick (ed.), *Wandering Stars: Russian Emigré Theater, 1905–1940* (Iowa, 1992), pp. 18–21; Laurence Senelick, *Cabaret Performance: Europe 1890–1920. Songs, Sketches, Monologues, Memoirs* (New York, 1989), pp. 144–6.

15. Golub, pp. 145–90.

16. Michael Green, 'Boris Pronin, Meyerhold and cabaret: some connections and reflections', in Russell and Barratt, pp. 66–86.

17. Senelick, *Wandering Stars*, p. 40.

18. Marjorie Hoover, *Meyerhold and his Set Designers* (New York, 1988), pp. 10–20; Marjorie Hoover, *Meyerhold: The Art of Conscious Theater* (Boston, 1974), pp. 51–74; K. Rudnitsky, *Meyerhold the Director*, tr. George Petrov, ed. Sydney Schultze (Ann Arbor, 1981), pp 49–76.

19. Kholodov, pp. 165–6; Hoover, *Meyerhold and His Set Designers*, pp. 20–49; Rudnitsky, *Meyerhold the Director*, pp. 77–130; K. L. Rudnitskii, *Russkoe rezhisserskoe iskusstvo, 1898–1907* (Moscow, 1989), pp. 308–64; K. L. Rudnitskii, 'V teatre na Ofitserskoi', in L. D. Vendrovskaia and A. V. Fevral'skii (eds.), *Tvorcheskoe nasledie V. E. Meierkhol'da* (Moscow, 1978), pp. 137–210.

20. Kholodov, p. 387.

21. Hoover, *Meyerhold: The Art of Conscious Theater*, pp. 75–83.

22. Mokul'skii and Markov, vol. IV, p. 883; Kholodov, pp. 393–5; Nick Worrall, *Modernism to Realism on the Soviet Stage* (Cambridge, 1989), pp. 21, 24.

23. Worrall, pp. 24–30; Alexander Tairov, *Notes of a Director*, tr. William Kuhlke

(1969), pp. 39–65 (quote from p. 59); K. Rudnitsky, *Russian and Soviet Theater 1905–1932*, tr. Roxane Permer, ed. Lesley Milne (New York, 1988), pp. 15–19.

24. Performed at the Luna Park Theatre, St Petersburg, 2–5 December 1913; libretto by Kriuchenykh, prologue by Khlebnikov, music by Guro's husband Mikhail Matyushin.

25. K. S. Malevich, *Za 7 dnei*, 28 (15 August 1913), quoted in E. Rakitin, 'How Meierkhol'd never worked with Tatlin and what happened as a result', in *The Great Utopia: The Russian and Soviet Avant-Garde 1915–1932* (New York, 1992), p. 649; David Elliott, *New Worlds: Russian Art and Society 1900–1937* (London, 1986), pp. 13–14; in Stephanie Barron and Maurice Tuchman, *The Avant-Garde in Russia, 1910–1930: New Perspectives* (Los Angeles, 1980): Jean Claude Marcade, 'K. S. Malevich: from Black Quadrilateral (1913) to White on White (1917): from the eclipse of objects to the liberation of space', pp. 20–4; Michail Grobman, 'About Malevich', pp. 25–7; and Magdalena Dabrowski, 'The plastic revolution: new concepts of form, content, space and materials in the Russian avant-garde', pp. 28–33. Velimir Khlebnikov, *The King of Time: Poems, Fictions, Visions of the Future*, tr. Paul Schmidt, ed. Charlotte Douglas (Cambridge, Mass. 1985), p. 4; Steven A. Nash, 'East meets West: Russian stage design and the European avant-garde', in Nancy Van Norman Baer (ed.), *Theatre in Revolution: Russian Avant-Garde Stage Design 1913–1935* (New York, 1992), pp. 103–6.

26. Katherine Marie Lahti, 'Mayakovsky's Dithyrambs', (Ph.D. dissertation, Yale University, 1991), pp. 82–160.

27. Vyacheslav Ivanov, 'Thoughts on symbolism' (originally published 1912), tr. Samuel Cioran, in Carl Proffer and Ellenda Proffer (eds.), *The Silver Age of Russian Culture* (Ann Arbor, 1975), pp. 32–9.

14 Revolutionary theatre, 1917–1930

ROBERT LEACH

The achievement of the revolutionary theatre was to find a new and hitherto untried way of constructing drama; its tragedy was that the way was blocked and barred before its end was known. Born in the intense suffering and struggles of the revolution and the Civil War, growing up during the risky and heady insecurity of Lenin's New Economic Policy and the titanic struggle between Stalin and Trotsky, it was snuffed out by the growing might of the new tyrant, whose eccentric attitude towards drama and theatre was consistent only in its abomination of anything experimental or new. But in 1917 and for a few years thereafter, the way seemed open for a genuinely democratic re-examination of every aspect of social and moral life, and the theatre became perhaps the most important forum for this re-examination. It was carried on with passionate sincerity and at times absurd absolutism, but its very intensity guaranteed its significance.

The first clear demonstrations of what the new drama might be like came on 7 November 1918, when Vladimir Mayakovsky's *Mystery Bouffe* was presented in a production by Vsevolod Meyerhold at the Theatre of Music and Drama Conservatory in Petrograd and on the same day at the Vvedensky People's House in Moscow, Vasily Kamensky's *Stenka Razin* received its premiere in a production by Arkady Zonov and Vasily Sakhnovsky. These were brash, noisy, 'popular' epics, peopled by grotesque caricatures and peppered with eye-catching and unexpected stunts, popular sloganising poetry and a brassy and unrepentant iconoclasm. They may be regarded as the visible tip of a vast iceberg, a veritable 'theatre epidemic', which gripped Russia immediately after the revolution, producing a popular, participatory movement of unequalled magnitude and vitality. The Proletkult (Proletarian Cultural and Educational Organisation), whose self-appointed task was to provide working-class and peasant people with the means to fulfil their artistic or creative urges, had literally hundreds of theatre groups performing improvised and agitational plays across the country, and this national organisation was complemented by the independant local groups attached to factories, villages, social clubs and so on.

The Bolshevik government struggled to contain the theatre explosion. Within its Commissariat of Enlightenment, headed by Anatoly Lunacharsky, himself a playwright, it set up a Theatre Division (TEO) under Olga Kameneva (Trotsky's sister and Bolshevik leader Kamenev's wife), and put Meyerhold in charge of the Petrograd branch. He and Kameneva worked to put all theatres, including the former Imperial Theatres, the Art Theatre and more, under their own radical leadership, in effect to nationalise them, but on their terms. Meyerhold wanted nothing less than a revolution in the repertoires, acting styles and organisations of all theatres. Unfortunately for him, in May 1919 he was struck down by tuberculosis and left Petrograd for the south to recuperate. In June, perhaps seizing the chance of Meyerhold's absence, the leaders of the mainstream theatres, including Stanislavsky, and Aleksandr Yuzhin of the Maly Theatre, enlisted Lunacharsky to defend them. With Lenin's backing, he sacked Kameneva, taking her place himself, and set up Tsentroteatr, which awarded 'academic' status, large subsidies and artistic freedom to the major theatres, and a lesser position, with smaller subsidies and less freedom, to the others.

Proletkult, which was seen as a threat to the Bolshevik Party itself, became a special target of Lenin's ire: in the spring of 1920 he tried to make it an extra-mural branch of the Commissariat of Enlightenment, and when that made no difference to its soaring popularity and dynamic and attractive activities, he used a party faction within it at its national conference in October 1920 to take control both of its central committee and its philosophy, which was thereafter to be subordinate to that of the party. The new party-approved chairman, Valerian Pletnev, within a few months had himself fallen foul of the Bolsheviks' tireless appetite for power, and the vendetta against the Proletkult was pursued relentlessly for several more years.

Running parallel to the Proletkult, but using mostly displaced but not disaffected professional actors, was Terevsat, the theatre of revolutionary satire. The brainchild of Mikhail Pustynin, the director of the local branch of the Russian telegraph service, Rosta, in Vitebsk, Terevsat's activities began as a means of spreading news and propaganda to those who were illiterate or otherwise unable to read the newspapers. The format which the group quickly developed was similar to a revue or cabaret, and usually included songs, comic grotesqueries mocking the enemies of the revolution, exhortatory sketches and dramatisations of political events, such as Pustynin's early piece, *The Blockade*. Other favourite items included 'tantomoresques', poster-like animated cartoons, made by cutting out the head and hands of a life-size drawing and having the actor stand behind and insert his own head and arms through the holes; folk dance; gymnastic group movement; and scenes centring on the popular traditional puppet, Petrushka, sometimes played by a live actor. Thus, in a collage of brief, unconnected items, structured according to the format of a revue, these 'living newspapers' kept their audiences informed about and engaged with the issues of the day.

Terevsat began in Vitebsk, but was soon to be seen on tour in the countryside and at the Civil War front. The resemblance to the old strolling troupes of players was clear, their popularity as great. In 1919 they were invited to perform in Moscow, and in April 1920 they moved there permanently, acquiring the Nikitsky Theatre in November of that year thanks to the intervention of the recovered and returned Meyerhold. Meanwhile, other groups calling themselves theatres of revolutionary satire sprang up across the country, using the same format, even sometimes the same scripts, as the original troupe. Encouraged by Lunacharsky, Terevsats were established in many places, including Baku, Nikolaev, Kaluga, and, notably, Petrograd, where Nikolai Petrov, with Yury Annenkov and Nikolai Evreinov, ran a company. The end of the Civil War largely undermined the *raison d'être* of the Terevsats and most of them disappeared in the early 1920s, but they were important, not only because they gave employment to out-of-work performers but, more significantly, because they developed a form, the living newspaper, which clearly influenced the development of revolutionary theatre, and indeed is perhaps not completely worked out now.

Meanwhile, the bubbling popular participation in theatre found a new outlet in 'mass spectacles', specially-created dramas for performance by vast numbers of participants, presented usually on one of the new holidays of the Bolshevik regime. Taking themes such as the history of Marxism from 1848 to 1917, or the epic of popular rebellions from Spartacus to the Paris Commune, they consisted of largely symbolic actions by groups declaiming or moving in more or less synchronised fashion. The most spectacular of these was *The Storming of the Winter Palace*, created and directed by Nikolai Evreinov, with Yury Annenkov, Aleksandr Kugel and Nikolai Petrov as his assistants, and presented in front of the Winter Palace in Petrograd on 7 November 1920, the third anniversary of the events depicted. It was perhaps the most literal theatricalisation of a historical event ever staged, since those who had taken part in the events of 1917 were actively sought out and invited to play themselves – and many did. There were more than 8,000 participants, and an orchestra at least 500 strong, and the presentation was watched by more than 100,000 spectators.

The performance began at 10 p.m. with a single gunshot in the night. On one side of the emblematic stage, the Whites, under a clown-like Kerensky, were depicted as grotesquely foolish and greedy. Opposite them, across a bridge, were the Reds, workers toiling with pickaxes and mallets, who were stirred to revolution by a Lenin-like orator. Symbolic battle was joined on the bridge, the Whites were vanquished, and Kerensky and his ministers toppled over one another in a hilarious scramble to get aboard a car and flee across the square and into the palace itself. Crowds of Red soldiers flooded the square from all directions, and pursued the Whites into the building. Suddenly the Winter Palace itself was illuminated, and white blinds drawn over the windows were lit from behind to show shadow fights going on. The battleship *Aurora* fired her guns, signalling a deafening roar of artillery and machine-gun fire which lasted for two or three minutes. A huge rocket streaked to the sky. Victory. Silence. Then, massed voices began to sing *The Internationale*. The windows of the Winter Palace, which had gone dark, were now each lit with red stars projected onto the blinds, and a huge red banner was hoisted over the building. As the clown Kerensky fled, a firework display began.

The performance juxtaposed buffoonery and clowning, especially among the White crowds, with solemnity and an almost mysterious awe in a bustling, swarming, continuously energetic performance. It was naive, in a non-pejorative sense, and popular, and in its use of clown techniques for dramatic purposes capitalised especially on the work of Yury Annenkov, one of Evreinov's assistants, and Sergei Radlov, a former pupil of Meyerhold, and a director of mass spectacles himself (he was at the time director of the Theatre of Popular Comedy). Annenkov had created a notorious 'circusisation' of Tolstoy's anti-alcohol play, *The First Distiller,* in Petrograd in 1919, and Radlov mounted a series of commedia dell'arte-inspired productions, which used circus performers and improvisational techniques, chases, slapstick and crude jokes, to forge a style like 'a Russian *lubok* passed through the prism of futurism'.[1]

Meyerhold himself had used circus devices in his production of *Mystery*

Bouffe. In autumn 1920, he had returned to Moscow, having lived through some hair-raising episodes of the Civil War on the Bolshevik side, and had been put in charge of the reinvigorated Theatre Department, Tsentroteatr having been dissolved in the meanwhile. He immediately declared the need for an 'October revolution in the theatre'. Ignoring the 'accies' (academic theatres) as too powerful to touch for the time being, he proceeded to create a block of theatres that would support him. With Valery Bebutov, he amalgamated three struggling but progressive groups at an old operetta house, the Zon Theatre, under his own leadership, and called it the RSFSR Theatre No. 1. Evreinov was invited to take over RSFSR Theatre No. 2, which Meyerhold created from combining the Red Army Theatre and the former Nezlobin Theatre. Evreinov refused to co-operate, but this did not stop Meyerhold, who made the Korsh Theatre into RSFSR Theatre No. 3, Fyodor Chaliapin's Studio into No. 4 (Chaliapin having emigrated), and the Moscow Terevsat into RSFSR Theatre No. 5. This was the point when it was presented with the Nikitsky Theatre.

Meyerhold was also largely responsible for a renewal of the languishing Proletkult's theatre work in Moscow, providing it with a Central Arena Theatre, and setting up a 'Ton-Plas' Studio under Evgeny Prosvetov, to investigate ideas of collective creation through rhythmic movement and choral speech. The 'tonal plastic' performance of a piece entitled *Labour* met with some success, being a sequence of stylised free dances interspersed with choric verses and *tableaux vivants*, but the independent thinking and expansion of non-traditional dramatic work which characterised Meyerhold's period as head of TEO did not last long enough to enable his reorganisations to come to much: in February 1921 he was demoted and TEO itself had much of its power removed, and the following month Meyerhold resigned from the department.

His RSFSR Theatre No. 1 continued for a few months more, however. It had already mounted a controversial production of a play by the Belgian Symbolist Emile Verhaeren, *The Dawns*, which Lenin's wife had excoriated, despite its considerable popularity with audiences. Now Meyerhold presented a new version of Mayakovsky's *Mystery Bouffe*, whose rewritten Prologue was virtually a manifesto of the new theatre he and the author were bent on creating:

> For other theatrical companies
> the spectacle doesn't matter:
> for them

the stage
is a keyhole without a key.
You look – and what do you see?
Uncle Vanya
and Aunty Manya
parked on the sofa as they chatter.
But we don't care
about uncles or aunts:
you can find them at home – or anywhere!
We, too, will show you life that's real –
very!
But life transformed by the theatre into a spectacle most extraordinary![2]

This 'most extraordinary' spectacle was, according to Ilya Ilinsky, 'a major cultural event, and the whole of Moscow's attention was chained absolutely to it' when it opened at the Zon Theatre on May Day 1921.[3] At the end of the performance, the audience stamped and cheered, Meyerhold and Mayakovsky took repeated bows, and one spectator wrote, forty-five years later, that it was 'difficult to recall another performance which was greeted with such enthusiasm'.[4] *Mystery Bouffe* is an allegory of the revolution: the 'Unclean' overthrow their 'Clean' masters, and go through Hell, Heaven and the Land of Chaos, to reach the Promised Land of electricity and socialism in a genuinely moving and uplifting finale. Its naivete provides part of its undoubted theatrical power – it dramatises the feeling Wordsworth expressed:

Bliss was it in that dawn to be alive,
But to be young was very heaven![5]

Mayakovsky deployed a startling array of devices which Meyerhold's production enhanced to create a glittering spectacle. Clowning and other 'antics appropriate to the theatre'[6] took place on a stage which seemed to spill out into the auditorium, and were performed by a gallery of grotesques who were as entertaining as they were unexpected. The play was constructed as a series of dynamic moments, each of which was presented with great intensity in its own terms. Each was placed next to another intense moment, to which it was thematically, though perhaps not logically, related so that a dazzling montage of movement and dramatic virtuosity was achieved.

The impact of *Mystery Bouffe* was not unlike that achieved by the post-

1917 productions of Evgeny Vakhtangov, whose 'fantastic realism' was an attempt to find a middle way between the psychologism of the Moscow Art Theatre, where he had trained, and the stylisation of the RSFSR Theatre No. 1. In fact, his last four productions used many of the typical techniques of the revolutionary theatre and were probably closer to the style of Meyerhold than Stanislavsky, with their distorted sets, and grotesqueries which ranged from improvised clowning to passionate intensity. 'Theatre is theatre,' he wrote in 1921, words which Meyerhold could easily have endorsed. 'A play is a performance.'

Vakhtangov's acceptance and endorsement of the revolution was perhaps a romantic gesture by one who was fundamentally apolitical. But the productions which he mounted in 1921 and 1922 were of central significance to the theatre of their time. The first of these chronologically was Maeterlinck's *The Miracle of St Anthony*, with which the theatre on Arbat now known as the Vakhtangov Theatre opened on 29 January 1921. Here, characters were deliberately depersonalised, and the whole production was organised rhythmically, which was especially effective in the weird, Hoffmanesque crowd scenes. *Erik XIV* by August Strindberg, which Vakhtangov also presented in 1921, was dominated by a single performance, that of Michael Chekhov as Erik. Markov commented on the vital physicality of this performance, its 'every movement and gesture; the posture of his body in space; the hand which darted out and remained suspended in the air; the hopeless melancholic gaze of the morbidly wide-opened eyes upon the elongated, wondering face; the thin hands and feet slipping from the silver garments; the sudden uplifts and plungings of the timid and bold movements'.[7]

In 1922 Vakhtangov staged *The Dybbuk* by S. Ansky, for the Jewish Habima Theatre. The play, which concerns traditional Jewish beliefs about demonic possession, as well as Jewish law and financial dealings, seems far removed from the realities of Russian life under Lenin, but at least one critic, Mikhail Zagorsky, found it revealed something about the essence of contemporary revolutionary reality. As Leye is liberated from the dark forces which possess her, Zagorsky 'recognized the deep meaning of the mythos now being created . . . this production reveals the meaning of building and destruction, of abandoning historic tradition for the sake of the victory of love . . . In a sea of powerful emotions – of love stronger than death – a centuries-old social system disintegrates.'[8] Vakhtangov used mime and dance, as well as weird musical effects, and staged the second act as a kind of beggar's holiday, accelerating in pace and crescendoing in volume as Leye's fate is inexorably sealed. Where Meyerhold had created a uniquely varied gallery of grotesques in *Mystery Bouffe*, Vakhtangov created his festive beggars as a group, each more repulsive than the last. They were overwhelming: poverty-stricken, diseased, deformed, they were a kind of equivalent of Aeschylus's Eumenides, but the stylisation which Vakhtangov employed was rooted in ancient Jewish, not Greek, rituals which underpinned the play, and found further expression in the drab colours – black-grey, dark grey and occasionally white.

In *Princess Turandot* by Carlo Gozzi, presented at the Third Studio of the Moscow Art Theatre, he went to the opposite extreme. Here a cascade of brilliant colours, characters ripe with *joie de vivre*, and a hallucinatory, distorted setting, transported the spectator to some imagined world of revelry, light and laughter, implicitly an evocation of what post-revolutionary Russia might become. Using the tricks and techniques of the commedia dell'arte with more sophistication and more assurance than Radlov at the Petrograd Theatre of Popular Comedy, Vakhtangov nevertheless shared the excitement other directors felt for popular forms. This production attempted to use that tradition as earnestly as Dostoevsky used the tradition of the popular detective tale to create his major novels. So dance, music, stunts, *lazzi* and bad jokes combined to create a celebratory, inventive and energetic performance. But it also contained demystifying elements which were to become part of the characteristic armoury of the revolutionary theatre. At the start of the play, Tartaglia, Truffaldino, Pantalone and Brighella introduced themselves to the audience, then two of the comedians parted the curtains and the rest of the troupe came through. The bare stage was covered with apparently random strips of bright cloth. Suddenly, to fast, exhilarating music, the actors spread across the stage, picked up the pieces of ribbon and playfully added them to their costumes. They finished dressing at the same time, came to the front to sing a chorus number, and disappeared. The comedians were left clowning. Only then did apparent stage hands appear to change the scenery, or rather, set up the first scene. The overt theatricality added both resonance and joy to the audience's response. Unfortunately, although Vakhtangov was still alive when the first performance was given, he was too ill with cancer to attend, and shortly afterwards he succumbed to the disease.

Almost exactly two months after *Princess Turandot's* theatricality had captivated Moscow audiences, Meyerhold's still more theatrical production of *The Magnanimous Cuckold* by Fernand Crommelynck received its premiere. Since losing the RSFSR Theatre No. 1 in September 1921, Meyerhold had been in charge of the State Directing School, but had continued to work at the same time with a number of young 'Meyerholdites' at the Free Meyerhold Workshop. Early in 1922, when the Zon Theatre had again become vacant, Meyerhold had formed the Actors Theatre and repossessed the Zon. The production of *The Magnanimous Cuckold*, however, was significant not merely because it was the first production of what became the Meyerhold Theatre, but because its startling brilliance was the outcome of Meyerhold's new attempts to codify his practice in the school and the workshop. It was in fact the first production to use his new system of 'biomechanics'.

Meyerhold arrived at this system by way of Diderot, who suggested that 'At the very moment when [the actor] touches your heart, he is listening to his own voice . . . He has rehearsed to himself every note of his passion . . . He knows exactly when he must produce his handkerchief and shed tears.'[9] Mediated by Coquelin, this enabled Meyerhold to produce a formula which suggested that unlike other artists, the actor was both the controller and the instrument of his art. He must therefore learn absolute control of his instrument – his body – so that it would obey precisely the requirements of the brain, intellect and imagination. 'The first principle of biomechanics', he wrote, 'is: the body is a machine, and the person working it is a machine-operator.'[10]

This language, typical of the constructivist phase of Russian social and artistic development, should not be allowed to obscure the practical achievements of the system, especially the extraordinary acrobatic and clowning skills, the extreme physical flexibility and agility. The central exercises of biomechanics – 'Shooting from the Bow', 'Throwing the Stone' – are carefully crafted and executed *études* which use the basic movements of the action to create a dance-like fantasy on the theme. To shoot from a bow, for instance, an archer must lean forward with the left hand thrusting the bow out, lean back to take an arrow from the quiver on his back, lean forward to fit the arrow to the bowstring, lean back to draw the bowstring, and so on. Such movements executed by an agile and graceful actor-performer through a series of planes and directions, demonstrate both physical control and expressiveness, and also how the body functions in space and time. This can then move outwards, towards clowning and tumbling or alternatively towards the disciplines of gymnastic or acrobatic work. And if the correct physical control has been established, the performer can actually move between clowning, acrobatics, dance and, most crucially, stillness, with maximum rapidity and ease.

This could be seen in the very first moment of *The Magnanimous Cuckold*: when Stella and Bruno burst onto the stage, Bruno flees to the top of the stage construction and turns to catch his wife, and together they slide helter-skelter down the chute, crying 'Wheee!' and laughing like schoolchildren just liberated from lessons. That stage construction was designed by Lyubov Popova – a 'machine for acting', it was designated – and consisted of an infinitely flexible series of platforms, doors, steps and slides, with a series of wheels which spun like propellers and conjured associations not only with the mill where the action was supposed to take place, but also with a children's playground, not to mention the trestle stage of the itinerant commedia dell'arte. The whole confection blended popular tradition with radical modernism in a completely original, but thoroughly arresting way.

A third production from 1922 which combined the high spirits of the victorious revolutionary with modernist staging and an acknowledgement of traditional, especially commedia dell'arte, acting techniques, was *Girofle-Girofla*, presented by Aleksandr Tairov at his Kamerny Theatre on 3 October 1922. Tairov, though as apolitical as Vakhtangov, had welcomed the revolution which he saw as refreshing the tiredness of tsarist Russia, and his Kamerny Theatre, which had been struggling, was awarded 'academic' status in 1920. Nevertheless, as his *Notes of a Director* make abundantly clear, he was by nature an experimenter. He wished for a 'synthetic' theatre which would unite naturalism with symbolism, for he declared, like the other radicals of the theatre of the revolutionary period: 'Theatre is theatre.' To him, this implied the need to 'theatricalise the theatre', which could be achieved by the actor and director finding and exposing the 'rhythm of the action'.[11]

Tairov's production of *Princess Brambilla* by E. T. A. Hoffman in 1921 had shown his mastery of the rhythmic virtuosity required by the modernist commedia, and now *Girofle-Girofla* took this further. Like *Princess Turandot* and *The Magnanimous Cuckold*, *Girofle-Girofla* is careless, light-hearted, even rapturous, but spiked with tragedy at its heart. Designed by Georgy Yakulov, with trapdoors, platforms, folding screens, revolving doors and ladders, the production was the epitome of 'theatricalised theatre'. 'The

30. Nikolai Tseritelli and Alisa Koonen in Eugène Scribe's *Adrienne Lecouvreur*, 1921.

result', wrote one observer, 'was a genuine masterpiece of the theatre arts, the most ebullient buffonade that the Soviet theatre has ever known.'[12]

Later Tairov productions of the 1920s – *The Man who was Thursday, St Joan, The Hairy Ape, Desire under the Elms* and Hasenclever's *Antigone* – were significant for introducing the best of Western drama to Moscow, but were in consequence less close to the heart of the revolutionary theatre. His designer and actor, Boris Ferdinandov, felt impelled to break away and found his own Experimental-Heroic Theatre which aimed for a social and political relevance Tairov's work never achieved. Where Tairov's acting school was comparatively eclectic in its curriculum (for example, it included improvisation, dance, acrobatics and gymnastics, and juggling, as well as speech, diction and theatre history), Ferdinandov sought the 'fixed laws' of theatrical presentation, and taught 'metro-rhythmics', and the 'synthetic-theatrical gymnastics of the Experimental-Heroic Theatre'. However grandiose these terms and however high-flown Ferdinandov's ambitions, he created a number of brilliant productions together with his collaborator, the poet Vadim Shershenevich, culminating in the latter's satirical detective thriller, *The Lady in the Black Glove*, which was in some respects like a Keystone Cops movie, with a great deal of breathless chasing over ladders, horizontal bars and similar gymnastic equipment.

More sensational, and perhaps more significant, was the work of Nikolai Foregger, whose Theatre of Four Masks had operated in the sitting-room of his own home in the immediate post-revolutionary years. In 1921 he opened a new workshop, MastFor (Masterskaya Foreggera), where he developed his own system of theatrical and physical training, known as TePhyTrenage. Like Meyerhold, he divided the actor's functioning into two – that of the body, which must be like a machine, and that of the controlling brain – and developed a large number of exercises that enabled his actors to present programmes that mixed acrobatics, dance and stylised acting.

MastFor first made its name with comic, satirical parodies of current theatrical hits. *Even One Operetta is a Stumbling-block for a Wise Man* parodied Ostrovsky's *Even a Wise Man Stumbles*, for instance, and *The Rhinoceros* (*Nosorogie*) made fun of *The Magnanimous Cuckold* (*Rogonosets*). Probably of more significance were MastFor's 'parades' – cabaret-style miniature dramas, mostly written by Vladimir Mass, and organised musically at 'an American tempo' with characters deriving from Foregger's updated commedia of 'four masks'. These included the Female Communist in leather jacket and with brief-case under her arm; the Mystical Intellectual, an overblown Symbolist Poet; the Militiaman, a comic Soviet policeman; and the NEPman, ostentatiously 'nouveau riche'; as well as the inevitable Red Clown, Auguste, everybody's scapegoat. The parades were comic and satirical, featuring unexpected plot twists and plenty of slapstick. Mass based the best known, and probably the best, of them on Mayakovsky's poem, *Kindness to Horses*. An actor in a horse's head entered, and fell over. This was the cue for a variety of social types, such as a Braggart Soldier from the Russian Civil War and a 'Soviet Miss' in miniskirt and high boots, to respond to the pathos of the fallen beast. Its recovery was marked by a dynamic, celebratory and satirical cabaret.

In all his shows, Foregger's company danced – often the most modern, Western, 'decadent' dances, like the tango, the foxtrot, or the shimmy. Their most original dance, however, which gained the director-choreographer notoriety and international notice, was the 'machine dance', first shown on 13 February 1923. Using performers in tight black-and-white leotards, he created a kaleidoscope of mechanical patterns the like of which had never been seen before. The dancers ran onto the stage, rapidly formed a pyramid or similar 'construction' and to the accompaniment of a 'noise orchestra' – drums, a Jew's harp, the shaking of bags of broken glass, the clanging of metal objects, whispers and shrieks from the players themselves – they gradually stirred into mechanical motion. Their arms, or legs, sometimes their whole bodies, made pistons, gear-levers, crankhandles. In 'The Transmission Belt', for instance, two men stood about two metres apart with their arms out. As they rotated on the spot, their arms formed sprockets for a chain of actresses, the drive belt, to go round. Everything was performed in strict tempo and with maximum precision, and was expressive not only of the machine age the country was attempting to enter, but also, and more importantly, of the new yearning for organisation and productivity after the chaos and decline of the revolutionary Civil War. All these – parodies, parades, dances and sketches – combined to form an evening's revue-style entertainment, a series of numbers adding up to a montage of apparently unrelated items.

In terms of dance, Foregger was probably the most original choreographer in the early Soviet period, if only because he was so much more extreme than Gorsky, Goleizovsky, Lopukhov and others. His work was thought of as the high point of 'eccentrism', epitomised by the Poet in *Kindness to Horses,* whose costume consisted of two completely contradictory halves – a peasant's cap and smock on one side, a smoking jacket and top hat on the other. The designer for this was Sergei Eisenstein, the future film director, who also worked briefly with the leading eccentric group in Petrograd, known as Feks, the Factory of the Eccentric Actor. Under the leadership of Grigory Kozintsev and Leonid Trauberg, Feks presented their own outrageous version of Gogol's *Marriage* in September

1922. This was a fantastic kaleidoscope of theatrical wizardry, with dance, acrobatics, melodrama, clowning and even film sequences, succeeding one another in helter-skelter fashion, all played in front of a character representing Gogol sitting on a chamberpot wired to an electric point. In the end, he expired pitifully and in despair. Their second show, *Foreign Trade on the Eiffel Tower,* followed the same pattern, and was supposedly adapted from *Hamlet.* Soon after this, Kozintsev and Trauberg were invited by Sevzapkino to make a crazy comedy film, and they never returned to the theatre. Many years later, Kozintsev wrote an explanation of his and similar theatricalisations, which gives a key to the meaning and success of these works: 'It was a case of trying to find [theatrical forms] which could convey the intense sentiment of the new life. Unless this last point is recognized, our creations of the period would become incomprehensible. All these experiments, all these quests for new forms came because we had an intense feeling of an extraordinary renewal of life.'[13]

Eisenstein's own theatre work was even more significant in this context. He had studied for a year under Meyerhold, whose State Directing School had been absorbed into the new State Institute for Theatrical Art, GITIS, which for a time operated as an umbrella organisation for several workshops, including those of Ferdinandov, Foregger and Meyerhold. Eisenstein was Meyerhold's assistant on his next production after *The Magnanimous Cuckold,* a radical reworking of the gloomy nineteenth-century satire, *Tarelkin's Death,* now made carnivalesque, spectacular and dynamic. The setting consisted of a series of free-standing pieces, painted brilliant white and resembling gymnasium equipment more than stage scenery. These pieces, however, were constructed in such a way as to be able themselves to joke practically with the actors: at a climactic moment, a large trap-like cylinder actually devoured Brandakhlystova, the washerwoman. This part was played in the Meyerhold–Eisenstein production by the youthful male actor, Mikhail Zharov, in a theatrical travesty which was its own practical joke on the audience. The whole was further demystified in the interval, when actors played catch with spectators, and papier mâché apples were let down from the ceiling on strings, while big placards were flown in with slogans such as 'Death to the Tarelkins! Make way for the Meyerholds!' The show was structured round a series of chases using bladders on sticks, trapezes and so on to create a rhythm which mocked tsarist bureaucracy, the subject of the play, with the naive and youthful vigour of the new Soviet state.

Shortly after this, the GITIS organisation broke up in rancour. It was almost as if the celebratory period in the young Soviet Union was finished, to be replaced by something less attractive. Eisenstein moved to the first Workers Theatre of the Proletkult, almost all that was left of that once thriving organisation, while the Zon Theatre was given to Meyerhold exclusively, and renamed the Meyerhold Theatre. Here his first production was an adaptation by Sergei Tretyakov of Marcel Martinet's play, *Night*, now renamed *The World Turned Upside Down*. Tretyakov made a 'montage' of the text, reducing the five long acts to eight self-contained episodes, in order, he said, 'to lift the playgoer out of his equilibrium so that he will not leave serene, but ready for action'.[14] The aim signifies the new era. The production also marked a new creative playmaking process based less on an all-powerful director, and more on the equal contributions of writer, director and designer. All the revolutionary theatres had dominant directors, some of whom had used designers imaginatively, especially Vakhtangov and Tairov, while others, notably Foregger and Ferdinandov, had worked closely with writers. In *The World Turned Upside Down*, Meyerhold's work was complemented by Tretyakov's script and equally by Lyubov Popova's constructivist setting, so that this work was the result of three artists' almost equal collaboration. Popova, who had earlier designed *The Magnanimous Cuckold*, here moved a stage further, centring her conception on the use of space, but now not shaping it through the creation of objects within it, but rather letting it be itself. Moreover, anything which entered the space – telephones, typewriters, lorries, projection screens, and so on – did so as themselves, not as symbols of something else, or as representatives of reality: they were real. *The World Turned Upside Down* was thus a significant step in more than one new direction.

Meanwhile, Eisenstein was also employing Tretyakov to adapt Ostrovsky's *Even a Wise Man Stumbles*, which he planned to stage in the 'real' space of a circus ring. In Tretyakov's version, called simply *A Wise Man*, Glumov, the central character, was made into a White Clown, his mother into a Red Clown, and the action was transferred to Paris where the characters became Russian émigrés from the revolution. The circus idiom reached its climax when the villain, Golutvin, decided to return to Moscow, which he did over the heads of the audience on a tightrope. Glumov, less daring, went 'by the back way', leaving his mother, the Red Clown, on stage alone: 'Everybody's gone. But they've forgotten somebody,' she mutters, parodying Firs at the end of Chekhov's *The Cherry Orchard*.

Glumov's servant returns down the tightrope, holding onto a pulley by his teeth. The two clowns have a water fight, then the Red Clown turns to the audience and shouts: 'The end!' Fireworks explode under the seats of the spectators.

The production, a '*succès de scandal*', provoked Eisenstein into writing what is probably the most important theoretical justification of revolutionary theatre, 'The Montage of Attractions', published in *LEF* magazine in the summer of 1923. In this, he argues that the basic unit of the dramatic presentation is – or should be – the 'attraction', 'any aggressive moment of theatre' which will produce some kind of 'emotional shock' in the spectator. A series of such attractions are put together to create an 'effective structure' which 'moulds the audience in the desired direction'.[15] This is the 'montage' – in effect, a sophisticated rhythmic configuration, quite different from the usual type of dramatic construction.

This provocative formulation was the starting point for Eisenstein and Tretyakov to begin a period of intense practical research and thinking. With the rest of the company of the first Workers Theatre of the Proletkult, they worked out a system of 'expressive acting', developed partly from a study of the work of Jacques-Dalcroze and Bode, with which to present the new kind of play. Stricter than Tairov's system, less eclectic than Meyerhold's biomechanics, less diffuse than Foregger's TePhyTrenage, and more applicable than Ferdinandov's metro-rhythmics, expressive acting basically teaches the actor 'perfect' movement, and then how to deform that perfection so that it becomes expressive. Eisenstein pointed out that a person walking with perfect agility and athleticism down the road may express less in his walking than one with, say, a slight limp. The fruits of this conception can still be seen in Eisenstein's early films, which he made after staging two more provocative plays by Tretyakov, *Are You Listening, Moscow?* and *Gas Masks*. The latter acquired a certain notoriety because Eisenstein, in the continuing search for 'real space', presented the play in an actual gas works in Moscow. This was a mistake – the play's 'reality' lay paradoxically in its theatricality – but the experiment may have helped to direct the revolutionary theatre back to more conventional playing spaces.

Gas Masks attempted to dramatise an incident from real life, which Tretyakov had read about in a newspaper. It owes a clear debt to the 'living newspaper' devised by Terevsat, so that it is no surprise to find that Tretyakov was a critical sympathiser of the movement which took up this form, and which was in some senses the heir to both Proletkult and Terevsat, the Blue Blouses. Created by a journalist with a keen feeling for theatre, Boris Yuzhanin, and making their debut in October 1923, the Blue Blouses developed 'living newspaper' techniques for their tendentious and propagandistic revue-style presentations so successfully that in a very short time, there were Blue Blouse groups operating all over the country. They were touring troupes, some of them professional supported by the trade unions, but mostly amateur, and they performed in workers' clubs, factory canteens, in the reading rooms of peasant villages and other similar venues. By the mid 1920s they published a magazine, *The Blue Blouse*, which contained actable scripts, photographs, suggestions for staging, and so on, as well as theoretical discussions. In 1927 they reached the height of their renown in a strikingly successful tour of Germany, where groups in imitation of them sprang up like mushrooms.

However, by then Stalin had won his victory against the Left Opposition and times were changing rapidly. That same year the Communist Party instigated an enquiry into the Blue Blouse organisation to assess how it could be used, not to stir up debate, which is what a montage of attractions tends to do, but for ends the party would determine. In 1928 the *Blue Blouse* magazine was closed down, and Yuzhanin was replaced. The troupes themselves were ordered to concentrate on propagating the party line and, after 1930, to praise Stalin specifically. With self-motivation no longer permitted, groups simply disbanded, and the Blue Blouse movement faded away.

A similar tale of Communist domination was increasingly evident in the theatres themselves. In 1927, Michael Chekhov, Vakhtangov's Erik XIV, was denounced as 'a "sick actor" who spurted a mystical infection toward the entire Soviet theatre'.[16] He was apparently due to be arrested in 1928, but fled from Moscow the day before this was to be carried out. His absence from his native Russia, and his partially successful later career in the West, did nothing to dim the memory of his best performances, which had struck a particular chord with the audiences of revolutionary times, however 'mystical' they may have been. Many remembered his performance as Khlestakov, for instance, in Stanislavsky's production of *The Government Inspector* at the Moscow Academic Art Theatre in 1921,[17] when his performance carried many of the hallmarks of revolutionary theatre – despite Stanislavsky's apparent lack of sympathy with this style: 'Chekhov's Khlestakov now dived underneath the table three times in search of money, now skipped across the stage like a young goat, now lusting for the mayor's wife, gnawed the leg of a chair, now mocking Khlopov, moved a burning candle about right under his nose. Countless mischievous, eccentric pranks followed one after another, forming themselves into the dodging confused line of behaviour of the unprepossessing, snub-nosed official from Petersburg.'[18]

Although times were harsher for revolutionary theatres (often damned now as 'formalist') after Stalin's ascendancy was confirmed, there were still astounding performances which used the old revolutionary energy and spectacle to make their impact. A brilliant example, and one which may be compared with Michael Chekhov and Stanislavsky's achievement of 1921, was Meyerhold's own *The Government Inspector*, first performed in December 1926. Set inside an ominous semicircle of polished mahogany doors – fifteen of them in all – the scenes were played on small trucks wheeled on and off to make unexpected close-ups, the stage only occasionally opening up for full use, as it were, in long shot. The scenes of Khlestakov, played by the spindly Erast Garin with a doughnut in his lapel, idly mistaking the mayor's wife's finger for the sugar, and spooning it into his teacup; of the corrupt officials spying on Khlestakov through all those nightmare doors; and of the myriad of fantasy hussars serenading the mayor's wife, played by Meyerhold's wife, Zinaida Raikh, and even committing suicide for her sake, have luckily been preserved on film, and something of Meyerhold's extreme theatricalism can be perceived.

Meyerhold's production of *The Government Inspector* caused a furore in theatre-going Moscow. This was, however, as nothing compared to the storm provoked by Igor Terentiev's production of the same play at the Leningrad House of the Press the following year. Meyerhold's nightmare was here rendered down to irreverent farce, and in place of the polished mahogany doors, Terentiev used five tall, free-standing cubicles. When the play began, the town officials were apparently in the cubicles, and from their groans one understood they were in toilets. Later, Khlestakov took the mayor's wife, and then his daughter, into one of the cubicles, and again the noises, this time squeals of delight, which emanated therefrom told what was going on within. Meyerhold's ending, whereby the characters metamorphosed into tailor's dummies in a *coup de théâtre* which staggered the audience, was matched by Terentiev's finale, when the townspeople froze and Khlestakov reappeared, and read with cool irony Gogol's character notes about each.

The apparent rivalry between Meyerhold and Terentiev reached its climax over the production of what was to prove Sergei Tretyakov's last play, *I Want a Baby*. The play centred on Milda, the party worker-type with jackboots and a brief-case under her arm, who thinks to serve the party by giving birth to a perfect proletarian baby. After a series of debilitating, horrific and hilarious episodes, she achieves her aim and becomes pregnant. But in a dream at the end of the play, the monstrousness of her project, its desiccated inhumanity, is evoked, and we see a society robbed not only of ugliness, but of comfort, compassion and fun as well. According to the author, the play was an attempt to 'provoke the healthy discussion which society needs' on the subjects it raises, such as the rational organisation of society, sex and the morality of genetic engineering, and the position of women and their rights in a progressive society.[19]

The themes are important, but the play, a montage of attractions which includes both farce and tragedy, a satirical ballet of 'The Emancipation of Women' and a gang rape, was banned, and despite a thorough rewriting was still disallowed until Meyerhold suggested that he and Terentiev submit alternative schemes for a production to the censorship committee. This they did, and although Tretyakov himself expressed a preference for Terentiev's conception, Meyerhold's plan was allowed to pass. It had a design by El Lissitzky which used not only the stage, but also the theatre's galleries and gangways for the action, and seated the audience around the interior, thus providing them with the means to join in what was happening. With underfloor lighting and slogans round the walls and gallery railings, it was cetainly spectacular, but according to one critic, it was more than this, for Lissitzky here 'fused architectural and theatrical elements together to create a new concept of the theatrical stage and the theatrical interior'.[20]

But in spite of obtaining permission for this production, the design remained unrealised, and the play unstaged. The Zon Theatre's state of repair made it virtually untenable, and Meyernold had been promised a new theatre. *I Want a Baby* was therefore postponed until this was completed. It never was. The unfinished *I Want a Baby* seems even in its title to embody the yearning for a future which revolutionary theatre was denied. The nearest the theatre came to achieving some fitting culmination to its ten-year experiment, therefore, was probably seen in some of Meyerhold's other productions, even though by the early 1930s he had no permanent theatre of his own. Perhaps the most notable of these were of the last two plays by Mayakovsky, *The Bedbug* and The *Bathhouse*. The first of them is now the better known: it satirises Prysipkin, a 'former worker and former Party member, currently a fiancé' who gets married, but in the drunken revelry of the wedding reception, the restaurant is burned down. The water used to put out the fire then freezes. Fifty years later, when a thaw sets in, the deep-frozen Prysipkin is uncovered and resuscitated. He is of course completely out of step with the fearsome, automated future society.

Mayakovsky, however, is less concerned with the overt meaning of the story as with the implicit theatricality of the dramaturgy. It is spectacular, naive, and uses broken rhythms to surprise the spectator, which was what appealed to Meyerhold. As far as the acting was concerned, Mayakovsky insisted, the characters must have 'no biographies'. 'Everything must be understandable. No psychologising.'[21] The style derived from 'the little genres – circus, variety stage, music hall', noted Vladimir Lyutse, a former student of Meyerhold, who directed the premiere in Leningrad. 'The actor's performance is created through the solving of a series of physical problems.'[22] The actor was required constantly to change genres, even while on stage: at one moment a singer, then a dancer, an acrobat, a dramatic actor, and so on. And not only must the actor be able to effect these transformations, but often he is required not to 'be' what he is showing, but to create an exaggerated parody of it. These demands fully reveal the purpose of the biomechanical training.

It also suggests that the production was constructed rhythmically. In this, the music by the young Dmitry Shostakovich was central. Already becoming embroiled in controversy about his brilliant atonal opera, *The Nose*, itself a late flowering of revolutionary theatre on the opera stage, and warned that if he did not 'recognize his false step . . . his creative work is headed for an absolute dead end',[23] Shostakovich nevertheless managed to respond to Meyerhold's contention that 'in *The Bedbug* there are a number of extraordinary shifts from one episode to another in which we feel the best rhythmic modulations of Shakespeare'.[24] Thus, in the wedding scene itself, Shostakovich created a smoochy foxtrot, which was then picked up by the off-stage band and put into the relative major key to become 'stormy' and 'grotesque'. Quite quickly, the theme was 'devoured by wild, unthinkable collisions between ever-stronger sounds'.[25] The music itself effected the transition to the future.

The music thus became not simply a means of moving from one attraction to another, but an attraction in its own right. Lyutse noted that 'a

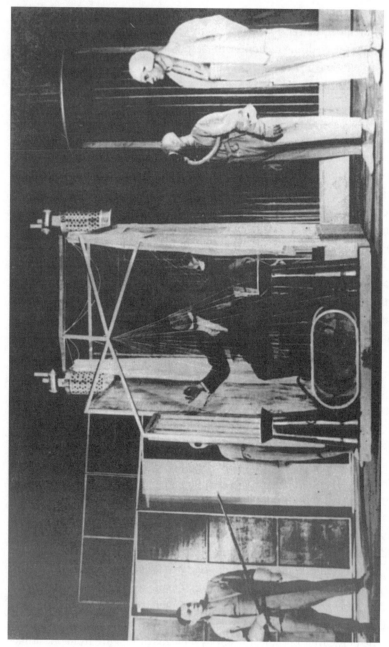

31. A scene from Vladimir Mayakovsky's *The Bedbug*, directed by Vsevolod Meyerhold, Meyerhold State Theatre, 1929.

production which is properly faithful' to the author's intentions 'will be built as a montage of attractions',[26] and, according to *Pravda*'s reviewer, Meyerhold's production achieved this: '"Psychology" is completely absent. The action proceeds by shocks and merrily. The laughter is by no means Chekhovian, but is the harsh, rather coarse, uncompromising laughter of a social activist, political laughter which has its own form.'[27] The designers also made their own independent contribution to the montage. For the 'reality' of the first part, 'Kukriniksy' dressed the characters and decorated the stage with 'real' clothes and properties, bought in Moscow shops. Rodchenko's clinical, desiccated future presented in the second part of the play was wholly different: white and austere, it was a world quite incapable of dealing with the venal Prysipkin. It was his nightmare which Rodchenko presented.

Prysipkin's horrified vision, of course, was as nothing compared to the reality which overtook Russia, and notably its revolutionary artists, in the 1930s and 1940s. Seeing the drift of events, perhaps, the closing of many doors, Mayakovsky committed suicide in 1930. In the following decade, Shostakovich, Eisenstein, Rodchenko and others were effectively silenced. In 1937 Tretyakov was arrested and killed. Meyerhold's theatre was never built, or rather, was turned into the Tchaikovsky Concert Hall, while his company was disbanded, and he himself arrested in 1939. When Meyerhold was shot in prison on 2 February 1940, the rich promise of revolutionary theatre had reached the bloody end of its road.

Notes

1. E. Kuznetsov, quoted in D. Zolotnitskii, *Zori Teatral' nogo Oktiabria* (Leningrad, 1976), p. 246.
2. V. Maiakovskii, *Mystery Bouffe*, in G. Daniels (tr.), *The Complete Plays of Vladimir Mayakovsky* (New York, 1968), pp. 45–6.
3. I. V. Il'inskii, *Sam o sebe* (Moscow, 1984), p. 198.
4. A. Fevral'skii, *Vstrechi s Meierkhol'dom* (Moscow, 1967), pp. 185.
5. W. Wordsworth, *The Prelude*, Book 11, lines 108–9.
6. See R. Leach, *Vsevolod Meyerhold* (Cambridge, 1989), passim.
7. P. Markov, 'Pervaia studiia MXT', in *Pravda teatr* (Moscow, 1965), p. 308; quoted in L. Black, *Mikhail Chekhov as Actor, Director and Teacher* (Ann Arbor, 1987), pp. 18–19.
8. Quoted in N. Worrall, *Modernism to Realism on the Soviet Stage* (Cambridge, 1989), p. 122.
9. C. Diderot, 'The Paradox of Acting', in T. Cole and H. K. Chinoy *Actors on Acting* (New York, 1970), pp. 164–5.

10. V. Meierkhol'd, 'Printsipy biomekanika', *Teatral'naia Zhizn'* (Jan 1990), p. 24.
11. Alexander Tairov, *Notes of a Director*, tr. William Kuhlke (Coral Gables, Fla., 1969), p. 142.
12. N. A. Gorchakov, *The Theater in Soviet Russia* (New York, 1957), p. 228.
13. Quoted in L. and J. Schnitzer, *Cinema in Revolution* (London, 1973), p. 94.
14. Quoted in P. Nizmanov, 'The Soviet theatre today', *International Literature* (July 1933), p. 140.
15. Richard Taylor (ed.), *S. M. Eisenstein: Selected Works*, (3 vols., London, 1988–96), vol. I, p. 34.
16. Black, *Mikhail Chekov*, p. 20.
17 In 1920 the Moscow Art Theatre (MAT) became the Moscow Academic Art Theatre (MXAT) and was subsidised by the central government instead of the Moscow city council. After 1920 it was still popularly called the 'Art Theatre', but later it became known as MXAT (pronounced 'mu-hat').
18. K. Rudnitskii, *Russian and Soviet Theatre* (London, 1988). p. 52.
19. S. Tretiakov, *Slyshish' Moskva?!* (Moscow, 1966), p. 198.
20. C. Lodder, 'El Lissitzky's set for Sergei Tretyakov's *I Want a Child*, and constructivist stage design', unpublished paper given at a conference, 'Tretyakov: Brecht's teacher', at the University of Birmingham, Jan 1989.
21. 'Poet v teatr', *Literaturnoe Obozrenie*, no. 11 (1978), p. 109.
22. *Klop* (Gosudarstvennyi Bolshoi Dramatich. Teatr. Filol., Leningrad, 1929), p. 10.
23. Quoted in F. K. Prieberg, '"The Nose" by Shostakovich' (Ariola Eurodisc, 89 502 XFR).
24. A. Gladkov, 'Meyerhold speaks', in E. and C. R. Proffer (ed.), *Russian Futurism* (Ann Arbor, 1980), p. 218.
25. K. Rudnitsky, *Meyerhold the Director*, tr. George Petrov, ed. Sydney Schultze (Ann Arbor, 1981), p. 445.
26. *Klop*, p. 10.
27. *Pravda*, 24 Feb 1929.

15 The theatre and Socialist Realism, 1929–1953

INNA SOLOVYOVA

TRANSLATION BY JEAN BENEDETTI

Soviet theatre historians correctly described the year 1929 as a more significant watershed than 1917. In the years that followed the October Revolution the leading personalities, writers, directors, actors remained the same. While, in that year, some dramatists (Aleksei Faiko, Nikolai Erdman, Vselvolod Ivanov) faded from view, and one or two newcomers made their appearance (Aleksandr Afinogenov, Vladimir Kirshon, Vsevolod Vishnevsky, Nikolai Pogodin), essentially the most performed writers were still Leonid Leonov, Boris Romashov and Bill-Belotserkovsky. It was the same with directors. Despite his heart attack in 1928, Stanislavsky continued to supervise new MXAT productions. Nemirovich-Danchenko, Meyerhold, Taïrov were all at the height of their powers. The off-shoots of the Art Theatre, The First and Second Studios, the Second Art Theatre remained a dominant influence. Two former pupils of the First Studio, Aleksei Diky and Aleksei Popov, had come to artistic maturity. Ilya Sudakov, a product of the Second Studio, who had directed *The Days of the Turbins* (1926) and *The Armoured Train* (1927), was instrumental in creating a new repertoire. The Second Art Theatre, under Bersenev, Sushkevich and Birman maintained its individual artistic policy. Vakhtangov's influence was still strong and his successors, young and old, such as Yuri Zavadsky, Ruben Simonov and Boris Zakhava, continued to maintain the highest professional standards. Nikolai Petrov, noted earlier for his wide range and the effortless manner in which he moved from Expressionism to drawing-room comedy, moved with equal ease in 1928 to Soviet propaganda plays on the same stage, with the same company. The cast-lists remained the same. Such new faces as there were did not produce any kind of radical change or break-through.

In his pamphlet *Our Policy for the Theatre* Robert Pelshe, a critic and party apparatchik, stated ruefully that no one in the Bolshevik party had come properly to grips with the theatre after the Revolution and that 'during the first five years after the Revolution the same old repertoire went on regardless'.

This was not entirely the case. The government had set up a committee, the Glavrepertkom, to supervise repertoire as early as 1923 and it had by no means been idle. Nemirovich-Danchenko stated, without comment, in a letter of the same year: 'it bans a play when it considers it counter-revolutionary, or when it isn't Soviet enough, or when there's a tsar (*Snow Maiden*) or a figure of authority (*The Governor*) or when the past is beautiful or there's a church (*A Nest of the Gentry*) or whatever'.[1] The Glavrepertkom cooperated with the GPU (later to become the KGB) but still had not managed to gain full control or impose a single ideology

Artists had their own agenda on which there were two items: self-preservation and self-transformation, both pursued with equal vigour. It is essential to grasp this willingness on the part of artists to change, develop and transform in response to a new society. In a private letter Nemirovich-Danchenko wrote that thanks to the Revolution he had been able to change in the way he wanted. He was prepared to excuse the inadequate technique, the crude ideas of the writers he was working with provided, like Kirshon and Afigonenov, they were rooted in nature.

The crucial dilemma for the party was to determine how far it could give free rein to natural creative processes, even when they were moving in the direction it wanted. Natural, spontaneous creativity is the last thing a totalitarian régime wants from an artist, because the creative act (like life) is innately non-totalitarian. Consciously or unconsciously, there is something in art which resists ideology. A study of Russian theatre in the 1930s and 1940s enables us to discover just what that 'something' is.

Pelshe's article expresses irritation and frustration at the capacity of art to resist pressure, its refusal to be steamrollered, its capacity to bounce back. Later in his article he takes the Art Theatre, in particular, to task for ideological back-sliding. How could a theatre which had presented *The Armoured Train*, to mark the tenth anniversary of the Revolution, first stage Bulgakov's *The Days of the Turbins*, which many considered sympathetic to the counter-revolutionary White Guard, then *Flight*, as well as *The Embezzlers* and *Untilovsk* which dared to suggest there was corruption in the local government? And who wanted Chekhov? This was not the repertoire of the new Soviet Union. 'This . . . unquestionably reveals the political opposition of petit-bourgeois elements in our society and their hostility to progressive proletarian-socialist ideology.'[2]

Pelshe's article also gives us a foretaste of the dead jargon which the theatre had to learn to decipher after 1929, the watershed year, the year in which everything changed. The limited mixed economy Lenin had introduced under the New Economic Policy was replaced by the first Five Year Plan, a command economy with centralised control, that gave priority to the development of heavy industry and imposed the collectivisation of agriculture at the cost of millions of lives. The ruthless and deliberate construction of communism was under way. Trotsky and his followers had been ousted from the party leadership, internal conflict had been eradicated. Stalin was gathering the reins of power ever more tightly to himself.

1929 was also the year in which Lunacharsky was sacked. In May 1927 Lunacharsky had still thought it necessary to bring his underlings to heel and remind them that the theatre 'was a delicate matter'. Should it be ill, it needed 'a real doctor, not a horse-doctor'.[3] The days of such tact were over. He was replaced by Bubnov, an ex- soldier whose sole talent was for giving orders. Even Lenin's widow, who worked in the people's commissariat, and knew how to be tough, was shocked by the tone that was being adopted.[4]

The party machine was efficient and well-oiled by the beginning of the 1930s. Anyone in control could guarantee to steamroller anything with greater and greater ease and that included the arts which had, like industry and agriculture, to be brought into line with the new policy. They were part of the construction of communism.

A major factor in keeping the theatres in line was their financial dependence on the state, the only patron of the arts remaining after the Revolution. The state was, on occasion, a generous benefactor and its generosity was supposed to elicit feelings of gratitude (Stanislavsky and Nemirovich-Danchenko expressed this sentiment quite sincerely).

The Agitprop Section of the Central Committee summed up the situation:

Under the dictatorship of the proletariat, when theatres are the property of the Soviet government . . . when we hold the means to regulate and direct their activities, such as state subsidies and the Glavrepertkom, all theatres . . . can move more or less quickly in a socialist direction, they can and must undergo a period of ideological and political reconstruction.[5]

Production budgets and salaries were decided centrally. This was nothing new for those who could remember the old tsarist bureaucracy. But the creative process was also now defined centrally and that was new. The new policy for the arts was Socialist Realism, a term that first came into usage in 1932.

Opening the First Congress of Soviet Writers in 1934, the Secretary of the Central Committee of the Communist Party, Zhdanov spoke of the need to know life so as to be able to portray its revolutionary development properly: 'Truth and historical concreteness of artistic portrayal must be combined with the task of ideologically transforming working people and educating them in the spirit of socialism. We call this method of writing Socialist Realism.'

To know life and portray it correctly – who among those who adhered to the traditional principles of Russian realism could object to that? But the words that followed deprived actors and directors of any possibility of holding on to the fundamentals of their art. Any attempt by an artist to create a separate, aesthetically self-sufficient inner world, any claim to the intrinsic value of the creative act, or the imagination, was outside the limits prescribed to Soviet artists.

Socialist Realism, the fundamental principle of which was drawn from Lenin's essay, *Party Organization and Party Literature*, entailed a specific selection of the material to be represented and a specific approach to it. The art it created was posited as the inheritor of the 'fertile aesthetic tradition of all world art'. In the theatre, this 'fertile' tradition was declared to be the tradition of Russian realism, going back to Shchepkin and successfully developed by the Art Theatre.

In his speech Zhdanov also quoted Stalin's definition of artists as 'the engineers of the soul'. Just as the Five Year Plan would transform the economy, so Soviet artists would transform the attitudes of their fellow citizens and help forge the New Man. In the crude materialist ideology that was being created notions of the unconscious and latent content were rejected. Human nature was the product of social forces. Change the forces and you changed man. Nature, human and otherwise, could be controlled and manipulated. This principle found its most extreme expression in the genetics of the biologist, Lysenko, who claimed he could produce new species in one generation and so increase productivity several fold. This delusion, fanatically defended by the party ideologues, ruined Soviet agriculture for decades. But the concept of centralised, planned control over all human activities, including the arts, was too attractive to be abandoned easily.

In its role as a contributor to the construction of communism, the theatre was only to present positive values. Everything was to be done to encourage belief in the party and its policies, which ensured the future happiness of all good Soviet citizens.

Few at the time realised the full implications of Zhdanov's speech, which amounted to a total reversal of previous policy. The avant-garde was now under fire. The classics were reinstated and Chekhov, whom Pelshe had so confidently dismissed as irrelevant, once more became a key author.

Between 1934 and 1938 the theatres were reorganised. The Proletkult theatres had already been abolished in 1932, although they had actually ceased to be of any real significance much earlier. The Association of Proletarian Writers (RAPP) was also disbanded to be replaced by the Writers' Union. In the process of producing a monolithic party, it was, ironically, the so-called 'hard left' that was the first to suffer.

The main attack, however, was reserved for the avant-garde. The enemy was now Formalism. What was meant was not the highly sophisticated body of theory that critics like Viktor Shklovsky had developed. It was a crude blanket term that could be applied whenever the party leadership felt so inclined. Any overt concern with aesthetic problems rather than with 'the task of ideologically transforming working people' was condemned as 'Formalist'.

Socialist Realism was also marked by a tone of high seriousness. By the mid-1930s, the hammer also began to fall on art which was undoubtedly true to life but accused of being petty, puny and quite incapable of portraying the revolutionary development of life. Many small theatres suffered because they had built a repertoire out of humourous, true-to-life revues, of comedies, melodramas and entertainments about ordinary Soviet life, which were classed as non-ideological and therefore, once again, non-Soviet. Playwrights with a gift for farce or situation comedy or wit or humour or simple theatricality had their lives ruined. Vasily Shkvarkin was a typical example. He started his career in the theatre as a warm-hearted humorous professional, giving traditional characters like the fool, the innocent, the good-natured rogue a Soviet flavour, and traditional situations a new twist. His sketches and satirical revues which had undoubted success with audiences were taken apart every time by the party press as 'limited' and 'mere entertainment', 'a distorted picture of Soviet man' etc. Small wonder that he lapsed into deep depression.

The party had its own concept of 'entertainment'. In 1936 a festival of art from all the republics in the USSR was organised in Moscow. It was crowned by gala concerts and receptions in the Kremlin for artists and government leaders at which awards were distributed. The party knew how to reward the worthy as well as chastise the dissident.

Everyone was aware that there was a new party line on art but no one could be sure what it was. The decisions that came from on high were arbitrary. There was no apparent logic or consistency to them. Artists attempted to read the signs, to guess what the party line on any particular work or issue would be. And to guess wrongly now entailed far more than the vilification Bulgakov had had to suffer after *The Days of the Turbins*. It entailed, in the growing atmosphere of terror, arrest and imprisonment and possibly torture and death. Lunarcharsky's successor had been an early victim. Within months of being appointed he was declared an enemy of the people and quickly shot. That was the pattern: a People's Commissar one year, a traitor the next.

This was the period in which the Communist party was being ruthlessly purged. One after the other the old Bolshevik guard came forward at their show trials and confessed to crimes against the state they had not committed and were then taken away and shot. Actors, writers, directors and musicians lived in a state of constant fear. The ways of the party, like the ways of God, were inscrutable and the Kremlin shrouded itself in an atmosphere of quasi-religious mystery.

Artists had to learn to read the signs, to construct a possible 'line' out of hints. An opportunity came in 1936 with the creation of the title People's Artist of the Soviet Union, awarded to 'those most prominent in the arts'. This would show who was in favour and who was not. The initial list was short and significant. Nemirovich-Danchenko who was included, alongside Stanislavsky, Kachalov and Moskvin wrote: 'I understand why Meyerhold isn't on it. That indicates the line.' The line was also indicated by the conferment of the title on old artists: on Maria Blumenthal-Tamarina, who had recently appeared at the Maly, on Ekaterina Korchargin-Aleksandrovskaya, who had been performing at the former Aleksandrinsky, now Pushkin theatre, for more than twenty years. Both were expert in realism, inventive and sincere interpreters of Ostrovsky, and had recently appeared in Soviet plays. Korchargin-Aleksandrovskaya played the Bolshevik, Clara, in Afinogenov's *Fear*, in 1931, the nurse Khristina Arkhipovna in Aleksandr Korneichuk's *Platon Krechet* in 1935. Blumenthal-Tamarina had played the mother of the heroic pilot, Motylkov, in Gusev's *Glory* in 1936.

The line was also evident in the award of the title to Boris Shchukin, who had worked with Vakhtangov. He was not only a man of rare talent but Russian to the core. His acting fascinated by its overt theatricality and its trueness to life, its strength that was learned 'from living'. He played Tartaglia, the stammerer, in *Turandot* and Lev Guzyck Sinichkin in Lensky's vaudeville. He also played in Gorky's *Egor Bulychov and Others* (1932). As the cancer-ridden, depressed, roguish merchant, who asks God, 'Why do people have to die?' he lived the philosophical dilemma powerfully, his body and mind seething with indignation, unable to reconcile himself to his approaching end. As an actor he was undoubtedly a genius. However, to the perceptive mind the 'line' was clear: Shchukin was being honoured for his roles as Bolsheviks – Pavel Suslov in *Virinea*, Pavel in Leonov's *The Badgers* and the captain of the cruiser in Boris Lavrenev's *Breakup*, who goes over to the revolutionaries, and for the builder, Ermolai, in Pogodin's *Tempo*. And for Lenin in *The Man with the Rifle* which he was already rehearsing (he played it in 1937).

National theatres received encouragement. In the Ukraine Saksargansky became a People's Artist, as did Khorava and Vasadze in Georgia.

Nemirovich-Danchenko was not surprised by Meyerhold's absence but he was by Oleg Leonidov's. Leonidov was a senior member of the Art Theatre, a major tragic actor. The MXAT management thought it was a clerical error and took steps to get it rectified. Barely two months passed before Leonidov was named People's Artist in a decree dated 1 November 1936. The real reason, which was kept hidden, was anti-semitism. It was, however, many years before the government would come out into the open.

Not only was it impossible to anticipate who would be attacked, it was impossible to foresee when the blow would fall. It could come out of a clear sky. The Second Art Theatre was taken completely unawares by the decision, taken by the People's Commissars and the Central Committee of the Communist Party, and published in *Izvestia* on 28 February 1936 to close it down. What comes across in Sofia Giatsintova's memoirs, written late in life, is not so much suffering from old wounds, or indignation at the arbitrariness of it all, but bewilderment. Why were they closed down? Ivan Bersenev had taken the theatre over after Michael Chekhov, the 'defector' as he was labelled, had emigrated in 1928, and seemed to have put the theatre out of danger. The traditions of the First Studio – *Cricket on the Hearth* still in the repertoire, a new version of *Twelfth Night*, with sets by Favoysky and with Giatsintova as Maria and Durasova as Viola, staged in 1933 – were squared with the demands of a new age. The Second Art Theatre had found a talented writer who gravitated towards psychological realism and was at the same time a reliable communist: Aleksandr Afinogenov. His *Crank* (1929) is about an enthusiastic builder working in the back-of-beyond, with Azarii Azarin as Volgin, Serafima Birman as Troshchina and Giatsintova as Sima. Though later productions – Karavaeva's *The Homestead* (1930), Mikitenko's *Shine, Stars* (1930) and *A Matter of Honour* (1931) were less successful, they were still on the plus side, Soviet material with a Soviet purpose. And if the gloomy tone of the historical tragedies that were staged – *Peter I* (1930) with sets by Ignaty Nivinsky, and the revival of the *Death of Ivan the Terrible* (1934) – ran counter to the socialist realist drive for optimism, that was surely compensated for by the sparkle and joy of *Twelfth Night* and the renaissance colours of Fletcher's *The Spanish Curate* (1934) with sets by Lentulov and Giatsintova as Amaranta and Birman as Violanta. On his return to the USSR from Italy, Gorky started on a new version of *Vassa Zheleznova* for Birman, with her razor-sharp inner technique ('I'm a tight-rope walker, not a pedestrian'). The Second Art Theatre's last production, Deval's *Plea for Life* (1935) with the highly popular Ivan Bersenev as Pierre Massoubre and Giatsintova as Genevieve, had an extremely enthusiastic press. Favourable critics presented it as an exposé of bourgeois society. Then the lightning struck out of a clear sky.

This closure, however, was not an isolated incident. It marked the beginning of a virulent campaign against the Formalists. An article entitled the 'Second Art Theatre' appeared in *Pravda* on the same day as the announcement in *Izvestia*, alongside a devastating attack on Shostakovich, 'Muddle not Music' and 'Balletic Lies'. The day before Stanislavsky had been asked to write a letter in the theatre's defence, despite the fact that he had considered his ex-pupils to have betrayed everything artistically he held most dear, he agreed. But the letter was never sent. It was made quite clear to him it would do no good. To this day no clear explanation of the reasons for the closure has been forthcoming.

The clouds could gather for a long time and loom threateningly as with Meyerhold's theatre, Gostim. Of the twenty-six plays it staged the bulk were by Soviet writers. Four new works were performed in 1929: Mayakovsky's *Bedbug*, Selvinsky's *The Second Commander*, Bezymensky's *Shot* and the review *A Window on our Country*. Mayakovsky's *Bathhouse* followed in 1930 and Olesha's *A List of Blessings* and Vishnevsky's *The Last Fight* in 1931 and German's *Prelude* in 1933. In 1937 Gostim staged Evgeny Gabriolovich's *One Life*, an adaptation of the novel *How The Steel was Tempered*. Nikolai Ostrovsky, who wrote the novel on his sick-bed, blind and paralysed from wounds he received in the Civil War, became a martyr and saint in the communist calendar, a classic of Soviet literature. None the less, Gostim was accused of being out of touch with Soviet life, of having a predilection for writers who were enemies of the people and of being opposed to the general drive towards Socialist Realism.

On 17 December 1937, *Pravda* published an article 'An Alien Theatre'. On 7 January 1938, the government committee with responsibility for the arts decreed the closure of Gostim as a theatre that had adopted 'a totally bourgeois formalist position, not in keeping with Soviet art'. Its artistic director was arrested on 20 June 1939, tortured and shot. The leading actress, Zinaïda Raikh[6] was later murdered in her apartment in mysterious circumstances.

Life continued somehow under the clouds. Executions began, then were stopped. 'Justice', it seemed, was being tempered with mercy. Then the thunder would roll again, but then the lightning would cease. The story of Aleksandr Taïrov and the Kamerny theatre is a prime example.

If anyone reached the watershed year ill-equipped to 'reflect Soviet reality' it was Taïrov. Indeed, he was even openly mocking the government. In 1928, the Kamerny put on Bulgakov's *Purple Island*. The action of this satire takes place in a theatre where they are talking about submitting an ideologically sound play about a mass uprising on a non-existent and uninhabited island to the Repertkom. It was after that episode that Stalin called the Kamerny ' a really bourgeois theatre'. Sentence was thus passed in 1929. Execution only came much later in 1950.

True the theatre mended its ways and the mockery stopped. Plays were

32. Vsevolod Vishnevsky's *An Optimistic Tragedy*, directed by Aleksandr Tairov. Kamerny Theatre, 1933.

staged that fell into line with other new works extolling the Revolution and the heroic construction of socialism: Semionov's *Natalya Tarpova* (1929), Nikitin's *Line of Fire*, Kulish's *Sonate Pathétique* (1931), Pervomaisky's *Unknown Soldiers* (1932), Kaverin's *Taming of Mr Robinson* (1933). These weak productions were followed by the success of Vishnevsky's *Optimistic Tragedy* of 1933.

It was a success and saved the theatre's reputation. The flood of accusations of bourgeois aestheticism and hostility to Soviet reality was stemmed. But it was also a success artistically. The play, which concerned a state of anarchy in the navy and a female commissar triumphing over it by force of will, was seen as fundamental to the Kamerny's programme and its task of presenting emotionally lived forms. Expressive physical shapes were found for a revolutionary explosion – tight circles swirling downwards as in a crater. The theatre had found the right space for tragedy, its speech, music, light, rhythm, its brevity and scope.

Taïrov was apparently sufficiently in favour to be asked to welcome the participants on behalf of all theatre people at the 1934 Writer's Congress. But Taïrov did not know what the party line was any more than Alisa Koonen, his wife.

Execution again seemed imminent in 1936. A decision was taken by the Central Committee with regard to Taïrov's production of *Heroes* (words by Demyan Bedny to the music of Borodin's parody opera of the same name). Writing in the spirit of his usual antireligious sketches and revue items about the conversion of Rus, Bedny failed to detect the military, patriotic shift in party policy and his work was condemned as 'a distortion of our national past'. Taïrov was described in even tougher terms: the theatre in general was 'out of line politically'. In August 1937, the company of the Realistic Theatre, which had also been attacked with equal severity for 'Formalism', was merged with the Kamerny, together with its director, Okhlopov. The newcomers were aliens and the atmosphere deteriorated. Internal conflict grew. The quality of productions suffered. Mdivani's *Alkazar, Honour, Battalion Goes West* (1936, 1938, 1942), Yanovsky's *Thoughts about the Ukraine* (1937), Zhatkin and Vechoya's *Kochubei* (1938), adapted from a novel by Perventsev about the Civil War, bore a superficial resemblance to the theatre's policy of 'romantic drama' but were empty and worthless. For ten months, from the autumn of 1939 the theatre went to the Far East on military service.

While they were there, Alisa Koonen rehearsed the part of Emma

Bovary which she premiered in 1940. In Flaubert's novel, which she adapted herself, Koonen emphasised the incompatibility of Emma's exalted world with the mundane world around her with the inevitable resulting catastrophe.

On their return after their evacuation, Taïrov staged *The Seagull* with Koonen. She was fifty-six, and made no attempt to appear, or play, younger than she was. She gave a concert-version about the fame and fortune Nina blindly followed as an actress. After *The Seagull* came Ostrovsky's *Guilty Without Guilt*, with Koonen as Kruchinina, seen as a romantic novella about a great actress. The roles Koonen acted formed a triptych, glorifying tragic art. After that, a full stop.

After the war they staged Bergoltz and Makagonenko's *Faithful Hearts*, Kozhevnikov and Prut's *The Fate of Reginald Davis*, Yakobson's *Life in the Citadel*, and Vasilev and Elston's *Actors*. But neither these characterless works nor Ilya Erenburg's *The Lion on the Square* with sets by Robert Falk, nor an efficient production of Gorky's *Old Man*, nor Isaev's and Maklyarsky's effective war-time detective play *Unsung Heroes*, bore any relation to the theatre as it had been. The real Kamerny was no more, but they put it down as though it were.

In September 1947, the Central Committee's official journal *Culture and Life* published an article on the Kamerny, entitled 'Bourgeois Theatre in a Blind Alley'. The last production, *Lady Windermere's Fan* (1949), was banned. On 25 June 1949, Tairov was thrown out of his own theatre (officially he was offered a post as a regular director at the Vakhtangov Theatre). The Kamerny was closed in 1950 and a newly constituted company was named the Pushkin Theatre.

According to legend, the place was cursed. And when Vasiliy Vanin agreed to run the theatre he died before he could direct or act in a single play.

But it was not only 'bourgeois' theatres which suffered. Others, which apparently conformed to party policy were eliminated. There seemed to be an intention to break the existing pattern of theatrical provision and reshape companies. Actors of diametrically opposite styles were forced together; those specialising in psychological depth and subtlety were put side by side with others of a broader, cruder approach. This was the case when actors from the disbanded Second Art Theatre were simply incorpo-rated willy-nilly into the MGSPS (Moscow Region Professional Union

Theatre). Any real kind of artistic unity was impossible. The theatre was destroyed in the mid 1930s, although it was not 'Formalist' either in its work or intent. On the contrary, its declared intent was to play for audiences of workers. Unlike the Proletkult theatre it selected easily comprehensible forms and rejected 'bourgeois' psychology, preferring 'our' authors writing about 'our' lives.

A major theme in the plays of the 1930s was the 'miraculous smelting'. That was the title of one of Vladimir Kirshon's plays. In 1931, Aleksei Popov had produced Nikolai Pogodin's *Poem of the Axe*. The theme in both is research: the proposition is that sooner or later a new metal will be smelted. It will be indestructibly hard and suitably malleable. The idea of a wonder metal, a crucible in which different substances combine to create something uniquely superior, went hand in hand in people's minds in the 1930s with the idea of 're-forging'. Beneficial hammer blows would knock undesirable human material into another, better shape. 'Re-forging' is an all-embracing theme. It unites the various episodes in Pogodin's *Aristocrats* which deals with the 're-forging' of criminals and saboteurs into shock-workers building the White Sea–Baltic canal. 'Re-forging' underlies a series of plays which show how people who only yesterday were uncertain about their ideological choices are turned into ideal Soviet citizens.

In his Notebooks[7] Stanislavsky outlines a plan: 'Hand the annexe over to Meyerhold once we have merged our two companies.' He indicated a rough idea of how to manage the two buildings and divide up the responsibilities: 'I will create a company (of re-experiencing) for him. He will create a company of biomechanics and I'll work as a director.' 'A common management for both theatres. Nemirovich-Danchenko, Meyerhold and I will have artistic control, the administration – Arkadier + Radomyslensky + Torsky.'

Meyerhold knew of these plans and, in August 1937, discussed them enthusiastically with his colleagues, describing them as a possible means of salvation.[8]

The desire to create some kind of all-inclusive theatre, a 'wonder alloy', a single artistic language in which everyone could express their most meaningful and sacred feelings was part of Stanislavsky's nature.

The problem of reconciling the logic of art, the logic of the individual destiny of great artists with 'our policy for the theatre' and the dogma of Socialist Realism is not an easy one to resolve.

2.

We must now consider how the dogma of Socialist Realism affected the *practice* of theatre in the USSR of the 1930s and 1940s. Its values were no longer private but public and open. Its distinguishing marks were clarity, truth-to-life, moralism, hard-line didacticism and a striving for clear-cut simplicity.

Adjectives like elusive, oblique, fluid, rare, sensitive, mutable, airy, melting are no longer part of the critical vocabulary. All these qualities had practically disappeared from the stage, which was distinguished by its power, vitality, its pictorial and emotional energy.

Artists were attracted by the clearness, the openness of the world. No one, apparently, was attracted by its hidden side. Tragedy was something that arrived from elsewhere. It was no accident that of all Shakespeare's tragedies the favourite was *Othello*. Stanislavsky worked on his last production plan in 1929–30 while being treated abroad after his heart attack. There is nothing in the Moor's goodly, open courageous nature (or, for Stanislavsky, in the nature of man in general) that could make a response to Iago's vile 'lures'. Evil is something that comes from the outside. It is not revealed from within. It is almost a misunderstanding.

What theatres wanted most was to resolve misunderstandings. The wonderful cycle of Shakespearean comedies in the 1930s, the productions of Spanish classics that accompanied it, were swept along by the energy with which a satisfactory dénouement was sought. The world was simple, architectural, open, transparent, and was reflected in the sets Vadim Ryndin designed for Vakhtangov Theatre's production of *Much Ado About Nothing*.

Cecilia Mansurova and Ruben Simonov not only played Beatrice and Benedick's exchanges with grace and energy as a love game, they were brought together by a common willingness to defend Hero's good name, and the world's good name. Hero was guiltless, but so was the world.

In *As You Like It* at the Ermolova Theatre the world was not entirely good. But there was somewhere to run to, away from those places where evil existed. The fairy-tale, lyrical world of the Forest of Arden was more real than the real world. And so, everything in the set was real. The directors, Khmelev and Knebel asked the designer for natural products, straw, new wood, chamois leather, skins. Everything was light, golden brown, in natural forest tones. A place to live, a *locus amoenus*.

It was a style in which there was a place for joy but none for irony. Thus the approach of the Theatre of Comedy in Leningrad, which was determined by the personality of its director, Nikolai Akimov, a man of brilliant, cold, shining intellect, an elegant thinker with a hint of a smile, lyrical and imaginative at the same time, clearly fell outside the boundaries set by Socialist Realism. There was a certain logic to his being removed as director in 1949.

Theatrical style between 1930 and 1950 moved from restrained, almost austere, large-scale, terse, monumental forms where all the richness lay in the riotous play of light, colour and emotions, to verbose, overdecorative productions which lost their sincerity, severity and stability. This style had its high points, and brought masterpieces to the stage (*Resurrection* and *Enemies* which Nemirovich-Danchenko directed at the MXAT in 1930 and 1935), and its low points (*The Salvo of the Aurora* directed at the MXAT by Kedrov in 1952 by which time it had run itself out).

We need to place this style in its world context. Unquestionably, there are many similarities between Soviet art and the art of Hitler's Germany but also, surprisingly considering Soviet isolationism, with stylistic trends in England and the United States. Both English and Russian theatre historians have noted a marked break in the 1930s in Britain with earlier experimental productions and a revival of a national tradition, a return to classical theatre.[9] They noted the return of the worship of courage as a virtue. This was also happening on the Russian stage. It would be easy to confuse descriptions of favourite Soviet actors with those of popular English actors, to mistake the Georgian actor Khorava's vigorous and joyful call to battle as Othello with the young Laurence Olivier in his athletic, martial Hamlet of 1935, with his angry outbursts and bounding, steel-like body.

Biographical and historical plays and the bio-pic similarly grew in importance both in Russia and throughout the world. The films of William Dieterle and John Ford's *Young Mr Lincoln* display the same characteristic features as Russian bio-dramas of the 1930s and 1940s: the search for documentary truth with an inviolable core structure: idealised, larger-than-life leading figures in a 'normal' context. Considerations of plot regularly had to give way to the theme of an anti-hero; the theme of a vocation, a kind of conversion, a journey through temptation and doubt, victory over self and the rebirth of a sense of duty. True, in the Soviet Union, the circle of heroes was still restricted to revolutionaries and the soldiers of the Civil

War (Furmanov's *Chapaev*, Vslevolod Ivanov's *Parkhomenko*) but the circle soon widened. Pushkin and Lermontov were staged (Globa's *Pushkin* at the Ermolova, Paustovsky's *Our Contemporary* at the Maly and Lavrenev's *Lermontov* at the MXAT). So were the encyclopedist Lomonosov (in a play by Ivanov at the MXAT) and Michurin, the geneticist (in Dovzhenko's *Life in the Light*).

It is tempting to find parallels in the way the theme of future war arose. This was the subject of Bulgakov's *Adam and Eve*. In 1941 Afinogenov wrote *On the Eve*, in which he pictured an attack on the Soviet Union and the presumed heroism of the Soviet people.

At the end of the 1930s, artists in western Europe as well as in Russia began to feel they were living in a period when war was imminent. This realisation, which proved correct, drew young audiences to a writer who launched his career with a 'war theme' presentation at the Lenin Komsomol Theatre. His name was Konstantin Simonov.

We should, perhaps, note that at the time when Simonov wrote *The Man from Our Town* he was translating Kipling's verse. Kipling who had but recently been banned in the Soviet Union as the minstrel of Imperialism attracted readers by his cult of the soldier, of masculine patience in war, and by his strong rhythms and his belief in an ideal.

Restraint, reserve, a slightly bogus machismo and toughness, a deliberate terseness of utterance, minimal gestures, designed to conceal rather than reveal but at the same time hint at inner heroism, that was the lexicon of Simonov's productions when the world was on the brink of war. These plays concern people born to fight, and their love. Love recaptures its absolute value, the plot is subordinated to it. The meaning of life consists in doing one's military duty as a real man and then returning to a woman whose duty it was to wait and understand a man of war.

In the 1941 production, the Man from Our Town was played by Vladimir Solovyov, who went to the TRAM school, an actor with a considerable talent for theatrical 'clarity'. Ivan Bersenev, who had been in charge of the Lenin Komsomol Theatre since 1938, directed. In his productions and his later performances as an actor, he combined psychological truth with an accessible loftiness of tone and attitude (Gergel and Litovsky's *My Son* in 1939, Gorbatov's *Fathers' Youth* and Rostand's *Cyrano de Bergerac* in 1943).

He staged two other productions in these immediate pre-war years, as if to counter the macho approach and Simonov's non-theatrical style. One of them, fortunately was based on a play by an author with whom he had been associated in his earlier successes, Afinogenov – *The Crank* at the Second Art Theatre and *Hallo Spain* at the MGSPC, or Mossoviet Theatre, which he had joined after many complex wanderings, and in which he now staged Afinogenov's latest work. Afinogenov had been through a great deal, too. He was killed during the bombardment of Moscow in 1941. After the rousing success of his play, *Fear* in 1931, he voluntarily withdrew his next play, *The Lie* (1933) which had earned Stalin's disapproval even in manuscript form. He expected to be arrested throughout the Great Terror, but survived. In 1941, his *Mashenka* was premièred. It was the moving story of the friendship of a young girl of 14 and a lonely old scholar. Lyubimov-Lanskoi played the old man and Marietskaya the fourteen-year-old girl.

At the beginning of the 1930s Afinogenov went after a rigid kind of 'Ibsenism', in box sets, examining a tight circle of characters, concentrating on concepts (the concept of fear in *Fear*, of lying in *Lies*, of death in *Far Away* of 1935). He was a man of his time in his concerns. But even in *Mashenka* with its Dickensian tone, its tenderness, its choice of characters, their age – very young or very old – when he stands apart from any ideology, he is still a man of his time.

Before falling in love with *Mashenka* Moscow had given its heart to Aleksei Arbuzov's *Tanya* (1939), which Andrei Lobanov staged at the Theatre of the Revolution with Maria Babanova in the lead. The sad story of charming Tanya, who loses her husband, then her child, had its share of moralising. She is punished for locking herself in the ephemeral, fragile world of a home for two, where all is tenderness. Babanova did not argue with the moral of the play, but played the mind of character closest to her.

Having worked with Meyerhold, she was expelled from Gostim at the height of her success. In her later roles she returned to the theme of rejection, repudiation, the orphan: Coga, the boy left alone with a strict father in Faiko's contemporary melodrama *The Man with the Briefcase*; Larisa, shamelessly abandoned by her lover in Ostrovsky's *The Dowerless Girl*; Tanya, who loses her love. She played these roles 'without sentimentality', with an austere elegance and dry eyes.

Lobanov's production of *Tanya* was doubly important at the end of the 1930s. It told the moving 'story' of one young woman with a consummate sense of theatre as theatre. The success of *Tanya* showed that independence was possible, not by engaging in a polemic with the party line but by side-stepping it.

Arbuzov went on to show through his own life that there were, indeed, times when the party turned a blind eye and even enjoyed it. That, in essence, was his story. He was first and foremost a man of the theatre. He worked in theatres in Leningrad and Moscow from the age of fifteen. In 1935, his plays, *The Long Road* and *Six Lovers* were staged. In 1939, following the rousing success of *Tanya*, he gathered a group of young people around him, the 'Arbuzov Studio', the first after the break up of its predecessors. It was there that *The Town at Dawn* was jointly written and performed. The members of the studio went back to the subject matter of pre-war, official theatre – the heroes of socialist construction, the war against sceptics and spies. They were looking not for a new relationship to the object but new methods of creative working, including improvisation and the free play of the imagination, rather than a new relationship to established themes. The wish to combine the time-honoured rules of traditional genres with theatrical freedom is the determining factor in Arbuzov's later work. Trouble passed him by. He was a genuine professional. It is difficult to find another Russian author, who, year in year out, for half a century enabled the theatre to do new work, never doing the same thing twice, while always being true to himself. *The Immortal* was widely performed during the war. In the post-war years, *Encounter with Youth* had a marked success. *Years of Wandering* was staged in the early 1950s. Arbuzov was constantly in the repertoire in the early 1960s with *An Irkutsk Story* and *The Lost Son*. He had strong and permanent links with the Vakhtangov Theatre and later with the director, Anatoly Efros (*My Poor Marat* 1965, *The Happy Days of an Unhappy Man*, 1969, *Tales of the Old Arbat*, 1970, *Memory*, 1981). His wide range of interests and his talents as a teacher led him to create a writers' studio from which a new style emerged with talented dramatists like Petrushevskaya and Slavkin. The Lenin Komsomol Theatre's production of his play *Cruel Games* in 1978 showed the influence of his students.

Arbuzov, however, the only Soviet dramatist to enjoy commercial success in the West, was the exception to the rule. The rule was Lobanov, the director of *Tanya*.

Lobanov, a director of undoubted talent, was discovered after his productions at Ruben Simonov's studio (Ostrovsky's *Artists and Admirers* in 1931, an audacious and convincing *Cherry Orchard* in 1934 and a controversial, ironic interpretation of Gorky's *Children of the Sun* in 1937). Lobanov directed in many other theatres, from Zavadsky's studio to Children's Theatres, of which there were several in Moscow. As well as precise, original creative ideas Lobanov had many ways of unlocking actors' individuality. That, too, was evident in *Tanya* in which everything was built around the central role. Nikolai Khmelev, who was running the Ermolova Theatre, invited Lobanov to direct J. B. Priestley's *Time and the Conways* (1940). Khmelev's pupils and Lobanov found common ground in their use of analysis through action and their liking for a style that was extremely true-to-life and entertaining. When Khmelev died in 1945, Lobanov took over the theatre, so beginning a ten-year period in which it was pre-eminent in Moscow, the best it had known. The life he showed in his productions had a familiar look and feel but at the same time filled with theatrical energy and light. The staging was vivid, intelligible and constantly changing, as were the voices and the dialogue. The audience could grasp all the nuances, all the details of the feelings of the leading characters as they developed both in contemporary plays (Malyugin's *Old Friends*, 1945 and Panova and Dar's *The Sputniks*, 1947) and classics (Ostrovsky's *Easy Money* and *Slaves*, 1945 and 1948 and Gorky's *Summerfolk*, 1949). Lobanov's natural predilection for biting, nettling truth sooner or later had to invite attack.

His career was cut short after he directed Leonid Zorin's *Guests* in 1954, a play in which the defects of the social structure of the Soviet Union were brought into focus. Reviews and articles thundered their disapproval. Lobanov had to quit, suffered a heart attack and died soon after.

The fate of other, genuinely loyal Soviet artists was even more dramatic.

We only have to recall the shooting of Vladimir Kirshon, a man whose sincerity once delighted Nemirovich-Danchenko. The fate of those like Pogodin, who had engaged, with cheerful pugnacity, in a major debate about dramatic form with Afinogenov and Kirshon in the early 1930s, is no less instructive.

Nikolai Pogodin began his career as a journalist. Until 1930 he was a roving correspondent for *Pravda* and his travels provided the material for his early plays: *Tempo* (1930) was preceded by short pieces about tractor-makers and the heroic *Poem of the Axe* (1931). He wrote *The Poem of Steel* (1927) about the foundry-workers from Zlatoust. The play about the frontier guards, *Silver Gorge* (produced in 1939), was preceded by articles entitled *Far East*

Frontiers. His work for *Pravda* not only provided him with stories and characters – the residents of workers' hostels, trades-union activists, engineers – but determined the journalistic nature of his early plays – the opening of car conveyor-belt (*My Friend*, 1932) or the opening of the White Sea–Baltic canal (*Aristocrats*, 1934). The subject-matter of these early plays was fresh and modern and there was an evident enthusiasm for facts. He was thrilled by the scale of the construction plans and the speed and enthusiasm with which they were fulfilled. In the debate about the path soviet drama should take, Pogodin rejected the 'domestic play', the usual subjects love, jealousy, betrayal, just as he rejected the 'Ibsen' problem play. He was closer to the popular entertainments and Agitprop theatre of the Civil War period. Later he tried out various forms but the form which was most natural to him was the fast-moving constantly changing chronicle. He tried to adapt this form to historical-revolutionary drama (*The Man with the Rifle*, 1937, *Kremlin Chimes*, 1942). His natural craving for living fact constantly distanced him from the semi-official press. He was reprimanded for his plays *Courage* (1930), *The Moth* (1939), *Boatwoman* (1943), *We Three go to the Virgin Lands* (1955). The articles in which he tried to find some kind of meaning to which he tried to conform caused him great personal damage. The effort to trust the dictatorship turned him into an opportunist (the 'anti-American' play, *Missouri Waltz*, 1949; the glorifying of Boshyan, the pseudo-scientist and follower of Lysenko, *Breaking Lances*, 1953).

Fate linked Pogodin with the director, Aleksei Popov whose life was not dissimilar. He grew up in the Volga with a working-class background and became a draughtsman. He admired the MXAT from afar, auditioned in 1912 and was accepted. He acted at the First Studio. He was soon committed to the notion of art's responsibility to life. Stanislavsky called him an 'ideological dreamer', when he left Moscow and went out into the 'sticks' to teach amateurs and workers and then started an experimental theatre in an attempt to develop the moral and artistic principles of the First Studio. In 1924, he returned to Moscow and joined the Vakhtangov Theatre. He sincerely and genuinely believed that the Revolution had liberated the people and removed the gap between a cultural élite and the masses. He detested the world of those who had rejected the Revolution, hence his disagreement with Bulgakov whose *Zoïkina's Apartment* he staged as a satire. He felt the same about Olesha's *The Conspiracy of Feelings* of 1929. He was attracted by other things – a 'positive dynamic', the world turned upside down. In Seïfullina and Pravdukhin's *Virinea* he overcame the episodic, fragmentary nature of the adaptation of a story about the Siberian country and made 'the excitement of ideas' the common source of energy for the production and for the actors. He staged Lavrenev's *Breakup* (1927) and Kataev's *Avant-garde* (1930) which were preliminary sketches for his later productions about construction workers. He had to stop work on Pogodin's first play, *Tempo*, because rehearsals had begun at the Vakhtangov Theatre which he left. But he took Pogodin's second play with him to the Theatre of the Revolution and went with the author to the Urals, into factories. The principles of 'open staging', with its free structure, and shock montage technique attracted Popov not so much because they created new theatrical problems but because, they enabled him to add in a vivid sense of a colourful, forward-moving, populous reality which revelled in its own abundance. Although morose and given to doubt by nature, Popov believed that conviction and good spirits were the essential attributes of art. The rhythm and atmosphere of his productions of Pogodin's *Poem of the Axe* (1931), *My Friend* (1932), and *After the Ball* (1934) were full of joy and humour. There were no threatening notes.

Popov was excited by the possibility of passing from joy to tragedy in the abundance of life in *Romeo and Juliet* which he staged in 1935. In radiant, passionate and chaotic Verona, Mikhail Astangov, who played Romeo, was surprisingly close to Hamlet, as he analysed his gloomy premonitions. Popov suffered a serious personal crisis before he finished the production. He left the Theatre of the Revolution.

From 1936 to 1958, he was in charge of the Central Theatre of the Red Army. The nature of this establishment was determined by the limited, specialist, practical functions the state ascribed to the theatre. The first production was devoted to local events. The army had an unlimited budget. It created a wonderful company, engaged the finest professional directors and early on a departure from purely military subject-matter was viewed with indulgence. Popov staged *The Taming of the Shrew* in 1937. He saw the battle between Katarina and Petruchio as a game between two strong people who were willing to love each other. That game became part of a feeling of the fullness of life, of general affection and humour. But official indulgence had its limits. The theatre had been created to play a military and patriotic repertoire. And Popov with his personal sense of duty turned to suitable plays: Bakhterev and Razumovsky's *Captain Suvorov* (1939),

Perventsev's *Winged Breed* (1941) and later Stein's *The Admiral's Flag* and Vishnevsky's *Unforgettable 19th*. To Popov it might have seemed that his problem was the unbelievable size of the stage which was built with battle scenes in mind, and on which even tanks and cavalry could be deployed. But the problem was not really the size of the acting area but the speciousness of the broad 'historical canvas' that had to be staged. For a patriot (and Popov had that 'secret glow of patriotism' Tolstoy spoke of, which is shy and hates display) it was intolerable to have to deal with pseudo-patriotic, military show-pieces.

Popov and his actors managed to develop that 'secret glow of patriotism' in their war-time productions – in a heroic comedy, written in verse, Gladkov's *Long Long Ago*, in 1942 and in the courageously panoramic *People of Stalingrad*, an account of the battle on the Volga by the war-correspondent, Chepurin, in 1944. He staged three more productions with Chepurin – *The Last Line* (1948), *Conscience* (1950), *Vernal Stream* (1953). In these semidocumentary plays, and in Vinnikov's *The Steppe is Wide*, he tried to discover the breath of life.

The more effort artists had to make, to take on board the tasks the Communist Party assigned them and combine them with their own creative impulses, the more dramatic their fate. That was the state of affairs in the theatre which the Soviet authorities praised the most, the Art Theatre.

We cannot fail to see an organic movement towards a new style in the work which Vasily Kachalov did here over the years. His first roles after his return from the foreign tour in 1924 show an obvious gravitation towards work on an epic scale, so that he could observe the general historical and philosophical panorama from a considerable distance and justify what would appear appalling if seen close to. In his solo programmes were Blok's *The Twelve* and *The Scythians* and speeches from Byron. He rehearsed the role of Aeschylus' Prometheus and played Aladin in Ivanov's *Armoured Train 14–69* (1927) on a similar scale. In is experiments with the epic there is a growing absence of detail and a kind of ironic psychology. That was the way he played the hypocritical wind-bag Zakhar Bardin in Gorky's *Enemies*. His masterpiece was Chets ('a character based on the author'), in Tolstoy's *Ressurection*, where his ironic attitude towards social construction could not conceal an inexhaustible Tolstoyan – and personal – feeling and enthusiasm for life. An undying note of love of life and confidence in it was evident in the last role Kachalov played when he was sixty-three – Chatsky in a new production of *Woe from Wit* in 1938. It coloured his reading of verse in solo performances (Pushkin, Blok, Mayakovsky, Esenin etc.).

Less and less was left of what was considered Chekhovian gentleness in the acting at the MXAT. It was no accident then that a new actor, Mikhail Tarkhanov, Ivan Moskvin's brother, was so much needed at MXAT, with his experience of working-class audiences, his boldness, his unusually brash colours, the improbability and persuasiveness of his characters – like the baker, Semeonov in the play based on Gorky's *Among the People* (1933). A traditional Chekhovian actress like Olga Knipper-Chekhova, combined elegance of form in her new roles with a mocking smile directed towards her characters. It may well be that a taste for life and a wish to settle oneself comfortably and cosily was very like Olga Knipper in life – she was sharp and mocking on stage and showed the same qualities in Nadezhda Lvovna, the refugee White Guard in *The Armoured Train 14–69*, Maria Aleksandrovna in *Uncle's Sleep*, adapted from Dostoievsky (1929) Countess Charskaya in *Resurrection* with her bird-like nature, and the well-groomed liberal, Polina Bardina in *Enemies*.

Nikolai Khmelev had already been noticed in the Second Studio where he found strong expressionistic forms for 'villains' (Spiegelberg in Schiller's *The Robbers*, Ushakov in Smolin's historical melodrama, *Elizaveta Petrovna*). The role of Aleksei Turbin, in 1926, set the new style of acting for the MXAT, creating characters of maximum intensity and precision. He defined the question he faced: 'What kind of choreography do I have here?' His solution was remarkable for being both paradoxical and thoughtful. He liked to alter his tasks. He played Prince K., in *Uncle's Sleep*, adapted from Dostoievsky, as a mechanical, deranged, unhappy, painfully disjointed being. In Kataev's *Embezzlers* (1928), his Vanechka was masterly – a simpleton, caught up in a wave of poetic feeling and the accelerating rhythm of adventure. Cast as the engineer Sholte in the same play, he created a tough, cold, terse embezzler who was coming to the end of his escapade. In the same year (1935) he played the doomed, saintly Tsar Fyodor and the prosecutor Nikolai Skrobotov in Gorky's *Enemies*, not only creating two different human types but respecting the philosophies of two diametrically opposed plays which were both equally important in the repertoire of the Art Theatre in the 1930s. Other roles he played were Storozhev, the kulak in Virta's *Earth*, and Karenin in *Anna Karenina* (both in 1937), which were almost grotesques, and after them Tuzenbakh in *The Three Sisters* (1940) a role without a trace of toughness, always physically truthful as when waiting for the holiday in Act 2, or waiting for Irina in the street on a mild winter night, in the warm snow so as to take her home after work, or his premonition of death, the sleepless night before the duel, the need for approval – 'I haven't drunk any coffee today'. His last role was Ivan the Terrible in Aleksei Tolstoy's *Difficult Years*. He died the day of the first run-though.

No less tense and brief was the life of another actor, Boris Dobronravov, who also died suddenly. He started by understudying the sharp-edged character roles which came quite naturally to him, like the brash young shop-assistant Narkis, who was his landlady's lover, in Ostrovsky's *Burning Heart* in 1926. During the foreign tour of 1922–4 he was confronted for the first time with roles which made other demands – masculine restraint, intense lyricism (Alyosha in *The Brothers Karamazov*, Petya Trofimov in *The Cherry Orchard*). When he came to work on Captain Myshlaevsky in *The Days of the Turbins*, Dobronravov combined his own gift for humour, broadness, living authenticity with an heroic interpretation 'à la MXAT'. Dobronravov was an actor of rare masculine charm and attractiveness. Soviet writers relied on him and he invested their positive heroes with these qualities – the Bolshevik, Mikhaïlov in Kirshon's *Bread* (1931), Listrat in *Earth* (1937), the front-line soldier Safonov in Simonov's *Russian People* (1943). When he played classic roles at the MXAT he did not break with tradition but in roles like Vasily Pepel in *The Lower Depths* and Lopakhin in *The Cherry Orchard* he revealed an inexhaustible desire for good and a store of inner strength. His Vanya in the 1947 revival of *Uncle Vanya* was enchanting.

Unquestionably, the most remarkable actress of the 'second generation' was Alla Tarasova. Twice she became Moscow's darling. The first time in 1916 when as a student of the Second Studio, she captivated everyone as the schoolgirl Finochka in Gippius's *Green Ring* and the second time in 1937 when she played Anna Karenina. She played this role with exceptional economy, avoiding detail. 'Blazing passion', that was the director's overall suggestion, the 'blazing passion' of a woman being consumed by fire under the cold, indifferent gaze of uniformed, golden, velvet, granite-stone Petersburg. The 1930s and 1940s were genuinely happy times for her. Stanislavsky directed her as Negina in *Artists and Admirers* (1933); Nemirovich-Danchenko provided her with extremely subtle scores as

Tatyana Lugovaya in *Enemies* (1935), and as Masha in *The Three Sisters* (1940). The affectionate, betrayed character of Yulia Tugina in Ostrovksy's *Last Sacrifice* ended this happy period.

Both Tarasova's directors prized her capacity for emotion, her strength, and the simplicity of her interpretation which was integrated and not over-burdened with detail. Lacking their guidance in her later roles, she coarsened her gifts: she was either too emotional or too statuesque. Her official status as 'leading actress' of the Art Theatre and of the Soviet state, a title she received after being publicly applauded by Stalin in *Anna Karenina* (according to TASS), her political career (deputy in the Supreme Soviet), were of little benefit to her. The Chekhov roles she played in her youth (Anya, Sonya) overshadowed those she played later – Elena Andreevna in *Uncle Vanya* (1947), Ranevskaya in *The Cherry Orchard* (1958), Arkadina in *The Seagull* (1960). Her performances in Surov's *Green Street* (1948), and Virta's *The Conspiracy of the Doomed* (1949) were as predictable as the writing. Even in her best later roles, such as Maria Stuart in Schiller's tragedy (1957), she lacked the depth of artistic insight of Angelina Stepanova, who played Elizabeth opposite her.

Angelina Stepanova joined the Art Theatre in 1924. She was the devoted pupil first of Stanislavsky, who directed her as Mary in Dickens's *The Battle of Life* and played opposite her in *Woe from Wit*, and then of Nemirovich-Danchenko. The influence of the Vakhtangov school, where she did her early training, can be detected in her acting. While staying in character, she gave great clarity of form; she combined psychological depth with boldness of outline, for example, the single-mindedness with which she played the nub of a character, be it Betsy Tverskaya with her cold, corrupt joie de vivre in *Anna Karenina*, or Irina in *The Three Sisters*, with her uneasy, expectant and disappointed belief in life. Her characters were sharply, sometimes bitingly portrayed – Mariette in *Resurrection* (1930), Betsy in *The Fruits of Enlightenment* (1951), Kalerya in *Summer Folk* (1953). In lyrical roles she avoided sentimentality and was mentally alive. She had a precise sense of genre – old-fashioned melodrama as Henriette in D'Ennery and Cormon's *The Gérard Sisters*, or drawing-room comedy as Gertrude in Wilde's *An Ideal Husband*. She had a feel for what Stanislavsky called 'a writer's special quality'. She used Gorky's individual creativity when she played Shurka in *Egor Bulychov* (1934) and found the right answer for the ardent and overt theatricality of Korneichuk's plays (Lida in *Platon*

Krechet, 1935). Her outstanding performance as Queen Elizabeth in *Mary Stuart* (1957) at the same time solved the problem of 'Schiller in the Art Theatre'. Her basic gifts were a feeling for theatrical form, a capacity for analysis, elegance and economy, hidden lyricism and humour.

Stepanova's own dramatic, brilliant story, as one of the most beautiful and intelligent women in the Moscow of the 1930s could provide material both for the novelist and the historian. Her correspondence with the playwright Nikolai Erdman is a monument to the period.

In the 1930s, the Art Theatre had a staggering wealth of gifted actors, almost too many. The company was swollen three times by the arrival of actors from theatres that no longer existed – first from the Korsh Theatre, then from the Second Art Theatre and finally a few people from Meyerhold's theatre.

It was not easy for the core members. Vera Sokolova's talents were not properly used. She was an elegant, delicate, iridescent personality. She had to share the role of Elena which she played at the première of *The Days of the Turbins* with far too many other actresses and there were no new roles for her. Vera Popova wiled away many weary years of idleness after she joined MXAT from the Korsh Theatre. Her profound sense of drama and boldness of characterisation, her expressionistic intensity of rhythm and psychological mobility, which made her one of the finest interpreters of the plays of Eugene O'Neill, were not called upon. Also in the Art Theatre with her was Vasily Sakhnovsky, with whom she had done some of her best work (including Katerina in *The Storm*) but his fate was yet another indication of the overcrowding, the surplus talent in every square metre of the building.

Sakhnovsky was one of the most interesting Russian theatrical minds. His artistic policy, which he set out in his pamphlet 'The Art Theatre and Romanticism on Stage: a Letter to Stanislavsky', was emphatically opposed to flat naturalism. He put his ideas into practice in the short-lived theatres he created, the Exemplary (1919) and the Moscow-Dramatic (1922–3), where he staged *The Storm* with Popova as Katerina and Igor Ilinsky as Tikhon. In 1924 he revived the Komissarzhevskaya Theatre, which he had created before the war with Fyodor Komissarzhevsky, where he staged an adaptation of *Dead Souls* with Mikhail Astangov as Chichikov, and *The Case* and *Tarelkin's Death* by Sukhovo-Kobylin. But the theatre went out of business in 1925 and after a year working in various companies, he was invited to join the Art Theatre. 'That's quite something!' was Nemirovich-Danchenko's judgement, who happened to be in Hollywood at the time.

The idea was that Sakhnovsky should go back to the Art Theatre to work on writers who excited him (Gogol, Sukhovo-Kobylin, Ostrovsky) and Russian tragic satire. However, the actors who began to work on *Tarelkin's Death* felt so depressed by his cold, biting sarcasm they stopped work. Stanislavsky was enthusiastic about his staging of Leonov's *Untilovsk*, in which Sakhnovsky saw oversize characters and the richness of provincial longings and desires, but the play, rehearsals for which spread over two years, was a failure. In the adaptations of *Uncle's Sleep* and *Dead Souls*, the Art Theatre management were so high-handed in interfering with Sakhnovsky's directorial and philosophical ideas that everything was radically changed. Having entrusted him with this work, they could not quite come to terms with his gifts. In 1938 he staged another play by Leonov, *The Polovchansky Gardens*, an agonizing work in which the cosmological and chthonic images, which always fascinated this writer, are linked to the spy-mania of the time and stories of attempts to sabotage the USSR's military power.

It would be superfluous to ask why Sakhnovsky and Popova did not leave the Art Theatre. It had already been canonised and being within its walls was safety in itself. And vice versa, leaving it, even unintentionally, was to reject favour and all that that entailed. In October 1941, as the Germans approached the capital, MXAT left Moscow but Sakhnovsky was seriously ill and stayed behind. He was immediately arrested. The theatre management had to take strong measures to save him but he came out of prison and returned to his work on *Hamlet*, begun in collaboration with Nemirovich-Danchenko. After Nemirovich's death he continued alone. Sakhnovsky died suddenly and with his death work stopped for good. Dmitriev's set-model survives, a huge circular structure, a crude black castle, seen as though from some strange distant spot. An ice-bound platform on the battlements, winding corridors, dark empty stone niches.

The Art Theatre emerged from the 1930s with three major projects, only one of which came to fruition: *The Three Sisters*, a new production of Chekhov's play after almost forty years, on the stage on which it was first performed. It had an open, ever deepening space, enigmatic, barely perceptible turning of the revolve, and seemingly unplanned moves. The unifying factors were dreams of the future, or memories of the past, a celestial haze enfolding genuinely living people. All this occurred in the 1940 production with inexplicable naturalness, as though nothing but this miracle were possible. The themes of suffering, endurance and hope were one with the changing seasons, with the humble suffering of nature. Klaudia Elanskaya, Alla Tarasova and Angelina Stepanova did not play Olga, Masha and Irina but the intimacy, the inseparability, the unity of three people in total, loving sympathy with each other. The theatre of the living touched its highest point and almost became liturgical drama. Yet in 1940, this term could not be used as an expression of praise.

Two other projects got no further than the drawing board: *Hamlet* and *Antony and Cleopatra*. The fact that *The Three Sisters* could be produced at all was something of a miracle. But the miracle could not go on, nor could productions of Shakespeare. And that was not just because Nemirovich-Danchenko died.

3.

The dogmas of Socialist Realism, handed down from on high, were not open to question at any time in the Soviet era. But the rigour with which they were applied differed according to the times. The only period that can really be compared to the active savagery of the early 1930s, was inaugurated with the pronouncement by the Central Committee of the Communist Party of 26 August 1946 'On the Repertoire of Dramatic Theatres and the Means of Improving it', and reached its height with the publication in *Pravda* on 28 January 1949 of an editorial on the machinations of 'stateless cosmopolitans', who were 'antipatriots'. The ostensible target was theatre critics, who hardly merited being singled out as the beginning of party's clean-up campaign. But 'cosmopolitan' was a code word for Jewish. Officials began revealing actors' real, or Jewish, names, by 'opening brackets' as they put it at the time. Thus in the case of Leonidov, in official papers or questionnaires the words 'real name Wolfenson' appeared in brackets after his stage name. The anti-semitism of ten years before was beginning to show its face. 'Cosmopolitan' was an ingenious choice of word since it suggested both the corruption of foreign influences and less than total allegiance to the Soviet state. And, indeed, in its invectives the party charged artists with 'using the Soviet stage as propaganda for reactionary bourgeois ideology and morals, an attempt to poison Soviet consciousness with a world-view hostile to Soviet society and to revive the last vestiges of capitalism both in the mind and in reality'. Soviet plays, it was stated, only represented about 30 per cent of plays in the repertoire, the rest being taken up by 'foreign bourgeois authors'. They poisoned the mind. No one dared open their mouths to explain that plays like the adventure story *The Tales of Marguerite de Navarre* or Labiche's little farce *The Money Box* were hardly malign. One of the most talented young actors of the 1940s, Andrei Popov made a lively début in the Labiche. Both productions were accused of being dangerous examples of ideological decadence. The Communist Party suppressed light foreign plays which the public enjoyed, just as it suppressed the first stirrings of contemporary comedies of Russian life. Theatres were warned that 'among native Russian works there are weak, ideologically defective plays . . . A grotesque caricature is being offered of the Soviet people, who were presented as primitive, uncouth, with low tastes and manners . . . These plays are a misrepresentation of Soviet life.'

Accordingly, there was a drive for plays which would give a correct – i.e., joyful, overblown – picture of Soviet life. The Central Committee forced theatre managements to provide no fewer than two, or, better, three 'new, high-quality plays with themes ideologically and artistically relevant to Soviet life, each year'.

There was a rush of writers eager to provide acceptable plays to fill the gap left by the unacceptable. The best theatres in Moscow were thrown open to them and those who won approval could count on being shown on hundreds of provincial stages. There was also the distant prospect of the Stalin prizes (established in 1939 for his 60th birthday) which represented a handsome sum of money, not to mention an improvement in social status for the prize winners which pushed them into positions of responsibility in the artists's unions.

It is not difficult to understand why those professional theatre critics who had not entirely abandoned their standards resisted this assault. They were, in consequence, the first to be crushed.

Those engaged in the frightening and ever widening battle against the cosmopolitans were colourful individuals. They banded together to exterminate their enemies but once the hunt was over and they had celebrated their success, they indulged in feudal strife among themselves. Sometimes there was poaching on other people's 'sacred' territory but in general that was not approved of. The agreement was that each theatre should cultivate its own author and the author should stick with it. Aleksei Surov, for example, was the protégé of the Ermolova theatre.

Like Pogodin, he had been a journalist. His play, *Far from Stalingrad*, which the Ermolova accepted, was a story of daily life in a factory during the war and had an air of reality. It was warmly approved by the collective and, in Lobanov's production, gave the actors the opportunity to work towards real not theatrical stage action. Surov's later career was as typical as it was shocking. Officially recognised as a paragon of Socialist Realism, he became very active in the 'struggle against the cosmopolitans', some of whom were his recent collaborators, whom he then turned into unacknowledged 'ghost' writers. His *Green Street*, an exposé of the 'cringing attitude towards the West', was staged at the MXAT in 1948, *The Insult* at the Mossoviet in 1948 and, in 1950, *Dawn over Moscow*, which represented the high point of good fortune in Soviet reality. *The President's Compatriot*, also known as *The Demented Haberdasher* (1950), was one of his 'anti-American plays'. He was one of the few people who, as a result of events following the death of Stalin, was called to account by his aggrieved 'ghosts'. He was expelled from the Writers' Union and stopped working in the theatre. However, in 1982 his request for reinstatement was accepted and he died a member of the Writers' Union.

Anatoly Sofronov began his career at the same time as Surov. His first plays were performed in Moscow in 1948 – *In One City, A Moscow Character. In Our Time* and *Varvara Volkova* followed in 1952 and 1953. He was a master of all the techniques of traditional popular theatre in its special Soviet and crudely ideologised version and his plays were widely staged. He managed to preserve the position he achieved both socially and in the Party after the 'struggle against the cosmopolitans' had shown his ability to get his opponents publicly denounced. His power was bolstered not only by the fact that he had been the editor of the biggest mass circulation magazine, *Ogonyok*, for many years but by the fact that he was friends with the upper echelons of government. The paradox was that for all their ideological pretensions, his plays were, in fact, rather pleasant light comedies, like *A Million for a Smile* (1959) and a trilogy about a proud, capricious countrywoman, the cook Pavlina (1959, 1961, 1964) or high melodramas, like *The Heart Knows no Farewell* (1954), *The Son* (1966), *The Inheritance* (1969), which provided opportunities for showy acting and entertaining spectacle.

The third person forced into the repertoire by the powers that be was Nikolai Virta. After the staging of *Earth* Virta was more and more drawn to a monumental style, celebrating the heroism of the Bolsheviks. *Days of Greatness* (1947) showed Stalin as a victorious commander. *Our Daily Bread* (1948) was a paean of praise to Bolshevik leadership in the countryside during the war. *Conspiracy of the Doomed* (1949) showed those who opposed communism in Europe as criminals and traitors. All were awarded Stalin prizes. Assaults by ideologically unswerving, socially close, sterile, talentless people were not new. Remember the attacks by RAPP on the Art Theatre at the beginning of the 1930s which Stanislavsky managed to drive off. But this time its automatic power of recovery did not work. Worn-out material and destruction from within took their toll.

The destruction of the Russian theatrical tradition, the break in continuity, was evident as was straightforward deprofessionalisation.

As the 1940s turned into the 1950s productions by Surov, Sofronov and Virta were forced on theatres and Romashov, Perventsev and Mdivani were added, possibly out of a desire to offer a broader choice. The Art Theatre engaged all three.

We need to examine why this cycle of events was more artistically destructive for the Art Theatre than, for example, the Maly, which also staged Romashov's *Great Strength* (1947) and Perventsev's *Southern Junction* (1948), which lauded Stalin's military gifts, Sofronov's *A Moscow Character* (1948) and *No Other Way to Live* (1952) and the inevitable *Conspiracy of the Doomed* (1949), Vishnevsky's *The Unforgettable 19th*, about Stalin's leading role in the Civil War (1949), and Mdivani's *People of Good Will* (1950) in which, using thinly disguised pseudonyms, North Korea's struggle against the South was praised.

No matter how many of these plays were in the Maly repertoire Varvara Ryzhova maintained her masterly style of acting, her freedom, warmth and humour when she played Anfisa Tikhonova in *Wolves and Sheep*, or Ulita in *The Forest*. Similarly, Evdokia Turchaninova never lost her elegance, clarity, musical richness of voice and tone, her genuine grandeur when she played Bogaevskaya in *Barbarians*, or Murzavetskaya in *Wolves and Sheep* (1944), Anna Dmitrievna in *The Living Corpse* (1951), and Mrs Higgins in the brilliant, exemplary staging of Shaw's ever-popular drawing-room comedy *Pygmalion*. From 1943 onwards she had great success in this small role with Darya Zerkalova and Konstantin Zubov, who played the two leads. The Maly and the former Aleksandrinsky suffered less from the corrosive effect of appearing in atrocious plays, which almost changed their very nature, than the Art Theatre.

In this period Mikhail Kedrov was the artistic director of the MXAT. He staged his first production there in 1933 with an adaptation of Gorky's novel *Among the People* and, in 1935, worked on *Enemies*. In 1936 Stanislavsky took him into his Opera-Dramatic Studio and rehearsed him as Tartuffe. He then staged the production after Stanislavsky's death. His best productions were Kron's *Deep Drilling* (1943) and *The Fruits of Enlightenment* (1951). He was a disciple of the so-called 'method of physical action', the only approach he acknowledged. Displaying a rare intransigence when it came to working method, Kedrov was indifferent to the ideology of the plays he had to put on. Besides Chekhov, Ostrovsky and Shakespeare (*Uncle Vanya*, 1947, *The Forest*, 1948 and *The Winter's Tale*, 1958) he staged the apologia for Stalin *The Salvo of the 'Aurora'* in 1952 and the hasty responses to the regular political campaigns and trials *Green Street*, and *A Stranger* by Simonov.

When he was rehearsing his last experimental production, *Tartuffe* in 1937, Stanislavsky suggested to Vasily Toporkov it was possible to go on believing passionately, joyfully in spite of all the evidence to the contrary. Orgon, as played by Toporkov, was not blind, but a man learning to believe despite the evidence of his own eyes. His Orgon believed to the hilt, rejoiced in anything that made belief difficult, and exaggerated the virtues of anyone who could believe in the saintly Tartuffe despite his excesses ('I believe because it is absurd').

Later Toporkov played a character similarly possessed by lies and nonsense, the spiritualist, Krugosvetlov in *The Fruits of Enlightenment* (1951) with his contemptuous pity for sceptical rationalists. But, when working on Mikhalkov's *Ilya Golovin*, this talented and upstanding actor found himself having to say, 'I believe because it is absurd'. But how else was he to stage this shameless piece and play the lead role of the composer (intended to be Shostakovich) who lost touch with the people but was brought back into line by party critics?

The less rubbish theatres staged, the less they were corrupted. The first plays, in the mid-1950s, to celebrate the return of the genuine, professional virtues of Russian theatre were written either by long-standing silent opponents of the Soviet 'grand style' or by completely new authors. But many more years had to elapse before the dominance of Socialist Realism came to an end.

Notes

1. Nemirovich-Danchenko, *Selected Letters*, 2 vols. (Moscow 1979), vol. II, pp. 277–8.
2. Robert Pelshe, *Our Policy for the Theatre* (Moscow and Leningrad, 1929), p. 90.
3. Minutes of Agitprop meeting, 1927, p. 243.

4. Cf. her letter to Stalin, 5 July 1937.
5. Quoted in V. Zhidkov, *Theatre and the Age, from the Revolution to Perestroika* (Moscow 1991), p. 130.
6. Meyerhold's second wife. Meyerhold was arrested in 1939 and shot in 1940. Raikh's murder followed shortly after.
7. MXAT Museum, Stanislavsky Archive N263, p. 34.
8. See V. E. Meyerhold, *Stat'i, Pis'ma, Rechi, Besedy* (Moscow, 1968), vol. II, p. 570.
9. Robert Speaight, *Shakespeare on the Stage* (London, 1973); J. C. Trewin, *Shakespeare on the English Stage* (London, 1974); Aleksei, Bartoshevich, *Shakespeare on the English Stage* (Moscow, 1985).

16 The 'thaw' and after, 1953–1986

BIRGIT BEUMERS

The thaw: Khrushchev's Years of Liberalisation

The 'thaw' after Stalin's death in 1953 derived its name from literature (Ilya Erenburg's novel *The Thaw*, 1954), and affected cultural life in several particular ways. The theatre experienced the thaw in two phases.[1]

The 'first thaw' started with an editorial in *Pravda* on 7 April 1952 attacking the 'drama without conflict' theory of Nikolai Virta and Boris Lavrenev (a theory postulating that socialist realist drama cannot contain conflict) and calling for playwrights to express the truth and to strike against any negative aspects of Soviet life. In 1953, Glavrepertkom, the Central Repertoire Board which controlled the theatres, was abolished, and its functions were taken over by the newly formed Ministry of Culture. The theatres were monitered by their literary advisers and an Artistic Council, and these were supervised by Glavk, the Central Directorate of Culture of the Moscow City Council, and the RSFSR and USSR Ministries of Culture, which in their turn were subordinate to the Central Committee of the Communist Party. Control and censorship were thereby divided between several authorities, which theoretically introduced more democratic structures, but in practice placed power in the hands of innumerable bureaucrats.

The 'second thaw' in the arts was heralded by an editorial in *Kommunist* in 1955, which favoured diversity in the arts, and attacked the theory of 'drama without conflict' as well as the levelling and uniformity evident in a theatre that had been dominated by the Stanislavsky system. At the same time, the rehabilitation of Meyerhold led to a revival of his productions of Mayakovsky's satires (*The Bathhouse* in 1953, *The Bedbug* in 1955, and *Mystery Bouffe* in 1957); they were staged by Meyerhold's pupil Valentin Pluchek at the Satire Theatre. The Stanislavsky system was challenged openly by the Vakhtangov Theatre's directors, Boris Zakhava and Ruben Simonov, who called for a synthesis of the acting methods of *perezhivanie* (experience) and *predstavlenie* (representation).[2]

Whereas the 'first thaw' affected dramatic writing, it was only the second that concerned the theatre arts. Both precede the event which marks the thaw in politics, the XX Party Congress of February 1956, during which Khrushchev admitted in his 'secret speech' to the falsification of history, and dismissed the cult of personality. However, Khrushchev's liberalism was met by a strong Stalinist opposition, as demonstrated by the violent crushing of the attempted revolution in Hungary in November 1956. Khrushchev's fight for his liberal pro- gramme against the old Stalinists was reflected in the USSR's cultural politics, repressive one day and liberal the next: for example, in 1958 Aleksandr Tvardovsky was reinstated as editor of the literary magazine *Novy Mir*, while Boris Pasternak was forced to refuse the Nobel Prize for Literature.

The thaw bore upon the theatre most noticeably at two points during the Khrushchev era: at the beginning and at the end, in the seasons 1956/7 and 1963/4.

THE FIRST LIBERAL WAVE OF 1956–1957

This wave manifested itself in terms of both appointments and repertoire. The Leningrad director Nikolai Akimov returned as Chief Artistic Director to the Leningrad Theatre of Comedy after his dismissal in 1949; Maria Knebel, actress and director, and pupil of Stanislavsky and Michael Chekhov, became Chief Artistic Director at the Central Children's Theatre; and Valentin Pluchek was appointed Chief Artistic Director of the Satire Theatre. In 1957 the Berliner Ensemble toured Moscow and Leningrad, acquainting the Soviet audiences with Brecht's epic theatre. The Vakhtangov Theatre, whose theatrical and fantastic production style had suffered badly from the levelling in the arts, was able to revive some of Vakhtangov's productions. Meyerhold's pupil Nikolai Okhlopkov, in charge of the Mayakovsky Theatre (formerly Theatre of the Revolution), returned with Aleksandr Stein's *Hotel Astoria* to the platform theatre, as well as reviving his 1935 production of Pogodin's *Aristocrats* (1956).

Two events in the 1956/7 season had long-term significance for the Soviet theatre: in Moscow, Oleg Efremov's foundation of the Sovremennik Theatre; and in Leningrad, Georgy Tovstonogov's designation as Chief Artistic Director to the Gorky Bolshoi Drama Theatre.

Maria Knebel and the Central Children's Theatre

The importance of Maria Knebel as theatre theorist and practitioner is often underestimated. Her work as teacher and director has influenced

33. Oleg Efremov and Mikhail Kozakov in Viktor Rozov's *Alive Forever*. Sovremennik Theatre, 1964.

greatly those directors who adhered to the Stanislavsky tradition, but who were to modify and develop it along the lines of Michael Chekhov (whose works were not published in the Soviet Union until 1986). Knebel invited her pupil, the director Anatoly Efros, and the actor Oleg Efremov to join the Central Children's Theatre.

The plays of a new generation of playwrights, most importantly Viktor Rozov, gave the impulse for young directors to explore the psychological realism of Stanislavsky. Rozov's plays with mainly young protagonists offered themselves to a theatre which wanted to create a hero with whom both actor and audience could easily identify psychologically. His plays were first staged by Efros at the Central Children's Theatre with a young graduate of the Moscow Art Theatre school, Oleg Efremov, playing the leading parts. *Good Luck to You!* (1954) impressed by its natural acting and by the contemporaneity of both actors and characters. Efros later directed *In Search of Joy* (1957), in which the hero demolishes a piece of furniture, symbol of the petty bourgeoisie, with his father's sabre. This gesture of cutting – into the air – became typical of Efremov's Sovremennik Theatre. At the Central Children's Theatre, Efros was primarily interested in investigating Rozov's 'young boys', children on the way to adulthood, and their revolt and protest during the process of inner liberation. He combined an abstract set with psychological realism in the acting.

The Sovremennik Theatre

The Sovremennik Theatre sprang up as a 'Studio of Young Actors' from the MXAT school under Oleg Efremov, opening in 1957 as the 'Studio Theatre Sovremennik' with Rozov's *Alive Forever*. Efremov and his acting class separated from MXAT, which was unable to resolve problems of collective leadership or make contact with its contemporaries. The name 'Sovremennik' (The Contemporary) referred to the fact that the audience, the actors and the playwrights all belonged to the younger generation.

Efremov had started acting at the time when monumental realistic sets were losing favour. He did not aim at outward verisimilitude, using neither make-up nor elaborate costume, nor any effective *mise-en-scène*. He preferred non-realistic, associative sets, although this can partially be ascribed to financial difficulties. Young actors like Galina Volchek, Evgeny Evstigneev, Oleg Tabakov and Lidia Tolmacheva were able to bring their personalities into the role: Efremov's psychological realism implied that the actor's personality remains visible as he lives through the character's train of thought and identifies psychologically with him. The actors shared their views with the other members of the ensemble, and this homogeneity in the group was vital for the theatre: 'A theatre is a community of people, who breathe the same air and share the same ideas. Theatre is ten hearts beating in unison, ten minds searching for answers to the questions of life which worry each of us individually. A theatre collective is an artist.'[3]

The actors were united with the audience in their desire to find and express the truth. Although the theatre refrained from breaking the 'fourth wall' with devices like the entrance through the auditorium or direct address to the audience, the theatre shared views (rather than space) with the audience, creating a mental and psychological rather than physical link. Efremov consciously combined the conventionality of the set with the authenticity of a way of life, an everyday realism for the psychological portrayal of the character. He tended to subject the interpretation of a play to the theme of truth and responsibility.

Apart from Rozov's dramatic writing, other new playwrights also found their way on to the stage of the Sovremennik, such as Aleksandr Volodin and the British 'angry young men'. In Volodin's *The Appointment* (1963), Efremov dwelt on the theme of man's responsibility for his existence, broadening the meaning of 'appointment' to a universal level. Efremov began to exploit some theatrical devices to great effect; for instance, the role of the two chiefs was played by one actor (Evgeny Evstigneev), making them exact replicas of each other to caricature the uniformity of the bureaucratic apparatus. With this production Efremov achieved a transition from moral ethics to social issues, from a black-and-white character portrayal to more subtle psychological differentiation.

So far Efremov had used neutral scenic spaces without placing much emphasis on set design, making his theatre appear less aesthetic. From 1965 onwards, Pyotr Kirillov, Sergey Barkhin and Mikhail Anikst worked at the Sovremennik, creating neutral, multifunctional, but aesthetically appealing set designs. The production of Rozov's *The Traditional Reunion* (1966) reflected the new image the theatre had found. The production, staged by Efremov in a confessional and lyrical mode, showed a capacity for psychological differentiation. The audience, never integrated before, had a function in the production: some famous members of the audience were called up ad hoc as if they too were invited to the get-together of the old schoolfellows. Kirillov's set consisted of two lines of school desks, which could serve as office desks or tables. Efremov, again, used a new theatrical device: shadow theatre. Silhouettes of contemporary youth danced behind screens as the reunion was taking place. The parallel between past and present was also drawn in another scene: the schoolchildren of the present were photographed in the same position as the schoolfellows of the reunion. For the first time, Efremov restructured a text, here making it centre around Agnia Shabina (Lidia Tolmacheva), who had sacrificed her love for Sergei Usov (Evgeny Evstigneev) to her career. The theatre protested against the suppression of feelings, against the waste of life for the sake of social rewards. The production was controversial for this interpretation and for the challenging integration of the audience into the production. The breaking of the fourth wall, the barrier between stage and auditorium, was feared by the bureaucrats of the Directorate of Culture, who often removed addresses to the audience.

The Sovremennik's relationship with the authorities, that is, the Central Directorate and the Ministry of Culture, was not an easy one. Interpretations were often criticised, the repertoire, with too many contemporary plays (including one by Vasily Aksenov who later emigrated), was overseen with great suspicion. Aleksandr Galich's play *Matrosskaya Tishina*, which dealt with a Jewish family during the war and in the 1950s, when they come out of a camp, was banned after the final dress rehearsal in 1957 although it had been passed by Glavlit (the literary censorship).[4] The reality of the 1950s may have been fit for printing, but not for representation on stage at a time when ideology was being tightened in preparation for the fortieth anniversary of the revolution.

Efremov spent his last years at the Sovremennik on the production of a historical trilogy, investigating the psychological motivation of revolutionary figures from the Decembrist uprising of 1825 to the Bolshevik revolution. When Efremov left the Sovremennik to become Chief Artistic Director at MXAT in 1970, he took many actors with him, breaking the ensemble apart.

Georgy Tovstonogov and the Bolshoi Drama Theatre in Leningrad
In 1956, Georgy Tovstonogov was appointed Chief Artistic Director to the Bolshoi Drama Theatre in Leningrad. Tovstonogov, born in Georgia and educated at the Lunacharsky State Institute for Theatrical Art (GITIS) in Moscow under the director Aleksei Popov, had been at the head of the Theatre of the Lenin Komsomol in Leningrad since 1949, developing a style which merged the concepts of Stanislavsky and Meyerhold, mixed

conventionality with authenticity, and combined figurativeness with psychological analysis.

Tovstonogov's was an actor's theatre. The director did not impose an idea on the actor, but had a concept of the production as a whole. He relied on the actor's talent for improvisation to develop the role psychologically, giving him liberty to change the part. Tovstonogov showed an outstanding capacity to bring out the talent of the young actors he gathered at the theatre; particularly Tatyana Doronina, Emilia Popova, Zinaida Sharko, Kirill Lavrov, Sergei Yursky, Innokenty Smoktunovsky, and Evgeny Lebedev. In the late 1950s and early 1960s, he often created his sets himself; on other occasions he worked with established set designers (Semyon Mandel, Sofia Yunovich, Vladimir Stepanov) and for the musical arrangements with M. Tabachnikov.

Tovstonogov's use of theatrical devices was balanced, because purposeful. His productions showed a harmony between historical and contemporary meaning, between the objective and the subjective, the historical and the personal, which created an ambivalent and objective meaning. The audience was addressed for the purpose of initiation (rather than challenge) in prefaces to the productions. The device of 'quoting' other productions was used occasionally, as for example in Vishnevsky's *Optimistic Tragedy* (1955) with a reference to the set of Tairov's production, or *The Government Inspector* (1972), which echoed the famous Meyerhold production in its use of social masks. The action evoked emotion from the tension between growing oppositions with an interest in the process rather than the result, in polyphonic rather than linear development. Tovstonogov favoured non-dramatic literature and perceived the play as a scenario or a musical score. For Tovstonogov, 'a theatre director is not a *metteur en scène*, but the author of a production. The possibilities for a director in the interpretation of a play today are unlimited.'[5]

Tovstonogov's repertoire included contemporary plays by Volodin and Rozov, Aleksandr Gelman and Eduard Radzinsky; the classics of Gorky and Chekhov; prose adaptations of Sholokhov, Tolstoy and Dostoevsky. His production of Dostoevsky's *The Idiot* (1957) was innovative in centring around Myshkin rather than Nastasia Filippovna, as most other theatrical versions of the novel had done. Myshkin (Innokenty Smoktunovsky) was interpreted as a person capable of resurrecting broken links between man. Naive, good and natural, yet unable to save the world, his illness stemmed from his incapacity to complete his mission to bring good to the earth. In Griboedov's *Woe from Wit* (1962), Tovstonogov continued the line of interpretation of a lonely individual with good intentions towards the surrounding world: Chatsky was an intelligent and sensitive young man who spoke to an understanding audience, but nobody on stage wanted to listen to his reason.

Tovstonogov's interest in non-dramatic literature, in polyphonic structure and cinematic possibilities made him turn to Sholokhov's novel *Virgin Soil Upturned* (1964), in which he developed the technique of having the narrative parts and inner monologues read by Smoktunovsky, thereby preserving their original function. Other cinematic techniques included a 'light curtain' to separate episodes; the voice-over, fading voices, and leaving the interlocutors to gesture as the voice of the author resumes his narrative position; and the use of music to build up tension, as in the cinema.

Without Tovstonogov's production of *The Three Sisters* (1965) none of the later, controversial Moscow productions of Chekhov would have been possible. The sisters were isolated on stage, speaking to themselves and the audience, rather than each other: between them, everything had been said already. The house with all its interior detail was open and transparent to the audience; an alley of birches was visible in the background. In Sofia Yunovich's set, the exterior and the interior were united. Nature appeared as indifferent and beautiful, embracing man: man came from nature and would return to it (as Tuzenbakh does when leaving for his death in the duel). A revolving platform several times moved characters to the front, and brought the three sisters to the audience at the end. The curtain went down, separating the sisters from the stage and uniting them with the audience, spatially breaking the fourth wall. Tovstonogov explored the characters psychologically and enhanced their motivations by using theatrical devices. With his production, Tovstonogov investigated the origin of a wall of non-communication and protested against indifference and inertia. His production was innovative in its interpretation of the play in terms of the absurdity of existence, expressed in moderate rather than challenging terms, with understanding and sympathy. Hence Tovstonogov's relatively unchallenged position: few conflicts arose with the authorities, the director was allowed to stage productions abroad, the theatre was even permitted to tour Western countries.

THE SECOND LIBERAL WAVE OF 1963–1964

A second liberal wave started in 1963 with the appointment of Andrei Popov to the post of Chief Artistic Director at the Central Theatre of the

Soviet Army, which he revived with his own productions and those of Maria Knebel, Boris Lvov-Anokhin and Leonid Kheifets. The Sovremennik was officially established as the Moscow Sovremennik Theatre (making it eligible for more subsidies) in 1965, at a time when MXAT's reputation rested entirely on its old 'star' actors, and when the Maly Theatre was damaged by an exodus of actors despite the attempt to revive it by inviting directors from other theatres. A similar situation occurred at the Pushkin Theatre in Leningrad, where Leonid Vivien was not replaced after his death, leaving the theatre to become a museum of old productions.

Two events in the 1963/4 season were to determine the theatrical life of the decade: Anatoly Efros was appointed Chief Artistic Director of the Theatre of the Lenin Komsomol, which was in a desolate state, with neither an audience nor a good repertoire; and Yury Lyubimov was made Chief Artistic Director of the Taganka Theatre, in an equally desolate state, and moreover, located outside the centre of Moscow.

Efros at the Theatre of the Lenin Komsomol

Efros had gained most of his experience working on contemporary drama, and at the Theatre of the Lenin Komsomol he continued staging plays by Viktor Rozov, Aleksei Arbuzov and Eduard Radzinsky. He developed a repertoire almost entirely based on contemporary drama: Rozov's *On the Day of the Wedding* (1964), where the heroine's revolt against her marriage out of duty was represented formally by her breaking free from the set (designed by N. Sosunov and V. Lalevich), which consisted of tables and chairs arranged for a wedding party. Efros started to work with the concept of 'psychophysics', where movement has the function of making inner psychological changes visible. Radzinsky's *104 Pages about Love* (1964) opposed rationalism (at the time of what was called in the USSR the 'scientific-technological revolution') to emotional behaviour, and explicitly talked about sexual relationships. The play met many objections from the Directorate of Culture. Radzinsky's *A Film is Being Shot* (1965) was equally criticised for outspoken sexuality, taboo on the Soviet stage. Arbuzov's *The Promise (My Poor Marat)* (1965), about a woman who chooses her husband out of duty rather than love (she marries him after he has been injured during the Leningrad blockade), saw love triumph at the end. Most controversial were Efros's interpretations of two classics: Chekhov's *The Seagull* at the Theatre of the Lenin Komsomol in 1966 and *The Three Sisters* in 1967 at the Malaya Bronnaya.

Efros's *The Seagull* was condemned for its unorthodox interpretation of Chekhov in terms of 'lack of communication', perceiving Chekhov as a predecessor of the Western theatre of the absurd (with no equivalent in the Soviet Union, since a socialist society could not have such a phenomenon). All the characters were tense; they shouted and screamed at each other, revealing hatred rather than love, egoism rather than compassion. Treplyov was the central figure: a young boy, starting his artistic career in a hostile environment. This atmosphere derived from the lack of meaning in life, the lack of communication, but it stood in sharp contrast to the commonly accepted readings of Chekhov. 'Efros rejected the accepted idea about a relatively medium room temperature in Chekhov's plays, raised the tone, turned on the rhythm, sharpened the situations. The classical "Chekhovian dialogue" falls apart, from all corners of the stage wailing, shouting, groaning, hysteric sobbing can be heard. Hence the impression of troublesome everyday life in a communal flat.'[6] Furthermore, the play was set in a neutral and un-Chekhovian set, without lake, trees or estate, but only new wooden boards – the product of the cut trees of *The Cherry Orchard* (design by N. Sosunov and V. Lalevich). The stage was encircled by a wooden fence, and the little platform for Treplyov's play was made from boards, looking like a scaffold. It was the combination of the interpretation and the set both striking a contemporary note which made the production so controversial.

Similarly, in *The Three Sisters* the tone of the production was one of bitterness and disappointment. The interpretation of Vershinin and Tuzenbakh caused most controversy. Tuzenbakh sang, danced to a waltz, and was either drunk or asleep throughout the play. His only moment of sobriety was in his remark 'What does it all mean?', revealing his utter existential despair. Vershinin appeared as timid, but animated by his love to speak nicely. As Konstantin Rudnitsky remarked, all that was said in the play about the meaning of life, about recognising the present and looking into the future, was placed between brackets of parody and comedy (Tuzenbakh) and melancholic timidity (Vershinin).[7] The set, by V. Durgin, was designed in the Russian *style moderne*: the ornamentation of the Moscow Art Theatre interior was reproduced and enlarged in the centre, with golden leaves decorating the flowers. This set could also be taken as an ironic reference to the outmoded Art Theatre productions of Chekhov.

At the Theatre of the Lenin Komsomol Efros developed the use of *mise-en-scène* to express the inner conflict of the characters. The scenic space was conditional and neutral, giving no exact location. Efros involved the actor in the process of creating a role and used the method of 'demonstration', in which the actor approaches the part after analysing it structurally with the director before rehearsals proper begin. Efros worked closely with the actors Nikolai Volkov, who was tall, representing the weak, masculine hero; Lev Duov, short, who portrayed childish cleverness and often played the fool or the clown; and Olga Yakovleva, doll-like with a fragile voice. They left with him for the Malaya Bronnaya in 1967.

Lyubimov's Taganka

Yury Lyubimov was an actor at the Vakhtangov Theatre when he started to teach at the Shchukin School, which is annexed to the Vakhtangov. For his students' degree project he produced Brecht's *The Good Person of Szechwan* (1962), and successfully managed to come to terms with the Brechtian epic theatre. The production was met with hostility by the faculty board of the school for breaking so obviously with realism, but after a most favourable review by the highly-placed writer Konstantin Simonov in *Pravda*, it was officially acknowledged.[8] The successful translation of Brecht's epic theatre onto the stage was helped by the fact that the actors were students unspoilt by the 'system'. Lyubimov had noticed the dangerous uniformity in Soviet theatre and abhorred the use of make-up, costume and decorative props. Lyubimov took with him a group of students from the school when he was put in charge of the Taganka Theatre of Drama and Comedy in 1964.

The Good Person of Szechwan was set on a bare stage (again, as with the Sovremennik, partially due to financial limitations). A portrait of Brecht and a notice saying 'Street Theatre' were placed on the sides of the stage, and panels indicated locations. Songs were used to alienate and to comment; a musical rhythm set the pace of the production. Choreographed movement and dance frequently replaced verbal action. The Gods who fail in the play to help the prostitute Shen Te lead a good life were presented as bureaucrats whose unwillingness to help bring about change made it necessary for the individual to act. In order to be successful, the individual must be in solidarity with the people: man was perceived as a member of a broad social movement, active and capable of doing good. The link with the audience was emphasised; the audience was appealed to and apportioned an active role in the process, making both man and the world good.

The productions that followed *The Good Person of Szechwan* contained a strong sociopolitical element, building contacts with the audience. The theatre perceived society – a group of individuals, and the audience as part of it – as a generator of social and political change. Lyubimov touched on several themes of sociopolitical significance in his early productions.

The range of theatrical devices was fully explored in the initial years, but especially vividly in *Ten Days that Shook the World* (1965), based on John Reed's account of the revolution. This production used clowning and mime, created with the help of circus artists, and presented the revolution through symbols or images, such as the rising of the red flame of the revolution itself. The beating on the anvil was a symbol of the power of the workers to spark the revolutionary fire. The imprisonment of the revolutionaries was represented by the prisoners holding their arms in the form of a rectangle around their faces, which were lit by a spot, creating the impression of heads behind bars. Shadow play showed the 'shades of the past': several typical members of the old society passed behind a huge white screen that stretched the whole height of the stage. Three Red Guard soldiers had their shadows enlarged to a size that even extended over the screen, almost wiping away all the 'elements' of the past. Light created images, such as prison bars. A 'light curtain' (bulbs in the stage floor projecting to the balcony) distanced stage events. Brecht's alienation effects were successfully used: songs commented on the action; projections of Lenin created a documentary atmosphere; placards indicated the place of action. The production started in the foyer, decorated with red banners bearing revolutionary slogans; the audience tickets were impaled on bayonets by Red Guards. The audience was asked upon leaving to vote for or against the production by inserting their tickets into either a red or a black box. The integration of the audience into the festive revolutionary atmosphere served to deprive history of its magnificence, and private life of its seclusion.

Galileo was much more straightforward in terms of theatrical devices: the set, designed by Enar Stenberg, consisted of walls of egg carton with windows cut into the carton where needed, which could be moved to form narrow streets or rooms. Basically and simply, the walls indicated whether the space was open or closed, oppressive or liberating, private or public. Two choirs, one of monks and one of Pioneers, illustrated Galileo's inner conflict. In the montage of Vladimir Mayakovsky's poetry *Listen!*, Mayakovsky was played by five actors to illustrate a multifaceted personality. Enar Stenberg's set consisted of cubes painted with the letters of the alphabet, reflecting the 'constructivist' approach to poetry and allowing for the formation of words as well as space. With the unorthodox reading of Mayakovsky as a man torn between revolution and the need for love, the theatre encountered difficulties with the Central Directorate of Culture. However, the Taganka Theatre had a very strong Artistic Council composed of leading members of the intelligentsia, which made disputes with the authorities long-winded, but nonetheless helped to pass many controversial productions. The continuous conflict with the authorities forced the theatre into a 'negative' form of appeal: it challenged the audience to reject the behaviour and the ideas presented on the stage. The warning to watch out for 'false friends' in *Tartuffe* for the first time shattered the notion of a homogenous social movement. *Tartuffe* was staged unconventionally in two ways: the set by Mikhail Anikst and Sergei Barkhin parodied the clichéd fixation of character; all the actors emerged from flexible portraits of the characters in the play. Moreover, Molière's conflict with the archbishop and the king over *Tartuffe* was used as a prologue to the production; permission had to be obtained from the archbishop and the king, marionettes in golden frames at the sides of the stage.

Lyubimov's is clearly an author's theatre: the director composes or adapts texts and imposes his personal interpretation on the production. As did Brecht in his epic theatre, Lyubimov wishes to create an awareness in the spectator of being in the theatre. The actor is not required to pretend or to evoke emotions in himself artificially, but to bring his own personality into the role and react both to the role and to the audience. In Lyubimov's theatre, the actor is an executor of the director's will.

After the thaw: the reaction after 1966

A reaction had begun already under Khrushchev with the campaign against 'parasites', which led to the arrest of the Leningrad poet Iosif Brodsky in 1964. In 1965, Andrei Sinyavsky and Yuly Daniel were arrested for publishing their works abroad under the pseudonyms Abram Terts and Nikolai Arzhak. During the XXIII Congress of the Communist Party in 1966, several critical and controversial productions were banned. *The Fallen and the Living*, Lyubimov's montage of war poetry dwelling on the fate of the young poets who sacrificed their lives, was permitted only after numerous viewings and the support of a Politburo member. Tvardovsky's *Tyorkin in the Other World* was removed from the repertoire of the Satire Theatre for the duration of the congress; Tvardovsky himself had to resign as editor of *Novy Mir* in 1970. *A Film is Being Shot* was excluded from the repertoire of the Theatre of the Lenin Komsomol. In 1967 Solzhenitsyn wrote a letter against censorship to the IV Congress of the Writers' Union and was ousted from the union. Fyodor Burlatsky and Len Karpinsky, editors of *Komsomolskaya Pravda*, published an article in which they favoured a liberalisation of cultural politics with regard to the theatre; they were dismissed from the editorial board of the newspaper.[9] Yury Rybakov was removed from the magazine *Teatr* in 1969 for his liberal editorial politics. The liberally orientated writers Evgeny Yevtushenko, Viktor Rozov and Vasily Aksenov were dismissed from the editorial board of the journal *Yunost*. This wave of reaction in the cultural sphere ran parallel to the Soviet intervention in Prague in August 1968. The atmosphere was best reflected in Yury Zavadsky's production of *Crime and Punishment,* with the title *Petersburg Visions* (1969), at the Mossoviet Theatre. The set, by Aleksandr Vasilev, reflected the gloomy and ghostly atmosphere of Dostoevsky's Petersburg. The central character, Raskolnikov, was interpreted as a man who had played with an idea imposed by the outside world. The design, with an atomic mushroom for the finale, underlined the danger of ideas. The theme of the danger of ideas imposed from outside would change in the 1970s to that of the destructive power of ideas created by man himself. Zavadsky's interpretation clearly showed the limits of this: it was possible to condemn the outside environment, capitalist society (of Raskolnikov's Petersburg or 1968 Prague), for creating ideas which destroy mankind. But it was not yet time for the interpretation Lyubimov was to offer ten years later, that of man crippled by ideas he has forged himself.

In 1967 Efros was dismissed as Chief Artistic Director of the Lenin Komsomol Theatre for 'ideological shortcomings' and given the inferior post of staff director at the Moscow Drama Theatre, later called 'Malaya Bronnaya' from its location, as with Lyubimov's 'Taganka', properly the Theatre of Drama and Comedy. Efros's productions of *The Promise* and *The Three Sisters* were banned in 1968. He ran into further difficulties with *Seducer Kolobashkin* by Radzinsky, about a modern Don Juan, which was considered an unsuitable concept for a socialist society.

At the Taganka, the authorities refused to pass Lyubimov's production of Boris Mozhaev's *The Tough: From the Life of Fyodor Kuzkin*. The production was reviewed several times by the Central Directorate and the Ministry of Culture, once in the presence of the minister of culture, Ekaterina Furtseva. Lyubimov was dismissed, but thanks to the support of the Artistic Council was reinstated in office. The conflict reached its climax in 1975, when a delegation of collective-farm workers and representatives of the Ministry of Agriculture was invited to a viewing by the Ministry of Culture to ban the production from the stage for good. *The Tough* asserts that action and resistance are needed even if the system remains unchanged. The collective-farm worker Kuzkin fights to be allowed to work outside the farm, since he cannot live on the income from his farm work. He wins the fight against a bureaucracy which is caricatured to the extreme. The production was banned: officially because it did not correspond to what the Soviet officials perceived as the truth of life on the collective farm (a delicate issue because of its inefficiency); unofficially, because the bureaucrats reviewing the production had recognised themselves in those caricatured on stage.

THE STAGNATION OF THE 1970S

Cultural policy continued along a reactionary line in the 1970s, particularly with regard to Lyubimov and Efros. The XXV Congress of the Communist Party of 1976 promoted the 'production theme' in drama, compelling playwrights to show the hero at work. Since such plays were not very attractive, the theatres instead proceeded to adapt prose works. There were hardly any changes in the appointments of chief artistic directors. However, young directors started to work under the auspices of the established theatres, which opened so-called 'small stages' in the late 1970s for experimental work, allowing also for a more intimate contact with the audience. Anatoly Vasilev, Kama Ginkas and Roman Viktyuk worked at MXAT, Garry Chernyakhovsky at the Mossoviet Theatre, Lev Dodin at the Maly Theatre, and Mark Rozovsky at the Bolshoi Drama Theatre.

At the same time, the old guard was replaced by established directors. Andrei Goncharov, succeeding Nikolai Okhlopkov, managed to maintain the standard of both ensemble and repertoire at the Mayakovsky Theatre by encouraging young directors to experiment. But Evgeny Simonov, succeeding his father Ruben Simonov, failed to maintain the standard of the Vakhtangov Theatre, even though some interesting productions resulted from his collaboration with the actor Mikhail Ulyanov.

Efremov at the Moscow Art Theatre (MXAT)

Efremov had demonstrated his closeness to the MXAT tradition with his emphasis on psychological realism, but moved away from the external realism of the set design. At MXAT, he successfully introduced a generation of young dramatists into the repertoire, especially Aleksandr Gelman and

Mikhail Roshchin, whose plays dealt with the inner conflicts of contemporary men resulting from work. Efremov investigated work ethics in relation to the individual conscience in his productions, which often caused controversy. He attracted talented artists to MXAT: Innokenty Smoktunovsky and Tatyana Doronina from the BDT, Evgeny Evstigneev from the Sovremennik, and Andrei Popov, Ekaterina Vasileva, Oleg Borisov and Aleksandr Kalyagin of the young MXAT generation.

Efremov was the first director to stage successfully Aleksandr Vampilov, whose plays were discovered in the late 1970s. In *Duck Hunting* (1979) Efremov showed the continuous downfall of the hero, Zilov (played by Efremov himself), whose tragedy was underlined by a restructuring of the text: the production started with the end, Zilov's funeral, to give a retrospective account of the events of the past with the psychological motivation of self-analysis. Efremov worked with the Taganka's designer, David Borovsky, for this production, with a tree under polythene as a metaphor for man's estrangement from nature.

Efremov also enriched the repertoire with a new range of interpretations of Chekhov: *Ivanov* (1976), with Smoktunovsky in the lead and an abstract set designed by Borovsky; and *The Seagull* (1980), which in 1970 he had staged at the Sovremennik. In his earlier production of *The Seagull* the heroes failed to communicate and the atmosphere was doomed by sterility, reflected also in the set by Sergei Barkhin in which the exterior intruded into the interior. Now, the production underlined closeness and confidence, the permanent attempt to reach happiness in the future. The colourful and decorative set by Valery Levental, where the lake reflects onstage in mother-of-pearl green and red, and gulls can be heard, was more Chekhovian and poetic than the earlier version.

When the Art Theatre had to move to its new building on the Tverskoi Boulevard, the bond with the audience, so vital for Efremov's approach, was broken, and MXAT started to ossify.

Lyubimov and the Taganka

At the Taganka Theatre, the productions of the 1970s reflected political stagnation: the theatre presented a tragic perception of the individual as alone in a hostile and evil society, pushing the audience into a passive role. In the late 1970s, the isolated individual withdrew into himself and the human conscience emerged as the dominant theme in Trifonov's *The Exchange* (1976) and *The House on the Embankment* (1980).

Artistically speaking the ensemble was encouraged to take on outside work: many actors, for example Alla Demidova and Valery Zolotukhin, established themselves in the cinema or in literature. Vladimir Vysotsky was well known as a 'guitar poet' whose songs were illegally circulated on tapes. His Hamlet, which he played in a torn, black jumper, reciting in his coarse voice Pasternak's Zhivago poem 'Hamlet' to guitar accompaniment at the beginning of the production, was remarkable in two ways: both Vysotsky's music and Pasternak's *Doctor Zhivago* were officially prohibited.

A perfect symbiosis between director and designer was reached in this period, when Lyubimov worked with David Borovsky. Borovsky only works with natural material and authentic objects, an approach which ideally matched Lyubimov's concept that there should be nothing 'false' on stage. A preoccupation with image and form dominated Lyubimov's approach to the theatre. Lyubimov and Borovsky created a central metaphor, which concentrated the contents of the literary material in a formal image: 'In art, the truth of everyday life is not in itself important, but the artistic image; the underestimation of the role of form in search of imagery is a strange but widespread prejudice. The psychological mood of the actor, if not expressed in a clear scenic form, is unconvincing and diffuse to the audience.'[10]

Borovsky condensed the central idea in Lyubimov's often overflowing theatricality into a straightforward image, without which the productions would not work: in Boris Vasilev's *But the Dawns Here are so Calm. . .* (1971), it was a truck to transport the women soldiers, which could be dismantled into boards to cross the swamp or to represent head stones when the women died. In *Hamlet* (1971), it was the curtain, woven of thick yarn, representing fate: it swayed across the stage with such force as to tear people away or throw them into the grave, a patch of sand at the front stage; the costumes were of the same texture. In *The Exchange* (1976) the furniture clustered on the front stage narrowed the room and reflected the small space given to the old human values of the protagonist Dmitriev in Soviet society, which (represented by ice-skaters) occupied the whole of the back stage. The old world with its furniture was wrapped in polythene at the end. *The House on the Embankment* (1980) was represented on the stage by its glass-panelled lift shafts, behind which all that happened in the past (that is, in the protagonist's memory) took place, limiting his present space to a narrow corridor on the front stage.

Lyubimov also started a close collaboration with the composers Alfred Schnittke and Edison Denisov during this period. They provided musical

34. A Taganka Theatre production of *Hamlet* with Vladimir Vysotsky as Hamlet, 1972.

arrangements, which Lyubimov used to pace the rhythm of the action, to set the accents, and mostly to provide opposing forces with their individual leitmotifs.

The conflict with the authorities sharpened at the beginning of the decade: the production *Protect Your Faces*, based on Voznesensky's poetry, was closed because the authorities would not tolerate the experimental character of a production in which Vysotsky sang 'The Wolf Hunt' and in which the palindrome '*a luna kanula*' (and the moon sank) was taken to refer to the Soviet failure to perform a manned landing on the moon before the Americans. Bulgakov's *The Master and Margarita*, which had been published only in 1966, somewhat miraculously passed the Central Directorate when Lyubimov used old parts of set designs and thereby managed without a budget. Lyubimov used all his theatrical imagination and paid homage to a writer for whom artistic truth could not be destroyed. Once passed, the production was pulverised in the press.[11] Similarly, the 'battle' around *The Queen of Spades* was fought in the press: Lyubimov had been invited to stage the opera at the Palais Garnier in Paris in 1978 in a new version designed to bring the romanticised libretto by Modest Tchaikovsky back to Pushkin's story (instead of dying, the protagonist goes insane). After Lyubimov had criticised Soviet cultural politics in the French press, Algis Zhuraitis (conductor of the Bolshoi Theatre) published an article in *Pravda*, in which he attacked Lyubimov and the composer Alfred Schnittke for 'destroying the great heritage of Russian culture' by turning the opera into an 'Americanised musical'.[12] The Ministry of Culture cancelled the production.

Efros at the Malaya Bronnaya

At the Malaya Bronnaya, Efros worked mainly on classical drama, giving many comic texts a tragic dimension in his interpretations. Efros developed his method of structural analysis for the exploration of character psychology, and his concept of the necessity for the psychological motivation of movement on stage, 'psychophysics'. 'On the whole, theatre is close to ballet in my opinion. It must have the same plastic expressivity of relations between two or more people. Only there is the word as well. . . . Every difficult and deep thought must be expressed with theatrical means: not only in the inner action, but in the movement, in the outer dynamics.'[13]

For Molière's *Don Juan* (1973) Efros found an interesting psychological explanation for Don Juan's death from the touch of an old man rather than the commander: Don Juan expected death so much that he projected its arrival into the old man. Efros interpreted Don Juan not as a seducer, but as a representative of a philosophy of negation and scepticism. His discussions with Sganarelle were conducted across the auditorium to open the dialogue, spatially breaking the fourth wall. The set, by Borovsky, was charged with metaphorical significance: a broken-down barn as metaphor for Don Juan's soul, and broken stained glass in a carriage wheel representing his broken faith.

Gogol's *Marriage* (1975) acquired a tragic dimension thanks to the exploration of the characters' psychology. Levental's set consisted of frames, one containing a carriage (Podkolyosin's flight), the other a sofa, a table, and a cage with parrots (Agafya Tikhonovna's existence) encircled by portraits of St Petersburg life. The set reflected Efros's tendency to perceive dialectically and draw his characters clearly, often as polar opposites. His concept of exterior expression of psychological process was developed in the device of animation: Agafya's suitors were described by Fyokla and came alive in Agafya's imagination differently from the way they would later appear in reality.

Efros perfected his method of structural analysis for a clear-cut image of character and externalisation of psychological motivation, which he taught at the Theatre Institute and which greatly influenced Anatoly Vasilev.

Tovstonogov at the Bolshoi Drama Theatre

From 1972 onwards, Tovstonogov worked with the set designer Eduard Kochergin. As does Borovsky, Kochergin works from basic natural material, such as wood or paper (never industrial products such as metal or plastic) to create monochrome spaces. For musical arrangements, Tovstonogov collaborated permanently with S. Rozentsveig.

Tovstonogov developed his repertoire in the direction his previous work had suggested. This was relatively unaffected by politics and censorship, and he was able to complete his Gorky cycle, return to Chekhov and pursue the line of prose adaptations with Sholokhov's *The Quiet Don* (1977), set on a stage covered with soil ploughed in front of the audience (design by Kochergin).

A remarkable production of this decade was the adaptation of Tolstoy's *Strider (The Story of a Horse)* (1975). The production had been initiated by Mark Rozovsky, a journalist who, from 1958 until its closure in 1970, had headed the Moscow University Theatre 'Our House' where he had explored many of the theatrical devices also seen in the Taganka Theatre. He had been invited to the Bolshoi Drama Theatre's small stage, opened in 1973, for a production of his musical *Poor Liza*.

The set by Kochergin was made of sack-cloth, referring to '*kholst*' (canvas) in the name of the horse (Kholstomer), and was draped around the stage. Patches in the sides could be undone and opened, as in the scene of the death of the horse, when red roses were revealed – a colourful and poetic image for death. The costumes were made of the same material, and the actors playing horses wore leather straps around head and body as a harness, thus imprisoning the body. Colour was only used in the costumes of the human beings. Each actor developed the horse's movement for himself; again the director showed reliance on his actors. Tovstonogov used many of his cinematic devices, such as the preface: the production started with a disembodied voice that read a text by Tolstoy on the importance of form in art. The narrative stance is particularly interesting in the story, because it is told by the horse Kholstomer. Tolstoy employs this in order to estrange the point of view. In the production, Evgeny Lebedev played the horse Kholstomer and at the same time assumed the narrator function for his dreams. A choir present on stage described the horses and implicitly compared the situation with the human condition. The choir did not, as in Brecht, identify or comment, but it linked episodes and drew analogies between man and horse. Roles were doubled to enhance parallels. Imagery in the scenes of violence and death represented events: Kholstomer's death was shown by having red ribbon come out of his mouth.

Tovstonogov interpreted the condition of the horse as a tragic metaphor for human life, creating at the same time an allegory for the deformation of nature by claiming it as human property. His interpretation showed his concern with the universal and the general rather than with explicit social criticism.

Theatre of the Lenin Komsomol

Mark Zakharov was appointed Chief Artistic Director to the Theatre of the Lenin Komsomol in 1973. He created a wide-ranging repertoire, including musical productions (*Troubadour and his Friends* in 1974, and *Till,* by Grigory Gorin, also in 1974), political documentaries by Mikhail Shatrov, contemporary plays by Arbuzov and Petrushevskaya, and classics in contemporary interpretation. He built up an ensemble with many actors known from their work in the cinema, such as Inna Churikova, Aleksandr Abdulov and Oleg Yankovsky. Zakharov reached his peak as a director only in the 1980s (with set designer Oleg Sheitsis) with the musical *Perchance* by Voznesensky and Rybnikov (1981) and Shatrov's *Dictatorship of Conscience* (1986).

The Stanislavsky Theatre

In 1977, Andrei Popov was appointed Chief Artistic Director at the Stanislavsky Theatre. He took with him his pupils Anatoly Vasilev, Iosif Raikhelgauz and Boris Morozov.

35. Anastasia Vertinskaya and Vladislav Lyubshin in Molière's *Tartuffe*. Moscow Art Theatre, 1981.

Two productions by Anatoly Vasilev revived the theatre artistically and brought back some of its forgotten actors such as Albert Filozov, Elizaveta Nikishchikhina and Yury Grebenshchikov. Vasilev uses the actor like wax in his hands, creating a psychologically and physically real character on stage, behind which the personality of the actor is effaced. In 1978, he staged Gorky's *Vassa Zheleznova* (1905 version) with the architect and set designer Igor Popov. The space of the theatre is of vital importance to Vasilev's productions, even if the set does not impose itself on the spectator. Here, the stage was narrowed by walls and furniture, open only to the top, where a cage with Prokhor's beloved pigeons hung. Prokhor's death from a heart attack was caused by the feathers of his birds being thrown at him. The theme of human cruelty and disintegration was dwelt upon in the production.

Even more spectacular – due to the use of jazz music, condemned in the 1950s and 1960s as decadent – was *A Young Man's Grown-Up Daughter* (1979). The play, by Viktor Slavkin, is about the meeting of old university friends, now in their forties, who used to be jazz fans and *stilyagi*. Two levels of time are contrasted: the present of the seventies and the past of the 1950s, which is expressed through the jazz music. The everyday realism of the set is given a theatrical conventionality by the arrangement of the fifties furniture diagonally across the stage, as if it were a room with its walls unfolded.

Due to internal quarrels Vasiliev left the Stanislavsky Theatre and was offered the small stage at the Taganka Theatre where for several years he rehearsed Slavkin's next play, *Cerceau*, which premiered in 1985 and is often regarded as the best production of the 1980s. A forty-year-old man invites some colleagues and neighbours for a weekend at his dacha. After a series of excursions into the past, initiated by dresses, letters and the game of *cerceau* found in the attic, the tragic isolation of each of them becomes apparent; they part at the moment when they could actually share their lives with each other.

THE BEGINNING OF THE 1980S

Between Brezhnev's death in November 1982 and Gorbachev's accession in April 1985, there was no clear line, liberal or repressive, in cultural politics, owing to the quick change of leaders. Only Lyubimov's dismissal and forced exile in 1984, immediately after Andropov's death, brought out the difference between Andropov's reformist attitude and the conservatism of Chernenko. Lyubimov was not allowed to return until 1988, while Efros, who had been forced to take over the Taganka when several other directors had refused to do so for ethical reasons, died of a heart attack in 1987. With Tovstonogov's death in 1989 and Efremov's psychological realism unable to respond to new developments, the old avant-garde left the stage to a new generation of young directors who had been experimenting under the guardianship of the 'masters'. They emerged with Gorbachev's *glasnost* and *perestroika,* which started first and foremost with the arts.

Notes

1. Jürgen, Rühle 'The Soviet theatre', in A. Brumberg (ed.), *Russia Under Khrushchev* (London, 1962), pp. 489–528.
2. *Teatr* 8 (1956) and 1 (1957).
3. Oleg Efremov, 1962, quoted in Raisa Beniash, 'Efremov', *Portrety rezhisserov,* (Moscow, 1972), p. 185.
4. Aleksandr Galich, 'General' naia repetitsiia', in *Vozvrashchenie* (Leningrad, 1990); also in ... *Ya vernus'* ... (Moscow, 1993).
5. G. A. Tovstonogov, *Krug myslei* (Leningrad, 1972), p. 28.
6. K. L. Rudnitskii, *Spektakl' raznykh let* (Moscow, 1974), pp. 146–7.
7. Ibid., p. 156.
8. K. Simonov, 'Vdokhnovenie Iunosti', *Pravda*, 8 December 1963.
9. F. Burlatskii and L. Karpinskii, 'Na puti k prem'ere,' *Komsomolskaia Pravda*, 30 June 1967.
10. Iurii Liubimov, 'Algebra garmonii,' *Avrora*, no. 10 (1974), p. 60.
11. N. Potapov, '"Seans chernoi magii" na Taganke', *Pravda*, 29 May 1977.
12. Algis Zhuraitis, 'V zashchitu "Pikovoi Damy",' *Pravda*, 11 March 1978.
13. Anatolii Efros, 'Ia – za takoi teatr. . .', *Literaturnaia Gazeta*, 21 September 1988.

17 Russian theatre in the post-communist era

ANATOLY SMELIANSKY

TRANSLATED BY STEPHEN HOLLAND

I.

It is interesting to compare the legacies of two epochs of Russian theatre history: firstly the Soviet decade (1917–27) and secondly the so-called post-Soviet decade, which began in the mid 1980s and could now in the mid 1990s celebrate an anniversary.

The specific circumstances under which Soviet theatre began to emerge after the revolution and the Civil War are well known. The state nationalised the theatres, taking upon itself responsibility for their financing. All aspects of theatre production were brought under the strictest ideological control – from what we might call the manufacture of a drama right through to the launching of productions and the process of publicising them. However, despite the censor's squeeze (to which, by the way, Russian theatre was completely accustomed) and the state's regulation of art, the post-revolutionary decade turned out to be unusually productive. 'The energy of delusion' brought to life masterpieces of the revolutionary stage. We need only mention Mayakovsky's *Mystery Bouffe*, Crommelynck's *The Magnanimous Cuckold*, Ostrovsky's *The Forest* and Gogol's *The Government Inspector* (Meyerhold productions), Gozzi's *Princess Turandot*, Strindberg's *Erik XIV* and Ansky's *The Dybbuk* (Vakhtangov productions), Tairov's production of Racine's *Phèdre*, Stanislavsky's versions of *A Passionate Heart*, *The Days of the Turbins* and *The Marriage of Figaro*, as well as *Hamlet*, and Andrei Bely's *Petersburg* and Sukhovo-Kobylin's *The Case*, all brought to the stage by Michael Chekhov. The list could be continued.

And it is not only these performances, mounted on the whole by artists who had matured before the revolution, that should be remembered. During those years the life of the theatre called out to new generations of dramatists, actors, directors, theatre artists and composers, for whom utopian ideas of rebuilding the world became the pretext (both positive and negative) for developing those major dramaturgical ideas that have by and large shaped the face of world theatre in our century.

In this respect the epoch ushered in after April 1985 did not produce anything of theatrical importance remotely comparable. Here we have the first paradox which the historian of the Russian stage needs to make sense of.

The most recent Russian theatre has developed in uniquely complex historical conditions, which we need, albeit briefly, to recall. The period of delight and euphoria which began with Gorbachev's 'thaw' very quickly became one of decay, disintegration and disappointment. Freedom overtook the country 'from above', and it fell upon utterly unprepared soil; there were neither democratic institutions, nor the habits of life under a parliamentary system. Nor was there any respect for private property, a vital condition for laying the basic social foundations of durable democratic states. The new state took shape amidst chaos. The power of the emboldened 'democratic' official fused instantly with the power of the mafia (in this latest era's dictionary of most frequently used journalistic and everyday words, the blurred concept of the 'mafia' undoubtedly occupies first place). The police state collapsed, but from the ruins a very strange social phenomenon arose, unparalleled in history (just as the very process of moving from socialism to capitalism itself has no precedents).

On the eve of 1995 (as though to mark the fifteenth anniversary of the invasion of Afghanistan) Russian political history described an astonishing about turn: the campaign in Chechnya began. The Caucasian war was perceived by many as some sort of overall legacy of the post-Soviet decade during which blood and freedom had become inextricably linked. Aleksandr Gelman, one of the dramatists who defined the repertoire of the seventies and eighties, summed up the mood in our society with the greatest sincerity and exactitude:

> Many things came together in this unexpected onslaught upon
> Chechnya, but the main thing to emerge was the crushing sense of
> defeat, which had been building up gradually, growing year after year
> throughout the whole of that decade. There was no war of course, no-
> one was conquering us. But many felt suffocated by a sense of defeat. A
> defeat without war, without blame. After all, had not our people
> achieved a great, non-violent victory over a totalitarian regime? Had
> they not contributed to the peaceful liberation of the peoples of

Europe, been involved in the peaceful reunification of the two
Germanies and secured for the first time in history, if I am not mistaken, the peaceful redrawing of European frontiers?. . . The whole
world felt relief, joy, but back in our country many people, ordinary
people at that, not those in power, experienced a soul-destroying
sense of defeat.[1]

A blundering Russian government enjoying no support from its people and
which was not restrained by one productive policy, the scattered outbreaks
of bloody violence around the country, corruption on a scale hitherto
unseen, the marginalisation of a former world power (the Mexican soap
operas filling the nation's television screens seemed to reflect Russia's slide
into third-world status) – it was against this backdrop and in such a set of
circumstances that a new Russian art was developing.

The rapture of freedom fairly quickly turned into the savagery of basic
capital accumulation with contract killings, plush presentations, verbiage
and other delights described in their time by the Russian classics. It was no
coincidence that Aleksandr Ostrovsky became one of the most frequently
staged dramatists in the new Moscow. *Easy Money, Wolves and Sheep, Guilty
Without Guilt* – the titles of these dramas and comedies, written in the
middle of the last century and familiar since childhood, sparked with a
new-found pointed meaning.

As the shape of things to come became clearer, so the legacy of Soviet
theatre began to be experienced nostalgically. The loss of Anatoly Efros
(1987) and Georgy Tovstonogov (1989), leaders of the Russian stage from
the 1960s to the 1980s, left a gaping hole. It became clear that under repressive conditions in Russia a uniquely great theatre had been created which
had fulfilled its historic task. Bled dry by the censor, extremely narrow in
its thematic concerns, separated by an 'iron curtain' from the development
of world theatre – nevertheless the best achievements of Russian theatre
had expressed and shaped the spiritual life of its own society. Recalling
Stanislavsky, we could say that this was a theatre which possessed a transcendent goal. Not for nothing did the founder of the Moscow Art Theatre
so love that word 'transcendent'.

In circumstances of relative freedom Russian theatre lost its special
significance. It disappeared along with the 'transcendent political power'.
'Transcendent theatre' became simply theatre. All manner of spiritual
activities experienced this lowering of status. The circulations of the 'better

newspapers' fell from 20 million down to a few thousand. Great literature, banned for decades and suddenly unloaded in one fell swoop upon the head of the dazed reader, gave way to the gutter press. The cheapest examples of American trash wasted no time in taking over the artistic market. 'Evil has never been so sexy,' proclaimed the television advert for some bestseller, addressing itself to a country gone mad, unable at this point to set limits for itself. Soviet literature had been crowded out, but it had given up its seat not to a new Russian literature but to that mass demand which, obeying all the laws of the free market, had rushed in and swamped us.

Dramatists, actors, directors, writers, who, in the absence of this free-for-all, had considered themselves the spiritual shepherds of the people, began to lose their way. Their books were no longer bought, their productions became part of an impoverished Russian 'leisure time'. Everything began to show its true colours. Not a happy sight – especially from the standpoint of those utopian notions about the country, with which the liberal Soviet intelligentsia had sustained itself.

That theatre should be condemned to a secondary role as one arm of the contemporary entertainment industry, long since the case in countries with a sound tradition of democracy, was something entirely new for those involved in Russian theatre and was keenly felt. Freedom of artistic effort was no longer perceived as something exceptional and beneficent: people quickly grew accustomed to it as they do to the presence of air (whose lack they notice only when they begin to suffocate). Furthermore, the absence of censorship allowed an orgy of base instincts: those market regulators 'supply and demand' began to dictate their own terms to the life of the theatre. The majority of Moscow theatres, in an attempt to survive, began to surrender their premises to the 'new Russians' (as the newly created businessmen were being called). Inside theatres casinos were opened, night clubs, foreign currency offices. Heavy with symbolism, signs saying 'Exchange' adorned the entrances to the leading theatres of Russia. If the country was changing its spots – well, the theatres would, too. In the midst of all this, it was not particularly clear what was changing into what or by what route. A loss of social status in tandem with a loss of a secret feeling of 'leadership' which had been written into the genetic code of those concerned with artistic creation in Russia – this was one of the most important outcomes of the 'exchange'.

Naturally this is a formulaic, inevitably schematic overview of the actual process. What this formula does not include is those who were not disappointed and did not experience the 'numbness of defeat', but to whom, by contrast, was offered a historic chance. Their voice was barely audible during those years, but nevertheless it was heard. Sergei Zhenovich, and Vladimir Mashkov, the young theatre formed with students of Pyotr Fomenko, these were each significant and substantial realities in the new life of the theatre.

Neither was the 'disappointed' generation all of one hue. Directors of this generation mounted a series of important productions reflecting the transitional times. The art of Pyotr Fomenko and Kama Ginkas, of Lev Dodin and Anatoly Vasilev, of Oleg Efremov and Mark Zakharov – for all the variety and spread of their abilities – did still answer the challenge of a troubled time. Very often the productions actually carried this disturbance within themselves, in their very artistic construction and tone. With the disappearance of the Soviet transcendent theatre came the difficult birth of another language, another method of relating to the public, another type of theatre as yet unnamed.

2.

The first sign of a new theatrical era was the division of the Moscow Art Theatre (MXAT) instigated in the spring of 1987.

The Art Theatre had always mirrored events in the country. Mikhail Bulgakov, who dedicated to this theatre his *Memoirs of a Dead Man* (known in English as *Black Snow*), captured splendidly this very characteristic. His pen transformed the picture of an independent theatre with its secret, semi-mystical structure, managed by a petty and stupid tyrant, into a microcosm of the Stalinist state. As it was in the past, so it was also in more recent times.

The conflict in the Art Theatre was born of *perestroika*, which unleashed, as it were, the theatre's sleeping forces, both productive and destructive. It was the first clap of thunder that allowed us to guess the course of the storm. The sequence of events was unusually straightforward and one that had already repeated itself at various levels of Soviet society. The enormous troupe, which at the moment of schism numbered 160 artists, was to all intents and purposes unemployable. Many actors had not set foot on a stage for months, if not years, yet regularly received their wages and associated benefits. All the attempts of Oleg Efremov to reform the theatre (he became director of MXAT in the autumn of 1970) foundered not only on the blind opposition of the 'lower echelons' but also on the visible displeasure of the 'higher echelons', who saw the theatre as a special emblem of the state.

Actors at the theatre could always exert direct influence over important party officials, who, at the necessary moment, would always stymie any attempt at reform. The theatre had fossilised inside its own inert structure, an emblem of our whole society. Everyone had got used to this, had learned to live with it and even to profit from the situation.

Oleg Efremov believed in the idea of *perestroika* immediately and precipitately. The party leader spoke the language of the sixties, which the director understood. Gorbachev tried to refine the idea of revolution and secondly to refine the idea of Stanislavsky. *Perestroika* at MXAT led to Efremov's suggestion that the troupe be divided into two halves, so that each half would have the opportunity to demonstrate its right and its ability to be involved with art. Those who demonstrated their entitlement were destined to enter the bright edifice of communism, that is to say the historic building of the theatre itself, which at that very time was getting ready to receive audiences after many years of repairs.

A national scandal erupted, started of course by those who considered themselves the undoubted losers in this reformist action. The squabble, which in earlier times would never have gone beyond the four walls of the theatre (such a thing had not even happened when Stanislavsky asked Stalin to poke his nose into reform of the theatre's troupe in the mid 1930s), was picked up by the newspapers. The public began to follow with amazement this unique politico-theatrical show, which in many ways pre-empted the historical spectacle unfolding in the country at large. In essence, the division of the Moscow Art Theatre, the instantaneous collapse of an organism that had taken a whole era to develop, became the model for the swift and rapacious breakdown of the Soviet empire.

The schism immediately acquired an ideological hue. The two halves of MXAT began to oppose each other as 'genuinely Russian' and 'non-Russian', one democratic, the other reactionary. In the spring of 1987 the conflict was taken all the way up to the Politburo (in Soviet times MXAT's problems were always resolved at the highest level). A decision was made very much in accord with the way things were developing in the country, that is, there was a complete fudge. It was decided, as an experiment, to divide the MXAT into two theatres, but both would still be housed under the same world-renowned roof.

As a result, the second MXAT, or the female one as it is called in Moscow, came into being. The actress Tatyana Doronina, who had no connection either with the director or with the art that had become synonymous with the name of MXAT, received into her jurisdiction half of the troupe and a building in the centre of Moscow. On the pediment of this building she very quickly displayed all the Orders of Lenin and of the Red Banner of Labour, which, in its time, the Soviet government had bestowed upon MXAT. Next, the two MXATs parted company over their names: one became the Chekhov Art Theatre, the other – the Gorky (the symbolism of the writers' names was also deeply politicised).

The two theatres were supported by different political forces and practised different artistic policies. The Chekhov MXAT developed with great difficulty, trying to find its place in contemporary society. Oleg Efremov responded to the Gorbachev thaw with a production of Aleksandr Misharin's *Silver Wedding* (1986). This production began a sequence of theatrical advertisements for the idea of *perestroika*, amongst which were *The Dictatorship of Conscience* by Mikhail Shatrov in the Lenin Komsomol Theatre (director Mark Zakharov), and *Speak!*, a play by Aleksandr Buravsky adapted from a story by Valentin Ovechkin. These productions enjoyed immense success largely because of their superficial verbal brilliance. However, Efremov very quickly sensed the change in the taste of a public which had had its fill of political comment and uncensored boldness. When he put on at MXAT in 1991 Aleksandr Solzhenitsyn's play *The Conquerors' Feast*, a piece about life in the camps under Stalin banned for three decades, the production seemed not even to register with the public. Very likely an instinct for self-preservation was at work here: people were reluctant to pick over an old carcass when everywhere was littered with so many fresh ones.

Then Efremov changed direction drastically towards the Russian classics, sensing that here lay the only good spiritual soil. *The Cherry Orchard* (1989), *Woe from Wit* (1992), and *Boris Godunov* (1994), in which Efremov played the leading role, were milestones along this road, but were very variably received by the Russian press.

The Gorky MXAT also tried to respond to contemporary events. Perhaps its most controversial statement was the production *Batum* based on a play by Mikhail Bulgakov about Stalin. The play, commissioned by MXAT and written towards the end of the 1930s, was earmarked for the sixtieth birthday of the people's leader but was banned. Thereafter worldwide there was no attempt to mount it: the play remained as a monument to the faintheartedness of a remarkable writer who was simply attempting to survive. The world premiere of *Batum* took place on the stage of the

Gorky MXAT on 7 November 1992, the 75th anniversary of the October Revolution, and turned into a political demonstration: the auditorium greeted rapturously the generalissimo in his white single-breasted jacket, as his wise gaze pierced the distance. The brass section of the orchestra thundered and a powerful choir brought fanatics to their feet with the words of the banished Soviet anthem:

> Stalin has raised us to be loyal to our nation
> For our toil and our exploits he is our inspiration.

The two MXATs became a sign of dual time, the new emblem of Russian theatre. They face one another from across each side of Tverskoi Boulevard – one of the main streets in Moscow. They stand like two columns of demonstrators, one with red flags, the other with a tricolour. This opposition will no doubt last just as long as the opposition in our fractured country is unable to break with its Soviet past.

3.

The division of MXAT was only the beginning. One after another, Moscow theatres began to split up and collapse in its wake. The demise of the Taganka Theatre was certainly the most significant for the fate of Russian theatre.

In the autumn of 1983, when Yury Lyubimov, founder and artistic director of the Taganka Theatre, was in London staging *Crime and Punishment*, he began a public row with the leadership of the Soviet Union, demanding that they lift a ban on productions of *Boris Godunov* and *Vladimir Vysotsky*. As a result of this argument he lost his Soviet citizenship and was ostracised by the state: the director's name was removed not only from the posters but even from the programmes for the productions he had staged (the plays themselves continued to run during all of this!). The banishment lasted several years. From 1984–7 Anatoly Efros was director of the Taganka Theatre. His arrival was met with blunt opposition by Lyubimov's troupe, who continued to hope for a miracle. In January 1987 Efros died suddenly, and the Taganka Theatre began to fight for Lyubimov's return.

And the miracle happened (very much in the style of all those miracles which occurred back then in Gorbachev's Russia). In May 1988 the former director of the Taganka arrived back in Moscow on an Israeli passport and at the personal invitation of one of his actors, Nikolai Gubenko (who had played Tsar Boris Godunov). He returned to a different country; just how different took him some time to understand. He resurrected the banned productions. They did not pass unnoticed, but neither did they make many waves. In the new circumstances the measure of what might be considered a real event had altered. Lyubimov and his theatre had grown accustomed to working with the sense of an external enemy, one who, to a certain extent, defined both the style of Taganka productions and, in a manner of speaking, its lifestyle. This was the style of a permitted dissidence, which in the new circumstances had lost all meaning.

The first production put together under the new conditions and designed to speak artistically to them was *The Suicide* by Nikolai Erdman (1989). For all manner of reasons the choice of play was a matter of principle. Banned personally by Stalin at the beginning of the 1930s (both Meyerhold and Stanislavsky had wished to stage it at one and the same time, the latter considering it as great a piece as Gogol's *The Government Inspector*), Erdman's comedy was the production dream of the great Russian directors. Yury Lyubimov had one further personal motivation for its staging: Nikolai Erdman had been his friend and one of those 'allies at court' for the Taganka in its formative years. Thus the production became a duty of memory and emotion whose accountability was greatly increased in the face of the new historical situation.

The simple theme of how Semyon Podsekalnikov, an ordinary Joe, threatens his wife with his own suicide and then receives dozens of suggestions outlining under what philosophical circumstances and because of whom he ought to quit this life was elaborated in just the way Gogol developed the plot of *The Government Inspector*. 'These days, citizen Podsekalnikov, anything you might think of while you're alive, you can only say when you're dead.' This line encapsulated the world of Erdman's comedy, projected onto the backdrop of the pivotal late 1920s. The whole country, representatives of all its classes, address themselves to our man in the street and bogus suicide Semyon Podsekalnikov. Each puts forward his own version of why Semyon ought to do away with himself and what last will and testament he ought to leave. Underneath the parodic choir of doubles and mimics can be heard the repressed hubbub of voices of a real country and its people gone mad at this abrupt turning in history, which at the time Stalin called 'the year of the great turning-point'.

Yury Lyubimov and his designer David Borovsky hung across the stage a huge sheet showing the face of Karl Marx. The leader of the world's proletariat took an active part in the proceedings. Sometimes his eyes would sparkle (to highlight a particular point): from his beard little suicide notes were retrieved. Upstage, in front of Marx, stood a railway handcar. A wooden monument, it was a tower on which were acted out not scenes from the play but from its author's life in exile in the camps. From the tower of the camp the playwright often looked down compassionately at his hero, the little man of the Soviet epoch. In some sense they were made equals, levelled under the wheels of the prison cart and the beard of the German intellectual looking out over millions of Podsekalnikovs and Erdmans.

Through tragicomedy Lyubimov was trying to tackle his favourite theme of death. For in this country just simply to die like that, without any transcendent purpose, somehow also seemed impossible. Everyone wants Podsekalnikov to die 'philosophically' and heroically. But in the Taganka production Podsekalnikov could not destroy himself. The desire to live, even just to fill his stomach, was too strong. Vitaly Shapovalov (in the leading role) was above all a person alive. Small-minded, insignificant, devoid of ideals, cowardly, but alive. You needed to be steeped in our past to understand that 'sense of dislocation' Lyubimov was attempting to create. The utopian dream of those in power was above all else to eliminate what Russia called the petty bourgeois and the Philistines. In order to crush people under a new ideology you needed to drag them out of their homes, defame the poetry of the family and all the other simple joys of ordinary existence. Erdman – perhaps without wishing to – definitively described in his comedy how our world was neatly turned like a greyed collar: we were left an existence but our life was destroyed.

Lyubimov mounted a production about how life which is truly alive can be murdered at various levels including the protoplasmic one of Podsekalnikov. That was how the production was conceived. But it was acted in a very different way. The director's freedom clashed with what might be called the inertia of the style. All the scenery for the play, the devices of both director and actors, even the way the production related to its audience, all bore the stamp of the old Taganka, that is to say of a theatre always keeping a hidden enemy in mind. If we are to believe the journalist from *Soviet Culture* who reported on rehearsals of *The Suicide*, the director was begging actors to play it so that 'they would be closed down'.

But there was no-one around to close them down.

At the end of the 1920s Nikolai Erdman wrote a highly prophetic fairytale. In it the keys of a piano raged against the pianist who struck and oppressed them. The pianist justified himself in this way: 'Only when you are struck do you give out any sounds. If no-one hits you, you'll remain silent.'

The phenomenon of 'transcendent theatre' was very much dependent upon this paradox. The 'sounds' of art were often produced in response to monstrous blows of power. Many remarkable directors, dramatists, actors and whole theatres were shaped under this regime. Tragically, the theatre needed to be freed from within. A change in artistic mentality was required. But the energy to achieve this was lacking. After *The Suicide*, Lyubimov staged several more productions, including Boris Pasternak's *Dr Zhivago* with music by Alfred Schnittke. But even this production passed practically unnoticed in the new Moscow. The artistic crisis coincided with an organisational one. Nikolai Gubenko, who, apart from the unbanned *Godunov*, had managed to play the real role of the last minister for culture of the Soviet Union, became embroiled in a bitter and protracted conflict with his former teacher, the founder of the Taganka. The end result was that within the theatre two separate troupes formed under the same roof. Neither troupe turned out to be viable. Lyubimov did not give up the threatre but tried to work at the same pace as before, mounting operas in the west and new productions on the old stage of the Taganka which he inherited after the company split. It was there in the 90s he produced *Medea* and *Elektra* and it is there that he will mark his 80th birthday by directing *The Brothers Karamazov*. His productions still bore the name of the theatre, the Taganka, but the once glorious, the real Taganka, had faded and died with the period in which it was born.

4.

Some theatres died, others were restored to a new life. It was during those years that the Maly Theatre in Petersburg acquired a worldwide reputation under the leadership of Lev Dodin. The theatre world judged what was going on in Russian drama by the wandering splinter of the Maly. This theatre was possibly the first to overcome that 'mentality of the prisoner' ingrained in the whole of our society (to use Bulgakov's phrase writing to Stalin about his desire to set eyes on an unattainable Paris). Flying Dutchmen from Petersburg, they freely cross our border, tirelessly travel back and forth, evoking rapture in some, envy and amazement in others. The difficulty here is not one of visas and passports, rather of a certain type of artistic existence which could only evolve during troubled times. Many artists do indeed live in just this way, pursuing two differing regimens, in two linguistic and cultural contexts, and, just as importantly, using two different currencies. They work as it were in Russia, but they earn their means of existence in the West.

The danger of such a dichotomy was certainly not perceived immediately. I remember only the prophetic statement by Anatoly Vasilev, one of the most talented directors of the post-Lyubimov generation, after he had travelled round half the world with a production of *Cerceau* in the mid 1980s: 'A month of touring in the West and you no longer have Russian theatre.'

Lev Dodin's theatre is trying to survive. Its double life was initially even a cause for celebration. In the production *Brothers and Sisters* (the first example of Dodin's work to play in Europe and America) the West discovered the so-called 'transcendent theatre' of Russia which seemed to belong only to the mythical days of Stanislavsky. Extended over two nights, the fate of the countryside under Stalin after the war unfolded on an epic scale. This was done not only in shocking detail and with penetrating insight into the human soul, but also extremely theatrically. Essentially the production became a powerhouse of striking theatrical metaphors which overcame social and linguistic barriers.

The actors in *Brothers and Sisters* were yesterday's students, who played the roles prepared for them extremely well. Working in the post-Efros and post-Lyubimov era of theatre (the two most influential tendencies in Russian theatre since Stalin), they were obliged to define themselves as one or the other. Lev Dodin's direction became, in one sense, the art of mediation, of the attempt to create a synthesis which does not recognise the boundaries between 'own' and 'other'. In this respect the director relived the fate of Vakhtangov, who tried to find the golden mean between Stanislavsky and Meyerhold at the beginning of the 1920s.

As usual, new dramatic purposes began to take shape around the new 'theatricality'. No-one seemed worried by the vague and well-worn nature of this concept. Lev Dodin tried to affirm the idea of a theatricality, which could overcome all stylistic and thematic barriers, in strikingly different areas of drama: Dostoevsky, Kleist, Eugene O'Neill, and Chekhov were some facets of this sought-after 'theatricality'.

The most impressive (and the simplest) attempt at a dramatic treatment of post-Soviet life came in a production of *Gaudeamus*. The improvisations on the theme of life in an army construction battalion (the play was based on *Combat* – a story by Sergei Kaledin) rested on a paradoxical collective decision. Dodin compressed the gloomy and bitter Soviet army reality into sweet, crystalline wafers (quite obviously we could only take this medicine in such a form). Reality was chopped up, prepared and shaped into little parables, rituals and musical sketches, which were called upon to tease out eternal biblical themes in contemporary life. The enormous and infectious energy of the young actors, the garishness of the figurative metaphor, all the other devices of contemporary theatricality became the means by which 'music lessons' were extracted from the depths of a hopeless every-day life. The darker life is, the more joyful art. This was a hopeless opti-mism, helping us to survive and to resist chaos and corruption.

As they travelled around the world, the theatre evolved a particular crea-tive rhythm. At specific moments the Russian minstrels cut short their 'flight' and returned, as it were, to their native 'lair' in Petersburg. Cancelling evening performances, the actors rehearsed day and night to create a new repertoire. The premieres often took place not in Russia but in France or Germany, as happened for example with *The Devils*, sponsored by the town of Braunschweig.

The most important production for Dodin, and his response to the new historical situation, was this ten-hour adaptation of Dostoevsky's classic anti-revolutionary novel, *The Devils*. The previous regime had not allowed Dostoevsky's novel on the stage since 1917. Back then they had supposed that the heirs of the 'devils' – the Bolsheviks – might have taken offence. The production was several years in preparation. Dodin bided his time, clarified his ideas, sharpened his focus. The premiere of *The Devils* second-guessed the collapse of the Soviet Union, as Meyerhold's *Masquerade*, also in rehearsal for five years, heralded the end of the tsarist empire. At the start Dodin had wanted to settle accounts with the past. But he ended up aston-ished before the present. Everyone was amazed. The unhappy insight that the 'devils' exist within us and always will, regardless of changes in the political climate, was the main message of a directorially ascetic produc-tion. The stage was transformed into the location of tense spiritual relation-ships, where emphasis was laid on Dostoevsky's words, on the psychological justification of the huge monologues stripped of any exter-nal theatricality whatsoever.

As I have already said, Lev Dodin's theatre became the first Russian theatre for many decades to come into close and protracted contact with what Russians call Western theatre, which includes that of Europe, and the USA and Canada. Diaghilev's seasons in Paris, tours by the Meyerhold and Kamerny theatres, the two-year journey of MXAT through Europe and

America with its old productions created at the start of the century were essentially the limit of any real Western acquaintance with the phenomenon of twentieth-century Russian theatre, given the impenetrable wall of Stalinist times and then the decades of manoeuvrings by officials allowing into the West only what seemed necessary to them for propaganda purposes. The Maly Theatre in Petersburg not only toured endlessly in the West, it also began to create new works both in collaboration with Western producers as well as directly commissioned by them. Not just *The Devils*, but also *Claustrophobia* and *The Cherry Orchard* came into being this way. They had their premieres in Paris during a 1993–4 Russian season.

For all its similarity to the 'Diaghilev seasons' the new 'Russian season' in Paris was not a revelation in artistic terms. Rather it was a demonstration that Russian theatre still existed, that it had not lost its energy and was capable of depicting the country or its current state of disintegration. Success in Paris, it must be said, was not necessarily followed by success back in the home country. Quite the reverse: the double life of Dodin's theatre aroused widespread opposition from Russia's nascent theatre criticism. His art began to be seen as 'made to measure', intended for another type of spectator and sensibility (this was said particularly about *Claustrophobia*). There was much here that was unjust, provoked by the discord of the 'troubled times' the country was experiencing.

However, there was another issue. That type of metaphorical theatre, at the heart of which lies strongly politicised emotion and which formed the basis of *Claustrophobia,* had ceased to be experienced with the same keenness. What is more, its social diagnosis seemed wide of the mark. It was not 'claustrophobia' but fear of isolation, the horror of life without boundaries or limits, without a past or a future that had overwhelmed us. The terrible scenes created by the Petersburg actors, which had such a strong impact in Europe, made little impression on the Russian public, who reacted to them as though under anaesthetic.

In essence, during the period we have surveyed, the Petersburg Maly remained almost the last example of the type of theatre which had reigned supreme in twentieth-century Russia. It was a repertory theatre living according to strict artistic and ethical rules. Holding on to these rules under the conditions of early capitalist accumulation turned out to be a matter of unbelievable complexity. From all of this stemmed the expectations, the insults and the demanding tone directed at the theatre. Dodin's theatre was not only expected to secure success, triumphs and good productions. It was also asked to deliver a shock and a 'transcendent meaning' which were probably no longer attainable. Because when all is said and done this 'transcendent theatre' was the product of a lack of freedom, in which actor and audience had been united by a single emotion and a shared memory.

5.

A freedom which revealed Russian artists to the world and concealed them from Russia was a paradox not only at work in Lev Dodin's theatre. Another fairly complicated example was the fate of the School of Dramatic Art, a theatre founded by Anatoly Vasilev in the middle of the 1980s. Having initiated during the early years of freedom the practice of round-the-world tours (as well as *Cerceau*, a production of Pirandello's *Six Characters in Search of an Author* had also enjoyed huge success in the West), Anatoly Vasilev fairly quickly desisted from this. He personally sometimes mounted productions 'on the side', such as his Comédie Française production of Lermontov's *Masquerade*, which roused the indignation of the French capital, but he was not able or did not want to prolong the life of a classical-style repertory theatre. He did not want to turn a Russian repertory theatre into a respectable commercial enterprise. Instead he began to realise 'projects' as he liked to call them. Anatoly Vasilev's school started up in the centre of Moscow, on the very same Povarskaya Street where once Stanislavsky and Meyerhold had organised their first experimental workshop, which changed the course of Russian drama. Possessed of a formidable ability to formulate his theatrical ideas and to organise them into a coherent statement, Vasilev would often explain the nature of his investigations. He worked in the sphere of Russian psychological theatre which he drastically restructured. Through his teacher, Maria Knebel, Stanislavsky's first apprentice, he had inherited a direct legacy from a common forefather. He tried to fuse psychological insight as an acting technique with the West's centuries-old tradition of playfulness. In his workshops he tried to base his ideas on the stuff of world literature, from Plato's *Socratic Dialogues* and Pirandello's and Molière's plays right through to those 'devils' of Dostoevsky. He repeatedly affirmed the possibility of a 'theatre without spectators' (the effect of a picture in a gallery). He elaborated so-called 'vertical theatre', which demands a genuinely liberated artist and a person capable of improvising and of relating not only to colleagues and the public but also to some higher force for which he must be the conduit. Vasilev hated the Russo-Soviet bourgeoisie of *perestroika* and its celebrity-actor practitioners (he called them 'portraits') who had very little to say after the dismantling of all those cages in which the artist was supposed to work. In some essential way Vasilev's school recalled Jerzy Grotowski's famous Polish workshop, most importantly in its understanding of the act of theatre as a phenomenon with consequences far beyond the boundaries of art, and connected to the deepest events in our spiritual life. To all intents and purposes it is still the same 'transcendent' theatre in the most literal sense of this word.

Students from all over the world beat a path to Vasilev's basement on Povarskaya Street. Yet in Russia virtually nothing was known of this. There were no marketing slogans there, and the experimental 'projects' or 'The Glass Bead Game' (to use the title of a famous German novel) awoke no special interest in free Moscow.

6.

Theatre is searching for a new vindication. It has infiltrated rooms, basements, the corridors of theatre schools and canteens, any nook or cranny where it might be possible to preserve the cadence of the human voice and to test once again its relationship with the public. Into the space left once the country had ceased to be a huge resonator for 'transcendent theatre' have stepped room-sized productions which try to ignite the sparks of a new theatrical faith. And faith is the word here. Religion if you will: not only is the language of Russian theatre breaking down, but also the whole structure, the whole 'body'.

Kama Ginkas belonged to the same generation as Lev Dodin and Anatoly Vasilev. He had lived through the same years of homelessness in the catacombs of Soviet theatre. He shared the same fervent belief in the director as the theatre personified (this he took from his apprenticeship under Georgy Tovstonogov). He too had long gaps in his life without productions, and had placed remarkable productions stealthily like cuckoos into the nests of other theatres. He shared the same theatrical faith which turned out to be no easier to defend in a situation of freedom than before.

Kama Ginkas did not establish his theatre conventionally. He also started to live in two worlds, working a great deal outside Russia and staying little in Moscow. But almost every piece was a real event, a challenge to generally accepted notions. He refused to depict the truth on stage with 'truthful' methods. He had long ago begun the search for the means to express theatrical truth, that is to say that quality of acting already attained by both Dodin and Vasilev. His most characteristic method of expression was to connect the audience unwittingly, through paradox, irony and parody, to the most powerful sources of human emotion. Whether he was staging Dostoevsky's *Notes from Underground* or Aleksandr Galin's *Tamada*, Chekhov's *Ward Six* or Dostoevsky's *The Idiot*, he opened up the writer's world through a theatrical playfulness which he considered to be the universal language of proper and resourceful human communication. There were no restrictions upon this playfulness: he once called one of his best productions, based on *Crime and Punishment*, *Let's Play Crime*.

The scene is a room, outside the footlights. The Helsinki actor Marcus Grot (a Finnish Swede) plays Rodion Raskolnikov, his hair crew-cut and prickly, in a long black visibly ill-fitting coat and boots that suggest both the clown and the prison-camp inmate. He does not speak, just mumbles incomprehensibly in some cryptic mixture of Russian, Swedish and Finnish. Every so often some sort of Russian word tries to form itself out of the syllables. This disconcerting, playful, almost circus-like idea quickly finds an inner justification. Such a Raskolnikov swiftly jolts us out of our mechanical reading of the classical text and brings us face to face with the searing message of the book.

A raving young man is trying to explain himself. It appears that the boy has travelled to the time of the great revolution in our country, where they should be able to understand his simple ideas about 'ant-hills' and 'trembling creatures'. It is surely just a matter of finding the words and fitting a meaning to them. But he cannot communicate! The plot twists and turns like a duel of words. Tragicomic misunderstandings continually arise, because the Western maniac in the circus boots has ended up not in a country of revolution, but in one of ordinary citizens, all the 'reds' here have long ago been wiped out, and there remains only one person, Porphiry Petrovich, an investigator who understands Raskolnikov without recourse to words (portrayed excellently by Viktor Gvozditsky).

Kama Ginkas's premise, seemingly, was that the spectator (not only the Russian one) had lost faith in all language. His productions conveyed the truth about human relationships independently of language: thus, for example, Sonia Marmeladova reads the parable of the raising of Lazarus to the pitiful Raskolnikov. She makes him understand the Bible story with a striking simplicity which touches directly his suffering soul as though bypassing the outward shell of words. Inside this shell of sound Ginkas always discovered a theatrical energy he could release. The methods he used were frequently shocking. Theatrical play worked alongside a refined and considered naturalism, without which of course it would have been impossible to produce a real effect on the audience. And he certainly achieved effects: in their own way Ginkas's productions became a touchstone for the Russian stage.

7.

So far we have discussed the supreme examples of the Russian stage. But theatre life in times of freedom and restriction does not, as we know, consist solely of masterpieces. It is defined also by what is simply fashionable, by what the public, who (in the words of Pushkin) are the making of dramatic talents, go to see. It was during these very years, not far from Moscow, that Roman Viktyuk's star was in the ascendant. A director from the Soviet fringe, a typical marginal, he blossomed in the new climate. Jean Genet's *The Maids*, Nabokov's *Lolita*, and *Madame Butterfly* were just about the most notable premieres during those years. Their success was like that of a well-timed quotation. Roman Viktyuk first forged what the West calls 'gay' art. The hitherto banned subject matter, allied to a brilliance and dynamism of expression, entranced Moscow. Within this now permitted domestic rebellion could also be found the spirit of freedom, including theatrical freedom. The rebellion did not last long. Roman Viktyuk began to repeat himself, the banned and the 'marginalised' became a commonplace, and he had no other distinct theatrical idea in reserve. Nevertheless his productions, staged in various theatres, and then also his newly created Viktyuk Theatre, became the enzyme producing what the West calls commercial art.

This type of art is also multi-layered. The combined weight of the Soviet press obscured this until the end. Emancipation gave to each artist and every theatre their own particular profile. To this we owe the phenomenon of Mark Zakharov and of Lenkom (the Lenin Komsomol Theatre), which he headed.

A sixties man, if we looked at his director's passport, it was indeed at the end of the sixties that he staged his best production. *A Profitable Post*, based on Aleksandr Ostrovsky's play, was the confession of a generation. The play concerned a young man faced with the choice between a government official's career, bribes and the possibility of saving his soul. The hero of the production, played by Andrei Mironov, one of the most popular actors of his generation, miraculously walked a tightrope between honesty and

36. A scene from Jean Genet's *The Maids*, directed by Roman Viktyuk, 1988.

baseness, did not fall off and so bequeathed his most difficult of balancing acts to many of those who were forced to live and accomplish things under the circumstances of the so-called 'stagnation'. The production was banned, but for many years Zakharov was firmly labelled unorthodox or dissident.

Within the framework of the then regime dissidence required a perpetual moral balancing act. Like the hero in *A Profitable Post* the director pulled off this circus act not just successfully but also with a certain panache. When, in the late 1970s, he headed the Lenin Komsomol Theatre, he very quickly made it one of the most popular in Moscow. It was a second-order theatre, after Lyubimov, Efros and Tovstonogov, but it had its own character and repertoire. Mark Zakharov was the first to have the courage to create, together with the composer Aleksei Rybnikov, the Soviet rock operas *Yunona* and *Maybe*. He 'discovered', as they used to say then, Lyudmila Petrushevskaya: *Three Girls in Blue*, with Inna Churikova in the leading role, was a revelation. Always on a tightrope, he tried to make Soviet dramaturgy his own, staging plays about Lenin and much else in this vein. At the same time even productions about the leader of the revolution needed to show his dissident credentials. In fact this was not all that difficult: anything that veered even subtly from the official line was considered unorthodox. This was exactly what shaped the life of Mikhail Shatrov with his plays about the leader of the revolution upon which bans were constantly being placed and then lifted.

During the Gorbachev thaw Mark Zakharov became the undisputed leader of the renewed theatre. Quite a creditable writer, with an undeniable sense of humour, he immediately fired off some broadsides with a series of reforming articles, in which he outlined how policed was the life of the theatre, and how in turn this mirrored remarkably well the general state of the country. He inspired the so-called experiment (1986–8) when, for the first time in the history of the Soviet regime, a string of theatres were allowed to choose their own repertoire and to take responsbility for their own financial policy. Zakharov's productions from those years turned out to be the most resonant reformist thrillers, from which the idea of cleansing the revolution of its filth, sounded loud and clear. As the curtain fell on the eighties, Mark Zakharov created one of his most significant productions, *A Prayer for the Dead*, an adaptation by Grigory Gorin of Sholom Aleikhem's novel *Tevye the Milk-seller*, in which Tevye was played marvellously by Evgeny Leonov. The production was a landmark both in our theatrical and in our social consciousness, yet, in its attack on nationalist discord and bloodletting, was after the moment even as it was delivered to us. Events were taking the worst possible turn, and pleas from the theatre fell upon deaf ears.

The end of *perestroika* came with the putsch of August 1991. Mark Zakharov was one of the first to offer his services to the new authorities. On a television show he publicly burned his party card, then took his place in the so-called presidential advisory group. He was, it appears, the first theatre director after Meyerhold (once the head of the theatre section of the People's Commissariat of Enlightenment) to gain such close proximity to the ruling elite. The Lenin Komsomol Theatre became Lenkom and as Lenkom it did indeed become the new 'court' theatre, adroitly adjusting itself to the new market realities. It was the first to open a foreign exchange office, the first to acquire a night club. Indeed the changing situation was reflected in the very substance of the productions. In the perceptive and clever *Marriage of Figaro* (1993) the French revolution provided only the amusing background to the heroes' amorous intrigues. Only paper fireworks exploded from the threatening canons, and a well-endowed young woman strode back and forth upstage parodying the famous picture of Eugène Delacroix, 'Freedom on the Barricades'.

The fraternisation of former opponents of the regime with the new authorities utterly destroyed the age-old tradition demanding that the Russian artist maintain a distance between art and the powers that be. Mark Zakharov bravely did away with this tradition, supposing that the authorities really had changed their spots. In his wake, not a few veterans of the banned dissident community went and asked for their own 'profitable posts'. The campaign in Chechnya brutally curtailed this 'honeymoon' between artists and government. The leaders of the country once again considered themselves to be manning the barricades, resurrecting an historical tradition. It is likely that the director of Lenkom, the most successful theatre in the new Moscow, also experienced that 'crushing sense of defeat', which took over as by far the most prevalent emotion of the time.

8.

At history's turning-points theatre embraces that which it knows best. It begins to talk about itself. This was the origin of the Vakhtangov Theatre's production *Guilty Without Guilt*, Pyotr Fomenko's version of Aleksandr Ostrovsky's play. Mounted in the cramped space of a theatre buffet, for audiences of a few dozen, the production possessed exceptional theatrical power and acquired that transcendent meaning which forms the life-blood of Russian theatre. Pyotr Fomenko, like Mark Zakharov, had his theatrical passport issued in the sixties. But the theatrical blood in his veins belonged to other times. He focused all the skills of his generation, including the civic ones, and transformed them into one sense: a sense of theatre. And of one special, undoubtedly doomed theatre at that. An avid interest in the evil lurking in all aspects of life, the eccentric depiction of the basic human feelings at their most extreme, from the ecstasy of love to the automatism of physical lust, and a complexly organised hierarchy of spiritual values hidden behind an exaggerated set were enough. Such differences from the 'grand style' of post-Stalinist theatre made Fomenko an outcast or, more exactly, a rolling stone.

He criss-crossed the length and breadth of our theatrical territory. He tried to accommodate his natural talent to the prevailing circumstances, staging Braginsky, Trenev and Mikhalkov (alongside Shakespeare, Camus and Giraudoux). He too walked on a tightrope, deformed himself and agonised, tried on many different masks and took on many roles, amongst them artistic director of a Soviet theatre, the Leningrad Theatre of Comedy, with all the ensuing consequences for his spiritual and physical health. Despite immense efforts he was not able to realise his dream of building a home for his own theatre. But his vision of theatre he did preserve.

Fomenko somehow gave life's bitter medicine a good shake before he used it on stage. He was preocupied with that moment where 'reality' is transformed into art. His preferred genre was mystery bouffe: life, that is, taken to its breaking point. The business of acting was one part of this global mystery bouffe and in his view could not be categorised solely as a profession. Acting was a way of life and, perhaps, a road to salvation. 'Artists are an impoverished bunch,' asserts a rich provincial landowner and adorer of actresses (in the new Russian – a sponsor) in the play *Guilty Without Guilt*. He then gives two definitions of his concept. 'Europeans would mean proletarians, but in our native language we Russians would call them the birds of the sky: where seed is scattered, they peck, where not – they starve.'

Pyotr Fomenko staged Aleksandr Ostrovsky's melodrama about the life of Russian provincial actors in the very same theatre where, in 1922, as winter drew to an end, Evgeny Vakhtangov created his masterpiece, *Princess Turandot*, just before he died. The hackneyed melodrama with its sense of everyday life behind the scenes and its 'guiltlessly guilty' boy, stretching out his little hands to his actress mother who has cast aside her offspring, gave us a definitive Russian Princess Turandot for the new historical conditions. Using the melodrama of a classic native dramatist the theatre celebrated in its own way the 'end of ideology'. Long buried emotions were all unearthed at once. Fomenko gave us a water of life – the urgency of emotional experience, feasts for our eyes, parodies, romances, tears and all the other 'antics appropriate to the theatre' – and all this with such a light touch, with a freedom and genuineness impossible to resist. It was what they call 'breathing easy'. In the midst of historical turbulence the actors uncovered for us the original forgotten shape of normal life. They played as if inspired, as they had never played before, as though intoxicated by some wonderful potion. Endowed with our comedic memory, Fomenko made sure each of his actors could really make an impact. Within the overall 'grand performance' he arranged smaller ones: to each of his actors he gave a few heightened seconds, when theatre, public, life itself belonged only to him. Everyone was treated the same, from the young actors I watched for the first time to the stars I watched as though for the first time. In its own special way art had set them all on an equal footing, and, if not all, still many clichés were rooted out, amongst them even the Vakhtangov Theatre's own trademarks which the actors themselves satirised in this production. A play about the theatre of life and life in the theatre hit the historical nail on the head with such unerring accuracy, that a straightforward production was transferred into a ground-breaking one.

The idea we see in Hamlet, that actors are the mirrors of humanity, occurs even in the Russian theatrical backwaters. The bearers of this reflectivity are of course unaware of their task, so completely obsessed are they with matters backstage. The comedians greedily peck the seed scattered by the dramatist and multiplied a hundredfold by a contemporary director who has himself pecked at the stuff for so many decades. They have nothing in their lives except this eternal 'seed': regardless of how anyone acts, or how they are received, or who bends whom to whose will. They suppose that souls in this world are also allocated a part ('You know, for an actor, I'd have said a soul was a bit superfluous,' one comic decides bitterly. 'For comedians that's true, but there are other parts you know,' replies an aggrieved lover-hero). And these comedians and first lovers live by the rules of the plays they perform, and start up monstrous intrigues and wound the heart of a person as easily as they would hit a cardboard target. They make no distinction between cranberry juice and real blood.

In *Guilty Without Guilt* everyone reflects this old theme of life off-stage, but the most incisive of all have been two women, two actresses, working at two different poles of acting and unfettered theatricality – in this production played by Yulia Borisova and Lyudmila Maksakova. The actress Lyudmila Vasilevna Maksakova plays the actress Nina Pavlova Korinkina with great bravado. She plays the role impudently, without make-up and without any tranquillisers, with an excess comparable to the merciless public experiment on herself. So much harder becomes Borisova's task –

not to play anything, to portray at this bazaar not an actress, but a person, or more accurately, someone who is both actress and person, endowed with a soul and compassion and capable of investing her role with the most intimate of feelings. After some years even Stanislavsky will grace this spiritual centaur with the name of 'person-role', a strange sounding concept yet one which has taken root in Russian theatre.

The 60-years-young Fomenko, who, through these years of *perestroika* had been recharging his batteries not at meetings but in the student lecture hall, creating perhaps the best director's workshop in the country, felt the inner ferment of the times. Somehow he understood that only a short historical divide separated Ostrovsky's comedy about the theatre, written shortly before his death, from the explosion in the very quality of Russian actors (and indeed of the whole nation!) produced by the merchant's son and attentive spectator of Ostrovsky's plays who took the theatre pseudonym of Stanislavsky. 'I am a fellow artist, or better still, your fellow craftsman. Which do you think: fellow artist or fellow craftsman?' Who is it that engages with the actress Kruchinina – Grisha Neznamov or Kostya Alekseev-Stanislavsky? And does not this hate felt by the founder of the Moscow Arts Theatre for the 'bird-like' in the artist, does not the torment of uniting the 'bird-like' with the human, the creature with the creator, become the main engine of his own destroyed life? For in another language or jargon 'person-role' is nothing other than 'God-person'. The 'buffet' masterpiece of the Vakhtangovites was illumined from within by the light of great theatrical themes living not so much in Ostrovsky's actual text as in the memory of the genre.

Pyotr Fomenko and the artist Tatyana Selvinskaya went beyond this and transformed the usual theatrical world of Ostrovsky. Not for us the shabby walls and peeling wallpaper of actors' dressing rooms (as indicated by the dramatist). Playing with our preconceived notions, they sat us down in the cramped little room of Lyuba Otradina, which will become the artist Kruchinina's room. Then they transferred us to the buffet, separated off from the 'life' of the street by small many-coloured blinds, which are now opened, now closed, as though they were confining themselves within the conventionally theatrical little world. The playful ambiguity is echoed throughout the whole stage set; high up the chandeliers have been draped with different coloured materials, and the provincials themselves, with the help of similar light, motley capes, remind us of the characters in Italian commedia dell'arte.

However, this is not an Italian, but a very Russian, Muscovite carnival, with all the anguish of Russia, its drunken romances and belief in goodness knows what. And when they took each other by the hand, those tragedians and comedians, those 'mummies' and 'mumsies', and skipped around in a circle, gasping with you (this *mise-en-scène* runs right through the whole of Fomenko's production), the common thread joining the epochs of Russian theatre was suddenly made tangible. They are running around the same magical circle as the one the linked actors danced in the Art Theatre's fairy-tale about the 'bluebird', and again in the old Italian tale appropriated for the needs of the revolution by the dying Vakhtangov. But what kind of music was it that sounded then, what was it they so rejoiced over in the winter of 1922? What came out of the Civil War and the famine, that made it possible once again to bless life? It is hard to say, all the more so since their presentiments deceived them, and the death of Vakhtangov himself during the celebrations seemed far more prophetic than the literal meaning of their production.

Art, like the country in which it exists, searches out new ways of surviving. The small show in the buffet of the Vakhtangov Theatre revealed its transcendent theatrical meaning. If you like, Fomenko's production became the long-awaited sign and symbol of the inner freedom we were finding. And part of that freedom was theatrical. The director had guessed the general mood. His devices restored what pathos had destroyed. Through Ostrovsky he called to us and helped us understand, that we were still alive, that theatre was still alive, that the plague had apparently passed on. These comedians, these 'jesters' felt the change in the historical weather with a startling and intuitive keenness.

Why? Precisely because they are the birds in the sky.

Note

1. Aleksandr Gelman, 'Integrity is when people are Intact', *Moskovskie Novosti*, 25 December 1994.

18 Russian theatre and Western theatres

ROBERT LEACH

The question may legitimately be asked at the end of such a lengthy survey as this: what relevance has Russian theatre to us in the West? What has it all to do with us? After all, the Russian repertoire barely impinges on our theatres, though readers of earlier chapters, such as that of Professor A. D. P. Briggs, may regret this. Nevertheless, it is true that though Gogol's masterpiece, *The Government Inspector*, has a sure and lasting place in the world repertoire, his other dramatic works are virtually ignored, and the work of his contemporaries, Griboedov, Lermontov and even Pushkin (apart from Musorgsky's opera of *Boris Godunov*), are almost wholly unknown. Turgenev's *A Month in the Country* is also reasonably well known beyond Russia's borders, but Turgenev's other dramas are not, and nor is the vast, varied and often brilliant *œuvre* of Aleksandr Ostrovsky. Again, Chekhov's dramas are very widely performed, and Gorky's, too, are known in some parts of the West, but the dramatic work of some of their no less interesting contemporaries, such as Aleksandr Blok, are not. From the post-revolutionary period, a few apparently anti-Bolshevik pieces, such as Erdman's *The Suicide* and Bulgakov's *The Days of the Turbins*, have had their day, without their genuine complexities ever being really considered, while other playwrights of the period – Babel, Mayakovsky, Tretyakov – remain largely unread and unperformed in the West. And the same is true of later plays by writers as diverse as Solzhenitsyn, Shatrov, Vampilov and Petrushevskaya.

The neglect of many of these plays, especially in the English-speaking West, is shameful, because of their enormous dramatic potential. But the reason for studying Russian theatre and drama is the same as the reason for reviving some of these plays: they grow out of a theatre whose continual primary emphasis has been on the art of the actor. That is why the Russian theatre not only still has something to teach us, but has in fact taught us so much already, that almost all the performance techniques which are known in the West today derive from models developed in Russia.

Consider the case of dance. In the five years before the First World War, the Western world came to recognise Russian performance as probably the most spectacular example yet seen of what could legitimately be called 'total theatre'. Diaghilev's Russian seasons in Paris wrought this transformation single-handed: he presented Russian opera, featuring the charismatic and brilliant singer Fyodor Chaliapin, and, even more impressively, ballet, choreographed by Mikhail Fokin, with settings by Leon Bakst and Alexandre Benois. Though the dancers – Anna Pavlova, Tamara Karsavina and Vaslav Nijinsky – created continuing amazement, the décor and costumes initially at least made an equal impact. The first ballets Diaghilev mounted were restagings of known works. It was in the creation of original work, however, that his company made their enduring mark, beginning in 1910 with *The Firebird*, with music by Igor Stravinsky, settings by Aleksandr Golovin and choreography again by Fokin. One observer of the first night of this ballet exclaimed of the audience, when Nijinsky and Karsavina entered, 'Good Lord! I have never seen such a public. You would have thought their seats were on fire!'[1]

The Firebird was followed in 1911 by *Petrushka* and in 1913 by *The Rite of Spring*, all using Russian folklore, legend and peasant belief to create a stunning and overwhelming new dimension in stage art. Partly this was achieved by the visual beauty of the décor: according to Fokin, the garden created by Aleksandr Golovin for *The Firebird*, for instance, was 'like a Persian carpet interwoven with fantastic vegetation, and the architecture of the castle was unbelievably sinister-looking. All the scenery was in dark tones, with the golden apples shining eerily.'[2] Besides this, Stravinsky's music penetrated the Russian experience with a vivid intensity never before heard – cold, yearning, and fearful. And finally the choreography by Fokin broke new ground, which he later justified as being based on 'the laws of natural expression', which he contrasted with the stereotypical gesture and movement of earlier ballets.[3] Yet Fokin's work was eclipsed by that of Nijinsky, who choreographed the sensual and shocking *L'Après-midi d'un faune; Jeux*, the first modern-dress ballet, which wittily dissected love through the metaphor of a game of tennis; and most startling of all, *The Rite of Spring*, in which he used Dalcroze eurhythmics as the basis for a primitive and relentless pagan dance, which climaxed with the sacrifice of a young girl who dances herself to death in order to rejuvenate the earth. The hand-painted costumes, the beads and headbands, the wailing or threatening music, and the curious wooden quality of the dance, suddenly exploding into frenzy, mark this as one of the few genuinely original theatre works of the twentieth century. Its appearance confirmed Russia's place at the pinnacle of theatrical achievement, especially in ballet, a position retained over the decades not only by works of almost comparable power, such as Nijinsky's sister's *Les Noces*, but also by a stream of matchless dancers and choreographers who followed Nijinsky – Leonid Massine, George Balanchine, Mikhail Baryshnikov, and finally, perhaps the greatest of all, Rudolf Nureyev.

If these men, and other Russian émigrés, disproportionately influenced Western dance, the influence in the West of Meyerhold and the theatrical revolutionaries who supported him in the development of political and epic theatre is perhaps more to be expected. This is often reckoned to have begun with the work of Erwin Piscator in Berlin, but it is worth noticing that his productions for the Proletarian Theatre and then the Central Theatre, were based in naturalism, which admittedly was occasionally interrupted, or at least jolted, by a kind of anarchic, Dadaist streak. The Proletarian Theatre's manifesto at its foundation, indeed, proclaimed that while wishing to break the bourgeoisie's cultural stranglehold, it still intended to preserve 'the eternal works which sublime spirits, past and present, have bestowed on mankind'.[4]

It was only after news of the Russian revolutionary theatre's extraordinary experiments, especially those of the mass spectacles and the work of Meyerhold and Eisenstein, had reached Germany that the political theatre began to change. Piscator always denied the Russian influence on his work, but the fact is that he was extremely pro-Soviet from 1918 onwards, and he had many connections with people such as Bernard Reich and Asya Lacis, German theatre practitioners and communists, who were working both in Russia and Germany. One of his closest collaborators, Alphonse Paquet, whose play, *Flags*, was the first which Piscator described as 'epic' when he staged it in 1924, had been to Russia, as had other friends and collaborators, such as George Grosz and Franz Jung. Moreover, Aleksandr Tairov's Kamerny Theatre had made a deep impression on the German radical intelligentsia when they had appeared in Berlin in 1923. Piscator's denial smacks of disingenuousness.

As a matter of historical fact, virtually all the features of 'epic theatre' usually associated with Weimar Germany, especially Brecht and Piscator, had appeared on Meyerhold's stage: the half-curtain, the use of projections, the lack of concealment for lighting and even the theatre's brick walls, the snapping on and off of the house lights, bright stage lighting, the use of music and song, the use of few but telling properties, the refusal to 'identify' the actor with the part, the formal groupings on the stage, the deconstruction of the narrative line into episodes or chain-links, the propensity to adapt given texts, and, as Brecht propounded, 'montage' not 'growth', and 'each scene for itself' in a 'narrative', not 'one scene making another' in a 'plot'.[5] These are the principles behind a great deal of dramatic creation, both by playwrights and directors, especially in the second half of the century when Brecht's influence became so noticeable in Western theatre. His debt to Meyerhold and the Russians has never been fully recognised.

Also in the area of political theatre is the twentieth-century phenomenon of 'agit-prop' – theatre of agitational propaganda. As a distinct theatrical form, it can still be found in fringe performances across the world, though often shorn of its specifically political intent. It originated in Russia immediately after the Bolshevik revolution, when the communists realised that duty coincided with expedience in the spreading of news and political ideas. The 'living newspapers' of Terevsat were original in conception, and were taken up and developed by the Blue Blouses. When the Moscow troupe of the Blue Blouses toured Germany in 1926, they were received with amazement and acclaim. The embryonic 'workers' theatre' groups, struggling like all amateurs to create a convincing naturalism, saw in this new form something much more dynamic which was also within their compass.

Large numbers of 'Blue Blouse' troupes sprang up across Germany, with programmes like those of their Russian counterparts, as this one of the Red Rockets group from 1928: (1) The Rocket Song – entrance; (2) The Stupefaction Crusade of the Salvation Army; (3) Political Couplets; (4) The Political Musical Clock; (5) The Wonder Horse Called 'The Great Coalition'; (6) Political Jazz; (7) Nigger Song; (8) Workers' Songs; (9) Knock-out – a Boxing Match; (10) Songs Ridiculing the Constitution; (11) Pinkerton – an Opera; (12) Capital and the Press.[6] Such a programme, politically rather than aesthetically inspired, was typical of the German workers' theatre movement, which published a magazine for adherents, *The Red Megaphone*, and which was brilliantly captured on the film made in 1932 by Brecht, Ernst Ottwalt and Slatan Dudow, *Kuhle Wampe*.

Whereas by 1930 the agit-prop movement was dying – or being strangled – in Russia, it was reaching its height in the West at the time of *Kuhle*

Wampe. In 1930 an International Workers Theatre Movement was established, and in 1931 a group of English working-class amateurs visited Germany. They in turn were profoundly impressed. 'When we got home we decided to try ... building up a show from different items, and working to break down the barriers between players and audience ... Before then, we had just been one main group in London. Very soon we had some ten groups in London, and all over the country from Bristol to Dundee, from Rochdale to Reading, new groups were formed.'[7] One of these, the Red Megaphones of Manchester, metamorphosed into the Theatre of Action under Ewan MacColl and Joan Littlewood, becoming after the Second World War, Theatre Workshop, probably the most influential avant-garde company in British theatre history. Other London workers' theatre groups coalesced into Unity Theatre which opened in 1936 and which performed in Britain for the first time works by Brecht, Odets, O'Casey, Sartre and, among Russian premieres, it introduced plays by Shatrov to London. Among those who cut their professional teeth with Unity were Bill Owen, Alfie Bass, Maxine Audley, Ted Willis and Lionel Bart,[8] while those who graduated from Theatre Workshop to make a significant impact on the British theatre are almost too numerous to mention: Patience Collier, Harry Corbett, Miriam Karlin, Billie Whitelaw and Barbara Windsor are a randomly chosen few.[9]

Agit-prop found fertile soil in other countries during the Depression years of the 1930s, too. The International Union of Workers' Theatres had committed memberships from Czechoslovakia, Belgium, Bulgaria, Poland, Japan and other countries. In France, the movement was surprisingly weak, whereas in Poland and Romania there were strong agit-prop movements in spite of authoritarian and neo-Fascist regimes.[10] In the USA, the Federation of Workers' Theatres organised some 400 different shows in 1931 to 1932 and became the main provider of talent later in the decade for the socially and politically oriented Federal Theatre Project, which set in motion the careers of, among many others, Orson Welles, Hallie Flanagan, Will Geer, John Huston, Virgil Thomson, Arthur Miller, Marc Blitzstein and Elmer Rice. Of course Russian theatre was not directly responsible for the careers of these artists, but they were part of a movement, one strong root of which could be traced back to Russia.

Exactly contemporary with the overtly political theatre movement, which originated in Russia, was the growth of the influence of Stanislavsky and the Moscow Art Theatre in the West, although untangling how this came about is no easy business. After the revolution numerous displaced Russians visited and emigrated westwards. Among theatre practitioners was the singer, Fyodor Chaliapin, who left despite flattering treatment from the Soviet government; others included the Bat, or Chauve-Souris, cabaret theatre, and that master of the cabaret form, Nikolai Evreinov. But these found the going tough. True, Nikita Balieff's Bat made an extremely favourable impression when it first arrived in 1920 in Paris; it did equally well in London, and in New York its initial run of six months on Broadway received the ultimate accolade of an invitation to the White House from President Coolidge. But by the end of the decade, it had sunk into oblivion, and Balieff was unable to transfer his talents to other theatrical enterprises. The mercurial Nikolai Evreinov, too, had some successes, fitfully, over the two decades after his emigration in 1925, but his originality as writer, director and theatre theoretician was never properly appreciated in the West.

More successful, and more significant for the West, was Fyodor Komissarzhevsky, who left Russia in 1919. In 1925 he was appointed to the tiny theatre, formerly a cinema, in Barnes, west London, and here, in a remarkably short space of time, he made a major impact on British theatre by presenting Anton Chekhov's plays in a way quite startling to English play-goers. Chekhov was largely unknown in the West, but Komisarjevsky, as he now called himself, found a way to present the plays which maximised the tragicomic ambivalence which lies at their heart:

> I have seen nothing more lovely in the theatre than the stage pictures Komisarjevsky created on that cramped little stage at Barnes. His productions were as satisfying to the ear as they were to the eye. His use of subtle variations of tempo, modulation of tone and delicately timed pauses was far in advance of anything in the English theatre of that time.[11]

In his company were John Gielgud, Martita Hunt, Claude Rains, Charles Laughton, Jean Forbes Robertson, and more: all leaders in the British theatre in the following decades, so that although Komissarzhevsky went on to work in Stratford and London, Rome, Vienna, Paris and New York, it is unlikely any of his later work was as influential as those two years in Barnes.

Yet if Komissarzhevsky contributed one more significant Russian element to the development of theatre in the West, it was nothing to that of the Moscow Art Theatre, the reverberations of which can still be felt after more than seventy years. During the Civil War, the Art Theatre found itself split into two groups, one of which was outside Bolshevik-controlled territory. It included Kachalov, and Olga Knipper, Anton Chekhov's widow, as well as Maria Germanova, Andrius Jilinsky, Vera Solovyova and others. While some of these, including Kachalov and Knipper, responded to Moscow's urgent demand that they return in 1922, some did not, and founded the Prague Group which continued to try to uphold the parent company's ideals with a surprising degree of success for a decade or so. Undoubtedly, their presence in Eastern Europe through the 1920s was significant in the development of the theatre there, seen most notably in the work of Karel Hugo Hilar, whose expressionism became tempered by a more 'truthful' approach at that time.

The main body of the Art Theatre, however, was in Moscow still, and it was from there that Stanislavsky led them on their most memorable tour of the West, from 1922 to 1924. The Art Theatre astounded its audiences, first in Europe, and then even more deeply, in USA. In New York especially, the critics' encomia drew capacity audiences of spectators who knew no Russian but remained spellbound by the performances. Members of the theatre profession responded even more enthusiastically. John Barrymore, who was playing Hamlet on Broadway at the time, asserted that this was 'the most amazing experience I have ever had by a million miles in the theatre', while an appreciative critic noted:

> We have yet to hear an American actor who does not say that they are greater than the critics and ourselves have pronounced them to be. So hard-boiled an American artist as Mr Frank Keen for instance, sits night after night in rapt observation of them [and] we have seen Miss Ruth Draper and many others in what we believed were tears of approbation.[12]

The American theatre, its own mediocrity exposed by this extraordinary level of achievement, determined to emulate the Art Theatre.

When the Moscow company were rather bad-temperedly summoned back to Moscow by Nemirovich-Danchenko, they left behind the first version of Stanislavsky's book, *My Life in Art,* and, perhaps more importantly, several of their number who decided to defect. While the book outlined their mentor's struggles and developing ideals, it was in fact the players who were most influential in steering the course which mainstream

Western dramatic theatre was to take for the rest of the century. First among these was Richard Boleslavsky, originally Polish, who had been through the Art Theatre and its First Studio in Moscow, had worked with the Prague Group and in 1922 and 1923 was able to work again, both as actor and director, with the parent company and with Stanislavsky himself. As soon as the Art Theatre company left American shores, Boleslavsky signed a deed with Miriam Stockton which established him at the head of a new American Laboratory Theatre, dedicated to the dissemination of Stanislavsky's ideas in the USA. Working with Maria Ouspenskaya, who had also elected to stay, for six years he planted the most significant seeds which were to grow into the American 'method' in its broadest and most diverse sense.

Boleslavsky approached the task of teaching acting with a thoroughness learned from Stanislavsky but virtually unheard of in the West. Something of this is preserved in his short book, *Acting, the First Six Lessons*, first published in 1933, by which time he himself had left New York and was working in Hollywood, where he was to die in 1936. The first six lessons focus on: Concentration – Boleslavsky insists that the actor must concentrate as unrelentingly as the pilot of an ocean-going liner or a biologist with a microscope, the object of his concentration being not the tides or the plasma, but the 'human soul'; Emotion Memory – like Stanislavsky, he asserts that outward circumstances remembered can evoke inward feelings, which can then be controlled and used by the sensitive actor; Dramatic Action – sometimes known as the 'through line', Boleslavsky uses images of the spine and ribs, the trunk of a tree and the branches, the string and the beads, to suggest the relationship between the actor's large purpose and the individual incidents which make up the dramatic action; Characterisation – he insists on the need for the actor not to find a characterisation too early, and that it is 'largely a question of rhythm . . . the character's rhythm must infect yours', the actor's; Observation – here the actor is encouraged to observe life around him systematically since from this he will learn how life proceeds, what is sincere and what is insincere; finally, Rhythm – according to Boleslavsky, the actor should be asking not 'What is the theme of the play?' but stating, 'This is how the theme perseveres or does not persevere through all obstacles.' The distinction is both subtle and significant, especially as the answer lies in the rhythm of the play. [13]

Boleslavsky's whole project moved acting in the Western world into an entirely new dimension, and his work was complemented not only by

Maria Ouspenskaya and, later, by Maria Germanova and Tamara Kaikarkhanova, at the American Laboratory Theatre in New York, but also by Ivan and Maria Lazariev in Chicago, Lev Bulgakov in New York, and others. Of course, how true what was taught in America was to Stanislavsky may be questioned: Boleslavsky and the others knew the system at a particular point in its development, before Stanislavsky himself had finally reached any definitive conclusions. It was, moreover, their interpretations of what the master taught. Boleslavsky, for instance, put much emphasis on emotion memory, and worked at it with non-verbal exercises and improvisations, at a time when Stanislavsky was moving away from these techniques. The difficulty of remaining faithful to Stanislavsky was further aggravated by inappropriate translations or wrongly accented language. What Stanislavsky calls, with graphic elegance, a 'bit' of a scene or play, is still frequently – and confusingly – referred to in the USA as a 'beat' and there is a remarkable lack of clarity in distinguishing between 'affective' and 'effective'.[14]

Nevertheless, the influence of Boleslavsky's Stanislavsky was pervasive, and almost entirely beneficial. This was because the work deriving from the Moscow Art Theatre focused on the actor as the central artist in the theatre, of greater significance than either the playwright or the director. It was notably reinforced during the 1930s by the work of two other ex-Moscow Art Theatre actors who began working in USA, Andrius Jilinsky and his wife, Vera Solovyova. Both had worked for years with the Art Theatre, but arrived fresh from the company of Michael Chekhov, which coloured their Stanislavsky-based work in unexpected ways. For Jilinsky, 'truth' on stage was the actor's highest aim, as he explained: 'If you want to create truth on the stage, you must be acquainted with your own truth, and the truth of your life. It is something that belongs not only to the tradition of acting, but to the moral content of the theatre.'[15] To some extent, Jilinsky refined Boleslavsky's ideas, emphasising the need to learn to concentrate with each of the five senses, inculcating the actor's responsibility to his colleagues on the stage, as well as his responsibility towards the play, and setting greater store by physical action than Boleslavsky did. He constantly warned against 'playing', insisting that each action must be accomplished simply and truthfully, without 'marking' or 'indicating', and suggested that the actor's most telling creative energy is released in the process of overcoming obstacles which stand in the way of his achieving his objective.

Jilinsky founded the American Actors' Company, where his work was clearly rooted in the principles of the Art Theatre. One principle which was not easily assimilated in the West, especially perhaps in the USA, was that of the 'ensemble', yet without a permanent company working and learning together, the Moscow Art Theatre could not have achieved the standard which had so impressed the West. Perhaps the first conscious attempt to create such an ensemble came with the founding of the Group Theatre by a number of practitioners including Stella Adler, Lee Strasberg and Harold Clurman who were associated with the old Theatre Guild, but who had also worked with Boleslavsky in his American Laboratory Theatre. Others who worked with the Group were Morris Carnovsky, Franchot Tone, Cheryl Crawford, Clifford Odets, Elia Kazan, Ruth Nelson, Mordecai Gorelik, Lee J. Cobb, Karl Malden, and many more. Although the Group was riven by dissent in 1934 when Stella Adler returned from working with Stanislavsky and proposed that a version of his 'method of physical action' should supplant the centrality of the emotion memory and other kinds of exercise for the 'inner' self in the Group's philosophy, and although it existed for a mere decade, yet the Group's influence on American acting was profound.

It was complemented by the influence of the followers of Michael Chekhov. Though coming, like Boleslavsky and Jilinsky, from Stanislavsky's Art Theatre, Chekhov was more brilliant and less stable than either. He left Russia in 1928, under the impression, perhaps correct, that the secret police were about to arrest him. Working first with Max Reinhardt in Berlin, and later with Georgette Boner in Paris, with the Lithuanian National Theatre and others, his first years of exile were nevertheless frustrating and failed to fulfil his desire to codify his ideas through the typically Russian way of teaching in a school and working with a theatre company simultaneously. In New York with his Moscow Art Players in 1935, he received an invitation from Beatrice Straight to create a drama section in the utopian experiment then being conducted at Dartington Hall, in England, by Leonard and Dorothy Elmhirst (Beatrice Straight's step-parents). With Deirdre Hurst and Straight, and alongside Kurt Jooss's dance company and other experimental projects in holistic agriculture and cottage industries, Chekhov was at last able to begin to develop his own system.

When war threatened, Chekhov, Hurst and the whole establishment moved to Ridgefield, Connecticut, near New York, where they established the school anew, and added a touring theatre company. A second Chekhov Studio was opened in New York, but by 1943 the war was disrupting life in the USA, too, and the Studios were disbanded. Chekhov himself moved to the west coast. Here he continued teaching and also played a number of film roles, including the psychoanalyst in Hitchcock's *Spellbound* for which he received an Academy Award nomination. In America his pupils included, among others, Hurd Hatfield, Yul Brynner, Ford Rainey, Jack Palance, Anthony Quinn, Gregory Peck, Mala Powers and Marilyn Monroe.

He also evolved his own method out of what he had learned from Stanislavsky, and especially out of Stanislavsky's system as developed by Sulerzhitsky and Vakhtangov at the First Studio, and then modified by his own nomadic life and work. He paid much attention in his system to the 'exterior' of the actor, his physicality: 'If there is one aspect of acting that is the foundation of Chekhov's system, it is the actor's physicality.'[16] Then he attempted to fuse together the actor's exterior physicality and the inner self of his emotions, memories, ideas and spirituality, largely by use of what he called the 'psychological gesture'. This was a very particular movement or gesture discovered by the actor which physicalises the character's psyche. Thus, says Chekhov, 'Through the experience the Psychological Gesture offers him, the actor enjoys the organic process of gradually "becoming" a character.'[17] This holistic approach, derived as much probably from his contact with Leopold Sulerzhitsky at the First Studio immediately before the Bolshevik revolution, as from his later conversion to Rudolf Steiner's 'anthroposophy', led him almost entirely to excise from his system such Stanislavskian techniques as 'sense memory' and 'emotional recall', and to substitute the less tangible 'imagination', and the accompanying 'atmospheres and qualities', which suffuse his work, and give it its special quality. In fact, for the practising actor, Chekhov's ideas often blow a fresh and invigorating breeze into the more usual Stanislavskian work, and his ideas have grown in influence since his death in 1955.

Nijinsky and Nureyev, Meyerhold, the Blue Blouses, Komissarzhevsky, Stanislavsky and his followers, Boleslavsky and Jilinsky, as well as Michael Chekhov, have created the styles we expect to see in the performance of almost any kind of play, film, or television drama. Only in the area of the surrealistic or absurdist play is it possible to discount the Russian influence on twentieth-century Western theatres. The reasons for this dominance are various and perhaps arguable. Partly it is a result of the theatrical history discussed in this book: the encouragement of permanent ensembles from the beginning of the Imperial Theatres, for example, and the generous subsidies from the tsar's exchequer or the private merchant's bank account, enabled the dramatic and theatrical arts to grow steadily and cumulatively. There are also the temperaments of the leading practitioners: Stanislavsky and Meyerhold, so different in so many ways, were both restless geniuses who would have made their mark wherever they had lived. But it may be permissible to suggest also that the reasons have some connection with the political repressions the Russian people have suffered through the centuries. The iconoclastic spirit first identified in this book by Catriona Kelly in chapter 1 has never been quite eradicated by successive tyrants, and the theatre has honourably kept the flame alight, if sometimes only flickeringly, through the decades.

But it is not so much the overt dissent or satire, or even the double meanings and deft defiances of plays and performances, impressive though the range of these may be, that are the root of the Russian theatre's influence. The performers and teachers discussed in this chapter are also significant because their work demonstrates that theatre carries a truth more potent and more profound than is evident in the mere content of the play. The art of acting which the Russian masters addressed with an integrity and passion hardly dreamed of in the West, is itself a source of joy and wonder. Just as we look at Monet's painting not in order to know what a poppy field looks like, but because we respond to the higher world which art images, and gives life to, through colour, composition, brush technique and so on; so we go to great acting to see how life can be imagined, though now not by paint and canvas, but perhaps even more tellingly, by actions performed in time and space. Acting gives us a notion of what life might be, what the human body and the human spirit can conjure.

The systems of Meyerhold and Michael Chekhov, Fokin, Stanislavsky and the rest are important to us because they have helped talented performers in the West who had no such system, to become theatre artists. As Shakespeare pointed out, actors are 'the abstracts and brief chronicles of the time'. The Russian masters learned to create performances which would in themselves speak to audiences caught up in the whirlwinds fanned by despotism, and their discovered techniques helped their spectators to stand proud. They were among the few who were able to nourish hope. That, finally, is what we all have to learn from the vicissitudes of the history of the Russian theatre.

Notes

1. Tamara Karsavina, *Theatre Street* (London, 1950), p. 154.
2. Aleksandr Shuvalov and Victor Borovsky, *Stravinsky on Stage* (London, 1982), p. 21.
3. Selma Jeanne Cohen (ed.), *Dance as a Theatre Art* (London, 1977), pp. 102–8.
4. Erwin Piscator, *The Political Theatre*, ed. Hugh Rorrison (London, 1980), p. 37.
5. Bertolt Brecht, 'The modern theatre is the epic theatre', in John Willett (ed.), *Brecht on Theatre* (London, 1964), p. 37.
6. Richard Stourac and Kathleen McCreery, *Theatre as a Weapon* (London, 1986), pp. 109–11.
7. Tom Thomas, 'A propertyless theatre for the propertyless class', in Raphael Samuel, Ewan MacColl and Stuart Cosgrave, *Theatres of the Left, 1880–1935* (London, 1985), pp. 89–90.
8. See Malcolm Page, 'The early years at Unity', *Theatre Quarterly*, 1:4 (1971), pp. 60–6.
9. See Howard Goorney, *The Theatre Workshop Story* (London, 1981), pp. 211–13.
10. See Philippe Ivernal, 'Introduction', in Denis Bablet (ed.), *Le Théâtre d'Agit-Prop de 1917 à 1932*, (Lausanne, 1977), pp. 13–14.
11. Norman Marshall, *The Other Theatre* (London, 1947), p. 219.
12. Quoted in Christine Edwards, *The Stanislavsky Heritage* (London, 1966), p. 232.
13. Richard Boleslavsky, *Acting, the First Six Lessons* (New York, 1949), passim.
14. See, for instance, Mel Gordon, *The Stanislavsky Technique: Russia* (New York, 1987), p. 228; Andrius Jilinsky, *The Joy of Acting* (New York, 1990), p. 114.
15. Jilinsky, p. 10.
16. L. Black, *Mikhail Chekhov as Actor, Director and Teacher* (Ann Arbor, 1987), p. 49.
17. Michael Chekhov, *On the Technique of Acting* (New York, 1991), p. 62.

A history of Russian theatre

Select bibliography

I. GENERAL

Al'tschuller, A. Ia., *Teatr proslavlennykh masterov: Ocherki istorii Aleksandrinskoi stseny*, Leningrad, 1968.

Al'tschuller, A. Ia. (ed.), *Ocherki istorii russkoi teatral' noi kritiki*, 3 vols., Leningrad, 1974–9.

Belinskii, V. G., *O drame i teatr*, 2 vols., Moscow, 1983.

Belova, L. A., *Russkii dramaticheskii teatr*, Moscow, 1976.

Bolkhontseva, S. K., *P'esa i spektakl'*, Leningrad, 1978.

Cooper, M., *Russian Opera*, London, 1951.

Evreinov, Nikolai, *Istoriia russkogo teatra*, Letchworth, 1955.

Istoriia russkogo dramaticheskogo teatra, 7 vols, Moscow, 1977–87.

Kelly, C., *Petrushka: the Russian Carnival Puppet Theatre*, Cambridge, 1990.

Khalizev, V., *Drama kak iavlenie iskusstva*, Moscow, 1978.

Leifert, A. V., *Balagany*, Petrograd, 1922.

Lifar, Serge, *A History of the Russian Ballet*, London, 1954.

Luchanskii, M. S., *Fedor Volkov*, Moscow, 1937.

Petrovsaia, I. F., *Istochnikovedenie, istoriia russkogo dorevoliutsionnogo dramaticheskogo teatra*, Moscow, 1971.

Rabinovich, A., *Russkaia opera do Glinki*, Moscow, 1948.

Shcheglov, I., *Narodnyi teatr*, St Petersburg, 1898.

Slonim, Marc, *Russian Theatre from the Empire to the Soviets*, New York, 1962.

Surkov, E. D., *Chto nam nekuda?*, Moscow, 1986.

    Na dramaturgicheskie temy, Moscow, 1962.

Syrkina, F. Ia. and Kostina, E. M., *Russkoe teatral'no-dekoratsionnoe iskusstvo*, Moscow, 1978.

Taruskin, R., *Opera and Drama in Russia*, Ann Arbor, 1981.

Warner, Elizabeth, *The Russian Folk Theatre*, The Hague, 1977.

Zguta, Russell, *Russian Minstrels*, Oxford, 1978.

2. FROM THE EARLIEST TIMES TO THE END OF THE EIGHTEENTH CENTURY

Aseev, B. N., *Russkii dramaticheskii teatr ot ego istokov do kontsa XVIII veka*, Moscow, 1977.

Berkov, P. N., *A. P. Sumarokov*, Moscow and Leningrad, 1949.

Evgrafov, K., *Fedor Volkov*, Moscow, 1989.

Istoriia russkoi dramaturgii XII-pervaia polovina XIX veka, Leningrad, 1982.

Kuz'mina, V. D., *Russkii demokraticheskii teatr XVIII veka*, Moscow, 1958.

Lehmann, D., *Russlands Oper und Singspiel in der zweiten Hälfte des 18 Jahrhunderts*, Leipzig, 1958.

Perets, V. N., *Starinnyi teatr v rossii, XVII–XVIII veka*, Peterburg, 1923.

3. NINETEENTH CENTURY

Alpers, B., *Teatr Mochalova i Shchepkina*, Moscow, 1979.

Al'tschuller, A. Ia., *Aleksandr Evstaf'evich Martynov, 1816–1860*, Leningrad, 1959.

Al'tschuller, A. Ia. (ed.), *Vera Fedorovna Komissarzhevskaia: pis'ma aktrisy, vospominaniia o nei, materialy*, Leningrad, 1964.

Anikst, A., *Teoriia dramy v rossii ot Pushkina do Chekhova*, Moscow, 1972.

Bakhtiarov, A., *Briukho Peterburga*, St Petersburg, 1888.

Baring, M., *The Mainsprings of Russia*, London, 1915.

Ben'iash, R. M., *Pelegaia Strepetova*, Leningrad, 1967.

Brianskii, A. M., *Vladimir Nikolaevich Davydov*, Moscow, 1939.

Danilov, S. S., *Russkii dramaticheskii teatr XIX veka*, Moscow, 1957.

Davydova, M. B., *Ocherki po istorii russkogo teatral'nogo iskusstva XVIII–nachala XX v*, Moscow, 1974.

Dmitriev, Iu. A., *Tsirk v Rossii ot istokov do 1917*, Moscow, 1977.

Dmitriev, Iu. S., *Mochalov – akter-romantik*, Moscow, 1961.

   Russkie tragiki kontsa XIX–nachala XX veka, Moscow, 1983.

Dmitriev, N., *Opernaia stsena Moskovskogo imperatorskogo teatra*, Moscow, 1897.

Drizen, N. V., *Sorok let teatra: vospominaniia 1875–1915*, St Petersburg, 1916.

Durylin, S. N., *Mariia Nikolaevna Ermolova, 1853–1928*, Moscow, 1953.

Eikhenbaum, B. M., *Drama Lermontova*, Leningrad, 1961.

Gordin, M. A., *Vladislav Ozerov*, Leningrad, 1991.

Gozenpud, A., *Russkii opernyi teatr XIX veka*, 3 vols., Leningrad, 1969–73.

Grigor'ev, A. A., *Teatral'naia kritika*, Leningrad, 1985.

Iuzhin-Sumbatov, A. I., *Zapiski, stat'i, pis'ma*, Moscow, 1951.

Kara, S. S., *Varlamov*, Leningrad, 1969.

Karatygin, P. A., *Zapiski*, Leningrad, 1970.

Khaichenko, G., *Russkii narodnyi teatr kontsa XIX–nachala XX veka*, Leningrad, 1975.

Lakshin, V. Ia., *A. N. Ostrovskii*, Moscow, 1982.

Lotman, L. M., *Ostrovskii i russkaia dramaturgia ego vremeni*, Leningrad, 1961.

Mann, Iu. V., *Komediia Gogol'ia 'Revisor'*, Moscow, 1961.

Medvedeva, I. N., *Ekaterina Semenova: zhizn' i tvorchestvo tragicheskoi aktrisy*, Moscow, 1964.

   'Gore ot uma' na Russkoi stsene, Moscow, 1987.

Mochalov, P. S., *Zametki o teatre*, Moscow, 1953.

Pazhitnov, L. N., *A. P. Lenskii*, Moscow, 1988.

Petipa, Marius, *Russian Ballet Master, The Memoirs of Marius Petipa*, ed. Lillian Moore, London, 1958.

Petrovskaia, I., *Teatr i zritel' provintsial'noi Rossii*, Leningrad, 1979.

Poliakov, M. Ia., *Russkaia teatral'naia parodia*, Iskusstvo, 1976.

Poliakova, E. I., *Teatr L'va Tolstogo*, Moscow, 1978.

Rassadin, S. B., *Genii i zlodeistvo, ili Sukhovo-Kobylina*, Moscow, 1989.

Rodina, T. M., *Russkoe teatral'noe iskusstvo v nachale XIX veka*, Moscow, 1961.

Rudnitskii, K. L., *A. V. Sukhovo-Kobylin: ocherk zhizni i tvorchestva*, Moscow, 1957.

Rybakova, Y., *Komissarzhevskaia*, Leningrad, 1971.

Shakh-Azizova, T. K., *Chekhov i zapadnoevropeiskaia drama ego vremeni*, Moscow, 1966.

Shchepkin, M. S., *Zhizn' i tvorchestvo*, 2 vols., Moscow, 1984.

Schneiderman, I. I., *Mariia Gavrilovna Savina, 1854–1915*, Leningrad, 1956.

Senelick, Laurence, *Russian Dramatic Theory from Pushkin to the Symbolists*, Austin, 1981.

   Theatre in Europe: A Documentary History, 1746–1900, Cambridge, 1991.

Stanislavskii, K. S., *Khudozhestvennye zapisi, 1877–1892*, Moscow, 1939.

Syrkina, F. Ia., *Russkoe teatral'no-dekoratsionnoe iskusstvo vtoroi poloviny XIX veka: ocherki*, Moscow, 1956.

Wiley, R. J., *Tchaikovsky's Ballet*, Oxford, 1985.

Worrall, Nick, *Nikolai Gogol and Ivan Turgenev*, London, 1982.

Zhikharev, S. P., *Zapiski sovremennika: vospominaniia starogo teatral'a*, 2 vols., Leningrad, 1989.

Zograf, N. G., *Aleksandr Pavlovich Lenskii*, Moscow, 1955.

   Maly teatr v kontse XIX–nachale XX veka, Moscow, 1966.

   Maly teatr vtoroi poloviny XIX veka, Moscow, 1960.

4. TWENTIETH CENTURY

Abalkina, N., *Nasledie Stanislavskogo i praktika sovetskogo teatra*, Moscow, 1953.

Alpers, B. V., *Teatral'nye ocherki*, 2 vols., Moscow, 1977.

Alpers, B., *The Theater of the Social Mask*, New York, 1934.

Alpers, B. (ed.), *Sovetskaia dramaturgiia*, Moscow, 1934.

Autaut-Mathieu, Marie-Christine, *Le théâtre soviétique durant le dégel, 1953–64*, Paris, 1993.

Bablet, Denis (ed.), *Le Théâtre d'Agit-Prop de 1917 à 1932*, Lausanne, 1977.

Bakshy, Alexander, *The Path of the Modern Russian Stage*, London, 1916.

Barron, Stephanie and Tuchman, Maurice, *The Avant-Garde in Russia, 1910–1930: New Perspectives*, Los Angeles, 1980.

Beaujour, Elizabeth K., *The Invincible Land: A Study of the Artistic Imagination of Iurii Olesha*, New York, 1970.

Benedetti, Jean, *The Moscow Art Theatre Letters*, London, 1991.

   Stanislavski, London, 1988.

Benois, Alexandre, *Memoirs*, 2 vols., London, 1964.

Berkovskii, N. Ia., *Literatura i teatr: stat'i raznykh let*, Moscow, 1969.

Beumers, Birgit, *Yury Lyubimov at the Taganka Theatre 1964–1994*, Amsterdam, 1997.

Bialik, B. M., *Gorky – Dramaturg*, Moscow, 1962.

Black, L., *Mikhail Chekhov as Actor, Director and Teacher*, Ann Arbor, 1987.

Boleslavsky, R., *Acting, The First Six Lessons*, New York, 1933.

Borovsky, Victor, *Chaliapin, a Critical Biography*, London, 1988.

Bowlt, John E., *Russian Art of the Avant Garde: Theory and Criticism, 1902–1934*, New York, 1988.

Bradshaw, M. (ed.), *Soviet Theaters 1917–41*, New York, 1954.

Braun, E., *Meyerhold: A Revolution in Theatre*, London, 1994.

Braun, E. (ed.), *Meyerhold on Theatre*, London, 1969.

Buckle, Richard, *Diaghilev*, New York, 1979.

Nijinsky, London, 1971.

Bugrov, B., *Geroi prinimaet reshenie*, London, Moscow, 1987.

Bulgakov, Mikhail, *Black Snow*, London, 1967.

Bushueva, S. K. (ed.), *Russkoe akterskoe iskusstvo XX veka*, St Petersburg, 1992.

Carnicke, S. M. *The Theatrical Instinct*, New York, 1989.

Carter, Huntly, *The New Spirit in the Russian Theatre*, London, 1929.

Chebotarevskaya, T. A. (ed.), *Dramaturgiia i vremia*, Moscow, 1974.

Chekhov i teatr. Pis'ma, fel'etony. Sovremenniki o Chekhova-dramaturge, Moscow, 1982.

Chekhov, M., *Lessons for the Professional Actor*, New York, 1985.

Literaturnoe nasledie, 2 vols., Moscow, 1976.

To the Actor, New York, 1953.

Clayton, J. Douglas, *Pierrot in Petrograd*, Montreal and London, 1993.

Collins, Christopher, *Life as Theater*, Ann Arbor, 1973.

Dana, H. W. L., *Handbook on Soviet Drama*, New York, 1938.

Demidova, A. S., *Vladimir Vysotskii*, Moscow, 1989.

Derzhavin, Konstantin, *Kniga o Kamernom teatre*, Leningrad, 1934.

Eder, Boris, *Jungle Acrobats of Russian Circus*, New York, 1958.

Efros, A., *Kamernyi teatr i ego khudozhniki 1914–1934*, Moscow, 1934.

Efros, A. V., *Prodolzhenie teatral'nogo rasskaza*, Moscow, 1985.

Professiia – rezhisser, Moscow, 1979.

Repetitsiia – liubov' moia, Moscow, 1975.

Efros, Nikolai, *Teatr 'Letuchaia mysh'' N. F. Baleva*, Petrograd, 1918.

Evreinoff, Nicolas, *The Theatre in Life*, London, 1927.

Evreinov, N. N., *Teatral'nye novatsii*, Petrograd, 1922.

Fedorov, A. V., *Teatr A. Bloka i dramaturgiia ego vremeni*, Leningrad, 1972.

Fokine, Michel, *Memoirs of a Ballet Master*, London, 1961.

Garafola, Lynn, *Diaghilev's Ballets Russes*, Oxford, 1989.

Garin, E., *S Meierkhol'dom*, Moscow, 1974.

Gershkovich, Alexander, *The Theater of Yuri Lyubimov*, New York, 1989.

Golovashenko, Iu. A., *Rezhisserskoe iskusstva Tairova*, Moscow, 1970

Golub, S., *Evreinov: The Theater of Paradox and Transformation*, Ann Arbor, 1984.

The Recurrence of Fate: Theatre and Memory in Twentieth Century Russia, Iowa, 1994.

Gorchakov, N., *Stanislavsky Directs*, New York, 1954.

The Theater in Soviet Russia, Oxford, 1957.

Gorelik, Mordecai, *New Theaters for Old*, London, 1947.

Gorfunkel', E. I., *Smoktunovskii*, Moscow, 1990.

Gourfinkel, N., *Le Théâtre russe contemporain*, Paris, 1930.

Gozenpud, A., *Russkii opernyi teatr na rubezhe XIX–XX vekov i F. I. Shaliapin*, Leningrad, 1974.

Green, Michael (ed.), *The Russian Symbolist Theater: Plays and Critical Texts*, Ann Arbor, 1986.

Gregor, Joseph, and Fulop-Miller, Rene, *The Russian Theatre*, London, 1930.

Grigoriev, S. L., *The Diaghilev Ballet, 1909–1929*, London, 1953.

Hammarstrom, David L., *Circus Rings Around Russia*, New York, 1958.

Hoover, Marjorie, *Meyerhold: The Art of Conscious Theater*, Amherst, Mass., 1974.

Meyerhold and his Set Designers, New York, 1989.

Houghton, Norris, *Moscow Rehearsals*, New York, 1936.

Return Engagement, New York, 1962.

Il'inskii, I. V., *Sam o sebe*, Moscow, 1984.

Imikhelova, S. S., *Sovremennyi geroi v russkoi sovetskoi dramatugii 70-kh godov*, Novosibirsk, 1983.

Iufit, A., *Revoliutsia i teatr*, Leningrad, 1979.

Iufit, A. (ed.), *Russkii sovetskii teatr, dokumenty i materialy, 1917–1921*, Leningrad, 1968.

Iur'ev, Iu. M., *Zapiski*, 2 vols., Moscow, 1963.

Iurskii, S. Iu., *Kto derzhit pausu*, Moscow, 1989.

Iuzovskii, Iu. I., *Maksim Gorkii i ego dramaturgiia*, Moscow, 1959.

O teatre i drame, 2 vols., Moscow, 1982.

Jilinsky, Andrius, *The Joy of Acting*, New York, 1988.

Kachalov, V. I., *Vospominaniia, pis'ma: Sbornik statei*, Moscow, 1954.

Karlinsky, Simon and Heim, Michael (eds.), *Anton Chekhov's Life and Thought*, San Francisco, 1975.

Karsavina, Tamara, *Theatre Street*, London, 1930.

Kashina-Evreinova, Anna, *N. N. Evreinov v mirovom teatre XX veka*. Paris, 1964.

Kastorskii, S., *Dramaturgia M. Gorkogo*, Moscow, 1963.

Kaun, Alexander, *Leonid Andreyev: A Critical Study*, New York, 1924.

Kaverin, F. N., *Vospominaniia i teatral'nye rasskazy*, Moscow, 1964.

Kaye, Phyllis J., *American Soviet Playwrights Directory*, 1988.

Kerzhentsev, P., *Tvorcheskiy Teatr*, Petrograd, 1920.

Kleberg, L., *Theatre as Action*, London, 1993.

Kleberg, L., and Nilsson, N. A., *Theater and Literature in Russia, 1900–1930*, Stockholm, 1984.

Knebel', M. O., *Vsia zhizn'*, Moscow, 1969.

Komisarjevsky, T., *Myself and the Theatre*, London, 1929.

Komissarzhevskaia, V. F., *Pis'ma aktrisy; vospominaniia o nei; materialy*, Moscow, 1964.

Koonen, Alisa, *Stranitsy zhizni*, Moscow, 1975.

Krymova, N. A., *Imena: rasskazy o liudakh teatra*, Moscow, 1971.

Kryzhitskii, Georgi, *Dorogi teatral'nye*, Moscow, 1976.

Kugel', A. P., *List'ia s dereva: vospominaniia*, Leningrad, 1926.

　　Teatral'nye portrety, Leningrad, 1967.

Kuziakina, Natalia, *Theatre in the Solovki Prison Camp*, Amsterdam, 1995.

Law, Alma and Gordon, Mel, *Meyerhold, Eisenstein and Biomechanics*, London, 1996.

Law, Alma and Goslett, Peter, (eds.), *Soviet Plays in Translation*, 1981.

Leach, Robert, *Revolutionary Theatre*, London, 1994.

　　Vsevolod Meyerhold, Cambridge, 1989.

Leonard, Charles, *Michael Chekhov's To the Director and Playwright*, New York, 1963.

Levin, Dan, *Stormy Petrel: The Life and Work of Maxim Gorky*, New York, 1965.

Liubimov, I., *Le Feu Sacré*, Paris, 1985.

Lordkipanidze, Nateli, *Rezhisser stavit spektakl'*, Moscow, 1990.

Lunacharskii, A., *Teatr i revoliutsiia*, Moscow, 1924.

McLeod, Joseph, *Actors Across the Volga*, London, 1946.

　　The New Soviet Theatre, London, 1943.

Magarshack, David, *Stanislavsky on the Art of the Stage*, London, 1950.

Maliutin, Ia. O., *Aktery moego pokoleniia*, Leningrad, 1971.

Margolin, S., *Pervyi rabochii teatr proletkul'ta*, Moscow, 1930.

Markov, P. A., *O teatre*, Moscow, 1977.

　　The Soviet Theatre, London, 1934.

　　V khudozhestvennom teatre: kniga zavlita, Moscow, 1976.

Meierkhol'd, V. E., *Perepiska, 1896–1939*, Moscow, 1976.

　　Stat'i, pis'ma, rechi, besedy, 2 vols. Moscow, 1968.

Metcalfe, Amanda, *Evgenii Shvarts and his Fairy Tales for Adults*, Birmingham, 1979.

Mgebrov, A. A., *Zhizn' v teatre*, 2 vols., Moscow, 1929–32.

Mikhailovskii, F. N., (ed.), *Moskovskii Khudozhestvenniy teatr v sovetskoi epokhi*, Moscow, 1974.

Mironova, V., *Tram*, Leningrad, 1977.

Moldavskii, D., *S Maiakovskim v teatre i kino*, Moscow, 1975.

Moskovskii khudozhestvenniy teatr v sovetskoi epokhi (materialy i dokumkenty), Moscow, 1974.

Moskvin, I. M., *Stat'i i materialy*, Moscow, 1948.

Nemirovich-Danchenko, V. I., *O tvorchestve aktera*, Moscow, 1973.

　　Rozhdenie teatre, Moscow, 1989.

Nijinska, B., *Early Memories*, London, 1982.

Ninov, A. A., (ed.), *Russkii teatr i dramaturgiia nachala XX veka*, Leningrad, 1984.

Okhitovich, L. (ed.), *Kamernyi teatr: stat'i, zametki, vospominaniia*, Moscow, 1934.

Petrov, N. V., *50 i 500*, Moscow, 1960.

Petrovskaia, I. F., *Istochnikovedenie istorii russkogo dorevoliutsionnogo dramaticheskogo teatra*, Leningrad, 1971.

Picon-Vallin, B. (ed.), *Liubimov. La Taganta, Les Voies de la création théâtrale*, vol. 20, Paris, 1997.

Pitcher, Harvey, *Chekhov's Leading Lady*, London, 1979.

Poliakova, E. I., *Stanislavskii – akter*, Moscow, 1972.

Proffer, Ellenda, *Bulgakov: Life and Work*, Ann Arbor, 1984.

Proffer, Ellenda (ed.), *Evreinov, a Pictorial Biography*, Ann Arbor, 1981.

Radlov, S., *Desyat' let v teatr*, Leningrad, 1929.

   Stat'i o teatre, 1918–1922, Petrograd, 1922.

Ripellino, A. M., *Maiakovski et le théâtre russe d'avant-garde*, Paris, 1965.

Roberts, Spencer E., *Soviet Historical Drama: Its Role in the Development of a National Mythology*, The Hague, 1965.

Rodina, T. M., *Aleksandr Blok i russkii teatr nachala XX veka*, Moscow, 1972.

Roslavleva, Natalia, *Era of the Russian Ballet*, London, 1966.

Rozovskii, Mark, *Teatr iz nichego*, Moscow, 1989.

Rudnitskii, K. L., *Russkoe rezhisserskoe iskusstvo, 1898–1907*, Moscow, 1989.

   Spektakl' raznykh let, Moscow, 1974.

Rudnitsky, K., *Meyerhold the Director*, Ann Arbor, 1981.

   Russian and Soviet Theatre, London, 1988.

Russell, Robert, *Russian Drama of the Revolutionary Period*, London, 1988.

Russell, Robert, and Barratt, Andrew, *Russian Theatre in the Age of Modernism*, London, 1990.

Sats, Natalia, *Zhizn' – iavlenie polosatoe*, Moscow, 1991.

Sayler, Oliver M., *Inside the Moscow Art Theater*, New York, 1925.

   The Russian Theatre, New York, 1922.

Schouvaloff, Alexander and Borovsky, Victor, *Stravinsky on Stage*, London, 1982.

Schuler, Catherine A., *Women in Russian Theatre*, London, 1996.

Segel, Harold B., *Turn-of-the-Century Cabaret*, New York, 1987.

   Twentieth Century Russian Drama, New York, 1979.

Senelick, Laurence, *Cabaret Performance: Europe 1990–1920. Songs, Sketches, Monologues, Memoirs*, New York, 1989.

   The Chekhov Theatre, Cambridge, 1997.

Senelick, Laurence, (ed.), *Wandering Stars: Russian Emigré Theater, 1905–1940*, Iowa, 1992.

Shakh-Azizova, T. K., *Chekhov i zapadnoevropeiskaia drama ego vremeni*, Moscow, 1966.

Sherel', A. A. (ed.), *Meierkhol'dovskii Sbornik*, 2 vols., Moscow, 1992.

Shub, Iu. G., *Andrei Popov*, Moscow, 1989.

Simonov, Reuben, *Stanislavsky's Protégé: Eugene Vakhtangov*, New York, 1969.

Smelianskii, A. M., *Klassiki i Sovremennost'*, Moscow, 1987.

   Nashi sobesedniki, Moscow, 1981.

Smeliansky, Anatoly, *Is Comrade Bulgakov Dead?*, Methuen, 1993.

Solov'eva, I. N., *Nemirovich-Danchenko*, Moscow, 1979.

Solov'eva, I. N., and Shitova, V. V., *Stanislavskii*, Moscow, 1985.

Souritz, Elizabeth, *Soviet Choreographers in the 1920s*, London, 1990.

Stanislavskii, Konstantin, *An Actor Prepares*, London, 1988.

    Building a Character, London, 1988.

    Creating a Role, London, 1988.

Stanislavskii, K., *Moe grazhdanskoe sluzhenie rossii*, Moscow, 1990.

    My Life in Art, Harmondsworth, 1967.

Stark, Edward, *Starinnyi teatr*, Petrograd, 1922.

Stites, Richard, *Russian Popular Culture: Entertainment and Society Since 1900*, Cambridge, 1992.

Stroeva, M. N., *Rezhisserskie iskaniia Stanislavskogo 1898–1917*, Moscow, 1973.

    Rezhisserskie iskaniia Stanislavskogo 1917–1938, Moscow, 1977.

Tairov, Alexander, *Notes of a Director*, Miami, 1969.

Taylor, Richard (ed.), *S. M. Eisenstein: Selected Works*, 3 vols., London, 1988–96.

'*Teatr', kniga o novym teatre: shornik statei*, St Petersburg, 1908.

Titova, G. V., *Tvorcheskii teatr i teatral'nyi konstruktivizm*, St Petersburg, 1995.

Tovstonogov, G. A., *Krug myslei*, Leningrad, 1972.

    Zerkalo stseny, 2 vols., Leningrad, 1984.

Trabskii, A. Ia., (ed.), *Russkii sovetskii teatr, dokumenty i materialy, 1921–1926*, Leningrad, 1975.

Turovskaya, M. I., *Ol'ga Leonardovna Knipper-Chekhova*, Moscow, 1959.

    Pamiati tekushchego mgnoveniia: ocherki, portrety, zametki, Moscow, 1987.

Uvarova, E. M., *Estradnyi teatr: miniatiury, obozreniia, miuzik-kholly 1917–1945 gg*, Moscow, 1983.

Vakhtangov, Evgenii, *Sbornik*, Moscow, 1984.

Valenti, M., *Vstrechi s Meierkhol'dom*, Moscow, 1967.

van Gyseghem, Andre, *Theatre in Soviet Russia*, London, 1943.

Van Norman Baer, Nancy (ed.), *Theatre in Revolution: Russian Avant-Garde Stage Design, 1913–1935*, London, 1992.

Vendrovskaia, L. D. and Fevral'skii, A. V. (eds.), *Tvorcheskoe nasledie V. E. Meierkhol'da*, Moscow, 1978.

Vendrovskaia, L. D. and Kaptereva, G. P., *Evgenii Vakhtangov*, Moscow, 1984.

Verigina, V. P., *Vospominaniia*, Leningrad, 1974.

Vilenkin, V. Ia., *Kachalov*, Moscow, 1976.

Volkov, Nikolai, *Meierkhol'd*, 2 vols., Moscow, 1929.

von Geldern, James, *Bolshevik Festivals*, San Francisco, 1993.

Wiener, Leo, *The Contemporary Drama of Russia*, Boston, 1924.

Worrall, Nick, *Modernism to Realism on the Soviet Stage*, Cambridge, 1989.

    The Moscow Art Theatre, London, 1996.

Wright, A. C., *Mikhail Bulgakov: Life and Interpretations*, Toronto, 1978.

Zakhava, Boris, *Vakhtangov i ego studiia*, Leningrad, 1927.

Zharov, M., *Zhizn', teatr, kino*, Moscow, 1967.

Znosko-Borovsky, E. A., *Russkii teatr nachala XX veka*, Prague, 1925.
Zolotnitskii, D., *Akademicheskie treatry na putiakh Oktiabria*, Leningrad, 1982.
    Budni i prazdniki teatral'nogo Oktiabria, Leningrad, 1978.
    Zori teatral'nogo Oktiabria, Leningrad, 1976.
    Sergei Radlov: The Shakespearian fate of a Soviet Director, Amsterdam, 1995.

Index